GLENN M. VERNON, Ph.D., Washington State University, is Professor and Head of the Department of Sociology and Anthropology at the University of Maine. He previously taught at Brigham Young University, Central Michigan University, Auburn University, and McMaster University, Canada. In addition to the many articles he has written for leading journals in the fields of religion and sociology, he has also authored a textbook on the sociology of religion.

HUMAN INTERACTION

An Introduction to Sociology

GLENN M. VERNON
University of Maine

THE RONALD PRESS COMPANY · NEW YORK

Library of Congress Catalog Card Number: 65–17095

PRINTED IN THE UNITED STATES OF AMERICA

To my mother
ROSELTHA BINGHAM VERNON
and my father
the late WILLIAM M. VERNON

Preface

This text has been written with the hope that several things could be accomplished. An effort has been made to use symbolic interactionist theory as the orienting framework into which a body of sociological knowledge is integrated. Attention is focused upon three closely interrelated facts: (1) the manner in which the symbols man uses are related to his behavior, (2) the "inter-" or social aspect of behavior, and (3) the dynamic, emergent aspect as well as the systematic, orderly aspects of behavior. It is felt that "interaction" is a more useful concept than that of the "group" for many sociological purposes, since it calls attention to what man does rather than what he has or what he "is." Attention is paid to man's behavior in speaking, thinking, and communicating—those processes in which his use of symbols is so heavily involved.

The concepts used are amenable to scientific research. If the student is to learn to think sociologically, it is important for him to know how the sociologist acquires his knowledge through the medium of research. It is even more basic, however, that he know how to ask questions that can be researched. This involves an awareness of the types of questions that can be answered with the use of scientific method and those that cannot. This, in turn, requires that the student be equally aware of the fact that any phenomenon can be viewed or studied in any number of different ways and that the answers secured be always relative to the method used to secure them.

In any case, knowing how to ask sociological questions is the first step. The acquisition of this understanding is a major goal of the text. Coupled with this, of course, is the obvious intent of providing the student with enough of the substantive content of sociology to make the structure of sociological knowledge "become alive."

Symbolic interactionists are particularly aware that the concepts one uses in any behavior influence his own experiences in the world. Sociologists and sociology students are no exception. Efforts have been made to use basic terms that can be defined operationally for scientific research, fully recognizing that such concepts may be defined quite differently by others who employ them. Within the symbolic interactionist framework, these definitions permit accurate identification of empirical phenomena for oneself and for others, and greater certainty of the ingredients being put into the "sociological gristmill." Following such a procedure one can talk about the phenomena that are the subject of his research; he is not limited to considering the phenomena as "pointing to" or being an "indicator of" some non-empirical and observable thing.

Discovering how to ask sociological questions and how to look at behavior sociologically can be a stimulating, thought-provoking experience. Becoming aware of another way of viewing behavior; discovering relationships, to use Poincaré's expression, "between characteristics long known, but wrongly believed to be strangers to one another," can be exciting. It is hoped that the student who uses this text will be able to gain insight into some of the exciting perspectives possible through such study.

The chapters have been organized into a pattern whose structure is consistently enlarged upon as additional concepts are provided and integrated into the developing picture.

The text itself is a result of considerable interaction—most of it symbolic. Although some of the ideas presented are original, most have come from the "common storehouse." The presentation of these ideas, however, is in a relatively original form.

Appreciation is expressed to Robert L. Stewart who read parts of the manuscript and made valuable suggestions. The comments and reactions of the students who have been exposed to the manuscript in various stages of completion have been most helpful and are appreciated. Mrs. Judy Smart and Mrs. Mary Lou Hodge spent many hours typing the manuscript and providing secretarial help. Their contributions are acknowledged with thanks. To my wife, June, and to Greg, Becky, and Paul, who have graciously lived with "the book" and also contributed to the final form in many ways, including editing of parts of the manuscript, great appreciation is expressed.

Glenn M. Vernon

University of Maine
  February, 1965

Contents

III. CULTURAL DEFINITIONS

IV. THE INTERACTION PROCESS

Past Experiences. Socialization Involves Interaction. Early Stages in the Socialization Process. Conscious and Unconscious Socialization. Society, Subgroups, and Individuals. Technics of Socialization.

V. DEMOGRAPHIC AND ECOLOGICAL FOUNDATIONS OF INTERACTION

VI. SYSTEMS

VII. SOCIAL CHANGE

Part I

Introduction

Sociology Defined

Why sociology? As long as man has been man he has concerned himself with questions about his own behavior and has provided many elaborate (and some not so elaborate) explanations. What justification, then, is there for the development of sociology when many other answers are already available?

A major conclusion of sociology, if we may disregard traditional norms and introduce our subject matter with a conclusion, is that only when people share common definitions of the terms they are using can their interaction proceed smoothly and effectively. Students and professors of sociology are no exception. The interaction (symbolic interacting, in this case) between author and student will be facilitated if a working definition of sociology is established early. This is the goal of our introductory chapter. The full significance of the term "sociology" will most likely not be acquired from this first chapter, but will be gained only after a study of the entire text together with additional outside readings. Recognizing this, however, we will lay the foundation for such understanding by providing a short definition of sociology, followed by a somewhat extended discussion of its major aspects.

DEFINITION OF SOCIOLOGY

Our short definition of sociology: *Sociology is the scientific study of human interaction.*

Human Interaction

Let us develop this definition by first turning our attention to the term "human." Sociology is a study of man, and we are consequently not directly concerned with the study of lower animals. The study of other animals such as chimps and rats is an area of interest to some scientists and provides valuable information about chimps and rats. Such concern, however, is foreign to sociology. This position stems from two major factors. First, there is the matter of time and ability. It is impossible for one man or group of men to study all things. Some division of labor has to be established if any extensive research and study is to be undertaken. In this sense the division is an arbitrary one—sociologists have decided to study human behavior rather than any other form of behavior.

A second more important reason for thus limiting the area of concern is an awareness of the differences that exist between the behavior of man and that of the other animals. To equate human behavior with non-human behavior overlooks these basic differences—a major one of which is man's ability to utilize symbols. This

3

will be discussed extensively as we move into our subject. We start out, then, with the premise that man is a unique being, whose social behavior can be most adequately understood by paying attention to man himself. Sociology is the study of *human* interaction.

Let us turn now to the second half of the phrase "human interaction," subdividing the word "interaction" and discussing first the "inter." "Inter" suggests that we are concerned with actions that take place between and among individuals. *Interaction occurs when we have human beings taking each other into account or having a reciprocal influence upon each other.* Interaction, then, is a *group* or a *social* concept in that it always involves more than one individual. Groups are composed of interacting individuals and may vary in size from two individuals (a dyad) on up. Thus, a couple out on a date is a group. A family, a neighborhood, a community, a nation, a peer group, a delinquent gang, or a class in sociology are all groups, and all are subject matter for sociological investigation. A glance through the chapter headings of this text will further suggest the group orientation of sociology. This group orientation is frequently used to distinguish sociology from psychology, which is more oriented toward the individual.

At one time serious attention was given to the question whether a group is a "thing," or an entity which could be studied as such. Sociologists today do not concern themselves with such a question and would, in fact, raise the obverse question whether the group or group experiences are not the major reality in the lives of everyone. Once you move above the biological level, it is difficult to say much about an individual as an individual without a group connection or social implication. Once you start to talk about an individual and you pay attention to something other than his biological makeup the dimensions most often taken into account involve the ways in which the individual relates himself to others. Most of our "individual" behavior involves interaction with others, reflects interaction with others, or stems from interaction with others.

The study of sociology sensitizes the student to the fact that human beings are almost always functioning as members of a group. The behavior of an individual is but one part of a larger system of behavior which involves others and in which those involved exert an influence upon each other. On a more complex level, various systems of behavior also reciprocally influence each other. A common tendency of many people when they explain or analyze behavior is to pay attention to the individual involved and to push the others involved in the situation into the background where they can be relatively ignored. Sociology reverses this tendency and brings the social background into sharp focus, and in so doing it views the individual as part of the whole picture—but only one part, influencing but also being influenced by the others. The sociological position suggests that to do otherwise overlooks the basic quality of human behavior—its social nature.

Let us look now at the second half of the word "interaction." "Action" suggests that we are concerned with what man does. We study man's behavior, including his verbal behavior. Sociology seeks answers to the question why man *behaves* the way he does. We will pay attention to regularities in behavior, but it is well to remember that behavior is a dynamic phenomenon. Behavior is a constantly changing phenomenon, in which, of course, regularities and uniformities can be discovered and studied. In this sense human interaction is an on-going process (a term which we will use frequently), in which various elements (variables or units) are constantly in the process of becoming something else. Change is probably the most constant aspect of human behavior. Consistencies in the change, however, can also be identified and studied. Various types of processes (interaction) will accordingly be identified and studied.

Unless specifically stated otherwise, when we use the term "behavior," it is *social* behavior to which we refer. Of course while social behavior is taking place, other behavior is taking place within the individuals. Hearts are beating, digestion occurs, cuts heal, cells grow and die, biochemical and electrical processes take place, and atoms, as well as neutrons and protons, move in particular manners, to mention a few types of such behavior. The type of behavior in which we are interested, however, is social behavior—individuals taking each other into account.

There are two other terms related to interaction which we will have occasion to use. Sociologists talk about the *structure* of human interaction. In doing so they are emphasizing the uniformities found therein. A study of human interaction is essentially a study of the arrangement or relationship of various units. Sociologists identify many different "units" in social structure which will be examined as we proceed through the text. One illustration, however, is the relationships between professor and student in a sociology class. Such behavior is patterned, or structured, as evidenced by the fact that it is the professor who always (or most always) does certain things, such as deliver the lecture, and it is the student who does certain other things, such as take class notes on the lecture.

The other term is "function," which refers to what happens when certain arrangements or relationships occur. Thus, in the classroom situation a major function of student–teacher interaction is the transmission of knowledge about, say, sociology, from teacher to student. However, the student who is at all familiar with classroom interaction is aware that much more happens in a classroom than just the transmission of sociological (or other) knowledge. One of the goals of the sociology of education, in fact, is to determine some of these results or identify some of the *functions* of this type of interaction.[1] Throughout the text, the functions of various elements of interaction systems will be discussed.

[1] Sociologists and anthropologists who have given particular attention to such factors have been collectively called "functionalists." Attention to such aspects will be woven into the entire body of this text, with Chapter 20 providing a more detailed analysis thereof. For further discussion of the "Functional School," see Nicholas S. Timasheff, *Sociological Theory* (Garden City, N. Y.: Doubleday and Co., Inc., 1955), chap. xvii.

SOCIOLOGY COMPARED TO OTHER DISCIPLINES

Sociologists, then, are concerned with the study of human interaction. A moment's thought, however, will make one aware of the fact that they are by no means unique in this concern. Almost everyone everywhere has had an interest of one type or another in social interaction. Such interests have been extremely varied. Some have been concerned with influencing the behavior of others, some with how to "win friends and influence people," how to get away from others, how to defeat others, how to "win souls for God," how to get more work from employees, how to write poems, stories, or essays about others. Thus, the statement that sociologists are concerned with human behavior or human interaction is such a broad statement that, if left unqualified, it does not really tell us much about sociology.

Among those who have given attention to the area of human behavior are the following:

Man-in-the-street	Novelist
Poet	Historian
Philosopher	Psychologist
Religionist	Anthropologist
Lawyer	Economist
Legislator	Political scientist

If all of these others have given attention to human interaction and have provided man with answers about himself it is legitimate to raise the question whether sociology has anything to contribute that would justify its existence as a separate discipline. Does sociology make any contribution or provide any insight that is not already to be found in the works, of those in these other areas?

The answer is "Yes." The distinction between sociology and these other disciplines, however, lies not in the broad subject matter (the social behavior of man) but in the approach used in studying this subject matter. The approach of the sociologist is quite different from that of the philosopher, the religionist, the poet, the novelist, the legislator, the reformer, or the man-in-the-street. A major difference was indicated in our introductory definition, which identified sociology as the *scientific* study of human interaction. A second distinguishing characteristic is that sociology views human behavior as being essentially social in nature, or that it consists of individuals relating themselves to each other. Any *one* individual is but one part of the larger interaction system.

The ramifications of these statements are so extensive that a full chapter will be devoted to an elaboration of each of them. At the moment, we merely indicate that our method of study is the scientific one, and further, that this is one distinctive feature of sociology when compared with the other approaches just enumerated.

Sociology, however, is not the only approach that uses the scientific method in the study of human behavior. Other disciplines such as psychology, anthropology, economics, and political science all share this characteristic to one degree or another. Thus, our understanding of just what sociology is is far from complete until we distinguish sociology from these other areas of study.

Figure 1.1 Human interaction takes many forms. People can relate themselves to each other in many different ways, as suggested by the painting *Children's Games* by Peter Breughel the Elder. (The Bettmann Archive, Inc.)

Anthropology is frequently subdivided into physical anthropology and social or cultural anthropology. Physical anthropology is quite foreign to sociology in that its major concern is with the biological origins of man and with variations, including racial ones, in the human species. Attention is also given to the study of fossil men and to the characteristics of lower animals. Social or cultural anthropology, however, has much in common with sociology. Both are group-oriented and study the social interactions of human beings. Anthropology, however, has concerned itself more with pre-literate (primitive) groups and the historical development of man, whereas sociology has directed its attention more to contemporary groups. The basic concepts of both disciplines are much the same. Sociologists frequently draw upon anthropological studies in order to make comparisons with modern societies and to elaborate further the concepts under consideration. This text will follow this pattern.

Economics is the study of how men make their living, with specific attention being given to such things as supply and demand, cost, price, investments, and savings. Political science is a study of a specific kind of behavior—one that is political in nature, with attention being given to types of government and their various subdivisions. Traditionally political science has emphasized the legal and the administrative aspects of government.

The concern of sociology is broader than that of either economics or political science. The sociologist is looking for regularities which are characteristic of *interaction in general;* the economist and the political scientist are much more specific in their orientations. The sociologist is concerned with both the economic and the political dimensions of social behavior but not exclusively so. His interest includes other behavior such as familial, educational, and recreational. He is concerned with human interaction in general. Sociology, then, can be called a *generalizing science,* as contrasted with these other sciences, which are more particularizing.

This distinction also holds true for history and sociology. Whereas history concerns itself with the study of specific events and provides historical explanations, sociology is not so much concerned with any one specific event as with the characteristics that different events have in common. History, for instance, studies the family patterns found in colonial America. Sociology attempts to discover the characteristics which all families, including colonial and contemporary families as well as those among the Eskimo groups, have in common.

Sociology is a generalizing discipline. History, political science, and economics, by way of contrast, concentrate their attention upon more specific areas. In some respects the sociologist can provide us with an understanding of the broad foundations which underlie the more specific areas. Specialized courses in these various areas also are generally provided in the sociology departments of American universities and colleges. These include the sociology of the family, political sociology, sociology of work or industrial sociology, sociology of religion, and sociology of deviant behavior.

The distinction between psychology and sociology has already been suggested. Psychology is more individual-oriented. Greater attention is also given to biological factors in psychology than in sociology. Psychologists have also studied animals at the non-human level. Social psychology is somewhat of a meeting ground between these two disciplines, with the definition of social psychology being frequently given as the study of the influence of the group upon the individual, where psychology studies the individual and sociology the group.

PURE AND APPLIED SCIENCE [2]

An understanding of the traditional difference between a pure and an *applied* science will also

[2] The pure–applied distinction is not as clear as it may appear in this discussion. See, for instance, the President's Science Advisory Committee, "Scientific Progress, the Universities and The Federal Government" (Washington, D. C.: Government Printing Office, 1960). For a discussion of clinical sociology, see James B. Taylor and William R. Catton, Jr., "Technical Problems of Clinical Sociology," *Sociological Inquiry,* XXXIII, No. 1 (Winter, 1963), 34–44.

Applied Sociology

In the army no one would think of adopting a new type of weapon without trying it out exhaustively on the firing range. But a new idea about handling personnel fared very differently. The last thing anybody ever thought about was trying out the idea experimentally. I recall several times when we had schemes for running an experimental tryout of an idea in the sociopsychological field. Usually one of two things would happen: the idea would be rejected as stupid without a tryout (it may have been stupid, too) or it would be seized on and applied generally and at once.

—Samuel A. Stouffer.*

enable the student to anticipate more accurately what will be covered in an introductory sociology text. Let us briefly explore this distinction. It might be well to state at the beginning of the discussion, however, that the lines which will here be drawn may not always be so clear when specific college classes are considered.

The pure scientist, whatever his area of interest, is concerned primarily with gaining understanding or knowledge. He is seeking knowledge for the sake of gaining knowledge. This knowledge-for-the-sake-of-knowledge orientation is one which is generally quite foreign to the average individual who will read this text. Most individuals want to know how the new knowledge will help them. How can it be applied to make the world a better place in which to live? The pure scientist, as a scientist, does not share this orientation. He is concerned only with questions such as the following:

Why does this happen in this particular way?

What would happen if these elements were combined in such and such a fashion?

What are the component parts of X and how are they related to each other?

What is the relationship between this and that?

What happens when I do such and such?

The applied scientist is interested in applying scientific findings to specific problems which are felt to be of pragmatic value to the scientist—or to those who pay the scientist his salary. The applied scientist is action-oriented. He is concerned with making better mousetraps of one type or another. He wants to make salt water drinkable or usable as irrigation water. He wants to improve rocket performance, to improve marriages, or to reduce employee absenteeism. He applies his knowledge in an effort to achieve a goal which he has accepted as desirable. Knowledge is a means to an end, but not an end in itself.

The findings of a pure scientist are in a sense a two-edged sword. They can be used to accomplish any goal to which they are applicable, regardless of whether these goals are defined as desirable or undesirable. The principles of atomic physics can be used to build bombs which destroy human beings or to power hospital ships which save lives. The findings of the social scientist can be used by management to manipulate employees, but they can also be used by employees to manipulate management. They can be used to build strong organizations or to destroy strong organizations.

Utility of Social Science

We already know a great deal more about man and his social relationships than most people in our casually patterned society are willing to use.

—Hadley Cantril.*

---

* Samuel A. Stouffer, "Some Observations on Study Design," *The American Journal of Sociology,* LV, No. 4 (January, 1950), 356.

* Hadley Cantril, "Don't Blame it on 'Human Nature'!" in John F. Cuber and Peggy B. Harroff, *Readings in Sociology* (New York: Appleton-Century-Crofts, 1962), p. 137.

SOCIOLOGY DEFINED 9

The pure scientist is not concerned *as a scientist* with how his findings will be used, although even here his research for pure knowledge may well rest upon an "applied" assumption that such activity will *in the long run* benefit mankind. Whether they actually do or not is another question and one, by the way, which the scientist *as a scientist* cannot answer for reasons that will be made clear in our subsequent discussion of values.

In the social sciences the applications of the findings of the pure scientist have been somewhat limited. This is not surprising in view of the relatively short time that the social sciences have existed. It seems safe to predict that more extensive application of existing and subsequent findings will be made in the future.

The pure–applied dichotomy can be illustrated as follows:

Pure Science	*Related Applied Science*
Astronomy	Navigation
Botany	Agriculture
Chemistry	Pharmacy
Geology	Engineering (petroleum)
Physics	Engineering
Physiology	Medicine
Sociology	Administration, social work, diplomacy, city planning
Zoology	Animal husbandry

Sociology, as the student will be exposed to it in this text, falls in the category of pure science. Our goal is to gain understanding of human interaction, or of man's social behavior. We are seeking knowledge, not treatment. The text is not designed to provide direct answers to the problems which beset society. The student who seeks such answers will not find them here. The information gained through such a study, however, can be utilized by anyone who does want to bring about social changes or to "improve" society.

In making this distinction, or in laying out our course of study in this way, we are not suggesting that one approach (pure or applied) is better than the other. All we are doing is establishing a division of labor and indicating what the "role" (to use a term to which we will return for extended discussion) of the pure scientist is.

Sociology then is a study of what *is*, not what *ought to be*. We are concerned only with trying to understand why human beings relate themselves to other human beings the way they do. We are not at all concerned with whether this is "as it should be." Why these limitations are imposed upon our study will become clearer as you read Chapter 2 on scientific methodology and Chapter 6 on values.

SOCIOLOGY AND COMMON EXPERIENCE

When we label sociology a scientific discipline we emphasize a crucial characteristic. While we have not as yet clearly stated what is specifically involved in the scientific method, it is desirable at this point to distinguish between scientific sociology and common experience or common sense. Our major purpose is to emphasize that these two are far from identical.

One of the basic premises of sociology, which will be explored in detail later, is that different individuals and/or groups may each view the same phenomenon in different ways, depending upon the experiences that each has had. The sociologist frequently views or interprets behavior quite differently from the commonly accepted views—or from common sense. Sociological interpretation and common-sense interpretation may sometimes harmonize, but they may also be contradictory. This need not necessarily disturb the student when he understands how the contradictory answers are derived. We should not in fact be surprised that different methods do not always produce identical results.

Let us look briefly at some of the characteristics of common sense. Common sense is frequently given a vague and over-simplified expression. Many popular sayings are of this type, but are repeated by some individuals as though they represent unqualified universal truths.

Note, for instance, the following contradictory adages:

Look before you leap.
He who hesitates is lost.

Repeat a lie often enough and people will believe it.
Truth will prevail.

Out of sight, out of mind.
Absence makes the heart grow fonder.

East is east, west is west, and never the twain shall meet.
We're all brothers under the skin.

You can't make a silk purse out of a sow's ear.
Clothes make the man.

Opposites attract.
Birds of a feather flock together.

The sociologist as scientist attempts to qualify his statements, specifying, for instance, under what conditions opposites tend to attract and under what conditions "birds of a feather flock together." The student in his study of sociology should develop the habit of asking himself and others the question, "Under what conditions is such and such true?" (This may not help his popularity on campus if he does it too often in social intercourse but this further indicates the differences between sociology and common sense.) In most interaction those involved do not want to be as specific as does the sociologist. To be so would, they feel, impose limitations upon their behavior that would make them uncomfortable. Common sense, then, facilitates certain types of interaction.

Common sense may contain many beliefs that are false according to scientific information. At one time it was widely believed that the world was flat; this, however, did not make the world flat. That people have believed something for years and acted accordingly does not make the belief scientifically true. The fact that early Americans doubted that the average female—because of her "innate inferiority"—could do col-

lege work as well as the average male did not prove the innate (biological) inferiority of the female.

Sociology is not the same as common sense. Sociologists provide scientific checks for common sense. Many people, however, may not want such checks. Sociologists may, in fact, get into "hot water" when they challenge beliefs that have been widely accepted.

The distinction between common sense and sociological sense becomes clearer when it is recognized that "experience with" something does not necessarily produce scientific knowledge about this something even though "experi-

---

Common Sense

It is common sense that leads us to think that the earth is flat; that two plumb lines are parallel (they are both directed toward the center of the earth and consequently form an angle); that motion in a straight line exists; which is absolutely false as we have to take into consideration not only the motion of the earth around its axis and around the sun, and that of the entire orbit of the earth, but also the motion of the whole solar system toward the constellation Hercules, etc. As a result a bullet, or an airplane, which seems to move in a straight line with respect to the earth, for a certain length of time, in reality follows a trajectory more closely resembling a kind of corkscrew with respect to a vaster system of reference, the nearest star, for instance. Common sense tells us that the edge of a razor blade is a continuous straight line, but if we examine it under a microscope it resembles the wavy line drawn by a child. Common sense tells us that a piece of steel is solid; X-rays show us that it is porous, and the modern theories of matter teach us that it is in reality made up of trillions of animated, miniature universes having extraordinary rapid movements and no contact with each other.

—Pierre Lecomte du Noüy.*

---

* Pierre Lecomte du Noüy, *Human Destiny* (New York: David McKay Co., Inc., 1947), pp. 5–6.

ence with" may have built up a store of common-sense answers.

Since there are any number of things one might know about man's behavior and any number of ways of gaining such information (or information about anything else, for that matter), it follows that all experiences do not produce the same knowledge. Studying man scientifically is a unique experience. Because Citizen Jones has had considerable experience with upper-class people, it does not follow that he necessarily has scientific knowledge about them. On another level, the fact that Housewife Jones has had experience with electric refrigerators does not make her an electrical engineer. She may, in fact, have had years of experience with refrigerators without ever really understanding very much about refrigeration. Co-ed Jones is not necessarily an authority on mechanics just because she has had long experience of one type or another with cars. The fact that an individual has had considerable experience with a minority group, say, the American Indians, does not mean that his understanding of Indians is a scientific one. Ample evidence indicates that individuals with much experience with certain types of people may, in fact, believe many things about their behavior that are quite contrary to scientific findings. It is likewise true that having had extensive experience with yourself does not mean that you have scientific knowledge about yourself. The student who goes through a college course in sociology or psychology may find that his interpretations of his own behavior change considerably as he progresses through this study.

If our premise about the relationships between science and common sense is true, the typical student can anticipate having some of his beliefs about human behavior challenged and others confirmed. When such contradictions arise, the student should approach the situation with the questions: "How does the author of this text support his premise?" "What proof is there on this issue?" One of the basic purposes of science is to provide individuals who have conflicting views with a method of resolving their differences, so long as these dif-

ferences apply to an area to which the scientific method is applicable.

To repeat, the scientific study of human behavior is a unique experience. To have had many non-scientific experiences with people does not qualify a person as a *scientific* student of human behavior. Becoming a social scientist is a long, difficult process.

ALL SOCIOLOGISTS ARE NOT EQUALLY SCIENTIFIC

The scientific orientation which has just been discussed has not always been as pronounced in sociology as it is today. Early sociologists were more "armchair-oriented," although they did begin to pay attention to social variables which had escaped the attention of others. Although there can be no question that sociology

---

Revised Maxims

Penny wise is inflation foolish.

Waste not and there will be no work.

A dollar saved is a quarter earned.

Honesty is the best policy without general coverage.

What goes up must come down—if it can solve the re-entry problem.

If Detroit had meant people to walk, it would have manufactured shoes.

Eyesight is only skin-deep.

Why start at the bottom of the ladder? Take the escalator.

A rolling stone gathers no pension.

Early to bed and early to rise, probably indicates unskilled employment.

A taxpayer and his money are soon parted.
                                    —John Ciardi.*

---

* John Ciardi, in *Saturday Review* (May 26, 1962), 194. Used with permission.

has moved strongly into the scientific "camp," the student should remember, as he begins to explore sociological journals and books, that not everyone who carries the title of "sociologist" is equally scientific. Our subsequent discussion of just what it is that makes a study scientific should help the student in his evaluation of writing and research to decide whether an author is scientifically oriented or not.

SOCIOLOGY IS A NEW AREA OF STUDY

Historically, sociology is one of the newer disciplines. The establishment of separate sociology departments in American universities was initiated in 1876, in France in 1889, and in Great Britain in 1907. Universities in Poland and India took such steps after World War I, Egypt and Mexico in 1925, and Sweden in 1947.[3] In the United States, sociology was first accepted at Yale, Columbia, and Chicago. It spread throughout the midwest and then gradually across the entire country, until today all major universities include sociology as an area of study.

Sociology acquired its name from the nineteenth-century Frenchman Auguste Comte, who felt that the various sciences followed one another historically in a logical sequence, with the science of human behavior appearing last. While it may be questioned whether the sequence Comte outlined is or was inevitable, the area of social behavior is one of the last to which man has turned his scientific curiosity. This may have stemmed from a fear of what he might find, from a feeling that human behavior was so different from other areas that the scientific method would not apply, from the assumption that society already had the important answers about human behavior and that further research in the area was unneces-

---

[3] *Teaching in the Social Sciences* (Paris: UNESCO, 1954), p. 23. For an account of the development of sociology in the United States, see Roscoe C. Hinkle, Jr., and Gisela J. Hinkle, *The Development of Modern Sociology* (New York: Random House, Inc., 1954).

Public Acceptance of Sociological Findings

Should . . . systematic inquiry only confirm what has been widely assumed . . . [the sociologist] will, of course be charged with "laboring the obvious." He becomes tagged as a bore, telling only what everybody knows. Should investigation find that widely held social beliefs are untrue . . . he is a heretic, questioning value-laden verities. If he ventures to examine socially implausible ideas that turn out to be untrue, he is a fool, wasting efforts on a line of inquiry not worth pursuing in the first place. And finally, if he should turn up some implausible truths, he must be prepared to find himself regarded as a charlatan, claiming as knowledge what is patently false. Instances of each of these alternatives have occurred in the history of many sciences, but they would seem especially apt to occur in a discipline, such as sociology, that deals with matters about which men have firm opinions presumably grounded in their own experiences.

—Robert K. Merton.*

---

sary, or from any number of other sources. Whatever the reasons, the scientific study of social man by man is of fairly recent origin and Comte was an early advocate of this study.

Comte also called attention to the fact that man's study of man has typically proceeded from the theological approach to the scientific approach. This pattern was evident in early American sociology; many of the early sociologists came to sociology from religion.

Subsequent chapters will point out that the introduction of new elements into an on-going social system frequently produces difficulties and necessitates a readjustment of the whole system. Anything new runs the risk of being misunderstood, of being challenged and being

---

* Robert K. Merton, "Notes on Problem-Finding in Sociology," in Robert K. Merton, *et al.* (eds.), *Sociology Today* (New York: Basic Books, Inc., 1959), xv–xvi.

labeled a "disturber in Israel." The history of sociology is a case in point. The introduction of sociology into the academic world, as well as into the broader society, has not been accomplished without difficulties. Well-established disciplines have questioned its worth. Established alignments of academic areas have had to be changed to permit its introduction. Administrative problems have been created. Questions are still being raised in the 1960's as to whether sociology is *really* a science, and sociological answers are still viewed with skepticism in some other areas. Understanding this, the student should not be particularly surprised if he finds that the analysis of human behavior provided in some particular college class does not coincide with that given in his sociology class. To expect such harmony from the various areas, each with its own unique approach, suggests a lack of understanding as to just what a university is as well as the level of achievement in the various areas.

The new product "sociology" has had to compete with the better-established "brand names" not only in the university but also in the marketplace. Employers have at times been hesitant about hiring students with a sociology major because they did not fully understand what sociology was. Much of this introductory "spadework" has already been accomplished, but being new, sociology is still in the "process of becoming." The student may find it interesting as he progresses through this text to compare his understanding of sociology with that of individuals from his parents' generation.

Since the science of sociology is still young in comparison with other sciences, many changes will likely be introduced as new research is undertaken and as new theories are developed. Certainly sociology in mid-twentieth century is quite different from sociology when Cooley, Sumner, Small, and other early American sociologists were introducing it to American college students. Sociologists today are not in complete agreement about all aspects of their area of study. Many lively controversies have not by any means been resolved.

SOCIOLOGY IS A DIFFICULT SCIENCE

Many characteristics of sociology make it a difficult area of study. We have space to look briefly at a few of them.

Sociology studies values. By values we mean, in over-simplified terms, the ideas people have about what is good and what is bad. One of the most difficult aspects of the study of sociology is the manner in which sociologists handle values. This aspect is so broad and crucial, in fact, that we will later devote an entire chapter to the subject. Here we will merely point out that the social scientist studies the values that people accept—such as the belief that it is good to marry primarily for love, or that gambling is evil—without concerning himself with whether these values are right or whether the group should accept these values. Many people feel, however, that since the social scientist studies values such as these, he is, in fact, challenging or questioning their ideas about what is good and bad. In reality he is not. It is difficult, however, to limit one's study of values, as does the sociologist, to identification of values without going beyond this to the question whether particular values are the correct ones. Since the sociologist is not concerned as a scientist with the question as to which values are the right ones, it is difficult for the beginning student to think in a similar manner and eliminate such considerations as he does his sociological explorations. Further, just to study commonly accepted values may cause some people to look with suspicion upon the one doing such a study.

The value of sociology is questioned. The student beginning his study of sociology as a science is faced with many problems which do not confront the student of a physical science. The chemistry student, for instance, is not faced with the question whether or not it is moral to study chemicals and manipulate chemicals in a particular way. The physics student lives in a society which generally feels that using the scientific method in the study of the physical world is desirable and practical. Our society agreed some time ago that it prefers to study chemicals scientifically rather than to rely upon philosophical speculation, pray to a supernatural source, or rely upon political or other authority to secure answers in this area. Sociology does not receive the same degree of social acceptance.

Sociology and common sense do not always agree. Sociology may challenge beliefs about aspects of human behavior that have previously been accepted without question. Many individuals find such questioning uncomfortable to live with. One way to escape such uncomfortable situations is simply not to engage in scientific study, but rather to accept the premise that one already has the answers (the really important ones, anyway) and thus strive to defend them against any evidence that contradicts them. Individuals with this orientation question the importance of sociological investigation and may directly or indirectly impede research and study.

The sociologist in a sense studies himself. Because the researcher is also the researched and we, as sociologists, are directly or indirectly studying ourselves the study of sociology is difficult. Some persons have taken the position that it is impossible, under these conditions, to engage in any meaningful and accurate research. Man studied almost everything else with his scientific method earlier and more extensively than he studied himself. The scientific study of man may challenge some cherished beliefs that we have about ourselves and thereby become threatening to us. Learning how to study oneself and one's groups scientifically is a difficult task that requires effort and time.

Terms are difficult. Even the term "sociology" is sometimes confusing. A sociologist may be equated with a "socialist." Of course there is no relationship between these two terms. Sociology is an area of study, whereas a socialist is one who endorses a particular type of government. Our discussion of pure and applied scientists has suggested that as pure scientists we are not concerned with attempting to establish any particular type of government. If

The Sociologist

. . . The sociologist . . . is a person intensively, endlessly, shamelessly interested in the doings of men. His natural habitat is all the human gathering places of the world, wherever men come together. The sociologist may be interested in many other things. But his consuming interest remains in the world of men, their institutions, their history, their passions. And since he is interested in men, nothing that men do can be altogether tedious for him. He will naturally be interested in the events that engage men's ultimate beliefs, their moments of tragedy and grandeur and ecstasy. But he will also be fascinated by the commonplace, the everyday. He will know reverence, but this reverence will not prevent him from wanting to see and to understand. He may sometimes feel revulsion or contempt. But this also will not deter him from wanting to have his questions answered.

—Peter L. Berger.*

this distinction between the role of scientist and the role of citizen is a confusing one at the moment, our subsequent chapter on roles should help to clear it up.

Sociologists have also utilized in their work terms that have already been given other non-sociological definitions by society. The student should be alert to the fact that key sociological concepts have unique definitions, even though they carry common labels. Confusion results from concluding that the familiar definitions of such terms as culture, role, society, and institution are the same as the *sociological* definitions.

SOURCE MATERIAL

Our discussion of science and common sense has already implied that most popular magazines containing articles written for the average person are usually not adequate sources of

* From *Invitation to Sociology,* by Peter L. Berger. Copyright © 1963 by Peter L. Berger. Reprinted by permission of Doubleday & Co., Inc.

scientific information about human behavior. Such sources tend to over-simplify and are not accurate enough for scientific purposes, even when they present the findings of scientific research.

This text will refer to many of the major sociological works; the instructor will, no doubt, add more. In addition to these sources, the student is referred to the following journals in which he can find reports of current research and thinking in the area of sociology. A perusal of any of these journals will suggest areas of specialized interest in sociology as well as the methods utilized in studying these areas.

American Catholic Sociological Review
American Journal of Sociology
American Sociological Review
Annals of the American Academy of Political and Social Science
Behavioral Science
British Journal of Sociology
Current Sociology
Journal of Abnormal and Social Psychology
Journal for the Scientific Study of Religion
Marriage and Family Living
Midwest Sociologist
Pacific Sociological Review
Review of Religious Research
Rural Sociology
Social Forces
Social Problems
Sociological Abstracts
Sociology and Social Research
Sociometry
Southwest Social Science Quarterly
trans-action

VALUES OF STUDYING SOCIOLOGY

The major goal of sociology is to gain an understanding of the social behavior of man, or how man relates himself to other men (the structure of society) and the results of such interaction. In pursuing this goal, the student can expect to find in this text (1) generalizations about such interaction (sociology is a generalizing science), (2) reports of research, theory, and other information supporting these generalizations, all of which should serve to

(3) increase his understanding of his society in particular and of societies in general and of himself as an interacting member of society.

SUMMARY

We have defined sociology as the scientific study of human interaction. Our discussion of the key concepts "scientific," "human," and "interaction" emphasized (1) that the scientific nature of sociology distinguishes it from such approaches as the literary, religious, philosophical, judicial, and common-sense; (2) our concern with "human" behavior excludes any extensive consideration of the behavior of lower animals; and (3) most behavior of man is social behavior in that it involves interaction with others. In that we study interaction, our approach is called *interactionism* (anti-reductionism) with the term identifying the level at which research, theory, and discussion will be placed. It is recognized, of course, that study at other levels is done for other purposes. From our sociological perspective, however, such study remains tangential rather than central to the type of answers we seek.

The scientific nature of our study is shared by other social sciences. Brief distinctions were accordingly provided between sociology and psychology, anthropology, economics, and political science, which emphasized the interactionist perspective of sociology and its generalizing nature. We further classified sociology as a pure rather than an applied science.

The distinction between scientific answers and common-sense answers was discussed, with emphasis upon the fact that disagreement is frequently found. This is so because not all experience is *scientific experience* and not all knowledge is scientific knowledge. Scientific sociology, then, provides only one of many different answers available today as to why man does what he does.

Being a relatively new area of study, sociology has had its "growing pains" in establishing itself in both the academic and the non-academic world. Some problems still exist.

Sociology is a difficult area of study because, in addition to the reasons enumerated above, it studies values and involves a person in studying himself. Confusion sometimes exists between the common and the sociological meaning of some of the basic terms used.

In his study of sociology the student may expect to gain, from the generalizations and research reports presented, increased understanding of the interaction which takes place in society in general as well as in the particular society of which he himself is a part.

QUESTIONS

1. What is the basic thing to which sociologists pay attention in their study?
2. What type of answers does a generalizing science seek?
3. What are the major goals of sociology?
4. Can scientific answers be provided to questions about what society should do? Why?
5. How is sociology different from social work?
6. What is the difference between pure (basic) and applied science?
7. How do you explain the fact that the answers to questions about human behavior which college students receive in various classes do not always harmonize?
8. Explain the statement that sociology is not the same as common sense.
9. When faced with contradictory statements about human behavior, how does the sociologist attempt to resolve the conflict?
10. Why should the introductory sociology student be careful how he defines sociological concepts?

PROJECT

Examine a current issue of one of the journals listed in the chapter and list the various types of subject matter discussed.

SUGGESTED READING

CAMERON, WILLIAM B. *Informal Sociology.* New York: Random House, Inc., 1963; Paperback, SS21.

COOLEY, CHARLES H. *Social Organization.* New York: Charles Scribner's Sons, 1920.

COSER, LEWIS A. (ed.) *Sociology Through Literature.* Englewood Cliffs, N. J.: Prentice-Hall, Inc., 1963.

HINKLE, ROSCOE C., JR., and GISELA J. HINKLE. *The Development of Modern Sociology.* New York: Random House, Inc., 1954. Chap. vi.

INKELES, ALEX. *What Is Sociology?* Englewood Cliffs, N. J.: Prentice-Hall, Inc., 1964.

LIPSET, S. M., and NEIL J. SMELSER (eds.). *Sociology: The Progress of a Decade.* Englewood Cliffs, N. J.: Prentice-Hall, Inc., 1961.

LUNDBERG, GEORGE A. *Foundations of Sociology.* New York: The Macmillan Co., 1939.

LUNDBERG, GEORGE A. *Foundations of Sociology.* New York: David McKay Co., Inc., 1964. A revised and abridged edition of Part I of the Macmillan 1939 publication.

MERTON, ROBERT K., LEONARD BROOM, and LEONARD S. COTTRELL, JR. (eds.). *Sociology Today.* New York: Basic Books, Inc., 1959.

MILLS, C. WRIGHT. *The Sociological Imagination.* Fair Lawn, N. J.: Oxford University Press, 1959.

PARSONS, TALCOTT. "Some Problems Confronting Sociology as a Profession," *American Sociological Review,* XXIV, No. 4 (August, 1959), 547–559.

WILLIAMS, ROBIN M., JR. "Continuity and Change in Sociological Study," *American Sociological Review,* XXIII, No. 6 (December, 1958), 619–633.

Part II

The Sociological Approach

2

The Norms of Science

Many different answers are available to questions about human behavior. How can one know which of these answers are secured scientifically and which are not? Even more important, how can one tell when the same individual is speaking as a scientist and when he is not?

INTRODUCTION

Human interaction is a complex phenomenon involving many interrelated elements, one of which is man's knowledge. The study of this particular phenomenon and of how it is involved in his behavior is called the sociology of knowledge, and includes such topics as the identification of various types of knowledge, the processes by which knowledge is acquired, and its organization and distribution. This chapter is a part of the sociology of knowledge: attention is centered on the process by which one type of knowledge—scientific knowledge—is acquired.

A major conclusion of the sociology of knowledge is that the type of answer one gets to a question is always relative to the method he utilizes to secure that answer. Different methods of investigation do not always produce identical answers to the same question. Parents, for example, do not always arrive at the same answers as their children concerning such questions as the worth of a new piano, whether children should eat all the candy they want, how long it would take to travel 1,000 miles by car,

or even what time of day it is. Children do not use the same method or take into account the same variables as adults.

In Chapter 1 a major distinction was made between the sociologist and the philosopher, theologian, novelist, poet, or lawyer, in the method each uses in coming to a decision about the behavior of man. Sociology attempts to be scientific in its approach; these other disciplines follow another, non-scientific approach. Since the approaches are different, the answers derived by these different disciplines are also frequently different.

This chapter is designed to provide a broad understanding of the rules of science so that the student can understand the answers provided by the scientific method. Subsequent discussions of the sociological explanations of man's behavior will be more understandable if we clearly indicate the advantages and the limitations of the scientific method; it cannot be used to secure *all* of the answers in which one might be interested. The student should also understand some of the qualifications surrounding the available scientific answers and the several steps involved in securing those answers. He may

American Scientists

During the past three centuries world population has doubled every 10 or 15 years. But the portion of the population composed of scientists of all kinds has increased 10-fold. Because of this exponential growth, 90 percent of all scientists who ever lived are alive today.

It is further estimated that 75 percent of those who write one scientific paper let it go at that, whereas 10 percent of the authors are highly prolific and produce approximately half of the world's scientific literature.

—Paul Zinner.*

do some tentative thinking as to just how he would go about checking scientifically some aspect of behavior in which he is interested.

We might digress briefly to comment on the word "norms" used in the chapter title, and indicate that in many areas of human behavior man develops shared ideas on how certain things should be done, and evaluates behavior—at least in part—by these expectations. "Norm" or "norm definition" is the sociological term which has been used to label such expectations. The rules and regulations of scientific endeavors are an illustration of "norms" and the term is an appropriate one to apply to the material discussed in this chapter. Anyone who wants to do scientific work has to learn the norms or norm definitions of science before he can very effectively "play the role" (to use another term which will be discussed in greater detail later on).

SCIENCE IS METHOD—NOT CONTENT

If "science" is a term which can properly be used to describe such varied disciplines as chemistry, astronomy, biology, psychology, anthropology, and sociology (and many others), what is the element shared by all of these disciplines and identified by use of this term? The

common element is the method utilized in coming to decisions about subject matter. It is not *what* one studies that makes a study scientific; it is *how* one studies whatever he studies. Science refers to method of study, not content of study.

The scientific method is a way of understanding some phenomenon; it is not the manner in which this phenomenon behaves. A rock falling from a cliff does not behave scientifically in following the law of falling bodies. The individual determining its rate of fall, however, behaves in a scientific manner. Likewise, the study of delinquent behavior does not make the delinquent behavior scientific, nor does the scientific study of religion imply that religious behavior is *ergo* scientific behavior. Further, the terms "natural science" and "social science" are somewhat misleading because by using the words "natural" and "social" to qualify "science" it may seem that science is either natural or social rather than the subject matter to which the scientific method is applied. The distinction may also be misleading if one concludes that the social behavior of man is somehow "unnatural." [1]

In any case, it is the method of study which is identified when a discipline is labeled "scientific."

SCIENTIFIC METHOD REQUIRES RELIANCE UPON EMPIRICAL PHENOMENA TO TEST AN HYPOTHESIS

To come to a decision about his subject matter, the scientist investigates something which exists outside of himself and is available to his senses. Such phenomena are called empirical phenomena. He does not come to a decision on the basis of his internal "feelings" or because he "believes in" something. Rather he manipulates or observes the empirical objects of study and on the basis of what happens to these empirical objects comes to his decision about them. Scientific answers are obtained

---

* Paul Zinner, "The Noise Level of Science," *American Scientist*, LI, No. 3 (September, 1963), 238A.

[1] Harry Alpert, "The Fallacy of the Misplaced Qualifier," *American Sociological Review*, XXV, No. 3 (June, 1960), 406.

from empirical phenomena available to others, through a method available to others; they are not "private" answers.

As a simple illustration, if a scientist wants to determine how many teeth a horse has, he does not come to a conclusion by sitting down and logically reasoning that a horse must have a certain number of teeth. Rather, he counts the teeth of horses. Or, if he wants to find out something about the family behavior patterns of mid-century Americans, he does research on family behavior patterns, rather than making a decision introspectively.[2]

The scientist cannot study fairies or ghosts, since there is nothing in the empirical world which he can investigate in such a study. He cannot see, feel, weigh, or in any other manner observe or manipulate ghosts in order to come to a decision about them. The realm of the supernatural, which is an integral part of religion, also falls outside of the realm of science. If one wants answers to questions about angels *per se*, he cannot secure them through scientific study, since there is no empirical phenomenon available. Angels are by definition not observable—they are superempirical.

An important distinction should be emphasized at this point. The scientist can study ideas (definitions) about such things as angels and ghosts through either the verbal or the written symbols (language) of man. These are empirical and thus fall within the limits of his scientific study. Obviously, studying ideas about ghosts and studying ghosts *per se* are two different things. The first falls within the domain of science, the second does not.

Further, some of the concepts used in popular explanations of human behavior have to be discarded by the scientist because there seem to be no empirical phenomena available if he wants to study them. Let us use the concept "instinct" as an illustration. Assume (as it was held at one time) that human behavior is caused by instincts that exist inside of man. If a scientist is to support this premise, he is faced with the question of deciding how he is going to observe an instinct. To what does he pay attention? How does he look at, hear, weigh, or feel this "thing"? How does he check to see whether, in fact, instincts do "cause" human behavior? If he is going to pay attention to empirical phenomena he finds that as far as he can tell there just are no such "things" as instincts. He rejects this concept, then, just as the physical scientists rejected the concept of phlogiston which was presumably a "thing" which caused wood and other combustible substances to burn. His explanations of human behavior cannot involve this concept if he wants to stay within the bounds of science. One can, however, stay within the bounds of science and say that some behavior pattern is *instinctive*. All that is said here is that the behavior is unlearned. The term is used in a descriptive sense, and nothing is said about what *caused* the behavior.[3]

The scientific method of study is by no means the only one available to man. Other methods, such as philosophical or common-sense methods, are frequently used to secure many of the answers in which man is interested. Such methods may utilize concepts which the scientific method cannot.

Empirical phenomena are external to the scientist, and they are available to his senses. If he cannot establish sensory contacts with these objects, even though they may exist independently of him, such objects are not empirical, as we are using the word, and consequently are not available for scientific study. If it is true, for instance, that a supernatural realm which is different from the natural realm does exist, but in a form different from the natural, this realm would be non-empirical. As our chapter on religion points out, aspects of religion dealing with the supernatural are not capable of scientific investigation, since the phenomena involved

---

[2] It is recognized, of course, that in the last measure the "decision" to which he comes is an "internal" or individual thing, and in this sense his method is that of introspection. However, it is important to recognize that in science the manipulation or observation of some aspect of the empirical world is a necessary antecedent condition to his "internal" decision-making.

[3] See George A. Lundberg, *Foundations of Sociology* (New York: The Macmillan Co., 1939), pp. 10–11.

are non-empirical (*non-* or *super*natural). It might help to reiterate that stated *ideas about* the supernatural are empirical and can be studied scientifically.

Another point should be added: beliefs or definitions are developed through sensory experiences of one type or another, or through contacts which are "available to the senses." Contact with *ideas about* ghosts or angels, however, is quite different from contacts with angels or ghosts *per se*. Further, just because all experience is sensory it does not follow that in all experience the human individual behaves scientifically. Scientific behavior requires that one pay attention to empirical phenomena—those external to the researcher and available to his senses. Both aspects of the definition of "empirical" are necessary.

What, then, are the major empirical phenomena to which the sociologist pays attention? *Human beings interacting with each other.* Special attention is given to verbal or symbolic interaction, thereby including within our area of study the ideas or definitions which man has about the world and about others involved in the interaction of which he is a part. Other objects are, of course, also involved.

Since the scientist pays attention to empirical phenomena which exist outside of the researcher and are available to his senses, he is wary of using his own personal experiences, in which scientific research was not involved as the basis for conclusions. As one gets involved in scientific research, it becomes clear that individuals, on the basis of their own experiences, have come to all sorts of contradictory conclusions about the universe in which they live and the people who interact therein. However, a strong personal conviction that the world is flat does not make the world flat. Or, just because one's personal experiences have led him to conclude that punishment is the most effective way to get children to conform to socially approved norms, it does not follow that punishment does, in fact, produce these results.

Restricting decisions to the results obtained when empirical phenomena are manipulated in an objective manner reduces the likelihood that decisions will be made on the basis of non-scientific "personal" experiences. Such restrictions likewise increase the possibility that other scientists can and will check these observations in their verification endeavors, and thus detect any tendency to "see what we want to see" in observations of the empirical world. The sociologist as a scientist, then, is not concerned with whether he or anyone else "believes in" his conclusions, in the sense that one believes in a particular value position or a religious dogma. He is concerned with the empirical evidence that has a bearing upon a question, recognizing that such evidence may even contradict certain beliefs.

The beginning student should be aware that some of the conclusions to which he has come on the basis of his own past experiences may not coincide with the conclusions presented by the sociologist. Conflicts stemming from such different interpretations can sometimes be resolved by raising the question a scientist would: "Upon what evidence have these contradictory conclusions been based?" Advancement in developing the skills of the sociologist (playing the role of the sociologist) will, in fact, be facilitated, if the student develops the habit of consistently asking: "Upon what evidence does this conclusion rest?"

When conflicting answers are available, those who are willing to accept scientific evidence are willing to alter their decisions accordingly. Those who are not willing to accept scientific evidence—and there are many in this category—may maintain their previous decisions despite scientific evidence to the contrary. Illustrations of this behavior are found every day in the average individual's experiences. There are, of course, important types of decisions upon which no scientific evidence can be obtained. These of necessity must be reached by some method other than the scientific. Decisions about the supernatural realm *per se* and about "goodness and badness" are in this category.

What has been presented here is a somewhat idealized statement of the behavior of scientists. Scientists themselves have frequently resisted scientific advancement. Vested interests de-

Symbols and Science

The symbols man uses at first to represent the world are oral, and very little scientific development is possible as long as this is true. Many of the things that scientists wish to communicate simply cannot be adequately transmitted through oral language. The structure of the idea which scientists must communicate is so complex that it cannot be matched in a succession of acoustic stimuli. Consequently, the language of science must increasingly consist of written graphic symbols, which provide an enduring instead of an immediately vanishing stimulus, and offer possibilities of arrangement (tabulation, etc.) that cannot be communicated in oral language.

—George A. Lundberg.*

velop within scientific areas. Scientists get involved in the social structure of a university, a research agency, or a business enterprise, and engage in activities to enhance their prestige. For these and other reasons resistance sometimes exists within the ranks of scientists themselves.[4] To find such a situation on a college campus may be disturbing to the student. For those who find themselves in an atmosphere of resistance, one approach to any problem of this kind is to ask "Upon what evidence do these contradictory conclusions rest?" and resolve the disagreement on the basis of this evidence. From such procedures are neophyte scientists developed.

Because an individual is scientific in his decisions about the empirical world, it does not follow that he is scientific in all of his decisions. An individual is not scientific, for instance, in deciding to become a scientist or in deciding to study economic behavior rather than political behavior. Science is a method of coming to a

decision about the empirical world external to the scientist, but not about the behavior of the scientist himself. Just because an individual is scientific in his research about atoms or human groups, it does not follow that he is scientific in *all* of his behavior, such as in deciding which girl he will marry, which car he will drive, which church he will attend, or whether he will eat pork chops or chop suey for dinner. The scientific method, in fact, cannot be used in obtaining many important answers even though it is a scientist who makes the decision. Further, a decision to use any particular method of study is arrived at through some method other than the scientific one.[5]

SCIENTIFIC METHOD INVOLVES BEING OBJECTIVE

Objectivity is the ability and willingness to study the empirical phenomena of a given field without prejudice or bias.[6] The scientist wants to discover the characteristics of the world as they are, not as he might wish them to be, or to discover the characteristics which obtain completely independently of himself. His effort is to discover what these characteristics would be if he, in fact, did not exist. Presumably, two atoms of H and one atom of O will, when combined, produce water regardless of who observes them or of the beliefs and opinions of observers. The scientist seeks such information. Being objective involves trying to discover what is "out there" regardless of what goes on "inside" the researcher. In a technical sense, this is most likely a goal impossible of achievement, since it is logical to assume that the mere fact of observation is a variable involved in the situation. This is particularly true of human behavior. The scientist, however, attempts to standardize the influence of the observer upon the behavior

* George A. Lundberg, *Foundations of Sociology* (New York: David McKay Co., Inc., 1964), p. 57.

[4] See, for instance, Bernard Barber, "Resistance by Scientists to Scientific Discovery," *Science,* CXXXIV (September, 1961), 596–602.

[5] LaMar T. Empey, "Pure Science and Sociology," *Sociological Inquiry,* XXXIV, No. 1 (Winter, 1964), 3–12.

[6] See Max Weber, *The Methodology of the Social Sciences,* trans. by Edward S. Shils and Henry A. Finch (New York: The Free Press of Glencoe, Inc., 1949), "Objectivity in Social Science and Social Policy," pp. 49–112.

under observation. Further sophistication in research techniques may include methods of taking the process of observation into account in explanations of the observed behaviors.[7]

Being objective involves coming to a decision on the basis of what happens to the empirical phenomena under investigation after the study has been done, rather than reaching the decision on some other grounds, such as preconceptions, loyalty to others or to certain goals, emotional attachment to others or to ideas, etc. If one is objective, he waits until after the study is done and then comes to his decision on the basis of the empirical data. The antithesis of objectivity is characterized by the statement: "Don't bother me with the facts. I've already made up my mind."

Objectivity is possible in scientific investigation, partly because of the requirement of restricting attention to empirical phenomena. If one's attention is restricted to the empirical world, he is able to meet this requirement of objectivity by coming to his decision on the basis of what happens to this empirical world. If, however, we attempt to come to decisions about non-empirical "things" such as heaven or hell, goodness or badness, beauty, etc., then it is impossible to meet the requirements of objectivity. Such endeavors require that some other method be used; one method is reliance upon *authority*. Thus, if one wants to decide whether the Mona Lisa is a beautiful picture, one way to decide this is to ask the authorities in the field of art. If one cannot agree with the authorities, or if the authorities do not agree among themselves, these differences of opinions cannot be resolved by the scientific method. This is one reason, of course, why there is so much disagreement on matters of beauty and why we are more likely to develop a universal science than a universal religion.

Being objective is a behavior pattern that is not particularly easy to acquire. Much of our

experience, in fact, prepares us to be subjective. The development of group attachments, as well as personal likes and dislikes, hinders one in his efforts to be objective. Most of us have all sorts of preferences and loyalties which we feel called upon to defend. We may have some strong convictions, for instance, that our group is the best group (the sociological term for this is "ethnocentrism"), that certain things are good and certain things are bad, that we should do certain things and avoid other things, etc. Actually, none of these conclusions can be arrived at scientifically. They are, however, extremely important dimensions of human behavior.

The scientific method cannot be used in making such decisions, but it does not require anyone to abandon such beliefs, and neither does it say that it is wrong to have any of these beliefs. All that is asked is that the researcher does not let these definitions influence his observations and conclusions. He is asked to be objective.

At this point we can anticipate a future discussion of roles. We are saying that when one plays the role of a scientist he is expected to behave in a manner which in some respects is quite different from other role behavior—that of a father, child, citizen, or fraternity member. The behavior appropriate for one role may be quite inappropriate for another. We are merely specifying one of the role requirements of the scientist.

Even more important, however, is the fact that human beings tend to see what they have been prepared to see or what they want to see, and thus, very literally, may not see what is "right before their eyes." This point will be discussed in some detail in a subsequent chapter, and if the statement seems a bit unrealistic the student is asked to reserve final judgment until after the supporting evidence has been presented. We can anticipate this evidence somewhat by briefly suggesting here that the behavior of an individual under hypnosis provides supporting evidence that is sometimes dramatic. The hypnotized individual can see, hear, or feel what he is told to see, hear, or feel. In one degree or another, much of our behavior

[7] See, for instance, Theodore M. Mills, "A Sleeper Variable in Small Group Research: The Experimenter," *Pacific Sociological Review*, V, No. 1 (Spring, 1962), 21–28.

is like this, and to develop the ability to view the world as it is, rather than as one may wish it to be, or has been previously taught that it is, is frequently difficult.

To develop the quality of objectivity several things can be done. Understanding of what objectivity is and to which aspects of life it can be applied is the first requirement. Constantly asking oneself upon what evidence a conclusion rests also helps. If the conclusion is derived from empirical research and is supported by the behavior of empirical phenomena, then it is likely to be objective.

Measuring devices of one type or another are also helpful. To find out how tall an individual is, it helps if one has a yardstick. To find out how heavy a piece of rock is, it helps to have a scale of some sort. If it is being questioned whether a particular society has anti-American attitudes, it helps to have an anti-American attitude "scale" to use. To find out the intelligence quotient of an individual or a group, I.Q. tests are helpful. Such tools increase the likelihood that the researcher will be objective. Illustrations of the types of tools used by current social scientists will be found throughout this text. We might suggest, however, that most tools in use at this time are rather crude, with the conclusions derived from their use likewise being rather crude.

Our discussion of the requirements for observation or manipulation of empirical phenomena has implied one of the basic postulates of scientific procedure. The scientific method rests upon the assumptions that *uniformities* do exist in the universe and that they can be detected by objective observation. If uniformities did not exist in whatever was studied, about the only conclusion the scientist could reach as a result of his studies would be that he could not come to any definite conclusions using his method.

VERIFICATION

Reliance upon empirical phenomena, observed objectively, permits and facilitates the next requirement of the scientific method—veri-

fication. Scientists are constantly checking and rechecking each other's work. Only when particular results have been verified by others does the scientist conclude that he has discovered a scientific *truth* or *law*. Many journals publish the findings of scientific research, usually indicating the steps the scientist went through in order to reach his conclusions, so that other scientists can verify his research and relate it to other research and theories being used. Conferences wherein scientists report their research serve a similar function.

Where verification is not obtained, the scientific method requires a re-examination of the methods, tools, and theories involved, in an effort to "iron out" the difficulties and perfect the conclusions.

DEFINITIONS OF TERMS

Scientific achievement is related to the exactness with which significant terms can be defined. Obviously, verification of previous work is handicapped to the extent that there is uncertainty as to just what was done or what was studied. Interpretation of research is likewise hampered to the extent that unclear concepts are involved. The scientist accordingly attempts to specify precisely the meaning of the terms he uses. Sometimes he must develop new terms to stand for the objects, the processes, or the relationships involved in his research. Or he may take terms which already have one or more definitions established and more or less accepted, and provide yet another technical definition. Confusion sometimes results when nontechnical definitions are used in interpretation or in subsequent research. As was pointed out in the previous chapter, in the development of sociology several terms of this latter type have been used. The student should be aware that his understanding of sociology will be more complete if he makes sure that he does not confuse the technical sociological definitions with the more common definitions. Terms such as "culture," "society," "conflict," "role," and "group" are of this type.

Operational Definitions

Precision of meaning is increased if the scientist utilizes operational definitions, that is, if he specifies the operations or the sequence of steps he has used in observing particular phenomena. Thus, in a study of adult criminals, the scientist must first specify clearly how such criminals are to be recognized. One definition that has been used is that a criminal is anyone who has been adjudicated by the courts of the land. The operations involved, then, in identifying such individuals are to examine court records and on the basis of this examination distinguish criminals from non-criminals. The question may arise, however, as to the classification of adults who have broken the law but never been brought to court, or maybe not even been detected. Also, who is an adult and who isn't? Obviously, more refined definitions must be developed. The relevant point here is that the scientist must clearly specify the operations he goes through, in order to identify and define his universe of study. On his delineation of his work will depend its subsequent verification as well as the interpretation of his conclusions.

In setting up his research, the scientist is constantly concerned with the question: "To what and in what manner do I pay attention if I am going to study such and such?" Only when this question is clearly answered can he proceed with his research. This problem of operational definitions in the social sciences is highlighted by the question: "To what empirical phenomena do I pay attention if I want to study such things as mind, attitude, instinct, ego, superego, conscience, and emotions?" If an operational definition cannot be established, this should cause the scientist to question seriously the utility of such terms for his research, and should lead to the conclusion that perhaps many of the commonly accepted concepts are not usable in scientific endeavors. We have previously indicated that in sociology the empirical phenomena to which we pay attention are human behavior (plus empirical objects). The utility of our concepts, then, is enhanced if they are defined in terms of the human behavior involved therein.

PREDICTION

A major goal of the scientist is to study the relationships between empirical units. Once particular relationships have been established, he is then able to predict (within the limits of his data) subsequent relationships between these or similar units. Thus, the social scientist can predict such things as what will happen to the divorce rate in America during depressions or periods of prosperity. Similar predictions can be made with reference to crime and delinquency rates. He is able to predict the increase in the divorce rate that will result from an increase in interfaith marriages.

In the physical sciences and/or the social sciences, such predictions rest upon the condition that other variables will remain constant or fairly constant. The law of falling bodies, for instance, is true only in a vacuum. Under other conditions (and not many bodies fall in a vacuum outside of the laboratory) adjustments may have to be made if the prediction is to be at all accurate.

Cult of Unintelligibility

With the increasing complexity of scientific research, a long program of rigorous training is necessary to test or even to understand the new scientific findings. The modern scientist has necessarily subscribed to a cult of unintelligibility. There results an increasing gap between the scientist and the laity. The layman must take on faith the publicized statements about relativity or quanta or other such esoteric subjects.

—Robert K. Merton.*

---

* Robert K. Merton, *Social Theory and Social Structure* (rev. and enlarged ed.; New York: The Free Press of Glencoe, Inc., 1957), p. 546.

So far, the social sciences have not reached a stage of scientific advancement that enables them to do extensive prediction. Future studies should increase this ability. It should be emphasized, however, that human behavior is predictable. It is not uncommon to hear the suggestion, when sociology is labeled a science, that it can never be a science because human behavior is so unpredictable. This is not true. To provide some illustrations, which will be expanded considerably throughout the entire text, the sociology professor at the typical American university can predict with a high degree of accuracy that his students will show up at his classroom at the prescribed hour and will enter the room prepared to listen to a lecture or participate in a discussion on sociology. Further, they will carry on the discussion in the English language, and their notes will be written on their notebook paper from left to right. He can predict how they will be dressed, and also that no one will show up for class in the nude.

It is also possible right now to predict with some certainty that on December 24, American children will be looking forward to receiving Christmas gifts and not valentines, and that on February 14, there will be no decorated Christmas trees in American homes. It is unlikely that Christmas carols will be sung at the Easter church services, and parents who would never think of letting their children "beg" from their neighbors, on an autumn evening will help their children dress up in ridiculous clothes and allow them to threaten their neighbors with a trick unless they are given a treat.

Not many Americans will *want to* shoot off fire crackers in December, although many will *want to* in July. Further, it is a safe prediction that not many American males will *want to* study hard to become witch doctors, although a certain percentage will *want to* study hard to become medical doctors or doctors of philosophy.

Actually, if the student will stop and analyze his own behavior, he will soon conclude that he is constantly predicting or anticipating the behavior of others and that he does so with a fairly high degree of accuracy. In terms of subsequent discussion he is constantly engaging in the process of "taking the role of the other" and adjusting his own behavior accordingly. In fact, social behavior is possible only because we are able to predict the behavior of others.

Recognizing this, a major goal of all scientific work is to be able to predict events upon the basis of antecedent research. In the study of human behavior, this appears to be an obtainable goal.

VALUE DEFINITIONS

How the sociologist handles value definitions is a key factor in deciding whether he is scientific or not. This value dimension is closely related to the qualities of empiricism and objectivity, previously discussed. An extended discussion of value definitions will be found in a subsequent chapter. Here we will merely relate in a broad manner how such definitions are related to the scientific method.

Briefly, value definitions are statements as to the relative worth of things. Our discussion will be primarily concerned with moral worth—whether some thing or some practice is defined as good or bad. The statement that cheating on a college exam is wrong is a value statement. The statement that it is good for children to honor their parents is also a value statement. Value definitions indicate the moral evaluation of something.

Science requires attention to empirical phenomena which exist outside of the individual and are available to his senses. Goodness and badness, then, as these terms are generally defined, cannot be studied by the scientist. Why? Because there is nothing empirical which one can investigate if he wants to study goodness. One cannot see, touch, feel, weigh, or taste goodness. The term "goodness" has no empirical referent. The scientist, then, is not concerned with whether something is good or bad. He cannot provide scientific answers to moral questions, although others playing different nonscientific roles, especially religious leaders, can do so. Answers to such questions can most assuredly be found, but not in science.

Science is amoral or non-ethical. One cannot be scientific in determining the accuracy of value definitions, although the scientist can study the value definitions that people endorse. The scientist can, for instance, study the values of Group X. He can find out whether they feel that capital punishment is good or bad. He is studying the behavior of the people involved—whether Group X defines this particular behavior as good or bad. He is not studying goodness or badness *per se*.

This discussion emphasizes one of the limitations of science. People who want answers to value questions cannot secure them through the scientific method. Since science requires empirical objects to study, it avoids values *per se*, and since the scientific method requires objectivity (lack of bias or prejudice—or, in part, lack of value judgments) the scientist avoids letting his value definitions enter into his observations and conclusions about his empirical objects of study. He tries to see what is there, independent of himself, rather than what his particular values might predispose him to see.

One of the most difficult aspects of being objective is to approach a study indifferent to whether the subject matter is good or bad, but concerned only with the empirical evidence. The physical scientist, for instance, is not concerned with whether it is good or bad for an airplane to be able to fly, but only with the variables that affect such a phenomenon. The social scientist, likewise, is not concerned with whether divorce is good or bad as he studies the factors related to divorce rates. He is not concerned with whether it is "good" to graduate from college when he studies the social factors affecting academic achievement. He is not concerned with whether Negroes should live next door to whites when he studies race relations. As the discussion of the pure and applied sciences in the previous chapter has suggested, the pure scientist is only trying to understand why specific things happen—not whether they are good or bad. Some things, of course, happen because those involved hold certain value positions. This the sociologist takes into account, but he does not attempt to determine whether these value positions are right or wrong.

EXACTNESS

Being exact generally increases the utility and the accuracy of prediction of a scientific study. Exactness *per se*, however, does not make something scientific, but exactness incorporated within the scientific method increases understanding.

Popular discussions frequently make extensive use of dichotomies. A dichotomy is a classification that divides whatever is under consideration into two—and only two—categories. It is either hot or cold, heavy or light, good or bad, black or white, big or small, virgin or non-virgin, etc. A dichotomy is an either–or statement. The scientist attempts to avoid dichotomies as much as possible because of their inexactness. If we divide everything into either a black or a white category, we ignore all the shades of grey in between. Or to take an illustration more closely related to the academic

---

Science and the Puritan Ethos

The Puritan ethic, as an ideal-typical expression of the value-attitudes basic to ascetic Protestantism generally so canalized the interests of seventeenth-century Englishmen as to constitute one important element in the enhanced cultivation of science. The deep-rooted religious interests of the day demanded in their forceful implications the systematic, rational, and empirical study of Nature for the glorification of God in His works and for the control of the corrupt world.

—Robert K. Merton.*

---

* Robert K. Merton, *Social Theory and Social Structure* (rev. and enlarged ed.; New York: The Free Press of Glencoe, Inc., 1957), pp. 574–575.

life of the student, if at the end of the sociology course all the students are divided into two categories—"passed" or "failed"—such a classification fails to distinguish between the different degrees of passing and lumps together the straight A student with the lowest C student. More meaningful studies can generally be done if measures more precise than dichotomies are used. Thus, rather than saying that a student is either tall or short, we can say that he is 5 feet 6½ inches tall, if we have a yardstick to use. Rather than saying that a student is "dumb" or "smart" we can determine that he has an I.Q. of 123. Scales which permit the researcher to distinguish differing degrees of the same condition are more useful to the scientist than dichotomies because they permit greater exactness. A scale that permits such distinctions of degree is called a *continuum*. Continuums will be used more extensively in the social sciences as they are developed and standardized, or when their utility in terms of prediction or understanding is demonstrated. Again, anticipating a future discussion, we can say that the behavior of any group is limited by the concepts and the tools it has developed. Sociologists as a group are no exception. They behave in terms of the concepts they have developed. Most sociologists today would agree that the discipline could use new concepts and new insights into human behavior. Great recognition is awaiting the sociologists who are creative enough to invent new concepts, or to show us how to look at or pay attention to human behavior in a different manner. Lundberg has indicated, for instance, that "sociologists are beginning to realize that improved symbolic instruments and tools may be as important in unscrambling human relations as are electron microscopes and cyclotrons in physics." [8] Development of new tools permits the development of new concepts and new research techniques. The reverse is also true in that the development of new concepts may lead to the development of new tools whereby the definition of the concept is standardized and involved in on-going research.

Exactness is also increased if the scientist, particularly the social scientist, qualifies his statements so that they are not more general than the data warrant. Thus, when he talks about groups, only a few broad statements about *all* groups can be made. If his evidence is drawn from middle-class American males, he cannot generalize to *all* males, or even to all American males. A study of twelve-year-old boys at a scout camp cannot generalize to all boys, or even to all twelve-year-old boys. The results of a study done in 1964 may not be applicable to the same group in 1974. Studies which find that something happens "on the average" cannot be generalized to include "all" of whatever is studied. Averaging "washes out" differences which are there in "all" cases. It is easy for one not trained in scientific work to generalize beyond his data.

CORRELATION

It is also easy to misinterpret the correlations which are frequently reported in scientific research. A correlation suggests that two variables are "co-related," or that the relationships studied are such that changes in one variable are associated with changes in another. A simple and familiar example is the correlation that exists between the height of human beings and their weight. Generally, as height increases, weight also increases. This relationship is sufficiently consistent that, with a certain margin of error, the weight of an individual can be predicted by knowing his height, and while the prediction for one individual may be way-off, the predictions for a large group of people will be more accurate. The relationship wherein one variable increases as the other variable increases is known as a *positive correlation*. The relationship wherein one variable increases as the other decreases is referred to as a *negative correlation*. An illustration of a negative cor-

[8] George A. Lundberg, "Quantitative Methods in Sociology: 1920–1960," *Social Forces*, XXXIX, No. 1 (October, 1960), 24.

relation from the field of sociology is that between the amount of family income and the number of children in the family. On the average, the higher the income, the lower the birth rate.

To understand the work of the scientist, it is important not to misinterpret statements of correlation. Such statements merely indicate how two or more variables are related to each other, but do not indicate *anything* about *cause* and *effect* relationships. A high relationship between two variables, A and B, does not prove that one is the cause of the other. A may be the cause of B, or B may be the cause of A, or both A and B may be caused by C or some other factor.

CAUSE

Actually, the concept of "cause" is a difficult one to handle. In the realm of human behavior, it would seem to be grossly inaccurate to think in terms of single or unit causation—that *one* factor is caused by only *one* other factor. The concept of *multiple causation* is more accurate: a causal explanation of any single unit of behavior must take into account multiple factors. To explain even the relatively simple fact that a reader is currently reading this book would seem to require that a multitude of factors be taken into account if any adequate explanation is to result. A few of these would be the belief of the student that he should get a good grade in his sociology class, or his belief that it would please his parents were he to get a good grade in the class, which is related, of course, to his belief that it is desirable to obtain a college degree, which is related to his belief that with a degree he will be able to get a better job, which is related to his belief that maximizing his income is desirable, etc., etc., etc. These beliefs are all related in a causal manner to the fact that he was born in America where these beliefs are taught, which, in turn, may be related to the fact that his ancestors migrated to the United States back in 1875, which may be related to the social conditions in England at that time and so on and on and on. Human behavior is

Is It Logical?

Any system of logic is justifiable or true if it provides a set of postulates which are internally consistent, that is, from which propositions can be deduced without contradiction. It is precisely this practice which has marked the great epochs of science. The Euclidian geometry set it down as an axiom that only one straight line can be drawn through a given point parallel to a given straight line. Lobatchewsky chose to postulate that more than one such line can be drawn, and on this axiom proceeded to evolve what has come down to us as non-Euclidian geometry. Riemann in turn chose to postulate that no parallel line at all can be drawn parallel to a given line—a procedure which to the conventionally minded is simply false. Yet it was by proceeding on the Riemannian postulate that Einstein evolved the relativity theory. Each of these developments resulted from the difficulty of forcing increasingly adequate observations into the then existing verbal schemes.

—George A. Lundberg.*

an on-going process, with causal roots extending in many different directions and far into the past. To chop off arbitrarily a small portion of one root and say that this is *the* cause of some behavior pattern greatly oversimplifies human behavior. Popular thinking frequently follows unitary causation patterns. Social science, if it is to develop any degree of sophistication, must go beyond this. Elements of human behavior are too complex to be explained in terms of a single factor.

Actually, for a cause-and-effect relationship to exist between two factors, three conditions have to be present. If A is the cause of B: (1) A must exist prior to B, (2) B must change as changes occur in A, and (3) some sort of causal connection must be established between them. Because it may be established, for instance, that soon after a rooster crows the sun

---

* George A. Lundberg, *Foundations of Sociology* (New York: David McKay Co., Inc., 1964), p. 56.

comes up, this does not prove that it is the crowing of the rooster which causes the sun to come up.

REASON AND LOGIC

Since the scientific method requires the use of empirical evidence in coming to a conclusion, it follows that it does not rely exclusively upon reason or logic in this respect. While scientific answers are generally both reasonable and logical, it does not follow that everything that is reasonable or logical is therefore scientifically true. Actually, there are different types of reason and logic, and a logical statement may not be true when checked against empirical evidence. It may be logical to assume, for instance, that medical doctors, who are most familiar with the relationships between lung cancer and smoking tobacco, would stop smoking. Empirical evidence, however, does not support this conclusion.

SAMPLE DATA

In his studies, the social scientist frequently finds it necessary for a number of reasons to study sample data rather than the entire universe with which he is concerned. If he wants to gather some information about the student body of a particular university or college he may not have the time or the necessary money to interview the entire student body. Instead, he may study a sample of the students. In order for him to generalize to the larger group from his study of the sample of this group, it is necessary that his sample be *representative* of the whole group. If it is 100 per cent representative, any conclusions about the sample are equally true of the whole. With reference to such samples, it is representativeness that is of major importance, and not necessarily the size of the sample. A 50 per cent sample is not necessarily any better for scientific work than a 10 per cent sample, if the 10 per cent sample is representative of the larger group.

Selecting a representative sample of almost any universe is a complicated and difficult task, and is a subject discussed in texts and courses in research methods. We will not discuss the techniques here, but only recognize that samples are extensively used in scientific research. Statistical techniques have been developed whereby the researcher can determine the margin of error that exists in his generalizations from the sample data to the larger universe of study.

Sociology has already been described as a generalizing science. We are looking for information about social behavior in general. Studies are designed to secure such information. Individual cases, then, are of only limited utility to the sociologist. Such cases may be used to illustrate something but not to *prove* something. The case of the interfaith marriage of "Uncle John" and "Aunt Susie" which terminated in divorce does not *prove* that interfaith marriages, in general, end in divorce. Any particular case may, for one reason or another, be an exception to a general rule.

THEORY AND RESEARCH

Our previous discussion has emphasized that in his research the scientist pays attention to empirical phenomena. He does not, however, cease his labors once he has made his observations of such phenomena and recorded his conclusions. Obviously, no one piece of research can come to conclusions about all aspects of anything that is being studied. It is, in fact, physically impossible for anyone to pay attention to all aspects of the universe at once. We will in a later chapter treat more extensively this *selective perception*, indicating that man always selects, from the available aspects of the universe to which he could pay attention, a very limited aspect to which he does, in fact, pay attention. This is true of all perception, scientific and unscientific alike. Thus, the scientist is interested in tying his various perceptions or research conclusions into a larger scheme of things so that in some way they make sense to him. Once he begins to do this, he begins to develop a *theory* or a *system* of logically interconnected concepts.[9] His theories are founded in his research, but they go beyond this in an effort to "make sense" out of a configuration of his findings. In such efforts, he attempts to arrange the results of scientific research into categories that are meaningful to him, and then to arrange these new categories into further categories, of which each is felt to be a specific example. He then arranges these higher-order categories into other relationships, so that somehow much of the information available to him is given meaning. Theory development, may, of course, work in the reverse direction, wherein high-order categories are developed through one means or another, and then the various subcategories as well as given observations—scientific or otherwise—of empirical phenomena, are ordered into further subcategories. In any event, theories (and many different ones have been developed) are used by man in his efforts to bring order to his experiences. The order may, of course, be more a result of his systematic arrangement of concepts than reflection of the order found in the phenomena of study.

Many theories of human behavior have been developed; one has been given the label of "biological determinism." In greatly over-simplified terms, this theory rests upon the premise that the major or final "causes" of human behavior are to be found in the biological makeup of man, thus endorsing the conclusions that man behaves as he does because biological factors inside of him "force" him to. Among the many concepts woven into this theory is the concept of "instincts." Those who feel that mothers instinctively love their children are endorsing the biological determinism theory, in that they imply that there is a "mother-love instinct" inside of the mother which forces her to love her child.

Economic determinism is another theory which has had many followers. Basically, this theory interprets behavior in economic terms, viewing these as the basic "causes" of human behavior. Classical Marxism falls in this category.

It is doubtful whether any adequate theory exists which permits the categorization and organization of all aspects of behavior into a meaningful and consistent pattern. The student of society can expect that new theories will be developed in the future; some will be short-lived, but others may have a tremendous impact not only upon the social sciences but upon society at large, much as did the psychoanalytic theory initiated by Freud and fostered and changed by his many disciples.

The basic theory utilized in this text to tie the sociological findings into a somewhat consistent whole is symbolic interactionist theory. The student should recognize that while this theoretical approach is able to serve a unifying function in what seems to the author an adequate manner, it has some gaps and inconsistencies. It is likely that not all available research can be integrated therein, but it will be used as our integrating theoretical approach in the hope that it will adequately serve the purpose of this textbook and may be productive of further refinement in the field of sociology. The theory will be outlined and discussed as we move on through the text.

Another point about the scientific utility of theory should be made. Theory is a major source from which new hypotheses for scientific testing are derived. Before the scientist begins to do research with empirical phenomena, he has to decide to which aspect of the universe he is going to pay attention and how he is going to pay attention to it. The research is planned and organized before it is undertaken. This involves systematizing a series of concepts which then serve as the guidelines for actual research. In these activities "nothing is as practical as a good theory." The productivity of a scientist is related to the number of concepts with which he is familiar and his ability to visualize potential relationships between them.

Theory is also utilized extensively by nonscientists—even those who may deride the "egg-

---

[9] Robert K. Merton, *Social Theory and Social Structure* (rev. and enlarged ed.; New York: The Free Press of Glencoe, Inc., 1957).

heads" who concern themselves with theoretical considerations rather than "practical" day-by-day problems of life. Most decisions made by man in his day-by-day affairs are, in fact, firmly rooted in some theoretical assumptions, of which the "practical man" may be only vaguely aware—if at all. In fact, not concerning himself with these theoretical considerations may permit him to endorse conflicting behavior (including, of course, verbal behavior) without being troubled by these inconsistencies. He may, for instance, quote the conflicting adages given in the previous chapter, feeling that he has made a profound statement about human behavior, without the necessity of harmonizing the conflict involved.

In developing his theories, then, the scientist pays attention to the results of research with empirical phenomena, but theory-building has no such restrictions. Theory-building is involved in the role of the scientists, to be sure, but the method utilized in theory-building is not the scientific method that we have outlined. In developing theories, the scientist moves beyond his empirical evidence, developing concepts which, in fact, may have no empirical referent. The scientific method is a method of coming to a decision about the empirical world, not a method of developing theories about the empirical world. Theories are always tentative, not scientifically proven. A theory does not state scientific laws (although these may be involved therein) but rather provides tentative conclusions.

TRUTH, AS THE SCIENTIST SEES IT

The word "truth" as used in scientific discussions or writings needs to be clearly defined, to avoid potential difficulty. As applied to the scientific field, the term is much more tentative than most people generally define it in non-scientific work. There are, in fact, different types of truth—scientific and non-scientific.

To the scientist, "truth" basically means that conclusion which the empirical evidence supports *at the moment*. This, in effect, leaves the door open; new research tomorrow may change

scientific truth. Such truth is always tentative, and, accordingly, has been constantly changing. Science is skeptical; it is always questioning, and always ready to correct old data if justification can be found. Scientific truth as taught to college students during the 1960's is quite different from the scientific truth taught during the 1860's, and this is true of the physical as well as the social sciences. Religion, by way of comparison, frequently talks in terms of ultimate or final truth. Science does not. Thus, if one is seeking for ultimate or final truth, he will be disappointed if he turns to science for his answers.

There are many different types of knowledge (truth). There are many different methods for coming to decisions about practically anything. The decisions reached are always relative to the

---

Science and Society

...as Lynn White has written: "The modern outburst of scientific activity is not necessarily permanent. The cultural support which science enjoys today rests more on fear of foreign enemies and disease than upon understanding, and fear may not be a healthy or lasting foundation." We are certainly foolish if we draw much comfort from the fact that science and technology currently enjoy great prestige. Whole civilizations—and vigorous, sophisticated ones at that—have managed very well without scientific technology; for instance, the Roman Empire....

It seems to me entirely possible that our society, which, for whatever motives, has invested not only immense sums of money but large amounts of spiritual faith in what it uniformedly conceives science to be, may become as thoroughly disillusioned and rebellious toward scientific and technological authoritarianism as early societies became rebellious towards regal authoritarianism.

—Eric Hutchinson.*

---

* Eric Hutchinson, "Science and Responsibility," *American Scientist*, LII, No. 1 (March, 1946), 47A–48A.

method used. One should certainly not be surprised, then, if the answers given by the various departments and colleges on the university campus do not harmonize with each other. Religious, historic, literary, artistic, legal, and scientific truths may be "kissing cousins" in some respects, but such conclusions or truths are far from identical or even mutually supportive. To anticipate another future discussion, we have been emphasizing that there are any number of different ways of viewing and responding to the world in which we live. The terms we use prepare us very literally to see the world differently than do others who use different terms. We respond to the aspects of the world we do, in the manner which we have learned. Since each of us has had different learning experiences, we may view the same things somewhat differently. Likewise, since those in each academic discipline have had a different background or collective learning experience, they may, accordingly, view things differently.

In a previous section of this chapter, it was emphasized that any discipline provides specific definitions for the terms it uses. Here, then, is an illustration of this point. Truth means different things to different people. Scientific truth has the qualities we have just described.

RESISTANCE TO SCIENTIFIC TRUTHS

Since the differences just discussed do exist, it is not surprising that conflict and resistance have developed as various truths have been made known. Once "truths" have been accepted it is generally (but not always) difficult to change them. The experience of scientists illustrates this.

When hypnotism was first developed, for instance, a doctor was dismissed at University College in London for endorsing its study. And when James Esdaile reported from India in the 1840's the successful completion of over a thousand operations (one-third of them major operations) with the patients hypnotized and a death rate of only 6 per cent during or after the operations, his critics alleged that he had bribed his patients to sham insensibility. According to

one account, "It was because they were hardened imposters that they let their legs be cut off and large tumors be cut out without showing any sign even of discomfort."

Similar reactions met Harvey's discovery of the circulation of the blood, Pasteur's work on microbes, and Semmelweis's discovery that physicians themselves spread the infection of puerperal or childbed fever from one mother to another. And, at the first demonstration of Edison's phonograph, before the Paris Academy of Sciences, all the scientists present declared that it was impossible to reproduce the human voice by means of a metal disc. One man proposed to throttle the demonstrator. "Wretch!" said he. "Do you suppose that we are fools to be duped by a ventriloquist?"[10] It is difficult even for scientists sometimes to live up to the requirements of the scientific method.

Further, when anesthesia was first introduced in America in the 1840's, opposition was voiced by some of the clergy, on the assumption that pain was the direct consequence of original sin

---

Scientific Heritage and Dogmatism

However, when ideas, concepts and theories which have guided a man throughout his creative life break down, their change is not accepted like the harmless prank of a child who builds houses out of blocks, then demolishes them only to rebuild again. The conflict of scientific opinion is a sharp struggle. It entails abandoning views formed over a period of many years (or by memorizing the deductions of others as the cases may be) and this in some instances may be an extremely painful process. Indeed, it often implies renunciation of one's alter ego, coupled with mental anguish and disappointment and requires courage and determination.

*—V. V. Parin.**

---

* V. V. Parin, "Scientific Heritage and Dogmatism," *Soviet Review,* III, No. 8 (August, 1962), 55.

[10] See Ian Stevenson, "Scientists with Half-closed Minds," *Harper's,* CCXVII (November, 1958), 64–71.

and, therefore, must be endured. A young dentist who did some experimental work with anesthesia was threatened with prosecution and there was general condemnation of drugs that supposedly set aside the laws of God and man. One clergyman wrote of ether as a "decoy in the hands of Satan, apparently offering itself to bless woman, but in the end it will harden society and rob God of the deep earnest cries that rise in time of trouble."

TYPES OF RESEARCH

The sociologist engages in different types of studies. He may merely be hunting for information, insights, or suggestions for future studies. Such efforts can be called *exploratory*. He may seek to accurately *describe* certain phenomena, or he may as the previous discussion has suggested seek to establish relationships between variables by setting up hypotheses and systematically testing them. Each of these types of studies is valuable to the scientist for different purposes, and all fit into the over-all discipline.

The sociologist may conduct his studies in the natural setting of human interaction. He may study society as it is engaged in its day-to-day activities. He may do his work in the laboratory where he is able to gain greater control over the variables involved. He can, under these conditions, to some extent hold all but one variable constant and then check to see what happens as this one variable is changed. The sociologist may also pay attention to records kept by members of society. He may, for instance, secure data about marriages and divorces from the records of the appropriate officials in the various areas. He may study the records of industry, of mental hospitals, of schools, and of churches. He may utilize correspondence between individuals. He may do an analysis of the content of mass media, of plays, songs, or other written works. Limitation, to be sure, is found in certain types of information. However, this only means that the limitations have to be taken-into account, not that the data are unusable for scientific work.

In many of his studies, the sociologist utilizes statistics to help him come to decisions about his data. He has to be able to measure whatever it is he is studying and detect differences which are found there. He then has to decide whether these differences are significant differences, or whether they are only chance differences which might be reversed were he to repeat the study the next day. Statistics provide him with valuable tools in coming to such decisions. Also, various types of recorders and tabulators, including IBM machines, can be used to speed up his analysis and also to provide increased accuracy.

IS SOCIOLOGY A SCIENCE?

The final answer to this question is not available.[11] According to the discussion in this chapter, sociology is a science to the extent that the sociologist utilizes the appropriate method. Certainly this method has not always been used in all research. Much is labeled sociology that has not been developed in this manner. There is, in fact, disagreement even among those who call themselves sociologists as to whether sociology *should be* or should strive to be scientific. However, much of the body of knowledge which today goes under the title of sociology has been secured in a scientific manner. Familiarity with scientific procedures such as those outlined briefly in this chapter will help the student to decide whether any particular conclusions rest upon scientific evidence or not. There can be no question that sociology has been becoming increasingly scientific in approach, and this fact is reflected in our definition of sociology as the *scientific* study of human interaction. As was indicated in the preceding chapter, this would seem to be a major justification for the existence of sociology as a separate branch of study.

In various sections of this chapter, reference has been made to concepts and conclusions which will be discussed more extensively later on

11 See, for instance, Maurice Stein and Arthur Vidich (eds.), *Sociology on Trial* (Englewood Cliffs, N. J.: Prentice-Hall, Inc., 1963).

in the text. The purpose for introducing such statements in this chapter is twofold: (1) to sensitize the student to the terms as early as possible, and (2) more importantly, to emphasize that the concepts of sociology can be used in understanding the behavior of sociologists as well as the behavior of others. The scientific study of human interaction in general includes the study of the interaction of sociologists in particular.

SUMMARY

Since the method used is the factor which determines whether any study, including that of sociology, is scientific, the scientific sociologist must know the norms of science. While this chapter has not provided an extensive discussion of all of the steps involved in this method, it has provided information to help the student decide what types of questions can be answered scientifically, which should in turn help him decide when an individual is speaking as a scientist and when he is not. Not all of the questions in which man is interested can be answered scientifically, and not all of the answers provided by an individual who may be, among many other things, a scientist, are scientific answers.

To be scientific one must pay attention to empirical phenomena in an objective, verifiable manner with as high a degree of exactness as possible. Precision in the definitions of terms, which frequently requires an operational definition, is required. Generalizations to the larger group cannot be made from an individual case, but samples of the larger universe of study can be used in scientific research with the validity of the results being relative to the representativeness of the sample.

Since the scientist is restricted to empirical phenomena, he cannot provide answers about non-empirical "things" such as values and the supernatural. He can, however, take into account the definitions which man has about these phenomena by paying attention to the verbal behavior of man.

The existence of a correlation between certain variables proves nothing about the causal relationships between them. Further, the fact that a conclusion is logical or reasonable is not accepted as *proof* that it is scientifically true, since the scientist comes to his decision on the basis of what happens to his empirical phenomena of observation, not on the basis of logic alone.

Research frequently stems from theory and may also result in changes in theory. The methods of research as outlined in this chapter and the methods of theory-building, which were only briefly alluded to, however, are quite different, and should not be confused. Theories integrate the research findings into larger configurations which then provide increased meaning and may also stimulate future research. Individual research findings might, however, be integrated equally well into several different and even contradictory theories.

Scientific answers (laws, truths) are tentative, although even some scientists have difficulty accepting change.

QUESTIONS

1. What are the differences between scientific truth and other types of truth?
2. How does restricting one's study to empirical phenomena facilitate being objective and how do the empirical and objectivity requirements of science facilitate verification?
3. Discuss the place of skepticism in science.
4. Why is quantification important in scientific study?
5. Make a list of the major concepts you have used in the past to explain human behavior, and then indicate what one would pay attention to if he wanted to do scientific research relative thereto.
6. How is theory related to scientific work?
7. What do you consider to be the most difficult aspect of studying human behavior scientifically?
8. Do you think it is possible to be objective about non-empirical phenomena?
9. When scientists disagree about something, how do they attempt to resolve the disagreement?
10. If A is the cause of B, A should exist independent of and prior to B. Are there two separate and identifiable things referred to in the statement: "Sally brushes her teeth every morning because she has a habit of doing so"?

PROJECT

Provide three hypotheses about human behavior which could be tested by scientific research and three which could not be tested by scientific research.

SUGGESTED READING

BARBER, BERNARD. *Science and the Social Order.* New York: The Macmillan Co., a Collier Book, 1962.

BARBER, BERNARD, and WALTER HIRSCH (eds.). *The Sociology of Science: A Reader.* New York: The Free Press of Glencoe, Inc., 1962.

CHASE, STUART. *The Proper Study of Mankind.* Rev. ed. New York: Harper & Row, Inc., 1946.

LAZARSFELD, P. F., and M. ROSENBERG (eds.). *The Language of Social Research.* New York: The Free Press of Glencoe, Inc., 1955.

LUNDBERG, GEORGE A. *Can Science Save Us?* New York: David McKay Co., Inc., 1947.

LUNDBERG, GEORGE A. *Foundations of Sociology.* New York: The Macmillan Co., 1939.

LYND, ROBERT S. *Knowledge for What?* Princeton, N. J.: Princeton University Press, 1939.

MERTON, ROBERT K. *Social Theory and Social Structure.* Rev. and enlarged ed. New York: The Free Press of Glencoe, Inc., 1957.

MILLS, C. WRIGHT. *The Sociological Imagination.* Fair Lawn, N. J.: Oxford University Press, 1959.

PEARSON, KARL. *The Grammar of Science.* London: Walter Scott, 1892.

POINCARÉ, HENRI. *The Foundation of Science.* Ephrata, Pa.: The Science Press, 1914.

3

The Symbolic Nature of
Human Interaction

Given his biological makeup, how do you think man's behavior would differ from what it now is, if he could not respond to symbols or were suddenly unable to take symbols into account?

Man is frequently only vaguely aware of what is closest to him, and consequently may pay but little attention to it. For instance, it has been said that the last thing a dweller in the deep sea would be likely to discover is the water. He would become conscious of its existence only if he were somehow exposed to surface conditions where there was no water. The same would seem to be true of man's immersion in "the world of symbols." Throughout his history man has been but vaguely aware of how extensively he uses symbols, and knowledge of the full impact of this factor upon his behavior seems to have generally escaped him. He is not much aware of this influence until it is specifically called to his attention.

One of the most important capacities of the human being with normal biological equipment is the capacity to respond to symbols, to manipulate symbols, and to engage in symbolic interaction. Using language is a universal *human* characteristic, with each group having at least some distinctive language patterns of its own. Man lives in a symbolic world. People are con-stantly "throwing symbols back and forth at each other." If one stops wherever he is and looks around him, he will find that there are literally hundreds of things for which he knows a name and, further, that he knows how human beings use these things. The library at a university is a vast storehouse of symbols which students and faculty look at and then write or talk to each other about, with the writing and talking, of course, being further symbol manipulation. Symbolic interaction is a major activity at a university as, indeed, it is throughout much of one's lifetime.

While single symbols can be used in a meaningful manner, most symbols are actually used in combination with others. Most human behavior involves the use of systems of symbols. The language man uses is systematized. Part of the meaning of any single symbol, in fact, is derived from the larger configuration of which it is a part. The system becomes apparent as one thinks of the mathematical system he uses, and how the various units involved are related to each other in a particular way. Among other

38

systems man also develops systems of logic, poetic systems, musical systems, etc.

This chapter will explore the process of symbolic interaction with emphasis upon the manner in which man's behavior is influenced by the symbols he uses. Although much of the discussion will be presented in terms of single symbols, it should be remembered that its conclusions apply equally well to the more complex use of symbol systems.

SYMBOLS AND REFERENTS

Let us begin by defining "symbol." A symbol is a thing that stands for something else.[1] The major parts of this definition, then, are two "things"—separate and distinct, with one thing, however, standing for or representing the other. The first thing we will call the symbol, the second we will call the referent, or the thing to which the first refers.

There seems to be no limit to what sort of thing can be a symbol. The kind with which we are most familiar is the printed or spoken word. The printed words on this page are symbols. A gesture such as shaking the head successively from left to right can be a symbol, which may mean "yes" or "no" depending upon how you have learned to define it, or upon your society. The wedding ring, the national flag, the Christian cross, the notes on a page of music, the fra-

[1] Symbols are a particular type of sign. Lindesmith and Strauss define a sign as "a stimulus which calls for a response that is the same as or similar to the response previously evoked by some other stimulus." They distinguish between *natural* and *conventional* signs. A natural sign is a "movement, sound, smell, gesture, or any other stimulus which is perceived regularly to precede or be connected with something else. The natural sign and what it indicates occur together in the same space-time framework, and both are thus parts of a concrete situation.... By contrast, the conventional sign derives its meaning from social consensus and is 'movable' or arbitrary, in the sense that different signs (e.g., in different languages) may mean the same thing, and that the sign (e.g., a word) may be used in situations where the object referred to is not present." Symbols as we are using the word are *conventional* signs. See Alfred R. Lindesmith and Anselm L. Strauss, *Social Psychology* (rev. ed.; New York: Holt, Rinehart and Winston, Inc., 1956), pp. 53–56.

The Study of Symbols

To submit a person's language to ruthless analysis is quite generally regarded as a personal attack through the medium of sympathetic magic or otherwise. "Hair splitting," "garbling," "distortion" are favorite epithets for those who meddle with other people's language. Still more general is the feeling that "fine" points in linguistic tools do not matter, and are merely a way by which "smart alecks" call attention to themselves. This may be the case, of course. Nevertheless, a careful scrutiny of the fitness of our linguistic tools is perhaps of greater importance than a loquacious use of them.

—George A. Lundberg.*

ternity pin, the gun shot at the beginning of a race during a college track meet, a coat of arms—anything, literally any "thing," can be used as a symbol.

If, as has been suggested, there is no inherent relationship between the symbol and the thing to which it refers (its referent), then how do these two things get tied together? How, for instance, did the symbol "book" come to refer to objects such as the one you are reading? Why not reverse the symbol and call this type of object a "koob"?

Such connections are strictly arbitrary. Human beings simply decide in the process of interaction that some particular symbol will be used to refer to something else. Tying the symbol and the referent together, then, is a human behavior pattern. The connection between symbol and referent is a human product. Nothing functions as a symbol by itself. A "thing" is a symbol only when it is interpreted by someone as standing for something else. You can never tell which symbol will be used to refer to any particular referent, or which referent is labeled with which symbol, by paying attention to either the symbol or the referent. You can find this out

* George A. Lundberg, *Foundations of Sociology* (New York: David McKay Co., Inc., 1964), p. 51.

only by engaging in symbol manipulation of one kind or another—asking the people involved what connection they have decided upon. Later on, we will say that you can determine this relationship by paying attention to the culture of the group.

Meaning, then, is a human product. It does not reside in either the symbol or the referent. Providing meaning for symbols is a human behavior pattern. When concerned with finding out the "correct" meaning of a word, one does not pay attention to its referent. We ask others what the word means, frequently turning to an "authority" in this field, such as a dictionary. Feedback of one type or another is an important requisite of accurate communication. Validation of our own definitions by others serves to perpetuate them. Meaning is a social product, and it is the group that decides the "correctness" or "incorrectness" of any symbols.

CONSENSUS AND COMMUNICATION

Since the connection between symbol and referent is strictly arbitrary, it follows that groups or individuals can approximate accurate communication only when they share similar understanding of the symbols they use. All sorts of difficulties can result when people in discussions use the same symbols but each has a somewhat different meaning for these symbols. Parents and teachers spend a good deal of time making sure that the children of their group learn and use the symbols already standardized by the group. Students who want to get a high grade on a college exam should make sure that their definitions of the terms to be used on the exam coincide with those of their professor.

Accurate communication is also frequently hampered by the fact that the same symbol may have different meanings, as well as by the fact that different words may have the same meaning.

Human beings also develop special speech patterns wherein the words "do not mean what they say." Americans make frequent use, for instance, of phrases such as the following:

He has a heart of gold.

She let the cat out of the bag.

He kicked the bucket.

My heart is broken.

Don't beat around the bush.

We were scraping the bottom of the barrel.

Learning a foreign language frequently leads to humorous experiences when idioms such as these are interpreted literally.

Accurate communication is, indeed, a difficult process, in part at least because human communication is symbolic interaction.

Figure 3.1 Consensus must be obtained if symbols are to be used effectively. Learning how to use spoken symbols in the approved manner is not always easy. (Wide World Photos.)

TYPES OF REFERENTS

A symbol is something that stands for some "thing" else. Let us now explore some of the characteristics of the second "thing"—the referent. As with symbols, there is no limit to what a referent can be. For our purposes we will identify *three* major types of referents. Using a term we defined in our discussion of the scientific method, we can say that the *first* type of referent is an empirical one. This type of referent exists outside of and independent of the individual using the symbol and is available to his senses. The book you are holding in your hand is an example. Thus, if you want to teach a child what the symbol "book" means, you can point to an empirical object and say, "This is what I refer to when I say the word 'book'." The child can touch and see the empirical object. We run into some difficulties, of course, when we try to distinguish between a book, a pamphlet, a brochure, or a tract. But nonetheless, there are empirical referents for these symbols. In similar fashion you can teach a child what symbols such as "grass," "tree," "rain," "house," "car," or "hat" represent.

A *second* type of referent is the non-empirical one. If you want to teach others about the meaning of these symbols, you cannot point to the referents. You can teach about these symbols only by using other symbols. Let us briefly look at one category of non-empirical referent, the supernatural. The English language, for instance, contains the symbol "angel." If you want to teach a child about angels you have to resort to some technique other than physically pointing. You might suggest to the child that angels are like human beings, in some respects, but in the last measure you can only use other symbols to round out your definition or understanding of angels. Terms such as "gods," "devils," "angels," "spirits," "souls," "heaven," "hell," and "purgatory," are all of this type. Individuals and groups *may believe* that such terms refer to things having substance, or are not purely "figments of one's imagination," but when they attempt to "point to" or "touch" these things

Symbol–Referent Connection

And out of the ground the Lord formed every beast of the field, and every fowl of the air, and brought them unto Adam to see what he would call them: and whatsoever Adam called every living creature, that was the name thereof.

—Genesis 2:19.

we are forced to the conclusion that given man as he is now and this supernatural realm, whatever it may be, as it is now, these supernatural "things" are of a type different from empirical things. Whether these "things" have substances of a non-empirical nature is, of course, a question the scientist cannot answer. If this premise is accepted, it is accepted on the basis of faith rather than empirical evidence.

This difference among kinds of referent does not, however, stop man from applying symbols to the supernatural. Since man can respond to the symbol rather than the referent, he can talk about, think about, or in some other way take the supernatural into account in his day-by-day living. The universality of religion suggests how extensively man manipulates this type of symbol. An interesting question, then, upon which the reader may like to speculate is, "What sort of religious behavior would we find among human beings, if they could not respond to symbols?" Would it, in fact, be possible for man to be religious in the sense that we generally use the word today if he could apply symbols only to the empirical world?

Man also has the ability to utilize symbols for referents believed to be purely fictitious. Many novels, for instance, refer to purely fictitious places, people, and events. They refer to nothing in the empirical world. The novel, then, is a system of symbols. Individuals and groups may, of course, take the novel into account in any number of ways, even though its symbols have no empirical referents. In a similar category are such words as "ghosts," "gremlins," "fairies," "Santa Claus," and "Easter Bunny."

A *third* type of referent we will call an "imposed upon" or "evaluative" type. This type is also non-empirical. Our discussion in Chapter 2 of the non-empirical nature of values has anticipated our discussion here. This type of symbol can be used with reference to both the empirical and the non-empirical world, although it does not refer to any empirical quality of either. It is involved in the way man interprets or evaluates such phenomena. An example can illustrate this type. Let us analyze the statement that "Picture X is beautiful." Is this quality we call "beauty" an empirical dimension of the picture? Where is the beauty? Can you point to it, touch it, weigh it? The answer is "No." Beauty is not an empirical thing. The same picture may be evaluated as beautiful by one individual and as ugly by another, and you cannot resolve this difference by looking at the picture. Beauty is a concept man uses when he evaluates the picture. It is a dimension man "superimposes" upon the picture. As Shakespeare said, "Beauty lies in the eyes of the beholder."

Other dimensions of a similar nature are goodness, badness, righteousness, evilness, ownership ("mineness" and "yourness"), and economic value ("dollar-and-centness").

Man, then, is able to decide upon certain standards through the manipulation of symbols and then apply these standards in his behavior. Much of his activity involves learning the standards appropriate to his group and applying them to the various situations in which he participates.

In addition to the use of symbols with non-empirical referents as just discussed, symbols can be used to refer to relationships between empirical things as well as relationships between symbols that have no empirical referent. Man also develops symbols that facilitate his manipulation of symbols. Words such as "of," "therefore," "however," "plus," and "minus" order man's symbols into particular patterns.

In our discussion thus far we have identified the following types of symbol–referent combinations:

1. Symbols with empirical referents.

2. Symbols with non-empirical "things" as referents.
   a. Symbols referring to "things" believed to be fictitious.
   b. Symbols referring to "things" believed to have substance but of a non-empirical type, as the supernatural.
   c. Symbols that permit man to evaluate his phenomena of concern in terms of some man-made criteria such as beauty or goodness, which, as popularly used, refer to non-empirical qualities of empirical phenomena.

For ease of communication throughout the remainder of the text we will use the following designations:

ER symbols = symbols that have an empirical referent (No. 1 above).

NER symbols = symbols that have no empirical referent (No. 2 above).[2]

Human beings learn to use both types of symbols (ER and NER) and usually engage in be-

---

[2] The labels "ER" and "NER" are used to qualify *symbols* rather than *referents* to which they more accurately refer (all symbols are empirical), because most of our subsequent discussion will be in terms of symbols rather than referents. Further, however, in the second category above (NER) the referents are non-empirical "things," and, therefore, our scientific limitation which requires attention being paid only to empirical things, excludes our consideration of these "things." We can, of course, pay attention to the empirical symbols involved. A major point that our subsequent discussion will bring out is that it is misleading to use concepts such as goodness and beauty as we typically do, since to do so encourages one to think that these are, in fact, qualities of the objects thus classified. Actually, to talk about the referents of these terms (goodness and beauty, etc.) as "things" to which the symbols refer is also misleading since it encourages the same type of conclusion (that goodness is a "thing"). We will, however, use the definition of a symbol as something that refers to something else and distinguish between ER and NER symbols, calling attention thereby to the fact that all types of NER symbols, as far as we can tell scientifically, really have no "thing" to which they refer—at least not an empirical thing.

havior that involves both types, mixing the two together and rarely if ever, unless specifically asked to do so, separating them. It is no wonder, then, that individuals frequently come to the conclusion that the two types of symbols rest equally upon empirical foundations.

One of the reasons why more attention is not given to these different types of symbols is that as yet the English language appears to have provided no labels by which they can be distinguished. Leslie White, in 1959, wrote:

> Now it turns out that there is a class of phenomena, one of enormous importance in the study of man, for which science has yet no name: this is the class of things and events consisting of or dependent upon symboling. It is one of the most remarkable facts in the recent history of science that this important class has no name, but the fact remains that it does not.[3]

The phenomena to which he refers are what we have called NER symbols, which in this text are distinguished from ER symbols to call attention to the two types of phenomena.

In the United States today it is not infrequently concluded that because a scientist is an authority on one aspect of the empirical world, he is, therefore, an authority on the nonempirical world as well. Those who do so fail to recognize that different methods are required to come to decisions about these different types of phenomena.

The young child first learns to use ER symbols accurately, and then as facility in their use is developed, he develops the ability to use NER symbols in a socially approved manner, frequently, however, making mistakes for which he is corrected. The young child is not concerned with, nor can he be taught much about justice, monetary values, morality, beauty, and algebra. His concern in life is restricted mainly to the empirical physical world, many aspects of which he is only vaguely aware of. Only as symbol manipulation becomes somewhat sophisticated does he move to NER concerns.

[3] Leslie A. White, "The Concept of Culture," *American Anthropologist*, LXI (1959), 227–252.

Communication in Dancing

How does the college co-ed follow her dancing partner at the Homecoming Dance? How does she know when he is going to turn, back up, or do the latest popular step?

He generally tells her what he wants her to do without saying anything directly about it. He constantly communicates with her and she with him. Such communication is interaction with gestures. Dancing teamwork requires fairly accurate encoding, transmission, and decoding of symbols even though not a word is spoken.

Man's behavior always involves the empirical world but certainly is not restricted to it. In a sense, he also develops a vast social or symbolic world that he superimposes upon his physical world. He develops culture, which involves, in addition to direct definitions of the empirical world, definitions about justice, morality, logic, reason, goodness, badness, evil, monetary systems, arithmetic, mathematics, algebra, trigonometry, superstitions, myths, and religion. These concepts are not, of course, mutually exclusive. Their NER symbol systems provide man with many of the important criteria he applies in coming to decisions about his life.

It should be clear that the accuracy of man's knowledge about the empirical world is not necessarily affected by or related directly to his definitions about NER symbol systems. Combining H_2 and O presumably produces water, regardless of whether this is thought to be good or bad, moral or immoral, logical or illogical, reasonable or unreasonable, worth \$5 or 5¢, or just or unjust. These are considerations of a different type, and cannot be resolved with respect merely to the H_2 or the O, either separately or in combination. At the social level, if broken homes are a major cause of juvenile delinquency or if the suicide rate of a nation is related to its religious characteristics, the relationship exists regardless of whether such a situation is defined as good or bad, moral or immoral, logical or illogical, reasonable or unreasonable, of value to know or valueless to know, or just or unjust.

Jumping to the conclusion that because one knows something about an empirical phenomenon one therefore knows something about the relationship of the NER systems to this empirical phenomenon evidences a basic unawareness of the difference existing between the two.

A further comment may be in order concerning non-empirical referents. In our discussion of the scientific method we emphasized that we can be scientific only about empirical phenomena. How can human behavior be studied scientifically then, if so many of man's symbols have no empirical referent? The answer to this question is that in his study of human behavior the scientist pays attention only to these symbols—not to the referents. He takes into account man's definitions about goodness and badness, gods and devils, beauty, etc. These are empirical. These he can get at, primarily by talking to people about them. As a scientist he is not concerned, however, with the question whether any particular definition is the "true" or the "real" definition, or which pictures "really" are beautiful, or which definition of god is the "true" definition. If an individual wants an answer to such a question he cannot get it by using the scientific method.

Since a symbol refers to things other than the symbol *per se*, it should be clear that the symbol is not the "other thing." Korzybski [4] has emphasized this point by indicating that a symbol is somewhat like a map that portrays a particular territory. A map of the State of Utah is not the State of Utah; it is only a man-made representation. The map can call our attention to but a limited number of features of the territory involved. A map can never say all there is to say about a territory. Neither can the map accurately duplicate the territory—it can only represent the territory (referent).

The same is true of symbols. Symbols do not fully describe or duplicate the referent. Any

particular symbol can call attention to and label only limited aspects of the referent (selective identification). To begin to describe or represent all aspects of any referent would take thousands of symbols. Any referent can be classified and considered in any number of ways.

PLANS OF ACTION

Our discussion of symbols so far has implied that in symbol manipulation man's symbols merely serve as labels for different aspects of his world, enabling him to communicate about them. This, however, is only part of the picture. Man's response to symbols is more extensive than this. As we learn the names used to refer to certain objects, we also learn how man is expected to relate himself to these objects. Our definitions of symbols, or our understanding as to what symbols mean, generally include this other dimension—what man should do *about*, *to*, or *with* their objects. Our definitions include "plans of action." Part of our definition of "chair" is that it refers to a certain type of object *upon which one sits*. The "upon which one sits" is a plan of action, a part of our definition of "chair." A spoon is an object with which one eats certain types of food. A wedding ring is an object one wears on a certain finger. A secretary is, among other things, an object (human, to be sure) to whom one dictates letters. A college professor is, among other things, an object (individual) from whom students receive lectures. A good practice is one the individual should try to incorporate into his behavior. These examples are, of course, much simplified.

We have previously indicated that the connection between referent and symbol is a man-made one. Man has to be taught that the symbol "chair" refers to objects with certain characteristics. What we have been saying here is that the learning process goes beyond this. Children, for instance, are not only taught the group names for objects but in the process are also taught how they should relate themselves to these objects. The label and plans of action get tied together in the definition.

---

[4] See A. Korzybski, *Science and Sanity* (Ephrata, Pa.: Science Press, Inc., 1933).

The meaning of any ER symbol may also include an evaluative or NER dimension. Again using our example of "chair," use of the label may, in addition to sensitizing the user to its referent and plans of action, sensitize him to any evaluative aspect he has learned to associate with it, such as its beauty, economic value, or morality or immorality. Three major components of the "meaning" of a symbol are:

1. Referent identification,
2. Plans of action, and
3. Evaluation aspects involving NER symbols

When we are confronted with a strange object (including another human being) one of the first questions we generally try to answer about the object is "What is it?" Once we have answered this question or decided which label we will use, we have generally also answered the question as to how we should treat it, or how we should relate ourselves to it. When thrown into contact with strangers most of us try as soon as possible to find out *who* they are or *what* they are (or to label them), in part, at least, so that we will know how we should treat them as well as how we can expect them to treat us. Since these relationships between symbol and plans of action are arbitrary, it follows that considerable variation is found between the plans of action developed by various groups. The meaning (definition) or the plan of action associated with any symbol is the reaction the individual makes to that symbol.

Some authors make a distinction between what they call "extensional *meaning*" and "intensional *meaning*." Extensional meaning, they hold, is the meaning found in the empirical world, and the intensional meaning is the meaning provided by man. In our discussion it seems more appropriate to say that all meaning is intensional or provided by man. What they call "extensional meaning" we have identified as "empirical referent" but we have also emphasized that man's definition or the meaning of any empirical referent is man-made (intensional). We will talk about different types of referents but only one type of meaning—that supplied by man.

STIMULUS–RESPONSE PATTERN

The fact that man's behavior involves the use of symbols is closely related to the stimulus–response patterns of human behavior. To label human behavior as a "stimulus–response pattern," however, is an over-simplification. Man does not respond directly to a stimulus, but rather to his definition of that stimulus. Man is constantly engaged in the process of naming things, or of "tacking labels on things." Once a label has been applied, man's behavior follows the plan of action he has learned as appropriate to the label. Human response to stimuli, then, is not a $S \rightarrow R$ pattern, but rather:

$$Stimulus \longrightarrow Definition \longrightarrow Response$$

In order to understand human behavior, we need to know what definitions an individual applies to objects (including other human be-

---

Gestures

Perhaps my interest began with the young catatonic woman who broke through a period of completely blocked communication and obvious anxiety by responding when I asked her a question about her feeling miserable: She raised her hand with her thumb lifted, . . . isolated from the four hidden fingers. I interpreted the signal with, "That lonely?," in a sympathetic tone of voice. At this, her facial expression loosened up as though in great relief and gratitude, and her fingers opened. Then she began to tell me about herself by means of her fingers, and she asked me by gestures to respond in kind. We continued with this finger conversation for one or two weeks, and as we did so, her anxious tension began to decrease and she began to break through her noncommunicative isolation; and subsequently she emerged altogether from her loneliness.

—Frieda Fromm-Reichmann.*

---

* Frieda Fromm-Reichmann, "Loneliness," *Psychiatry,* XXII, No. 1 (February, 1959), 1.

ings) with which he is involved. These definitions identify the aspect of the object to which attention is being paid. If we want to know why a prospector reacts to the rapid clicking of his Geiger counter in a particular way, we have to take into account the meaning of the rapid clicking to the prospector—or how he defines this stimulus. If we want to understand a student's reaction to a D on his grade card, we have to consider how he defines a D.

Figure 3.2 Gestures are symbols with which man can communicate as shown in this drawing of the New York Stock Exchange in 1901 by S. M. Stone. (The Bettmann Archive, Inc.)

The importance of definitions in human behavior is suggested in the following story:

Sharing a railway compartment were an American grandmother, her young and attractive granddaughter, a Romanian officer, and a Nazi officer. As the train passed through a tunnel, no one spoke but they all heard a loud kiss and a vigorous slap. After the train emerged from the tunnel nobody spoke but the following reactions occurred:

Grandmother: What a fine girl I have raised. She will take care of herself. I'm proud of her.

Granddaughter: Well, grandmother is old enough not to mind a little kiss. Besides, the fellows are nice. I'm surprised what a hard wallop grandmother has.

Nazi officer: How clever these Romanians are. They steal a kiss and have the other fellow slapped.

Romanian officer: How smart I am! I kiss my own hand and slap the Nazi.

Response to the same empirical stimulus may be quite different for different individuals, since man responds to his definition of the stimulus rather than directly to the stimulus *per se*.

DO WE LABEL AND THEN SEE, OR SEE AND THEN LABEL?

The fact that man's behavior is influenced by the symbols he uses to classify his world raises an interesting question. Does man see his world and after he has identified the characteristic in it apply the appropriate label, or does he attach the label (classify the object) and then see the qualities that he has learned to associate with the label? Is man, in fact, able to "see" the qualities the label calls for even though they may not be there empirically?

In a sense he does both of these things. Before he attaches a label to an aspect of his world, he sees something he feels justifies his applying the particular label. In a limited sense, then, he does first see, hear, or become aware of something to which he later applies his label. However, human behavior is much more complex than this. It is entirely possible for man to "see" what the label calls for even though it may not empirically be there. We actually see the sun and the moon "rise." Different people may witness the same accident but "see" quite different things. The student fan at a basketball game and a referee both "see" the same behavior on the playing floor, but they may also see it quite differently.

The fact that we tend to see the qualities we feel a label calls for is related to any number of experiences. For instance, if individuals have an idea as to how people whom they label "artist" are supposed to behave, then whenever they apply this label they tend to see the "appropriate" behavior patterns. If, for instance, artists are believed to be temperamental, then whenever someone defined as "artist" is encountered there is a tendency to interpret his behavior in a manner that harmonizes with this belief. Contrary evidence tends to be ignored or minimized, while supporting evidence is emphasized. This is called *selective perception*.[5]

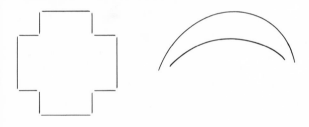

Figure 3.3

Individuals who have been exposed to stimuli that could be interpreted in different ways tend to recall the stimuli in such a manner that the appropriate aspects associated with the label are contributed by the individual. Students exposed to the stimuli in Figure 3.3, for instance, will frequently, when asked to reproduce the figure from memory, fill in the lines so that the figure is completed, or so that closure is obtained.[6]

To state the same point somewhat differently, once we have developed or accepted a "stereotype," or a standardized definition as to how some particular thing or person will behave, it is easy for us to interpret our experiences so that they harmonize with the stereotype. It is, of course, also possible through the learning experience to reinterpret or even abolish stereotypes. Here we merely emphasize that human beings respond in this way, and, further, that such behavior on their part is not "dishonest" behavior. The individual may very sincerely and with the best of intentions see that which his stereotypes call for.

If prejudice is defined as a particular type of pre-judgment, it follows that man is able to pre-judge something basically because he is able to manipulate symbols. He can use symbols and reach a decision about something he has never experienced directly. When he does have an experience with the object, he enters the experience all prepared to respond in a particular manner. Prejudice as defined above would be impossible if man could not use symbols.

EMERGENT NATURE OF HUMAN BEHAVIOR

This discussion leads us to another conclusion. If man can both see and then label, and label and then see, it follows that although there is a degree of consistency about human behavior, it is an on-going dynamic process. Human behavior is constantly changing. We are constantly interpreting and then re-interpreting. We may respond to an object one way today and another way tomorrow. Man is constantly labeling the things in his environment and attempting to engage in what seems to him the appropriate action. The on-going process of interaction, however, may result in re-labeling and adjusting to the new labels. Human behav-

[5] For a more extensive discussion of this area, see Eleanor E. Maccoby, Theodore M. Newcomb, and Eugene L. Hartley (eds.), *Readings in Social Psychology* (New York: Holt, Rinehart and Winston, Inc., 1958), chap. i; see also Charles E. Osgood, "Cognitive Dynamics in the Conduct of Human Affairs," *Public Opinion Quarterly*, XXIV, No. 2 (Summer, 1960), 341–365.

[6] See L. Carmichael, H. P. Hogan, and A. A. Walter, "An Experimental Study of the Effect of Language on the Reproduction of Visually Perceived Form," *Journal of Experimental Psychology*, XV, No. 1 (February, 1932).

ior in any particular situation reflects the past experience of the individual, including the definitions he has already acquired, the past experiences of the others involved, including their definitions, and the present conditions, i.e., human beings in interaction in a particular social situation. Out of the interplay of all these factors particular behavior patterns emerge. Human behavior is an on-going, emergent process.

SUBJECTIVE REALITY AND OBJECTIVE REALITY

Let us at this point review some of the points we have already made.

1. Human beings manipulate symbols.

2. Human behavior is not simple stimulus–response behavior, but rather human beings respond to the definitions or meanings they associate with the label or symbols.

3. Definitions attached to symbols may correspond somewhat to empirical qualities of the referent, but there is no necessary relationship between these two. Indeed, when defined properly, black may be seen as white.

This foundation, then, permits us to make another distinction which will be of major importance to us throughout our future discussions—between *subjective reality* and *objective reality*. Let us define these terms.

Subjective reality is what is defined as real by the individual doing the defining. Subjective reality is what an individual believes to be true. If I think a picture is beautiful, to me it is beautiful. If I think my child should be spanked, to me he should be spanked. If I think the door is open, to me it is open, even though it may empirically be closed. If Americans think they are the best people on the face of the earth, to them they are the best people on the face of the earth. If a professor thinks a student is cheating on an exam, to him the student is cheating on the exam. The important aspect of these sentences is the "to me" or "to them" qualifiers. Subjective reality is what the individual believes to be

real. It is the pattern of definitions that the individual accepts.

Objective reality is what is real, independently of how an individual defines it. It is what would be real even if the individual did not exist. People at one time believed the world to be flat. This was subjective reality. The shape of the world regardless of how they defined it is objective reality. At times people go through the process of sitting down on a chair they believe to be in the proper location to receive them (subjective reality). If the chair has been removed by a practical joker, the objective reality might be drastically different from the subjective reality. Objective reality refers to the empirical world as it exists, independently of how it is defined by man.

Returning again to our discussion about the types of referent that symbols may have, we can say that under objective reality we include the empirical world in its various aspects.

Subjective reality includes all that an individual defines as real. In reaching any decisions, subjective reality is everything that is real to the individual. Actually, all one knows is his experience. We do not, for instance, become directly acquainted with a table. We do not know the objective qualities of the table. All we know is our *reaction* to the table. Indeed, for the individual, it is impossible to separate his experience of the table from the table itself. All he knows is what he experiences. In this sense, then, the existence of objective reality is only an assumption upon which human behavior rests.

The scientific method, as we have outlined it, is probably the best method so far devised for harmonizing subjective reality and objective reality. When a group of scientists can come to agreement about the objective world, it would seem to be safe to conclude that their subjective reality corresponds fairly well to objective reality. The changes that have occurred in science over the years, however, lead one to be cautious about accepting such a conclusion.

Human beings, then, are capable of viewing their world in any number of ways. Whatever the view may be *to them* the real view is subjective reality. As far as human behavior is concerned subjective reality would seem to be one of the major factors to be taken into account if we want adequately to explain such behavior. Not to be concerned as to how those being studied define the physical world, other persons, the social situation, and themselves would seem to be overlooking the "cornerstone" of human behavior.

To talk about two types of *reality* that are possibly contradictory may be somewhat confusing. However, the word "real" does seem to be appropriate. Subjective reality is real *to the individual*. It would seem to be the only reality he ever knows. Available evidence strongly supports, on the other hand, the premise that there is an objective empirical world—which is real—outside the individual. With the qualifiers "subjective" and "objective" the word "real" seems to be an appropriate one.

This discussion of subjective reality adds depth to our previous statement that the scientific method involves empirical phenomena. Since human beings are capable of defining phenomena in any number of ways, the scientist does not accept the fact that people believe something to be true as *proof* that it is true. He comes to his decisions upon the basis of what happens to the empirical phenomena he is studying, not on the basis of beliefs or subjective reality of others.

Stated somewhat differently, the social scientist is so aware that a great discrepancy frequently exists between subjective reality and objective reality that he refuses to accept subjective proofs as adequate evidence that a statement *is* true. He seeks for non-subjective proofs and for verification by other competent observers. When there is general agreement, he accepts this as evidence that he is on the right track.

It does not necessarily follow, just because a word exists and can be involved in subjective reality, that there is a corresponding empirical referent in objective reality, although it is easy to believe that there is. This fact has contributed to problems in the development of the social sciences. Use has been made, for instance, of such concepts as "mind," "memory," "drive,"

Reality?

Locke, Berkeley, Hume, and Kant made us understand what the Greek atomists already knew: that sense experience is not the bridge which connects us with, but the abyss which separates us from, absolute reality.

—Alfred Stern.*

and "impulse" as though these were things that existed inside the individual. Since these "things" were believed to exist, it was easy to take the next step and attribute to them causative powers. People behaved in a particular manner, it was maintained, *because* of conditions of the mind, drives, or instincts.

Willingness to accept these terms as providing causal explanations of behavior has made it easy to stop at the level of the individual and not give attention to how the observable behavior developed or to the social conditions related to the behavior.

While the scientist strives to obtain as much knowledge as possible about his area of interest and to gain an accurate picture of objective reality, it does not follow that this is equally true of individuals playing other roles. In some situations, lack of accurate knowledge or ignorance of the facts by at least some of those involved may be defined as highly desirable. In an earlier chapter it was pointed out that acceptance of new scientific findings frequently has been difficult. For some, at least, accepting a new interpretation exposes a previous ignorance, which may be distasteful. To accept a new interpretation may, in fact, destroy illusions that have helped those holding them to adjust to their life situation. Under some circumstances accurate knowledge of the others with whom we interact may be disruptive to an established way of life. Some physicians are convinced, for instance, that some patients should not be told everything about their physical condition. Sub-

---

* Alfred Stern, "Science and the Philosophers," *American Scientist*, XLIV, No. 3 (July, 1956), 291.

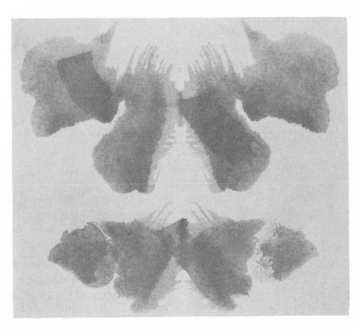

Figure 3.4

jective and objective reality most likely never completely agree.

In interpreting human behavior, then, it is sometimes as important to find out what an individual or group does not know as to find out what they do know.[7]

SYMBOLIC ENVIRONMENT OF MAN

Our discussion has suggested that man lives in a symbolic environment. The human baby is born into a world, the various parts of which have already been classified and have plans of action already developed by the group into which it is born. Most young children learn to classify their world in the manner upon which their parents or other significant adults have already decided, and then they learn to respond to the labels used in their efforts at classification in the manner upon which their parents or other significant adults have also already decided.

[7] See, for instance, Louis Schneider, "The Role of the Category of Ignorance in Sociological Theory: An Exploratory Statement," *American Sociological Review*, XXVI, No. 4 (August, 1962), 492–508.

It is difficult, if not impossible, to know how the world would appear to us if none of its parts were identified and labeled and we were thus unable to take these parts into account. It would appear something like the inkblot in Figure 3.4. At first glance it does not appear to be any "thing." Then as you begin to look at it you can see certain "things" that you can name. Here, of course, we rely upon previously learned concepts. However, once you name the aspect of the whole figure you are considering, you can talk to others about it, and in other ways take it into account. As a group of students discuss inkblots such as this it frequently happens that after someone has indicated he can see a "tux," or two flying witches, or two people playing leap-frog, others say, "Oh, yes, now that you call it to my attention, I can see it." They have an "Aha" experience and "discover" the thing.

Once parts of the universe are identified or once boundary lines are figuratively drawn around certain aspects of the universe and identifying names are given them, we can then take these things into account. We can talk to others about them and see how they are related to other things. We also tend to identify with any degree of specificity only those things for which our group already has names. The process of naming in a sense abstracts one small part from all the aspects of our world to which we could pay attention. In the process of naming, this part becomes "foreground" whereas other dimensions are pushed into the "background." Naming in a sense stops the on-rushing world, or at least a part of it, so that it can be evaluated.

In his experiences with his world, an individual tends to see only those things for which he has developed labels. He tends to see only the things he has been taught to see. When a professor of music listens to a symphony orchestra, he hears many different things from what is heard by the individual who has not learned to identify and label the elements of a symphony and the instruments of an orchestra. To the non-musician, many things that are sharp and clear to musicians are merged together into a much larger whole. The mother listening to her child give a public speech may hear many "mistakes" that others fail to hear. The auto mechanic likewise hears different things as he listens to the sound of the motor from what is heard by the non-mechanic driver. The artist sees different things in a picture than the non-artist.

The influence of symbols upon the manner in which we view our world is more extensive than most people realize. Many believe that symbols or names serve only to identify already existing "things" and that in the process of language-building we simply come up with sym-

bols that serve this identification purpose. The process, however, is much more complex than this. The world in which we live is capable of being subdivided into any number of different "things." Any object can be viewed as a composite of other small "things" or as an entity in itself. Almost anything we can think of is a part of a larger entity, which can also be identified, labeled, and responded to. A cell in the human body, for instance, can be responded to as an entity, or the organ of which it is a part can be responded to as an entity, with the cell being pushed into the background. We can go from the organ to the system of which it is a part, to the individual of which it is a part, to the nuclear family of which the individual is a part, to the larger expanded family of which it is a part, to the neighborhood, the community, the state, the region, the nation, the world, the universe, and presumably on to infinity.

Microscopes and telescopes have permitted us to respond to various aspects of our universe. The things identified in this discussion are things for which our group has already provided us with labels and thus about which we can communicate with a fair degree of accuracy. However, there are any number of different levels to which we could pay attention, any number of ways of classifying anything depending upon the characteristics to which one pays attention. The textbook you are currently reading, for instance, can be classified in any of the following ways, to list but a few, depending upon the "level of abstraction" involved:

A sociology text
A social science text
A college text
A book
Printed material
A man-made object
Non-living material object
Material object

It is important also to recognize that when we use words, we force the words into certain relationships to each other. It would be wrong, however, to think that the referents of these symbols have the same relationship to each other. They may, but on the other hand it is

Symbols and Symbols

*There is a difference between dividing 3173 by 49 and dividing MMMCLXXIII by XLIX—a difference which explains why many problems that high school students solve routinely today were beyond the powers of ancient Rome's most talented mathematicians.**

* *Fortune* (May, 1964), 194.

possible to combine symbols in ways which would be impossible for the referents. The objective world and its component parts do not necessarily relate themselves to each other in the way our language would lead us to believe they do. As a previous chapter pointed out, our language may provide us with only a two-fold distinction, and thus we may think and talk in terms of dichotomies when any number of shades of differences would be possible, if we had the terms.

From this discussion, then, it follows that the various languages of the world do not merely contain different names for the same things. In some respects they do, but different languages "cut up" the world differently. It is possible to say in one language what cannot be said in another. The Eskimos can talk about many more different types of snow than can a person using the English language. Arabs can identify many more different kinds of camel than a person using another language. American teenagers can talk about more different kinds of cars than can Eskimos. More than this, the English language contains many words borrowed from other languages because there was no English equivalent. The French word *"rapport"* is an example. One becomes impressed with the relativity of language when one tries to translate the words for colors from one language to another, even if the two languages are Indo-Germanic. The English words for colors distinguish spectrally by hue. The Greek words have to do almost entirely with depth and brightness, and you cannot find a Greek word for blue, although you can find one that sometimes means blue.[8]

Social systems of different groups may also be drastically different, with labels to identify the different parts. In effect, this entire book will enlarge upon this point. Here we merely emphasize that the physical world and the social world can be viewed in any number of different ways and that the labels used by a particular group of people reflect their manner

of viewing the world. One such point of view may be drastically different from that of some other group.

By learning a new language, particularly one not closely related to his own, a person also learns new ways of responding to the universe. One does not need to leave the university campus to demonstrate this. To an extent, at least, each of the disciplines on campus has its unique language. A course in geology in which the student learns the language of geology sensitizes him to aspects of his world that previously escaped him. A course in chemistry or physics brings certain other aspects of our world into sharper focus. The psychology student interprets human behavior differently than he did before he was provided with the psychology concepts and their accompanying plans of action. The same thing is true of almost all departments of a college. The aspects of life studied in each area all existed before the student took the course, but in many respects he very literally did not see them, or was not aware of them, because no one had called them to his attention and in the process supplied him with names so that he could identify them and respond to them.

Thus, by naming and classifying the various aspects of our environment, new modes of behavior as well as new possibilities for manipulating that environment are brought into existence. Individually and collectively we label the things we come to feel are important to us. Thus we are constantly paying attention to only a limited aspect of our universe. And what the individual pays attention to is basically that which his groups have decided upon.

New ways of responding to our world are constantly being devised. Learning to identify and respond to uranium, for instance, was a new development that has had profound impact upon the world. In the academic realm, learning to identify and respond to I.Q. has likewise had sweeping repercussions. Not many of us, however, take such "giant steps"; most of us, most of the time, confine ourselves to the terms with which our ancestors provided us. There are any number of different ways in which human behavior can be subdivided and studied by the

---

[8] Robert J. Oppenheimer, "Talk to Undergraduates," in Edward Hutchings, Jr. (ed.), *Frontiers in Science* (New York: Basic Books, Inc., 1958), p. 346.

social scientist. It would seem to be safe to predict that many of the concepts that will permit man to better understand man and to predict his behavior have yet to be formed. Possibly someone reading this text may contribute to just such a development.

One of the most important aspects of man's symbolic behavior is that he can produce symbols and respond to them without the referents present. Man can write checks, for instance, and use them to purchase goods at a store. The check is merely a piece of paper with some symbols on it. An absentee owner in New York can come to a decision about an employee in San Francisco and fire him or promote him without even being seen by the employee. A scientist can predict the next eclipse of the moon long before it ever occurs. We can send letters and telegrams around the world. And the student in a college mathematics class can spend his whole semester manipulating symbols (which have no empirical referents) according to an internally consistent system.

Man, of course, spends time manipulating the empirical world. He plants seeds, mines ore, and builds rockets. But even in these activities his manipulation of the physical world also involves symbol manipulation. Man spends much of his time in this manipulation of symbols, and the manner in which he does this has a profound influence upon his life. Man indeed lives in a symbolic world.

Symbols also permit man to engage in self-interaction. At first glance the term "self-interaction" appears to be contradictory. What is meant, however, is that man is able to both initiate the symbols and also receive them. He can speak and hear himself speak. He can then respond to his own initiated symbols. The same interaction seems to go on in the process we call thinking. The individual initiates the symbols and then responds to them. Most of us have had the experience of thinking about something and then developing feelings of happiness or sadness as a result of this thinking. We engage in self-interaction, or self-stimulation. Thinking would appear to be symbol manipulation or silently talking to oneself.

Systems of Truth

. . . the same relationship between man and the world [may] be conceived by means of different conceptual or symbolic systems . . . it is possible that several philosophical systems establish constructions equally free from logical contradictions and equally well applicable to the relations between man and his world. In realizing that these different philosophical systems are only different possibilities of conceiving theoretically the same basic relationships between man and the universe by means of different symbols, we must become more tolerant toward diverging systems and not think that one has necessarily been refuted by the other because the other appeared later in time. In some cases, it has been refuted, but in other cases it has not. If we would dogmatically affirm that the truth of a philosophical system consists in the fact that it is a copy of reality, then among the hundreds of systems the history of philosophy has produced there would be only one true system. Such an affirmation would be nonsense. But while only one system could be the right copy of reality, there may be many systems applicable to reality with the same degree of evidence.

—Alfred Stern.*

SYMBOLS AND INTERNAL PHENOMENA— "GETTING INSIDE OF THE INDIVIDUAL"

Because man is able to manipulate symbols he can also do another important thing. He is able to talk about his own behavior, including behavior that is emotional in nature. He is able to label internal behavior and processes and learn appropriate behavior to direct toward these behavior patterns. He is, for instance, able to identify certain internal conditions as hunger and tell himself that food will serve under normal conditions to relieve this condition. In like manner he learns to identify thirst, drug addiction,

* Alfred Stern, "Science and the Philosophers," *American Scientist*, XLIV, No. 3 (July, 1956), 288.

Some Language Differences

English has separate words for "pilot," "fly (n.)," and "airplane," but Hopi has only one. Eskimo has many words for different kinds of "snow" but English has only two. On the other hand, Aztec has only one basic word for our separate words "cold," "ice," and "snow." We have one word for "water," whereas, Hopi has two, depending on whether the water is stationary or in motion. English has such words as "speed," and "rapid," whereas, Hopi has no real equivalents for them and normally renders them by "very" or "intense" plus a verb of motion. English has separate terms for "blue" and "green," but only one term for all intensities of "black" short of "gray." Navaho, on the contrary, does not have separate highly codeable terms for "blue" and "green" but does have two terms for different kinds of "black." English has the generic term "horse" but Arabic has only scores of different terms for different breeds or conditions of horses. The kinship terminology in some languages is certainly vastly different (and in certain respects both more refined and more gross) than it is in English. In all of these cases, it is not difficult to relate the codifiability differences to gross cultural differences.

—Joshua A. Fishman.*

etc. He is able to talk about his feelings and indicate whether he has any emotional reactions when he views his national flag blowing in the breeze or hears his national anthem. He is able to tell himself and others how he feels about his wife or about his mother-in-law. And the student is able to tell his sociology professor how much he likes or dislikes sociology as an area of study, to say nothing about the teaching ability of the professor.

In this sense, then, we are symbolically able to "get inside" the individual and discover how he feels about things. More accurately, however,

* Joshua A. Fishman, "A Systematization of the Whorfian Hypothesis," *Behavioral Science*, V, No. 4 (October, 1960), 8–9.

we are able to pay attention to his verbal behavior and evaluate it not only in our day-to-day relationships with others (and ourselves) but also in scientific research. Verbal behavior is indeed one of the most important types of behavior for the social scientist. We have previously emphasized that our response to any particular stimulus is influenced strongly by the manner in which we define that stimulus. Verbal behavior is the major source of information about such definitions.

SYMBOLS AND LOWER ANIMALS

The ability to manipulate symbols is one of the major features or characteristics that distinguish human beings from the lower animals. Human beings live in a symbolic world, in a world "cut up" or subdivided in an intricate pattern, with the various units named or labeled and plans of action developed. Animals, it would appear, respond more directly to the world and do not superimpose upon it dimensions such as the religious or esthetic. Lower animals, however, apparently think. Lower animals do learn. How this is accomplished without symbols is at the moment an unanswered question about which we can only speculate.

INTERACTIONISM

Chapter 1 suggested that our approach to the study of human interaction would be that of the interactionist. This discussion of the symbolic nature of human interaction provides additional support to this position. If, as we have maintained, human beings respond to symbols (subjective reality) and if the definitions of symbols are learned, then it follows that conclusions about human behavior that fail to take this into account would be inadequate. Language is a social phenomenon. Learning symbols and their definitions is a social phenomenon. Using them is a social phenomenon. To attempt to reach conclusions about such phenomena by paying attention to any level other than the social—the individual, biological, atomic, or biochemical for instance—would seem, sociologically, to be relatively unproductive. Social behavior should be studied at the social level if sociological understanding is to be obtained.

SUMMARY

Since much of man's interaction is symbolic in nature (a characteristic that distinguishes man from other animals), an understanding what symbols are and how man uses them provides increased understanding of human behavior. Symbols have been identified as things that refer to other things. The man-made meaning or definition of symbols, however, is more extensive than mere referent identification. Meaning also includes the plans of action and the NER evaluations that man develops and associates with the symbols or labels he uses. The connection between referent and symbol with its accompanying meaning is an arbitrary one that man himself develops. Man's use of symbols is not restricted to ER symbols which identify aspects of the empirical world but includes use of NER symbols, which permit him to recognize dimensions such as the supernatural, fictions, and evaluative systems and mathematical systems that he develops. Further, there is no necessary mutually interdependent relationship between ER and NER symbols.

Human behavior, then, is not simply "stimulus–response" behavior, but rather "stimulus–definition–response" behavior since the behavior that man directs toward objects, including other human beings, stems more from the labels he applies with the accompanying plans of action (his subjective reality) than from the empirical qualities of these objects (objective reality). This permits man under the appropriate circumstances even to see what his label calls for, though it may not be there in objective reality.

A person's language influences how he experiences his world, and since any object can be viewed in any number of different ways, people with different languages have different experiences, and learning new languages or even new words permits one to respond to his world differently than he did before.

Symbols that may reflect objective reality with differing degrees of accuracy can be applied by an individual to himself, and to any of his internal processes of which he may be aware.

Applying symbols to one's world, deciding upon the accuracy of their use, adjusting to those symbols, and acting in such a way as to harmonize them—these constitute a dynamic process not rigidly predetermined, but, in part at least, emerging from the interplay of all the factors involved. Thus when we couple the term "symbolic" to another basic term, "interaction" (to which the next chapter will be devoted), and throughout the text talk of "symbolic interaction," it is a dynamic, emergent phenomenon to which we refer.

QUESTIONS

1. Explain the statement by Stern that "Locke, Berkeley, Hume, and Kant made us understand what the Greek atomists already knew: that sense experience is not the bridge which connects us with, but the abyss which separates us from, absolute reality."
2. Distinguish between ER and NER symbols.
3. Discuss: "Society exists *in* communication."
4. Distinguish between subjective and objective reality.
5. Explain how people with different languages experience their world differently.
6. Why is feedback important in accurate communication?
7. Where do the plans of action incorporated in the meaning of symbols come from?
8. How can "attitude" be defined so that it has an empirical referent?
9. Discuss the statement that any label only sensitizes us to but one small aspect of the phenomenon labeled.
10. How are symbols related to such things as daydreaming, fantasy, and reliving the past?
11. How do you react to the statement that the ultimate weapon may not be the bomb but may be the symbol instead?

PROJECT

Select an item from your campus setting and list the categories into which it can be classified. What does this suggest about the process of selective perception?

SUGGESTED READING

BROWN, ROGER. *Words and Things.* New York: The Free Press of Glencoe, Inc., 1958.

HAYAKAWA, S. I. *Language in Thought and Action.* New York: Harcourt, Brace & World, Inc., 1950.

LEE, DOROTHY. *Freedom and Culture.* Englewood Cliffs, N. J.: Prentice-Hall, Inc., 1959.

LINDESMITH, ALFRED R., and ANSELM L. STRAUSS. *Social Psychology.* Rev. ed. New York: Holt, Rinehart and Winston, Inc., 1956.

LYND, HELEN MERRELL. *On Shame and the Search for Identity.* New York: Harcourt, Brace & World, Inc., 1958.

MACCOBY, ELEANOR E., THEODORE M. NEWCOMB, and EUGENE L. HARTLEY (eds.). *Readings in Social Psychology.* New York: Holt, Rinehart and Winston, Inc., 1958. Particularly pp. 1–40.

MEAD, GEORGE H. *Mind, Self and Society.* Chicago: The University of Chicago Press, 1934.

ROSE, ARNOLD M. (ed.). *Human Behavior and Social Processes.* Boston: Houghton Mifflin Co., 1962.

SAPIR, EDWARD. *Culture, Language and Personality.* Berkeley, Calif.: University of California Press, 1958.

STRAUSS, ANSELM. *Mirrors and Masks.* New York: The Free Press of Glencoe, Inc., 1959.

WHORF, BENJAMIN LEE. *Language, Thought and Reality.* New York: John Wiley & Sons, Inc., 1956.

4

The Social Nature of

Human Behavior

Can you think of any behavior of man that does not directly or indirectly involve others? What happens to our explanations of human behavior if this social dimension is not included?

INTRODUCTION

We have defined sociology as the scientific study of human interaction, specifying, among other things, that being scientific in the study of this interaction requires that one pay attention to empirical phenomena in an objective, verifiable manner. An entire chapter has explored the significance of the fact that human interaction is basically symbolic interaction, emphasizing that man subdivides his world into various parts to which he gives names, and decides upon plans of action felt to be appropriate for the things he thus identifies. His response to the things surrounding him and affecting his daily actions stems from the labels he uses to identify them. There seems to be almost no limit to the ways in which the universe can be subdivided and labeled. Groups with different languages experience their world differently; conversely, to learn a new language or even new words permits one to respond to his world in a manner different from before.

The principle of selective perception applies to the study of sociology as it does to all behavior. It is literally impossible for any individual, and this of course includes the sociologist, to pay attention to everything at once. Attention is always focused upon limited aspects of the universe. This chapter will help the student identify and anticipate the limited types of phenomena to which the sociologist pays attention and the types of answers he can expect to obtain from a sociological study of these phenomena. The answers one obtains are always relative to the questions he asks, and to the phenomena to which he directs his attention in obtaining his answers.

SOME POSSIBLE PERSPECTIVES

Let us, then, briefly identify some of the different ways, scientific and non-scientific, in which behavior can be viewed (see Chart I).

Before proceeding with our discussion of the implications of analysis at these different levels,

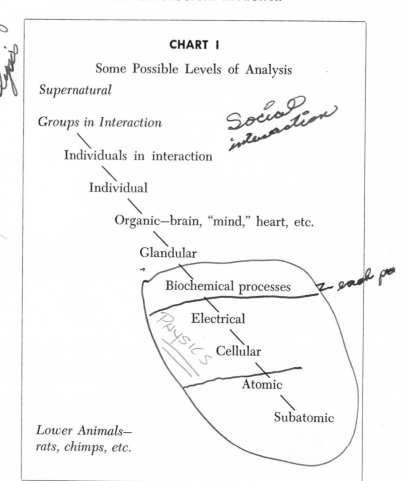

CHART I

Some Possible Levels of Analysis

Supernatural

Groups in Interaction

     Individuals in interaction

         Individual

            Organic—brain, "mind," heart, etc.

               Glandular

                 Biochemical processes

                   Electrical

                     Cellular

                       Atomic

                         Subatomic

Lower Animals—
rats, chimps, etc.

let us supply some labels to facilitate this discussion. We will call the approach which concentrates primarily upon interaction between groups and individuals "interactionism" or the "interactionist approach." We will use the term "reductionism" or the "reductionist approach" to identify all of the other approaches in which attention is *reduced* to some component part of the phenomena identified by interactionism— groups and individuals in interaction. In terms of Chart I, this includes those levels from the individual down to the subatomic. This obviously includes many different levels under the "reductionism" label, and consequently fails to call attention to many differences which exist within this broad category. The term "reductionism,"

however, will serve our purpose since our major goal is not to explore all of these differences, but rather to distinguish the sociological from the many other non-sociological approaches.[1]

[1] Smelser and Smelser define reductionism as an "attempt to translate, without loss, all statements at one analytic level into statements regarding the operations of variables at another level." Examples of reductionism would be the statements that "personality is nothing more than the subjective manifestation of social structure" or "social systems are nothing more than the objective manifestations of personality states. The general consequence of reductionist reasoning, if pushed far enough, is to deny the independent conceptual status of one level." Neil J. Smelser and William T. Smelser, *Personality and Social Systems* (New York: John Wiley & Sons, Inc., 1963), p. 12.

The term "anti-reductionism" has also been used as synonymous with interactionism. We will use both terms. It is obvious, however, that any of these other levels can, theoretically at least, be reduced for study purposes to smaller component parts, and that study which concentrates at *any* level is, in a sense, anti-reductionist to the lower levels. We will not use the term in that sense, but only as synonymous with interactionism. It therefore identifies an approach that involves paying major attention to individuals or groups in interaction.

Since we have defined sociology as the study of human interaction, our approach is that of the *interactionist* or the *anti-reductionist*, and since, as the previous chapter has pointed out, human interaction is symbolic interaction, the study of symbols is included under this label.

In this chapter we explore the basic premise that human behavior is a social phenomenon, and indicate how the study of the social aspects of such behavior falls within the domain of sociology.[2]

INTERACTIONISM—THE SOCIAL ASPECTS OF HUMAN BEHAVIOR

Individual and Society

A sociological perspective is obtained by paying attention to the way individuals and/or groups relate themselves to each other. Attention is not focused upon isolated individuals, since it is felt that to do so shuts out important aspects which help explain human behavior. The question can, in fact, be raised as to whether there is such a thing as an *isolated* individual, or more specifically *isolated individual behavior*. The behavior of an individual is viewed socio-

logically as being but one part of a larger social matrix, and from this perspective it is as inaccurate to describe behavior in terms of the single individual as it would be to describe a pair of scissors in terms of one blade. Human behavior involves individuals coming together, as do the blades of a pair of scissors, in a process of mutual stimulation. Interaction is a major characteristic of human behavior.

From this perspective, to separate the "individual" and "society," as is frequently done in discussions of human behavior, is unwarranted; "individual" *and* "society" implies that these are two separate and distinct entities, with the individual existing independently of society, as depicted in the following diagram.

Individuals do not exist in this manner. Every individual is a *part of* society. If all individuals were isolated there would be no society. Society is composed of *interacting* individuals, as shown in over-simplified form in the following diagram:

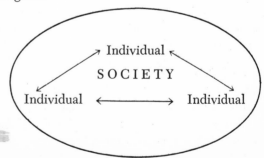

Knowledge of the nature of the relationships that obtain between individuals is necessary if we are to gain an adequate sociological understanding of human behavior. Explanations of behavior that are not based on social perspective are quite different from those that do. The narrowed perspective of individual studies and interpretations as contrasted with an interactionist perspective is suggested in the diagram that follows on page 60.

[2] For further discussion, see: Max Weber, *The Theory of Social and Economic Organization*, trans. A. M. Henderson and Talcott Parsons, edited with an Introduction by Talcott Parsons (New York: The Free Press of Glencoe, Inc., 1947), pp. 111–120; Bronislaw Malinowski, *Crime and Custom in Savage Society* (London: Routledge & Kegan Paul, Ltd.), pp. 39–45; and Talcott Parsons and Edward A. Shils (eds.), *Toward A General Theory of Action* (Cambridge: Harvard University Press, 1952), pp. 105–107.

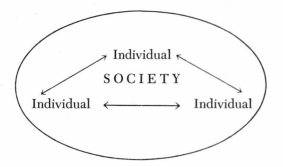

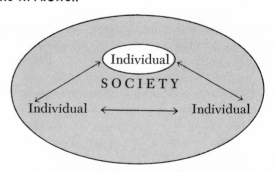

The contrast between the individual and the social perspective is clearly shown by Becker[3] in his discussion of deviant behavior. He points out that social groups create deviance by making the rules whose infraction constitutes deviance, and by applying those rules to particular people and labeling them as outsiders. From this point of view, deviance is not a quality of the act the person commits, but rather a consequence of the application by others of rules and sanctions to an "offender." The deviant is one to whom that label has successfully been applied; deviant behavior is behavior that people so label.

The social perspective also directs attention to groups of individuals interacting with each other.

Sociology enlarges upon the social perspective; it takes into account the setting or situation in which this interaction of individuals takes place. Situational factors are always involved in man's behavior and are thus included in sociological explanations. Climatic and geographical factors are some obvious illustrations of natural situational factors. Various social factors also are involved, many of which will be identified as we progress through the text. Situational factors *per se* and man's definitions of them are both involved in any interaction sequence.

Expectations and Interaction

The social nature of human behavior is further illustrated by the fact that behavior is generally, if not always, directed toward others. Man, in his behavior, is directly or indirectly "playing for a particular audience." The behavior of the individual is influenced by his awareness of the other or others toward whom it is directed. He tailors his behavior to mesh with that of the others involved. Waller[4] has pointed out, for instance, that "a girl who is called to the telephone in the dormitories will often allow herself to be called several times, in order to give all the other girls ample opportunity to hear her paged."

The individual edits his speaking and thinking to fit the situation, and an important factor involved in this "tailoring" process is the ideas (definitions) an individual has as to what others involved expect him to do. He also, of course, has some expectations as to how these others will behave. Decisions concerning the expectations of others are, of course, related to the expectations which the others have; and these in turn are introduced into the on-going behavioral sequence. Continued interaction reaffirms or discounts the expectations of interacting individuals toward each other, and the result may be modifications of behavior to adjust for these new perspectives. Behavior is constantly being adapted to the audience for whom it is intended. Understanding of human behavior is facilitated if we know, for instance, whether it is interaction between friends or foes, in-groups or out-groups, or any of the endless combinations of individuals and/or groups. And, as Parsons and Shils[5] have indicated, "Communication through a common

---

[3] Howard S. Becker, *Outsiders: Studies in the Sociology of Deviance* (New York: The Free Press of Glencoe, Inc., 1963), p. 9.

[4] Willard Waller, "The Rating and Dating Complex," *American Sociological Review*, II, No. 5 (October, 1937), 730.

[5] Parsons and Shils, *op. cit.*, p. 105.

system of symbols is the precondition of this reciprocity or complementarity of expectations."

The audience toward which the behavior of an individual is directed may, of course, be himself. We all do things for and to ourselves. An individual can initiate activity directed toward himself and can then respond to this self-initiated activity. This fact, however, does not invalidate the basic premise that behavior is directed toward some particular audience. It only identifies one particular audience. Behavior that is self-oriented may be quite different in certain respects from behavior that is oriented toward others. Most of us, by way of illustration, will generally tell ourselves (frequently this is done silently in the form of "thinking") things about others which we will not express publicly.

We have pointed out that man's behavior is usually not haphazard, undirected, chaotic behavior, but rather is orderly and systematic. This orderliness stems, in part, from the fact that social order is a group phenomenon. While it would theoretically be possible for an isolated individual to be orderly and systematic "all by himself," this is not possible for interacting individuals. Order under these conditions requires that those involved relate themselves to each other in systematic ways. Behavior and expectations must be at least somewhat harmonious if interaction

---

Individualist or Collectivist?

After all, even the philosophy of individualism is a philosophy of a collectivity. If it were not, it could not exist. The "individualist" found this philosophy a widely accepted belief in the social heritage into which he was born. He is not even an individualist in the selection of his philosophy of individualism. It was passed on to him along with his language, his religion, his mode of dress, and other patterns.

—Lawrence Guy Brown.*

---

* From *Social Pathology* by Lawrence Guy Brown. Copyright, 1942, F. S. Crofts & Co., Inc. Reprinted by permission of Appleton-Century-Crofts.

is to take place. The "other" is an ever present factor to be taken into account. The sociologist is interested in identifying this order or structure of interaction, as well as the factors that contribute to it. He is interested in determining the functional requisites for systematic human behavior, in finding out what individuals have to do to and for each other in order to maintain their systems of symbols and related behavior.

Some Major Definitions Involved in Interaction [6]

Our previous discussion of the symbolic nature of human behavior has emphasized that man labels portions of his universe and then responds to them according to the definitions that he has learned to associate with these labels. Four important definitions are involved in all interaction. They are presented here from the perspective of the actor.

1. The definitions man places upon the *situation* in which he finds himself, and in which his interaction takes place. He is aware (tells himself) that he is, for instance, attending a funeral, applying for a job, making love, behind the enemy lines, etc., and such awareness influences his behavior in this situation. He may, of course, misinterpret the situation and get into difficulty as a result thereof.

2. The definitions man places upon the *others* with whom he interacts in this situation. He defines these others as the mourners at a funeral, the personnel director of the company, his sweetheart, or an enemy soldier. Such definitions influence his behavior in that he engages in what are to him the appropriate plans of action to direct toward objects (human) thus labeled. The others involved in any sequence of behavior need not be physically present. Man can respond to symbols without the referents being present.

3. The definitions man places upon *himself*. He may see himself as a newspaper reporter at a funeral, an applicant for a position, an eager beau, or an espionage agent for his country. He

---

[6] Each of these definitions will be further discussed in subsequent chapters.

engages in behavior which he defines as appropriate for such an object—himself, with the proper label.

4. The definitions man places upon any non-human *objects* involved in the interaction, such as a casket, the Masonic ring on the finger of the personnel director, the diamond ring on the finger of his sweetheart, or the falling snow which is covering his tracks as he moves behind the enemy lines. Value definitions are an important type of definition attributed to these objects.

In the dynamic on-going interaction of life these definitions may, of course, be constantly modified, or at least different aspects of them may be taken into account. They may be systematized and related to each other in many different ways. Whatever the dynamics may be, it is sociologically important to pay attention to these factors (among others, of course) in our efforts to develop theories and explanations of human behavior. Human behavior is a social phenomenon. Individuals do not behave as isolated individuals, but rather as participants in on-going social behavior; even a hermit cannot be a hermit unless others stay away from him. From this perspective it would seem safe to conclude that "you can't be human all by yourself."

REDUCTIONISM

Reductionism Contrasted with Interactionism

Let us turn now to the contrasting reductionist viewpoint, in which the world is subdivided in a manner different from that just described. Included in this category, as Chart I has indicated, are explanations focused at such levels as the individual, biochemical, organic, cellular, atomic, and subatomic. All of these levels are obviously levels at which extensive study and research can be done. Experts in each area, in fact, spend their lifetime doing such study. The important question here is how phenomena at any of these levels are related to the social behavior of man.

There can be no question that individuals, biochemical processes, organs, cells, and atoms do exist and are all *involved in* man's social behav-

Figure 4.1 Physical interaction, as in this Maori greeting involving nose rubbing, is given meaning by the ones involved. It is the meaning that influences subsequent behavior. (The Bettmann Archive, Inc.)

ior. However, the fact that they are "involved in" behavior does not mean that study at any of these levels provides answers adequately to explain *social* behavior. Each of these factors may be a *necessary* element of this behavior, in that man could not behave as he does if these elements were not all involved, but they do not in and of themselves provide *adequate* answers about social behavior. Interacting human beings are something *more than* atoms, cells, organs, or *an* individual. They are social phenomena.

Explanations which involve only lower-level (non-social) factors as direct causative factors in social behavior are sociologically inadequate in that they fail to specify how the jump is made from the lower level to the social level. Explanations of social behavior in terms of interacting atoms, to take the extreme case, may show how atoms interact with atoms, but not how atoms interact with human beings or how human beings interact with human beings. Social behavior involves interacting atoms, to be sure, but it is more than this. It involves masses of atoms (human beings) interacting with other masses of atoms. It is highly doubtful, in fact, whether we can even say or think the same things about *human beings* using concepts appropriate to the atomic level that we can by using concepts appropriate at the social level. In order to conceptualize or visualize social behavior of man, one has to move to the higher level which, while it involves atoms, is concerned with a larger configuration of atoms which is considered as an entity.

The same thing is true of cells. Cells (composed of interacting atoms) interact with cells, not with the large configuration of cells of which a human being is composed. Organs (composed of interacting cells, which are composed of interacting atoms) interact with organs, not with other human beings directly. Biochemical and electrical processes (involving atoms, cells, and organs) take place within the individual, not between individuals.

Since humans in interaction are directly or indirectly involved with others it would seem that theories which stop at any of the non-social levels would fail to explain social behavior adequately. There is always the question, as has been previously stated, of how theory and research move from one level to another. Devereux [7] has suggested that it is impossible to think simultaneously in terms of two different frames of reference. How does one start out investigating atoms, cells, nerves, or organs, and end up talking about social behavior? Such an approach involves some big jumps which are generally not recognized by adherents of such theories or are glossed over without giving the impression that they are important.

If cells interact with cells, and atoms with atoms rather than with human beings, how then do human beings interact with other human beings? What is the connecting link? How do individuals influence each other? What basically is the mechanism of interaction? The connecting link is the *symbol*. Human beings define each other. An individual's particular definitions stem from his past experiences and from his definition of the current situation, including those cues presented directly or indirectly by the others involved. Social behavior, in oversimplified terms, involves human beings "throwing symbols back and forth at each other." Atoms and cells of one individual do not interact with atoms and cells of another individual; human beings interact with human beings and the connecting link between these individuals is communication. Direct physical contact is, of course, possible and is a frequent occurrence. However, even here, as has been already suggested, it is not the physical contact *per se* but rather the definitions of it that have the greatest impact upon man's behavior.

Behavior is viewed sociologically as emerging from the reciprocal give-and-take of interdependent individuals who are constantly adapting their behavior to that of the others involved. The

---

Interaction of Schizophrenic Patients

When patients are able to establish meaningful relationships with staff personnel, this facilitates meaningful relationships between patients. . . . If a patient likes his boss, it is possible that this is partly because the other patients like the boss as well and because patients are getting on well together. Interpersonal relationships have a habit of rubbing off on others in the same social setting whether these relationships be positive or negative.

—Robert A. Chittick, et al.*

---

[7] George Devereux, "Two Types of Modal Personality Models," in Smelser and Smelser, *op. cit.*, p. 25.

* Robert A. Chittick, *et al., The Vermont Story: Rehabilitation of Chronic Schizophrenic Patients* (Burlington, Vt.: Queen City Printers, Inc., 1961), pp. 40–41.

personality of the individual, or his distinctive ways of behaving, is viewed as developing and being reaffirmed in his on-going interaction with others. Sociologists pay attention to the interchanges that go on among human beings as they come into contact with one another, interchanges which are primarily symbolic in nature.

By its very nature, symbolic behavior is interactionist or social in nature. A second person is required not merely in the process of learning language, but as the indispensable and enduring condition of all symbolic behavior. The very act of symbolic formation, whether it be language, art, or thinking, is a formulation for *someone else*.

Individuals and Individual Differences

It is certainly not maintained here that individuals do not exist, or that there are no individual differences. Recognizing both of these facts, the important point here is that to study an individual without taking the situation and the others into account deletes important sociological variables from consideration. Individuals do not exist *in isolation*. Individuals do behave differently from other individuals; no two, in fact, ever behave in an identical manner. The behavior that is different is social behavior, and the difference is due in part to the fact that others are differentially involved in this behavior.

The interactionist perspective can be illustrated by an analysis of the following contrasting ways of viewing causality or responsibility for acts.

Individual Determinism

Individuals are seen as being independent, as "free agents" who make decisions and act individually. They have "free will." The individual is solely responsible for his own acts, and is rewarded or punished accordingly.

Societal Determinism

From this perspective, individuals do not make independent decisions or behave as "free" indi-

viduals. Society, rather, makes the decisions or establishes the patterns, and the individuals are merely "rubber stamps" of society. This type of thinking forces one to dichotomize society and the individual. It pays no attention to the fact that society is composed of interacting individuals, or that each individual *is* a part of the society of every other member. Some refer to this approach as "cultural determinism."

Interactionism or Interactional Determinism

From this perspective, individuals are viewed as mutually influencing each other. Society is, in fact, composed of interacting individuals; each has an influence, and each is at the same time being influenced by others. Individuals make choices or decisions all the time, but they are limited rather than "free" or unlimited choices. Decisions are limited by several factors: the symbols learned, situational factors, the behavior of others.

There is another aspect to be considered. Interacting individuals impose limitations upon each other, but interaction permits behavior which could never be engaged in by an isolated individual. It is doubtful if individuals could do many of the things which they usually do throughout the day if they were separated. Man is a social or interacting being.

In terms of causality or responsibility, from the interactionist perspective neither the individual nor the others with whom he interacts are *solely* responsible for some particular act. There is no such thing as a self-made man.

If we take the individual perspective and think in terms of individual responsibility, we are likely to conclude without considering the matter further that the individual is somehow compelled to engage in his behavior and that he will continue to do so. On the other hand, if we view, say, deviant behavior as behavior which arises in interaction with others, we become aware that changes in the interaction patterns may produce significant changes in the "deviant behavior." In a study of juvenile delinquents who "hustle"

Responsibility and Reward

When Standing Bear as a boy of about five killed his first bird, his father celebrated the event by giving away a horse to someone else, an old man who could never return the gift. . . . Individual achievement is completely obliterated here. Since the self is not distinguished, gratitude has no part in the picture; so that when a warrior gave a horse to the village crier for an orphan boy, he neither expected nor received thanks; on the other hand, a group of his village-mates formed a band to sing his praises.

—Dorothy Lee.*

adult homosexuals, Reiss [8] points out that the boys themselves are not homosexual. They engage in homosexual practices, but as a part of a delinquent pattern of behavior, and their behavior is governed by the norm definitions of the peer group in which they are primarily involved. When they get older and are able to make money in other ways—when according to group standards it is no longer appropriate for them to engage in such homosexual behavior—they stop their homosexual activity.

An individual is *a* causal factor (partly to blame or partly responsible) but so are the others with whom he has related himself and they likewise are partly to blame or to be praised. The American system of justice is built upon the premise of *individual responsibility.* At a college graduation ceremony the diploma is given to the *individual* and he is recognized for *his* achievements. Yet, parents, brothers, sisters, classmates, dorm mothers, teachers, administrators, and taxpayers have all been involved in the process.

* Dorothy Lee, *Freedom and Culture* (Englewood Cliffs, N. J.: Prentice-Hall, Inc., 1959), p. 62.

[8] Albert J. Reiss, Jr., "The Social Integration of Queers and Peers," in Howard S. Becker (ed.), *The Other Side* (New York: The Free Press of Glencoe, Inc., 1964), pp. 181–210.

The principle of multiple causation applies to human behavior, whatever the reward–punishment system a group may follow.

Interactionism leads to a rejection of a completely individualistic interpretation of behavior, but does not eliminate the individual from consideration. What we have done is to view the individual as but one part of the larger social matrix to which we pay attention.

A Symbolic Analogy

The significance of our discussion can be sharpened by the following analogy of the different levels of symbolic analysis. Three levels can be identified as follows:

1. Letter level, in which one pays attention to single letters such as O, G, D.
2. Word level in which one pays attention to a combination of letters such as DOG.
3. Sentence level, in which one pays attention to a combination of words, such as THIS ANIMAL IS NOT A DOG.

The crucial question here is whether one can come to the same kinds of conclusions from an analysis at any of these levels. Can one, for instance, pay attention to letters only, and come to a conclusion such as THIS ANIMAL IS NOT A DOG? Can one pay attention to just words (not combinations of words) and come to the conclusion that the label DOG is a wrong one? The answer would seem to be "no." Letters and words are involved in the third level, but it is more than just these. At the third level the lower-level elements are arranged in particular patterns from which new meaning is gained. A different type of phenomenon exists at the third level.

Carrying the analogy to another area, can one pay attention to bricks, boards, and nails, and talk or theorize much about rooms or houses? Or, can one talk about drops of water and say much about rivers or lakes? No. More inclusive, basically different concepts are needed.

Similarly, can one talk only about biological factors or about *an* individual and say much that is very meaningful about *human beings in interaction?* [9]

Reductionism at the Trait Level

Reductionist explanations are sometimes stated in terms of personality traits, which are viewed as entities or at least as consistent behavior patterns which an individual "carries with him" as a consistent part of his personality. Accordingly, an individual may be classified as being honest, dependable, and aggressive. Personality inventories make use of such terms, as do letters of recommendation. To view behavior in such a fashion, however, divorces it from the situations in which it takes place, and consequently shuts out an important sociological factor. Individuals, for instance, are not honest in the abstract (although they may endorse honesty in the abstract) but they are, rather, honest in particular situations and dishonest in other situations. A man who is "as honest as the day is long," if caught behind enemy lines in a combat situation, may lie in order to save his life, to get back to his own lines, or to prevent vital information from getting into enemy hands. He may expect to be rewarded and be rewarded for his effective lying, and feel proud of himself for what he has done. In less serious situations, one may tell a friend that she looks nice in a new hat without really being convinced that she does. Lying then is engaged in and appropriate in particular situations.

Making the unqualified statement that Citizen Jones is honest ignores the important sociological fact that honesty does not exist in isolation or in a vacuum. Honesty is always relative to a situation, and different individuals are honest or dishonest in different situations. The football player whom the coach describes as having an aggressive personality may be anything but aggressive as he presents a talk before his English class. People are aggressive only in certain situations, not in isolation. This is true of all personality "traits."

Coutu [10] has suggested that the use of the term "tinsit" might remind the user of the situational factor in the human equation. His point is that human "tendencies" do not exist independently but rather are always relative to a situation, and thus to talk of "tendencies" without taking into account the situational factors ignores an important variable. "Tinsit" then is short for "tendency in situation." Although the word has not been widely used, it is at least an effort to get social scientists to take a broader perspective in their analysis of human behavior. This is also the major objective of this chapter—to sensitize the student to the social aspects of behavior.

Empirical Biological Entities as Causative Factors

Reductionist explanations may involve the biological entities known to exist inside the human body. The biological sciences have identified the parts of the body—heart, lungs, liver—and specialize in the study of these organs. However, these do not seem to be involved in *social behavior* as *direct* causative factors. Man does, of course, have many processes going on inside of him all the time. His heart, stomach, and

---

Others Are Watching

The social nature of behavior is suggested when one considers how he might behave if he could spend, say, twenty-four hours completely invisible. And the social function or consequence of religion is also suggested when one considers the influence upon behavior of the belief that an all-powerful God is watching over you.

---

[9] Sherif and Sherif have indicated, "It seems to us that the notion of levels is a useful one in making interdisciplinary attempts really effective. It will give men working on human relations the realization that they are approaching similar or the same problems at different levels, which necessitate that each formulate its appropriate approaches, units of analysis, concepts in referring to events." Muzafer Sherif and Carolyn W. Sherif, *Groups in Harmony and Tension* (New York: Harper & Row, Inc., 1953), pp. 7–8.

[10] Walter Coutu, *Emergent Human Nature* (New York: Alfred A. Knopf, Inc., 1949).

kidneys, for example, are constantly functioning, but their functions do not directly produce any certain type of social behavior. People with an empty stomach may eat or may fast, depending upon how they define themselves and the situation. They may be hypnotized and told that they are not hungry and, when questioned later, report that they feel no hunger and when presented with food may refuse or decline to eat. An internal condition does not *directly* cause social behavior.

Rather, internal conditions are defined in the same way that other phenomena are defined. Man's reactions to them stem more from his definition of a condition than from the condition *per se*. It makes a big difference in his subsequent behavior, for instance, whether the individual defines himself as (1) being ill because of some disease germs which have found their way inside of him, (2) possessed by an evil spirit, or (3) under the influence of a magical spell initiated by his enemy. An individual can use many explanations to label the same internal condition. To understand human behavior it is important not only to know what the internal condition may be but *in addition* how an individual defines it. Man is more than just a biological being!

Non-empirical Internal "Entities"

Man's definitions of phenomena are not restricted by the empirical qualities observed. Man has used many symbols for which there are no empirical referents, and used them in ways which are very significant for his behavior. To return to the example used in the preceding paragraph, if one thinks that he is possessed by an evil spirit, the fact that there is no empirical entity to which the term "spirit" applies is of little consequence. *To him* (subjective reality) he is possessed by an evil spirit and he may engage in activities designed to rid himself of this spirit.

Various reductionist explanations of human behavior have made use of non-empirical concepts, frequently viewing them as being located somewhere inside the individual. Some of these non-empirical "things" are mind, instinct, drive, emo-

tion, habit, superego, attitude, and conscience. Note that all of these terms are nouns. Thus, according to English grammar they identify a "person, place, or thing." Since they are nouns it is easy to take the next step and attribute causative powers to these "things" and maintain, for instance, that Sally brushes her teeth every morning *because* of a habit. Or Johnny dislikes Jews *because* he has an anti-Semitic attitude. These are tautological and meaningless cause-and-effect statements because they fail to identify two "things," one of which could be the cause of the other. How, for instance, does one observe the "habit" to see if it *causes* Sally to brush her teeth every morning? Some define these terms as *processes* rather than things, which reduces the likelihood of attributing causative power to them. Using different labels would further reduce this practice.

Important questions which must be answered if one is to make *scientific* use of concepts such as these include the following: What are these "things"? Where do they exist? To what empirical object does one pay attention in order to study them? Can the concept be operationally defined? How does one know when his conclusions about them are wrong? How can others verify his conclusions?

While various theorists have viewed these "things" as causative agents of human social behavior, it is important to note that as yet no one has ever found any empirical evidence that these "things" exist inside an individual and are therefore available to "cause" behavior.

If, however, these words are changed from nouns to verbs or adjectives,' one does not as easily get into a semantic trap about "cause." If, for instance, one talks about instinctive or unlearned behavior rather than about "instincts"; about habitual behavior rather than "habits"; about emotional behavior rather than "emotions"; about remembering rather than "memory"; about making value judgments rather than a "conscience" he then neither says nor implies anything about what causes the emotional behavior or the particular value judgments. He is more likely to have seen such causes in previous behavior than to be attributing cause to some mystical non-empirical entity believed to exist inside of the individual.

Man seems frequently to have followed the noun orientation of his language and the previous beliefs and theories (culture) of his group, to have invented these "things" and then accepted the premise that they cause behavior. Rather than indicating that man behaves in a particular way and relating this behavior to past behavior, these mystical "things" have been invented and causative powers attributed to them. It is easy to believe what one wants to believe.

There can be no question that internal processes, particularly those involved in the brain, are involved in human interaction. The question raised here is relative to the usefulness of theories which would provide causative explanations in terms of variables such as "mind," "instinct," or "drives," which no one as yet has been able to find. It would seem to be more profitable to think and build theories in terms of what man

does and what he has previously done, recognizing that anything or any behavior is theoretically capable of being subdivided into smaller parts, and that at whatever level one wants to stop, there is still a lower level to which behavior could be reduced. The type of answers one gets are always relative to the level to which he gives attention. It is doubtful if similarly significant answers can be secured about man's *social* behavior at any of these non-social levels.

INTERACTIONISM AND REDUCTIONISM— SOME FURTHER COMPARISONS

Let us illustrate the reductionist and the interactionist approaches with the specific case of husband Jones kissing his wife good-bye as he leaves for the office. The contrasting ways in which the phenomenon can be explained are suggested in the following diagram:

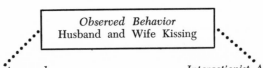

| *Observed Behavior* |
| Husband and Wife Kissing |

Reductionist Approach

Behavior explained in terms of internal conditions of husband and wife, including such "things" as:
1. Impulse
2. Drive
3. Attitude (defined as an internal condition)
4. Ego
5. Mind
6. Hormones

Interactionist Approach

Behavior explained in terms of antecedent learning experiences and current situational factors such as:
1. Previously seeing own father and mother behave in this way
2. Learned definitions as to how husband and wife should interact
3. Learning that kissing a loved one is a rewarding experience (not all societies define it this way)
4. Expectations attributed to others—husband believes wife expects and wants him to kiss her
5. Definitions of biological conditions — individual believes he will get an "emotional charge" from kissing this individual, or maybe tells himself, "I have bad breath this morning, so I'd better make it a 'quickie'."

Reductionists start out with the assumption that man's social behavior is biological in origin and accordingly turn their attention to internal variables, doing research and building theories accordingly. If empirical entities are not present adequately to explain the behavior, non-empirical entities (constructs) can be posited which help to round out this explanation so that it becomes acceptable to those postulating the theory.

Interactionists, while recognizing that internal biological processes are functioning and are involved in the on-going behavior pay major attention to social variables such as those identified in the diagram. Both factors are, of course, involved in the behavior. Different types of answers such as these—and others as well—are useful for different purposes. However, as Durkheim has indicated, "the determining cause of a social fact should be sought among the social facts preceding it and not among the states of the individual consciousness."[11]

SUPERNATURAL VARIABLES

Theories of behavior may involve variables believed to be supernatural in nature (see Chart I). Those who endorse such theories may, for instance, see "the hand of God" working as a causative factor in human behavior. Since supernatural factors are non-empirical or superempirical in nature, the scientist, with his empirical limitations, has to exclude them from his explanations of behavior. He can, of course, take into account the *definitions* which man has about the supernatural realm by paying attention to verbal or symbolic behavior, and this is what the scientific sociologist does. Theory and variables are kept at the natural—as contrasted with the supernatural—social level. The religionist who seeks different types of answers usually involves supernatural variables directly in his theories of man's behavior. The sociologist's approach, however, is different from that of the religionist.

The Cab Driver and His Fare

"In this business you've got to use psychology. You've got to make the ride fit the person. Now, take a businessman. He's in a hurry to get someplace.... With him, you've got to keep moving. Do some fancy cutting in and out, give the cab a bit of a jerk when you take off from a light. Not reckless, mind you, but plenty of zip. He likes that. With old people, it's just the opposite. They're more afraid than anyone of getting hurt or killed in a cab. Take it easy with them. Creep along, open doors for them, help them in and out, be real folksy. Call them 'sir' and 'Ma'am' and they'll be calling you 'young man.' They're suckers for this stuff, and they'll loosen up their pocketbooks a little bit."

—Fred Davis.[*]

Man's acceptance of explanations involving supernatural variables, since these are of the non-empirical type, facilitates his acceptance of explanations involving non-empirical internal entities such as the "mind." If it is felt that non-empirical variables are necessary to round out his explanations of his own behavior, it is easy to "find them" wherever man thinks they should be.

Sociological explanations at the social level may be unsatisfactory to those who have learned to view behavior primarily in terms of biological factors. These explanations may also be unsatisfying to those who have learned to rely upon religious or supernatural explanations, and may feel that some of the most important elements of behavior are being ignored. It is a sociological conclusion that we tend to see what we have learned to see and what we have been prepared to see. Our whole discussion in this chapter has been an elaboration of this premise; we have identified some of the different ways in which human behavior is capable of being viewed. Each approach has its adherents. Certainly no claim is

[11] Emile Durkheim, *Rules of Sociological Method* (New York: The Free Press of Glencoe, Inc., 1950), pp. 110–111.

[*] Quoted by Fred Davis, "The Cab Driver and His Fare," *American Journal of Sociology*, LXV, No. 2 (September, 1959), 164.

made that the sociological is the only way to analyze human behavior, nor that it is the most satisfactory way for all purposes. We have tried to make the student more aware of just what the sociological approach is and how it compares to other approaches to which he will be or has been exposed.

SUMMARY

The discussion of the symbolic nature of human behavior in this chapter has pointed out that phenomena can be viewed in any number of different ways. Human behavior is no exception. We have identified some of the different levels at which human behavior can be studied, from the supernatural to the subatomic. Study at each of these levels can, of course, provide answers which are valid for certain purposes. Behavior at each of these levels is also related to behavior at other levels. However, it is highly unlikely that study at any one level will produce the same type of answers as study at another.

The sociologist pays attention primarily to individuals and groups in interaction, and we have used the terms "social," "interactionist," and "anti-reductionist" to identify this level. The term "reductionist" has been used to identify study at any level lower than this. From this sociological perspective, attention is directed to the ways individuals and groups relate themselves to each other, with emphasis upon the definitions of "self," "others," "objects," and "situation," and the expectations stemming from these definitions, which are involved in this interaction. The individual and any of his personality traits are seen as always existing in a social situation, in which they influence, while they are influenced by, the others involved. The individual is *a part of* society.

The perspective of the sociologist excludes from direct study the biological entities inside the individual, but it does include the socially derived definitions which man applies to the biological functions. From the symbolic interactionist perspective, a question has also been raised as to the scientific utility of concepts involving non-empirical "entities" presumably existing inside the individual which have been woven into some reductionist explanations of behavior.

The sociologist's perspective also excludes direct concern with the supernatural realm, although again attention is paid to definitions about such phenomena. No attention is given to the study of lower animals.

Sociologists are basically concerned with the *social* behavior of man.

QUESTIONS

1. In what sense is the individual–group distinction a false dichotomy?
2. Do you see any incongruity when one person tries to persuade another to be "more individualistic?"
3. Discuss the statement: "You can't be human all by yourself."
4. How does the interactionist interpretation of behavior relate to the belief in free will, free agency, or individualism?
5. How many of the things you have done today do you think you would have or could have done without others being involved?
6. Explain the statement that behavior at non-social levels is involved in social behavior but does not adequately account for it.
7. Does the discussion in this chapter have implications for those engaged in professional education? In religious activities?
8. "Treat him as an individual" is a statement frequently heard. Exactly how does one do this?
9. How does the discussion in Chapter 3 as to how man uses symbols support the interactionist interpretation of behavior presented in this chapter?
10. Discuss the statement made by Cooley, the early American sociologist, that the individual and society are twin bred and twin born.

PROJECT

Observe your sociology class for one period and provide some illustrations of how its various members, including the instructor, influenced the behavior of others and the eventual outcome of the discussion.

SUGGESTED READING

BROWN, LAWRENCE GUY. "The Interaction Hypothesis," in JOHN F. CUBER and PEGGY B. HARROFF (eds.), *Readings in Sociology.* New York: Appleton-Century-Crofts, 1962. Pp. 108–112.

COTTRELL, LEONARD S., JR. "The Analysis of Situational Fields in Social Psychology," *American Sociological Review,* VII, No. 3 (June, 1942), 370–382.

COUTU, WALTER. *Emergent Human Nature.* New York: Alfred A. Knopf, Inc., 1949.

MEAD, GEORGE HERBERT. *Mind, Self and Society.* Chicago: University of Chicago Press, 1934.

MILLS, THEODORE M. "A Sleeper Variable in Small Groups Research: The Experimenter," *Pacific Sociological Review,* V, No. 1 (Spring, 1962), 21.

ROSE, ARNOLD M. *Human Behavior and Social Processes.* Boston: Houghton Mifflin Co., 1962. Pp. 3–19.

ROTTER, JULIAN B. "The Role of the Psychological Situation in Determining the Direction of Human Behavior," in RICHARD C. TEEVAN and ROBERT C. BIRNEY (eds.), *Theories of Motivation in Personality and Social Psychology.* Princeton, N. J.: D. Van Nostrand Co., Inc., 1964. (An Insight Book.) Pp. 8–181.

SHIBUTANI, TAMOTSU. *Society and Personality.* Englewood Cliffs, N. J.: Prentice-Hall, Inc., 1961.

STRAUSS, ANSELM. *Mirrors and Masks.* New York: The Free Press of Glencoe, Inc., 1959.

TURNER, RALPH H. "The Problems of Social Dimensions in Personality," *Pacific Sociological Review,* IV, No. 2 (Fall, 1961), 57–62.

5

Biological Foundations of
Human Interaction

As has been suggested, the making of value decisions is not the prerogative of science. Recognizing that the decision cannot be made scientifically it may still be insightful to consider which of the following two interpretations of behavior most enhances the evaluation of man: (1) He behaves as he does because biological factors force him to behave this way, or (2) He behaves as he does because he has learned to.

INTRODUCTION

If the social and symbolic aspects of human interaction occur as we have discussed them in the two preceding chapters, such behavior would have to be related to a particular type of biological makeup. Not all types of possible biological inheritance would permit man to behave in the manner we have been discussing. Whereas our major concern in this text is to study the social aspects of human behavior, this chapter will be devoted to an analysis of the biological foundation that makes this social behavior possible. Man is obviously a biological being. His biological makeup is intimately and intricately involved in all his behavior. Recognizing this, there remains the question as to what specifically are the influences of biological factors upon his social behavior—the old "nature–nurture" or "heredity—environment" question. The concern of this chapter is to explore the question as to how man's biological makeup or biological inheritance (original nature) is related to his social behavior.

BIOLOGICAL INHERITANCE

Certain human characteristics appear to be determined by biologically given factors. Once a particular egg and a particular sperm cell are united, many characteristics are determined by the chromosomes, genes, and DNA as they are brought together. Even here, "determined" may be too strong a word to use since the environment in which this union takes place and the fetus grows has a continuous influence upon the eventual characteristics of the being produced. No single factor, biological or otherwise, ever exists in isolation.

Recognizing this we can still say that biological factors basically account for such things as sex, general body build or somatotype, as some have called it, color of skin, and other racial characteristics, as well as the presence of normal biological equipment such as arms, legs, ears, heart, stomach, liver, and various glands. Deformities or deficiencies as measured by usual standards in any of these factors may also be biological in origin. No two individuals ever have identical biological characteristics; fraternal or identical twins are probably as much alike as it is possible for two persons to be. The brain, which is intimately involved in man's symbol manipulation, is likewise biologically provided, and it appears from available evidence that biological characteristics may impose limitations upon symbol use that are difficult if not impossible to overcome by any learning experiences. Many of those classified today as idiots and morons seems to have such limitations. It should be emphasized, however, that I.Q. tests and other such instruments do not directly measure any of these factors. I.Q. tests measure learned behavior, not biological capacity or potential. Past beliefs that one could safely infer one's potential from I.Q. tests have in recent times been seriously questioned by many, and successes in changing I.Q. scores by providing certain social experiences and by successful therapy efforts with individuals believed to be congenitally (biologically) incapacitated should make us a bit wary of attributing too much too readily to biological factors.

Much of the behavior of man's internal organs appears to be relatively unlearned or instinctive. Note that this does not say it was *caused* by instinct—only that it is unlearned. The normal human neonate does not, for instance, have to teach his heart to beat, his stomach to digest food, his glands to function, his lungs to extract oxygen from the air automatically taken into his body. He is prepared to do all these things. He is born with a functioning body. It should be clear that we are talking here about the biological makeup of human beings, not how the human beings thus constructed relate themselves to each other, which is quite different.

BIOLOGY AND SOCIAL BEHAVIOR

Human beings, of course, evidence considerable variation in their external and internal biological makeup, as a glance at any group of individuals will verify. Such differences are to one degree or another related to man's social behavior, and this chapter discusses some of these relationships. It should be made clear here, however, that these subsequent discussions are particularly applicable to humans who have the "normal" biological characteristics. In this whole text, we are primarily concerned with behavior of biologically normal individuals, and will not give extensive attention to the limitations imposed upon behavior by biological deviance.

Man's biological inheritance is a necessary requisite for his social behavior but in itself does not provide an adequate answer as to why man's social behavior is what it is. In order to understand social behavior, it is important to make a sharp distinction between (1) man's biological makeup *per se* and (2) what the individual does about this makeup, or his behavior with respect to it. The second factor is social, the first biological, and analysis of biological factors *per se* is analysis at a level different from that of social behavior.

In taking his own biological characteristics into account, man behaves in much the same way that he does when he considers any other factor. In a symbolic process, man labels and defines himself and his biological characteristics in much the same manner as for any other object. He does so in the manner that he has learned, paying attention to only those aspects to which he has learned to pay attention or to which he has become sensitized; selective perception is involved. There are most likely many biological aspects and processes extant in himself about which the individual knows little, if anything. What one does not know (ignorance) is as important in some respects as what he does know. The average layman, for instance, has not learned to pay attention to the same biological factors as has the physician, and he frequently interprets his own biological factors and functioning

The Placebo Effect

In 1794, Dr. Ranieri Gerbi, a professor at Pisa, published a manuscript describing a miraculous cure for toothache. . . . A worm species, called curculio antiodontaligious, was crushed between the thumb and forefingers of the right hand. The fingers then touched the affected part. An investigatory commission found that 431 of 629 toothaches were stopped immediately. Later, Dr. Carradori, court physician at Weimar, advanced the discovery by substituting a more pleasant ladybird, and an official commission confirmed the immediate relief of toothache in 65–70 per cent of the cases. (Emphasis added.)
                                        —Arthur K. Shapiro.*

quite differently than does his medical doctor. He, in fact, frequently goes to the M.D. to find out what "is wrong with" him or whether he is "in good health." The witch doctor may serve a similar function in some societies. None of us knows automatically how the body functions or what its different characteristics or symptoms mean. In a factory where carbon monoxide gas was escaping, for instance, each worker at first attributed his growing nausea to some personal illness, such as a hangover, or to not having eaten any breakfast.[1]

Man may be unaware of certain relationships between his biological makeup and his social behavior. Disease may be attributed to such things as evil spirits, magic spells, or the position of the stars in the heavens. He may see no connection between sexual behavior and conception, as in the tribe on the Island of Merlau which maintained that the first man to plant the leaf of a Cycas tree in front of the home wherein a babe was born was the father of that child.[2] An in-

dividual may by modern standards suffer a vitamin deficiency, but be unaware of it; he may be diabetic and be unaware of it and eat himself into the grave by consuming more sweets than his body can handle. The girl entering puberty may experience her first menstruation without understanding what is happening to her, as may the boy experience his first nocturnal emission without knowing much about it.

An individual deeply engrossed in some interesting task may have an empty stomach but not "be hungry" (tell himself that he is hungry) until the noon bell rings, whereupon he promptly gets hungry and hurries to his noon meal. An individual with a full stomach may "get hungry" when his favorite cookies have just been taken from the oven. The neophyte space traveler may be suffering from a below-normal oxygen supply and not recognize what is happening to him and may die right beside an oxygen bottle if he has not learned how to label his condition properly and the appropriate plans of action associated with the condition and the oxygen bottle. Also, it takes more than the normal intake of alcohol to make a person an alcoholic and more than a prescribed intake of drugs to make a person a drug addict.[3]

Then there are psychosomatic phenomena, wherein a biological condition such as a headache or a paralyzed arm, as far as can be determined, is not a direct result of any other biological factor but stems rather from social experiences, which in turn are related to a syndrome of definitions that appear to be "causing" the condition. And conversely, there is the placebo phenomenon, wherein people get well after taking a sugar-coated pill that in itself has no direct biological influence upon the illness or condition being treated.[4]

Man evaluates his physical characteristics according to standards he has learned through interaction with others; his behavior stems from

---

* Arthur K. Shapiro, "A Contribution to a History of the Placebo Effect," *Behavioral Science*, V, No. 2 (April, 1960), 112.

[1] Kurt Lang and Gladys Engel Lang, *Collective Dynamics* (New York: Thomas Y. Crowell Co., 1961), p. 105.

[2] Austin L. Porterfield, *Mirror, Mirror: On Seeing Yourself in Books* (Fort Worth, Texas: Leo Potishman Foundation, Texas Christian University, 1957), p. 145.

[3] See H. S. Becker, "Becoming a Marihuana User," *The American Journal of Sociology*, LIX, No. 3 (November, 1953), 235–252; see also A. R. Lindesmith, *Opiate Addiction* (Bloomington, Ind., Principia Press, Inc., 1955).

[4] See Arthur K. Shapiro, "A Contribution to a History of the Placebo Effect," *Behavioral Science*, V, No. 2 (April, 1960), 109–135.

the associated plans of action. He may accordingly define himself as being physically attractive or physically repulsive. He may define his red hair as a sign that he should be fiery and temperamental. He may define his dark skin as proof that he is "better" than others. Our previous discussion of NER symbols emphasized that such definitions have nothing to do directly with the characteristic being evaluated. There is no empirical referent for concepts such as goodness or badness. These are man-made standards and may be applied in any way man himself decides. A physical characteristic is not good or bad in itself, but only defined in this way by man. Such definitions, then, may vary from group to group and from time to time. Behavior involving such definitions evidences considerable variation, since they do not stem directly from any biological factor *per se*.

With reference to his biological characteristics or other factors, man's definitions and associated plans of action need have no necessary relationship to any empirical qualities of the objects defined. Subjective and objective reality frequently may be contradictory.

BIOLOGICAL DETERMINISM

Man has viewed the involvement of biological factors in his social behavior in many different ways. The label "biological determinism" has been applied to theories or views that see a direct causal relationship between biological factors and social behavior. Those who endorse variations of this view frequently make use of such concepts as "instincts," "drives," and "needs," which are seen as biologically given. Many types of human behavior have been interpreted as being caused by "instincts" and even today one hears talk of a "mother instinct" and an "instinct for self preservation" to mention but two. Sexual behavior has been seen as being caused by "drives" presumably located somewhere inside of the individual.

As was emphasized in the chapter on methodology, the sociologist attempts to be scientific and consequently restricts himself to the study of empirical phenomena. A question then is raised as to what empirical phenomena one pays attention if he wants to test scientifically hypotheses about instincts or drives. Can we be scientifically sure that a mother has an instinct inside that causes her to love her child, or that an individual has a sex drive that causes him to behave in a particular way? Unless such concepts can be operationally defined they are of questionable scientific utility.

Part of the problem about such concepts may stem from the language we use. The terms "drive" and "instinct" are nouns, and it is easy to conclude that since we have these words in our language they identify *empirical* things. The English language, as has been pointed out, has no way of consistently distinguishing terms that have an empirical referent from those that do not. Once terms are accepted as labels for empirical things, it is but one more step to attribute to them causative powers. It is scientifically more defensible to use concepts which can be operationally defined.

We can talk about "instinctive behavior," by which we mean behavior that is unlearned, without implying anything about what causes the behavior. The scientist is then likely to ask what does in fact cause the unlearned behavior, and may do research to find an answer. If, however, he concludes that the behavior is caused by instincts he has closed the door to research—he "knows" the causes already! Likewise, with reference to sexual behavior, we can determine: (1) the frequency with which certain behavior patterns occur, and (2) the frequency with which an individual tells himself that he wants sexual activity (by paying attention to his verbal behavior or by asking him) and relate both types of behavior to social variables without attributing any causative power to "things" that cannot be operationally defined.

NEEDS

The concept of "need" as a noun similar to "instinct" and "drive" also is a troublesome one. If this is a "thing," to what does the scientist pay attention when he wants to study it?

The concept has no predictive utility for the scientist. It is not useful if one wants to predict

A 1920 Statement About Behavior

A child acts as a human being rather than an animal because he inherits a human nervous system . . . is pugnacious and matter-of-fact because he inherits the nervous system of a male; he is a musician rather than a business man because he inherits the nervous system of a Bach.

A current is started in the retina of a nine-month-old baby by a glittering object held in front of him; compelled by the structure of his nervous system he must snatch at it, not because he wants it, not because he wills to do so, but because he is thus made, he cannot help it. Not at all a matter of volition, or of conscious attention, the act is merely a matter of the connections of neurons.

—Naomi Norsworthy and
Mary Theodora Whitley.*

future behavior rather than explain behavior that has already taken place. There is, of course, the problem just raised: what does one pay attention to if he wants to predict behavior on the basis of needs? But even if one infers the existence of a need, such inferences are not very useful for predictive purposes since these "needs" can each be satisfied in any number of different ways. The need for food, for instance, can be satisfied by beefsteak, fresh snails, or rotten eggs; or, for that matter, can be over-ruled by the need for recognition by the American teen-age girl who wants to maintain her school-girl figure, or by the religious need if one's religious prescriptions specify a fast.

Seeking a need-explanation of past behavior may be a stimulating pseudo-scientific activity for some, but when the concept is used in the manner we have discussed, it has no predictive utility. The scientific utility of the concept is further decreased by the fact that there has been no agreement as to exactly how many of these

* Naomi Norsworthy and Mary Theodora Whitley, *The Psychology of Childhood* (New York: The Macmillan Co., 1920), pp. 21, 23–24.

needs man has, and suggestions have ranged from two to over a hundred. This is not surprising in terms of the NER symbols involved.

The concept of need has utility for us, however, if applied in a different manner, as in the statement "*A* is needed to accomplish *B*." Used in this way, the concept is no longer a noun that presumably identifies a thing but a verb that connects two nouns or things. With reference to human behavior we can say that man is so constructed biologically that he needs food, water, oxygen, and elimination in order to survive. This, however, says nothing about how he gets the food, water, and oxygen, or how he eliminates. It says nothing about his *wanting* to do any of these things; it merely identifies a structural relationship between his biological makeup and the likelihood of his surviving. It is a statement about human beings similar to the statement that a car needs gas in order to run. It states a structural relationship, but nothing else. In like manner, we can say that a human group needs some sort of sexual activity if the group is to survive, which, however, implies nothing about actual behavior or the associated motivation.

Such need-statements do not imply that man always wants to do these things, or that such activities are always basic or primary and take precedence over other activities. Man may not want to survive, as witnessed by individuals and groups who commit suicide. Since certain behavior is necessary for survival, it would follow that individuals and groups that have survived have one way or another met these needs. Whoever fails to meet them does not last long. The groups available for the sociologist to study have worked out ways of meeting these survival needs, but it does not follow that the technics of meeting the needs are biologically given along with the biological conditions that establish them. These seem to be learned.

If when the term "need" is used it is always followed by a statement as to exactly what a thing or behavior pattern is needed for, there is little likelihood of reifying the term. Better yet, if the term "needed" is used instead of the noun "need," those involved are likely to inquire why a thing is needed or for what it is needed and then check the relationship between these variables, rather than to accept an unqualified "need" statement as telling us anything about human interaction.

ISOLATED AND FERAL CHILDREN

Dramatic evidence concerning the direct influence of biological factors upon behavior could be secured if a human child could at birth be isolated, somehow kept alive, and permitted to grow to physical maturity without any contact with other human beings. Although such an undertaking would appear to be impossible for several reasons, including our values, there are on record a few cases of individuals whose contacts with other human beings have been very limited. From these cases suggestive insights can be gained.

The two best authenticated cases are those of Anna and Isabelle.[5] Isabelle, an illegitimate child who lived virtually alone with her deaf-mute mother in an upstairs room for about six years, was discovered in 1938. She had had no chance to learn to speak, although she did use some gestures, and did make a "strange croaking sound." It was doubted at first if she could hear, and many of her actions resembled those of deaf children. She appeared to be "wholly uneducable."

However, skillful efforts to teach her to speak began to produce results and after about a week of intensive work, she made her first attempt at vocalization. She was putting sentences together in a little over two months. Nine months later she could identify words and sentences on the printed page, could write well, could add to ten, and could retell a story after hearing it. Seven months after that her vocabulary had grown from 1,500 to 2,000 words and she was asking complicated questions. When observed a year and a half after her discovery her I.Q. had trebled

and she gave the impression of being a "very bright, cheerful, energetic, little girl. She spoke well, walked and ran without trouble, and sang with gusto and accuracy." The turning point in her development seemed to be in gaining the ability to use symbols—learning that things have names and names "have things."

Anna's early experiences were somewhat similar to those of Isabelle. She was an illegitimate child who was given only a minimum of human care for almost the first six years of life. She did not make progress comparable to that of Isabelle. She may have had an inferior learning capacity, although this could not be determined since she did not have as extensive treatment as Isabelle, and she died in 1942 at about ten and a half years of age.

There are also stories about abandoned children who presumably lived with wild animals of one type or another. Such children are called feral children. The authenticity of these stories is open to question. They suggest, however, that if such an experience did occur such children would behave in the manner of the animals with which they were reared, and from which they would learn, most likely through a process of imitation. The story of Kamala, who was presumably found in India running with a pack of wolves, reports that she was brought to an orphanage run by a Reverend Singh, and that considerable time and effort was required to teach her to wear clothes, to sleep in a bed, not to pounce on chickens in the courtyard and tear them apart with her teeth, not to "bark" at the moon, etc. According to the story she did, through interaction with those at the orphanage, develop the ability to speak and to behave in the usual human manner. She died at the orphanage during her eighth year.[6]

There is also an account of a mother who during World War II kept her adult son sealed in a room and provided food for him through a dumb waiter. When the case was brought to light, he had apparently lost most of the behavior patterns we normally associate with

[5] Kingsley Davis, "Final Note on a Case of Extreme Isolation," *The American Journal of Sociology*, LII, No. 5 (March, 1947), 432–437. See also Bruno Bettelheim, "Feral Children and Autistic Children," *The American Journal of Sociology*, LXIV, No. 5 (March, 1959), 455–467.

[6] A. L. Singh and Robert M. Zingg, *Wolf-Children and Feral Men* (New York: Harper & Row, Inc., 1942).

human beings.[7] In 1956 there were reports in the popular press about a seven-year-old "chicken boy" in England whose 45-year-old widowed mother had kept him penned in her henhouse. He presumably grunted like an animal and could neither walk nor eat the usual human food. He got about by hopping like an ape.[8]

UNIVERSAL BEHAVIOR PATTERNS AND BIOLOGY

If social behavior were determined by biological factors, those who have essentially the same biological makeup should behave in essentially the same way. Males and females are everywhere distinguished by biological factors, although there are some who biologically do not fall exactly in either classification. Is there, then, any way of behaving that is exclusively female or male? To an extent there is, in that it is the female who provides the ova and gives birth to children and the male who provides the sperm cell for fertilization. The union of sperm and ova, however, is necessarily a social act. With modern technics of artificial insemination, however, it is not even necessary that the male who provides the sperm for fertilization ever have any physical contact with the female who subsequently bears his child, although an intermediary is required. With reference to childbirth, it may be the male who has morning sickness and among the Caribs and various of their South American neighbors it may even be the male who goes to bed following the birth of his child.[9] Parents may love their biological offspring, but they may with equal intensity love their adopted children; and biological or adopted children and parents may also hate each other.

There seems, in fact, to be no *social* behavior pattern that is exclusively male or female. Either sex may be aggressive or passive in sexual activity or any other activity. Either may be the

Culture or Biology

When informed that certain Tibetan tribesmen exist all winter without a bath, that the Caribs relish the eating of certain tree worms, that the Polar Eskimo eats decayed birds, feather, flesh, and all, the average American is inclined to be disgusted or incredulous. Yet one of the writers has seen aboriginal peoples in the jungles of South America who were nauseated by the taste of Grade A canned peaches, who laughed in derision at his practice of tooth-brushing, and considered the white man's firm refusal to pluck out his eyebrows an example of rank exhibitionism.

—John L. Gillin and John P. Gillin.*

breadwinner or the spouse who stays at home to take care of the house and children. Either may engage in hard manual labor or in more delicate tasks. Either may be the ruled or the ruler, leader or follower. With the anthropological evidence available we do not seem to find any specific social behavior patterns that are always associated with particular biological characteristics. Man is more than a biological being!

Biologically then, the normal human being comes into the world with the biological equipment for behaving in any number of different ways. He is biologically prepared to learn any language, or a language as yet undeveloped. He has the biological equipment to consume and digest any number of different types of food, to participate in any number of different types of recreation, earn a living in any number of different ways, relate himself in any number of different ways to members of the opposite sex, sexually and otherwise, and establish many different types of family relations. We might in a figurative sense say that at birth the newborn human being is a "mass of potential" capable of learning to respond in any number of different ways, and once any particular pattern is well learned he may feel it is natural or normal and maybe that

[7] Robert Bierstedt, *The Social Order* (New York: McGraw-Hill Book Co., 1957), p. 108.

[8] See *Detroit Free Press*, October 12, 1956.

[9] See E. Adamson Hoebel, *Man in the Primitive World* (New York: McGraw-Hill Book Co., 1958), p. 373.

* John L. Gillin and John P. Gillin, *Cultural Sociology* (New York: The Macmillan Co., 1948), p. 168.

the behavior is biologically given—that he "was made" to behave that way.

Which particular social behavior patterns are actually developed depends upon the social experiences the neonate has. Society is able to teach the newborn child any number of different behavior patterns.

OUR PERSPECTIVE

As we will view this nature–nurture relationship, the question as to which is more important, biology or social environment, is essentially a meaningless question when stated in terms as broad as this. Both heredity and environment are important in their own way. Both are related to man's social behavior. Man, in fact, could not behave as he does if either his biological makeup or his social environment were not as they are, or if they were to change in any significant manner. The relationship between these two factors is a reciprocal one.

When one asks "Which is more important?" he asks a value question, which can become scientifically testable only when our criterion of "importance" is operationally specified in such a way that it becomes empirically testable. We will not concern ourselves with this question, but with the scientifically testable questions as to the relationships found to exist between certain biological factors and certain social factors.

Figure 5.1 Biological characteristics alone do not determine behavior. What is "man's work" in one society may be "woman's work" in another. In Czechoslovakia most of the work in the fields is done by women. (Photograph by Tessore; copyright Camera Press Ltd., London.)

Multiple Causation

In our earlier discussions of the causes of human behavior it was emphasized that there are many or multiple factors causally related to any given behavior pattern. No behavioral sequence is *caused* by only one antecedent "thing." Biological factors are involved in any behavior but it should be clear that they are only one of many kinds of factors. Our previous discussion of the interactionist position or perspective indicated that biological factors were a *necessary* ingredient of social behavior, but that they did not provide a *sufficient* explanation of such behavior. Man is biological; but he is more than this, he is also social. It would appear that the human child at birth can do less for himself than any other newborn animal and cannot even keep himself alive without help. It would be impossible for him to behave as he typically does if he were not a part of a larger group with an established social system. Statements about social behavior that attribute major causative relationships to biological factors should be given only tenuous acceptance. As was indicated in an earlier discussion, high correlation between biological factors and social behavior should not be interpreted as proving that a causal relationship exists.

From our perspective, as outlined in the previous chapter, human behavior is viewed not as stemming directly from any biological condition *per se,* but rather as response to symbols. These symbols may be provided by the individual himself, either silently (thinking) or verbally, or by others. The biologically healthy man may wish to die (tell himself that he wants to die) and the biologically unhealthy man may wish to live. Efforts to remain alive or to take one's life do not stem directly from biological factors *per se,* but from definitions attributed to them. This would seem to be true of most, if not all, social behavior.

An analogy may sharpen this nature–nurture distinction. Think for a moment of the difference between a music box and a pipe organ. The music box when its lid is raised may play an intricate tune in a manner that appeals to many,

Disprove or Outgrow?

Apparently the resourceful man can always scare up enough backing for yet another inquiry into the alleged relationship between anatomy and criminality or between body chemistry and psychosis. Of course, we are not now, and probably never will be, able to disprove the relationship. But as Leslie White used to say, neither are we able to disprove the existence of Santa Claus. And he would add that sometimes science progresses not so much by disproving theories as by outgrowing them.
—Bernard Rosenberg, et al.*

but it plays the same tune over and over again each time the lid is raised, because it is so constructed that this is all it can do. The pipe organ, however, is so built that any number of different tunes can be played thereupon. What is actually produced depends upon two factors: (1) its mechanical construction, plus (2) the manner in which it is manipulated by the organist. If no one ever manipulates the keyboard the complex intricate mechanism may never even play a tune. If only those who know how to play "Chopsticks" manipulate the keyboard, "Chopsticks" is all that will ever come out of the organ. If, however, a virtuoso plays the organ the range of possibilities is vast.

The human being is like the pipe organ in the potential "tunes" his biological makeup is able to produce. Society, for the very young child, represents the organist. If the members of the society manipulate the child in a harmonious manner, the melody produced will be harmonious. However, just as the fingers of the organist may produce disharmony, so may the societal "fingers." The point is that the normal human neonate is so built that he can potentially engage in a multitude of different patterns, harmonious or otherwise, with the deciding factors as to which of the potential patterns he actually de-

* Bernard Rosenberg, Israel Gerver, and F. William Howton, *Mass Society in Crisis* (New York: The Macmillan Co., 1964), p. 7.

velops being the experiences he has with other human beings.

The analogy breaks down, however, for any but the very young child, since human beings are not just mechanically manipulated by "society." They *are* society. Each has an influence or some "say-so" about his own behavior as well as that of the others with whom he interacts. *Inter-action is always at least a two-way process.*

One further comment on values and biology. Some people hold the perspective taken here to be somehow degrading to man. Some feel compelled to "defend" man's instincts. One student suggested, for instance, that if God gave instincts to lower animals he could certainly have given them to man. The goal of this text is not to defend any value position, since such a goal is beyond the methods of science. It should be clear from our discussion, however, that a biological inheritance that would permit man the flexibility we have discussed is certainly more intricate and complex than one with biologically built-in predetermined patterns. Whether flexibility and high potential are desirable, however, is also a non-scientific value question.

usual complement of internal organs and glands, are biologically given. These, however, provide the foundation for subsequent social behavior, they do not determine it. Evidence concerning isolated and feral children support this position, as does the fact that no social behavior patterns have been found to be universally associated with any particular biological characteristic, such as sex.

In this area as in others, man develops labels with accompanying plans of action for biological characteristics, and his related behavior, including "want to" or motivational behavior, stems from the way these factors are labeled rather than from biological characteristics *per se*. Perception is selective and man sees and interprets as he has been taught, emphasizing certain aspects and ignoring others. Various causal interpretations are possible. Subjective and objective reality in these areas may evidence discrepancies.

Biological determinism (a reductionist approach), including instinct theories, does not adequately explain social behavior. "Need" interpretations are likewise inadequate unless couched in some variant of "X is needed in order to accomplish Y."

Neither biological inheritance nor social experience is more important than the other in human behavior. Each is a necessary ingredient of the behavior equation, and each has a reciprocal relationship with the other. It is important, however, to recognize the fact to which sociology sensitizes us, that man is more than just a biological being—he is also a social being.

SUMMARY

Biologically, the human body is multi-potential. We could not use symbols in the manner we have described if this were not so. Such individual features as sex, body build, racial characteristics, and capacity to learn, as well as the

QUESTIONS

1. If the symbolic interactionist is correct in his interpretation of the influence of symbols upon behavior, what kind of biological makeup would man logically have to have for him to behave in this way?
2. Distinguish between the two statements: "Behavior X is instinctive"; "Behavior X is caused by instincts."
3. In what ways might the symbols man uses restrict biologically given potentials?
4. What influence do biologically given factors have upon social behavior?
5. Why is it more meaningful to say that "X is needed in order to accomplish Y" than to talk about "needs" in the abstract?

6. Why is the question "Which is more important, heredity or biology?" a meaningless question when so stated?
7. Explain the difference between "drive" (1) as a description of behavior, and (2) as a cause of behavior.
8. Relate the two concepts "multiple causation" and "biological determinism."
9. How would you go about scientifically determining how many needs man has?
10. How does man know what to do about any given internal condition?

PROJECT

Interview ten freshmen who are non-sociology students, asking them to explain (1) why there are more males than females in America in the medical and engineering professions, (2) why homosexual individuals behave as they do, and (3) why mothers love their children. Identify any aspect of biological determinism involved in their answers.

SUGGESTED READING

DEXTER, LEWIS A. "Heredity and Environment Re-explored," *Eugenics Quarterly,* III (June, 1956), 88–93.

DOBZHANSKY, T. G. *Mankind Evolving: The Evolution of the Human Species.* New Haven: Yale University Press, 1962.

DUNN, L. C., and T. DOBZHANSKY. *Heredity, Race and Society.* Rev. ed. New York: The New American Library of World Literature, Inc., 1960.

KLINEBERG, OTTO. *Negro Intelligence and Selective Migration.* New York: Columbia University Press, 1935.

KRETSCHMER, E. *Physique and Character.* London: Routledge & Kegan Paul, Ltd., 1925.

LA BARRE, WESTON. *The Human Animal.* Chicago: The University of Chicago Press, 1954.

LEE, DOROTHY. "Are Basic Needs Ultimate?" in *Freedom and Culture.* Englewood Cliffs, N. J.: Prentice-Hall, Inc., 1959. (A Spectrum Book.) Pp. 70–77.

LINTON, RALPH. *The Study of Man.* New York: Appleton-Century-Crofts, 1936.

MONTAGU, M. F. ASHLEY. "Constitutional and Prenatal Factors in Infant and Child Health," *Human Development,* Selected Readings by MORRIS HAIMOWITZ and NATALIE HAIMOWITZ. New York: Thomas Y. Crowell Co., 1960, pp. 124–144.

SHAPIRO, ARTHUR K. "A Contribution to a History of the Placebo Effect," *Behavioral Science,* V, No. 2 (April, 1960), 109–135.

Part III

Cultural Definitions

6

Culture

It has been suggested that the concept of "culture" has had as great an impact upon man's thinking as did the findings of Copernicus and Galileo. Such a concept should be clearly defined. If the sociologist is to be scientific, there should be some empirical phenomena to which he pays attention when he studies culture. What are they?

The chapter on the symbolic nature of human life has emphasized that man collectively develops a complex and intricate system of symbols with which he labels the aspects of his universe to which he has become sensitized, and then patterns his behavior according to the plans of action he has learned to associate with those labels. In this chapter, we turn our attention to a more extended discussion of the accumulation of definitions held by any particular group.

For how many different things does the typical American know the appropriate name and the plans of action? A few minutes of thinking will make one aware of the tremendous number of labels he has learned. One unabridged dictionary, for instance, identifies approximately 600,000 words. No one person, of course, is familiar with all of them, but during a typical day the average individual identifies thousands of different empirical objects, including other human beings, for which he knows the name and the appropriate behavior patterns. In addition, he has a vast storehouse of information about symbols which have no empirical referent (NER symbols) which are incorporated into his way of life, and

must be taken into account in one way or another. We will use the label *culture* to refer to this vast accumulation of definitions.

When we refer to the culture of a group, we are not using the term in its popular sense; we are not referring to the practice of listening to classical music, the appreciation of art, or the technique of holding one's tea cup with the little finger extended and curved. We are using the term in a technical sociological sense; this chapter is in effect an extended definition of that term.

CHARACTERISTICS OF CULTURE

Culture is the sum total of the definitions known to a group,[1] and therefore identifies an

[1] Not all sociologists and anthropologists define culture in exactly the same way. Some add to the system of symbols that we have called culture either one or both of the following: (1) man-made objects and (2) learned behavior patterns, as did Sir Edward Tylor, the British anthropologist, who gave us the concept. See *Primitive Culture* (London: John Murray, 1891). The term "superorganic" has also been used by some to refer to culture. See, for instance, A. L. Kroeber, *The Nature of Culture* (Chicago: The University of Chicago Press, 1952).

extremely complex phenomenon. To gain comprehension of some of its characteristics we shall discuss the term "culture" in detail.

Culture is man-made. This point was emphasized in our discussion of symbolic interaction when it was stated that the attachment of symbols to referents and the development of accompanying plans of action was a human phenomenon. Definitions do not just exist "out there" in the empirical world waiting for man to discover them; rather, they are developed by man himself.

Culture is learned. The definitions which man uses in his interaction are not acquired through biological transmission. They are man-made and accordingly man learns to use symbols and to follow the plans of action associated therewith. To the learning process we will give the label "socialization" and will devote an entire subse-

quent chapter to a discussion of this process. In discussing culture here, we are more concerned with the fact that culture is learned and with the content of what is learned rather than with the learning process *per se.*

Culture is learned through human interaction. Definitions are developed, standardized, and reaffirmed for the group in the dynamic give-and-take of social life. Only when there is relative consensus concerning definitions can social interaction proceed with any degree of facility. Culture, then, is transmitted from one individual or group to another, but the transmission is a social, not a biological one. Consider for a moment the newborn infant. He is born into a group which already has decided how to label the various aspects of the world and how man relates to them. His group has its way of life well established. It has already decided in varying degrees many important things about the future life of this child such as the type of language he will speak, the food he will eat, the type of education he will receive, the type of vehicles in which he will travel, the type of God he will worship, the type of courtship patterns in which he will engage, and many other similar decisions. His parents are, of course, the major representatives of the larger group in the early socialization of the child, with his exposure to the larger society gradually expanding as his years increase. A major activity of parents and teachers is to make sure that new members of the group learn to experience their world more or less in the way the larger society does. This is accomplished by providing the new members with the set of definitions or culture which the society has developed and using sanctions of one type or another to insure acceptance of these patterns by the child.

Culture is the common property of the group. Culture is a group phenomenon; it is shared. No one individual, for example, knows all of the definitions contained within the American culture, or any other culture for that matter. Members of the group are constantly dying and leaving the group while new members are coming into the group through birth or immigration, yet the American culture remains fairly constant. The death of all of those who die today does not

---

Different Definitions of Culture

The complex whole which includes knowledge, beliefs, art, morals, law, custom and any other capabilities and habits acquired by man as a member of society.

— E. B. Tylor, an English Anthropologist.

The continually changing patterns of learned behavior and the products of learned behavior (including attitudes, values, knowledge, and material objects) which are shared by and transmitted among the members of society.

— John F. Cuber.

Those historically created selective processes which channel man's reactions both to internal and external stimuli.

— C. Kluckhohn and W. H. Kelly.

That complex whole that consists of everything we think and do and have as members of society.

— Robert Bierstedt.

The socially transmitted system of idealized ways in knowledge, practice, and belief, along with the artifacts that knowledge and practice produce and maintain—as they change in time.

— Arnold Green.

materially alter the sum total of the definitions in the American culture. These definitions are the common property of the group, and are used in the interaction in which they engage. Since culture is a group phenomenon, its consideration falls clearly within the interactionist perspective. If we narrow our field of vision to include only the individual and consider the total definitions with accompanying plans of action which are learned by a particular individual, we have moved from *culture* to the *personality* level.

Culture is cumulative. Each newborn child comes into a group which has numerous definitions already standardized. In this sense he is a recipient of the results of thousands of years of previous interaction. Newton indicated his awareness of this fact when he stated, "If I have seen farther, it is by standing on the shoulders of giants." Most of us do not fully appreciate how extensively we are indebted to our ancestors for our current way of life. From this perspective there would seem to be no such thing as a self-made man.

The historical foundations of the culture of any group extend many generations into the past, having been repeatedly passed from father to son. To paraphrase a biblical quotation, we can say that the culture of the fathers shall be visited upon the heads of their children for many generations. The origin of many cultural patterns is lost in antiquity. In a figurative sense, culture can be viewed as the "memory" of the human race. In conforming to culture we imitate our ancestors; in conforming to fashion we imitate our contemporaries.

Culture is constantly changing. No culture remains completely static. Human interaction is a dynamic phenomenon with new or relatively new elements constantly arising. In the stresses and strains of keeping a social system functioning, new ways of "cutting up" the world are constantly being developed in man's efforts to secure desirable goals. The American culture of 1965 is in many respects recognizably different from that of 1955 and drastically different from that of 1865. Some types of changes are readily accepted; others are fought with great zeal. However, change is an ever present phenomenon, and

man's definitions of his empirical and non-empirical world are always subject to change.

Culture provides man with plans of action. This point has been briefly stressed in our previous discussion of symbols. Definitions of particular labels not only provide referent identification, but also include plans of actions felt to be appropriate to address to the objects (including human beings) concerned. An object called

Figure 6.1 Memory of the human race. Culture can be preserved for generations yet unborn, as shown in this stone tablet from ninth-century Babylon. (The Bettmann Archive, Inc.)

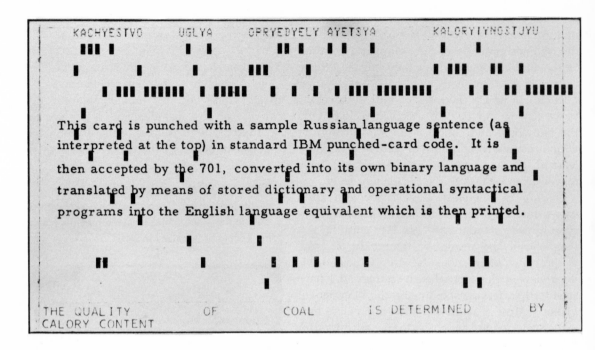

KACHYESTVO   UGLYA   OPRYEDYELY AYETSYA   KALORYIYNOSTJYU

This card is punched with a sample Russian language sentence (as interpreted at the top) in standard IBM punched-card code. It is then accepted by the 701, converted into its own binary language and translated by means of stored dictionary and operational syntactical programs into the English language equivalent which is then printed.

THE QUALITY   OF   COAL   IS DETERMINED   BY
CALORY CONTENT

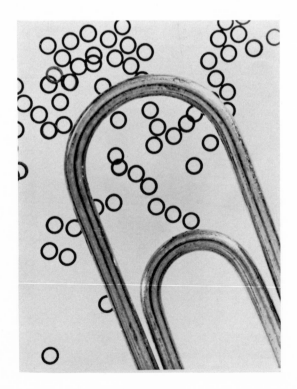

Figure 6.2 Symbol storage may be accomplished by use of IBM cards or by use of "memory rings" used in a computer. The tiny rings are made of ceramic and iron oxide compounds, each measuring thirty-thousandths of an inch in diameter, and are shown at left with a standard paper clip to indicate relative size. (Wide World Photos.)

a telephone is used for certain purposes but not for others, as is an object called a necktie. It is doubtful that these two plans of action are ever confused. In this sense, the culture of the group contains blueprints for future action, or we may say that the culture contains the script we follow in the "play of life." The culture contains prescriptions for behavior, so that many aspects of man's behavior are predictable before they happen. Many important decisions about how man should relate himself to specific objects are made for him long before he is born. The average unmarried college student, for instance, has already developed some fairly clear ideas as to how he will have his as-yet-unconceived child behave. Most of us generally follow the prescribed plans of action contained in our culture. Not to do so is to invite public sanctions of one type or another.

Culture includes both ER and NER definitions. Each group not only identifies the empirical objects involved in its definitions, but also develops an extensive system of symbols which have no empirical referents. These include religions, values, beliefs, fictions, norms (folkways, mores, and laws, discussed later on), mathematics, beauty, etc., which are used in making decisions. Both types of symbols are intermeshed into the functioning of the group. Culture includes both types.

Previous discussion has already indicated that while the sociologist studies the non-empirical systems that a society develops, he takes an amoral position and does not attempt to say which of these systems is the correct one. Such a decision cannot be made scientifically because of its non-empirical nature. Such systems, however, are an important part of the culture of any group and thus are related in important ways to the behavior of its members.

Culture includes motivational elements. Culture contains definitions not only about what the group wants its members to do, but also about what it wants its members *to want to do*. Motivational aspects of behavior then are incorporated into the culture of the group. If the American way of life is to persist, new members of the group must be taught not only how Ameri-

---

Recreation or Sin

A highly intelligent teacher with long and successful experience in the public schools of Chicago was finishing her first year in an Indian school. When asked how her Navaho pupils compared in intelligence with Chicago youngsters, she replied, "Well, I just don't know. Sometimes the Indians seem just as bright. At other times they just act like dumb animals. The other night we had a dance in the high school. I saw a boy who is one of the best students in my English class standing off by himself. So I took him over to a pretty girl and told them to dance. But they just stood there with their heads down. They wouldn't even say anything." I inquired if she knew whether or not they were members of the same clan. "What difference would that make?"

"How would you feel about getting into bed with your brother?" The teacher walked off in a huff, but, actually, the two cases were quite comparable in principle. To the Indian the type of bodily contact involved in our social dancing has a directly sexual connotation. The incest taboos between members of the same clan are as severe as between true brothers and sisters.
—Clyde Kluckhohn.[*]

---

cans behave but *to want to behave* in this way and to want to do the things that are necessary for the preservation of the group.

Culture involves emotional behavior. The plans of action associated with any object (including human) may specify how one manipulates this object directly, and also the type of feelings or emotional reactions one is supposed to experience in his relations to it. An individual observing an object defined as sacred is supposed to have feelings of awe and respect, while the same individual observing or maybe even hearing of behavior defined as vulgar or immoral is supposed to have feelings of disgust or abhorrence.

Certain Indian groups were, according to their culture, never supposed to show outward signs

[*] Clyde Kluckhohn, *Mirror for Man* (New York: McGraw-Hill Book Co., 1949), p. 26.

of grief, whereas the Chinese were expected to do just the opposite, as is indicated in the following quotation from an old Chinese book which was "required studies for women."

If your father or mother is sick, do not be far from his or her bed. Taste all the medicine yourself. Pray your god for his or her health. If anything unfortunate happens, cry bitterly. Otherwise, do not let your teeth be seen when you smile, and do not show your unhappiness easily.

Further, it may be defined as appropriate for those of one sex publicly to engage in certain types of emotional behavior, such as crying, whereas the same conduct is inappropriate for the opposite sex.

Culture is integrated or systematized. Man does not just develop a series of unconnected definitions about his world; he attempts to interrelate the various definitions, or at least many of them, in ways which appear to him to be logical and reasonable. He develops symbol systems wherein part of the meaning of each symbol stems from the manner in which it is related to the other symbols in the system. As has been indicated, both ER and NER symbols are interwoven in these symbol systems. The various parts of a culture tend to "hang together" or are mutually supportive. It is doubtful whether any system has been developed which has been completely consistent. However, since the definitions of a group are woven together into a somewhat consistent pattern, it follows that the behavior of its members will also be organized or systematized. Man's social order, whatever it may be, is a man-made order. It stems from the culture he has developed.

CULTURE AND CULTURE OBJECTS

We have defined culture as the man-made definitions which are the common property of the group. In addition to the development of definitions, man also makes various empirical objects which he then involves in his way of life. These man-made objects, including such things as a rocket, a loaf of bread, or a town hall, we will refer to as cultural objects. We contrast

them with natural (non-man-made) objects such as rocks, the moon, or wild flowers.

Some sociologists and anthropologists include cultural objects and behavior patterns including definitions (verbal behavior) under the heading of culture. The labels "material culture" (culture objects) and "non-material culture" (definitions) are sometimes used. Since it appears useful to keep these different types of phenomena separate, we will distinguish between culture (definitions) and cultural objects. We will, of course, take both definitions (culture and cultural objects) into account in our discussions of human behavior. It should be recognized also that whenever man pays attention to cultural objects, his responses are related to the labels which he places on the objects—or to the culture (definition) of his group. In our earlier discussion of how man uses symbols, it was pointed out that man may respond more to the symbols (labels) with which he identifies an object than

---

Cultural Variability

A Fijian buries his aged mother alive as a mark of duty and love.

An Australian Arunta lends his wife to a guest and is motivated to write neither tragedy nor comedy about the results.

The inhabitants of New Guinea practiced boy infanticide, while in Tahiti, the natives practiced girl infanticide.

The Andamanese put the secret burning of wax above theft, lying and murder in their criminal code as the worst crime of all.

In showing affection Maori rub noses; the Australians rub faces; the Chinese place nose to cheek; Westerners kiss; but some groups practice spitting on the beloved.

*—Austin L. Porterfield.** [*]

---

[*] Austin L. Porterfield, *Mirror, Mirror: On Seeing Yourself in Books* (Fort Worth, Texas: Leo Potishman Foundation, Texas Christian University, 1957), pp. 145–146.

to the object *per se*. If, because of his definition, he has come to believe that an object has characteristics which it in fact does not have, he may still "see" these characteristics in the objects with which he is involved.

SUBCULTURES AND PERSONALITY

Any group, particularly one as large as a society, can usually be broken down into smaller component parts or subgroups. Such divisions can be made along any lines that permit meaningful distinctions, such as religious, socio-economic, occupational, or regional. Such subgroups then share subcultures, being like the larger group in certain or maybe in most characteristics, but unique in that they share some unique definitions and thus behave in distinctive ways.

In the United States, we can identify some subcultures as Protestant, Jewish, or Roman Catholic; upper-class, middle-class, or lower-class; southern, western, or New England. All that we say of culture is also true of subcultures except that the group to which the subculture applies is smaller than the society, to which culture applies.

The number of subcultures into which a large culture can be subdivided is almost unlimited. Each individual member of a society could be considered as having a subculture, since even at the level of the individual we find an accumulation of definitions with accompanying plans of action, which are taken into account in his behavior. When our focus of attention is at the individual level, however, we will call this individual culture "personality." Personality is to the individual as culture is to the group. Culture is the collective expression of personality, whereas personality is the individual expression of culture.

No two individuals or groups ever have identical exposure to the culture of the larger society. No two individuals or groups ever learn exactly the same thing. Selective exposure to culture is one of the reasons why differences in behavior exist.

CULTURE, SOCIETY, AND INTERACTION

Culture, then, is not a mystical "thing" that exists independently of human beings. It is not a mystical *force* which causes people to behave in particular ways. Culture does not *determine* behavior—we do not endorse the position of cultural determinism. Human behavior is certainly influenced by the definitions people hold, and acceptance of some definitions is more restrictive than acceptance of others; but interaction is a dynamic process involving constant assessment of the behavior of all involved.

There would seem to be nothing gained by positing culture as a mystical entity which we then try to weave into the explanations of behavior. Man is the active causal agent, not culture.

The sociologist in his study of culture is concerned with human behavior and basically with verbal behavior. Although we can infer definitions from non-verbal behavior, once we rely primarily upon such inferences we open the door to almost unlimited speculation and make verification difficult. Usually, to find out how individuals or groups define anything, they should be asked in an appropriate manner and under conditions which have been found to produce no efforts at deception.

Obviously, then, most learning is restricted to acquisition of definitions which are already incorporated within the culture of the group. Some do, however, go beyond current cultural systems. Creativity and innovation are ever present, even though they may develop slowly.

A distinction between culture and society is useful for some purposes. Culture has been defined as the total definitions held by a particular group. When our attention is focused upon the definitions, we are investigating culture. However, when our attention is focused upon the group, we are considering society. A society is a group of people who share a common culture or common definitions to such a degree that the individuals involved can interact with at least relative effectiveness over a period of time. Defined in this way there cannot be a group unless culture is also present; neither can there be culture unless the group is present. In a sense, culture and society are different sides of the same coin.

We can, of course, distinguish between "society" as a concept and a society such as the American society, just as we can distinguish between "culture" and a culture. When we talk of the American society, we are talking of a particular group of people. When we talk of the American culture, we are talking about the accumulated definitions (including the plans of action involved therein) held by this group. The concept of "society" is used in relating a body of definitions to a particular group of people. This is one way of dividing groups of definitions into meaningful categories. Interaction involves members of a society mutually influencing each other, partly on the basis of the shared definitions they hold, and partly on the basis of their dynamic interpretations of the sequence of behavior in which they are involved.

Using the "society" concept also permits us to discuss and study cultural change. The group or the society is capable of developing new culture or cultural innovations; it is through the interaction of the members of society that new definitions are developed and standardized. New definitions do not arise from the interaction of already existing definitions per se, but from the interaction of people. Creativity is a societal process. The extent of change for any group is, of course, limited.

Three basic concepts in our discussion are:

1. Society—a group of interacting people.
2. Culture—definitions, including plans of action, learned by the society.
3. Interaction—the behavior of the members of the society, which is related to the culture of the society.

Interaction, which is learned (and is included as a part of culture by some authors), is more than just definitions—it is the enacting of the plans of action incorporated in these definitions. We enter our interaction sequences with a vast storehouse of definitions upon which to draw as

"Culture" as a Part of Culture

In the years to come it is possible that this discovery of the human origin and development of culture will be recognized as the greatest of all discoveries, since heretofore man has been helpless before these cultural and social formulations which generation after generation have perpetuated the same frustration and defeat of human values and aspiration. So long as he believed this was necessary and inevitable, he could not but accept this lot with resignation. Now man is beginning to realize that his culture and social organization are not unchanged cosmic processes, but are human creations which may be altered.

—Lawrence Frank.[*]

we define the "others," ourselves, and the objects involved in our behavior. We pattern our behavior to harmonize more or less with these definitions. There is, however, a further dynamic emergent quality. We are constantly appraising the adequacy of our definitions on the basis of what others do and what happens to us. Individuals apply definitions; re-evaluate their appropriateness as the interaction progresses; make decisions about how others are defining the same situation, the "others," and the objects involved; and anticipate the eventual influence of such definitions upon future behavior. This is a dynamic human process. Interaction is an emergent phenomenon in that all its aspects are not rigidly predetermined.

Culture provides a foundation out of which interaction emerges, but it does not predetermine exactly what will take place. Human beings are not the equivalent of a complex computer that has *all* aspects of behavior predetermined or mechanically programmed into it. There is more predetermination in human behavior than many would like to believe, especially those who have learned to view behavior

[*] Lawrence Frank, as quoted by Clyde Kluckhohn in H. Laurence Ross (ed.), *Perspectives on the Social Order* (New York: McGraw-Hill Book Co., 1963), p. 106.

in strongly individualistic terms and thus see what they have been prepared to see. Human interaction, however, includes an emerging, dynamic "human" element. Society is composed of inter*acting* beings.

In popular literature and discussions and in some professional writing as well, the two terms "culture" and "society" are used somewhat interchangeably. It is not uncommon to find foreign groups referred to as foreign cultures. Such terminology, while it discourages the use of exact definitions, should not cause any serious problem; if we have identified some distinct group, we can be sure that they have a distinct culture. One cannot exist without the other.

CULTURE AND SOCIAL ORDER

The order found in the social relations of man is an order which is put there by man himself. Behavior follows the patterns outlined in the plans of action which are a part of culture. One of the consequences or functions of culture is the establishment of orderly interaction. Interaction is ordered because the symbols that man uses are ordered, and the types of order vary from society to society, as does the culture.

Since behavior is orderly, one familiar with the culture of the group can, to a certain degree, predict its future behavior. The same thing is true at the personality level. If one knows the culture of the group or of the individual (personality) he can anticipate both the behavior of others and their anticipation of his own behavior. Orderly interaction then is possible.

Since there is no inherent relationship between the symbol systems (with accompanying plans of action) used by man to identify his world, and the objective reality in which a society functions, the order that man produces is a relative thing. Sumner, a nineteenth-century American sociologist, indicated that each society evidences a "strain toward consistency." Lack of complete consistency is sometimes referred to as a condition of "disorganization."

While the harmony among the various parts of a cultural system is never completely consist-

ent, and the behavior of the various individuals in the social system is, consequently, never completely harmonious, there is a relative harmony and the various elements of these systems tend to be mutually supportive. In broad terms, the familial, educational, economic, religious, and governmental elements at the societal or individual level tend to support each other. Conflicts are found, but through interaction each group or person is constantly in the process of resolving such conflicts and thus removing or reducing extant inconsistencies. The Congress of the United States, to mention one functioning entity in the American society, is constantly revamping the governmental aspect of our society in an effort to make our laws (one type of norm definition) and our interpretation of them harmonize more fully with existing conditions. Each individual reading this book can provide illustrations of how his college experiences have been integrated into his behavior patterns (thinking and social) so that their various aspects are somewhat consistent. It would be safe to predict, in fact, that the whole college experience will involve a continued effort to harmonize apparent and real conflicts so that a relative degree of harmony in the life of the student can be achieved. Those unable to do so will probably leave the college society, willingly or by invitation, and may be better able to harmonize the various aspects of their life elsewhere.

Complete harmony is rarely realized by any society or individual, but is a goal toward which societies and individuals usually strive.

UNIVERSALS AND VARIABILITY

All societies contain certain cultural elements in common. The existence of such universals reflects the fact that there are certain things a group must do if it is to maintain its existence *as a group*. These are sometimes referred to as "functional requisites." [2] For a group to exist,

2 The functional requisites of a society will be discussed in some detail in a subsequent chapter.

Partial List of Items Found or Dealt With in Every Known Society

age-grading	housing
athletic sports	hygiene
bodily adornment	incest taboos
calendar	inheritance rules
cleanliness training	joking
community	kin groups
organization	kinship nomenclature
cooking	language
cooperative labor	law
cosmology	luck superstition
courtship	magic
dancing	marriage
decorative art	medicine
divination	modesty concerning
division of labor	natural functions
dream interpretation	mourning
education	numerals
eschatology	obstetrics
ethics	penal sanction
etiquette	personal names
faith healing	population policy
family	property rights
feasting	puberty customs
firemaking	religious ritual
folklore	residence rules
food taboos	sexual restrictions
funeral rites	soul concepts
games	status differentiation
gestures	surgery
gift giving	tool making
government	trade
greeting	visiting
hair styles	weaning
hospitality	weather control

—George P. Murdock.*

for instance, there must be interaction among its members and, incorporating what we have said about man's biological makeup, this interaction must be symbolic interaction. Every society has a language of some sort; language is a cultural

* George P. Murdock, "The Common Denominator of Cultures," in Ralph Linton (ed.), *The Science of Man in the World Crisis* (New York: Columbia University Press, 1943).

universal. There is, of course, considerable variation among specific languages, but language *per se* is universal.

In some way the group must keep its members alive or it cannot continue as a group. Food-gathering, food distribution and preparation are universals, in that all groups have developed such plans of action. In an industrialized society, such food-gathering may directly involve only a visit to the corner supermarket; however, indirectly the wage-earner's occupation is involved. Thus, in broad terms, we may include food-gathering under the broad heading of economic activity.

Food-gathering is a cultural universal, although any particular society may provide alternative ways in which the task is performed. The value system may also attach greater rewards to certain methods than to others. Specialties also are developed in this area.

Other universals include family, governmental–political, educational, and religious interaction.

LOWER ANIMALS AND CULTURE

To the question of whether animals possess culture we answer "No." The use of symbols is a human phenomenon. This is in fact a major distinguishing feature between human and non-human behavior. This explains, in part, the fact that sociology is restricted to the study of human behavior; although similarities between man and the lower animals do exist, human interaction is a unique phenomenon to which generalizations cannot be applied from the study of other animals which do not share man's ability to manipulate symbols. Lower animals communicate, but their communication is not symbolic communication. Lower animals learn, but they do not learn to use symbols, nor do they learn from the use of symbols. Further, the learning that they do dies with them, since they have no ability to record this learning in the form of symbols that will be available to future generations of animals. Humans have culture; lower animals do not.

CULTURE AND BIOLOGY

Since culture is learned, it need not have any particular relationship to the empirical world. It may not, for instance, accurately reflect environmental conditions. Some men, for instance, may sincerely believe that the sun and the moon "come up" and circle the earth, even though this is quite contrary to the scientific conclusion that the earth turns and the sun and the moon do not go around it. There is also no consistent relationship between the culture of the group and the biological health of its members. The culture of a group may be productive of conditions of physical health or of ill health. Individuals and groups following the "script" of their culture may engage in behavior which is quite contrary to the maximization of health. People may starve to death even though there is food available which could easily sustain life, as has occurred in India where the cow is defined as sacred and is therefore not considered to be "food." Most people would rather die than eat human flesh; cannibals may not share this revulsion, since they possess a culture different from that of the major societies today. In addition, various rites in which people participate may include such practices as flogging, burning, mutilating or tearing of flesh, and the forced ingestion of various types of food and drugs.

Different groups even have different concepts of what constitutes "good health," or different value scales which consider the maintenance of biological health as a prized goal or as being of only minimal importance when other more highly prized goals are threatened, as in the case of religious martyrs. The biological features of man can be defined in any number of ways—as indeed can anything.

The relationship between culture and biology, however, is a reciprocal one, with each imposing limitations upon the other. Biology presumably makes it impossible for man to fly or to remain under water for any length of time unaided by any cultural object. The eating of certain types of materials will bring an end to life, as will engaging in certain acts. Females can give birth to babies but cannot provide sperm cells to be used in the process of fertilization. Some individuals seem to be biologically incapable of learning much of the content of the culture of the group even though the culture is available to them.

Conversely, defining biological features in particular ways may prohibit their development. Before the American female was defined as being constitutionally equal to the male, she was denied admission to college and to certain professions. Religious proscriptions or union regulations may restrict the number of biologically capable individuals who can develop their potential along certain professional lines. Culture and biology, then, may impose limitations upon each other.

The newborn child, of course, has no voice in the biological equipment he inherits from his parents, nor in the social culture he inherits from his society. He comes into the world with both of these inheritances provided for him. However, he soon becomes an *active* agent in the interaction of which he is a part.

CULTURE AND GEOGRAPHY

An understanding of the symbolic nature of man's behavior leads one to realize that geographic factors do not directly cause any group to behave in some particular way. If the group is not aware of the presence of some geographical factor, such as gold ore, its existence will have limited—if any—influence upon the life of the group. The factors of which a group is aware can be defined in many different ways. They may be "sacred" and thus worthy of, preservation and worship, or "secular," to be used or consumed as fully as possible. Man develops a whole system of NER symbols which have no direct relationship to geography, such as his system of value, beauty and esthetics. Geographical factors are *limiting* factors, but not *determining* factors. One cannot make gold coin out of sandstone (limiting) but he can define either gold or sandstone as being of great value, since the value is not an empirical quality of any geographic factor. An understanding of culture leads to the rejection of a geographical–deterministic theory of human behavior.

CULTURE AND THE PREDICTION OF HUMAN BEHAVIOR

The chapter on the scientific method has indicated that prediction is one of the goals of science, and the chapter on the biological makeup of man has indicated that biological factors are necessary in the behavior of man, but they alone are not sufficient to provide an adequate explanation of man's behavior. One cannot predict the future social behavior of an individual with much success by studying only man's biological makeup. Social behavior can, however, be predicted with some accuracy by directing attention to the culture of the group. Familiarity with the American culture, as we have seen, permits one to predict many things about the behavior of students in an introductory class in sociology at a typical college. There is little about the social behavior of an individual that can be predicted from an examination of his biological makeup. Examination of the culture of the group, however, permits relatively accurate prediction of much of the behavior of even its as-yet-unborn members.

Our previous discussion of man's use of symbols has indicated that different groups subdivide their world in different ways, so that those with different languages actually experience the world differently. Members of the subgroups have experiences which harmonize with the culture of the group, but they are different experiences, not just the same experiences tagged with different labels. Observers of a society different from their own are thus unable to comprehend the full meaning and significance of what they are seeing. We can interpret behavior only by using the concepts and symbols with which we are familiar. We see what we want to see or what we have learned to see. An account of foreign travels given by a tourist to his friends upon his return home may be a very inaccurate descrip-

Geography and Behavior

In the Great Lakes region, farmers have limited agriculture to a certain range of possibilities, mainly involving cereals and livestock. But if some of our ancestors at the dawn of civilization had not chosen to domesticate certain grasses as cereals and certain four-footed animals as livestock, but, instead, had chosen to develop fungus growths or edible insects as a basis of productive culture, our mode of life might be now utterly different in ways which the natural environment might support as well as it does our present agriculture, or conceivably better.

—Samuel Koenig, et al.[*]

tion of the way life is experienced by the natives of Timbuktu, even though he reports what he actually saw.

SUMMARY

In this chapter we have used the term "culture" to identify the totality of the definitions (both ER and NER) held by a group. Culture is not some mystical entity existing somewhere "out there"; it is a phenomenon that can be studied scientifically by investigating the verbal behavior or written records of a group. This man-made culture is learned through interaction and is consequently a group phenomenon that changes and expands from generation to generation. The plans of action involved in these definitions specify, with varying degrees of exactness, how individuals should relate themselves to each other under specific circumstances. These specifications include the motivational and emotional aspects of behavior.

The culture of a society, which contains both universals and specifics, is a complex configuration of definitions that tend to be integrated and

[*] Samuel Koenig, Rex D. Hopper, and Feliks Gross (eds.), *Sociology: A Book of Readings* (Englewood Cliffs, N. J., Prentice-Hall, Inc., 1953), p. 19.

systematized; the social behavior that is built upon this cultural foundation also tends to be integrated and systematized. This is a major reason for the predictability of human behavior.

Two important concepts are related to culture: "society," which identifies the group holding the definitions, and "interaction," which identifies the actions engaged in by the group as they apply these definitions. Interaction, which is a dynamic concept, rejects a strict cultural determinism and substitutes instead a "cultural influence" perspective.

Subgroups within a society share unique subcultures, and each individual has his own unique configuration of definitions. The definitions shared by all are a major integrating factor of any group.

Definitions about biological and geographical factors are included within the culture of the group, and there is no necessary "determining" relationship between these factors and man's social behavior, although they do influence such behavior. The fact that lower animals cannot engage in symbolic interaction prohibits them from developing an "animal culture."

Each of the subsequent chapters in Part III is devoted to an analysis of a particular type of definition. Our understanding of culture will accordingly be expanded as we direct our attention to discussions of value definitions, norm definitions, role definitions, self definitions, and definitions of the situation.

QUESTIONS

1. Distinguish among society, culture, and interaction.
2. To what does one pay attention if he wants to study culture?
3. Make five statements about the culture of your sociology class.
4. The last chapter discussed needs. What connection do you see between needs and culture?
5. What is meant by the statement that "Culture is a blueprint for living"?
6. In what respect is culture a group phenomenon?
7. How does an understanding of culture help one understand the behavior of man?
8. Can an individual believe in both "free will" and "culture"?
9. Explain the statement: "If I have seen farther, it is by standing on the shoulders of giants."
10. How is culture related to motivation?

PROJECT

Make twenty predictions about what will take place in your next sociology class. Bring these to class and determine the percentage of the predictions which come true. How was culture related to your successes?

SUGGESTED READING

BEALS, RALPH L., and HARRY HOIJER. *An Introduction to Anthropology*. 3d ed. New York: The Macmillan Co., 1965.

GOLDSCHMIDT, WALTER (ed.). *Ways of Mankind*. Boston: Beacon Press, Inc., 1954.

HOEBEL, EDWARD ADAMSON. *Man in the Primitive World* 2d ed. New York: McGraw-Hill Book Co., 1958.

HONIGMAN, JOHN J. *The World of Man*. New York: Harper & Row, Inc., 1959.

JAEGER, GERTRUDE, and PHILIP SELZNICK. "A Normative Theory of Culture," *American Sociological Review*, XXIX, No. 5 (October, 1964), 653–669.

KLUCKHOHN, CLYDE. *Culture and Behavior*. New York: The Free Press of Glencoe, Inc., 1961.

KROEBER, A. L., and TALCOTT PARSONS. "The Concepts of Culture and of Social System," *American Sociological Review*, XXIII (October, 1958), 582–583.

LEE, DOROTHY. *Freedom and Culture*. Englewood Cliffs, N. J.: Prentice-Hall, Inc., 1959.

LINTON, RALPH. *The Tree of Culture*. New York: Alfred A. Knopf, Inc., 1955.

MERTON, ROBERT K. *Social Theory and Social Structure*. New York: The Free Press of Glencoe, Inc., 1949. Pp. 217–264.

MURDOCK, GEORGE P. "The Common Denominator of Cultures," in RALPH LINTON (ed.), *The Science of Man in the World Crisis*. New York: Columbia University Press, 1945.

7

Value Definitions

Can you discover whether a sunset, a painting, or a particular girl is beautiful by paying attention to these phenomena directly? Is beauty a quality of any of these things? If so, to what specifically does one pay attention in making decisions about beauty?

Chapter 3 emphasized that man, in his social behavior, is not restricted in his use of symbols to those that have an empirical referent. Symbols with no empirical referent, or NER symbols, have also been developed and utilized by man. This chapter is basically an extension of this discussion with emphasis upon one type of NER symbols, i.e., value definitions.

Chapter 6 defined culture as the accumulation of definitions that a group has developed and that are involved in the on-going behavior of the group. This chapter is an extension of that discussion in that we now turn to one of the major components of culture—value definitions. All that we have said about culture in general is true of value definition in particular. Let us look further, then, at value definitions.

Value definitions specify the relative worth that man attributes to or imposes upon various aspects of his universe. Homans [1] and others

use the term "sentiments" to identify this same phenomenon. Value definitions permit man to rank or locate things along some value scale. In one way or another value definitions specify that X is more desirable than Y. Man has developed many different types of value systems. One of these is the moral values system, which is generally stated in terms such as goodness, badness, evilness, wickedness, righteousness, justice, sacredness, etc. Although much of our discussion will be presented in terms of goodness and badness, all that is said about goodness and badness can be applied to these other terms as well. The following are examples of value definitions:

1. Lying while under oath is wrong.
2. It is good that children obey their parents.
3. Communists are bad.
4. Cheating on your income tax is bad.

Statements that specify plans of action, directly or indirectly, reflect value definitions. Such statements are called norm definitions or just norms and are of such importance to the sociologist that

[1] George Casper Homans, *Social Behavior: Its Elementary Forms* (New York: Harcourt, Brace & World, Inc., 1961).

an entire chapter will be devoted to them. Here we merely point out the relationship between value definitions and norm definitions and illustrate it by stating the norm definitions that follow from acceptance of the above-listed value definitions:

1. You should not lie while under oath.
2. Children should obey their parents.
3. Communists ought to be put in jail.
4. Do not cheat on your income tax.

The labels "good," "bad," "moral," "immoral," and other similar terms used in making value statements have no physical referents—they are NER concepts. Goodness or badness is not a quality of any object or behavior pattern *per se*. For instance, if one were to endorse the premise that money is evil, he could never prove this by paying attention to the physical properties of money *per se*. He could detect its color, weight, or size by relying upon the empirical characteristics of money, but he would be unable to detect its goodness or badness by looking at the money, since this is not a quality of the money but rather a particular way of defining or evaluating the money. Value definitions are applied by human beings to objects; they are not "in" the objects. Value definitions are a social product.

This can be illustrated by an analysis of so-called bad and good words. In the American society, for instance, "hell" and "damn" have been defined by some as bad words. Does this badness, then, stem from any quality of the word *per se*? No. Such a dimension is attributed to the word by man. This is suggested by the fact that "bad" words may at a later time be redefined and become socially acceptable and hence become "good" words. If the badness were a quality of the word *per se*, such transitions would not be possible.

Something, then, is good to a particular individual or group only because it is defined as good. Goodness is a quality imposed upon or attributed to the physical world by the one doing the evaluating.

If man could not utilize symbols he could not do this evaluating. Without the aid of symbols

---

Like Putting Water in a Kettle?

. . . values attributed to any object—like "good" or "hateful"—really are not "in" the object. In having an experience one does not put value into it like water into a kettle. Value is not an element; it has to do with a relation between the object and the person who has experiences with the object. . . . Value as a relation is easily seen in conjunction with such an adjective as "useful"—useful for whom, under what conditions, for which of his purposes? Precisely the same is true whether the object is a thing or an event and whether the value is "useful" or "sinful."

—Anselm Strauss.*

---

he could not be told by others or could not tell himself that something is good or bad. Without symbolic interaction man would live in an amoral world—being unaware of any moral distinctions. Lower animals, who live in just such a world, since they cannot use symbols, do make distinctions between objects—they do make choices—but not on the basis of a value decision as man does. A dog does not try to justify his aggressive behavior toward other dogs or toward human beings. Man, however, does provide justification which involves value definitions for his aggressive behavior toward others.

Judgments concerning beautifulness and ugliness are in the same category as judgments of goodness and badness. These are dimensions that man invents and then takes into account in his social relationships. Beauty is not an empirical quality of anything, but rather as Shakespeare has indicated, "Beauty lies in the eyes of the beholder." One cannot discover beauty by paying attention to the empirical object believed to be beautiful. You must first know how people (including yourself) define beauty before you can decide whether an object "is" beautiful. But even then you cannot discover whether the object

---

* Anselm Strauss, *Mirrors and Masks* (New York: The Free Press of Glencoe, Inc., 1959), p. 24.

is beautiful; you can only discover how people define it. You cannot see, feel, touch, smell, or in any such manner detect beauty, since it is not a quality of any object. It is a quality attributed to or imposed upon objects, relationships, or concepts. It is a man-made dimension. One man may think, for instance, that his wife is beautiful, while another may define her as homely. The difference is not in the woman but in the men doing the evaluating. Statements about beauty of a woman really don't tell us much about the woman involved, but only about the person, male or female, making the evaluation. Alfred North Whitehead emphasizes this point when he states:

Nature gets credit which should in truth be reserved for ourselves: the rose for its scent; the nightingale for his song; the sun for its radiance. They should address their lyrics to themselves, and should turn them into odes of self-congratulations on the excellency of the human mind. Nature is a dull affair, soundless, scentless, colorless; merely the hurrying of material, endlessly, meaninglessly.[2]

Value definitions of an economic type which in the United States may be stated in terms of dollars and cents are of the same kind as definitions of goodness and beautifulness. The subjective non-empirical nature of this dimension is shown by the fact that in one store a unit of clothing may be "worth" $50.00, whereas in another store the same make of suit may be "worth" $100.00, and during a sale the "worth" of a suit is different from what it was the day before the sale. The "$50.00-ness" is not a quality of the suit; it is man's evaluation of the suit.

The manner in which we typically speak of goodness, badness, beauty, and dollars-and-cents-ness, suggests an interpretation of these dimensions contrary to what we have been discussing. In a sense our language patterns are misleading in that they may lead us to believe we have identified something which we have not. For instance, we typically make a statement to the effect that "Miss America is beautiful." The use of the verb "is" according to our rules of lan-

guage leads one to think that the statement tells us something about Miss America. This statement says that Miss America *is* beautiful. Our discussion, however, has indicated that beauty is not a quality of the object, but rather a way of defining or evaluating it. A more accurate statement, then, would be "Miss America appears beautiful to me," or "I would define her as being beautiful," or "She has those qualities which correspond to my ideas of beauty." In such statements the language emphasizes that it is the one evaluating the object who makes the decisions about beauty, and not any characteristic of the object *per se* which is identified.

The same thing is true with reference to dollars-and-cents, and goodness and badness evaluations. To state that "cheating is bad" easily leads one to believe that the badness is a quality of the cheating. To state that "honesty is the best policy" leads one to believe that the "bestness" is a quality of being honest. If, when one wants to pay attention to such dimensions, he were to link the evaluation with the *evaluator* rather than the *evaluated,* such an arrangement of symbols would more accurately reflect the objective reality involved. Use of the term "value definition" rather than just "value" facilitates such efforts.

The view of goodness or badness being not a quality of an object, but rather a quality attributed to it, has not been widely accepted. Among the Trobriand Islanders, to take a primitive tribe as an example, goodness is felt to be an element that goes into the making of various things. Objects that are believed to contain this substance are felt to be good; objects without it are not good. To them goodness is similar to magical potency. It is a component of the *vaygu'a,* a certain class of objects that are of no utility but are of supreme value. Thus, whenever a malignant spirit, in the shape of a snake or land-crab, is found near or in the village, such *vaygu'a* are put before it, not as a peace offering, but to impart, it is believed, to the spirit some of the goodness contained within them and so make it benevolent. When a man is dying or dead, his body is surrounded and covered with *vaygu'a* which are afterwards removed. Also, a certain

[2] Alfred North Whitehead, *Science and the Modern World* (New York: The Macmillan Co., 1925), p. 80.

class of yams—yams received or to be given as a gift—is believed to contain goodness. These are believed to be so full of goodness that every year, though gift yams form easily half the yam supply of Trobrianders, the magician works spells over them so that men should lose all interest in consuming them. This magic is believed to take away people's appetites or make them develop an abnormal yearning for the uncultivated products of the bush while the gift yams are "anchored" to the yam house and rot unconsumed through the year. At every opportunity, both the *vaygu'a* and the gift yams are handled and otherwise touched, since they are believed to give pleasure and satisfaction through their goodness.[3]

A modern parallel to this type of thinking is found in the following statement in a 1960 textbook in social psychology.

[3] D. D. Lee, "A Linguistic Approach to a System of Values," in Theodore M. Newcomb and Eugene L. Hartley (eds.), *Readings in Social Psychology* (New York: Holt, Rinehart and Winston, Inc., 1947, pp. 219–224.

Figure 7.1 Making a value decision. (Wide World Photos.)

Values are objects, ideas, or beliefs which are cherished. In America, such things as money and social position are valued highly, but we also have many values which are not economic; beauty is valued, as is art, music, and philosophical speculation.[4]

Some of the logical difficulties in defining goodness as a quality of the object rather than a way of defining the object can be seen in this quotation. It is first stated that values are objects, and then, in the next sentence it is said that "such things as money and social position are valued highly." These two sentences are mutually contradictory. The first indicates that the objects are values; the second that the objects are valued. These say quite different things. If the value inheres in the object, it is not at the same time a quality attributed to or imposed upon the object by the valuer. Further confusion is added in this text when at a later time it is indicated that "science itself *is* a value." Such confusion could be avoided if it were recognized that goodness (even though this is a noun) is not an empirical dimension of anything.

Since the value dimension is a non-empirical one, it is possible for man, individually and collectively, to cut up or subdivide the value aspect of his world in any number of different ways. In terms of an over-simplified dichotomy, it permits him to include under the label "good" or "bad" things which evidence almost unlimited variation as far as their physical or empirical characteristics are concerned, since using such concepts permits man to move to a non-empirical level of abstraction. Thus, such diverse practices as spanking one's child, destroying a neighbor's property, using a "vulgar" word, driving at a certain speed on a modern highway, and telling a lie before a court of law can all be lumped together under one label and classified as bad.

Applying the "bad" label, of course, provides some broad plans of action for all these behavior patterns. The plan of action which generally goes along with the label "bad" is that such be-havior is to be avoided. Using such categories permits a great simplification of behavior, since the same plan of action can be felt to be appropriate for a great diversity of things.

Those who are involved in socializing new members of a society to conform to the culture of the group also find that such efforts may be facilitated by the use of such evaluations. To have the young child, for instance, identify objects and practices as "bad" leads him to the "to-be-avoided" plans of action—if he has properly learned his "lessons." Further, since value definitions have no empirical referent, youngsters who are not as sophisticated as adults can usually find no acceptable way to challenge the value decisions of adults who generally speak of goodness and badness with the same degree of assurance and finality that they use in their references to such empirical things as cars, food, and Aunt Maggie.

Young children, and others as well, soon come to recognize, perhaps but vaguely, that value definitions are different from definitions that involve empirical referents. It is easy to conclude that they are superempirical or supernatural in nature or origin. Further, adults or leaders not wishing to have value decisions appear to be strictly arbitrary to their children or followers (and maybe even to themselves) may attribute the origin to a source beyond them, such as society, or to a supernatural source such as God. In either case, the responsible "other" is not immediately available for consultation as to a validity of value definitions. This makes the initiation of change difficult or unlikely.

Of course, this non-empirical nature of value definitions may also facilitate the introduction of new value definitions for those who claim to have supernatural endorsement for the proposed values. The advocates of the status quo can marshal no *empirical* evidence that the new values are right or wrong—only that they are different. Proposed value changes are more likely to be accepted if the one making the proposals has a position of authority.

This discussion of the nature of value judgments leads to the conclusion that an individual who may be an expert in coming to decisions

---

[4] Jack H. Curtis, *Social Psychology* (New York: McGraw-Hill Book Co., 1960), pp. 138–139.

about the empirical world is not by virtue of this fact also an expert about the non-empirical world—or about values. Decisions about the empirical world are secured, of course, in many different ways. Today, however, it is the scientist who is generally acknowledged as the expert in this realm. One way or another he manipulates the empirical world and then on the basis of what happens to the empirical phenomena of consideration comes to a decision. Such training, however, does not qualify him as an expert in the value area. Because a man is a qualified chemist or physicist does not make him, for instance, a qualified administrator, who is called upon to make frequent value judgments. If he is *also* a good administrator it is because he has had training or experience beyond that of a chemist.

Figure 7.2 Value does not reside in the object and may change with time. Any object, including a stock certificate, is valueless by itself. (The Bettmann Archive, Inc.)

VALUE DEFINITIONS AND SCIENCE

Our earlier discussion about the scientific method emphasized that this method requires that the researcher pay attention to empirical phenomena which are available to his senses. This, then, imposes limitations upon what can be accomplished with this method, as Albert Einstein suggested when he said, "The knowledge of (scientific) truth is wonderful, but it is so little capable of acting as a guide that it cannot prove even the justification and value of the aspiration toward that very knowledge of truth."[5] This poses a question about the procedures of the social scientist who studies human behavior. If value definitions are one of the important aspects of such behavior and if goodness or badness is not an empirical quality of anything, how, then, does the scientist handle values? If science is a technique for determining facts or for gaining knowledge about the empirical world, it is obviously not a method for providing answers about goodness and badness *per se*. Our earlier discussion of the scientific method emphasized that the scientist, in his role as a scientist, is not concerned with what ought to be, but rather with what is. What, then, does the social scientist do with values?

He does not leave values completely alone. The value area, in fact, is one of the most important to which he pays attention. What he does, however, is study the *value definitions* that people have. He is not concerned, for instance, with the question as to whether cheating on an examination *is* bad, since this is a scientifically unanswerable question. He is concerned, however, with the question as to whether the students at X University define cheating on exams as bad. In the second illustration, he is concerned with the behavior of man, including his verbal behavior. This is his area of competency. The social scientist studies the value definitions that people have and relates these to other behavior, but he does not attempt to decide as a scientist

[5] Alfred Stern, "Science and the Philosopher," *American Scientist*, XLIV, No. 3 (July, 1956), 281–295.

Teachers and Value Judgments

The professor should not demand the right as a professor to carry the marshal's baton of the statesman or reformer in his knapsack. This is just what he does when he uses the unassailability of the academic chair for the expression of political or cultural-political evaluations.

—Max Weber.*

whether these value positions are the right or good ones to have, or whether any value definitions are valid.

The social scientist, then, treats value definitions as data which he studies, and he may do this in any of the following ways:[6]

1. *Identify values.* He may merely list values, pointing out, for example, that Group A believes in infant baptism.
2. *Determine intensity of values.* He may measure how strongly an individual or group of individuals accepts certain values. Thus, he may point out that certain groups disapprove of divorce more strongly than do other groups.
3. *Compare values.* He may show that Group A believes that dancing is good and wholesome whereas Group B has as one of its values that dancing is evil and immoral.
4. *Determine the influence of values upon behavior.* He may study how the value definition that sex is immoral influences the outcome of marriage.
5. *Determine how behavior influences values.* He may study how participation in a delinquent subsociety, say a teen-age gang, influences the values of an individual.
6. *Determine or study the source of values.* He may study how the value that democracy is the best type of government developed in America.
7. *Study value conflicts.*
    A. How Group A's values conflict with Group B's values.

* Max Weber, *The Methodology of the Social Sciences* (New York: The Free Press of Glencoe, Inc., 1949), p. 5.
[6] Glenn M. Vernon, *Sociology of Religion* (New York: McGraw-Hill Book Co., 1962), pp. 9–10.

B. How the various values of particular individuals or groups may conflict with each other —how economic values may conflict with religious values.

C. How previous values may conflict with present values. He may study how early American beliefs about bundling conflict with present evaluations thereof.

D. How values held by individuals or groups conflict with the actual behavior of these individuals or groups. For example, how an alcoholic may believe that his drinking is harmful and bad, while at the same time he continues to drink.

8. *Study the process by which values are acquired.* This would include study of the whole process of socialization.

9. *Study value changes* and the various factors related to such changes.

None of these activities requires the social scientist either to endorse or reject any particular value definition—a task for which he as a scientist is unqualified. Thus, he may use value definitions as *data* in his scientific studies. In this sense value definitions are an important part of the material that the social scientist studies.

ORIGIN OF VALUE DEFINITIONS

A point of interest to the social scientist is the question as to the origin of value definitions and the process by which individuals or groups come to endorse particular value positions. As to the origin of value definitions, it is obvious that such definitions are learned and that they are learned through interaction with others. Although value definitions are constantly changing, just as culture of which they are a part is constantly changing, most people accept the value definitions endorsed by the significant groups to which they belong or hope to belong. Most of our value definitions, then, come out of the common culture storehouse. Exactly how a particular value selection is made and reinforced is the question before us now.

Since value definitions cannot be discovered from an examination of any empirical qualities of the objects to which they are applied, it follows

that the individual or group does not come to value decisions through such a procedure. Since value definitions are of the NER type it also follows that consensus about them must be secured through methods other than those used with ER type definitions. Consensus in the value definition area is, in fact, difficult to achieve, and great variability is evidenced. Since consensus cannot be secured through observation of the empirical phenomena evaluated, it follows that the *social relations* which support or discount particular value positions would be of major importance in such activities, as, in fact, they are. Human beings tend to share the value positions of those who are important to them. They tend to adopt the value definitions of those with whom they have developed or hope to develop satisfying relationships. Particular value definitions are accepted not because of any quality of the objects being evaluated, but because of the type of relationships which the evaluator has with others. Value definitions grow out of association with others, and acceptance of common value definitions is one of the things that hold a group together. The use of value definitions permits individuals to make certain types of distinctions between things that they have learned to take into account. The maintenance of the group as a functioning entity is facilitated by sharing such definitions.

What we have been saying is particularly true of the young child. As the individual matures, however, he may come to disassociate the value definitions from their originators and develop an allegiance to the set of value definitions or standards *per se*, which he may attempt to maintain regardless of the behavior of the originating group. In Riesman's terms, such an individual becomes "tradition directed." As most individuals grow into adulthood they move somewhat in this direction. What happens is that the social origin and the group endorsement or reinforcement are pushed somewhat into the background. They are still there, however. As such individuals change group allegiance and/or membership, the set of value definitions acceptable to the individual will most likely undergo change in a subtle or a more dramatic manner.

A second important method of coming to a decision about value definitions is to accept certain sources as authoritative. Since value definitions are imposed upon the physical world, it is not surprising that authority is frequently utilized in efforts to secure acceptance of certain sets of definitions. Religious functionaries are frequently accepted as authorities upon questions of goodness and badness. For the Roman Catholic, the pope is the final earthly authority and if he defines something as good, then to the devout Catholic it *is* good. For others a particular set of scriptures may be accepted as the final authority. To the fundamentalist Christian if the Bible says something is good, it is good and this definition is accepted without question. Those who question an "authority" question related value assertions.

In the realm of the arts, critics assume the role of the authority figure and exert considerable influence upon the decisions of others as to whether a particular film, for instance, is worthy of 4, 3, 2, or 1 "stars."

Reliance upon authority in matters of values is just another example of the previous point that it is man's relationship with other men that provides him with his values. We are generally willing to accept as an authority those sources which our significant others accept. In the last measure, value definitions are learned through and re-inforced (or undermined) by the interaction in which man engages.

Adherence to or endorsement of any particular set of values may involve a rational, logical element. Individuals may think through what sort of values they will endorse. Teachers, clergymen, parents, and scoutmasters, to mention but a few, may engage in extensive teaching activities in which the logical dimension of a particular value position is stressed. Most people, in fact, like to feel that their value definitions are firmly rooted in logic. However, since values have the origin they do, it is entirely possible for an individual or a group to endorse a value position in the face of logical evidence to the contrary. It is possible to maintain, "I don't care what they say; I still *feel* that this is right." Even though a particular value configuration is "proved" by some

logical or rational procedure to be "wrong," man may still endorse and protect it. He may, in fact, develop new sets of logical and rational underpinnings to support the values that he "knows" to be true. We shall discuss this point more extensively when we turn our attention to prejudice and ethnocentrism.

Since man lives in a symbolic world, he develops his own systems of logic and rationale. Such systems do not exist "out there" waiting for man to discover them. Man develops his own systems of logic. It is therefore possible for different systems of logic to be developed by different groups and individuals and also for different groups and individuals at different times or under different circumstances. It is important to understand that values may be maintained or retained even though they can be "proved" by one means or another to be illogical or irrational. Stemming as they do from satisfying human relationships, the conviction that they are "right" may be of sufficient intensity to override any logical proofs to the contrary. An individual may say, pointing to his heart, "I just know inside of me that this is right." Contrary logical evidence may not shake such a conviction.

When it is suggested that science cannot determine whether something is good or bad, such a statement does not incorporate the idea that definitions about goodness and badness should therefore be abolished. The scientist asks no such thing. Indeed, the study of sociology makes us aware of the fact that the preservation of any society is, in part, dependent upon the existence of value definitions that are shared by the group. Just because something cannot be done scientifically does not mean that it cannot be done by some other method. The scientific method can be used to obtain certain types of answers, but it cannot be used to obtain other types, of which answers about the validity of value definitions are a major illustration.

The following statement overlooks the point we have been making: "A sociologist who believes that people must believe in the validity of values but that such values actually have no validity must either deceive his public or help in dissolving the forces which hold society to-

Values in Text Books

The authors of a sociology text state "In our book we quite frankly and openly make certain value judgments. For example, we make no secret of the fact that we would like to see eliminated or reduced such phenomena as crime, war, and substandard housing ... but probably few social scientists would disagree with these judgments whatever their ideological position. We hold that these value judgments are no more unscientific than the medical scientist's judgment that tuberculosis is an evil which should be eliminated." *

The point overlooked is that neither the value judgments of the medical scientist nor these authors are scientific. The results of the research about tuberculosis remains the same whether the disease is defined as an evil or as a righteous phenomenon.

gether."[7] When we say that the validity of value definitions cannot be scientifically verified we are not saying that there are not other non-scientific ways of doing so. Science can provide us with certain types of answers, but certainly not with all types of answers.

The following conclusion by a popular columnist evidently stems from a lack of an understanding of the limitation of science in the value area: "The Sociologists are addicted to the statistical method, which leads them to describe as 'normal' whatever is widespread. What 'everybody is doing' is *all right* if it does not go too far."[8] Studies that show what is "normal" tell us nothing about the *rightness* or *wrongness* of the behavior.

* From comments by Mary Elizabeth Walsh and Paul Furfey in reply to a review of their book. See *American Sociological Review*, XXV, No. 3 (June, 1960), 407.

[7] William L. Kolb, "Values, Positivism, and the Functional Theory of Religion: The Growth of a Moral Dilemma," *Social Forces*, XXXI, No. 4 (May, 1953), 305–311.

[8] Dorothy Thompson, "Is America's Moral Code Breaking Down?" *Ladies' Home Journal* (June, 1960).

PREJUDICE

There are some important implications of this discussion of values for the study of prejudice. If prejudice is defined as acceptance of some premise in the face of objective evidence to the contrary, or in Allport's words, "thinking ill of others without sufficient warrant," then the label "prejudice" would seem to be the wrong term to apply to value definitions, since such differences do not stem from any empirical characteristics. Value premises cannot be found to be objectively inaccurate when compared with some empirical criteria. They are only wrong when compared to an arbitrary standard—a man-made standard rather than one inhering in the physical characteristics of any object or behavior pattern. In what sense, then, is prejudice "without sufficient warrant"?

An illustration may serve to sharpen the discussion. An individual may have anti-Negro prejudices with a content something like this. "Negroes are inferior to whites because their capacity to learn is inferior (less than) that of whites, or because they do not have the physical endurance of whites." The accuracy of such beliefs can be checked by paying attention to empirical phenomena. It could, for instance, be determined objectively whether Negroes or whites, as a group, are able to do certain tasks longer than the other group, when given equal opportunities, or whether under similar conditions one group was able to learn more than the other. The belief that one group is superior to the other, then, could be empirically tested. If the empirical evidence did not support the belief, and the belief were then maintained despite such evidence, the belief would meet the criteria of "prejudice" stated above.

But what about those who accept the belief that the Negro is inferior to the white, without attaching this belief to any physical characteristics of the Negro or white: "The Negro just isn't as *good* as the white." What about the individual who, when shown empirical evidence that Negroes and whites as groups have equal intellectual and physical potential, maintains that this is all the more reason for not giving the Negroes equal opportunity with the whites since this would invariably lead to their becoming equal to the whites in all areas of learned behavior. His definition of inferior or his criterion of inferiority is quite different from that of the first individual described above. The first belief in inferiority can be objectively verified; the second cannot. The second is strictly subjective. It is a definition imposed by man upon objects, not a quality of these objects.

If ease of communication is our goal, it would appear that it could be furthered by applying different labels to these two different types of behavior. We could distinguish between the following:

Prejudice$_1$—a belief maintained despite empirical evidence to the contrary.

Prejudice$_2$—a belief maintained despite the beliefs of others to the contrary.

Prejudice$_2$ involves, of course, differences in beliefs about non-empirical phenomena. In this sense, then, anyone who holds to a set of beliefs different from ours is prejudiced. However, as seen through the eyes of the other, it would be we who are prejudiced—not he. Such differences can easily lead to the "I'm right, you're wrong" type of argument for which there is no empirical method of settlement. Our thinking in this area would most likely be more effective if we used the label "prejudice" to refer to the first type of definition and "value judgment" to refer to the second.

Prejudice of the first type is a frequent human phenomenon. Since man responds to symbols rather than to the referent these symbols stand for, it is entirely possible for him to sincerely believe things about others which have no empirical foundation. He may, in fact, go further than this, and "see" what his prejudices call for. He may selectively ignore contrary evidence and pay attention only to supporting evidence. Since social behavior is basically symbolic behavior, changing of prejudice as well as value judgments is frequently difficult.

ETHNOCENTRISM

"Ethnocentrism" is a sociological term that is closely related to our discussion of value judgments. Ethnocentrism involves strong positive value judgments about one's own group and its culture. It involves more than just the belief that "my way is the good way," although this is a part of it. It also involves being unable to see any perspective other than one's own, because one's learning experiences have not prepared one to do so.

In learning the way of life of his group, the process to which we will later apply the label "socialization," the young child is taught in such a way that he believes, at first at least, that his is the only way of life. He learns his language with its built-in ethnocentrism. He learns his norms, his religion, etc., which are generally not taught as but one of the many ways to do such and such, but rather as "the" way. In many ways members of groups are taught that too high a degree of tolerance or acceptance of others is disloyalty. Obviously, the way of life of a society such as the United States could not be maintained unless most members, most of the time, shared common definitions that their way was the best way, or at least an effective way to get things done. Not only does the child learn these things, but even the manner in which he is taught them leads him to believe that other ways are inferior or maybe even dangerous. Ethnocentrism is also taught and reinforced through such things as the songs that he sings, the jokes that he learns to define as funny, the TV programs he

---

Ethnocentrism and the Golden Rule

The Golden Rule tells us to "treat others as you would have them treat you." This is an ethnocentric statement since it assumes that your way is the best way. A less ethnocentric statement would be to "treat others as they would like to be treated."

views, and the radio shows to which he listens, the movies, the mass media, and even advertising. In this sense much ethnocentrism is "caught," not taught. Even the terms that we select to refer to particular groups or behavior patterns reflect our ethnocentrism. Cohen has provided the following illustration: [9]

Favorable or Upgrading	In-between or Neutral	Unfavorable or Downgrading
discreet	cautious	cowardly
careful	meticulous	fussy
warmhearted	sentimental	mushy
courageous	bold	reckless, foolhardy
open-minded	liberal	unsound
humanitarian	idealist	do-gooder
business executive	employer	boss
pilgrim	migrant, refugee	alien
enlighten	report	propagandize

It is not maintained here that ethnocentrism is bad. This in itself would be a value judgment, which falls outside the realm of science. It should be recognized, however, that it would be difficult to maintain a society over a period of time without ethnocentric definitions on the part of its members. Since human beings do not have biologically built-in factors that make them participate effectively in a group, it follows that they have to learn to *want* to belong and to cooperate effectively with the members of the group. They have to learn to define the group goals and activities as being desirable. In a sense, they have to make the group goals their own goals. Ethnocentrism, then, includes what is popularly called group loyalty, *esprit de corps*, school spirit, and dedication.

Developing ethnocentric definitions tends to strengthen the group, and in times when the very existence of the group may be threatened, as in wartime, such definitions take on increased meaning. Strong ethnocentrism, however, may de-

[9] Felix S. Cohen, "The Reconstruction of Hidden Value Judgments: Word Choices as Value Indicators," in Lyman Bryson, *et al.* (eds.), *Symbols and Values: An Initial Study,* Conference on Science, Religion, and Philosophy (New York: Harper & Row, Inc., 1954), pp. 545–561.

Ethnocentrism

According to Eskimo beliefs, the first man, though made by the Great Being, was a failure, and was consequently cast aside and called kob-lu-na, which means "white man"; but the second attempt of the Great Being resulted in the formation of a perfect man, and he was called In-nu, the name which the Eskimo give to themselves.

When anything foolish is done, the Chippewas use an expression which means "as stupid as a white man."

When a Greenlander saw a foreigner of gentle and modest manners, his usual remark was "he is almost as well-bred as we," or "He begins to be a man, that is, a Greenlander."

The savage regards his people as THE people, as the root of all others, and as occupying the middle of the earth. The Hottentots love to call themselves "the men of men."

The aborigines of Hayti believed that their island was the first of all things, that the sun and the moon issued from one of its caverns, and man from another.

—Howard Becker and
Harry Elmer Barnes.*

velop certain "blind spots" in the perspective of the individual or group. It may lead to a rejection of other patterns of life that might be as effective or even more effective than those already established. Ethnocentrism encourages members of the group to reject other groups as being not just different but inferior, and it hinders the sharing of ideas and skills by different groups. Whether these goals are desirable ones, however, is again a value judgment that highly ethnocentric groups would no doubt reject.

Tolerance itself can be valued highly, and groups can be taught to be tolerant one of the

* Howard Becker and Harry Elmer Barnes, *Social Thought from Lore to Science,* Vol. I (2nd ed.; Washington, D. C.: Harren Press, 1952), pp. 17–18.

other. The idea of cultural pluralism endorsed by some suggests that differences are recognized but are valued, in part, for their being different. Different societies evidence different degrees of tolerance of differences. Ethnocentrism is a relative thing.

SUMMARY

Value definitions are a part of culture. Since they involve only NER symbols, such labels do not identify any empirical aspect of the objects evaluated but are rather a classification developed by man to distinguish or label certain objects toward which he has decided it is appropriate to direct certain plans of action. Contrary beliefs exist, however, despite the lack of empirical proof, to the effect that values do, in fact, reside in the objects thus labeled.

Because of this NER characteristic, scientific decisions can be made only about the symbol systems that involve values but not about the correctness of the system. In other words, the scientist can determine whether a group *defines* something as bad but not whether it *is* bad. Scientists, being experts in the empirical world, are not, because of this training, also experts in dealing with non-empirical values. Since the correctness of a value position cannot be determined by observation of the empirical phenomenon involved, value judgments develop and gain their support from the type of relationships that exist within the group. An individual tends to support the values of his significant others or his reference group. Since there is no necessary relationship between his subjective reality and objective reality, we may, however, develop many different types of justifications for the maintenance of a particular value position.

"Ethnocentrism" is a sociological term that identifies value judgments to the effect that "my way is the best way."

"Prejudice," when used without qualification, as a term to identify beliefs that are maintained despite evidence to the contrary may include judgments about empirical as well as non-empirical phenomena. Greater precision in thinking could result from using terms that distinguish between (1) beliefs held despite empirical evidence to the contrary and (2) beliefs held despite value judgments to the contrary. If the term "prejudice" were restricted to the first type of belief, "value judgment" could be used for the second.

The major goal of this chapter has been to provide understanding of value definitions *per se*. A subsequent chapter on motivational behavior will expand this discussion and direct attention to the process of making value decisions.

QUESTIONS

1. To what does one pay attention if he wants to study beauty?
2. How are value definitions related to culture?
3. We have said that value definitions cannot be proved to be correct by the scientific method. Does this mean, then, that they cannot be proved by another method?
4. Discuss the statement "Good is an irreducible and indefinable quality."
5. Does being scientific require that one give up his value definitions?
6. Discuss the statement that "value definitions are the data that the sociologist studies."
7. What difficulties might arise from using the word "goodness" as a noun?
8. Distinguish between the two types of prejudice discussed in the chapter.
9. Define ethnocentrism.
10. Analyze the process by which you arrive at a value decision and identify the factors which you took into account.

PROJECTS

Provide three statements about human behavior *involving value definitions* that could be tested scientifically and three that could not.

Identify ten different value definitions that are related to your being currently enrolled in college.

SUGGESTED READING

ADLER, FRANZ. "The Value Concept in Sociology," *The American Journal of Sociology*, LXII, No. 3 (November, 1956), 272–279.

ALLPORT, GORDON W., P. E. VERNON, and G. LINDZEY. *Study of Values*. Boston: Houghton Mifflin Co., 1952.

BARTON, ALLEN. "Measuring the Values of Individuals," *Research Supplement to Religious Education*, LVII, No. 4 (July–August, 1962), S–62–S–97.

BELSHAW, C. S. "The Identification of Values in Anthropology," *The American Journal of Sociology*, V, No. 6 (May, 1959), 555–562.

CATTON, WILLIAM R., JR. "A Theory of Value," *American Sociological Review*, XXIV, No. 3 (June, 1959).

GORDON, ROBERT A., *et al.* "Values and Gang Delinquency: A Study of Street-Corner Groups," *The American Journal of Sociology*, LXIX, No. 2 (September, 1963), 109–128.

KLUCKHOHN, FLORENCE R., and FRED L. STRODTBECK. *Variations in Value Orientations*. New York: Harper & Row, Inc., 1961.

KOLB, WILLIAM L. "Values, Positivism, and the Functional Theory of Religion: The Growth of a Moral Dilemma," *Social Forces*, XXXI, No. 4 (May, 1953), 305–311.

PERRY, R. B. *Realms of Value: A Critique of Civilization*. Cambridge: Harvard University Press, 1954.

SZASZ, THOMAS S. "Bootlegging Humanistic Values Through Psychiatry," *The Antioch Review* (Fall, 1962), 341–349.

8

Norm Definitions

Can you think of any of your usual experiences in which you do not, when you enter the situation, have at least a rough idea as to how the others involved will behave and also how you think they will expect you to behave?

Our previous discussions of the nature of symbols have emphasized that the meaning man associates with the symbols he learns generally includes plans of action that he has learned to accept as being appropriate for the object (whatever it is) to which he applies the label. The plans of action, then, specify how one is expected to relate himself to such objects, and conversely, how one can expect the object to relate itself to him. (These objects may, of course, be other human beings.) The expectations as to how inanimate objects will relate themselves to man are fairly consistent and usually present no great problems. The expectations with reference to animate objects, especially other human beings, however, may be extremely varied and necessitate all sorts of continuous adjustments on the part of the individual in his social behavior.

The discussion of norm definitions in this chapter is an expansion of this previous discussion of the symbolic nature of human interaction in that we will examine certain of these plans of action. The term "norm" has been given two different meanings. It has been used to refer to the behavior patterns that are "normal," customary, or usual. If one wants to find out what the norms are, he watches what people do and one way or another "averages out" the differences and thus discovers what the average member of the group does, or what the members of the group "normally" do. One of the norms of students in your class, for instance, is to be seated before the class bell rings. The term has also been used to refer to the expectations that are held with reference to others. In this sense the students are expected to be in their seats before the bell rings, which is saying something quite different from the above statement—the students *are* normally in their seats before the bell rings. Homans, using this definition, says:

A norm, then, is an idea in the minds of the members of a group, an idea that can be put in the form of a statement specifying what the members or other men should do, ought to do, are expected to do, under given circumstances.[1]

[1] George C. Homans, *The Human Group* (New York: Harcourt, Brace & World, Inc., 1950), p. 123.

112

It is the second definition that we will use, and in order to give emphasis to the fact that it is the expectations to which we refer we will depart from customary usage and use the term "norm definition" rather than "norm," as most texts do. Using this label also clearly includes "norm definitions" under our heading of "culture," which we have defined as the totality of the definitions held by a society. This chapter, then, is a discussion of one aspect of culture. It considers one type of definition, while the following chapters in this part of the text will each discuss other types of definition.

Norm definitions are plans of action felt to be appropriate for certain purposes and are thus related to the larger "definition of the situation." Norm definitions are expected behavior patterns. Other terms which have been used to refer to what we call norm definitions include rules, regulations, customs, taboos, conventions, etiquette, blueprints, script, and laws.

Any definition is related to a particular object. The object to which norm definitions are applied is man. Our discussion assumes that this is understood. Norm definitions apply to most human beings in most situations. They are very general in nature although there are most likely exceptions for most such definitions. Role definitions, which will be discussed in the next chapter, are more restricted in applicability. Once it is determined that an object is a person, the norm definitions specify the behavior patterns which are generally expected.

Any society develops a vast number of norm definitions. In America, for instance, letters are supposed to be written from left to right on the paper, to start somewhere near the upper left-hand corner, generally include the word "dear" in the salutation even though the addressee is a perfect stranger, and terminate with "sincerely yours" or some similar expression. At a football game, which is more likely to be played in the fall than in the summer, the fans are expected to dress in "sports" clothes rather than formal attire or swimming suits and to behave in a manner different from that of the football players. Most Americans know, in general terms at least, what types of behavior are expected at a church

supper, a junior prom, and while deer hunting. In those situations with which we are most familiar we know what the expected behavior is for those involved—including, of course, ourselves. We have learned the norm definitions. In strange situations, such as when traveling in a foreign country or visiting a strange church, the average person does not know the norm definitions with any degree of assurance and may, as a consequence, feel uneasy and insecure.

Norm definitions are a group rather than an individual phenomenon in that they are plans of action specifying how individuals interact with or relate themselves to each other. The previous chapter on the social nature of human behavior emphasized that most individual behavior is but one part of a larger system of behavior. Norm definitions are an integral part of this larger system, which facilitates the interaction, as will be discussed in greater detail later.

The norm definitions found in any specific group are extremely varied and are involved in the group behavior in many different ways. In order to further delineate this broad concept, let us distinguish between several different types of norm definitions and discuss some of the various characteristics of each type.

FOLKWAYS AND MORES DEFINED

Different norm definitions have been distinguished in terms of the degree of intensity or the associated value definitions. Some, for instance, are felt to be extremely important, while others are felt to be of only minor significance. Norm definitions can be arranged along an intensity continuum or a value scale as follows.

High Intensity ⬚ MORES

Low Intensity ⬚ FOLKWAYS

Norm definitions of high intensity have been given the label "mores" while those of lesser intensity are called "folkways." Mores are defined by the group as being very important or as having high value. We are particularly ethnocentric about our mores. These high-value definitions stem from and are reinforced by the fact that such definitions generally involve a supernatural or religious element, in that the group defines the behavior patterns incorporated in the mores as having in addition to social approval, supernatural approval. The mores of the group are frequently the subject matter of sermons preached by religious leaders. Those who accept them believe not only that their fellowmen expect them to do these things, but that whatever supernatural beings they accept also share these desires. Even where the mores are not related to the formal religion of the group, they are still considered to be somehow different from the folkways. They are "must" behavior and the group accepting them generally exerts great effort to assure conformity. Enforcement of the mores is facilitated if the group believes that they have supernatural endorsement or that they are inherent in the "very nature of things."

Folkways, while defined as appropriate and desirable behavior, are not felt to be as important as the mores. The supernatural element may be minimized or absent. Efforts are made to get members of the group to follow these expected patterns, but they are not as great as in the case of the mores.

Let us analyze some expected behavior patterns from the American society and see in which of these two categories they will fall. While dating, the American male is expected to help his female companion on with her coat; boy scouts are expected to help old ladies across the street; fans at a college football game are expected to cheer for their team; stamps are supposed to be placed on the upper right-hand corner of an envelope; and the average citizen is expected to use "proper" grammar when he communicates with others. All of these behavior patterns would be classified as folkways.

Americans are also expected to have certain parts of their bodies covered when they appear

Do Leaders Conform?

Something of a paradox exists in the prevailing treatments of conformity and status. Students of social psychology are likely to be left with the pat impression that the freely chosen leader conforms to, and perhaps, tenaciously upholds, the norms of his group. Yet this kind of leadership is also presented as a status sufficient to provide latitude for directing and altering group norms. . . . From . . . recent experimental work in this area, Dittes and Kelley have voiced a doubt that the relationship between conformity and status is ever a simple one. The evidence favors their assertion.

—E. P. Hollander.*

in public, be loyal to their country, stand when the "Star Spangled Banner" is played, avoid eating human flesh, and not take the life of other humans. Exception may, of course, be made as in the case of nudists, state executioners, and soldiers. However, under most circumstances behaving in the manner just described is felt to have the approval of society and God, and to be behavior which *has to be* performed if the society is to be maintained and not "degenerate." These are statements of "must" behavior. These are mores. (The singular of mores is "mos.") Conforming to the mores of the society is usually so extensive and so widely endorsed that such behavior is usually taken for granted. It may be felt to be in harmony with the very nature of man or even to be instinctive. Members of the group are expected to accept the mores without question. Any questioning that does exist is interpreted as evidence of degeneration or evilness.

An intensity continuum contains differing shades or degrees of intensity. All behavior patterns are not either folkways or mores; these two terms serve only to identify the two contrasting poles of the continuum. Such terms are broad and too inclusive for very meaningful research.

* E. P. Hollander, "Conformity, Status, and Idiosyncrasy Credit," *Psychological Review*, LXV (January, 1958), 117.

However, they do serve to help us identify differences in norm definitions, and these concepts will, no doubt, be further refined as sociological research and theorizing continue. Use of but two terms, such as folkways and mores, is dichotomizing, and the over-simplification that results from such dichotomizing was discussed in the previous chapter on methodology. Merton [2] makes a three-fold distinction when he talks of prescribed, preferred, and permitted behavior.

Further, not all behavior of any group is covered by the norms. Whether or not, for instance, the American male should put on his shirt before he puts on his trousers, or whether he should first put his left or right arm into his coat has not been specified in any norm definitions. Decisions with reference to such behavior are felt to be a matter of individual prerogative. Society can be said to be permissive about such behavior. Individuals may, of course, standardize their own behavior in these areas.

Since the plans of action which we have called mores and folkways are developed by man in his social interaction, it follows that any of them can be changed. The mores, however, are particularly resistant to change. Behavior that today may be a folkway may, over a period of years for one reason or another, evolve into one of the mores. A reverse transition may also occur.

Number of Norms

We do not have any reliable counts of the number of laws, but all observers seem to agree that the number of legally regulated activities is increasing in our society, which is one sign that our social order is growing and becoming more complex.

—Murray Gendell and
Hans L. Zetterberg.*

---

* Quoted in Murray Gendell and Hans L. Zetterberg, *A Sociological Almanac for the United States* (2nd ed.; New York: Charles Scribner's Sons, 1964), p. 7.

[2] Robert K. Merton, *Social Theory and Social Structure* (rev. and enlarged; New York: The Free Press of Glencoe, Inc., 1957), p. 133.

Thus, not many years ago it was against the mores for the American female to smoke in public, whereas today such behavior is given social approval. Norms are always relative to time and situation; they do not exist in isolation.

FOLKWAYS, MORES, AND LAWS—FORMAL AND INFORMAL DEFINITIONS

Norm definitions also vary according to the degree of formality associated with them. Expected patterns of behavior are frequently formalized and written down. Methods of gaining adherence to these definitions may also be formalized and written down, with specialized functionaries designated and empowered to utilize these approved sanctions. Definitions of this type are called laws.

In the American society, for instance, city councils and state and national legislators, to mention but three of the many such groups, may, in a formal deliberative manner, decide what certain definitions (laws) will be, and may establish law-enforcement bodies to enforce them.

A moment's reflection will make the reader aware that not all of the behavior patterns he is expected to adopt are established by his "duly-elected representatives." No legislative body, for instance, has passed a law specifying that it is the gentleman's responsibility and privilege to help his lady with her coat, and in America, until the early Mormons brought the issue to a head, no national laws had been passed prohibiting a man from having more than one wife. Both of these definitions, however, were a part of the American culture.

Each society may have informal, as well as formal norm definitions. In small, relatively primitive homogeneous groups, formal law-enacting groups may never even be established. The norm definitions, rather, are the product of the interaction of the members of the group. This is not to imply that the definitions may be any less binding. They are, in fact, likely to be more binding under these circumstances than under any other.

Informal norm definitions, which are sometimes called "crescive" norms, are developed in an informal manner. As people interact with each other, consistent patterns tend to develop. Generally, once a thing has been done in a particular manner, it is easier to do it that way again than to establish some new pattern. For example, if members of our group press their noses together in greeting, we come to expect that the next time we greet such members they will do the same thing. Likewise, if food has been gathered in a particular way, it is easy to follow the same pattern the next time food is sought. If a particular instructor behaves in a particular manner during the first class period, students may enter the class next time expecting him again to behave in this way. Standardized ways of behaving develop when we come to feel that others expect us to behave in a particular manner.

Once a pattern is well established, it is easy to take the next step and give these patterns moral overtones and define them as sacred. Any efforts to digress from them may be viewed as wrong, evil, or of the devil.

Small homogeneous societies that have endured over a period of time have usually developed their norm definitions in this informal manner. There is, in fact, in such a society, no need for a formal law-enacting body, since everybody except the young already know the important definitions that are applicable in the great majority of situations. In such a society change occurs slowly, and thus changes in the norm definitions can be initiated slowly and without much disruption. Such a society has come to be called a "sacred society," which label implies that the whole way of life, including the norm definitions, is defined as sacred and, therefore, there is little likelihood of extensive change. Man is generally reluctant to change anything he defines as sacred, be it one particular definition or his entire way of life.

By way of contrast, in the contemporary United States, which is called a "secular society," the society is so complex and heterogeneous, with so many divergent subgroups each with some unique definitions of its own, that some sort of formal law making and law enforcing is required if the entire group is to be welded together and function as an entity. The complexity of the configuration of norm definitions of a society is related to the *number* of subgroups. Formal laws may be developed at various levels, such as the national, state, county, and city. Various other groups of a familial, religious, recreational, or economic nature, to mention but a few, are also involved. The United States consists of a configuration of interrelated subgroups with considerable overlapping of membership.

In such a society, change is so prevalent that the group cannot wait for informal processes to establish effective norm definitions and enforce them. Formal agencies are established to meet these conditions. In such a society, formal laws take on increased importance, although the informal norm definitions are not by any means abolished. A democratic society, such as the United States, accepts the major premise that the laws of the group can and will be changed as the members of the group in rational discussion decide to do so.

Where both types of definitions exist, this raises the question as to the relationship which each has to the other. Let us now turn our attention to this relationship.

RELATIONSHIPS OF FOLKWAYS, MORES, AND LAWS

Many types of relationships are possible between the formal and informal norm definitions. For instance, some mores and some laws may be mutually supportive. The laws under these circumstances will be defined as good, moral, possibly "God-given," worthy of the support of the members of the group. To violate such laws would, accordingly, be defined as immoral as well as illegal. Law-enforcement officers do not experience much difficulty enforcing such laws, since most people want to conform to these standards and may exert considerable informal efforts themselves to assure such conformity on the part of others.

Laws and mores, however, may also be mutually contradictory. A group may feel that

Enforcing the Norm Definitions

*In 1961 American cities had 1.9 police depart-
ment employees per 1000 population and no
less than 3.85 million arrests. To maintain the
external defense of its social order, the U.S.
in 1961 maintained 2.5 million men in its military establishments about a third of whom
were based abroad.*

—Murray Gendell and
Hans L. Zetterberg.*

the "local customs" (mores) are more important
and moral than the formal laws of the larger
society. Laws that contradict the mores are defined as immoral, as against the conscience of
man (or at least "my" portion of man) and,
therefore, not worthy of obedience. It is under
these conditions that people are apt to make
statements to the effect that you "can't legislate
moral standards or attitudes." When the United
States Supreme Court handed down the verdict
that school integration in the United States must
be accomplished, the negative reaction of many
of the "segregationists" to such an interpretation
of the laws illustrates the conflict just described,
and the subsequent efforts of such individuals
and groups to avoid complying with the law
illustrates the strength of the mores of such
groups.

Indeed, it has been suggested that when the
mores are adequate, laws are unnecessary, and
when the mores are inadequate, laws are useless.

Various relationships are also found between
folkways and laws. Where they are mutually
supportive no social problems arise; however,
where contradictions occur, those involved may
attempt to harmonize the two. Under such circumstances, since the folkways fall well down on
the intensity continuum, the likelihood of changing them is much greater than it is for changing
the mores, which are particularly resistant to
change.

* Quoted in Murray Gendell and Hans L. Zetterberg,
A Sociological Almanac for the United States (2nd ed.;
New York: Charles Scribner's Sons, 1964), p. 8.

In an urbanized, industrialized society such as
the United States, in which hundreds of different
laws are passed by the national legislature alone
every year, it is likely that many of them are defined as being relatively devoid of any direct
connection with the informal norm definitions.
It is even possible to find mutually contradictory
laws.

There is an additional type of norm definition
to which brief attention should be given in order
to round out the typology we are using—the so-
called "common laws." This label refers to norm
definitions which have developed in an informal
manner but which have become so well established and intermeshed with formal laws that
formal sanctions may be utilized to enforce them.
The fact that formal sanctions may be used in
enforcement efforts, means, however, that the
common laws will be specifically stated in records such as court decisions and thus these norm
definitions do take on at least a semi-formal
status.

JUSTIFICATION OF NORM DEFINITIONS

In a secular society where laws are enacted
through a deliberative process of some kind, it is
generally easy to find an answer to the question
why these formal norm definitions are adopted,
since such questions are involved in the very
process of law enactment. Whether or not the
public justification for such laws and the private
justification of the lawmakers coincide is, however, frequently an open question. Certainly any
specific law may have any number of different
justifications.

In a sacred society justification for the norm
definitions is generally well established and well
known. However, it is important to recognize
that in many cases the justification may have
developed only after the norms were well established, and it is likely that the justification for
any particular definition may change as other
conditions change. The reason we give today
for shaking hands in greeting may not be the one
used to justify the practice when it was first
established. Many feel that the simple justification, "This is the way we have always done it," is

not adequate, and they therefore develop elaborate and involved explanations that justify the established practices.

Since human behavior is symbolic behavior, man is able to develop symbol systems (subjective reality). Although they may be sincerely accepted, they need not necessarily correspond with objective reality. Beyond this it is important to recognize that the justification for any act does not lie in any empirical aspect of the act *per se.* Justification is not an empirical quality of anything; it is rather a way man has of evaluating, defining, or interpreting behavior. The development of various different justifications for the same behavior, as well as subsequent changes in established justifications, is facilitated by this non-empirical characteristic.

Value judgments are frequently involved in the justifications of the norm definitions, and since these involve NER symbols, it is not surprising that great variability is found in such explanations. Our previous discussion of the mores indicated that strength is added to the norm definitions when members of the group accept the belief that these definitions have supernatural endorsement. Such believers easily accept the belief that "since this is the way God wants us to behave, this is the way I want to behave." Religion, then, is also frequently involved in the justifications that man provides for his norm definitions.

POSITIVE AND NEGATIVE NORM DEFINITIONS

Norms may vary in the manner in which they are generally stated in that they may prescribe that a particular thing be done in a specific way. These we will call "positive norm definitions." Or they may specify that particular things should *not* be done at all or maybe should not be done in specific ways. These we will call "negative norm definitions" or taboos. Of the Ten Commandments those which specify that "thou shalt not . . ." fall in the latter category, while the commandment for children to honor their parents is an example of a positive norm definition. Many

positive or negative norm definitions could be restated in a reverse manner, thus reversing the appropriate label.

SPECIFICITY

Norm definitions may also vary in their degree of specificity. Some may specify in great detail exactly what is to be done, whereas the expectations involved in other definitions may be understood only in very broad terms. Norm definitions, then, can also be ranked along a specificity continuum. The norm definitions for the typical college graduation ceremony fall near the high specificity end, whereas those involved in an informal group discussion among students in the spring sunshine on the campus lawn fall near the other pole. Army regulations, at the high pole, are usually very specific as to just how army personnel of various ranks or positions are expected to relate themselves to each other.

NORM DEFINITIONS AND SOCIAL ORDER

A major source of the order that is found in human interaction is the body of norm definitions that are developed by the group. Since man does not have biologically built-in motors or drives that force him to relate himself to others in an orderly manner, it follows that the order must be social in origin. Existing social orderliness stems in part from the fact that the group members have a common culture including common expectations or plans of action. Let us consider, for example, a family in which the behavior is usually orderly. The members, in the course of interacting with each other over a period of time, develop a set of norm definitions or expectations so that each knows, within limits, of course, what the other will most likely do under certain circumstances. Each member usually sleeps in the same bed each night and usually even on the same side of the bed. Each member has his "place" at the dinner table. Mother knows which of her family members is likely to enjoy eating certain types of foods, and the family members know what mother is likely to prepare for specific meals. Each learns what he can expect of the other and patterns his own behavior accordingly.

More than this, each member has some ideas as to just what the other members expect him to do under certain circumstances. An important factor influencing family interaction is the set of expectations which each has about himself and the others involved. Continued interaction confirms these expectations or perhaps produces some modifications. Certainly an individual who cannot adequately anticipate the behavior of others is likely to have some difficulties in his interaction, and efforts may be taken by the group to correct these "deficiencies." In any event, these expectations are one of the sources of the orderliness found in family interaction, and the same is true of larger groups.

Norm definitions that provide guidelines for behavior reduce the number of individual decisions that must be made in interaction. Without them, as MacIver and Page [3] have indicated, "the burden of decision would be intolerable and the vagaries of conduct utterly distracting."

In specifying expected behavior, the norm definitions indirectly also indicate what is taboo or inappropriate. The individual then knows what requests others may *not* properly make of him. Norm definitions provide protection from certain types of power relationships and provide a means of escape from certain types of more personal involvement. Individuals who are

[3] R. M. MacIver and C. H. Page, *Society: An Introductory Analysis* (New York: Holt, Rinehart and Winston, Inc., 1949), p. 207.

Figure 8.1 Taboos or negative norm definitions specify what should not be done. (Wide World Photos.)

Norm Definitions and Behavior

A Canadian student reports: "At Teachers College we were told: ...

... Return exams quickly for maximum learning—none were returned in less than five weeks and some were not returned at all.

... Allow free expression of opinion and ideas—I was called a 'stupid idiot' when I asked one master a question. ...

... A student should compete with himself not with others—we were in competition with the whole student body. ...

... 'never teach in a negative manner' ...."
                                        —Glenn M. Vernon.*

treated with strict politeness or rigid adherence to the norm definitions are discouraged thereby from attempting to place a given relationship on a more personal basis.[4]

The orderliness or the systematic aspect of interaction, however, is never complete. There are limits to the accuracy of our expectations as well as to our behavior. All interaction has an emergent aspect in that those involved are constantly engaged in interpreting their own behavior as well as that of others in a particular situation and deciding on the basis of these definitions what their subsequent action will be. The emergent aspect is always there, but the point being made here is that this emergent aspect grows out of the common expectations of the members, and these common expectations set limits and serve to channel the emerging behavior in particular ways.

The extent of the orderliness of behavior is also limited by the fact that man is capable of developing inconsistent definitions. The multitude of definitions he develops usually contain many inconsistencies, particularly in a secular society. Norm definitions are also relative to the situation and definitions felt to be appropriate in one situation may not apply in another. Further, definitions developed at one period of time may not harmonize with those developed later.[5]

The principle of socio-cultural compatibility applies here, however, and the various norm definitions do evidence a "strain toward consistency." Groups are constantly in the process of working out inconsistencies in their interaction patterns. Indeed, without a minimum of consistency, you would have no social order—only chaos. The cohesiveness or solidarity of any society is related to the number of norm definitions that have society-wide acceptance.[6]

A situation for which norm definitions have not been developed for the major types of interaction, and in which those involved have no or only few definitions to guide their behavior, as in times of crisis, has been called a condition of *anomie* or "normlessness."[7]

To further complicate the picture individuals and groups frequently develop systematic ways and means of evading some of the norm definitions; they develop "norms of evasion." The average motorist enjoys the story of the motorcycle patrolman who had stationed himself behind a sign board so that he could spot speeders while being undetected himself. After a period of time during which all the cars seemed to be going at the proper speed, he headed back down the road and found that some enterprising friend of motorists had posted a crude sign along the side of the road reading "cop hiding behind billboard ahead." Many are willing to help others avoid getting caught for violation of some traffic laws.

* Glenn M. Vernon, "Our Schizoid College Culture," in *Introductory Sociology*, ed. by John R. Christiansen (Dubuque, Iowa: Wm. C. Brown Book Co., 1963), p. 360.

[4] For a discussion of these points, see John W. Thibaut and Harold H. Kelley, "On Norms," in E. P. Hollander and Raymond G. Hunt, *Current Perspectives in Social Psychology* (Fair Lawn, N. J.: Oxford University Press, 1963), pp. 447–454.

[5] See Dick Hyman, *It's Still the Law* (New York: David McKay Co., Inc., 1961).

[6] See E. Adamson Hoebel, *Man in the Primitive World* (New York: McGraw-Hill Book Co., 1958), p. 168.

[7] For a discussion of anomie, see Merton, *op. cit.*, pp. 131–194.

The expectations of the university culture generally include regular student attendance at classes. Some students, however, may spend considerable time and effort devising ways of getting out of class. While teaching an off-campus class in a nearby high school, the author recalls seeing a sign posted in front of the school building reading "No parking between 8 A.M. and 5 P.M." The students in the class, however, knew that after school was out at about 3:30 they would not receive a ticket for parking there. Consequently the curb in front of the school building was frequently full long before five o'clock, with the cars, on one occasion, including even a police car. Groups may, then, develop systematic ways of evading some of their norm definitions and may provide justification which appears logical to them, both for the norm definition and for the evasion. Such behavior is possible for symbol users.

ENFORCEMENT OF NORM DEFINITIONS— SANCTIONS

Once norm definitions have been established for a group, there is the question as to how group members are induced to conform. This is basically the problem of social control. Since man has no biologically given "conformity drive" the inducement must be social in nature. Actually, there are many social factors involved in the process of getting group members to abide by the rules (culture) of the group. One of the most frequently used techniques is the development of sanctions or norms of sanction that specify what individuals can expect to happen if they disregard the established norm definitions. With reference to the formal laws of the group, we have already indicated that specific agencies are usually established with varying law-enforcement powers.

No such formal provisions are made for enforcing the informal norm definitions, the folkways and mores, unless they coincide with the laws. Informal means are usually developed, however, and may in fact precede the formal sanctions. These may include, among other things, simply talking to offenders in an effort to

---

Examples of Patterned Evasion of Norm Definitions

Prior to the repeal of the 18th amendment, bootlegging and speakeasy industry despite prohibition.

Political graft, "fixing" and "status justice" despite belief in impersonal, disinterested governmental services.

Prostitution despite family mores to the contrary.

"Cribbing" despite belief in classroom honesty.

"Void" divorces and the "alimony racket" despite legal rules regarding divorce.

Fee-splitting among doctors, ambulance chasing among lawyers, despite professional codes of ethic to the contrary.

Some business advertising and financial transactions ("business is business") despite ethical concepts of truth.

—Robin M. Williams, Jr.*

---

encourage conformity, giving them the "silent treatment," depriving them of privileges, expelling them from the group, etc.

In simple terms, imposing sanctions involves giving those concerned certain rewards (positive sanctions) or certain punishments (negative sanctions). What is defined as a reward or punishment may, of course, vary from group to group.

Religion may be involved in the sanctions used, and for those who accept the religious definitions the religious sanctions may be a very effective means of control. Religious definitions specify that the individual may, in addition to being subjected to society's sanctions, also be subjected to supernatural rewards and punishments. If one sincerely believes, for instance, that God will either reward or punish him for engaging in certain types of behavior, such a belief can be a

* Adapted from Robin M. Williams, Jr., *American Society* (New York: Alfred A. Knopf, 1956), p. 357.

potent source of control. Religious definitions, including value definitions, also provide moral justification for the utilization of sanctions, specifying that it is good or moral to do such and such —even to take the life of the offender under certain circumstances.

There are many subtle factors involved in gaining conformity to the norm definitions. Teaching of the definitions may be done in such a way that those learning them are led to believe that they are the only way to accomplish a particular goal. The young child may not have learned that there are "many ways to skin a cat." There is also the process of habituation. A particular way may be the way we "have always done it," and therefore no one seriously questions it. Most people are also taught to desire order and predictability and therefore find that following orderly patterns makes them feel more comfortable with a resultant lack of desire to change established patterns. To the extent that individuals want to do what the norm definitions specify, orderly interaction can be obtained without the use of formal means of control. Simmel [8] indicated this in 1902:

> In the morality of the individual, society creates for itself an organ which is not only more fundamentally operative than law custom, but which also spares society the different sorts of costs involved in these institutions. Hence the tendency of society to satisfy its demands as cheaply as possible results in appeals to "good conscience," through which the individual pays to himself the wages for his righteousness, which otherwise would probably have to be assured to him in some way through law or custom.

One of the most potent rewards that a group can give the individual is the reward of high self-esteem or high positive self-definitions. If the group can get its members to believe that following specific patterns will make them "good," "superior," or "moral" and show by the manner in which it treats the individual that such definitions are, in fact, accepted by the group or at

---

Sanctions

It is a significant fact that in all human societies the negative sanctions are more definite than the positive.

—A. R. Radcliffe-Brown.[*]

---

least the significant others involved, it has gone a long way toward gaining the conformity. Conversely, to get members of the group to believe sincerely that following a particular pattern of behavior will result in a devaluation of the individual is a potent method of getting them to avoid disapproved behavior.

Many have pointed out the relative ineffectiveness of punishment as a method of gaining conformity as compared with positive rewards such as enhancement of self-definitions.[9] Continued conformity is more likely if an individual conforms because he wants to (tells himself that he should) than if he conforms because he is afraid to do otherwise. Once the potential threat is removed, behavior is likely to take some other path.

Since no society has as yet been able to develop a configuration of norm definitions that evidence complete internal consistency, it should be recognized that following a particular norm definition may, paradoxically, bring forth both reward and punishment. A devout religious student who meets the expectations of his social group on campus by hunting on Sunday may violate the expectations of his parents who are strongly opposed to such behavior on religious grounds. Reward by one group may be counterbalanced by punishment from another. Resolving such conflicts is one of the perplexities of human interaction.

The "norms" do not *force* people to conform. Norm definitions are merely expectations people have as to what is appropriate behavior in a given situation. Any forced conformity results from the actions of people, not from the "action"

---

[8] G. Simmel, "The Number of Members as Determining the Sociological Form of the Group," *The American Journal of Sociology*, VIII, No. 1 (1902–1903), 19n.

[*] A. R. Radcliffe-Brown, "Social Sanctions," in *Encyclopaedia of the Social Sciences* (New York: The Macmillan Co., 1934), XIII, 531.

[9] See, for instance, Homans, *op. cit.*, p. 26.

of norm definitions. People may force other people to conform; norm definitions cannot. Such definitions, however, are one of the factors involved in the orderly behavior of man.

This discussion of orderliness is not an endorsement: we have not been saying that orderliness is a desirable thing. This is a value judgment and consequently falls outside our realm of scientific competency. If one desires orderliness, however, the development of effective norms is a potent aid.

SUMMARY

The culture of every group includes, along with the value definitions previously discussed, configurations of positive and negative norm definitions, the major types of which are folkways, mores, and laws, which indicate with varying degrees of specificity the plans of action felt to be appropriate for particular situations. The mores, which specify the "must" behavior, are religiously reinforced and more rigidly enforced than folkways. The intensity with which a group feels specific definitions should be enforced, however, frequently changes with time. Laws, which contrast with mores and folkways in that they are formally enacted and enforced, evidence varying degrees of harmony with the mores and folkways, and when dissonance exists the mores are usually given precedence.

Conformity to norm definitions is encouraged by providing value definitions to justify them and by use of negative and positive sanctions.

Harmonious interaction stems, in part, from consistently related norm definitions. The orderliness of any group, however, is never complete, since some definitions are consistently evaded.

QUESTIONS

1. Distinguish between norm definitions and norm enacting.
2. How are norm definitions related to value definitions?
3. How are the concepts "norm definitions" and "free will" related?
4. Provide a sociological explanation for the fact that a group may formally enact some laws (norm definitions) which they fully intend to ignore.
5. Discuss the statement "The mores can make anything right."
6. How is religion usually related to the mores?
7. Why are laws that do not harmonize with the mores of a group so difficult to enforce?
8. Provide illustrations of behavior patterns that have (1) changed from folkways into mores and (2) changed from mores into folkways.
9. List several types of behavior for which your society has provided or developed no norms.
10. Most likely by the time the class reaches this section of the text the seating patterns in the class have become somewhat standardized. Briefly describe what has actually happened and indicate what sociological principle this class behavior illustrates.

PROJECT

Observe class interaction for a period and identify the different types of sanctions which (1) the teacher uses in interaction with the class and (2) the class uses in interaction with the teacher.

SUGGESTED READING

BLAU, PETER M. "Structural Effects," *American Sociological Review*, XXV, No. 2 (April, 1960), 178–193.

COOLEY, CHARLES H. *Human Nature and the Social Order*. New York: Charles Scribner's Sons, 1902.

DUBIN, ROBERT. "Deviant Behavior and Social Structure: Continuities in Social Theory," *American Sociological Review*, XXIV, No. 2 (April, 1959), 147–164.

DYNES, RUSSELL R., ALFRED C. CLARKE, SIMON DINITZ, and IWAO ISHINO. *Social Problems*. Fair Lawn, N.J.: Oxford University Press, 1964. Sec. II, pp. 51–396.

HOMANS, GEORGE CASPAR. *Social Behavior: Its Elementary Forms*. New York: Harcourt, Brace & World, Inc., 1961.

MACCOBY, ELEANOR E., JOSEPH P. JOHNSON, and RUSSEL M. CHURCH. "Community Integration and the Social Control of Juvenile Delinquency," *Journal of Social Issues*, XIV, No. 3 (1958), 38–51.

PARSONS, TALCOTT. *The Structure of Social Action*. New York: McGraw-Hill Book Co., 1937.

SHERIF, MUZAFER. *The Psychology of Social Norms*. New York: Harper & Row, Inc., 1936.

SUMNER, WILLIAM GRAHAM. *Folkways*. Boston: Ginn & Co., 1906.

WILLIAMS, ROBIN M., JR. *American Society*. Rev. ed. New York: Alfred A. Knopf, Inc., 1960. Chaps. iii and x.

9

Role Definitions

When he is single an individual behaves differently from when he is married; after being sworn in as President of the United States an individual has many responsibilities and privileges he did not have as President-Elect. Why? What changed— the individual or the label placed upon him?

Previous chapters have discussed value and norm definitions. This chapter adds role definitions as one of the important types of definitions involved in human behavior.

The label "role" is obviously a stage term; there is, in fact, a close parallel between the theatrical and the sociological use of the term. In commenting on the parallel, Goffman indicates:

The stage presents things that are make believe; presumably life presents things that are real and sometimes not well rehearsed. More important, perhaps, on the stage one player presents himself in the guise of a character to characters projected by other players; the audience constitutes a third party to the interaction—one that is essential and yet, if the stage performance were real, one that would not be there. In real life, the three parties are compressed into two; the part one individual plays is tailored to the parts played by others present, and yet these others also constitute the audience.[1]

[1] Erving Goffman, *The Presentation of Self in Everyday Life* (Garden City, N. Y.: Doubleday & Co., Inc. (an Anchor Book, 1959), p. xi.

If the "play of life" is visualized as taking place on the worldly stage, then each of us plays a unique role or configuration of roles in the ongoing drama. Carrying the analogy one step farther, throughout the college "scene" of this on-going drama, each individual who is one way or another related to the college plays a unique role. Throughout the day the freshman may play, among others, the role of a roommate, a sociology student, an English student, a study companion, a customer at the campus bookstore, a tennis player, a dating partner during the evening, and possibly a confidant or counselor (informal) to a close friend who has just received bad news from home. This chapter is concerned with an analysis of the role definitions or the "script" which is followed in each of these roles. A moment's analysis will reveal that the script changes as the student moves from one role to another, calling for different behavior, different dress, different vocabulary, and different emotional involvement. One behaves and is expected to behave differently while a sociology student than while a dating partner.

Three important dimensions of any interaction pattern are involved in an understanding of role definitions. From the viewpoint of the participants in the interaction, these can be stated in question form as follows:

1. What am I doing here?

2. What are the others doing here?

3. What are the characteristics of the situation in which our interaction is taking place?

Answers to these questions are found, in part, in terms of social roles. Let us turn our attention, then, to an analysis of role definitions—the first part of the "role triad" of role definitions, role playing, and role taking.

This discussion is in effect a continuation of the previous chapter on norm definitions, since role definitions are a particular type of norm definition. Norm definitions are defined as plans of action or expected behavior patterns felt to be appropriate for a particular situation. Role definitions are likewise plans of action or expected behavior patterns, specifying what should be done and how it should be accomplished. The distinctive characteristic of role definitions, as contrasted with norm definitions, however, is that these plans of action are associated with a particular position or office. Some sociological writers use the term "status" as synonymous with position or office. We will not use "status" in this respect because to do so would introduce confusion later when the term is used to refer to prestige or ranking.[2] Norm definitions, as contrasted with role, need not be tied up with a specific position or office. They are more general in nature, being applicable in any or many situations. For instance, the American norm definition that one should wear clothes in public applies to most roles. The concept "norm definition," then, is more general than "role definition."

Role definitions, like norm definitions, include an intensity or value dimension in the sense that they specify which of the many plans of action

incorporated in a particular role are mandatory, which are desirable, and which are optional. The various behavior patterns incorporated in a particular role definition are distributed along a value continuum so that some are "must" behavior, some are "desirable," and some are "maybe-if-you-care-to."

Other terms that could be used to identify the same thing we are calling role definitions include role expectations, role prescriptions, role meaning, and role blueprint or script.

Examples of positions for which role definitions have been developed are bank president, bank robber, janitor, lawyer, wife, student, mayor, and "hood." The role definition is the plan of action, specifying what is done. It is, in effect, a "job description." Thus, a janitor, among other things, sweeps the floor, keeps the building clean, and takes care of the furnace. Here, of course, we are talking about "a" janitor, or janitors in general, not about any particular individual such as Janitor Jones. Role definitions for specific positions are usually much more specific than for any position in general.

If one wants to do scientific research on role definitions, to what empirical phenomena does he pay attention? Such research basically involves paying attention to verbal or written statements. We may ask members of the group directly what the expectations are for a particular position. Some groups, of course, maintain written records of these role definitions in the form of job description, tables of organization, by-laws, and constitutions. Such formal statements may also be supplemented by a set of informal definitions developed in the process of the on-going interaction of the group. In studying role definitions we must, one way or another, ask those involved *what the definitions are*.

Different roles, of course, may vary in many respects, and a subsequent section will identify some of these major dimensions. Here we are primarily concerned with a discussion of the overall definition.

When an individual actually engages in or enacts the plans of action or script associated with any particular position, we will call his behavior "role playing." A subsequent chapter will

---

[2] See, for instance, Frederick L. Bates, "Position, Role and Status: Reformulation of Concepts," *Social Forces,* XXXIV, No. 4 (May, 1956), 313–321.

Figure 9.1 Patterned behavior and objects result from accepted norm definitions, as when they specify the use of a particular type of transportation as they do at Oberlin College. (Wide World Photos.)

discuss role playing in detail, as one of the basic interaction processes. We merely identify the term here because we will use it occasionally in our discussion of role definitions. Let us return, then, to further discussion of role definitions.

An important characteristic of the plans of action that we call role definitions is that they are definitely associated with the position or office, not with any individual who may, at the moment, be playing the role. The role of mayor of Home-

town, for instance, applies equally well to Mayor Jones who played the role last year, and to Mayor Miller, who is playing the role this year, as well as to subsequent mayors as yet unelected. While playing the role, particular individuals conform more or less to the prescribed plans of action, but the plans of action *per se* go with the office, not with the individual. How one individual plays his role may result in some revamping of the role definition, with the changes incorporated into the over-all configuration. They thereby become the expected behavior of anyone who subsequently plays the role. Role definitions, like norm definitions and other parts of culture, are constantly changing. Nonetheless, the role definition goes with the position, not with the role player.

ASCRIBED AND ACHIEVED POSITIONS

The role definitions or the plans of action associated with any particular position usually or frequently specify the process by which an individual becomes qualified to play a particular role. For some positions, the necessary qualifications are acquired through birth and are, therefore, conditions over which the individual has little, if any, influence, and which he is relatively powerless to change. The position of male and female falls in this category. In societies where royal families have been established, the child born to royal parents inherits a position of royalty by virtue of his birth, rather than any accomplishment on his part. Such positions are identified as *ascribed* positions. *Achieved* positions have the reverse characteristic that by meeting certain established criteria, an individual may achieve or acquire the position. The college student who prepares himself to be a high school teacher by taking the prescribed course at college, becoming certified, and then getting hired for a teaching position has achieved this position. The term applies regardless of the value attached to the position. The position of bank president and that of bank robber are both achieved or acquired positions.

Roles in Society

All the world is a stage,
And all the men and women, merely players,
They have their exits and their entrances;
And one man in his time plays many parts.
—William Shakespeare.*

---

* William Shakespeare, *As You Like It,* Act II.

In a small, stable, relatively primitive society many important aspects of life are decided by birth. The social structure of such a society contains many ascribed positions. By way of contrast, the social structure of large, urbanized, industrialized societies such as the United States or Canada contains many achieved positions.

FORMAL AND INFORMAL ROLE DEFINITIONS

Some norm definitions are formally enacted, whereas others develop informally in the process of interaction. A similar distinction can be made for role definitions. The student who gets a part-time job at a local industrial plant finds that the company leaders have already worked out in some detail exactly how he should dress, what he should do and possibly the sequence of his acts, when he should work or have his coffee break. Similarly, the student who becomes a fraternity president on campus finds that a script has been prepared for him to follow. Interaction takes place within these organizations more or less in harmony with these prepared definitions.

There is, of course, much more involved in the on-going interaction. Informal scripts are developed and it does not take the neophyte long to discover what the informal requirements are. He learns that sanctions of one type or another will be invoked against him if he fails to take them into account. Effective role playing involves harmonizing the two sets of requirements into a working plan of action. Employers who fail to recognize that the informal role definitions play an important part in the behavior of employees and consequently in the over-all functioning of the organization are blind to one of the social realities.

TYPES OF BEHAVIOR COVERED BY PLANS OF ACTION

The various behavior patterns incorporated in a particular role definition may be of several types. Each role definition has its unique configuration. Particular role definitions may, of course, emphasize only certain types. Some of the most frequently included types are these:

1. *Type of dress.* A secretary is expected to wear "office clothes," not formal dress or a swimming suit.

2. *Type of speech.* A Sunday School teacher is generally expected not to swear.

3. *Type of posture.* An Air Force cadet is expected to stand erect and maintain a "military bearing."

4. *Type of motivation.* A minister is expected to engage in a "labor of love." He is supposed to tell himself that this is the reason, or at least a major reason, for being what he is and doing what he does. University students are expected to strive to gain knowledge. They are expected to tell themselves that this is a major goal of their college activities. This, of course, is a type of valuing behavior—placing value definitions upon certain things or behavior patterns.

5. *Types of rights, duties, and privileges.* Only the company treasurer and a few other top-level officials have the right to open the company safe and remove money. Likewise, on an informal basis, only those who hold the rank of junior executive or above can properly call the president by his first name or his initials.

6. *Type of preliminary behavior or required characteristics.* Role definitions may specify certain types of preliminary behavior or required qualifications which are defined as necessary requisites to playing the role. A candidate for the presidency of the United States, for instance, is expected to be of a certain age and to be a citizen of the United States. Preliminary requirements may also include going through certain *rites of passage,* or rites of transition, which, when completed, serve to indicate that those involved are now qualified to engage in the appropriate role behavior.

Examples of rites of passage in the American society would be the wedding ceremony, which indicates to all concerned that the bride and groom are no longer single (that "single" is the wrong label to apply to them) but that they are now "man and wife." The inauguration ceremony of the President of the United States, the graduation ceremony at the college and the swearing-in ceremony of the armed services are other examples of formal rites of passage. The giving and accepting of a fraternity pin by a college couple is an example of an informal rite of transition. Such requirements are associated with achieved positions.

7. *Use of specific position (status) symbols.* The plans of action may specify certain position or status symbols, the use of which identifies the user with the position. An army officer, for example, wears his rank insignia to identify his position. Such symbols may be formally selected and decided upon by the group, or they may develop in the informal interaction of the group. Anything can be used as a position symbol, including types of clothing, a handshake, verbal behavior of one type or another such as a "password," and facial expressions. Whatever the symbol and whatever its origin, if it serves its purpose it gets incorporated into the plans of action that are connected with the specific position.

ROLES AND COUNTER-ROLES

Our previous discussions have emphasized that human behavior is a social phenomenon, since human beings are constantly interacting with one another. The role definitions involved in this interaction have to involve more than one individual. A major aspect of this involvement is the fact that role definitions specify how one individual is expected to relate himself to another, or how one office or position is related to another. Role definitions do not exist in isolation. Human behavior does not occur in isolation. Certain

Role Definitions in Music

Virgil Thomson once likened a musical score to a "design for execution" adding: "A musician's rendering of a composition is as individual an achievement as what a builder erects from an architect's plan or design." He concludes: "Music, like architecture, envisages from the beginning collaboration."

—Joseph Szigeti.*

role definitions, then, can be viewed as fitting together to form a larger whole or entity, of which any specific role definition is but one part and the complete meaning of which is understood only as it is related to other parts. Thus, we can, in simple terms, talk of roles and counter-roles, with each being reciprocal to the other.

An example of a configuration of counter-roles would be the roles of husband and wife. So many of the plans of action of a husband directly or indirectly involve the behavior of the wife that it is impossible to understand what a husband is and does without also understanding what a wife is and does. In fact, it is impossible, as the terms are usually defined, for a man to be a husband without someone else being his wife at the same time. The term "reciprocal roles" may also be appropriate to identify the role relationships just discussed. The "alter-ego" terminology of the Freudians identifies this interrelatedness.

The interrelationships of roles are usually much more extensive than the simple husband–wife dyad. To expand this same example, we can work into the configuration the role of child, mother, father, mother-in-law, father-in-law, and grandparents, which, of course, by no means exhausts the potential interrelationships. All of these role definitions are interconnected so that the role definitions of any one involves relationships with all of the others. A business, re-

ligious, or governmental organization likewise encompasses a complex configuration or gestalt of interrelated role definitions. Merton calls such a configuration a "role set."[3] Thus, in order to understand the behavior of Husband Jones you have to know, among other things, whether he is relating his behavior to his wife or to his mother-in-law, or, to complicate things even more, whether he is relating himself to his wife and his mother-in-law at the same time and thus for this interaction sequence letting his behavior toward each be mediated by the fact that the other is also involved.[4]

This discussion of roles and counter-roles is in effect an extension of our discussion in Chapter 4 about the social nature of human behavior.

ROLE DEFINITIONS AS A PART OF CULTURE

Since all the definitions which a group has developed are incorporated into the culture of the group, it follows that role definitions are a part of culture. All that we have previously said about culture can also be said about role definitions. Role definitions (and culture) are man-made. They are social in origin. Role definitions are constantly changing, although they do evidence considerable stability. Role definitions are transmitted from one generation to another; most of the role definitions in any society were established before any of the current members were a part of it. They are a part of the cultural heritage.

There is nothing inherent in the types of role definitions incorporated in any culture that makes it mandatory that they be this way. Just because this is the manner in which one group has cut up or subdivided its social world, it does not follow that this is the only way to do it, or that it *has to be* this way. There would, in fact, seem to be almost unlimited variability possible, given the

---

* See Joseph Szigeti, "Composer, Performer, and Audience" in *Conflict and Creativity*, ed. by Seymour M. Farber and Roger H. L. Wilson (New York: McGraw-Hill Book Co., 1963), p. 304.

[3] See Robert K. Merton, "The Role-Set: Problems in Sociology Theory," *British Journal of Sociology*, VIII (June, 1957), 106–120.

[4] Neal Gross, Ward S. Mason, and Alexander W. McEachern, *Explorations in Role Analysis* (New York: John Wiley & Sons, Inc., 1958).

right antecedent conditions. Changes in established roles, however, are strongly influenced by the past experiences of the group, and since roles are but one part of a larger configuration, the variability in terms of *likely* future change is rather limited. Role definitions generally change in the direction of the "cultural drift" already established by the group. Changes in certain roles will tend to produce changes in other roles, particularly counter-roles, so that in the long run the entire configuration changes in somewhat the same direction.

This, of course, does not eliminate all conflict. We are merely suggesting here that conflicts tend to be resolved in such a way that the larger configuration is maintained as a functioning unit. A subsequent section will be devoted to a discussion of role conflicts.

Role definitions are learned, as is the behavior involved in following this script. One has to learn how bank presidents, club presidents, and P.T.A. presidents are supposed to behave. Those who have been acquainted with particular definitions all their lives may decide that they "instinctively" know about these roles. Familiarity with a foreign country (society) will indicate how much learning has to go into finding out how people functioning in certain positions are supposed to behave, to say nothing of actually behaving in the appropriate manner.

ROLE DIMENSIONS

Various dimensions of role definitions can be identified, some of which will be discussed in this section. Variation among roles may be found along any of these dimensions.

Specificity

For some role definitions the plans of action may be specified in great detail; in others only a bare outline may be provided. The ritual of the Roman Catholic Mass, which is incorporated in the role definitions of certain functionaries, for instance, involves a high degree of specificity, as does the role of programmer (board-setter-upper) at an IBM computer center.

Within the broad requirements role definitions may include several alternative plans of behavior. The role definition of husband in the United States, for instance, specifies that he should be the major breadwinner of the family but provides considerable leeway as to how the "bread should be won." The role of half-back on the college football team provides alternate methods of securing the ball and disposing of the ball, all of which are acceptable to the officials. Using unapproved alternatives in a football game or in the game of life, however, is likely to result in sanctions being leveled against the one who does so. In stage terms, some role definitions permit greater "ad-libbing" than do others.

Breadth or Extensiveness

Some roles are general and permeate the whole or much of the behavior of the individual playing the role, whereas others are segmental, influencing but a small part of the individual's life. It is doubtful whether the royal family of England, the Roman Catholic pope, or the President of the United States ever "gets far away from the fact" that they are playing a particular role. The high school boy, however, who played second base on the neighborhood baseball team one afternoon, may, a week later, forget that he even occupied such a position.

Continuity or Permanence

Some role definitions such as sex roles and those associated with other ascribed positions influence an individual for long periods of time. Most people, for instance, play the same sex role for their entire lifetime. Other roles are transitory. The role of a guest at a dinner party is of short duration. Role definitions of the first type are sometimes called traditional roles.

Value Attached to Role Definition and Accompanying Position

Human beings can attribute value to anything to which they pay attention, including roles. Different values, then, may be attributed to different roles. This is one of the dimensions involved in the stratification patterns of a group, which will be discussed to some length in a subsequent chapter. An important aspect of a configuration of roles and counter-roles is the pattern of superordination and subordination. According to the plans of action certain roles are given greater prestige than others. People in certain positions are given the duty or responsibility for issuing orders whereas others are expected to execute the orders. Status symbols indicating the developed "pecking order" are also frequently specified.

Ease or Difficulty of the Plans of Action Involved

Great variability in the ease with which the plans of action can be enacted exists between roles. In the 1960's, for instance, the role of astronaut involved greater difficulties than the role of production line worker in a Detroit automobile factory.

Integration of Specific Role Definitions into the Larger Configuration

Some role definitions fit with greater consistency than others into the larger socio-cultural matrix.

ROLE DEFINITIONS, SOCIAL ORDER, AND PREDICTABILITY

Our previous discussion about the interrelatedness of the various role definitions in a culture leads us to our discussion here of social order or social organization. One of the problems to which scientists have turned their attention is the question of how social order comes about. The answer to this question is tied up with role definitions. Human behavior is ordered, in part, because man arranges the symbols he uses in a systematic manner; or to move to another level, because man develops role definitions (symbols) which provide for an orderly arrangement of behavior patterns. In a broad sense, role definitions specify a division of labor for the group. The definitions for the various positions or offices within any group specify who will do what and under what conditions. Role definitions provide interlocking plans of action so that a degree of

---

Social Power

Few problems in sociology are more perplexing than the problem of social power. In the entire lexicon of sociological concepts none is more troublesome than the concept of power. We may say about it in general only what St. Augustine said about time, that we all know perfectly well what it is—until someone asks us.
—Robert Bierstedt.*

---

harmony is present for the entire group. Any society that has persisted will have developed role definitions that provide for the functional requisites of society, such as keeping the members alive and functioning, for reproduction, education, and the governing of members. Social order is a human invention. It is something man develops, not something he discovers. The development of role definitions is an integral part.

One of the first things we generally want to know about a stranger, if we expect to have any sort of extensive, meaningful interaction with him, is "what" or "who" he is. By "what" or "who" we generally mean what position or positions he holds, or what roles he plays. Or more specifically, what role he is playing right now. We generally feel somewhat uncomfortable until we are able to "pigeonhole" or "label" the stranger. Once we have been able to apply a label that appears to be correct, we have provided ourselves with plans of action so that we feel we know what we can expect of the stranger (although once we begin to apply labels, he begins to lose some of his strangeness), and what we can expect him to expect of us.

To identify the stranger with a particular position or positions for which we know the appropriate role definitions is generally the first step in introducing order into interaction. Even applying the label "stranger" to the other person carries with it a plan of action, part of which we have just indicated.

* Robert Bierstedt, "An Analysis of Social Power," *American Sociological Review*, XV, No. 6 (December, 1950), 730.

Why do we introduce speakers at our public meetings or on radio or television? The listeners need to know how to relate themselves to the speaker. Knowing this the one introducing the speaker generally selects labels that he feels will encourage the audience to respond to the speaker in the manner felt to be most appropriate for the type of engagement in which they are involved. Research supports the premise that listener response to speeches varies with the label associated with the speaker. A speech believed to be delivered by the American president would be interpreted differently from the identical speech believed to be delivered by the Soviet premier. Knowing who or what an individual is, then, helps those interacting with him to put his behavior into a larger context and make sense out of the whole experience.

This explanation of the order in society implies a complementary type of biological makeup of the members. If the social order is something that man himself develops, then it follows that it could not at the same time be biologically given. For role definitions to function as we have indicated, man biologically would have to be at birth a "mass of potential" capable of acquiring any of a multitude of different patterns (including roles) rather than a being with instinctive (biologically built-in) behavior. The close relationship between norm definitions and role definitions has already been discussed. Our understanding of this relationship can be expanded by pointing out here that this discussion of the relationship between role definitions and social order is in effect a continuation of the discussion in the last chapter of the relationship between norm definitions and social order. Both norm definitions and role definitions are an integral part of social organization.

ROLE DEFINITIONS AND PERSONAL (INDIVIDUAL) ORDER

If personality is the individual aspect of culture, and if we think not in terms of the individual *and* society but rather that the individual *is* a part of society, and if we emphasize interaction as a key social process, then it follows that what we have just said about social order is

equally true of personal order. One of the reasons (although not the only one) why the behavior of an individual is orderly and predictable is that he applies role definitions to himself. The clerk at the "five and ten" does much the same thing from day to day in part because she is following a role definition. Other variables do, of course, enter in; they are related to how closely she follows the prescribed plans of action, an important one being role conflict, which will be discussed in the next section. Here we are concerned only with tracing the relationship between the consistent behavior of individuals and the role definitions they apply to themselves.

Some of the important self-definitions of any individual are the role definitions he applies to himself. Some of the most important things that one knows about himself are the roles he plays— a husband, a Christian, a Democrat, a United States citizen, a member of the labor union, or president of the Elks' Lodge.

ROLE CONFLICT OR DISSONANCE

The various aspects of role definitions and consequently of role playing may not be completely harmonious one with another, even though *in the long run* they tend to be. We will now turn our attention directly to an analysis of this conflict.

Since role definitions are a part of the man-made culture, and since many aspects of culture develop in a crescive or unplanned manner, it is not surprising that complete harmony does not always exist between the various parts of culture. Lack of complete harmony is also fostered by the constant change going on within any society. Dissonance, then, is an ever-present condition. Society and its culture are always in the process of becoming something else.

Some of the major types of role conflict can be identified as follows.

Conflict between role definitions that apply to the same individual. The same individual may be a Christian and a soldier, with the role of Christian specifying in over-simplified terms that he should love his enemy, "turn the other cheek," and give him the coat from his back. The role of soldier calls for him to hate his enemy and kill him as a member of a hated out-group. Some college students have reported conflict between their role as son or daughter in a particular family and their role as fraternity or sorority member. The student can probably provide many other illustrations of this type of conflict.

In a society such as the contemporary United States where individuals may belong to many different groups, in each of which they play different roles, conflicts are a frequent occurrence. This is particularly true because the membership of some of their various groups may have little overlapping.

Lack of Consensus on Specific Role Definitions

For many reasons different members of a group may not share the same ideas as to what is expected of them. The boss and his newly hired secretary may define the role of secretary in different terms. She may feel that a secretary should have a ten-minute coffee break every morning and afternoon, whereas her boss may not include such a break in his ideas as to how his secretary should behave. The president of the local Rotary Club may find difficulty in satisfying his fellow Rotarians if he does not play his role as they expect him to. Where this type of conflict exceeds certain boundaries of the group (and these boundaries may vary from group to group) efforts to bring about greater harmony will generally be initiated by some of those involved. Sanctions of one type or another may be imposed.

Lack of consensus may also exist between the formal plans of action as laid down by the constitution, by-laws, job descriptions, etc., and the informal prescriptions held by the members of the group. The shop foreman may be required "as a part of his job" to see that those working under him produce a certain amounts of "units" during the day and obey the company rules, while at the same time those under him expect him to be a "good Joe" and to overlook certain infractions of the rules. Harmonizing these conflicting expectations can be a difficult task and one which may create trouble for individuals who attempt to play such a role. Although there may be agreement on broad role requirements,

Formal and Informal Role Definitions

Bob Jackson, a new employee, was given a high stool, a large pan of small nail-like plugs and a large stack of plastic boards, each with 680 holes which were to be filled with these plugs. He was told by his boss to take his time until he caught on to the job.

After the boss had left Jackson alone, an old-timer, Ben Lewis, sitting at the same bench, remarked, "Did ya get that, boys? Take your time! Can you imagine the bull of the woods telling us that?"

Bob stayed at this job, and became faster and faster at inserting the plugs in the plug board until he could beat anyone on the job. Bob, however, never turned in any more work than anyone else, probably because he had been approached long before by one of the respected old-timers who had said, "Listen, kid, you're working on an hourly basis the same as the rest of us. You won't get any more dough if you turn in more work than we do, and besides, the boss will raise our quota, which means more work for the same money. Get smart, boy."

—F. K. Berrien and
Wendell H. Bash.*

the conflict may involve the alternatives to be used in meeting these requirements. Disagreement may involve means as well as ends.

Roles are constantly changing and new definitions are developed. Conflict may result from an uneven rate of change of role definitions for all involved. Changing definitions of Negroes unevenly accepted throughout the society have, for instance, been related to such conflict situations as race riots.

Conflict Between Role Requirements

The abilities and interests of certain individuals may be such that they are unable adequately

* See F. K. Berrien and Wendell H. Bash, *Human Relations: Comments and Cases* (New York: Harper & Row, Inc., 1951) pp. 302–303.

to play a particular role even though they may officially hold the position and may want to play the role.

SUMMARY

This chapter adds role definitions to value and norm definitions as an important part of culture. Role definitions are, in fact, norm definitions associated with a particular position. Role playing, to be discussed in detail later, is the process of enacting the role definitions. All role definitions include a unique configuration of many types and aspects of behavior, systematically arranged so that the parts are somewhat consistent with each other and with the counter-roles that

form a part of the larger system to which they all belong. Role definitions are, accordingly, related to personal and social order, which is incomplete to the extent that role conflicts of one type or another exist at either the personal or social level.

Role definitions may be developed formally and informally and the positions to which they apply may be either ascribed or achieved. Role definitions are, further, an important type of self definition.

Although there is a clear distinction between norm definitions and role definitions, for certain purposes they can be considered as a combined entity. We will, accordingly, frequently talk of "norm-role definitions" throughout the text.

QUESTIONS

1. Relate the two concepts (1) role definitions and (2) role playing.
2. Discuss how an understanding of role–counter-role definitions supports the interactionist perspective.
3. How are role definitions different from norm definitions?
4. How does an individual go about deciding which role definition he should follow?
5. When you get your first job after graduating from

college, how do you expect to find out what role definitions you are to follow?
6. How are role definitions related to value definitions?
7. If you want to study role definitions, to what do you pay attention?
8. How are role definitions related to social order?
9. How are role definitions changed?
10. How does the development of role definitions in the family differ from the development of role definitions in a business organization?

PROJECT

Do a study of a selected group of college students to determine what they consider to be the major differences they expect to find in the behavior of American males and females. Interview a foreign student and

determine the differences between the male and the female role definitions in his society and those in the American society.

SUGGESTED READING

COSER, LEWIS A., and BERNARD ROSENBERG. *Sociological Theory*. 2d ed. New York: The Macmillan Co., 1964. Pp. 259–300.

DYER, WILLIAM G. "Analyzing Marital Adjustment Using Role Theory," *Marriage and Family Living*, XXIV, No. 4 (November, 1962), 371–375.

GOFFMAN, ERVING. *Encounters*. Indianapolis: The Bobbs-Merrill Co., Inc., 1961.

GROSS, NEAL, WARD S. MASON, and ALEXANDER W. McEACHERN. *Explorations in Role Analysis*. New York: John Wiley & Sons, Inc., 1958.

HUGHES, EVERETT C. "Dilemmas and Contradictions of Status," *The American Journal of Sociology*, L, No. 5 (March, 1945), 353–359.

KOMAROVSKY, MIRRA. "Cultural Contradictions and Sex

Roles," *The American Journal of Sociology*, LII, No. 3 (November, 1946), 184–189.

MERTON, ROBERT K. *Social Theory and Social Structure*. New York: The Free Press of Glencoe, Inc., 1957. Pp. 368–387.

NEIMAN, LIONEL J., and JAMES W. HUGHES. "The Problem of the Concept of Role—A Re-survey of the Literature," *Social Forces*, XXX, No. 2 (December, 1951). Pp. 141–149.

SEEMAN, MELVIN. "Role Conflict and Ambivalence in Leadership," *American Sociological Review*, XVIII, No. 4 (August, 1953). Pp. 373–380.

STRAUSS, ANSELM L. "The Development of Conceptions of Rules in Children," *Child Development*, XXIII (1954), 193–208.

10

Self Definitions

The conceptions a person has of himself are obviously a very personal thing; yet this same set of definitions is also very much a social phenomenon. How can this be so?

INTRODUCTION

The totality of the definitions that make up the culture of a group is an extremely complex phenomenon. Previous chapters have discussed value definitions, norm definitions, and role definitions, each of which is an important subdivision of the larger culture that is related to human behavior in distinctive ways. Each of these types of definitions, then, is an important variable to which the sociologist pays attention in his efforts to understand human interaction. This chapter adds *self definitions* to the list as an important type of definition that is prominent in man's social behavior.

DEFINITION OF TERMS

In his behavior the individual labels and pays attention to various animate and inanimate objects, including, of course, other human beings. His attention, however, is not limited to those objects that exist independent of himself. The *individual* is also aware of the *individual* as an active agent in the interaction of which he is a

part. Self-awareness is a constant human phenomenon. It is with the labels the individual places upon the individual (upon himself) and their accompanying definitions that we are concerned in this chapter. These we will call "self definitions." In that such definitions are shared by the group, they are a part of culture. Any such definitions that are held only by the individual are a part of his personality or his individual culture.

In the literature of sociology and psychology many of the discussions of self definitions are couched in terms of "the self," rather than "self definitions." Recognizing this may help the student interpret outside reading in this area. Using this traditional terminology, however, may pose some problems, since "self" is a noun and may be interpreted as identifying an empirical object of some sort. Once we begin to think of the "self" as a thing we sooner or later are confronted with the question what this thing is and where it is located. We already have the term "individual" to identify the biological being, so the term "self" would appear to identify something other than the individual. What, then, is

135

this other "thing"? It is easy to take the next step and posit that the "thing" is located inside the individual and then perhaps attribute causative powers to it.

Use of the term "self definitions," in light of our previous discussions about definitions, does not lead to this "semantic trap." We are merely identifying a particular configuration of definitions—those held by an individual that have as their object the same individual. We will occasionally use the single term "self" in this chapter as we refer to other writings. When we do, it is "self definitions" to which we refer, not any mystical entity believed to exist inside the individual, or anywhere else for that matter.

Each individual knows himself. Self definitions are those definitions that have as their object the individual holding them. Self definitions, then, are all related to the object to which the individual refers when he uses the pronouns "I" or "me." They include conceptions about how the "I" or "me" is related to others and to various aspects of life, together with any value definitions attached to these conceptions. Self definitions may be thought of as a "map" which a person consults in order to take stock of himself and his position. Just as a map is a representation of some territory, so are self definitions a representation of an object—the individual holding these definitions. The map is not the territory *per se*. Self definitions are not the object *per se* (the individual), but rather ideas the individual has about himself.

The English language in some respects makes the defining of self definitions cumbersome in that we frequently have to use the word "self" in the definition as well as in the term. The "self" part of the word "himself," however, is used in a different sense than when it is used alone as meaning "the totality of the self definitions held by an individual." We will follow the standardized usage of "himself" and "ourselves."

Our understanding of self definitions may be increased if we return briefly to our previous discussion of symbolic interaction. That discussion pointed out that as the individual becomes socialized he learns to identify the various objects that exist in his environment and the agreed-

What Is the Referent?

The necessity of using the concept of self does not confer the privilege of misusing it. As we use concepts in our thinking, they tend to get firmer and harder. Thought about fluid events tends to curdle and form solid clots. Before long we begin to think of the self as if it were a lump in the personality. It becomes an entity so sharply bounded that arguments begin as to whether a certain piece of behavior belongs in the self or out of it, proceeds across an ego boundary, or involves a collision between the ego and something else. In the end the self is standing like a solid boulder of granite in the midst of personality, and one's thinking about it is as flexible as granite.

—Robert W. White.*

upon symbols to label them. He also learns through social interaction the appropriate plans of action addressed toward specific objects. He learns, for instance, that books are objects with certain characteristics that are used for reading purposes.

In like manner the individual becomes aware of himself (the individual) as an object with certain characteristics; this object has a specific name or label and it is appropriate to address certain plans of action toward it. He learns, for instance, that he is a male, a member of the Brown family, an American, etc.

It is obvious that the totality of the things one knows about himself is exceedingly complex. Just as a modern American teen-age boy may know many different things about a car and can talk for hours about it, so he may also know many different things about himself. Just as each of us may know many things about those with whom we are well acquainted, so we also know many things about the individual with whom we are probably best acquainted—"myself." Some of the major categories under which the many self definitions of the college freshman

---

* Robert W. White, *The Abnormal Personality* (3d ed.; New York: The Ronald Press Co., 1964), p. 145.

(and others as well) could be classified are the following:

1. Biological characteristics [1]
   a. He is a male.
   b. He is six feet tall.
   c. He has red hair.
2. Behavior patterns—ways in which this biological object is and can be involved in social interaction, such as
   a. How he relates himself to others, including his role-playing ability, and his awareness of the "resources" he has at his command. He has his ideas of what he can and can't do, such as
      (1) How he treats his mother.
      (2) How well he does on sociology tests.
      (3) What kind of football player he is.
   b. His thinking (defining) practices
      (1) How he labels the objects he is familiar with and the plans of action he relates to them.
      (2) The norm and role definitions he uses—what he defines as appropriate behavior for the specific conditions and positions.
      (3) His evaluating practices or his moral or esthetic standards, including, of course, his evaluations of his biological characteristics (No. 1 above—it is good to be a male and to have red hair) and of his behavior patterns (No. 2 above—he is an "A" student and lousy football player but is good to his mother).

Any and all of these types of definitions can be held by different individuals. Such definitions of the individual held by the individual are the self definitions we are discussing. Such definitions held by others are involved in the development of self definitions, as will be discussed presently, but they are not part of *self* definitions as we have defined the term.

Most individuals enter most social situations with fairly well-formed ideas (definitions) as to how they will behave. The football player, for

instance, knows whether he is likely to be able to kick a field goal or not. The college co-ed on the dance floor knows whether she will be able to follow most of her male dancing partners or whether she is likely to have difficulties. When called upon to make a public speech, most individuals know whether they will be able to do it or not. This is not to imply that such self knowledge is 100 per cent accurate, but only to suggest that the individual has a general idea as to what he can do and what he cannot. We can say that the individual has as a major component of his self definitions an awareness of the resources which he has at his command. He knows, within limits to be sure, what he can contribute to the on-going behavior sequences in which he is involved.

This is particularly true in highly structured situations where the norm definitions are clearly understood by those involved. In relatively unstructured situations most of us are generally not "too sure of ourselves." We may or may not be able to "do the job properly."

The on-going experiences of the individual may, of course, serve to reinforce already existing self definitions or to change them in one direction or another. The old adage that "nothing succeeds like success" emphasizes this point. It also follows that nothing fails like failure. Continued failures may cause one to wonder, "What good am I?" Unexpected successes or failures may produce extensive changes in self definitions.

Self definitions may also be value definitions. Value definitions used by an individual to refer to that individual, or the value aspect of self definitions, evidence all of the characteristics of other value definitions. Value definitions are a man-made dimension of human interaction. There is no empirical referent to whatever value system man uses. Thus, considerable variation in value definitions is found from individual to individual and from group to group. The value aspects of self definitions are no exception.

Various values can, accordingly, be attributed to any and all of the biological characteristics of the individual. James, for instance, suggests that there are certain biological aspects

---

[1] When William James talks of the "material self," this is basically that to which he refers. This is also the "organism" to which others refer.

which the individual generally holds most dear. One can easily, he suggests, have one's hair cut, unless it is an essential part of one's self (self definitions), but loss of toes, limbs, facial or genital parts may be unbearable.

Since value definitions involve NER symbols, it follows that no characteristic is inherently or always valued higher than another. Maintaining some biological condition, or even the preservation of the biological being, is not always defined as being the most desirable goal. Men endure hunger, pain, and deprivation even to the point of death in order to keep secrets, to protect comrades, to advance a particular cause. Why? In part, at least, because the maintenance of the self concept—as a faithful believer—is more important to the individual than mere physical survival.

It should be clear that the complex configuration of definitions which an individual has about himself is a dynamic, ever changing one. The individual does not have a file drawer of ready-made definitions which contains all of his ideas about himself and upon which he draws in a mechanical fashion in the appropriate situation. As we move from one social situation to another we may change our definitions. The principle of emergence applies to the use of self definitions.

SELF DEFINITIONS AND ROLE DEFINITIONS

When an individual provides for himself answers as to who or what he is, he frequently makes use of role definitions. When a man tells himself, for instance, that he is a father, a mechanic, a Baptist, a student, or an American, he is identifying one of the roles he plays.

One of the important component parts of the configuration of self definitions at any given time, then, is the role dimension. In order to engage in social interaction with any degree of facility individuals have to identify their roles properly. They have to tell themselves who or what they are at the moment. They have to answer the question, "What am I doing here?" A school teacher, for instance, who happens to have his own child as a student, usually tries to treat the child as a student rather than as a son or daughter. The teacher tells himself or reminds himself that while in the classroom he is a teacher and only incidentally a father. It is his role of teacher that is salient in this particular situation. When he leaves the classroom and possibly takes his son home with him in the family car, a distinct change in roles may occur. Each of the individuals involved applies a different definition to himself, and different behavior patterns follow as a consequence.

As we move through a day of social interaction we are constantly assessing the situation and identifying our role. We do not, of course, play the same role in all groups. In one group, Individual A may be the leader, in another a follower. If he does not clearly identify his role in each group and if the others involved do not define it in the same way, he is likely to run into difficulty in attempting to play the role.

"Non-Persons"

Goffman speaks of a category of persons who in some social encounters are treated as if they were not present, whereas in fact they may be indispensable for sustaining the performance. Although cabdrivers are not consistently approached in this way by fares, it happens often enough for it to become a significant theme of their work. Examples are legion. Maresca tells of the chorus girl who made a complete change from street clothes into stage costume as he drove her to her theater. More prosaic instances include the man and wife who, managing to suppress their anger while on the street, launch into a bitter quarrel the moment they are inside the cab; or the well-groomed young couple who, after a few minutes, roll over on the back seat to begin petting; or the business man who loudly discusses details of a questionable business deal.

*—Fred Davis.**

---

* Fred Davis, "The Cab Driver and His Fare," *American Journal of Sociology*, LXV, No. 2 (September, 1959), 160.

Whatever the dynamics of role playing may be, role definitions are an important component of self definitions.

Differential value is generally attributed to the various roles in any particular group. Some roles carry with them great prestige, others lesser prestige. Since value definitions are a man-made dimension and persist only so long as there is relative agreement upon them, the value aspect of various roles changes frequently. However, whatever value system is in effect at any particular time, the value associated with a particular role becomes infused with the self definition of the one playing the role. If the role of president of the university is one to which great prestige is attributed, then when John Jones becomes president of Hometown University, this prestige is generally attributed to him by others and may be incorporated by him into his self definitions. How well he plays his role is also involved in the amount of prestige he will enjoy.

Self definitions have many dimensions, an important aspect being the role definitions involved.

SELF DEFINITIONS AND PERSONALITY

If we define personality as the totality of an individual's behavior patterns, and include within this totality his verbal and thinking behavior patterns, it follows that self definitions as we are using the term are a part of personality. One behaves toward himself in particular ways. One tells himself things about himself. One evaluates himself. Such behavior patterns are one type of behavior in which an individual can engage. They are a part of his personality.

Defined in this way, it follows that the theory used to explain personality at the same time explains self definitions.

SELF DEFINITIONS AND POSSESSIONS

Since the individual learns to value himself and other objects through the same process, and since personality patterns tend to be somewhat consistent, it is not surprising that we can find relationships between self values and the values attributed to other objects. Strauss has indicated that what a man has is a fair index to what he is.[2] It may be difficult to maintain a particular self definition if one does not possess objects that one feels are consistent with it. In terms of social class definitions, for instance, if one does not possess the proper prestige or status symbols, others may not attribute the desired class position to the individual. The individual, in turn, by having neither the status symbols nor the requisite evaluations reflected to him from the others with whom he interacts, may experience a corresponding decrease in self values. In the American society status symbols such as money, a coat of arms, and antique furniture in the home are important in helping an upper-class individual retain his self conceptions, since they provide empirical evidence that he is what he thinks he is.

Likewise, change in self conceptions is likely to occur when one loses objects into which great investment (not necessarily money) has been poured, or in which the individual has a heavy emotional involvement.

Some have, in fact, included both the individual and his possessions under the label "self." William James talks of the "material self," which includes the organism *and* such things as his family, home, and the products of his labor, to the degree that one has "invested one's self in them."[3] This expanded definition of the self is different from the one we have been using—the individual as known to the individual. According to our definition, any "non-individual" objects would be excluded from our definition of the self. We have, however, indicated that there is a *relationship* between one's self conceptions and the objects he values, but there would seem to be utility in separating these two elements, especially for scientific purposes.

[2] Anselm Strauss, *Mirrors and Masks* (New York: The Free Press of Glencoe, Inc., 1959), p. 36.

[3] In William James, *Principles of Psychology* (New York: Dover Publications, Inc., 1950).

Figure 10.1   Changing role definitions as reflected in two school activities.   (Wide World Photos.)

One's self conceptions are involved not only in how one views his own objects, but all other objects as well. As Shlein has indicated: [4]

If one feels strong, a boulder is a weapon to push into the treads of an armored tank; if weak, the same boulder is a refuge to hide behind. If one feels sick and helpless, the nurse is a creature of mercy, appealed to for comfort. The same nurse may be seen as a temptress, to be sexually pursued, if the patient sees himself as well and sturdy.

How objects are obtained also tells us something about the self definitions of the individual involved. The methods an individual is willing to use to get money vary with the manner in which he defines himself.

ORIGIN OF SELF DEFINITIONS

How does an individual learn about himself? Where do self definitions come from? How does one fulfill the biblical command to "Know thyself"? This section is an exploration of these questions.

Suppose, for instance, you ask an average three-year-old child whether he is an introvert or an extrovert. He most likely will be unable to tell you because no one has told him whether he is one or the other. Or suppose you were to ask an average high school student whether he is mesomorphic, endomorphic, or ectomorphic. He most likely would not know for exactly the same reason. No one has defined the words for him, so he doesn't know. If a student were asked at the beginning of the semester what kind of a sociology student he was, he likewise would most likely not know, again because in many respects he does not yet know what a "good" sociology student is supposed to know. That which is true of these terms is also true of all others: we have to have words defined for us before we can use them; and if we do not have words with which to identify objects or

---

Origin of Self Image

Does one's self image correspond more closely to

1. *the group image of him or*

2. *his perception of the group's image of him?*

"No. 2" says research by Miyamoto and Dornbusch.*

---

behavior patterns, we cannot with any degree of facility take these behavior patterns into account.

Self definitions, then, are social in origin. The newborn child for all practical purposes has no self definitions. In only a most rudimentary sense is he aware that he exists. Only as he progresses through a period of physical maturation and social interaction does he begin to acquire self-conceptions or self definitions. These develop slowly as an organization of elements that must themselves have time to develop. A rudimentary form of bodily self-consciousness arises early in life. Then, somewhere around his fifth month, the baby discovers his hands. He may spend time just looking at them and waving them before his eyes, apparently being intrigued by the discovery that he can control them. When he crawls, and especially when he begins to walk, somewhere around the end of the first year, he bumps into objects and perfects his coordination and his bodily self-consciousness. Analysis of the verbalizations made by children from one month to four years in age has shown that children develop a growing sense of self-awareness as age increases.[5]

Experiences with other individuals, of course, play a major role in the development of the

---

* See S. Frank Miyamoto and Sanford M. Dornbusch, "A Test of Interactionist Hypothesis of Self-Conception," *American Journal of Sociology*, LXI, No. 5 (March, 1956), 399–403.

[5] Louise B. Ames, "The Sense of Self of Nursery School Children as Manifested by Their Verbal Behavior," *Journal of Genetic Psychology*, LXXXI, No. 2 (December, 1952), 193–232.

---

[4] John M. Shlein, "The Self-Concept in Relation to Behavior: Theoretical and Empirical Research," *Research Supplement to Religious Education*, LVII, No. 4 (July–August, 1962), p. S115.

child's self definitions. For most children it is other family members (or family substitutes) who are most intimately involved in the process. Since most social experiences, indeed most experiences, take place in a family setting, this would of necessity be the major source of early self definitions.

As the child matures, his scope of operation branches out beyond the confines of the family, and non-family individuals begin to have an impact upon his self definitions. Such non-family contacts may reinforce what the family has already told him, or they may provide contradictory definitions. One way or another, depending on many other factors, he will take these definitions into account. Not all social contacts are of equal importance in this process. Some are more significant than others. Selective perception is involved.

When a child can properly use the pronouns "I" and "me" he has a fairly well-established awareness of his own identity and of his separateness from the others in his environment. He is also aware of his ability to initiate action and is able to take some responsibility for what he says and does. Hearing his own words when he talks also facilitates the development of self conceptions.

As the child begins to move outside the family, his play groups enter into his self-development. A child cannot participate very effectively in a game unless he knows something about the rules of the game (culture), the others also involved in the game, and his own behavior. In this process, then, he learns about himself. Children in play situations may be very frank in their efforts to let others know how they are being evaluated. Verbal indicators may be reinforced by other physical behavior (sanctions) of one type or another.

As the child matures, he is caught up in a stream of history in which society begins to give him a place and of which he gradually becomes aware. He becomes part of society and acquires a personality. Eventually he becomes involved in the major social institutions such as marriage, religion, and education, and as he learns about the roles of others in these institutions he con-

comitantly learns about himself. As he becomes familiar with his cultural heritage he becomes familiar with his roles and their relationships. He learns how he fits into the over-all social system and the various subsystems of which the larger system is composed. A subsequent discussion of religion will indicate that he may also learn to view himself as being involved in a larger matrix which includes a supernatural realm.

Rudimentary aspects of this whole social process are suggested in the following statement by one of the author's students:

Drawing on my own experience and my childhood in Hawaii, I was amazed to discover that all my playmates and friends were not considered alike by my parents. Although the climate is more conducive to racial harmony and I did not learn the difference until I was about eight years old; nonetheless I spent about one year trying to understand and differentiate among people. It took constant effort to determine who was what and to learn the definitions belonging to each nationality group. At the same time, I learned also the definitions of my own nationality group—they being "haole." Until I learned these definitions, I felt myself no different from my cohorts, but with the teaching of my peers and the actions of my parents, I learned how to react within the narrow bounds of "haole" and also learned when to be proud of my racial characteristics and when to be ashamed of them.

There is an American saying that "A man is known by the company he keeps." What we have been emphasizing here is that he also *knows himself* by the company he keeps.

Each of us as we come into contact with others is constantly, one way or another, telling them something about themselves. We are constantly telling them, among other things, something about how well they are playing their role at the moment and how well they are conforming to norms that we feel are important. We also frequently invoke sanctions, formal or informal, to reinforce our ideas as to how the others are behaving. While we are telling others these things they are also providing us with similar interpretations of our behavior. *Interaction takes place.* In this manner self definitions are reinforced or rejected.

The process we have been discussing applies to both socially approved and disapproved definitions. The process by which a child learns that he is a juvenile delinquent or a "goof ball" and the process by which the adult learns that he is a criminal, a drug addict, or an alcoholic all follow the same social pattern, even though the content of the definitions may be different.

IMPORTANCE OF A NAME

In the development of self conceptions, an awareness that the child has a name which serves to distinguish him from all others is probably crucial. Having a name not only serves to distinguish him from other individuals, but also to locate him within a particular group—his family group. The "Jones" part of the name "Johnny Jones" is basically a group concept, which ties this particular individual not only to a specific group of living individuals but to a whole group of ancestors extending back into history.

In addition to the family name, many of the other names the child or individual learns to apply to himself are group concepts that serve to identify the individual within a particular group. The family name, of course, is one of the first he learns. He may later learn that he is an American or Canadian, that he is white, Negro, or mongoloid, that he is a Christian or a Jew, a Utahan, or a Californian, a "TEKE" or a

Figure 10.2 Change in self definitions may be widespread throughout a society and may both result in and result from social movements such as the woman suffrage movement. Parades such as this one in Washington, D. C., in 1913 sought public affirmation for the change. (The Bettmann Archive, Inc.)

member of some other fraternity, a fifth grader or a college freshman at State U. Once such a label is accepted by the individual, whatever he learns about the groups to which he belongs has important implications for his self conceptions. If a group to which he belongs is accorded high prestige by the society of which he is a part, the individual will usually generalize this prestige from the group as a whole to himself as an individual. Others will, of course, usually do the same thing and thus reinforce the self conceptions of the individual. Further, the knowledge that the members of, say, the ELITE fraternity have as to how members of this fraternity are supposed to behave becomes involved in an individual's decisions as to how he is supposed to behave. The same thing is true of all groups to which the individual belongs. The self concepts which an individual has are personal definitions, but many of them are at the same time group concepts which identify for the individual and the others involved the groups to which he belongs. Many of our most important self labels are group names.

Special names of endearment and particular behavior patterns such as fondling, kissing, and holding in the arms (our silent language), once the significance of such behavior is learned, also serve to tell the growing child something about himself. Behavior of the reverse type, such as rejection of one type or another, or exclusion from certain groups or activities, also enters into the development of self conceptions. Psychoanalytic interpretations of behavior are usually based upon the premise that it is the early experiences of this type that establish the pattern for future self conceptions even though an awareness of such experiences may have long since been forgotten. Psychoanalytic therapy thus rests upon efforts of the therapist to reconstruct such experiences and to interpret current on-going behavior in terms of them.

All that an individual learns about his groups and about himself is not necessarily consistent. Indeed, in a heterogeneous, rapidly changing society, he may acquire many contradictory definitions about himself. He may, in fact, sincerely want to be or to become contradictory things, or

---

Self-Fulfilling Definitions

It is interesting that the belief in the superiority of local ways of living [self-definitions] actually conditions the way of life. Springdalers make an effort to be friendly and go out of their way to help newcomers.

—Arthur J. Vidich and
Joseph Bensman.*

---

to engage in conflicting behavior patterns. Various self definitions do *tend to be* mutually consistent, and most individuals try with varying degrees of success to wipe out inconsistencies. Contradictions of one type or another, however, are found in the self definitions of most if not all individuals. Extreme contradictions are, of course, difficult to live with for the individual and the others with whom he interacts and may result in isolation or special treatment of one type or another.

Our major emphasis in this chapter has been upon the social nature of self definitions. Our approach here has been that of the interactionist. Such an approach makes us aware of the fact that the individual and society (and self definitions and culture) are different aspects of a single whole. Cottrell [6] emphasizes this point when he talks about the "self–other" system. Thus, while the self is a constant factor in the human personality structure, it is also central to an understanding of the prerequisites of society and culture. As Hallowell has indicated: [7]

A human social order implies a mode of existence that has meaning for the individual at the level of self-awareness. A human social order, for example,

---

* Arthur J. Vidich and Joseph Bensman, *Small Town in Mass Society* (Garden City, N. Y.: Doubleday and Co., Inc., 1958), p. 34. (An Anchor Book.)

[6] Leonard S. Cottrell, Jr., "The Analysis of Situational Fields in Social Psychology," *American Sociological Review*, VII, No. 3 (June, 1942), 370–372.

[7] A. Irving Hallowell, "Culture, Personality and Society," in A. L. Kroeber (ed.), *Anthropology Today* (Chicago: The University of Chicago Press, 1953), pp. 614–615.

is a moral order. If the individual did not have the capacity for identifying the conduct that is his own and through self-reflection, appraising it with reference to values and social sanctions, how would moral order function in human terms? If I cannot assume moral responsibility for my conduct, how can guilt or shame arise? What conflict can there be between impulse and standards if I am unaware of values or sanctions?

Self definitions, then, originate in the process of social interaction. We learn about ourselves, or we acquire our self definitions, through interaction with others.

Others serve as a mirror or a looking-glass (to use the term of Cooley, an early American sociologist), from which we constantly find reflected back at us images of ourselves. Self conceptions are at the same time both a very personal and a social phenomenon. So many of the satisfactions of human life result from the approval of the individual by others that it is unlikely that one can escape for long from the knowledge that what others think of us is important, not only abstractly but in many practical ways as well.

RELIGION AND SELF CONCEPTIONS

The religious component of the self definitions of an individual may be a very important one for the behavior of the individual. Religion involves definitions about what is believed to be supernatural and ultimate and, in addition, generally relates the moral or value dimension of life to these definitions. Much variability is found in the realm of religion because questions about the supernatural and ultimate values cannot be answered by paying attention to empirical phenomena. Whatever the specific content of these religious dimensions may be, they are an active ingredient in the interaction of the members of any society. Our concern with religion here is with the manner in which religion may affect self definitions. In concise terms, religion may expand self definitions to infinitely large proportions or contract self definitions to infinitely small proportions.

Experiences of one type or another may lead an individual to believe that his behavior is not only approved by his fellow men or at least his significant others, but that it is also approved by deity—by the highest source of which the individual is able to conceive. To feel that one's behavior is in harmony with such a source is usually productive of increased self-approval. To feel that God approves of your family life, business life, recreational patterns, sexual patterns, or political patterns, increases the positive valence.

On the other hand, religion may also be related to patterns the reverse of those just discussed. To accept the premise that there is a supreme being (or beings) interested in man and concerned with his behavior, and then to accept definitions that make your own familial, sexual, political, or economic behavior out of harmony, can produce negative self-evaluations. To feel that one is a sinner, and possibly doomed to an eternity of "burning in a lake of fire and brimstone" or some other "punishment" has an impact upon one's behavior quite different from that related to the reverse definitions.

Acceptance of religious definitions by the individual permits him to conceive of himself as being intimately involved with the supernatural. Man may accordingly see himself as having a destiny whereby his work is defined as being also God's work. He may feel that he has a calling. He may further feel that he will, in a life subsequent to this one, "dwell forever at the right hand of God." He may see himself as an important cog in a supernaturally originated scheme of life. New meaning may be added to his behavior as a result of the acceptance of religious definitions. Green [8] provides us with the following comparison:

Man you are a pustule that has arisen by chance upon the body of an inferior planet, says the atheist. Man you are the noblest work of God and you will be united with Him, says the theist.

It is not surprising that the last set of definitions is widely accepted.

Religion is also frequently involved in the development of definitions about the "ideal self,"

[8] Arnold W. Green, *Sociology* (3d ed.; New York: McGraw-Hill Book Co., 1960), p. 434.

or definitions about the characteristics the individual feels he should have or should acquire. Most people usually define their own behavior as something less than it should be. Most people have unrealized goals toward which they strive. Since religion incorporates definitions about the supernatural and the ultimate, it is not surprising to find it ultimately involved in these definitions about the ideal self.

Such discussions are frequently couched in terms of the development of a "conscience," which "tells" the individual whether he is bad or good. The requirements of the scientific method specifying that one pay attention to empirical phenomena lead us to reject the concept as one of scientific utility. The social scientist does not see human beings as having a "conscience" or an entity of some kind inside of them which makes moral decisions for them; rather, he pays attention to observable phenomena and sees *human beings* who make moral decisions. It is the human being who makes the decision on the basis of his past experience, rather than a mystical entity assumed to exist within him. There is no doubt that human beings do make moral decisions and that such decisions are intimately related to the self conceptions of those making the decisions. The point made here is that the "conscience" concept has no scientific utility.

Difficulty in Changing

Since religion includes the supernatural and ultimate dimensions, any aspect of life, including self definitions, to which it is applied becomes particularly resistant to change. If God is defined as the ultimate source of value definitions, and is further viewed as being unchanging, then it follows that such definitions will not easily be changed. If one sincerely feels that he has sinned and has consequently been rejected by his God, it is difficult to change such definitions. Even where the religious dogma includes provisions for forgiveness, it is sometimes difficult for individuals to decide whether such forgiveness is complete.

Once definitions of being forgiven have been accepted, however, they are accompanied by feelings of great relief and satisfaction. If God

Conversion

A second misconception about conversion is that when a person becomes partly converted, and then is "lost" he returns to his previous identity. This is probably not so, for if a man has wandered some way from his loyalties, it is doubtful whether he merely returns to them. As in brainwashing: once a man has absorbed a new vocabulary with which to name and perceive the world, including his own actions, he can scarcely tear the vocabulary out of his brain; nor, even if he wishes to, can he forget his most disloyal recent actions, such as the denunciation of his family.

—Anselm Strauss.*

is defined as a significant other, and one sincerely believes that he has returned to His good graces, his evaluation of himself has undergone tremendous changes in the process. The contrast between the new and the old self definitions may only serve to accentuate the new feelings of joy and satisfaction with the new self definitions. It is no wonder that those who believe that they have been "saved" or "forgiven" or "called" typically describe such experiences as being ones of great joy and exhilaration.

This process, of course, also works in the reverse direction. Belief that one has fallen from a condition of acceptance to one of rejection is accompanied by other derogatory self feelings and evaluations.

SELF-DEFENSE

Human beings are capable of establishing value definitions with reference to any aspect of their universe. Our chapter on value definitions emphasized that anything that man decides to take into account can be placed along a value continuum with "good" and "bad" at the two poles. Value definitions, like other definitions, are accompanied by plans of action felt to be

* Anselm Strauss, *Mirrors and Masks* (New York: The Free Press of Glencoe, Inc., 1959), p. 123.

appropriate. In simple terms, we generally seek things defined as good and avoid things defined as bad. Man may also engage in various activities to preserve what he has learned to value highly. This applies to his self conceptions as well as to anything else. Just as an individual may attempt to increase the value of his home by applying a coat of paint, by building it in the "right" neighborhood, or by including things of which others approve, so he may do these same kinds of things with reference to his self definitions. Just as an individual may pass laws to protect his home or belong to pressure groups designed to insure protection for his home, so he may engage in similar activities with reference to his self definitions. We may defend our self definitions from anything which we have reason to believe may be responsible for reducing their value.

It is impossible for human beings to pay attention to everything at once; at any given time we have to pay attention to only certain things while we ignore others. *Selective perception* is an important characteristic of all human behavior, including perceptions related to self definitions. We are constantly looking to others to detect the image they are reflecting back to us about ourselves, and we are also selective in the cues we pick up. Out of all the cues to which man could pay attention, he generally selects those which tend to enhance his self conceptions and conversely ignores or minimizes cues that would be self-degrading. There are, of course, limits to this process, and an individual may through one means or another have definitions forced upon him that he has been reluctant to accept. Common self-defense mechanisms which may be used with varying degrees of success include the following.

Provide Self-enhancing Definitions

Since man's definitions of the situation in which he finds himself and of the others involved are not restricted to any objective characteristics, he may provide definitions of the situation and of the others involved in such a way that the unpleasant or negative aspects are negated or at least reduced in intensity. Man sees what he has been prepared to see. Varying degrees of honesty may be involved. In many cases the distortion is not dishonest. If lying is defined as a conscious act of deliberate concealment of a known truth, much of this type of behavior does not fall under this heading—it is simply selective perception.

Self definitions may not be entirely consistent from one situation to another, and without knowledge as to how the individual defines the situations and his role, it may be easy to conclude that he is lying about his self definitions. Also, in the process of developing self definitions an individual may vary from one situation to another, not being certain at any particular time just what he is. We may conceive of ourselves as marginal in many respects—not completely "in" or completely "out" of any particular category to which we wish to pay attention.

Self definitions that vary considerably from the definitions held by the others involved are generally regarded as symptomatic of severe personality disturbance. Individuals holding such definitions may be defined as psychotic and be isolated from others and given special attention in an effort to bring their self definitions (and other perceptions of their world) into greater harmony with those around them.

Selective Association

We may choose the others with whom we associate so that the self definitions reflected to us in our social interaction will be positive and self-enhancing. A corollary of this technique is to *withdraw* from any situation in which one may be made to appear unfavorably. The individual's choice of associates is greater in the case of his peer group and other voluntary groups than in the case of his family, especially while very young. Where choice is possible we tend to avoid interaction that we feel will be self-degrading.

Diversionary Tactics

Where self definitions are threatened or challenged, the individual may change the subject

No Rites of Passage

Most provisional roles conferred by society— like those of the student or conscripted soldier, for example—include some kind of terminal ceremony to mark the individual's movement back out of the role once its temporary advantages have been exhausted. But the roles allotted to the deviant seldom make allowance for this type of passage. He is ushered into the deviant position by a decisive and often dramatic ceremony, yet is retired from it with hardly a word of public notice. As a result, the deviant often returns home with no proper license to resume a normal life in the community. Nothing has happened to cancel out the stigma imposed upon him by earlier commitment ceremonies...the members of the community seem reluctant to accept the returning deviant on an entirely equal footing. In a very real sense, they do not know who he is.

—Howard S. Becker.*

of the conversation, attack those who are felt to be belittling him, or create some other diversion that permits him to avoid self-degrading experiences. He may claim to be uninterested in those who negatively define him, or he may maintain to himself and to others that they are maladjusted themselves.

Develop "Protective Tariffs" or Rules of Etiquette

Most of the rules of etiquette of any group are designed to permit or facilitate social interaction with a minimum of threat to the self conceptions of those involved. They encourage those involved to reflect respect and approval to each other. Developing and enforcing such norms is another technique of self-defense.

Physical Combat

Physical fighting may also be involved in self-defense. Engaging in physical combat usually involves more than defending one's physical body

* Howard S. Becker, *The Other Side* (New York: The Free Press of Glencoe, Inc., 1964), pp. 16–17.

from harm. Self conceptions may also be protected through this process. One may fight to protect his honor, his manhood, his family, or his "good name."

The fact that there is a rather widespread belief that man has an "instinct for self preservation" supports the point being made here that human beings do generally try to maximize their self conceptions.

Even though self-defensive behavior is a common human experience, not all such efforts are equally effective. Self definitions can and do change in a negative direction. Human beings can learn to value themselves less and less. Individuals who once thought highly of themselves may learn to define themselves as of little worth. Individuals may, in fact, destroy themselves in cases of extreme negative definitions. Durkheim, an early French sociologist, identified different types of suicide and called the types related to increased devaluation of self concepts "egoistic" suicides. Particular religious experiences may lead to definitions of sinfulness, guilt, and shame. Significant failures may be the catalyst of self-reorganization in a negative direction.

Self definitions, then, can be changed in any direction, but human beings do generally engage in activities that serve to defend and enhance the self definitions they wish to maintain.

THE REAL SELF

Many discussions of self definitions have centered around the question of what is the "real" self of an individual. When an individual tells others something about himself, there may, for instance, be a question as to whether he is presenting his real self definitions. This is an important question, not only with reference to any on-going social interaction but also with reference to any research involving self definitions.

Discussions about the "real" self or the "real" anything for that matter frequently stem from a belief that in the world there exists a series of "things" that human beings merely label so that they can take them into account. According to this view the "things" exist independent of whether they are named by human beings. The view of the symbolic interactionist is contrary to this. The world in which we live is viewed as being capable of subdivision into any number of units or things depending upon the past experiences and the desires of the one doing the labeling. Further, any "thing" can be subdivided into smaller units that can be taken into account, or any "thing" can be combined with other things to form a larger whole that can be labeled and responded to as an entity. The leaf of a tree, for instance, can be subdivided into cells or atoms; or it can be viewed as but one part of a twig, a branch, the tree, the landscape, or as a green thing, a living thing, etc. Exactly where one draws his boundary lines is an arbitrary decision. The world then is "cut up" according to the symbols the group has learned to use, not according to some pre-existing pattern. In this sense, then, there is no "real" self which exists independent of whether man pays attention to it. Rather, human behavior can be "cut up" or subdivided into any number of meaningful patterns which can be labeled and responded to. In this approach, we have no concern with whether we are identifying the "real" self or not, but only with the question as to whether those concerned share a common definition for the terms we do use. Scientific utility of the term is increased, of course, if there is an empirical referent for it.

We have defined the "self" (self definition) as the individual as known by the individual. Whatever the individual thinks he is, *to him* (although maybe not to some others) this *is* what he is. Individuals may for some reason or other be reluctant to expose their self definitions to some other or to any others. This is one of the problems of social behavior and social research. However, in the last measure, when the individual tells himself or others what he is *with no intent to deceive,* this is his "real self."

Our previous discussion has emphasized the social origin of these definitions. What others mean to tell us about ourselves (objective reality from our perspective) and what *we think* they mean to tell us (subjective reality) may, of course, not be the same. Human beings frequently misinterpret the "message" of others. In cases of discrepancy, however, it is our subjective reality which influences our behavior. Whatever we think others are thinking of us, *to us* this is what they are thinking of us. Self definitions are built from these perceptions. Human beings operate on the basis of their subjective reality.

Just as subjective reality and objective reality need not necessarily agree, it is not surprising that the definitions of the individual by all others may not agree with his own. Some seem to have a hard time understanding how one individual can "like himself" so much when "in reality" (to them) he is a "despicable bore." If our theory about the social origin of the self definitions is correct, the definitions of the significant others and of the individual would coincide closely.

There is, of course, always the question whether the verbal responses given by an individual when he describes himself are accurate ones. For purposes of this discussion, we are defining the self as the individual as known by the individual with no intent to deceive anyone. Research involving self definitions must in one way or another come to grips with possible deception. Some social scientists such as Symonds and Hilgard are skeptical about the validity of the individual's conscious self-reports. Both believe that projective materials, clinical interviews, and external observations are more accurate methods of obtaining information about self definitions. They maintain that one's conscious self picture can be distorted by "unconscious" factors as well as by conscious defenses.

I'm Not That Way

A client says, "The real truth of the matter is that I'm not the sweet, forebearing guy that I try to make out that I am. I get irritated at things. I feel like snapping at people, and I feel like being selfish at times, and I don't know why I should pretend I'm not that way."
—Carl R. Rogers.*

---

* Carl R. Rogers, "Learning To Be Free" in *Conflict and Creativity,* ed. by Seymour M. Farber and Roger H. L. Wilson (New York: McGraw-Hill Book Co., 1963), p. 269.

In discussing this point, Shlein [9] makes the statement that "it is perfectly true that if one is to attach validity to self-descriptions one makes the assumption that the described truly knows himself and is willing as well as able to reveal what he knows." When Shlein says that "one makes the assumption that the described *truly knows* himself," he falls into the trap of assuming that there is a "true" or "real" self upon which all must or should agree. This also poses the question, then, of how one knows what this "real" self is. It would seem to be of greater utility to recognize that three possible variables can be measured and taken into account in research:

1. The individual as known by the individual. Thus, whatever he sincerely believes he is is his "self."

2. The individual as known by others.

3. The individual's responses to projective tests of one kind or another, which, in effect, is a subdivision of No. 2.

If we recognize that the three measures of the individual's behavior need not—indeed, most likely never will—agree completely one with the other, then we are prepared to proceed with our research in such a way that we take these differences into account. Each of these approaches taps different types of behavior. There would seem to be no justification for assuming that there should be 100 per cent agreement between them, although it certainly is a scientifically researchable project to determine the relationships that do exist between any of them and then attempt to account for the existing relationships.

If one subscribes to the theory that "unconscious" factors can distort perception, it follows that these unconscious distortions can occur when the individual describes himself and also when the observer describes the individual. Restricting attention to empirical phenomena and training in objectivity, however, can reduce such distortion. The more productive course is for the researcher not to concern himself with the question of whether or not the self definitions he identifies through some projective technique

[9] Shlein, *op. cit.*, p. S114.

or the self configuration the individual provides is the "real self." Why not just explore the relationships that obtain between answers given on a projective device and other types of behavior? As we have used the term "self definitions" the definitions provided by the researcher fall outside our meaning. We have restricted self definitions to the definitions of an individual *held by the same individual*—not by some researcher. This in no way belittles research involving any projective techniques, but rather sharpens the theoretical interpretation.

SUMMARY

In this chapter we have talked about self definitions and have related this discussion to previous discussions of definitions of which it is a part. We have avoided talking about the "self," which could easily be interpreted as identifying some mystical entity believed to exist somewhere inside the individual.

In the same way that an individual learns to provide labels for the objects he learns to take into account, he learns to provide labels for various aspects of himself, including his external and internal biological makeup and his behavior patterns, including his thinking patterns. Such definitions we have called self definitions.

Self definitions, which are constantly involved in an individual's behavior, include value definitions and role definitions and are related to the possessions of the individual. Such definitions are learned and reaffirmed through an empathic or looking-glass process by observing the others, particularly significant others, with whom one interacts. Such definitions change with the social experiences of the individual. Religion may be involved in this process and may expand or contract such definitions depending upon the evaluation thus provided. Such definitions when firmly established are difficult to change.

The names one places upon himself are important determiners of behavior in that they locate him within particular groups and provide value identifications as well as distinguish his unique aspects. Various techniques are used to defend prized self definitions.

Definitions of the individual by the individual may be different from definitions held by specific others, or definitions determined through projective techniques. To possess an understanding of each type of definition may be useful for certain purposes.

QUESTIONS

1. What problems might result in sociological research from using "self" as a noun?
2. To what does one pay attention if he wants to study self definitions?
3. Relate the concepts "norm definitions," "role definitions," and "self definitions."
4. Discuss the statement: "A man is known by the company he keeps, but he also knows himself by the company he keeps."
5. Discuss the statement that "religion expands one's self definitions to infinite proportions."
6. If you want to study the "real self" or "real self definitions," to what do you pay attention? How do you know it is "real"?
7. What are some of the ways in which one goes about protecting his self definitions?
8. Relate the concepts "self definitions" and "significant others."
9. Why is it difficult to maintain a set of self definitions if the others with whom you interact refuse to confirm these definitions?
10. How is selective perception involved in the development and maintenance of self definitions?

PROJECT

By this stage of your course in sociology you have reached some decisions about what kind of a sociology student you are—you have, so to speak, acquired some "sociology-student self conceptions." Analyze the process by which you have acquired these definitions. How has professor-student interaction been involved? How has student-student interaction been involved? What would have to happen during the rest of the course to make you change these definitions?

SUGGESTED READING

Couch, Carl J. "Self-Attitudes and Degree of Agreement with Immediate Others," *The American Journal of Sociology*, LXIII, No. 5 (March, 1956), 491–496.

Goffman, Erving. *The Presentation of Self in Everyday Life.* Garden City, N. Y.: Doubleday & Co., Inc., 1959. (An Anchor Book.)

Kuhn, Manford H., and Thomas S. McPartland. "An Empirical Investigation of Self-Attitudes," *American Sociological Review*, XIX, No. 1 (February, 1954), 68–76.

Lynd, Helen Merrell. *On Shame and the Search for Identity.* New York: Harcourt, Brace and World, Inc., 1958.

Mead, George H. *Mind, Self and Society*, ed. Charles W. Morris. Chicago: The University of Chicago Press, 1934.

Miyamoto, S. Frank, and Sanford M. Dornbusch. "A Test of Interactionist Hypotheses of Self Conception," *The American Journal of Sociology*, LXI, No. 5 (March, 1956), 399–403.

Reeder, Leo G., George Donahue, and Arturo Biblarz. "Conceptions of Self and Others," *The American Journal of Sociology*, LXVI, No. 2 (September, 1960), 153–159.

Stone, Gregory P. "Appearance and the Self," in Arnold M. Rose (ed.), *Human Behavior and Social Processes.* Boston: Houghton Mifflin Co., 1962. Pp. 86–118.

Strauss, Anselm. *Mirrors and Masks.* New York: The Free Press of Glencoe, Inc., 1959.

Sullivan, H. S. *The Interpersonal Theory of Psychiatry.* New York: W. W. Norton & Co., Inc., 1953.

11

Definitions of the Situation

Suppose you go home for a weekend, expecting your mother to greet you at the door, since she has written that she is anxiously awaiting your visit. When you arrive the door is locked, the car is gone, and the neighbors report that they do not know where she is. How do you go about relating all of the known factors so that they make sense to you? How do you define the situation?

A popular expression maintains that there is a time and a place for everything. Without endorsing the implied appropriateness of any existing relationships, we can recognize that everything that happens does so in a particular place and at a particular time and that these factors will inevitably be related to behavior. A major premise of sociological theory is that social behavior is always relative to:

1. The situation, or more specifically, the characteristics of the environment or the "life space" in which it takes place (objective reality), as well as

2. The definitions of the situation provided by those interacting therein (subjective reality).

Situational factors, which are related to interaction patterns, include the geographic and climatic factors, physical arrangement of objects

and people,[1] size of the group, time sequences involved,[2] and established social systems. Besides any direct influence these factors have, there is the additional influence of the definition of the situation. Situations typically persist in time or have a recurrent character. The people involved may use definitions learned in the past in their current efforts to define the situation. As the relationship between the actor and certain recurrent aspects of the situation becomes stabilized, interaction itself develops an orderly character, and interaction *systems* are established. Both the situation and the definition of the situa-

[1] See Bernard Steinzor, "The Spatial Factor in Face to Face Discussion Groups," in A. Paul Hare, Edgar F. Borgatta, and Robert F. Bales (eds.), *Small Groups* (New York: Alfred A. Knopf, Inc., 1955), pp. 348–353.

[2] See Wilbert E. Moore, *Man, Time and Society* (New York: John Wiley & Sons, Inc., 1963).

tion are involved in behavior. We will, however, in this chapter devote major attention to an analysis of the definition of the situation.

Previous discussions have emphasized the importance of definitions in human behavior. Definitions of the situation are a particular type of definition, to which all of our previous discussions apply, but of sufficient uniqueness to warrant the separate discussion here. The major uniqueness of this definition lies in its synthesizing aspect.

It is impossible to comprehend everything at once. The process of situational definition al-

ways involves selective perception. Such perception, however, involves processes different from those in single-object definition, about which much of our previous discussion has centered. Each of the chapters in this section has identified separate elements of the culture system (definitions) to which special attention has been given. None of these, of course, actually exists in isolation. It is sociologically sound to say that each has an influence upon each of the others, and further, that those involved in any related behavior may or may not be aware of all of the existing interrelationships. Interacting human

Figure 11.1 Behavior is relative to the situation. When looking for bargains, women may overlook factors with which they would be concerned in a different situation. (Wide World Photos.)

Re-interpretation

One study, conducted on a number of people undergoing psychoanalysis, turned up a wide discrepancy between what the subject recalls directly after dreaming and what he later tells his analyst he dreamed. Some dreams are entirely omitted in talking to the analyst, others suffer major changes, deletions, or embroidery.
—Lawrence Lessing.*

beings, however, make efforts, with varying degrees of sophistication, to integrate the various elements involved into some meaningful whole. These efforts at integration are a major concern of this chapter.

In defining the *situation* individuals pay attention to enough of the interrelated aspects to reach a decision about the broad situation of which each individual aspect is but one part. Defining the situation requires a synthesizing process of some kind, or what MacIver calls a "dynamic assessment" so that the various aspects to which attention is given are somehow tied together and viewed as a meaningful whole. Such definitions are involved in man's efforts somehow to make sense out of a configuration of things. The synthesizing process involves ignoring certain aspects and highlighting others, ignoring elements that are "out of place," defining dissonant factors as being unimportant for current purposes, or maybe not even seeing them. To a degree at least, we see what we are prepared to see.

Those who watch a stage drama recognize that the actors are each playing a stage role and response to the observed behavior is made accordingly. In a crime scene, for instance, no one from the audience rushes forward to attempt to stop the "murder." Performances in which the audience can forget the artificiality of the production and "lose themselves" in the play are defined as superior performances, but the audience can

rapidly be brought back to "reality." The behavior of the actors, the audience, ticket takers, ushers, and others involved is integrated so that the various parts fit together. The behavior of any of those involved makes sense *in that situation*. In a different situation a different interpretation would apply. One of the reasons the individual segments of behavior are meaningful is that they are related to the larger definition of the situation.

The influence of the definition of the situation upon interpretations of behavior is clearly seen in game behavior. Behavior involved in "playing a game" is different from that in the serious business of living. The importance of the definition of the situation in such behavior is shown in Goffman's analysis of how participants are willing to forswear for the duration of the game any apparent interest in the esthetic, sentimental, or monetary value of the equipment employed, adhering to what he calls the "rules of irrelevance."

It appears that whether checkers are played with bottle tops on a piece of squared linoleum, with gold figurines on inlaid marble, or with uniformed men standing on colored flagstones in a specially arranged court square, the pairs of players can start with the "same" positions, employ the same sequence of strategic moves and countermoves, and generate the same contour of excitement.[3]

In playing a game one figuratively places a "frame" around a configuration of immediate events, thereby determining the type of sense or meaning that will be accorded everything within the frame. Rules of relevance and irrelevance are strictly applied but, of course, only for the duration of the playing.

Once the situation has been defined, decisions can be made as to what behavior and objects can appropriately be woven into the interaction sequence and what cannot. "Slips of the tongue," "boners," or other behavior which is seen as inappropriate for the situation may be viewed as humorous, embarrassing, or in more severe terms, depending upon the extent to which it deviates from what is appropriate to that situation.

---

* Lawrence Lessing, "Sleep," *Fortune* (June, 1964), 125.

[3] Erving Goffman, *Encounters* (Indianapolis: Bobbs-Merrill Co., Inc., 1961), p. 20.

The relationship of the definition of the situation to behavior can be further illustrated by an analysis of the behavior of the new college student as he goes through the procedure of deciding what behavior is appropriate to each classroom situation. When he goes to his first English class, he begins to take into account various situational elements: a specific professor, a particular group of students, a set of texts and classroom equipment, a particular room in a particular building, and a particular time sequence. During the next few meetings the elements are viewed as somewhat discrete units, but after repeated class meetings the whole configuration is integrated into a somewhat consistent setting or situation in which his behavior takes place.

When he seeks the room for his first class, he takes note of the building, the room number, and the hour of meeting, as well as the new professor, so that he is sure that he is "in the right place" for his class. Later the procedure becomes routine and the transition from playing the role of an English student to playing his role as, say, a sociology student, is made unconsciously as he leaves the first classroom and moves to the second. When he does enter the sociology classroom, however, he is prepared to behave in a way appropriate to that particular setting. Decisions as to how he will behave are influenced not only by the situation in which behavior takes place, but by his definition of the situation as well.

The same thing is true of all behavior. Decisions as to how the individual will behave are related to his decisions about the situation in which he finds himself. Making interpretations of the behavior of others likewise involves paying attention to the situation in which their behavior takes place. And this is true of interpretations of past behavior and anticipations of future behavior, of self and of others.

Awareness of the influence which the definition of the situation has upon behavior has been shown in research [4] in which the respondents were asked to identify the situations under which they were most likely to become sexually aroused. None of the approximately 300 students participating reported any difficulty in identifying such conditions. Some of the answers given to this question are as follows. These were selected for their contrast effect.

1. When alone with a member of the opposite sex.

2. Dancing in a dark room, low lights, and dreamy music, with a person I like very much.

3. I become most aroused when I am in bed with my wife and in "hot" movies.

4. When sex is made smutty or filthy or terribly vulgar.

5. When my wife wears her red slip.

6. When seeing a very well-proportioned woman fully clothed or almost so.

We See What We Have Learned To See

Now this is indeed a curious thing. In the half a century or more that psychologists have been interested in predicting the behavior of human beings in complex social situations they have persistently avoided the incontrovertible importance of the specific situation on behavior. They have assumed that if they could only produce a somewhat better schema for attempting to describe an individual's personality from a purely internal point of view they could somehow or other overcome this failure to predict. So they have gone from faculties and instincts and sentiments to traits, drives, needs, and the interaction of these within the individual, producing schema for personality organization and classification of internal states, and ignoring an analysis of the psychological situations in which human beings behave.

—Julian B. Rotter.*

---

* Julian B. Rotter, "The Role of the Psychological Situation in Determining the Direction of Human Behavior," in Richard C. Teevan and Robert C. Birney (eds.), *Theories of Motivation in Personality and Social Psychology* (Princeton, N. J.: D. Van Nostrand Co., Inc., 1964), p. 164.

[4] Unpublished research by the author.

7. Certain provocative clothing arouses me quite thoroughly, especially clothing that requires much imagination. For example, I'm more aroused by a sheath dress than I am by a low cut dress.

8. (Female) When viewing very virile, sleek male animals such as horses or lions.

9. (Male) Naturally by handling the genital organs with sexual thoughts in mind.

10. (Male) Pornographic literature is what I have found that gets me sexually excited very rapidly.

11. The "hot" shows in Las Vegas seem to have *no* effect on me.

12. Seeing exposed parts of the female body.

13. I get sexually aroused more by females in sheer clothing than in the nude.

The view that sexual behavior is primarily biological in nature or is caused primarily by internal drives is difficult to maintain if, as these statements suggest, such behavior can be shown to be related to the situation.

Failure to relate behavior to situational factors may lead to difficulty in interpreting the behavior of others (role taking) among scientists and non-scientists alike. Scientific predictions always carry the provision "other things being equal." Once "other things" begin to change, the observed behavior may change also. Interpretation of various types of tests, such as personality tests and job aptitude tests, is more accurate if the interpretation is related to the situation. Behavior exhibited in the classroom or the counselor's office may not be exhibited in the home or the job situation.

Interpretations of tests which indicate that what is being tested is "the individual" rather than "the individual in a particular setting" leave out this important dimension. Testing obviously is not only an individual phenomenon but also a social or interactive phenomenon, involving a tester and the individual tested in a particular setting. This factor was ignored in a discussion of the use of drugs in which the statement was made: "It is now possible to act directly on the individual to modify his behavior instead of, as in the past, indirectly through modification of the environment." [5] Such a statement implies that the one administering the drug and the drug *per se* are not a part of the environment of the individual receiving the drug. For any individual, the medical doctor who administers drugs, or anything else for that matter, is a part of his environment and is an integral part of the interactive sequence. Behavior always takes place in a particular environment (situation) and is related to situational factors.

Situational factors may account for the fact that a test developed by the Air Force for radar mechanics with a high face validity was found to be non-predictive of the behavior of individuals on the job. Also, in studying the relationship between ethnocentric attitudes and rigidity in problem solving, significant results of a directly opposite nature have been found in different studies. [6]

Scores on intelligence tests have been found to be related to such factors as the examiner, the purpose of the test, the instructions, and the orientation of the examiner. [7] There is also suggestive evidence that answers given on projective tests are related to the sex and personality of the examiner as well as to the physical place of testing. [8]

SELECTIVE PERCEPTION AND SYNTHESIS

The definition of the situation is not something the individual discovers "out there" as he relates himself to others; it is, rather, a definition provided by the individual doing the defining. The

[5] John B. DeC. M. Saunders, in the Introduction to *Control of the Mind*, Seymour M. Farber and Robert H. L. Wilson (eds.) (New York: McGraw-Hill Book Co., 1961), p. xii.

[6] Julian B. Rotter, "The Role of the Psychological Situation in Determining the Direction of Human Behavior," in Richard C. Teevan and Robert C. Birney (eds.), *Theories of Motivation in Personality and Social Psychology* (Princeton, N. J.: D. Van Nostrand Co., Inc., 1964), p. 165.

[7] S. Sarason, "The Test Situation and the Problem of Prediction," *Journal of Clinical Psychology*, VI, No. 4 (October, 1950), 387–392.

[8] R. G. Gibby, *et al.*, "The Examiner's Influence on the Rorschach Protocol," *Journal of Consulting Psychology*, XVII (1953), 425–428; and E. E. Lord, "Experimentally Induced Variations in Rorschach Performance," *Psychological Monographs*, LXV, No. 10 (1950), 1–34.

fact that such definitions are provided is related to the fact that individuals expect to find order in their world. Any phenomenon, large or small, can be viewed in any number of different ways. The perceived order in the situation may not correspond to the relationships that actually obtain. The perceived order (subjective reality), however, becomes the "effective environment" as far as subsequent behavior is concerned. It is true of these definitions as it is of all definitions that constant assessments and reassessments are made as interaction progresses.

The synthesizing process by which the various elements involved are related to each other is suggested, in over-simplified form, by the manner in which distance is judged. In general, decisions about distance take into account the fact that other things being equal,

Far objects appear:	Near objects appear:
small	large
to move slowly	to move swiftly
bluish in color	bright in color
overlaid by near objects	to cover distant objects
blurred in outline	distinct in outline

Particular decisions about distance may involve synthesizing several of these factors in a manner similar to that suggested by Berrien and Bash: [9]

As I look out the window, a large tan automobile stands beyond a smaller blue car. The factors of color and size alone would indicate that the smaller car is the more distant of the two. These two cues are balanced by the single cue that the blue car appears to "cover" parts of the tan car. There is no hesitancy in my judgment of the relative distance of these cars, and I have not the slightest doubt that my judgment is "correct." The balancing of these contradictory cues takes place instantly.

Further suggestions as to the manner in which this synthesizing process works are provided in experiments using the stereoscope devised by a psychologist, Edward Engel.[10] In previous re-

[9] F. K. Berrien and Wendell H. Bash, *Human Relations: Comments and Cases* (New York: Harper & Row, Inc., 1951), pp. 54–55.
[10] Reported by Hadley Cantril, "Perception and Interpersonal Relations," *The American Journal of Psychiatry,* CXIII (1957), 119–127.

Synthesizing

. . . Pudovkin described a little experiment in film editing. A simple, passive close-up of the well-known Russian actor, Mosjukhin, was joined to three different strips of film. In one this close-up was followed by a shot of a bowl of soup on the table; in another it was followed by shots showing a dead woman in a coffin; in the third it was followed by shots of a little girl playing with a funny toy bear. The effects on an unsuspecting audience were terrific, according to Pudovkin. The public raved about the acting of the artist. They pointed out the heavy pensiveness of his mood over the forgotten soup, were touched and moved by the deep sorrow with which he looked at the dead woman, and admired the light, happy smile with which he surveyed the girl at play. But we knew that in all three cases the face was exactly the same.

—Charles E. Osgood.*

search the stereoscope was used to study binocular rivalry and fusion, using dots and lines or geometrical patterns upon which the attention of the one being studied was focused. Engel, however, used "stereograms" consisting of photographs, 2×2 inches, one of which was seen with the left and the other with the right eye. Using photographs of the members of the Princeton football team just as they appeared in the football program, he found that the person looking at the "two" photographs did not see two faces but a synthesized face. When the viewer was asked to describe the face he almost invariably described a composite created from the features of both pictures and incorporating those features of each that the viewer found to be most attractive and appealing.

Such synthesizing is an extremely complex process, in which many elements or units are viewed as being related to each other, as well as to the behavior at hand—whatever it may be.

* Charles E. Osgood, "Cognitive Dynamics in the Conduct of Human Affairs," *Public Opinion Quarterly* XXIV, No. 2 (Summer, 1960), 341–365.

Figure 11.2 Many factors are synthesized in deciding whether a situation warrants particular actions. (Wide World Photos.)

In defining the situation, attention is paid to such things as (1) empirical objects present, as well as those which are not present—at times what is not there is as important in the synthesizing process as what is there; (2) relationships between such objects, including, of course, the human objects involved. A particular item may be defined differently in conjunction with other items than when by itself. Part of the meaning of any item may derive from the larger pattern of which it is but one part. (3) Time sequences in which current factors are related to past as well as to future conditions. Behavior and other events are frequently viewed as comprising "episodes" or blocks of interrelated or interpenetrating elements, to use Parsons' terminology.

Efforts to define the situation usually involve reaching decisions about a series of items and events that are seen as being sequentially related. (4) Decisions about NER concepts or dimensions may also be involved, as in the case of the stereograms discussed above. Decisions about beauty, economic value, utility, or supernatural aspects may be involved. Homans [11] suggests the following as a generalization about human behavior:

If in the past the occurrence of a particular stimulus-situation has been the occasion on which a man's activity has been rewarded, then the more similar

[11] George Caspar Homans, *Social Behavior: Its Elementary Forms* (New York: Harcourt, Brace & World, Inc., 1961), p. 53.

the present stimulus-situation is to the past one, the more likely he is to emit the activity or some similar activity now.

(5) Decisions about the motives of individuals involved, which may, of course, include NER concepts such as those just listed.

Synthesizing is an acquired ability, and it follows that not everyone has equal facility and (in harmony with the major point of this chapter) that the same individual may not be equally effective in all situations. Some of the factors that appear to be related to synthesizing performance are the following.

1. *Limited information may be available about people and other objects involved.* Most likely there is a positive correlation between the amount of information available and the accuracy of the interpretation. Misinformation as well as ignorance of relevant factors would obviously be related. Making decisions with limited information or knowledge is like driving a car on a dark or foggy night. There are few cues to which you can pay attention and these can be misinterpreted. However, as Steiner has pointed out, accuracy of perception will materially affect social interaction only when such accuracy is relevant to the immediate interaction.

Glaser and Strauss [12] also point out that under situations defined as appropriate, pertinent information may be deliberately withheld from one or more of the participants, as in some doctor–patient relationships in which death is an immediate possibility. Such a relationship is called one of "closed awareness," which is contrasted with one of "open awareness" in which each "interactant" is aware of the identity of the other and also the identity imputed to him by this other. "Suspicion awareness" is a relationship in which one suspects the true identity of the other or of the other's view of him, without the other being aware of the suspicion; whereas "pretense awareness" involves a relationship in which both are fully aware of the identity of the other as

A War Situation

The captain was a Southerner in his mid-twenties. He had been a rifle company commander on the Western Front. He was very well liked by both his fellow-patients and by the hospital personnel. His outstanding personality traits were modesty and the friendliness and kindliness of his disposition. As a boy he had been fond of duck-hunting but had given up the sport because, as he said, "I didn't see much fun in killing." Once, during a discussion of war experiences, he told the following story:

He had commanded a company during the disastrous Battle of the Bulge, when the German Army had broken through the American lines in the Ardennes Forest. The Captain found himself cut off from the rest of our forces and surrounded by the enemy. His situation was desperate. He had only about forty men left, no food, little ammunition and no idea where the American lines were. In addition to these difficulties, his company had a large number of German-prisoners on hand. There was no way to get rid of the prisoners by sending them to a camp in the rear area. Guarding them with his depleted forces was out of the question.

Therefore, he determined to kill the prisoners. He and the sergeant took them out in the woods in small groups and shot them. Among the captain's group was a young boy, only about 15 or 16 years old. The captain concluded his story with this remark: "He was crying and begging me to save him and I was kind of sorry I had to kill him."

—Hadley Cantril.*

well as the identity the other imputes to him, but both pretend not to be. No doubt such relationships are each situationally relevant.

2. *Answers secured by inferences are often open to question.* This includes answers relative to motivational factors and answers about past

---

[12] Barney G. Glaser and Anselm L. Strauss, "Awareness Contexts and Social Interaction," *American Sociological Review*, XXIX, No. 5 (October, 1964), 669–679.

The Secret

An agreement or secret between two persons, ties each of them in a very different manner than if even only three have a part in it. This is perhaps most characteristic of the secret. General experience seems to indicate that this minimum of two, with which the secret ceases to be the property of the one individual, is at the same time the maximum at which its preservation is relatively secure.

—George Simmel.*

and future events. Inability to distinguish between inference and fact may likewise introduce confusion and inaccuracy. In the normal course of social events, many decisions are of necessity made on the basis of inference.

3. *Perception is always selective.* Some, however, is more so than others. Individuals may become "obsessed" with a particular concern or some particular aspect of interaction and consequently cannot see the broader picture. Many antecedent conditions may be causally related to such conditions.

4. *Lack of experience is involved.* To take an obvious example, children frequently have difficulty interpreting the behavior of adults, in part because they have not had the experience necessary to "understand what is going on."

5. *The concepts the individual has acquired are obviously involved in efforts to synthesize.* The previous statement that learning a language involves learning how to respond to the world applies to synthesizing activity as it does to all behavior. The novice who finds himself in a data-processing center has difficulty deciding what is going on, except in very broad terms, in part because he does not even know the names of the various units that are related to each other, to say nothing of the plans of action that have been developed. There is truth to the statement, "You can't enjoy the game without a program."

6. *Situational factors such as the degree of order which obtains are involved.* Confusion breeds confusion. Whether the situation is one of stress or relaxation is also relevant.

Two logically different processes may be involved in defining the situation. (1) Attention may be paid to the discrete elements and then the over-all picture is constructed to take them into account. This involves going from the particular to the general. (2) The larger configuration may be identified, possibly from paying attention to some limited aspects, and then relating the constituent parts to this larger definition. Piaget calls this latter process "syncrestic" thinking.

This second method of reaching decisions was found by Riddleberger and Motz [13] to be the one by which prejudiced individuals perceived American Negroes. From an analysis of the reactions given to a series of pictures they concluded that "subjects define an individual in terms of the total situation to a greater extent than in terms of any clues gained from the individual's facial or physical features."

VALUE DEFINITIONS

Value definitions may stem from particular situational definitions, but they may also contribute to or color such definitions. Environments and/or relationships that involved prized or valued objects may themselves be evaluated more highly as a result. This frequently happens with reference to prized religious objects or experiences. The high value, perhaps even sacredness, attributed to objects or individuals may be generalized to other environmental or situational factors. The physical area, for instance, where individuals are believed to have had a religious vision may take on a sacred aura and may become a shrine to which pilgrimages may be made. The same may be true of experiences with a loved one, which accounts in part for

* George Simmel (1858–1918), "The Significance of Numbers for Social Life," in A. Paul Hare, *et al.*, *Small Groups* (New York: Alfred A. Knopf, Inc., 1955), p. 13.

[13] Alice B. Riddleberger and Annabelle B. Motz, "Prejudice and Perception," *The American Journal of Sociology*, LXII, No. 5 (March, 1957), 498–503.

efforts to preserve souvenirs and mementos that have been associated with highly valued individuals or experiences. Efforts to recall or relive past experiences may, of course, be aided by paying attention to such physical phenomena.

Situational factors usually have a "qualifying" effect upon value definitions. Such definitions and related norm-role definitions are frequently stated and endorsed as absolutes: "Thou shalt not kill," "Honesty is the best policy," or "It is better to have loved and lost than never to have loved at all." These statements are absolute in that they are stated without qualification, implying that they apply equally to all situations. It is doubtful, however, if any individuals apply such value definitions in an absolute manner. One of the dynamic aspects of role playing and role taking, in fact, is relating the value definitions to the definitions of the situations and deciding which set of value definitions applies to which situation and which does not.

To illustrate this point with reference to the commandment "Thou shalt not kill," we can point to the fact that many people would qualify this to mean that under certain conditions (situations) such as in times of war, killing in defense of one's country is justifiable. States which have and use capital punishment obviously endorse killing under certain conditions. Killing in defense of one's honor or one's virginity has also been frequently approved. The Roman Catholic Church defines as justifiable a war with its attendant killing, under the following conditions: (1) when it is necessary to defend the rights of the state in grave matters; (2) when it is undertaken only as a last resort; (3) when it is conducted according to national and international law; and (4) when it is discontinued after satisfaction has been offered by the unjust nation.[14]

Groups, particularly religious groups, frequently talk of "eternal values" with the implication at least that the value definitions apply eternally and in all circumstances. Justice, beauty, and

Motive Decisions in Extreme Situations

The numerous accounts of concentration camp survivors bear a notable common theme: when asked what hope kept them going they replied, in the words of one, "to come out alive and unchanged."

. . . To the extent that it is literally true that the self-respecting individual guarantees, in some final encounter, to choose death over dishonor, it would seem that the limiting (ultimate) case on the continuum of extreme situations is not the one in which a threat to physical survival is carried out, but the one beyond it. That is, the threatened individual who commits an intolerably degrading act of acquiescence to preserve his life accepts a "fate worse than death"—a self altered and despised.

*—Bernard Rosenberg, et al.**

honor are frequently so classified. These are all NER labels, the content of which cannot be checked against any empirical phenomena. Continued acceptance of these as eternal value definitions is related to the fact that the NER label can be endorsed and viewed as "eternal" while the immediate content as to just what behavior is just, modest, fair, or beautiful can be changed as the situation changes—but all in the name of unchange. Religious leaders in their official role playing, and others in their everyday decisions, constantly make decisions as to which set of value definitions applies under which situations, and there are undoubtedly situations under which any particular "eternal" value definition is viewed as being inapplicable.

NORM-ROLE DEFINITIONS

Norm definitions apply to human behavior in general. Mores are more general than folkways and apply in most situations. Folkways are more situationally relevant and likely to be more often

---

[14] See Charles Samuel Braden, *War, Communism and World Religions* (New York: Harper & Row, Inc., 1953), pp. 250–255.

* Bernard Rosenberg, Israel Gerver, and F. William Howton, *Mass Society in Crisis* (New York: The Macmillan Co., 1964), p. 159.

A Time for Fun

A recent development in American culture is the emergence of what we may call "fun morality." Here fun, from having been suspect if not taboo, has tended to become obligatory. Instead of feeling guilty for having too much fun, one is inclined to feel ashamed if one does not have enough.

—Martha Wolfenstein.*

---

disregarded than mores. This applies, of course, not only to the individual's own behavior but also to his expectations of the behavior of others.

Role definitions, however, always carry the situational stipulation that the behavior applies only in those situations in which the individual occupies a particular position, or when he defines himself and is defined by others as playing a particular role. In other situations, different role definitions are applied.

An individual defines his position in terms of the situation. Changes in situational factors contribute to changes in role definitions. In a reciprocal manner, individuals define the situation from the perspective of a particular role. To Mr. X as President of the United States, the international situation may look different than to Mr. X as the private citizen. Likewise, to Mr. Y as the fraternity president, the college situation may look quite different than it does to Mr. Y as the unaffiliated college student. Lieberman's research documents this conclusion; he found that the definitions of workers changed rapidly as they moved to and from the positions of foreman and steward in an industrial bureaucracy.[15]

The relevance of the situation to decisions about the applicability of norm-role definitions is clearly seen in reaction to situational factors

* Martha Wolfenstein, "The Emergence of Fun Morality," *Journal of Social Issues* (Society for Psychological Study of Social Issues), VII, No. 4 (1951), 15.

[15] Seymour Lieberman, "The Effects of Changes in Roles and on the Attitudes of Role Occupants," *Human Relations*, IX, No. 4 (1956), 385–403.

defined as an "accident." The accident is usually viewed as an excuse sufficient to relieve one from the usually accepted norm-role obligations. It is a situational factor that permits one to ignore accepted behavior patterns and likewise to avoid societal sanctions. Justification for deviant behavior related to accidents may be enhanced by defining them as "acts of God," which, if the definition is accepted, relieves man of certain responsibility and, it is believed, places it upon a supernatural being.

SELF DEFINITIONS

"What am I?" is a general question that everyone answers; a more specific question is "What am I doing here?" The "here" part of the question relates the individual to the situation and involves decisions as to subsequent behavior. Individuals, for instance, who find themselves in a situation defined as one of debauchery, a sexual orgy, or a mob scene may make efforts to get away, so that they will not be identified by others or by themselves as being involved. They may not even want to watch the activity, possibly feeling that "nice" people don't do such things, and "nice" people don't want to be seen watching such events.

One way to protect valued self definitions is to avoid situations in which oneself or others may have reason to question the definition. If avoidance is impossible, another way to disassociate oneself from the situation is to use some symbol or use some behavior pattern that will communicate to others that you are not to be identified with the other participants. The distinctive dress of a minister, for instance, serves as a protection in that when it is identified in a situation that could be interpreted as "compromising," individuals are likely to take the costume into account and define the wearer's participation as being "in line of duty" rather than as a participant. He may be viewed as being there to help, rather than to participate. The uniform of the policeman may serve the same purpose. The message communicated by such symbols is essentially, "Don't apply particular situational cues to me."

The process by which an individual relates himself to the situation and reaches self decisions about behavior defined as appropriate to the situation is suggested by Griffin [16] in an account of his experiences while "passing" as a Negro in the South.

By dark I was away from the beach area and out in the country.

Strangely I began getting rides. Men would pass you in daylight but pick you up after dark.

I must have had a dozen rides that evening. They blear into a nightmare, one scarcely distinguishable from the other.

It quickly became obvious why they picked me up. All but two picked me up the way they would pick up a pornographic photograph or a book—except that this was verbal pornography. With a Negro they assumed they need give no semblance of self-respect or respectability. The visual element entered into it. In a car at night visibility is reduced. A man will reveal himself in the dark, which gives an illusion of anonymity, more than he will in the bright light. Some were shamelessly open, some shamelessly subtle. All showed morbid curiosity about the sexual life of the Negro, and all had, at base, the same stereotyped image of the Negro as an inexhaustible sex-machine with oversized genitals and a vast store of experiences, immensely varied. . . . I note these things because it is harrowing to see decent-looking men and boys assume that because a man is black they need show him none of the reticences they would, out of respect, show the most derelict white man.

The three important situational factors related to the decisions made by the white men were (1) the racial identification they attributed to the one with whom they were interacting (2) as a stranger; and 3) the anonymity of the "nighttime in a car" situation. In harmony with this conclusion, Festinger, Pepitone, and Newcomb found in their research that in situations of anonymity, individuals were less likely to conform to established norm-role definitions.[17]

SUMMARY

The definitions people use in their decisions about behavior include not only definitions of discrete items such as empirical objects, relationships, time sequences, NER concepts, and motives, but definitions that synthesize individual definitions into a larger configuration. The definitions of the individual items influence the definition of the situation, and the definition of the situation influences the definitions of the discrete items. Some interpretations of behavior, professional and otherwise, overlook this relationship, such as the interpretation of test results suggesting that all that is measured is "the individual," and interpretations of sexual behavior that do not take into account the fact that such behavior always has situational correlates.

Making situational definitions is learned behavior and is influenced by such factors as the accuracy and amount of information available, accuracy of the inferences involved, selectivity of perception, past experience, and concepts available for use. Making decisions about the situation may involve going from the general to the particular or from the particular to the general.

Value definitions may stem from and contribute to situational definitions, and situational factors are usually employed to qualify "eternal" values. Folkways and mores apply to most situations, whereas role definitions are always situationally relevant. The accident is a situational factor seen as justifying non-role-norm enacting, and individuals locate themselves in situations and apply self definitions that take the situational factors into account. In interaction, efforts are made, some more successfully than others, to integrate large configurations of factors such as these so that they all more or less make sense.

[16] John Howard Griffin, *Black Like Me* (Boston: Houghton Mifflin Co., 1961), pp. 84–85. (A Signet Book.)

[17] Leon Festinger, A. Pepitone, and Theodore M. Newcomb, "Some Consequences of De-Individuation in a Group," *Journal of Abnormal and Social Psychology,* XLVII, No. 2 (April, 1952), 382–389.

QUESTIONS

1. Distinguish between the situation and the definitions of the situation.
2. Relate the concepts: definitions of situation, and subjective reality.
3. Suggest a sociological explanation for the fact that analysis of situational factors by social scientists has been somewhat neglected.
4. In what way is testing both an individual and a social phenomenon?
5. What changes in the sociology class situation would lead you to conclude that you were in the wrong place some day when you came to class?

6. How can you tell whether any particular value definition is an eternal one?
7. Provide an illustration of how you or an acquaintance have used an "accident" as justification for not following norm-role restrictions.
8. How do you decide how to behave in strange situations?
9. From your school experiences provide illustrations of how situational factors have influenced your performance on tests.
10. How would you let a friend know that you felt that his behavior was not appropriate for some particular situation?

PROJECT

Listen to a short movie without looking at the screen and report the problems of trying to decide what is going on without the use of visual cues. Then look at the movie without any sound and report the interpretation difficulties experienced without verbal cues.

SUGGESTED READING

BALES, ROBERT F., and EDGAR F. BORGATTA. "Size of Group as a Factor in the Interaction Profile," in A. PAUL HARE, EDGAR F. BORGATTA, and ROBERT F. BALES (eds.), *Small Groups.* New York: Alfred A. Knopf, Inc., 1955.

BERRIEN, F. K., and WENDELL H. BASH. *Human Relations: Comments and Cases.* New York: Harper & Row, Inc., 1957. Pp. 40–69.

COTTRELL, LEONARD S., JR. "The Analysis of Situational Fields in Social Psychology," *American Sociological Review,* VII, No. 3 (June, 1942), 370–382.

MOORE, WILBERT E. *Man, Time, and Society.* New York: John Wiley & Sons, Inc., 1963.

NEWCOMB, THEODORE M. *Social Psychology.* New York: Holt, Rinehart and Winston, Inc., 1950.

ROTTER, JULIAN B. "The Role of the Psychological Situation in Determining the Direction of Human Behavior," in RICHARD C. TEEVAN and ROBERT C. BIRNEY (eds.), *Theories of Motivation in Personality and Social Psychology.* Princeton, N. J.: D. Van Nostrand Co., Inc., 1964. Pp. 162–183.

SARASON, S. "The Test Situation and the Problem of Prediction," *Journal of Clinical Psychology,* VI, No. 4 (October, 1950), 387–392.

SIMMEL, GEORGE. "The Significance of Numbers for Social Life," in A. PAUL HARE, EDGAR F. BORGATTA, and ROBERT F. BALES (eds.), *Small Groups.* New York: Alfred A. Knopf, Inc., 1955. Pp. 9–15.

STEINZOR, BERNARD. "The Spatial Factor in Face to Face Discussion Groups," in A. PAUL HARE, EDGAR F. BORGATTA, and ROBERT F. BALES (eds.), *Small Groups.* New York: Alfred A. Knopf, Inc., 1955.

THOMAS, W. I. *Social Behavior and Personality.* New York: Social Science Research Council, 1951.

Part IV

The Interaction Process

12

Socialization

Socialization is defined at times as the process by which the individual acquires his culture, or the process by which what exists outside the individual is "internalized" or placed inside of him. How useful for scientific research is the "internalization" concept? To what empirical phenomenon can you pay attention if you want to determine whether the culture of the group has been placed inside the individual? How might the process be defined to increase its scientific utility?

INTRODUCTION

The previous chapters have provided the foundation for our current discussion of the process of socialization. They have emphasized that human beings do not have any biologically built-in mechanisms which automatically direct their social behavior or drive them to participate in one group or another. Rather, the biological inheritance of the normal human being provides only the physical characteristics necessary for learning. Unique physical conditions may, of course, impose limitations upon subsequent learning. However, social behavior, particularly during the early years of life, is primarily learned from the others with whom one interacts. *Socialization* is the name used by sociologists to identify this learning process.

In broad terms, socialization is the process by which beings who are biologically human become socially human. It is the process by which man acquires his social behavior patterns. We do not, however, restrict the term to the learning experiences of the young child but use it to identify a life-long process. Socialization that involves the learning of a culture on the part of an individual or individuals already socialized in another society with a different culture is called *assimilation*. In a sense, assimilation is resocialization in that certain things are forgotten or given up while the new culture is being learned. The immigrant goes through such a process. An understanding of the socialization process is an important part of any comprehensive theory or explanation of human behavior. To gain such an understanding is the goal of this chapter.

FUNCTION OF SOCIALIZATION

The broad consequences (functions) of socialization are two-fold. In the first place, the individual learns how to behave in a human manner. Second, from the perspective of the larger group, the society, the function of socialization is the preparation of new members or potential new members to behave in the manner of that group—to do the thing the larger group wants done, to think (define) in the way the group desires, to interact in the approved manner, and further, to *want* to do these things. Integration of the individual into the group is a function of socialization. This function is particularly apparent with reference to the socialization experiences of the newborn child. His parents, as representatives of the larger society, generally make extensive efforts to teach their child to behave in the way they think he should and to place him in situations that will facilitate this learning. The child, of course, although he is actively involved in the socialization process, has only limited influence upon the direction this socialization takes. He comes into a group which has already decided how it expects him to behave. The original desire for assimilation is the desire of the group, not of the individual, although he also will acquire this desire (value definition) if the socialization is successful.

Conscious socialization efforts are usually future-oriented. Parents bring up their children on the assumption that they are anticipating the future of these children. They socialize their children to fit into a particular type of social system. The effectiveness of any particular socialization patterns is always relative to the extent to which future conditions can be accurately anticipated.[1]

Socialization into the society also involves being socialized into various subgroups within the society, with the over-all configuration being somewhat consistent, although dissonance or inconsistencies are always present to one degree or

Importance of Childhood

Many of the most important misconceptions concerning human behavior have materialized through thinking in terms of cause and effect. The idea that the first five years of a child's life are the most important is one of these. Too much emphasis has been placed on childhood experiences per se. In reality, subsequent experiences determine the importance of these early activities. They can have meaning in no other way. The individual is not a product of his childhood, but is the result of what adolescence, youth, and adulthood do to childhood experiences.

—Lawrence Guy Brown.*

another. Viewed through the perspective of the individual being socialized, the function of socialization is to secure entrance into and acceptance by his society and various subgroups.

From the societal perspective, socialization is the process by which many different individuals are prepared to play many different and varied roles and interact in such a way that the interrelated individuals and groups can function as a whole—as a society. Socialization that prepares every new member to be a "chief" is not very effective from the societal point of view.

This is not to imply that in all socialization experiences those involved consciously tell themselves that they are doing what they are doing for the reasons just enumerated. Whatever the immediate intended results may be, the over-all result is to make those involved sufficiently alike that they can function as interacting members of a group and sufficiently different so that the various behavior patterns needed to maintain the society are produced. Socialization efforts may, of course, fail. To the extent that they do the group becomes disorganized.

---

[1] See Yehudi A. Cohen, *Social Structure and Personality, a Casebook* (New York: Holt, Rinehart and Winston, Inc., 1961), chap. iii.

* Lawrence Guy Brown, "The Interaction Hypothesis," in John F. Cuber and Peggy B. Harroff (eds.), *Readings in Sociology* (New York: Appleton-Century-Crofts, 1962), p. 111.

WHAT IS LEARNED—CULTURE AND INTERACTION PATTERNS

Before turning our attention to the socialization process *per se*, let us briefly consider the content of the process. The symbols and their associated definitions with their plans of action which are included in the culture of the group, are, of course, the major part of what is learned in the process of socialization. The ability to engage in the plans of action incorporated in these definitions is also learned. We can, in fact, say that the individual learns how to learn. The young child, for instance, learns how to use symbols and then how to learn through subsequent symbol manipulation.

Through socialization, the individual learns how to interpret or label objects, the others with whom he interacts, himself,[2] and the situation, and how to re-label or re-interpret any of these elements as any of the others change, or as feedback[3] is provided. He learns how to apply value definitions and how to involve these value judgments in his on-going behavior.

Thus, socialization involves learning to want to do certain things and conversely learning to not want to do other things, on the basis of the value definitions involved. The motivational aspects of behavior are not biologically given, and given the right kind of socializing experiences and the supporting social structure, human beings can be taught to want to do almost anything. However, once particular motivational patterns are well established, they become difficult to change.

The content of socialization is always relative to the society in which it takes place. Our previous discussions of culture have emphasized the great variation found in the cultures of different groups. Depending upon the culture of the society certain individuals may be socialized to become, and to want to become, witch doctors, medical doctors, or doctors of philosophy.

SOCIALIZATION INVOLVES RE-INTEGRATION OF PAST EXPERIENCES

Socialization is a continuing process. The process, however, involves more than just the mechanical addition of new definitions and new behavior patterns to those previously learned. It involves a continued re-assessment, or re-orientation of past events so that in one way or another they can be harmonized with the current situation. The manner in which a five-year-old child experiences his Christmas may be quite different from the manner in which the same individual at age twenty-five, or age fifty-five "re-experiences" the Christmas. Past events are re-interpreted in light of the new experiences of the individual or group. Selective remembering constantly takes place. Some, for instance, tend to de-emphasize or forget unpleasant aspects of past experiences and recall nostalgically the "good old days." As one learns new interpretations of behavior, possibly religious, psychoanalytic, sociological, or psychological, past experiences are re-interpreted in terms of the new "insight."

Previous discussions of man's use of symbols have emphasized that man, in a sense, sees what he wants to see or experiences what he had learned to experience. The human process of remembering or recall provides an illustration of this phenomenon.

SOCIALIZATION INVOLVES INTERACTION

Socialization is a process in which those involved are all *active* participants. It involves interaction. Socialization in the college classroom, for instance, involves both teacher and student. As any student is aware, the teacher does not, in fact cannot, in a mechanical arbitrary fashion "pour" his information into passive, completely receptive students who accept it all without question. The condition of the students, which, of course, reflects current situational factors, is an

---

[2] The previous discussion of the origin of self definitions in Chapter 10 illustrates one type of socialization.

[3] "Feedback" means the introduction of information about a completed aspect of a process into the uncompleted process so that attention can be given thereto and adjustment made in the process if so desired.

important factor. Some of them may be so in love that they cannot concentrate, or they may be worrying about flunking out of college. A student may be so excited about the job he just secured that anything the professor presents at the moment does not even get in one ear so that it can go out the other. In addition, the behavior of the students reflects their many previous learning experiences.

Whatever these factors may be, they are related to the amount of learning that takes place. Socialization involves *inter*action, although the degree of active involvement may vary.

The same thing is true of the learning of the very young child. He may not have years of past learning, but his past learning (whatever it is) and his current condition are both involved in the socialization efforts of his mother and father. He is not just a passive sponge, receptive to anything others do to him. Selective perception and selective retention are involved in this as in all behavior. The child is an active agent in the situation. Socialization is a social phenomenon.

Not all learning, however, involves the *direct* and *immediate* involvement of others. As an individual matures and acquires abilities to manipulate symbols (to think) he may come to new decisions by himself. He may experiment with his universe or have unique experiences and from them he may learn. A Robinson Crusoe alone on an island may continue to learn without direct physical interaction with others. Such learning, of course, reflects and is built upon previous interaction experiences. One never gets very far away from his groups; they are always in the background. The individual thinks with their words and in general views things and events as he has been taught to.

Socialization is also accomplished through reading books, journals, and other written material, as any college student is well aware. In such experiences the "other" involved is also "once removed" or maybe "many times removed" from the immediate socializing experience. There are various types of learning, but interaction is directly or indirectly involved in most of them.

Since man is a symbol user, he is able to go beyond the behavior patterns just described and engage in that uniquely human process of "juggling symbols" to see what happens, or experimenting with symbols, arranging and rearranging them in his efforts to secure new insights and new knowledge. Such behavior moves from the realm of socialization *per se* to the realm of creativity—the process by which new culture and new behavior patterns are developed. A subsequent chapter will be devoted to this process.

EARLY STAGES IN THE SOCIALIZATION PROCESS

The socialization process for the very young child can be viewed as taking place in three somewhat distinct stages.[4] First, since the child in the early part of his life has not acquired the ability to manipulate symbols, the original learning (and this includes learning how to use symbols) is different from that which takes place after facility with symbols has been acquired.

Changed Socialization Patterns

Over the entire 25-year period studied, parent-child relationships in the middle class are consistently reported as more acceptant and equalitarian, while those in the working class are oriented toward maintaining order and obedience. Within this context, the middle class has shown a shift away from emotional control toward freer expression of affection and greater tolerance of the child's impulses and desires.
—Urie Bronfenbrenner.*

---

* Urie Bronfenbrenner, "Socialization and Social Class Through Time and Space," in *Readings in Social Psychology*, ed. by E. E. Maccoby, T. M. Newcomb, and E. L. Hartley (3d ed.; New York: Holt, Rinehart and Winston, Inc., 1958), p. 425.

[4] See Arnold M. Rose (ed.), *Human Behavior and Social Processes* (Boston: Houghton Mifflin Co., 1962), chap. i.

This original learning is most likely some variant of conditioning, imitation, trial and error, or a similar process found among other animals. Exactly what is involved is essentially unknown at the moment.

In the second stage, the infant acquires the ability to recall past events to some extent, possibly in the form of pictures. As these events take place again, such as in subsequent feedings by his mother, he is able to recall and anticipate the complete sequence of behavior when exposed to the initial part, such as the presentation of the breast or bottle. When, for some reason, the sequence is not completed, he may still be able to remember the complete sequence. The initial phase "points to" or "stands for" the whole sequence and thus lays the foundation for subsequent use of symbols which stand for particular referents. As the others with whom he interacts consistently place names upon the objects and the sequences of behavior involved in his life, he learns to substitute the common name for whatever has been involved in his previous recall. Once he learns that things and behavior can be named, he then discovers that by using the name or the label he is able to recall the appropriate sequence. He learns that things have names and that the names can be taken into account even though the referent is not present. He also learns that use of the appropriate sound will produce particular actions on the part of others. He learns that saying "wa-wa" will influence his mother in such a way that she gives him a drink of water. Vaguely at first but then more specifically he learns that sounds or gestures made by him are an effective way to influence the behavior of others.

In his initial efforts to associate names with referents he may not use exactly the same names as others of his group, because his world is unstructured and he has not acquired the abilities to pay attention to small details. However, the group to which he belongs, ordinarily a family, will usually exert efforts to assure that he learns the commonly accepted terminology.

In the third stage, the individual uses whatever acquired symbols he has to designate to himself and to others the aspects of his universe and the aspects of himself to which he pays attention. He becomes an increasingly active agent in the socialization process. He learns to identify himself as well as his internal conditions and can take into account and anticipate that others will also take into account his desires, wishes, or wants (value decisions). In this stage the accumulation of symbols expands rapidly, and as new symbols are learned new plans of action are associated with them and new ways of experiencing the world and of taking aspects thereof into account are acquired. It is in this stage that facility in the use of NER symbols is acquired.

Socialization continues throughout the lifetime of the individual. It would be inaccurate to conclude that behavior patterns are so well established at any given age that change is impossible. Social behavior is a dynamic process and it always has its emergent aspects. The rate of change, of course, varies from time to time and from situation to situation.

CONSCIOUS AND UNCONSCIOUS SOCIALIZATION

The socialization process is not restricted to behavior in which a conscious effort is made to teach others particular things or in which a conscious effort is made to learn particular things. It includes such behavior but is not restricted to it. In the process of interaction individuals may learn things that no one ever intended them to learn. Many important definitions and behavior patterns are "caught not taught."

This is particularly true of value definitions, since they involve NER symbols. We cannot experience "goodness" or "badness" directly since there is no empirical referent for these symbols. Learning to use these symbols, rather, is closely related to the experiences one has with others. When an individual has satisfying experiences with other persons, he will likely be receptive to their value definitions. In some cases, he may deliberately determine the value definitions of

What Is Learned?

The attachment of children to parents who by all ordinary standards are very bad is a never-ceasing source of wonder to those who seek to help them.

—John Bowlby.*

such groups and then give serious consideration to the possibility of adopting such definitions himself. In other cases the process may be less deliberate and those involved may be somewhat unaware of what is going on; but in the process of having satisfying relationships with the group and seeking to repeat the experiences, the acquisition of the appropriate value definitions may be somewhat incidental. Crystallization of such definitions may occur when the satisfying relationships are threatened, or when important decisions are made.

The acquisition of value definitions is usually not a "one-shot" phenomenon. Rather, experiences that support certain value definitions gradually provide the foundation out of which firm convictions are developed.

Each individual is but one participant in the larger social system, and he engages in many different but interrelated activities. Throughout his day and week he moves from one position to another, from one group to another, from concern with one subject matter to another. He plays many different formal and informal roles. The interrelations among all of these are not always apparent to him. One type of behavior may influence other types of behavior without his being specifically aware of this. Research by Aberle and Naegele [5] has shown, for instance, how learning to play an occupational role influences the manner in which fathers define their

children. Despite the fact that they were able to determine such a relationship, they report that:

It became clear in the course of research that the relationship which some fathers could see between their job situation and their behavior in the home was trivial, that some fathers could find no connection, and that still others flatly rejected the idea that there could be any connection.

Another process by which those being socialized may acquire definitions not consciously introduced into the interaction is suggested by Berelson and Salter [6] in their analysis of the content of 198 short stories selected from popular magazines. They found that although minorities were not openly and frankly depreciated in these stories, in nearly all cases members of minority groups were portrayed in roles that led to unfavorable comparisons with the "100 per cent Americans." The consistent depreciation of minority groups is implicit and indirect and it is seldom acknowledged or its implications discussed, but it is there and negative definitions of these minority groups may be acquired in the process of reading the stories even though the reader is unaware of them.

Becker and Geer [7] provide an illustration of another type of unconscious socialization as they trace the changes in idealism and cynicism as medical students progress through their training in medical school.

In the process of living with, going to school with, working with, playing with, worshipping with, or fighting with (against a common enemy) certain others we learn many things in addition to the things consciously and deliberately taught. Awareness of what one has learned may be crystallized only when the specific content is somehow called to attention or questions are raised about it.

---

* John Bowlby, *Maternal Care and Mental Health* (Geneva: World Health Organization, 1952), p. 69.

[5] David F. Aberle and Kaspar D. Naegele, "Middle-Class Fathers' Occupational Role and Attitudes Toward Children," *American Journal of Orthopsychiatry*, XXII, No. 2 (April, 1952), 366–378.

[6] Bernard Berelson and Patricia J. Salter, "Majority and Minority Americans: An Analysis of Magazine Fiction," *Public Opinion Quarterly*, X, No. 2 (Summer, 1946), 168–190.

[7] Howard S. Becker and Blanche Geer, "The Fate of Idealism in Medical School," *American Sociological Review*, XXIII, No. 1 (February, 1958), 50–56.

SOCIETY, SUBGROUPS, AND INDIVIDUALS

The process of socialization provides the individual with experiences that serve to identify or locate him in the larger society of which he is a part and also within the subgroups or subsocieties in which his interaction takes place. He will, for instance, at birth acquire a name. The surname will identify him with the group who shares this family name, and his given or "first" name will serve to distinguish him from the others who share the same surname.

He will learn that particular types of behavior are appropriate while interacting with members of one group but are inappropriate for interaction within other groups. One, for instance, is permitted and expected to do certain things in the family group that are inappropriate in the work group. He learns the appropriate labels to identify the behavior patterns and the objects significantly associated with each group.

Such distinctions are not easily acquired. The young child has difficulty understanding what it means to be an American, a New Yorker, a Presbyterian, a lawyer's son, to mention a few possibilities. It is not easy to understand how he can be all of these at once, and yet how, under certain situations and in certain types of interaction, one or the other of a combination of these identifications becomes salient and then fades into insignificance as he moves to other situations. Socialization into various groups goes on simultaneously, and as he matures his identifications generally move from a condition of hazy indistinct labels to relatively clear and distinct identifications. Since socialization is an on-going process, such identifications may, of course, be subject to change at any time, depending upon the experiences of the individual.

Socialization involves the rather difficult task of developing loyalties (value definitions) to the various groups with which one identifies himself, and further (and this is where the complications arise), integrating these value definitions so that they somehow make sense. The individual has to learn when to give precedence to the demands of the nation over the demands of the family, or when the demands or requirements of the peer group take precedence over those of the school or the family. He may attempt to harmonize loyalties to the family of orientation into which he is born with the family of procreation, which he establishes when he gets married.

Then, to complicate the situation even further, he has to learn when his loyalty to himself takes precedence over loyalty to various groups. He develops aspects of "individualism" which harmonize more or less with loyalty to the groups to which he belongs. He also has to learn how to "live with himself" when he conforms to the norm definitions of a group while at the same time he defines other patterns as personally more acceptable.

This is not a simple task in a heterogeneous society such as in contemporary United States or Canada. Resolving conflicting demands or expectations is a task not everyone works out with equal facility. When the conflict becomes intense, certain individuals may react in such a manner that they are defined as neurotic or psychotic and are placed in an institution that isolates them from the major society.

Socialization involves learning how to categorize individuals (including oneself) and groups and how to relate oneself and others. The definitions placed upon oneself are one way or another related to the definitions placed upon the various groups with which one is involved. Harmonizing these definitions is not always an easy task.

No two individuals ever have the same socializing experiences, and no two individuals ever develop identical personalities. Each of us has a selective exposure to the complete culture of any group and each of us engages in only selective or limited types of interaction within any group. Individuality as well as similarity is developed. To the extent that different individuals have been socialized in the same groups and have met similar problems they will engage in similar behavior and endorse similar values. No group can last long as a group without such similarities.

One method of increasing the degree of similarity for members of a group is to limit the contacts of its members with other groups. This, of course, curtails the possible exposure to conflict-

Figure 12.1 Different types of socialization. In anticipatory socialization, children learn about playing future family roles; in formal socializaton involving two generations (*opposite page*), Afghanistan educators study American classroom procedures. (Wide World Photos.)

ing or different patterns. Physical isolation, such as is maintained by some monasteries, also increases the likelihood of similar behavior of the group members.

Not all the groups that exist within a society are identical.

As an individual is being socialized into one group, he may be acquiring value definitions and behavior patterns that are at variance with those of other established groups. The child, for instance, who is taught Christian beliefs and ways of life is in the process taught behavior patterns in some respects at variance with Jewish or atheistic groups. Individuals who are socialized to conform to a criminal group are in the process taught to deviate from the larger society. Deviant behavior is learned through the same process as conforming behavior.

TECHNICS OF SOCIALIZATION

Socialization is a process that involves contacts of one type or another with others and includes various configurations of rewards and punishments (sanctions). The phenomenon of selective perception applies to this process, as it does to all behavior. Not all contacts with others are involved equally in socialization. Neither are all contacts with the same individuals or groups equally involved. Each individual and group establishes somewhat unique relationships with different individuals and groups. Some become more significant than others.

In the process of socialization individuals learn to consult the standards or the norm-role-value definitions of particular groups in their efforts to reach decisions about certain matters. The child may conclude, "My family believes this is wrong; therefore it is wrong," or "My family does it this way and I will do it in the family way." The groups to which one refers in making decisions are called "reference groups."[8] Individuals orient themselves by adopting reference group definitions. The same group may not serve as a reference group for all decisions. Further, a reference group need not be a group in which the individual has membership; it may be one in which he aspires to have membership or even one in which he believes he may never have membership. Reference groups are acquired through the socialization process and then become actively involved in subsequent socialization.

Homans[9] has suggested the generalization that the extent to which the norm definitions of a group are felt to be binding is related to the im-

---

Computer Learning

In 1963 a Civil Engineering freshman class at M.I.T. was assigned a problem of designing a ramp of a highway clover-leaf intersection. Using a computer and a special language the students had no trouble with the problem. They solved it in about twenty minutes including a few seconds of machine time, and one student voiced the general complaint that it was much too easy. The significant thing about this story is that the problem was a formidable senior-level task and had never before been given to freshmen.

—John Pfeiffer.*

---

* John Pfeiffer, "Machines That Man Can Talk With," *Fortune* (May, 1964), 198.

[8] For a discussion of Reference Group Theory, see Robert K. Merton, *Social Theory and Social Structure* (rev. and enlarged ed.; New York: The Free Press of Glencoe, 1957), pp. 225–386.

[9] George C. Homans, *The Human Group* (New York: Harcourt, Brace & World, Inc., 1950), p. 151.

portance the individual attaches to the group. Studies of small groups have shown that members of highly attractive groups tend to change their opinions upon discovering that the others disagree with them more readily than those in less attractive groups.[10]

Different processes are involved with different types of learning. Certain types of factual information may be learned as easily from a relative stranger with whom one has no intimate or emotional contacts as from a member of one's primary group. In college classes where the goal is merely to transfer a body of knowledge from one individual to others, an impersonal secondary-type of relationship may be very effective. For the learning of certain types of information an impersonal relationship may be the most effective, and establishment of a more personal, primary relationship would serve to inhibit such learning.

However, for learning which involves NER symbols, especially value definitions, the reference groups and significant others are usually very extensively involved. Such definitions cannot be learned from observation of any empirical qualities of objects to which such definitions are applied. These are imposed by man himself. The acquisition and maintenance of such definitions, then, results from satisfying relationships with significant others.

Socialization may also be accomplished through experience in certain interaction that anticipates some future event. Parents may prepare themselves for the subsequent growing up of their children and the "empty-nest period" by experiences in which the children are periodically away from the home at school or in the service. Such preparation has been called anticipatory socialization. The behavior of the young child as she plays that she is a mother (playing at a role), or what might be called socialization by analogy, may also serve as anticipatory sociali-

[10] See Leon Festinger *et al.*, "The Influence Process in the Presence of Extreme Deviates," *Human Relations*, V, No. 4 (November, 1952), 327–346.

zation. The games children and adults play may also serve such a function.[11]

Schools

In an industrialized, urbanized society such as the United States, where extensive and intricately complex information about many things is included in the culture of the group, technically trained individuals must be involved in the socialization process. Most parents do not know the basic knowledge required for entrance into many available occupations. They are unqualified to provide occupational training (socialization) for their children. As the degree of industrialization-urbanization increases, the extent of formal education given by professionally trained teachers also increases. The schools are also involved in the socialization process in less apparent (latent) ways. In that the individual spends more and more time in formal school activities, he will also spend more and more time interacting with his peers, not only in the classroom, but in many types of extracurricular activities as well. From such extensive interaction, intimate (primary) relationships are established, and out of these contacts important value definitions arise.

Mass Media

Under industrialized - urbanized conditions, where direct interaction can take place between only small segments of the society, systems of communication designed for mass consumption are developed. The extent of such systems in the United States is suggested by the fact that by the

---

Upon What Evidence? *

Train a child the way he should go and when he is old, he will not depart from it.—Proverbs.
Just as the twig is bent, the tree's inclined.—Pope.
The child is father of the man.—Wordsworth.
Give us the child for eight years, and it will be a Bolshevist forever.—Lenin.

1960's the telecommunication system was 40,000 times greater than at the end of World War II, and it included microwave systems that could process simultaneously 24,000 telegraph messages. Newspapers, magazines, radio, and television under these conditions become important media through which certain types of socialization take place.

SUMMARY

Socialization is the life-long process by which human beings transmit culture and learn particular behavior patterns required for societal perpetuation. In the socialization process the young child is not a passive but rather a dynamic agent, without, however, much experience or a language of his own to draw on. Socialization varies with the age of the learner and the content. This complex process includes conscious and unconscious aspects and involves experiences in various groups and with various media, all of which are not mutually consistent. Socialization includes integrating or harmonizing efforts on the part of those involved.

---

[11] For a discussion of anticipatory socialization, see Irwin Deutscher, "Socialization for Postparental Life," in Arnold Rose (ed.), *Human Behavior and Social Processes* (Boston: Houghton Mifflin Co., 1962), pp. 506–525.

* From Read Bain (ed.), *Sociology: Introductory Readings* (Philadelphia: J. B. Lippincott Co., 1962), p. 84.

QUESTIONS

1. Is it possible to talk about unconscious learning without positing an "unconscious" as a noun or thing inside the individual?
2. Analyze your learning experiences at college to see if you have acted as a "passive sponge" into which the instructor has been able to "pour culture."
3. What is meant by the statement that socialization is the process by which one becomes human?
4. How much choice will your children during their early years have in what they are taught?
5. By the time he reaches college, the American student has learned to speak English in the classroom and generally to want to speak English. Analyze your own experiences to determine if you can see some of the ways in which you have learned to *want* to speak English. What sanctions have been involved? How is the behavior of others involved?
6. List some of the conflicting things you have been taught in different groups.
7. Have you found what you are taught in your various classes to be completely consistent? Provide a sociological explanation for this.
8. Can you identify some "anticipatory socialization" in which you have been involved?
9. Can you provide an illustration of an early childhood experience which you interpret differently now than you did at the time it happened? Which is the "correct" interpretation? How do you know?
10. Compare the lecture method of teaching with the discussion method. Which have you found to be more effective? How do you explain this sociologically?

PROJECT

Analyze the experiences which you have had at college and distinguish between those which have increased your desire (motivation) to get good grades and those which have decreased this desire. See how your experiences compare to the experiences of other students.

SUGGESTED READING

BETTELHEIM, BRUNO. "Feral Children and Autistic Children," *The American Journal of Sociology,* LXIV, No. 5 (March, 1959), 455–467.

BOSSARD, JAMES H. S., and ELEANOR S. BOLL. *The Sociology of Child Development.* 3d ed. New York: Harper & Row, Inc., 1960.

DEUTSCHER, IRWIN. "Socialization for Postparental Life," in ARNOLD ROSE, *Human Behavior and Social Processes.* Boston: Houghton Mifflin Co., 1962. Pp. 506–525.

GERTH, HANS, and C. WRIGHT MILLS. *Character and Social Structure.* New York: Harcourt, Brace & World, Inc., 1953.

HONIGMANN, JOHN J. *Culture and Personality.* New York: Harper & Row, Inc., 1952.

MACCOBY, ELEANOR E., THEODORE M. NEWCOMB, and EUGENE L. HARTLEY (eds.). *Readings in Social Psychology.* New York: Holt, Rinehart and Winston, Inc., 1958. Pp. 335–370.

MILLER, DANIEL R., and GUY E. SWANSON. *The Changing American Parent.* New York: John Wiley & Sons, Inc., 1958.

PIAGET, JEAN. *Language and Thought of the Child.* New York: Harcourt, Brace & World, Inc., 1926.

SHIBUTANI, TAMOTSU. *Society and Personality.* Englewood Cliffs, N. J.: Prentice-Hall, Inc., 1961.

WRONG, DENNIS H. "The Oversocialized Conception of Man in Modern Sociology," *American Sociological Review,* XXVI, No. 2 (April, 1961), 187–193.

13

Role Playing and

Role Taking

What do you pay attention to when you make decisions about the meaning of the behavior of others? How, for instance, do you decide when an answer of "no" really means "yes"? How does the student decide what the professor really thinks of the answer he gives in the class discussion?

Two of the basic interaction processes are role playing and role taking, both of which fit together in a reciprocal manner, along with role definitions, which were extensively discussed in an earlier section of the text. We have referred to role definition, role playing, and role taking as the "role-triad."

Role definition was defined as the expected behavior or the plans of action associated with a particular position. Engaging in this expected behavior or following the script (role definition)—this we will call role playing or playing a role.

Other terms that have been used for this process are role performance, role behavior, and role enacting. Role definitions are static. Role playing is dynamic. Role playing involves enacting, performing, or engaging in the plans of action spelled out in the definition. This chapter is a

discussion of this process and the process of role taking, to which we will turn our attention later.

A SOCIAL PHENOMENON

Our discussion of role definitions emphasized that any given role definition is a part of a larger configuration of role definitions—a role set. As Merton [1] has indicated:

... the single status of medical student entails not only the role of a student in relation to his teachers, but also an array of other roles relating the occupant of that status to other students, nurses, physicians, social workers, medical technicians, etc.

[1] Robert K. Merton, *Social Theory and Social Structure* (New York: The Free Press of Glencoe, rev. and enlarged ed., 1957), p. 369.

Role playing always involves others, directly or indirectly. Here again the concept of interaction is an important one. Role playing always involves two or more individuals taking each other into account. Role playing may also be influenced by definitions of people not physically present—by people dead, not yet born, or even mythical. The student at college, for instance, may be influenced by his parents at home via letter (symbolic interaction) or by his thoughts as to what parental wishes might be in the situation under consideration. Boy friends away in the service may also be taken into account. Interactions of Christians in the twentieth century may involve ideas as to what Jesus Christ would have done under comparable circumstances; or, at the other extreme, they may be influenced by ideas about what their children, who are yet to be conceived, will want to do in the future. Role playing, then, involves efforts to integrate the behavior of two or more individuals into a complete and meaningful whole. It is a social phenomenon.

ROLE PLAYING IS A DYNAMIC, EMERGENT PROCESS

Role playing is a dynamic process. It involves applying labels to oneself, to others, and to the situation in which the interaction is taking place.

Individuals tell themselves what role they are playing at any given moment. As the individual moves from one role to another, he not only tells others of this but also makes himself aware of it. Sometimes this involves paying attention to the standardized starting procedures (rites of passage) such as watching the clock at the office. At one minute before eight, he is "off duty," but at eight sharp he is "on duty" or he has changed his role. Also, the fact that certain roles require certain types of dress or some other status symbol provides individuals with reminders as to what role they are playing at any given time. In playing familiar roles the process is usually not as consciously undertaken as this discussion suggests.

Labels

Many college students are bothered by the multiplicity of possible ways to address their teachers. Is he a Doctor? Many students call all college teachers "doctor" which is embarrassing to those who have not yet obtained that status symbol, or "union card." On the other hand, should he be called "doctor" when he is really a "professor"? Doctors are a dime a dozen on every campus. Even the lowly instructor is a "doctor" in first rate universities, but professors (at least "full" ones) are relatively rare.

—Read Bain.*

Such definitions provide the basic information upon which subsequent behavior is built. Role playing also involves selecting from the alternatives present the ones felt to be most appropriate and then enacting them.

Applying role labels facilitates organizing a whole sequence of on-going behavior in a meaningful manner. As Goffman [2] has indicated, "We do not take on items of conduct one at a time but rather a whole harness load of them and may anticipatorily learn to be a horse even while being pulled like a wagon." Role labels help the individual "make sense" out of the behavior of others as well as of himself. And even if an individual is not behaving according to any clear role definitions, others viewing his behavior and possibly interacting with him tend to view his behavior as though it were, in fact, patterned according to a role definition. It is easier to understand his behavior this way, even if the understanding is not entirely correct.

In some situations those involved initiate their interaction with clear role definitions for all concerned. When this is not the case, most people try early in the interaction to decide what the

* Read Bain (ed.), *Sociology: Introductory Readings* (Philadelphia: J. B. Lippincott Co., 1962), p. 184.
[2] Erving Goffman, *Encounters* (Indianapolis: The Bobbs-Merrill Co., Inc., 1961), p. 87.

Figure 13.1   Dual status (position) symbols identify the dual nature of the military chaplain. (Wide World Photos.)

appropriate definitions are, so that they can feel more sure of their own behavior and of that of others. When clear-cut cues are not available, the individuals utilize whatever cues are present and on the basis of preliminary assessment so order other evidence that it harmonizes with the first identified evidence. Since human beings can see what they want to see, interaction may involve distorted perceptions that are felt to support earlier interpretations.

The fact that others treat us as though we were playing a particular role may so influence us that we begin to behave in accordance with that role definition. Individuals who return from brief foreign travel may be asked so many questions about the society they visited and in other ways be treated as though they were "experts" that they begin to behave as though they were and may even come to define themselves as being such experts.

Role playing involves the constant assessment and re-assessment of the behavior of those involved in order to make sense out of an experience and to decide upon future plans of action. Decisions are constantly being made. While playing a role, the individuals first decide what the appropriate role definitions are, and how these are related to the larger social situation of which they are a part. Then, on the basis of these decisions and an appraisal of the on-going behavior, the individual decides what he will do. He may, for instance, decide to follow the role prescriptions to the letter, or he may feel that there are situational factors that justify departing from the formal role definitions. He may even abandon such definitions. Or, he may, on the basis of his interpretation of the behavior of others, decide that he has made an accurate interpretation of what he is supposed to do and proceed accordingly. He may, however, on the basis of such interpretation, decide that his initial appraisal was in error and re-define the situation and his role to harmonize with what he thinks others are doing and how he thinks they are defining the situation. A lengthy sequence of role playing involves many appraisals and re-appraisals of a multitude of factors. Such appraisals serve as feedback, which helps one to decide precisely what his "next move" will be. Previous plans are constantly being re-inforced or modified on the basis of what happens in the interaction sequence. Feedback from others is taken into account and may, following a decision that previous definitions were inappropriate, result in the application of new definitions.

Our own self definitions may be re-inforced or forcefully changed as others respond to us in particular ways. Statements such as "But you're not the president of the club" may thus serve to put an aggressive member "in his place." Re-assessment of one's self definitions is not always easy and may be accompanied by other definitions that impede subsequent interaction. Participants may feel unhappy, distressed, or threatened with a consequent lessened ability to interpret accurately the behavior of self and the behavior of others.

A Ready-Made Self

In performing a role the individual must see to it that the impressions of him that are conveyed in the situation are compatible with the role-appropriate personal qualities effectively imputed to him: a judge is supposed to be deliberate and sober; a pilot, in a cockpit, to be cool; a bookkeeper to be accurate and neat in doing his work. These personal qualities, effectively imputed and effectively claimed, combine with a position's title, when there is one, to provide a basis of self-image for the incumbent.... A self, then, virtually awaits the individual entering a position; he need only conform to the pressures on him and he will find a me ready-made for him.

—Erving Goffman.*

Role playing involves making value judgments about the objects and the others involved and weaving such assessments into the subsequent decisions as to how behavior should proceed. Since such judgments do not stem from the empirical qualities of anything evaluated, such a process is *ipso facto* a dynamic one.

Role playing also involves the selection and application of sanctions felt to be appropriate to the situation, in part upon the basis of these value judgments applied by others, as the participants make efforts to influence the outcome of the interaction. One of the most potent sanctions involved in any situation is to enhance or diminish the self definitions of those involved. Deciding upon the sanctions to be used and the method of application, then, is an integral part of the process of role playing.

Continued interaction patterns may result in the participants changing the definitions of what is appropriate or inappropriate behavior for particular positions. Role definitions may be changed and a modified content standardized if

* Erving Goffman, *Encounters* (Indianapolis: The Bobbs-Merrill Co., Inc., 1961), pp. 87–88.

sufficient support, both formal and informal, is provided. This process has been called "role making."[3] Such change is usually slow and gradual. Extensive overhaul of any particular role definition is difficult, and definitions, including role definitions, produce confusion and discord. Situational factors such as poor communication facilities may likewise be involved. Poor feedback reduces effective assessment of what is happening and thus impedes the interaction.

Continued playing of a given role molds the personality of an individual so that the behavior patterns become habitual and are accepted without question. Under such conditions the individual no longer has to tell himself consciously exactly what to do or how and when to do it. The individual may be relatively unaware that he is playing a role—he feels he is just behaving. However, when he is somehow forced to explain to himself or to someone else just what he is doing and why he is doing it, he begins to see relationships betwen his behavior and the position he occupies at the moment.

When entering into a new position, the appropriate behavior may be very consciously undertaken in a mechanical manner. The one playing the role may have only a vague idea as to how the role should be played. The role player may look to others or consult the office handbook in order to play the role properly.

Generally the employer provides some sort of training program for his new employees. Male students in an ROTC program spend hours and hours learning how to march and to give and receive commands. Fraternity or sorority pledges are given "learning experiences," presumably upon the assumption that they help the prospective member to play his or her role better after being initiated into the group with the appropriate rites of passage.

In a stable society, most members enter most situations with fairly clear definitions of the expected behavior. When the typical American college student attends the Junior Prom, he enters the ballroom ready to participate in the appropriate way. He dresses appropriately, he knows the ritual involved in taking care of the wraps (he even knows that on this occasion they are *wraps*, although the same clothing in other situations are merely *coats*), how dancing partners will be selected, the proper type of dancing, types of conversation in which to engage, etc. Throughout the week as he moves from the dorm to the classroom, to the football game, to the movie, and to church services on Sunday, he has a well-established awareness of the appropriate plans of action, and in most cases his behavior conforms, more or less, to these plans. He plays the appropriate role.

Role behavior, however, is learned behavior. Habitual patterns do not appear without the necessary learning experiences. In this respect, children frequently have difficulty understanding and playing roles appropriately. Johnny has to learn that mother behaves differently when she is functioning as president of the PTA than

---

Evasion

A study by a participant observer of a large airplane factory found that "The use of the tap is the most serious crime of workmanship conceivable in the plant. A worker can be summarily fired for merely possessing a tap. However, it is estimated that at least one-half of the work force in a position to use a tap owns at least one. Every well-equipped senior mechanic owns four or five of different sizes, and every mechanic has access to and, if need be, uses them."

—J. Bensman and I. Gerver.*

---

[3] Ralph Turner, "Role-Taking: Process Versus Conformity," in Arnold M. Rose (ed.), *Human Behavior and Social Processes* (Boston: Houghton Mifflin Co., 1962), pp. 20–40.

* J. Bensman and I. Gerver, "Crime and Punishment in the Factory: A Functional Analysis," in *Mass Society in Crisis*, ed. by Bernard Rosenberg, Israel Gerver, and F. William Howton (New York: The Macmillan Co., 1964), p. 142.

when she is playing the role of companion to her child. He has to learn that he is expected to behave differently when he is in church with his friends than when he is in the backyard "rough-housing" with them. Playing games with others generally helps develop the understanding of "expected behavior" and also the consequences of failure to live up to it. Games have rules, and others expect you to conform to them. Sanctions of one type or another may be imposed for failure to do so.

In similar manner adults who move rapidly from one social level to another may find that new roles have to be learned and old ones modified to become acceptable at the new level. At the beginning the expectations of those at the new level may not be very well known, with resultant social difficulties.

SOCIAL AND PERSONAL ORDER

Our previous discussions of norm definitions and role definitions have already indicated that social order or structure stems from the fact that such definitions are developed and related to each other in an orderly manner. Consistent behavior, then, results in part from the patterns found in such definitions.

But how does society get its people to play the roles necessary to the functioning of the society? Since human beings do not automatically engage in these behavior patterns, the members of the group must be taught to play the roles and also be taught to *want* to play them. This involves teaching them a particular value system so that certain goals are defined as good and desirable. It also involves providing certain sanctions whereby those who conform will be rewarded and those who deviate will be penalized. Sanction systems are extremely varied, but nonetheless they are useful in recruiting and maintaining the required role players for any system.

Some of the most attractive aspects of playing a particular role may appear when the individual is not actually playing that particular role, as when the surgeon is playing the role of fellow guest or motorist.

Goffman [4] suggests:

. . . often, it is precisely these unfocused consequences of a focused role that carry much of the reward and punishment of playing it—the situations of the policeman, the country nurse, and the minister are examples. One might almost argue that role-formation occurs to the degree that performance of a situated task comes to have significance for the way the performer is seen in other situations.

ROLE CONFLICT

The degree of order in any social system never reaches maximum level. Since role definitions, or at least many of them, are developed in an unplanned (crescive) manner and since all systems permit a certain amount of "ad-libbing," a certain amount of role conflict or social disorganization is always present. Throughout his lifetime, and even during one particular day, any given individual usually plays many different roles. Linton [5] has suggested that we can distinguish between roles in which the individual is actually engaged at the moment and those he plays at other times but in which he is not actually engaged. He has labeled the former "active roles" and the latter "latent roles." Conflict between active and latent roles is a frequent occurrence.

The methods of resolving role conflicts are varied. One method is to relate the behavior to the situation in which it takes place, recognizing that behavior felt to be appropriate for one role may be defined as inappropriate for another. This process is sometimes called "compartmentalization." Such a procedure can be illustrated by the student who while working part-time on the police force, stops his professor for speeding, and tells him, as he hands him a ticket, "I hate to do this, Professor Jones, but you know, *I'm only doing my job.*" He wants to make sure that the behavior is related to the proper role.

---

[4] Goffman, *op. cit.*, p. 150.
[5] Ralph Linton, *The Study of Man* (New York: Appleton-Century-Crofts, 1936).

A soldier may tell himself that as a soldier he is expected to kill and provide for himself acceptable reasons for doing so, such as preserving his own life or the life of his loved ones, including, of course, his buddies fighting at his side. After the war is over, he may give strong endorsement to peace and loving one's neighbor (and enemy) and be able to minimize the differences between his roles as civilian and soldier.

Conflict can also be avoided by the careful selection of roles so that maximum consistency can be obtained. An individual may decline to accept a position (play a role) in which he would be required to do things contrary to his religious convictions—such as working on a "day of rest." Or he may define the conflicts as irrelevant and thus experience little or no difficulty in living with the dissonance.

Where differing role definitions are accepted by the participants of an on-going relationship, such as husband and wife, or employer and employee, resolving the conflict may be attempted by techniques such as the following:

1. Apply a different role definition, so that differences are minimized.
2. Change role-playing behavior to coincide with role definition.
3. Change role-playing behavior to coincide with expectations of others.
4. Agree to disagree, to recognize that disparity exists, but define it as not being of sufficient importance to disrupt the existing relationships.
5. Improve social conditions to facilitate harmony. This may include such things as improving the accuracy of the feedback system, or development of adequate sanction systems so that participants will *want* to behave as consistency requires.
6. Create distracting conditions which effectively make role playing difficult or impossible. These conditions might include the development of psychosomatic illness or disturbances of one kind or another, or in extreme cases suicide, as a means of escape. Such adjustment techniques are generally defined as neurotic or psychotic.

UNSTRUCTURED OR MARGINAL SITUATIONS

It would be erroneous to conclude from this discussion that all behavior is role behavior, except perhaps in the very broadest sense. Some situations are relatively unstructured, and those involved are left "to their own resources." Society has not developed any clear-cut plans of action for such situations, except some rather general norm definitions (such as wearing clothes and preserving one's own life and that of others). Individuals moving from one position to another may define themselves and be defined by others as in a marginal position—not completely in or completely out of some well-established positions. The individuals may follow any number of plans of action depending upon personality conditions and situational factors.

ROLE TAKING (ROLE INTERPRETATION)

The remaining major concept of our role-triad is role taking, which is a shortened version of George H. Mead's terminology, "taking the role of the other." "Role interpretation" is another label for this phenomenon and one which we will here advocate as being a more appropriate label in terms of the already established meaning of the word "interpretation." The word "empathy," also frequently used as synonymous with role taking, may introduce confusion since there is another meaning of this word.[6]

Basically the process of role taking or role interpretation involves coming to a decision about the behavior of others. In our discussion of symbols, it was emphasized that man is constantly engaged in the process of "cutting up" his world, applying labels to the parts thus created, and then responding to these labels. In role taking, the universe being "cut up" is the behavior of others. Labels are put on these parts, and once this has been done, response can be patterned according to the appropriate plans of action in-

---

[6] Empathy or "feeling with" another should be distinguished from sympathy or "feeling sorry for" another.

corporated in the meaning of these labels. In simpler terms, we interpret the behavior of the others involved. We tell ourselves what it means. We explain to ourselves why another is doing what he is doing and possibly infer something about antecedent conditions and anticipate subsequent behavior. The process, then, by which one comes to a decision about the behavior of others is role taking or role interpretation.

Exactly how this interpretation is accomplished is not very well known. The process outlined by Mead,[7] called "taking the role of the other," suggests that the manner in which this is done, for the individual doing the role taking, is figuratively or imaginatively to put himself into the role of the other and look at the situation through the eyes of the other. Lindesmith and Strauss [8] describe the process in these words:

A person by imagining or actually using the gestures, postures, words, and intonations of someone else and by drawing upon his understanding of that person from past experience evokes in himself responses which approximate those of the other person. He thus "feels" his way into the other's views and by so doing makes predictions about the other's behavior. . . . He is greatly assisted in this process by knowledge of others' motives and of the symbols and values, in terms of which they act.

They further suggest that "in order to interact effectively and realistically with other persons, even in hostile relations, it is necessary to put oneself in their shoes."

Sarbin indicates that this process involves two distinguishable elements: (1) a hypothetical assumption ("Suppose I were John Doe?") and (2) a consideration of the consequences of the assumption ("What would I think and do if I were John Doe?"). The first, he says, establishes a set or an idea. This idea must then be maintained as it is elaborated in specific acts. This process may be illustrated by the way in which

---

Interpreting the Behavior of Others

. . ."Balis" or "usog" is a half-superstition ailment—any person, hot and tired, can inflict this ailment to somebody he or she sees or talks to. They say a person who is hungry is most susceptible to catching the ailment. They also say that some people have stronger "balis" than others; that is, they either can inflict it more severely or more readily. . . . Whoever catches it suffers from severe stomachache, his sweat coming out cold and clammy, hands and feet getting cold. . . . The pains will not subside unless the person who inflicted it puts his saliva, usually from betel nut chewing, on the sufferer's stomach. . . . Some people don't believe in this; doctors certainly don't. In our place, they have a test to know whether the stomachache is from "balis" or not. The small finger would be aligned with the ring finger—right hand, that is—and if the tip of the small finger goes beyond the last knot of the ring finger, it's "balis."
—Ophelia San Juan.*

---

military commanders of opposing forces in a war seek to anticipate each other's actions and to "out-guess" each other.

To state the same premise somewhat differently, this approach suggests that one way in which the individual interprets the behavior of others is to say to himself, "Now, if I were in his place, doing what he is doing, it would mean such and such." This is a process by which we interpret or gain understanding of the behavior of others.

Cooley,[9] in his discussion of the "looking-glass process," also utilizes this approach. He suggests that in the development of his self conceptions, the individual is constantly engaged in the process of looking at himself and evaluating

---

[7] George H. Mead, *Mind, Self and Society* (Chicago: University of Chicago Press, 1934).

[8] Alfred R. Lindesmith and Anselm L. Strauss, *Social Psychology* (New York: Holt, Rinehart and Winston, Inc., rev. ed., 1956), p. 386.

* Ophelia San Juan (a Filipino girl who assisted in some research); reported by Bartlett H. Stoodley (ed.), *Society and Self* (New York: The Free Press of Glencoe, 1962), p. 238.

[9] Charles Horton Cooley, *Social Organization* (New York: Charles Scribner's Sons, 1920).

his behavior through the eyes of the others with whom he interacts. Cooley visualizes these others as a "human looking glass" which reflects back to the individual the image which they have of him. He suggests that the manner in which one sees this image is by figuratively putting himself in the place of the others and saying to himself, "Now, if I were in his position looking at me and behaving in the manner in which he is behaving, my behavior would mean. . . ."

A second way in which decisions about the meaning of the behavior of others are reached is the direct interpretation of the behavior itself, in much the same way that we interpret other aspects of the universe. In the process of socialization we learn to identify those parts of the universe which our groups have labeled and called to our attention. The process of identifying these objects generally includes learning the associated behavior. Thus, we learn that pencils are objects with which one writes. Chairs are objects upon which one sits. Sociologists are objects who behave in such and such a manner. This process extends to identifying behavior patterns and attributing meaning to them. Thus, when we see the chairman of the PTA stand up in front of the group, we have learned to interpret such behavior as indicative of the fact that he or she is ready to speak.

What is being suggested is that the individual learns to identify behavior patterns *per se* rather than figuratively putting himself in the place of the other and thus "feeling" the behavior of the other.

In social interaction, we pay attention to things that exist outside of us (behavior patterns) and define them directly. According to this point of view, empathy or role taking is not the process of putting oneself in the place of the other, but rather the process of directly defining the behavior of others. One defines the behavior of others on the basis of what is known about these others, rather than on the basis of what is known about himself.

When we have trouble with our car, we do not say to ourselves, "Now, if I were a car, coughing and sputtering in this manner, I would be doing so because my spark plugs are corroded." What

we typically do is to say to ourselves, when a car, or more likely a specific car, behaves as it is doing, it means that the spark plugs are corroded. We might distinguish between these two processes by using Mead's original terminology "taking the role of the other" to refer to the first pattern and "role interpretation" to refer to the other.

The aspects of behavior in this interpretation are limited only by the concepts of the individuals involved. We can pay attention to any aspect of the behavior of others and decide its meaning. This, of course, includes motivational factors. We are, in fact, constantly telling ourselves why we think others do whatever they do. Such explanations may involve guesses as to the value judgments others are making, some of which may be felt to be neurotic or maybe even psychotic. Since value judgments cannot be observed directly, and since in much interaction time is not taken explicitly to outline the value judgments that underlie particular behavior patterns, such decisions are usually made by inference. Such a procedure frequently introduces inaccuracies into the behavior sequence. Attention may also be given to status symbols with the behavior interpreted so that it is consistent with the status associated with the symbol.

The process of selective perception we have already discussed as being involved in role playing is also involved here. Decisions about the behavior of others are generally reached on the basis of limited cues. Human behavior being what it is, it is possible for man to provide or to "read into" the behavior of others aspects or details sufficient to round out a picture to harmonize with the cues interpreted in the way they are. We try to make the behavior of others consistent with what we already know about them and the situation. Sometimes this involves providing (or inventing) aspects that are not actually there. This may involve organizing the behavior of the other around role definitions applied by the observer, even though such definitions might not have been involved in the behavior by the one being observed. For instance, when Dennis the Menace observes a fellow in uniform embracing a girl and comments to his companion, "Of course they are fighting; he's a soldier, isn't he?" we are provided with an illustration of this process.

COMPLEXITY OF BEHAVIOR INVOLVED

The complexity of the types of decisions involved in this process can be suggested by thinking in terms of two individuals, A and B. A may use this method in deciding questions such as the following:

A decides how he thinks B defines A.
A decides how he thinks B defines B.
A decides how he thinks B thinks A defines B.
A decides how he thinks B thinks A thinks B defines himself.
A decides how he thinks B thinks A defines A.
A decides how he thinks B defines C.

When we expand this dyad to include C, D, and E, the possible combinations of this type of role interpretation increase in geometric ratio. Such behavior may include decisions about (1) on-going behavior; (2) past behavior; and (3) projected future behavior, all of which the individual attempts to harmonize in such a way that they all make sense to him.

The process of role taking or role interpretation is not restricted to only one "other." A child may come to a decision as to how he thinks his parents (two individuals) define his behavior. A student may come to a decision as to what his "classmates" think of him. A teacher may decide how his "class" will react to the lesson he has prepared but not yet delivered. Or on the broader scale, society itself may become the "other" involved in this process and the individual may conclude that "Americans" would not approve of such and such behavior. When the other involved becomes the whole society or some major segment, we speak of this "other" as the "generalized other."

Decisions as to the acceptance or rejection of one's behavior by his society or some significant segment may be influential in the behavior of individuals. The "generalized other" is involved in the development of moral standards, since society is the larger entity to which one turns for moral decisions. In terms of the young child, it is the standards of society that he accepts as his own.

The process of role taking or role interpretation can be extended beyond society, to a realm believed to be supernatural. God may become a significant "other" in the lives of individuals. When this happens, an important decision involved in the on-going behavior of an individual is how he feels God defines this behavior. The

---

The Sounding Out Process

The sounding out process can be illustrated by the problem of the boss with amorous designs on his secretary in an organization that taboos such relations. He must find some means of determining her willingness to alter the relationship, but he must do so without risking rebuff, for a showdown might come at the cost of his dignity or his office reputation, at the cost of losing her secretarial services, or in the extreme case at the cost of losing his own position. The "sophisticated" procedure is to create an ambiguous situation in which the secretary is forced to respond in one of two ways: (1) to ignore or tactfully counter, thereby clearly channeling the relationship back into an already existing pattern, or (2) to respond in a similarly ambiguous vein (if not in a positive one) indicating a receptiveness to further advances. It is important in the sounding out process that the situation be ambiguous for two reasons: (1) the secretary must not be able to "pin down" the boss with evidence if she rejects the idea, and (2) the situation must be far enough removed from normal to be noticeable to the secretary. The ambiguity of sounding out has the further advantage to the participants that neither party alone is clearly responsible for initiating the change.
—James D. Thompson and
William J. McEwan.*

---

* James D. Thompson and William J. McEwan, "Organizational Goals and Environment: Goal-Setting as an Interaction Process," *American Sociological Review*, XXIII, No. 1 (February 1958), p. 30.

importance of symbols in this process is obvious. For most people God is not empirically present and not available to their "natural senses" for direct observation; therefore decisions about God as an "other" can be arrived at only through symbol manipulation.

ROLE TAKING INVOLVED IN ROLE PLAYING

The role-triad we have been discussing is not composed of mutually exclusive terms, but rather of terms all involved in any sequence of behavior. Thus, in order to play any role that involves another (and most of them do), it is necessary to be constantly engaged in the process of role taking. The husband and wife who are discussing the summer vacation may follow this pattern:

Husband speaks.

Wife interprets his behavior, including the verbal behavior, and on the basis of her interpretation of his behavior and other factors, she makes what to her is an appropriate response.

Husband, in turn, interprets the behavior of his wife, fits it into the context of the larger configuration (including his interpretation of his own behavior) of which it is a part, and makes what to him is an appropriate response.

Wife, in turn, interprets the behavior of her husband, fits it into the context of the larger configuration (including her interpretation of her own behavior, etc.) of which it is a part, and makes what to her is an appropriate response.

We not only interpret the behavior of the others with whom we interact, but we are also constantly interpreting our own behavior. This interpretation includes our telling ourselves the motives behind our behavior or telling ourselves why we are doing what we are doing.

ROLE PLAYING INVOLVED IN ROLE TAKING

It seems logical and theoretically sound that those who have played or play a particular role, say that of a school teacher, should as a consequence of this experience be better able than many others to interpret correctly the behavior of those who play this role. Mothers should, as a rule, be better able to interpret the behavior of other mothers. Criminals should be better able than non-criminals to "understand" the behavior of other criminals.

Likewise, those from the same society or subsociety should be better able to interpret each other's behavior than those from differing societies. Part of the difficulty of the young child in accurately interpreting the behavior of adults is that he has had no experience as an adult upon which to base his decisions. It is no wonder that he frequently has difficulty understanding why his significant adults behave the way they do! In this sense, then, role-playing experience is involved in the effectiveness of our role-taking or role-interpreting activities.

OTHER FACTORS RELATED TO EFFECTIVENESS OF ROLE TAKING

Sharing common symbols (language) also facilitates role interpretation. Barth,[10] for instance, has suggested that the different language behavior of American Negroes and whites may be one of the factors that contributes to misunderstandings between these groups.

Ability to interpret correctly non-verbal cues, such as a facial expression, a raised eyebrow, speed of speaking, intonation, or state of excitation also affects the accuracy of role taking. Counselors are presumably particularly adept in picking up these cues. Paying attention to what is not said in a situation may be as meaningful as paying attention to what is said.

The state of being of the one doing the role taking is also significant. Concern for one particular thing may take precedence over others and thus decrease sensitivity in other areas. Being uncertain of oneself or having unclear self definitions may contribute to giving so much attention to oneself that accurate interpretation of others is difficult. Illness may also reduce sensitivity.

[10] Ernest A. T. Barth, "The Language Behavior of Negroes and Whites," *Pacific Sociological Review*, IV, No. 2 (Fall, 1961), 69–72.

The types of relationships previously established with particular others are also important. We are better able to interpret the behavior of those with whom we have an intimate, close personal relationship than those with whom our relationships have been segmental and impersonal.

Various other situational factors may be involved, including the decision the individual reaches as to the degree of understanding the situation calls for. Interaction between a customer and a clerk in the local shoe store is accordingly not usually felt to demand as much understanding as that between the representatives of two governments negotiating the terms of a peace treaty.

Role interpretation is a learned process. Individuals are not born with the ability to interpret the behavior of others; rather, it is developed in the process of interaction with others in the same manner that other skills are acquired. Our previous discussion of man's use of symbols pointed out that symbolic interaction involves the steps of (1) encoding, (2) transmission, and (3) decoding, with all of these steps involving learned behavior. What we have been discussing here is the process of decoding, not only spoken or written words but also any other behavior to which one has learned to pay attention.

If such an ability is learned, then differing abilities are related to different social experiences, and facility could be improved through certain experiences. Foote and Cottrell have demonstrated, for instance, that married individuals can increase their facility in interpreting the behavior of their spouses by going through certain learning experiences.[11]

Professional training in this skill may also be given to certain individuals such as counselors, ministers, and medical doctors. It should also be recognized that some professional activities may call for only limited empathy or "feeling with" others. The policeman, for instance, may be inhibited in imposing social sanctions upon public offenders if he lets himself "feel sorry" with the one being arrested. The surgeon may be hampered in his surgical skills if he too strongly "feels with" the patient upon whom he operates.[12]

MEASURING ROLE INTERPRETATION SKILLS

To what does one pay attention if he desires to do research on empathic ability? Basically, verbal behavior. One way or another we have to ask those involved how they interpreted the behavior of others involved in some on-going sequence and then measure this answer against the interpretations of the same behavior provided by those actually playing that role at the time. In one such study, college students were asked following a date to answer these questions:

Check one of the following statements which best describes your feelings about going with this person at the time the arrangements were made for the date.

_____ (1) I was very satisfied.
_____ (2) I was satisfied.
_____ (3) I was neutral.
_____ (4) I was unsatisfied.
_____ (5) I was very unsatisfied.

Check one of the following statements which best described what you thought *your dating partner* felt about going with you at the time the arrangements were made for this date.

_____ (1) My partner was very satisfied.
_____ (2) My partner was satisfied.
_____ (3) My partner was neutral.
_____ (4) My partner was unsatisfied.
_____ (5) My partner was very unsatisfied.

Since both participants in the dating experience answered these questions about themselves and their dating partner, it was possible to determine how accurately each had interpreted the behavior of the other.[13]

---

[11] Nelson N. Foote and Leonard S. Cottrell, Jr., *Identity and Interpersonal Competence* (Chicago: University of Chicago Press, 1955).

[12] See W. Coutu, "Role-Playing vs. Role-Taking: An Appeal for Clarification," *American Sociological Review,* XVI, No. 4 (August, 1951), 182.

[13] Glenn M. Vernon and Robert L. Stewart, "Empathy as a Process in the Dating Situation," *American Sociological Review,* XXII, No. 1 (February, 1957), 48–52.

PLAYING AT A ROLE

At this point let us briefly introduce one other term. What label are we going to use to identify behavior such as that of the young girl who, while playing with her doll, makes believe that she is a mother and goes through the actions of dressing, feeding, and playing with her "baby"? Or the behavior of boys who play that they are cowboys and Indians? Behavior which has this make-believe quality we will call "playing at a role." [14]

One more point may also help to avoid confusion for those who are familiar with various therapy procedures. Moreno developed a counseling system wherein those involved, say a husband and wife, act out a hypothetical situation in front of an audience, which might be composed of on-lookers or of others in the therapy program. The man, for instance, may act out the role of the wife while the wife acts out the role of the husband; in the process they gain greater insight into their own marriage behavior. This acting is make-believe behavior and would fall under the heading of "playing *at* a role" as we have just defined it. The label which Moreno himself applied to this process, however, is role playing. The student should be aware that using the term in this manner is contrary to the definition which we have given in this chapter. Such are the problems of symbolic interaction.

SUMMARY

Role definitions provide plans of action. Enacting this script, or role playing, is not a mechanical process, but one which, while there are limitations, involves adapting the script to the situation and to the behavior of those playing or believed to be playing counter roles. This involves assessment and re-assessment of the accuracy of labels and plans of action being used plus other efforts to eliminate or reduce any of various

[14] Coutu, *op. cit.*

Role Taking and Playing at a Role

One late afternoon near the dinner hour, B knotted his face into something of a scowl, and pitched his normally low voice into something approaching an infant growl.

"I want some meat for my supper," he said to his mother. Then added, "I'm daddy and I've come home from work." The mother took the cue and addressed him as daddy, asked how his little boy B was, etc.

At the table he insisted on taking his father's place at the head of the table, assigning the displaced parent to the high chair. . . . He admonished "B" not to spill his "brown milk," referring to the father's coffee. He referred to his milk as "white coffee," saying only big people could drink white coffee. After the meal, B continued to act in his capacity as daddy and "read" a story to his "son" and finally undertook to put him to bed. The father finally balked at being put in the crib, giving as his reason that the crib might break down. The two then agreed to "pretend" to put the father in the crib.

—Leonard S. Cottrell, Jr.*

types of role conflict that may be present. It also involves making value judgments and the selection and application of sanctions felt to be appropriate. Role playing is a dynamic, emergent process.

Since role playing is learned, abilities vary with learning experiences, and not everyone has equal facility. Role-playing skill is related to role-taking ability.

Role taking is the process by which the behavior of others is interpreted. This is complex and inadequately understood and includes such things as "feeling with" the other and directly interpreting aspects of his behavior to which one

* Leonard S. Cottrell, Jr., "The Analysis of Situational Fields in Social Psychology," *American Sociological Review*, VII, No. 3 (June, 1942), 370–382.

is sensitized (selective perception). Role-taking ability is also learned and can, consequently, be changed. The "other" involved in this process may be a single individual or a group of individuals, even a society or a "generalized other." Role taking is involved in role playing, and role-playing experiences are related to role-taking skills.

Playing at a role involves a make-believe, cowboys-and-Indians element in that one goes through the motions of playing a role he is not actually playing at the moment.

QUESTIONS

1. How is role taking involved in role playing?
2. How are role definitions involved in both role taking and role playing?
3. If you want to study role-taking ability, to what do you pay attention?
4. How do the members of a basketball team decide what the other members of the team are going to do so that they can "play as a team"?
5. Relate the concepts of role taking and subjective reality.

6. How can one communicate disapproval of a friend's behavior without actually saying it?
7. Provide a sociological explanation for the fact that married individuals are frequently able accurately to anticipate the behavior of the other.
8. Provide an illustration of role conflict which you have experienced and indicate what you did about it.
9. How does taking a college test involve role taking?
10. How do you account for the fact that not everyone has equal role-taking ability?

PROJECT

Briefly outline a study which would permit you to distinguish between the role-taking ability of different individuals.

SUGGESTED READING

BATES, F. L. "Some Observations Concerning the Structural Aspect of Role Conflict," *Pacific Sociological Review,* V, No. 2 (Fall, 1962), 75–82.

BROWN, J. C. "An Experiment in Role-Taking," *American Sociological Review,* XVII, No. 5 (October, 1952), 587–597.

BURCHARD, WALDO. "Role Conflicts of Military Chaplains," *American Sociological Review,* XIX, No. 5 (October, 1954), 528–535.

FREIDSON, ELIOT. "Dilemmas in the Doctor-Patient Relationship," in Arnold M. Rose (ed.), *Human Behavior and Social Processes.* Boston: Houghton Mifflin Co., 1962. Pp. 207–224.

MEIER, DOROTHY L., and WENDELL BELL. "Anomie and Differential Access to the Achievement of Life Goals," *American Sociological Review,* XXIV, No. 2 (April, 1959), 189–202.

MERTON, ROBERT K. "Role Set: Problems in Sociological Theory," *British Journal of Sociology,* VIII, No. 2 (June, 1957), 106–120.

SARBIN, THEODORE R. "Role Theory," in Gardner Lindzey (ed.), *Handbook of Social Psychology,* Vol. I. Cambridge, Mass.: Addison-Wesley Publishing Co., Inc., 1954. Pp. 223–258.

STRYKER, SHELDON. "Role-Taking Accuracy and Adjustment," *Sociometry,* XX (1957), 286–296.

STRYKER, SHELDON. "Conditions of Accurate Role-Taking: A Test of Mead's Theory," in Arnold M. Rose (ed.), *Human Behavior and Social Processes.* Boston: Houghton Mifflin Co., 1962. Pp. 41–62.

VIDEBECK, RICHARD, and ALAN P. BATES. "An Experimental Study of Conformity to Role Expectations," *Sociometry,* XXII (March, 1959), 1–11.

14

Collective or Unstructured

Behavior

Suppose you were told by your roommate that he had taken a call for you, and all he could remember was that you were to go to a particular lecture hall on campus at 4:30. You show up at the appropriate time and find a few others there. How would you go about structuring the situation so that you could decide what to do? Several alternatives might be: (1) Sit down by yourself and watch the others to see what they are doing. If they all go down front, you go down front too. (2) Ask others for information. (3) See if you can identify a leader and ask him. (How would you identify a leader?) (4) Being uncomfortable in such a situation, you may leave to get away from the uncertainty, maybe telling yourself that you really should be studying for tomorrow's sociology exam.

INTRODUCTION

Previous chapters have emphasized that the norm-role definitions developed by a society provide plans of action its members are expected to follow; many of them are, in fact, followed by most of the members most of the time. However, the extent to which the plans of action apply to the interaction of society members is always relative. In some behavior, such as in religious rituals or a military parade, the behavior may be specified in great detail; in other role playing only broad outlines or guides may be given. Some degree of spontaneity is provided for and is, in fact, expected in most behavior. All behavior has its dynamic, emergent aspects with the amount of spontaneity being related to the existing socio-cultural conditions as our previous chapter on role playing–role taking pointed out. Changes in society and culture are the result.

This chapter devotes specific attention to un-structured behavior and is consequently a continuation of these previous discussions. Here, however, attention is focused upon the more unusual and in some respects more dramatic types of behavior such as mob and crowd behavior, the rumoring and propagandizing processes, fads and fashion, and broad social movements.

The interactionist sees all behavior as being essentially social or "collective" behavior in that more than one individual is involved. It is only the manner that varies from one type of behavior to another. The difference upon which this chapter focuses attention is the amount of structure in the interaction—not whether more than one individual is involved. The term "un-

structured behavior" may accordingly be more appropriate than "collective behavior" to identify our area of concern. However, since "collective behavior" is a widely used term, we will use both terms interchangeably. The term "un-structured" is, of course, used only in a relative sense, since there is no such thing as completely unstructured or structured behavior.

ROLE TAKING—REACHING DECISIONS

Those involved in interaction are constantly role taking or empathizing—making decisions about the meaning of the behavior of others. Decisions about the meaning of standardized or routinized behavior usually follow standardized patterns and are provided by those involved without difficulty or even much conscious thought. When situations are undergoing change, when crises develop, when strong leaders are no longer able to lead because of disability or death, when accepted value definitions are being challenged and changed, when physical upheavals such as earthquakes and tornadoes disrupt social as well as physical systems, the process of role taking or of deciding "what is happening" takes on new and difficult aspects. It is at such times that behavior becomes relatively unstructured and consequently more collective in nature. One structuring technic that frequently develops under these conditions is rumoring, to which we will first turn our attention.

Figure 14.1 Machines and motives may get involved in answers to the question: "Why did I do it?" (The Bettmann Archive, Inc.)

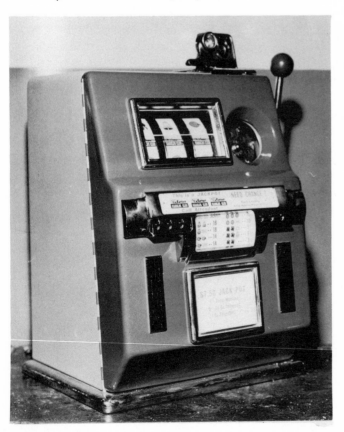

Rumoring

In terms of content, a rumor is information about some situational aspect which emanates from an anonymous source usually (1) by word of mouth or (2) by way of unidentified or informal channels.[1] The content may or may not be true,[2] although its truthfulness is generally at least somewhat questioned by those involved.

---

[1] Kurt Lang and Gladys Engel Lang, *Collective Dynamics* (New York: Thomas Y. Crowell Co., 1961), p. 53.

[2] Theodore Caplow, "Rumors in War," *Social Forces*, XXV, No. 3 (March, 1947), 298–302.

The Etiquette of Gossip

Like other small rural communities Springdale must face the classic problem of preserving individual privacy in the face of a public ideology which places a high valuation on positive expressions of equalitarianism and neighborliness. The impression of community warmheartedness which is given by the free exchange of public greetings and the easy way "everybody gets along with everybody else" has its counterpart in the absence of privacy implied by the factor of gossip. The observer who has been in the community for a length of time realizes that "everybody isn't really neighborly . . . that some people haven't talked to each other for years . . . that people whom you might think are friends hate each other. . . ." However, such statements are never made in public situations. The intimate, the negative and the private are spoken in interpersonal situations involving only two or three people. Gossip exists as a separate and hidden layer of community life.

—Arthur J. Vidich and Joseph Bensman.*

To refer to information as rumor is to express doubt about its validity. When one is inclined to believe what he hears but fears others may think it foolish, he may protect himself by passing the information along as "only a rumor." Gossip is similar to rumor.

Lang distinguishes rumor from news, which he defines as information which has a greater "ring of truth" and whose source is more likely known.[3]

How are rumors started and perpetuated? Shibutani[4] in a study of some fifteen hundred rumors concluded that rumor is facilitated when (1) individuals feel that they should be acting or getting ready to act, and when (2) there are shared wishes and fears or possibly vague expectations relative to some current situational factor, and (3) a desire for pertinent information relative to that factor and a dependence upon one another for this information. Available information may be incomplete, conflicting, or distrusted for various reasons. People may, in fact, be seeking a scapegoat for some unpleasant situation. Monotony and enforced inactivity may also be related, and rumors may result from nothing more than a desire for interesting conversation. Rumors may, of course, be "planted" by those who desire to achieve certain goals.

Whatever the specific content, rumors persist in part, at least, because they permit those involved somehow to make sense out of the behavior and the situation which concerns them. Perception and interpretation are always selective. Being the symbol user that he is, man is able to interpret behavior in many different ways. He is, in fact, able to see what he wants to see—within limits, of course. He is able symbolically to provide details in his interpretation which may not actually be there. Observation may, in fact, be inaccurate even when the observation and the reporting of it are almost simultaneous. Further, in reporting an incident to himself or to others, the restrictions of language and the effort to make the incident intelligible leads one to give a conventional form to the experience.

Further, man is constantly in the process of reinterpreting current and past events. History is in effect being constantly rewritten. One way to make sense out of unclear aspects of situations and behavior is to pay attention to rumors and then pass them along, edited, elaborated, or cut down to fit the known "facts." Rumors reflect the experiences, including the goals, of the group and the individuals from which they develop.

Three frequent content transformations of rumors as they are passed along have been identified by Allport and Postman as follows:

1. Leveling, or the deletion of aspects of the account, which, for some reason, are ignored or defined as unimportant.

* Arthur J. Vidich and Joseph Bensman, *Small Town in Mass Society* (Garden City, N. Y.: Doubleday and Co., Inc., 1958), p. 43. (An Anchor Book.)

[3] Lang and Lang, *op. cit.*, p. 51.

[4] Tamotsu Shibutani, "The Circulation of Rumors as a Form of Collective Behavior," unpublished Ph.D. dissertation, University of Chicago, 1948.

2. Sharpening, or emphasizing the points to which major attention has been given.

3. Assimilation, or reinterpretation of the information on the basis of the interpretors' experiences. In ordinary rumoring we find a marked tendency for the agent to attribute *causes* to events, *motives* to characters, and *raison d'être* to the episode in question.[5]

The development and acceptance of rumors are part of the process of collective behavior. Subjective reality being what it is, it follows that if rumors are accepted, the acceptors proceed with their behavior on the basis of the "truth" which they have. In fact, in certain respects, accepted rumors may become somewhat self-fulfilling prophecies.

Rumoring has been studied in "the field" of actual interaction and in the laboratory as well.[6] Aspects of the process can be demonstrated by the classroom or "parlor game" technic of having a group of individuals leave the room and return one at a time, with each retelling some particular story or incident to the one who follows him. Changes in the content of the story as it passes from one individual to another can be identified and analyzed.

Discontinuance of rumors is facilitated (1) when all members of the group have heard them, (2) by sudden changes in public interest, (3) by definite information which clears up the matter. Not all rumors are discredited and forgotten, however. Those that persist and are transmitted from generation to generation as a part of the culture become the legends or myths of that society and are accepted as being at least semi-official explanations of historic events.[7] They then, as Malinowski[8] has suggested, function to strengthen the tradition and endow it with a greater value and prestige by tracing the traditional beliefs back to a higher, better, and perhaps more supernatural reality of initial events.

Allport and Postman indicate that individuals whose "mental life" or patterns of thinking are either poorly structured, or else over-rigidly furnished with stereotypes and complexes are particularly susceptible to rumors. These may, of course, be poorly educated individuals.[9] The highly educated may, however, pass on certain types of rumors more than the less educated, since they are well informed on many issues which they define as worth thinking and talking about. Since they are well educated they have extensive verbal facility and are able to elaborate with ease.

Propagandizing

Use of propaganda is another technic of influencing the decisions of people. Propaganda is basically a conscious effort to get those involved to define events, objects, and goals in a particular way and to carry out the plans of action associated with such definitions. To some, the term "propaganda" carries negative connotations or implications—that is, it is viewed as an effort to get people to believe something or accept a definition which is wrong or at least not good for them, to get them to do something that they most likely would not do otherwise. Some distinguish propagandizing from educating, which is defined as the social transmission of facts and "correct" values. We will use the term with no evaluation, recognizing that what is defined as bad by one may be defined as good by another. Propagandizing is essentially a type of socialization; propaganda is the definitions, including the plans of action, which it is the goal of the propagandizers to get others to accept.

Propaganda invariably includes value definitions, since its goal is some action pattern. The previous discussions of value definitions and evaluating procedures are accordingly all related to the discussion here. Basically any effort, direct

---

[5] Gordon W. Allport and Leo Postman, *The Psychology of Rumor* (New York: Holt, Rinehart and Winston, Inc., 1947), pp. 80ff.

[6] Melvin L. DeFleur, "Mass Communication and the Study of Rumor," *Sociological Inquiry*, XXXII, No. 1 (Winter, 1962), 51–70.

[7] See Allport and Postman, *op. cit.*

[8] Bronislaw Malinowski, *Magic, Science and Religion and Other Essays* (Garden City, N. Y.: Doubleday and Co., Inc., 1954), p. 102. (An Anchor Book.)

[9] Allport and Postman, *ibid.*

or indirect, which may favorably impress those being propagandized can be effective. Some of the most frequently used propaganda technics include the following:

A. Associate the cause with existing value definitions.

  1. Use favorable words such as "justice," "mother," "home," "education"; avoid unfavorable words such as "cruelty," "communism," "murder."

  2. Use testimonials of individuals defined as important by the target audience, although the importance need have nothing directly to do with the immediate cause.

B. Speak in "glittering generalities" so that few can disagree.

C. Stack the cards, so that only details favorable to the cause are presented and present them in the most favorable manner.

D. Conceal exact identity and aims of cause.

E. Make audience anxious by suggested calamities which may result from failure to adopt the program.

F. Make a show of strength, to suggest that "everyone—but everyone" is jumping on the bandwagon.

G. Exclude competition, through whatever means will not hamper the cause.

H. Use whatever "propaganda of the deed" is available, so that the cause is provided with "action" support.

The effectiveness of any propaganda effort will be related to the manner in which it takes into account the composition, organization, susceptibility, and existing value definitions of the group toward which it is directed. It will be limited to the extent that the group has knowledge of relevant facts; by prevailing interests, prejudices, and established trends of the group; and by counter-propaganda.

Public Opinion Development and Measurement

A *public* is defined as all those who are concerned in one way or another (pro or con) with some particular issue. The issue may be of limited scope such as whether to install sidewalks along the north side of Union Street or of global scope such as whether to admit some particular nation to membership in the United Nations. A public may or may not be an organized group. Membership of a public may change and the degree of permanency will vary from public to public and for any particular public over a period of time.

Public opinion is the configuration of definitions held by a public concerning the relevant issue.

As the term is generally used, it does not involve opinions about just anything, but rather is restricted to value definitions about issues which are viewed as requiring conscious deliberation because decisions relative to them have not been previously determined. Questions exist as to which course of action the group should take with reference to the issue. A public opinion situation, as Lang and Lang have indicated, is one in which the behavior is not "scripted." The *public opinion process* involves all activities through which decisions about issues are reached.

If one wants to study public opinion he must study statements (verbal or written behavior) as to how aspects of the relevant issue are defined. An opinion may or may not be simply "for or against" the issue. Varying degrees of acceptance may be involved. Public opinion may fluctuate as other social factors change.

The behavior of publics can be contrasted with crowd behavior, which we will discuss later in the chapter. Crowd behavior involves individuals who are in close physical proximity and whose behavior is somewhat emotional; the behavior of a public, on the other hand, involves discussion and deliberation, which although it may at times be emotional is usually quite rational and unemotional. Members of a public need not be in physical proximity; they may, in fact, never see each other.

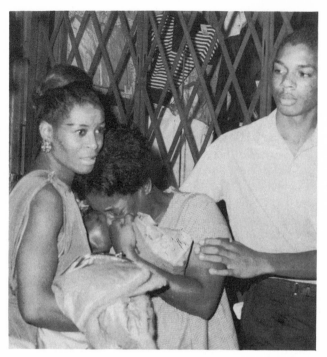

Figure 14.2 Taking the role of the other may lead to shared reactions or "feeling with" the other. (Wide World Photos.)

Any particular individual is likely to be a member of several different publics, giving attention to a particular issue as the situation seems to him to be appropriate. Although all members of a public usually do not know each other, they often react to an issue with the expectation that there is a group of others who will display reaction patterns similar to theirs and in support of their position.

Public concern for any particular issue may involve individuals and/or groups. On the issue of, say, the salary of teachers, the National Education Association may formulate and publicize an official opinion, as may a labor union or a parent–teacher association. Individual members of such groups may, of course, hold contrary opinions. The group's opinion may be taken into account by other groups and by individuals who are not members. Interaction between groups as well as between individuals may be involved in the development of public opinion. The opin-

ions of individuals and groups will frequently reflect the opinions of appropriate reference groups or significant "others."

Opinion Formation

The process of opinion formation involves all of the socializing agencies and processes which we have previously discussed. Reference groups and significant others are particularly involved, as are experiences which are unique to the particular individual.

Research in the area of opinion formation has identified "opinion leaders." Not everyone in a community has equal access to sources of information, nor an equal interest in seeking out relevant information and evaluating pros and cons. Those who are in such a position socially and geographically that they are the recipients and subsequent dispensers of such information are called opinion leaders. Research has indicated that much information relative to particular issues is, in fact, channeled through such individuals, who are accordingly in positions to edit consciously or unconsciously the content of the message as they receive and transmit it. They consequently become important factors in the whole dynamic opinion formation process.

Many members of the community turn to such opinion leaders to be told subtly or otherwise how they should define the situation, or what they should think about the issues at hand.

Information, including propaganda, transmitted via the mass media of the society is also involved in the opinion-formation process. Individual and group response to the mass media involves selective attention (and inattention) and selective perception (and ignoring), and consequently will vary from individual to individual and from group to group. The intent of the information dispenser may not be realized in the dynamic process of transmission and interpretation. Prejudiced individuals, for instance, or those who strongly endorse a value position may interpret the content of any anti-prejudice message in such a way that their prejudice remains undisturbed. We may hear and see what we want to.

Effect of Public Opinion

Public opinion is developed in situations, some aspects of which are unstructured. A major consequence of the development of public opinion is that structure may be provided thereby. Decisions may accordingly be made either by the whole group or by those in various power positions, who set into motion related social processes. Strong public opinion in favor of some behavior may result in laws being passed to assure that the desired behavior takes place. The development of strong opinion in favor of or against some behavior may provide the groundwork out of which folkways may become standardized and may in time evolve into mores. Our previous discussion of folkways and mores has indicated that their development is informal in nature. Public opinion formation is involved in this process.

Decisions made now, of course, influence future behavior and become the social facts of subsequent interaction.

In other areas, public opinion as expressed in the voting process determines who is elected to office and who is not, as well as whether a particular referendum is accepted or rejected.

This is not to say that public opinion is all that is involved in such activities—it is not. In fact, laws may be passed which are contrary to public wishes. Vested interest groups may have sufficient strength and/or political *savoir faire* to "stack the cards" in their favor in spite of contrary public opinion.

We should also be aware of the influence which public opinion polling *per se* may have upon subsequent opinion. Announcement of the results of such polls may help to create public opinion in support of the "public" opinion, or under certain circumstances may have a boomerang effect and help create a groundswell of opinion favorable for the underdog candidate or issue.

In a democratic society, public opinion may have more direct influence upon the societal behavior than, say, in a totalitarian nation. Democracy, in fact, rests upon the value premise that it is good for the members of society to be directly involved in the decision-making process. Further, a capitalistic type of economic structure encourages the involvement of the general public in decisions as to what will or will not be purchased and at what price. We should not be surprised if under such conditions men attempt to develop skills and technics designed to "win friends and influence people."

Another consequence of the process of public opinion formation is the emergence within the society of new groups that take into account the opinion lines or boundaries which are developed. Such groups may, then, engage in more formal actions to protect or perhaps to further what they define as important. Any society is a multi-group phenomenon. Public opinion formation is one of the factors involved in the kaleidoscopic patterns of groups with overlapping membership which develop in any society. Boundaries of "emotional contagion" are not set by physical proximity or even by group membership, but by limits of effective communication.

To summarize, we have indicated that in efforts to structure any behavior sequence individuals or groups give credence to rumors, gossip, propaganda, and the opinion of others concerned (public opinion). In addition to involving these definitions in his own interpretation, the individual may pay attention to the on-going behavior of the others with whom he is currently interacting and involve his interpretation of their behavior in his decisions as to what he himself will do. This may involve rational, conscious evaluation or may be spontaneous and unconscious. A factor involved in such interaction has come to be called "emotional contagion," or "emotional feedback." This phenomenon is found in the development of relatively unstructured crowd behavior, discussed in the next section. First, however, let us discuss emotional contagion *per se* and then relate it to the behavior of various types of groups.

Emotional Contagion. In situations where those involved are not sure exactly what to do or what is expected of themselves or of others, it is easy to become emotional or to engage in emotional behavior. With no clear cues from

Figure 14.3 Emotional contagion is evident in this painting of the celebration of the establishment of the Pony Express between St. Joseph, Missouri, and Sacramento, California, in 1860. (The Bettmann Archive, Inc.)

others as to what is expected, it is easy for some at least to "do what comes naturally." Individuals are then free or may feel free to give primary attention to behavioral factors which under other circumstances they have controlled or "repressed" as being inappropriate for those circumstances. As degree of structure decreases, the behavior alternates increase—within limits, of course.

If for some reason the behavior of certain members of the group becomes excited in that movement becomes rapid or somewhat random, talking becomes rapid and loud, faces become flushed, etc., others may see this behavior and follow suit. In terms of two individuals (and this, of course, greatly over-simplifies the situa-

tion), the pattern progresses something like this. A sees B engaging in excited, emotional behavior, and A's behavior as a result becomes more excited and emotional. B then sees A's emotional behavior and finds re-inforcement for his own behavior—he finds additional proof that there is something about the situation to get excited about. After all, others are excited too. So, his behavior becomes a bit more rapid, random, and high pitched. A then sees the increased excitement of B's behavior and becomes even more excited himself, with this increased excitement adding stimulation to B's excited stage and raising his level of excitement, and on and on in a cycle of mutual stimulation.

Religious Conflict

A church leader commented on a town meeting to discuss religion in the classroom, as follows:

"About 500 people were present, and most were out for blood. I wish I could communicate to you the abusiveness and violence in the air that night among the 'Christian' majority.... It was the mood of the western movie just before someone produces the rope, saying, 'We can handle this ourselves, boys—let's not wait for the sheriff.' This is no exaggeration. You just wouldn't have believed that it could happen in Hamden."

—Earl Raab.*

This process is magnified, of course, by the number of interacting individuals in the crowd.

As excited, emotional behavior increases, the crowd in effect gets prepared for some sort of action and is somewhat like "an accident or an incident looking for a place to happen." Under these circumstances various factors may be involved in the sequence of events which determines what the group eventually does. It is at this point that a leader may direct the group to the accomplishment of certain goals. If any individual or individuals present do things defined by the others as "leader behavior" or if they have symbols defined as "status symbols or leader symbols," they are likely to be called upon to structure the situation for the group. If clearly established leader behavior or symbols are not identifiable, then attention may be given to more subtle cues, and individuals who "look like they know what they are doing" may be "pushed" (reluctantly or otherwise) into leadership positions by the others, not only because they may want someone to lead them, but also because these incipient leaders have characteristics which lead others to expect them to take over the leadership of the group.

* Earl Raab (ed.), *Religious Conflict in America* (Garden City, N. Y.: Doubleday and Co., Inc., 1964), p. 206.

In spontaneous and unplanned collective behavior, leaders may arise from the interaction. It is also true, however, that situations may be carefully and deliberately planned so that certain "leaders" will be identified by the group. They can then lead the group in the accomplishment of goals which the leader and his cohorts had previously planned. Lynchings and riots may be of this type, although the majority of those involved and actually doing the "dirty work" may be unaware of the fact that they have been manipulated to further the goals of others.

Various leadership technics may be involved. The leader must first be accepted by the crowd as "one of us," even though a leader. He may encourage emotional behavior by use of rhythm, such as singing, clapping, swaying, band music, etc. Symbols may be employed to give crowd members a rallying point, or to increase "we" definitions. The leader may provide value definitions to justify on-going and projected behavior and may suggest means of accomplishing goals in harmony with these value definitions. Further dramatic behavior on the part of the leader may help to extend the emotionality of the behavior so that the group may increasingly define the situation as one which "demands" action.

Rumors may contribute to and be a product of emotional contagion.

Whatever the process by which the emotional behavior of the crowd is increased, the identity of the individual undergoes a transformation. Self identity increasingly becomes group identity. Lack of clear norm-role definitions contributes to the decision that the individual cannot be held responsible for his immediate behavior: How can one be accused of "breaking the rules" when there are no rules to break? The fact that others are present and doing the same things contributes to definitions of strength of the group and anonymity of the individual. Individuals are, of course, capable of engaging in emotional behavior when alone, but they are more likely to do so when caught up in the emotional, contagious behavior of the group. They may even, as many have testified, get caught up in spite of efforts not to. Man is a social being and his behavior is always relative to his situation.

CROWD BEHAVIOR—UNSTRUCTURED INTERACTION

We turn our attention now from the process by which definitions are secured to an analysis of the behavior of various types of groups which, among other things, take such definitions into account. We use the term "crowd behavior" to identify the broad category of such interaction. We define a crowd as a temporary collection of persons who react to a common focus of attention and engage in somewhat spontaneous interaction. The discussion will include the following types of crowd behavior:

1. Casual crowds
2. Conventional crowds or audiences
3. Expressive crowds
4. Acting crowds
   a. Mobs
   b. Rioting crowds
   c. Orgiastic crowds
   d. Panicking crowds

A crowd may form out of an organized group and conversely may develop into one. Crowds are constantly "in process"; they change frequently. They vary in size.

Casual Crowds

Groups watching a demonstration in a store window or the "sidewalk superintendents" at the local construction site are casual crowds. The actions of the members of such a crowd are not

Figure 14.4   Crowd behavior. The Great Methodist Camp Meeting, 1865. (The Bettmann Archive, Inc.)

preplanned, except in the broad sense that the general norm definitions of the society apply. Since they are together engaging in casual interaction, there is always the possibility that they may develop into an active crowd, such as a mob or a rioting crowd. Regulations which, in times of crisis, prohibit two or more people from collecting at any one place are designed to eliminate the possibility that casual crowds may become more active.

Conventional Crowds or Audiences

Conventional crowds or audiences are groups such as spectators at a football game, the persons gathered to witness the presentation of *Hamlet* by the university thespians, attendees at a PTA meeting, or delegates to a national political convention. Behavior of such groups is conventional in the sense that considerable interaction is patterned by established norm-role definitions, but a segment of behavior is deliberately left unstructured so that crowd members are sensitive to the behavior of others in decisions as to their own behavior. At a football game, for instance, the demonstrations of the crowd when a touchdown is made by the home team are somewhat, although never completely, spontaneous. Decisions to tear down the goal posts may arise from interaction following the winning or losing of the game. Audience reaction to the particular presentation of *Hamlet* depends upon factors which emerge from the on-going interaction, rather than from previously established norm-role definitions. Even here, however, culture is involved in that crowds in different societies "spontaneously" behave in different, somewhat traditional ways. It is the unstructured aspect of such behavior which leads to the inclusion of such group behavior in our discussion of "collective behavior." Emotional contagion is involved in such behavior.

Expressive Crowds

Expressive crowds are groups in which the members engage in behavior which is primarily defined as an end in itself rather than a means to some other end. Such groups do not disperse or direct their action toward some outside goal, but rather mill, jostle each other, possibly shouting, singing, or talking to each other. The behavior may be viewed as expressing or representing some "inner" feelings or emotions. The group at the college prom is an expressive crowd, in that they have congregated primarily to "express themselves" in acts of dancing. In some religious services people weep, laugh, twitch, or engage in other "spontaneous" behavior. Such groups are another example of expressive crowds.

Such behavior is never completely spontaneous, but is much more so than the behavior of other crowds.

Close physical proximity is an important factor in the development of emotional behavior in audiences or expressive crowds. An audience scattered over a large auditorium is not as responsive to the speaker as one in which the members are "rubbing shoulders" with each other. Revivalist speakers try to get their audience close to them, knowing that they will be better able to manipulate the group in the way they desire.

Acting Crowds

The major characteristic of an acting crowd is that attention and behavior are focused upon a particular goal. The selectivity of perception is heightened. The goal is defined in such a way that efforts to achieve the goal become emotional in nature, and those involved get "all wrapped up in" its accomplishment. They are influenced by the shouts and excited movements of others. Emotional contagion is particularly evident here. Such crowds are unstable and changeable, but members do not "let go" so much that they will literally do "anything." General norm definitions such as the wearing of clothes and the safety of the members of one's own group are still honored.

Mobs. A mob is a fairly unified crowd engaging in actions directed toward the accomplishment of some limited goal, such as the destruction of a building or a lynching. Such behavior is frequently very impersonal in nature in that it is directed toward any and all members of some particular group. Participants in one mob reported, "We didn't know him [the man killed]. He wasn't bothering us. But other people were fighting and killing and we felt like it, too." [10] As the term is generally used, the goal toward which the mob action is directed is one which would not have wide public approval. Consequently, such crowds are sometimes called "lawless" crowds. Such behavior may be technically against the established laws but have the support of the local mores. It would be safe to conclude, in fact, that mob behavior would not take place if there were not at least partial informal support for it. · A lynching can be avoided if enough people are opposed to it.

The aggression of mobs is always related to the social situation. Targets are socially defined. Scapegoating may be involved, and the aggressive behavior may be directed toward substitute targets when particular targets are not available.

Rioting crowds. Rioting is mob behavior but on a wider scale. It involves more than one group engaged in similar behavior in different places at about the same time. Rioting crowds, then, are influenced not only by the immediate local situational factors, but also by the society- or community-wide definitions and experiences which have made the broader situation "ripe" for some sort of action.

Research has indicated that active participants in race riots tend to be young, unmarried, lower class, and economically insecure.[11] Many of them have prior police records.[12] They are likely to be individuals with few responsibilities, many frustrations, and violent racial prejudices. They have bitter class hostilities, reject middle-class value definitions, and resent being lectured at and pushed around by authorities who represent the middle-class world from which they have been rejected.[13]

Orgiastic crowds. At times society may permit the relaxation of the norm-role definitions and allow or even encourage orgies of one type or another. Extensive drinking may be encouraged, sexual standards usually maintained may be rescinded "for the duration," and individuals may be encouraged to "let go." The goal of such behavior may be a "release of tension." That the orgy may be functional is suggested by LaPiere who indicates that with the curtailing of orgiastic demonstrations in the pubs of England by legal means, the frequency of wife-beating increased.[14]

Panicking crowds. A panicking crowd is a group in a state of collective retreat. The goal is basically to get away from something. Physi-

---

Lack of Leadership

In such stress situations, where the individual perceives only confusion, he may long for something or someone to provide standards of conduct. Thus soldiers caught in a hasty withdrawal of British forces after the breakthrough by Rommel's army in Libya, completely surrounded by confusion "bewilderment and fear and ignorance" wanted to receive orders. Here is the statement of a veteran wounded in the North Africa campaign: "One time we begged our lieutenants to give orders. They were afraid to act because they didn't have the rank. We took a beating while they were waiting for orders. . . ."

—Muzafer Sherif and O. J. Harvey.*

---

[10] Alfred M. Lee and Norman D. Humphrey, *Race Riot* (New York: Holt, Rinehart and Winston, Inc., 1943), p. 38.

[11] George Wada and James C. Davies, "Riots and Rioters," *Western Political Quarterly*, X, No. 4 (December, 1957), 864–874.

[12] Lee and Humphrey, *op. cit.*, pp. 80–88.

* Muzafer Sherif and O. J. Harvey, "Implications of Observations from Life Situations," in *Collective Behavior*, ed. by Ralph H. Turner and Lewis M. Killian (Englewood Cliffs, N. J.: Prentice-Hall, Inc., 1957), p. 53.

[13] Paul B. Horton and Chester L. Hunt, *Sociology* (New York: McGraw-Hill Book Co., 1964), p. 408.

[14] Richard LaPiere, *Collective Behavior* (New York: McGraw-Hill Book Co., 1938), p. 484.

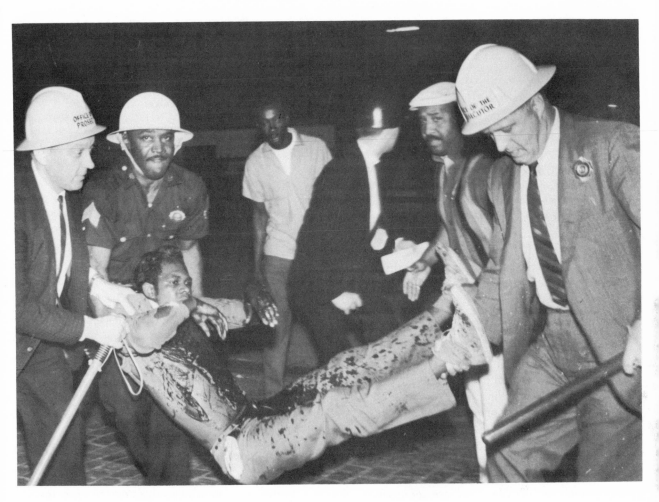

Figure 14.5 Riots may have bloody results. (Wide World Photos.)

cal survival may be involved, but preservation of economic or other social factors may also be important. Participants may define the situation in such severe terms that their behavior becomes, in fact, "terror behavior." They may be fearful and anxious of something. Emotional contagion is apparent in such behavior, since the efforts of others to get away may increase the sense of overwhelming danger. When a ship is sinking, when a theater is on fire (or thought to be on fire), when invaders are approaching, crowds may panic. With attention focused upon retreating, established norm-role definitions are in gen-eral ignored. The fact that everyone is or feels left to "look out for himself" is characterized by Lang as a condition of extreme "privatization."

Another type of panic behavior is immobility, in which efforts to escape take the form of either doing nothing except staying where one is or, in extreme cases, of refusing to think, speak, or take into account those around you—figuratively, a complete withdrawal (symbolic, not physical)—getting away from the situation by hiding "within oneself." Either type of retreat may be functional in that preservation of the individual may be accomplished.

The panic or retreat efforts may extend beyond the boundaries of an immediately interested crowd, as in the case of a radio program announcing an "invasion from Mars," in response to which hundreds of people fled or started to flee from a city.[15] "Mass panic" is a term used to label such behavior.

Many factors have an influence upon crowd behavior. Part of the explanation of such behavior lies in the socialization process itself. It would seem that no group has as yet developed a society in which the interaction was completely harmonious, so that all concerned individually and collectively were able to achieve all they desired. It would seem to be inevitable then that individuals would become dissatisfied with some aspects of life. Individuals and groups may become anxious or concerned as to whether they will be able to achieve goals upon which they "have their hearts set," plus many and varied minor frustrations. Under such circumstances, various types of adjustment are developed, not all of which turn out to be equally acceptable to those involved, even though they are somewhat forced to live with them. When these adjustment technics prove to be inadequate in the face of current situations, the individual may "go to pieces" and become more susceptible to crowd influences or collective influences. Such individuals, then, are more susceptible to crowd behavior. Laboratory research also supports the premise that the likelihood that students will engage in mob behavior decreases with increase in age, education, and intelligence.[16]

Crowd Control

Various technics have been found to be effective in controlling crowd behavior. Lohman,[17] a sociologist who has worked extensively with policemen, suggests the following:

1. Prevent crowd formation by promptly arresting and carrying off noisy trouble makers and ordering the onlookers to move on.

2. Meet any threatened disorder with an impressive show of force. Bring in enough police and equipment so that the use of force is unnecessary.

3. Isolate the riot area. Throw a police cordon around it, and allow people to leave but none to enter.

4. Diminish crowd by directing persons on fringes to "break it up" and go home. The crowd is thus stripped of support—potential and/or actual.

5. Train police to define maintaining the peace as an important part of their role, so that an officer's own prejudices do not lead him into the fatal error of ignoring attacks on those whom he dislikes personally.

Other procedures include distracting the attention of the crowd by one means or another and possibly redirecting it so that some particular action is avoided, plus removing the leaders if this can be accomplished without force. The crowd may, of course, disintegrate after the accomplishment of its goal, or as a result of some shocking experience which may bring the members "to their senses."

Unstructured situations are productive of change and change is productive of unstructured situations. New and distinctive patterns of defining and of behaving may be developed from such interaction, and may, of course, be evaluated in any number of different ways. Generally collective behavior, particularly crowd behavior, is seen as more likely to be productive of socially disapproved than approved behavior. However, behavior defined as heroic also results under such conditions. It is likewise true that the "hero" for one group is the "traitor" of another. Tremendous feelings of morale and group loyalty may be engendered by a collective behavior experience.

---

[15] Hadley Cantril, *The Invasion from Mars* (Princeton, N. J.: Princeton University Press, 1940). Reports on "The War of the Worlds," broadcast by Orson Welles in 1938.

[16] Norman C. Meier, G. H. Mennenga, and H. J. Stoltz, "An Experimental Approach to the Study of Mob Behavior," *Journal of Abnormal and Social Psychology*, XXXVI, No. 4 (October, 1941), 506–524.

[17] Joseph D. Lohman, *The Police and Minority Groups* (Chicago: Chicago Park District, 1947).

Fads, Fashions, and Crazes

On a less dramatic level, creativity resulting from various types of collective behavior is constantly being manifested. Fads, fashions, and crazes of one type or another spring up, run their course, and are replaced by others. Some types of such behavior and their associated products find their way into the more permanent behavior patterns of the group.

Fads and fashions, as a type of norm definition, are of temporary duration and are evaluated highly by the adherents, who may comprise only a small segment of a community or society. They are of such a nature that faddish or fashionable behavior does not involve much revision of the more established behavior patterns and is frequently somewhat cyclical or rhythmic in nature. When such behavior takes on great emotional investment, so that considerable time and energy are invested, the term "craze" is used. Fashions, fads, and crazes are not necessarily utilitarian or economically rewarding, but persist because they are related to other interests of those involved. Neither are any formal sanctions established to facilitate adoption of the appropriate behavior.

Conscious efforts involving propaganda and other mass media technics to initiate such behavior may, of course, be made, with financial gains

---

Fashions

We have found no evidence ... that fashions in given names are deliberately promoted. Among the names most common to girls born in Boston in the seventeenth century were Hannah, Abigail, Mehitabel, Bethiah, and Dorcas. Also fairly common were the "meaningful" names of abstract qualities: Mercy, Thankful, Desire and the like.

—Kurt Lang and Gladys Engel Lang.*

---

* Kurt Lang and Gladys Engel Lang, *Collective Dynamics* (New York: Thomas Y. Crowell Co., 1961), p. 477.

occurring to those who are able to "cash in" on the behavior. Not all such ventures succeed, however. The success or failure rests in part upon the decisions of many individuals who are in relatively unstructured situations which permit them to be influenced by a variety of impinging conditions, many of which are hard to predict. While there is much that is not known about such behavior, there is evidence to suggest that those who participate in a particular fad, fashion, or craze usually come from similar social circumstances, and that they tend to be somewhat uncertain about their own social status, which may encourage them to pay particular attention to those whom they define as leaders in one field or another. Adolescents of subordinate minority groups are particularly likely to be involved. New ways of behaving may develop from a desire to be somewhat different from others. They become fads and fashions when others want to conform—not deviate.

Each group and each stratum of a society has its own fashions and fads, and most persons are sensitive to changes in areas which are important to them. Fashions and fads are more common in a changing society like that of the United States than in a stable folk society.

Social Movements. Through the dynamic interplay of many factors, broad social and cultural changes may be set in motion. Scattered individuals develop somewhat the same interests and their satisfaction may necessitate important changes in the social structure. As these individuals through one means or another become aware of their common interest, they band together for mutual support. Relatively unstructured organizations may develop from such contacts; if continued support is found they may go through the institutionalization process and become increasingly structured. Local organizations may join together. Regional affiliations may be formed and a national organization may eventually be established. The major goal of such activities is change, and this includes not only change in interaction patterns, but in established value definitions as well. Social movement is the label for such changes; examples in the United States have been woman suffrage, prohibition, and civil rights.

VALUE DEFINITIONS

Structured or unstructured behavior (social organization or disorganization) can be evaluated in any number of ways. Some have called it "pathological"; others have viewed at least certain types as "progressive" in that they have caused certain changes defined as desirable to be introduced into society.[18] No evaluation is provided or intended here; our purpose is to try to understand such behavior.

Change can, of course, be valued in its own right. Yet, regardless of how unstructured behavior *per se* is evaluated, it is true that value definitions are inherently involved in such behavior. For one thing, the endorsement of certain value definitions may contribute to collective behavior, whereas endorsement of another set may discourage such behavior. Those, for instance, who strongly value a "free will" or a "rugged individualism" interpretation of human behavior tend to discourage the adoption of norm-role definitions which will highly structure behavior. The democratic government and capitalistic economic system in the United States, for instance, have incorporated such value definitions, and have developed harmonious norm-role definitions. However, when the freedom of those who endorse such positions begins to be curtailed by the "individualistic" behavior of others, it is not uncommon that they will seek to protect their own freedom by imposing social limitations upon the freedom of competitors. "What you have is negotiable, what I have is mine."

The degree of freedom or choice in any behavior, however, is always relative, and it is a safe sociological conclusion that most "free" people are not as free as they think they are. In fact, being free to do certain things usually involves being highly restricted in other areas.

[18] For a discussion of various approaches see Lang and Lang, *op. cit.*, chap. ii.

Individuals, for instance, are not free to carry on a discussion unless they restrict themselves to the use of the same language. It is sociologically more meaningful to ask what types of freedom are related to what types of social structure than to talk of freedom in the abstract.

Further, highly structured behavior derives in part from having a clear value structure which individuals endorse. Where value definitions are not clearly established, or where established value definitions are being questioned or challenged, the situation is ripe for collective action of one type or another.

Value definitions are likewise reflected in whatever collective behavior takes place. Rumors, propaganda, crowd behavior, fads, fashions, and social movements reflect the value definitions of those involved. Being NER in nature, value definitions are particularly susceptible to re-interpretation or re-editing, and the value structure imposed upon the behavior before, during, and after it takes place may be quite different.

NORM-ROLE DEFINITIONS

A major source of social order is the set of norm-role definitions which the group develops. Social order is man-made order. Behavior in any situation, then, can be as rigid or as unstructured as the group decides or as previous groups have decided. In a sense, groups even develop norms as to how extensively they want to *norm*alize their interaction. The extent to which those involved in any on-going interaction are able to make on-the-spot decisions concerning that interaction will, of course, vary. Decisions must constantly be made, however, as to whether norms have been developed to cover the situation, which norms are applicable, and whether their applicability continues as the interaction progresses. When interaction has been pre-planned, most people feel that it is easier to adapt themselves and their behavior to these plans than it is to "fly blind." It is not uncommon that simply the completion of previously decided-upon plans becomes a goal in itself—whatever the goal of the original plans may have been. This is sometimes referred to as efforts to obtain closure. Terminating incompleted plans in midstream may be a discomforting experience.

Collective behavior, then, is to some degree a part of all interaction, but begins to take on particular importance or begins to be more manifest under certain conditions such as: (1) when norms have not been developed to handle the interaction, (2) when established norm-role definitions for one reason or another no longer appear to be applicable to the on-going behavior, or some individuals want to evade them, or when (3) disaster or crisis makes it impossible or apparently impossible to enact the established norm-role definitions.

Mob and rioting behavior, the most dramatic and drastic types of collective behavior, are most likely to occur at places and times when interaction is least structured.[19]

It follows also that collective behavior may be productive of consensus concerning behavior so that new norm-role definitions are standardized.

SELF DEFINITION

The individual is always aware that he is involved in the collective behavior, and is constantly telling himself about such participation. However, since perception (of self or any other phenomenon) is always selective, self awareness is a relative thing. In rigidly controlled situations, the individual may de-emphasize self awareness and routinely go through the prescribed behavior or, in fact, may "have his mind on" things far removed from his current behavior. Likewise, in unstructured situations, the individual may, to a high degree, "forget about himself" and be so caught up in the on-going sequence, or pay so much attention to what is going on around him that he gets carried along with the crowd without strong self awareness. In the anonymity of a crowd, individuals may

---

Role Restrictions *

"After I heard the first explosion my first impulse was to go down to the docks and try to help there. But on the way down I saw two or three folks I knew who had husbands down there. I saw then that my job was with the families—not doing rescue work. I had a job that I was peculiarly suited for, prepared for, and I felt that I should do that."

---

feel little sense of individual responsibility.[20] A participant may, in fact, suddenly "come to his senses" and ask himself or others what he is doing there. He may, in retrospect, be surprised at his own behavior and possibly raise questions as to how he could have done a particular thing. This is reflected in the definition of a mob as a group in which "we all go crazy together."

Such experiences are productive of particular self definitions. Participation in a race riot or a lynching may serve to heighten one's awareness of his racial identity. Definitions of shame, guilt, or pride may result from such interaction. Efforts may be made to forget about—or to relive—the experience. Definitions as to one's strength, ability to endure pain, or susceptibility to "group pressure" may result. One does not, from the interactionist perspective, discover aspects of his "real self" through such interaction. What we have in collective behavior is just another illustration of the fact that behavior is always relative to the situation, and it consequently changes as the situation changes. All behavior is real behavior. Self definitions may be changed from collective experiences, but the resulting definitions are no more "real" than any others.

---

* Quoted by L. M. Killian in "The Significance of Multiple-Group Membership in Disaster," *The American Journal of Sociology*, LVII, No. 4 (January, 1952), 309–313.

[20] See Leon Festinger, A. Pepitone, and Theodore M. Newcomb, "Some Consequences of De-Individuation in a Group," *Journal of Abnormal and Social Psychology*, XLVII, No. 2 (April, 1952), 382–389.

---

[19] Lewis M. Killian, "The Significance of Multiple-Group Membership in Disaster," *The American Journal of Sociology*, LVII, No. 4 (January, 1952), 309–313.

Self definitions may be changed through another type of relatively unstructured interaction—nondirective individual counseling, or group therapy sessions. Experiences of this type, in which those involved are permitted to engage in relatively unstructured self analysis which at times may go to great "depth," usually terminate with the individual's applying a different set of labels to himself. Again, no set is any more "real" than another—they are all real, and may be all different. Any object, including the individual doing the defining, can be viewed in any number of different ways, and experience in an unstructured situation is productive of one type of definition.

SOCIALIZATION

Unstructured behavior does not result from "animal instincts" long repressed in one's "unconscious," but rather is behavior which people engage in under particular conditions. Actually, while certain past learned behavior may be defined as inappropriate or may not be taken into account as being even possibly appropriate for the situation, the behavior of people under crowd–mob situations is always at least partially structured and thus partially a result of learning. Those involved usually continue to wear clothes; they continue to speak and think in their native language, although shouts, cries, or groans, without using specific symbols, may serve to heighten the unstructuredness, in that this is verbal behavior for which only vague definitions have been previously provided.

The other side of the socialization process is also present in that collective behavior not only involves previously learned behavior to some degree, but is a part of the socialization process *per se*. From such experiences, individuals and groups develop new patterns and new value, norm-role, and self definitions. Many currently accepted patterns have originated through just such processes.

SUMMARY

In efforts to bring order to relatively unstructured interaction, attention may be given to rumors, propaganda, and the opinions of those concerned with a particular issue—a public. Out of interaction which takes these and other factors into account, and which may involve emotional feedback, decisions emerge which become involved in interaction. Unstructured behavior may occur in casual crowds, conventional crowds, expressive crowds, and action crowds—mobs, rioting crowds, orgiastic crowds, and panicking crowds.

Interaction patterns and related objects "catch on" and spread widely throughout a society and then usually dissipate—fads, fashions, and crazes, as well as the more extensive and more permanent social movements.

Collective behavior involves learned behavior and is productive of new insights and behavior patterns. It is always rooted in established value, norm-role, and self definitions, but may also be productive of changes, at times rather dramatic in any or all of these.

QUESTIONS

1. Why would it be unrealistic to think of a completely structured or completely unstructured situation?
2. How are role taking and role playing involved in collective behavior?
3. In what respects might a rumor become self-fulfilling?
4. Identify some of the propaganda technics used in the advertisements in a current magazine.
5. How can efforts to determine public opinion influence public opinion?
6. How do the cheer leaders at a college football game attempt to develop emotional contagion in the crowd?
7. Distinguish mobs, riots, and panic.
8. Identify a fad in which you have participated and decide what factors contributed to your participation.
9. How are social movements different from fads, fashions, and crazes?
10. How does the discussion of collective behavior in this chapter harmonize with the discussion in Chapter 4 of the social nature of human behavior?

PROJECT

Analyze the behavior at a religious meeting and identify any of the processes of collective behavior which were discussed in this chapter. Compare the analyses of different meetings provided by various students in the class.

SUGGESTED READING

ALLPORT, GORDON W., and L. POSTMAN. *The Psychology of Rumor.* New York: Holt, Rinehart and Winston, Inc., 1947.

BERELSON, BERNARD, and MORRIS JANOWITZ (eds.). The *Reader in Public Opinion and Communication.* (Rev. ed.). New York: The Free Press of Glencoe, 1953.

CANTRIL, HADLEY. *Gauging Public Opinion.* Princeton, N. J.: Princeton University Press, 1947.

HEBERLE, RUDOLF. *Social Movements.* New York: Appleton-Century-Crofts, 1951.

LANG, KURT, and GLADYS ENGEL LANG. *Collective Dynamics.* New York: Thomas Y. Crowell Co., 1961.

LAPIERE, R. T. *Collective Behavior.* New York: McGraw-Hill Book Co., 1938.

LEBON, GUSTAVE. *The Crowd.* New York: Compass Books, The Viking Press, Inc., 1960, paperback ed. Introduction by Robert K. Merton.

SMELSER, NEIL J. *Theory of Collective Behavior.* New York: The Free Press of Glencoe, 1963.

STRAUSS, ANSELM. "Research in Collective Behavior: Neglect and Need," *American Sociological Review,* XII (June, 1947), 352–354.

TURNER, RALPH H., and LEWIS M. KILLIAN. *Collective Behavior.* Englewood Cliffs, N. J.: Prentice-Hall, Inc., 1957.

15

Motivation

In courts of law, in family interaction, in religious behavior, and in moments of most intense self analysis, a question that keeps appearing is: "Why? Why did I (he, they) do it?" The question takes on particular importance when the behavior involved is defined as wrong. How can we account for the fact that human beings are able to do things which they define as wrong?

The concept of motivation has been of interest in many different disciplines and has been woven into the various theories of human behavior. Consequently, various definitions of "motive" have been employed by various people and today numerous interpretations are available to the customer in the "idea marketplace." Our discussion and definitions will harmonize with the symbolic interactionist perspective.

Motivation is accordingly defined as the explanations or reasons, frequently stated in terms of purposes, goals, or incentives, given by an individual to himself (subjective reality) as to why he behaves in a particular way. Such statements may be provided before, during, or after the related behavior. In actual interaction, such be-

havior is frequently silent (thinking) behavior. Research concerning motives, motive decisions, or motivational behavior, as we define these terms, requires that one pay attention to verbal (or written) behavior given with no intent to answer deceitfully some form of the question "Why did you do that?" or "What justification did you provide to yourself for doing such and such?" There is no inherent relationship between any particular act and any particular motive decision. Any act can be performed for any number of different motive reasons, and, likewise, any motive decision may be related to any number of different acts. It is important, therefore, to know how these variables are related by the individual involved. One way to determine this is, of course, to ask individuals to provide motive statements, as frequently happens in everyday interaction.

In research where such direct data are unavailable, an alternate procedure of inferring motivational elements through some role-taking procedure is used. Inferred motives are also frequently involved in counseling, clinical, or other applied approaches. It should be clear from our previous discussions, however, that the two approaches do not necessarily measure the same thing. In the first procedure, the individual provides answers about himself, whereas in the second the researcher provides answers about the individual. Some of the problems involved in the inference procedure are suggested by the fact that what is inferred seems always to fit into the frame of reference of the one doing the inferring, rather than that of the subject. Quite possibly the subject does not even know the concepts used by the clinician or the researcher to label "his" motives. The psychoanalyst, the religious counselor, or the clinical psychologist, it seems, consistently ends up with a motivational interpretation different from the others but consistent with the orientation of the one doing the inferring. Which, if any, of these motives (including that of the subject) is the "true" motivational pattern and which is a "rationalization" is open to question, and in any case depends upon how "true" is defined.

For certain purposes, however, each of these interpretations may be useful. Further, quite possibly the utility of such decisions for specific purposes such as counseling is enhanced if the client as well as the counselor is convinced that the same interpretation is, in fact, the "true" interpretation. Motivational phenomena, however, like all phenomena, are capable of being interpreted in many different ways, and the answers one gets are always relative to the method used to secure them. Our definition will be the one given above: we will pay attention to the motive definitions provided by the individual.

The fact that the motive decisions of an individual do not harmonize with the decisions of others analyzing the same behavior does not nec-

essarily invalidate either. Whatever the relationship may be between these two definitions, it is important to know how the individual defines his own behavior, and then how these definitions are related to other variables. It is the purpose of this chapter to explore such relationships. If direct and inferential motive behavior are to be studied, there would appear to be value in distinguishing between them, with identifying labels such as "self motives" or "direct motives" contrasted with "inferred motives." This would avoid calling either type the "true" motive while suggesting that the other is somehow untrue or unreal. Individuals may, of course, tell themselves one thing about their motive decisions and provide others with quite a different interpretation. This is another of the complexities of human interaction. Our concern here, however, is with motive decisions given to oneself *with no intent to deceive.*

Since we are here concerned with the self or direct motives, the material in this chapter is related to the previous discussion of self definitions provided in Chapter 10.

As has been suggested, answers to motivational questions can be secured about past, current, and future behavior. The answers which an individual gives to himself about the same behavioral sequence may be different under each of these conditions: (1) as he anticipates and plans his future behavior, including the time just prior to entering into the contemplated behavior, (2) as he enacts the behavior, and (3) as he reviews the behavior from some subsequent perspective. Individuals who have "found religion" may, for instance, find that current interpretations of past behavior may be quite different from the interpretations provided at the

---

Motives and Gifts

"It's not the price of the gift but the thought back of it that is important," is a familiar American value statement.

Suicide Motivation

In our model the "agent" of suicide is the "germ of the idea," the suicidal hypothesis. This is the belief that suicide is a good solution to life's problems which is always available when things become too difficult. No one commits suicide— I believe—who has not thought about it, no matter how briefly, and who has not thought specifically, "That's a good idea, I'll use it, sometime." A "suicidal hypothesis" must be developed and must germinate before a suicidal action can occur. The germination time may be extremely short and the "sometime" the next second. This seems to be true of impulsive suicides carried out under the influence of drugs, psychosis or alcohol.

—Elsa A. Whalley *

time the behavior actually occurred. As has been previously stated, history—personal or professional, and including motivational elements— is constantly in the process of being rewritten, and there most likely will never be one "true" historical account.

Labels. A methodological and conceptual problem which requires attention at this point has to do with the question of naming. Are we going to talk of *motives* (a noun) as things separate and distinct from behavior, to which causative powers can be attributed; or are we going to talk of motivational behavior, motive behavior, or motive decisions? If the "motive-thing" approach is used, one is immediately faced with the problem of deciding where these "things" (the motives) are located and how they can be observed. Those who follow this approach usually decide that the motives are located inside the individual as a part of an internal causative system and are consequently unobservable. "Thing"-names such as instinct, drive, need, or impulse are frequently used in this way. Pre-

* Elsa A. Whalley, "Religion and Suicide," *Review of Religious Research*, V, No. 2 (Winter, 1964), 95–96.

vious discussions have analyzed this approach, and have suggested reasons why it has not been followed in this text.

We will accordingly talk of motive decisions or motivational behavior. The phenomenon of observation, then, is one aspect of on-going behavior. Making motivational decisions is one of the many types of behavior of individuals as they interact.

Multiple causation. Over-simplified theories or unsophisticated interpretations of motivation at times lead to the conclusion that motivational decisions are *the* cause of behavior. When an individual sincerely tells himself, "I am going to get an A on this exam *because* it will please mother," or "I flunked the exam because the devil tempted me to go to the show last night rather than study," it is a motivational statement (as we have defined it) in that it involves what the individual actually tells himself as to why he behaves or behaved in a particular way. However, it is certainly not a *complete causal* statement.

Unit or singular causation statements ignore much more than they call to attention, as indicated in the discussion in Chapter 2. In human behavior (as in all phenomena) there are multiple causative factors operating. Our discussion here, then, should not be interpreted as implying that motive decisions are *the* cause of behavior, but only that this is an important type of causative phenomenon involved, along with many other causative factors, in human interaction.

There may be causative factors involved of which the individual is unaware. No doubt there are many. Such factors, however, would not be classified as "motives," as we are using the term. For therapy or other planned change purposes, it may be useful to get those involved to provide themselves with particular motive definitions, so that they *want* to do certain things. The point being made here, however, is that such definitions are not the *only* causative factors involved in the subsequent behavior. The therapist, for example, who succeeds in getting his client to develop a new set of motive defini-

tions is obviously a causative factor also. It is
easy to over-simplify causative relationships, including those dealing with motivation.

VALUE DEFINITIONS

The value definition is one of the most important types of definitions involved in motive decisions. An over-simplified view of such involvement is suggested in the statement, "I do (did,
or will do) this because it is good." While such
a statement may serve certain purposes, a more
accurate statement would be, "I do this because,
among many other things, it is good." The value
term "good" being NER, and thus without empirical limitations, can be a shorthand form for
saying, "My synthesis of many factors averages
out to this." Or at least when one is pushed to
defend his "good" evaluation, he can do so in
similar terms.

Despite its limited causal involvement, the
value dimension is of such importance that it
should be well understood. In the first place,
any phenomenon can be viewed in any number
of different ways, each of which may have a
value dimension. Value definitions can be applied, for instance, to many different aspects of
self definitions; "other" definitions; object, situational, relationship, goal, and supernatural definitions—to mention but a few broad categories.
Any one or a configuration of these potential
value definitions may gain saliency in any motive decision. Then, to complicate matters even
more, past, current, or future aspects of any of
these may be given attention in any particular
motive decision. When an individual emphasizes one aspect, he de-emphasizes another which
may appear to another observer to be more important. In any case, understanding the motive
decisions involved in any interaction involves
determining which aspect of the behavior is
being evaluated.

The value definitions of an individual or group
are not just a hodge-podge of unrelated single
definitions. In an effort to be consistent and to
be involved in an orderly manner with others,
the value definitions of each individual are or-

A Politically Oriented Motive Statement

*To those peoples in the huts and villages of half
the globe struggling to break the bonds of mass
misery, we pledge our best efforts to help them
help themselves, for whatever period is required
—not because the Communists may be doing it,
not because we seek their votes, but because
it is right.*

—John F. Kennedy, *Inaugural Address.*

---

ganized into some meaningful configuration. It
is doubtful if complete harmony is ever achieved
by any individual or group, but patterns are
established according to some intensity or saliency hierarchy. Some variation of the commandment, "Thou shalt have no other value
above *X*," with subsidiary "thou-shalts" and
"thou-shalt-nots" is woven into the culture of the
individual and the group. If value conflicts
arise, having an established value hierarchy facilitates conflict resolution. Establishing such a
hierarchy involves the application of value definitions to other value definitions, which is a complex, exclusively human, procedure. Religious
definitions figure prominently into established
hierarchies. Individuals frequently seek after
that which is "of God" (good) and seek to avoid
that which is "of the devil" (evil).

Religious involvement in motive decisions usually follows a particular pattern. Religion involves both overt behavior, which is defined as
being religious in nature, and verbal behavior,
or a system of theology or beliefs which is related to the overt behavior. Although both types
of behavior are religiously important, acceptance
of the theology is frequently viewed as being of
more importance than performing the overt behavior. Church members are not only concerned
with whether the individual attends church or
contributes his offerings, but they are also concerned with *why* such behavior is engaged in—
the "motives" back of it. Individuals are expected not only to do the "right" thing, but also
to do it for the "right" reasons. Full fellowship
in the religious group will usually not be ex-

tended to those who do not meet both require-ments. The individual who does all of the ap-proved acts such as, say, loving his family, but who has not convinced the group that he accepts the appropriate theology, will be viewed with skepticism. In certain respects, making the right motive decisions leads to acceptance even though the related behavior fails to conform to accepted standards.

Motive decisions are involved in religious be-havior and religious definitions may be involved in motive decisions about anything.

The popular expression that some act is a "necessary evil" illustrates the hierarchical ar-rangement of value definitions. The "necessary" aspect calls attention to one value definition and the "evil" definition calls attention to another. When early Christians defined marital inter-course in this manner, the "necessary" value called attention to the fact that sexual activity was recognized as necessary for group survival, and survival was a high-saliency definition. Sex-ual intercourse *per se*, however, was defined as "evil," but the higher ranking value definition in effect canceled out the lesser value definition. The "evil" definition may, of course, have added a bit of thrill value to the act by putting it in the category of "forbidden fruit."

In like manner, killing *per se* may be defined as wrong, but under invasion conditions, killing to preserve one's homeland may be valued suffi-ciently highly to counter-balance such negative definitions. Congressmen and fraternity mem-bers (in certain respects there is a close similar-ity) may not approve of a certain specific act, but may sufficiently value the "brotherhood" to vote affirmatively, in the name of brotherhood, for a disapproved act.

Individuals, then, are thoroughly capable of engaging in behavior which they define as wrong in one aspect if they can subordinate this evalua-tion to a higher ranking aspect which is affirma-tively defined. If planned change is to be ac-cepted by those for whom it is planned, the changes which may be disruptive and unaccepta-ble at one value level must be related to a level of values which will counter-balance this negative aspect. Such behavior may, of course, contribute

to subsequent definitions of guilt or shame which may be difficult to adjust to and may, under cer-tain circumstances, contribute to a subsequent rejection of the higher ranking values which at first overshadowed them.

Further complication is introduced when it is realized that despite the fact that value defini-tions can be and frequently are viewed as abso-lute, they are almost always relative to the situa-tion; there is probably an acceptable "excuse" for every "absolute" value definition. An excuse if accepted provides justification for not doing a particular act by invoking a value definition of higher intensity. Excuses are utilized in both formal and informal interaction. An act, then, may be viewed as right under one condition but wrong under another. Stealing may be defined as wrong under "normal" conditions, but under war conditions, stealing from the enemy is differ-ent—it is right. Time factors are also relevant: what is defined as right at one time is defined differently at another. The "evil" practice of female smoking in public changed into an ac-ceptable practice over the period of just a few years.

Statements that "X is good," which may lead one to believe that goodness is a quality of X, may facilitate the maintenance of social order, but may also make consistency appear as incon-sistency if interpretations fail to take into account the relevant situation and time factors.

Labeling something as good increases the like-lihood that motive decisions will take this label into account and that the definition will con-tribute in a causative way to the accomplishment of some goal. Such labeling does not, however, guarantee that the specific "good" act will be done. Human behavior is too complex for that.

It is, then, sociologically meaningful to seek to determine under what conditions a particular value definition is applied or takes precedence and under what conditions it is replaced by or subordinated to another. The motivational as-pects of behavior cannot be understood unless one knows to which aspect of the whole con-figuration each of those involved is paying atten-tion and where the applied value definitions fit into established value hierarchies.

Primary motives. Some discussions of motivation dichotomize primary and secondary, basic and not-so-basic, physiological and socially acquired motives. Such distinctions are of questionable utility if they lead to a conclusion that there is some universal motive-content pattern. Our discussion of the hierarchical arrangement of value definitions has indicated that some are given greater priority than others. However, it appears that man is capable of elevating almost anything to a top priority level. Certain things must be done *if* individuals are to survive, but this fact alone does not account for efforts to remain alive, nor does it mean that physical survival, individual or collective, is automatically given precedence over all other goals.

Figure 15.1 Rewards may be used to encourage individuals to want to do what others want them to do, as in teen-age driving competition, in which trophies and college scholarships are presented to winners. (Wide World Photos.)

Dorothy Lee, an anthropologist, has indicated:

. . . I know of no culture where human physical survival has been shown, rather than unquestioningly assumed by social scientists, to be the ultimate goal.[1]

Any goal, then, may become the top-level goal of an individual or group. Efforts to secure the goal may be so intense that other goals are subordinated, in which case behavior may be viewed as compulsive (the individual has a compulsion) or as "driven" behavior (he has a strong drive).

NORM-ROLE DEFINITIONS

Established norm-role definitions facilitate orderly interaction. If orderly interaction is desired, the establishment of a set of shared definitions is essential. However, such definitions facilitate what might be called "behavioral inertia," or the "tendency of a body (human, in this case) to continue in established patterns unless acted upon by some outside force." Established patterns lead to established expectations which together minimize the making of conscious decisions about behavior—including motive decisions. This involves the self-fulfilling aspect of expectations. If individuals treat each other as though they expect certain behavior from other persons this very treatment contributes to their behaving in the expected manner. Individuals expect things to be orderly, perceive them as orderly,

and tell themselves that they, too, should be orderly. Most people don't want to appear "scatterbrained"—even to themselves.

Under such conditions only rarely are questions raised, even to oneself, about motive decisions involved. Adults do not usually raise questions about why they speak English, or why they eat three meals a day, or why married couples regularly engage in sexual intercourse. Such behavior is defined as being normal or natural, maybe even biologically given, and thus not requiring motive decisions. Adults who speak a different language in regular social interaction, or who regularly eat more or less than three meals, or married individuals who refrain from sexual intercourse are frequently the object of the question, "Why do they behave *that* way?"

The "I don't know" answer of the child (and of some adults) given in response to the question "Why did you do *that?*" may be a sincere one. For some behavior, only when one is asked to identify the motive decisions involved does he give serious attention to such questions.

It would, in fact, be cumbersome to have to make motive decisions about much of the specific behavior in which we engage. Large configurations of behavior may be lumped under motive decisions: the statement, "I want to get my paycheck at the end of the month," with all its related motive decisions, can be subsumed under an "Ours not to reason why, ours but to do or die" approach. Only when, for some reason, those involved are called upon to defend the value premises involved do they give attention to the more specific motivational factors involved.

Frequently individuals, especially younger ones, are not aware that there are alternate ways of behaving and evaluating. If one has been taught that one way is *the* way and has had no opportunity even vicariously to experience alternate ways, it is easy to conclude that there may be biological or supernatural "forces" involved. One does "what comes naturally," and "natural" behavior requires no motivational justification.

The point is that well-established patterns tend to provide their own "motives." They tend to become "functionally autonomous," to use All-

---

Values and Values

A free choice implies a rejected as well as a selected value. What we want always conflicts with what we want.

—Samuel Z. Klausner.*

---

* Samuel Z. Klausner, "The Social Psychology of Courage," *Review of Religious Research*, III, No. 2 (Fall, 1961), 64.

[1] Dorothy Lee, *Freedom and Culture* (Englewood Cliffs, N. J.: Prentice-Hall, Inc., 1959), p. 72.

port's term.[2] Individuals engage in such behavior without consciously deciding that there are reasons to justify many aspects thereof, unless specifically pressed to do so.

Different role definitions specify varying concern with motive decisions. Clergymen, counselors, and lawyers are expected to pay particular attention to motive decisions. Motive information given to such individuals is frequently considered to be privileged information not to be divulged to others, although motive decisions may be revealed under conditions of anonymity in interaction with strangers.

Further motive definitions considered to be appropriate for one role or position may be seen as inappropriate for another. As one moves up the "ladder of success," his motive decisions are likely to change as his style of dress, his title, and his office location change. Acquisition of appropriate motive behavior or the potential for such change may, in fact, be seen as a necessary requisite for certain promotions.

SELF DEFINITIONS

One type of self definition in which everyone seems to be interested and about which we all reach decisions one way or another is the answer to the question "Why do I do what I do?" When the individual confronts himself with the question "What's wrong with me?" he is asking a motive question. We make motive decisions when we provide ourselves answers to questions such as "What am I striving for?" "What are my primary motives, desires, wishes, needs, hidden urges, etc.?" In our more serious moments we may ask, "What do I *really* want out of life?"

There are two aspects to such self questions: (1) Did I do (or am I doing) the right thing? (2) Did I do the right thing for the right reason? In many respects, the second aspect may have greater influence upon self definitions than the first. We are inclined to excuse behavior defined

---

Value Hierarchy of 2,000 College Students *

1. *Serving God, doing God's will.*

2. *Self-development—becoming a real, genuine person.*

3. *Promoting the most deep and lasting pleasures for the greatest number of people.*

4. *Fine relations with other persons.*

5. *Handling the specific problems of life as they arise.*

6. *Being able to "take it"; brave and uncomplaining acceptance of what circumstances bring.*

7. *Doing my duty.*

8. *Serving the community of which I am a part.*

9. *Overcoming my irrational emotions and sensuous desires.*

10. *Getting as many deep and lasting pleasures out of life as I can.*

---

as inappropriate in ourselves, and in others as well, if we are convinced that the motive decisions related to it were appropriate—if the "heart was in the right place."

Motive decisions may be related to the definitions one has concerning potential behavior. Decisions may be made in an effort to realize or "actualize" some potential one believes he has. In some cases, the individual may view this potential as a biologically given phenomenon which his behavior merely "actualizes," or helps develop. Others may take a more sociologically oriented view and see the ideas an individual has about his "ideal self" as being socially de-

---

[2] See Gordon W. Allport, *Personality* (New York: Holt, Rinehart and Winston, Inc., 1937), pp. 190–212.

* Quoted by Allen Barton, "Measuring the Values of Individuals," *Research Supplement to Religious Education*, LVII, No. 4 (July–August, 1962), p. S–73; from *Cooperative Study in General Education* (Washington, D. C.: American Council on Education, 1947).

rived. Whatever the origin, if an individual believes that he is destined to play some particular role or strongly desires to, these beliefs may be the focal point around which motive decisions are made.

Efforts to maximize self definitions involve motive definitions, although the route by which this maximization is sought is not always immediately apparent to the observer, as in the case of the individual who desires public recognition but seeks it in publicly disapproved ways—possibly after efforts to utilize more accepted channels have proved to be ineffective.

Motive decisions may also be influenced by efforts to maximize self evaluations. Since any particular behavior can be related to any number of motive decisions, it is easy to tell oneself—and be convinced of the truthfulness of the statement—that one's behavior is motivated by socially approved reasons. Our previous point that motive decisions are not the complete causative factor involved is pertinent here. Experiences which shatter such socially approved interpretations of one's motive decisions may be traumatic.

Motive definitions, then, are one of the many definitions an individual applies to himself. Decisions as to what type of a person one is are influenced by motive decisions, and conversely motive decisions are influenced by decisions as to what type of person one "really" is. Both decisions are involved in behavior.

SOCIALIZATION

Motivational behavior is learned, not biologically given. The discussion in Chapter 5 concerning the biological foundations of human behavior applies with particular cogency to the motivational area. Biological determinism's theories of motivation, stated in terms of instincts, needs, basic drives, etc., provide a contrasting interpretation, but one which does not harmonize with the symbolic interaction understanding. From our perspective, individuals are seen as providing themselves with explanations of their own behavior in the language they have learned, in the manner in which they have learned, and in terms of causative schemes they have learned to endorse.

If making motive decisions is learned behavior, it is *ipso facto* changeable behavior. Three types of change may be identified: (1) change in both motive decisions and the related behavior; (2) the related behavior may remain the same, or much the same, while the motive decisions related thereto change, as in the case of the individual who started going to church primarily for business reasons and ends up going for more "spiritual" reasons. Or, an individual who stops discriminating against minority group members in order to avoid legal sanctions may subsequently refuse to discriminate because he now defines such discrimination as morally wrong. (3) The motive decisions may remain the same while the related behavior changes, as in the case of the individual who continues to be politically active "because of his interests in good government," but his activity changes from involvement in one political party to involvement in another.

Changes in motive decisions may result from many experiences. One would be learning a different way of interpreting behavior in general and one's own behavior in particular. The

---

Making Motive Decisions

. . . on the battlefield . . . a terrified man may become even more afraid of running away, fearing what his comrades would think. Many apparently prefer to risk death than to have their friends look upon them as cowards. Men willingly make sacrifices only when the alternative is even more painful.

—Samuel L. A. Marshall.*

---

* Samuel L. A. Marshall, *Men Against Fire* (New York: William Morrow and Co., 1947), p. 148.

acquisition of new concepts and/or new theories of behavior may be involved. New experiences may lead to new self definitions including related motive definitions. Critical incidents may be productive of motive changes. Therapy of one type or another may provide new concepts and methods of self evaluation.

ROLE PLAYING AND ROLE TAKING

Reference Groups

Motivational decisions frequently involve taking into account relationships with particular groups. Some relationships are valued highly and others are given a lesser evaluation, while some are negatively evaluated. If a particular group is highly valued, *actual* or *potential* membership therein may likewise be highly valued. Decisions as to whether to follow some pattern of behavior, then, may involve answering the question, "Is this behavior approved by or in harmony with group *X*?" Individual decisions as to whether to follow a specific course of action may be reached by referring to the behavior or the norm-role-value definitions of such a group. "Reference group" is the term we will use to identify such groups, and "reference relationship" will identify such a relationship.[3] Motive decisions which involve a reference group or a reference relationship involve conclusions such as, "If group *X* approves, then I approve, or at least, I will conform." The decision of a Mormon not to smoke or of a Roman Catholic not to use birth control "because my church disapproves" illustrates such decisions.

The reference group may, of course, be "once removed" in decisions such as "I will not do act *X* because it is wrong, and it is wrong because my group (family, church, fraternity, political

party, etc.) disapproves." Likewise, a well-established reference relationship may not involve the actual process of deciding "Group *R* does such and such, therefore I will." Rather, the norm-role-value definitions of the group may be so well learned and accepted that decisions are made with reference to the standards of the reference group without the direct involvement of the specific group in the motive decision-making process.

It is usually easier to accept and live by a set of value-norm-role definitions if the others who are important or significant to us do likewise. The term "significant others" is frequently used to identify such groups or individuals. Reference groups are composed of significant others.

Making motive decisions is frequently difficult for marginal individuals, who are not securely in any particular group, or are possibly part-way in two somewhat conflicting groups, as in the case of the individual who is in the process of converting from one religious, political, or nationality group to another. Such an individual may be uncertain as to just whose confirming "vote" he seeks.

A reference relationship may obtain for a particular individual between himself and (1) a group in which he has membership, or (2) a group in which he does not hold membership but would like to, as in the case of the freshman who wants to become a fraternity member and makes his decisions in such a way that he sees his behavior as being imitative or worthy of a

---

[3] H. H. Hyman, "The Psychology of Status," *Arch. Psych.* (1942), 269, and Tamotsu Shibutani, "Reference Groups and Social Control," in Arnold M. Rose (ed.), *Human Behavior and Social Processes* (Boston: Houghton Mifflin Co., 1962), pp. 128–147.

Deans, Students, and Motives

When a student is "called on the carpet" by his college dean, it is frequently a motive decision that the dean seeks information about. "Why did you do _____?"

The student may provide one motive explanation for the dean, and another for himself.

The dean, knowing this, may discount the motive explanation, even as it is being spoken.

fraternity man. His decision as to just how a fraternity man should behave may, of course, be somewhat different from that of the actual fraternity members on campus. A reference group, in any case, is not necessarily a membership group.

Either of these relationships may be positive or negative. The statements above represent a positive relationship. A negative relationship (negative reference group) is just the reverse, in that motive decisions follow the pattern of, "If that is the way they (the negative reference group) behave, I want to do just the opposite." Such a relationship may acquire saliency through conflict of one type or another. Likewise, a diminution of conflict may be related to motive decision changes as is suggested in the statement of a rabbi in Sao Paulo, Brazil, that there is so little anti-Semitism there that it is difficult for him to keep his synagogue alive.[4]

Members of the reference group need not be directly involved in the interaction. A lower-class female planning to marry an upper-class male may, when interacting with other lower-class females, make motive decisions on the basis of how she thinks her upper-class future in-laws act or will act.

A person may also have a reference relationship with members of a group whom he has never seen or who are dead or perhaps never even existed in reality. This is the case with some people who people their world with imaginary groups [5] and may be labeled as insane by the larger society. Motive decision may also involve beings defined as supernatural—such as God. When the Christian tells himself, "I will do what Jesus would have done in this situation," he is thinking of such a reference relationship. The importance of symbols in such decisions is apparent.

The involvement of reference groups in motive decisions may vary with the type of society. In some cases, in fact, the whole society is the reference group.

In a stable, integrated, and relatively less differential society, there would probably be little necessity for the use of reference groups as a separate concept. Modern man, especially in Western societies, is caught in the throes of vertical mobility, in the "dilemmas and contradictions of statuses" and the painful predicament of marginality created by the demands and goals originating in diverse groups. The concept of reference groups forces itself through such facts. It becomes almost indispensable in dealing with the relation of individuals to groups in highly differentiated and poorly integrated societies, in the process of acculturation and experiencing the high tempo of transition.[6]

The "reference group at work" can be seen in an excerpt from Whyte's Street Corner study.[7] At one time, Whyte tells us, the Nortons were seriously interested in bowling, and the bowling performance became more or less the sign of distinction in the group. High performance was expected of the leaders and encouraged. But not so with members with relatively little rank, as in the case of Frank.

Frank was a good player in his own right, yet "he made a miserable showing" while playing in his own group. He said to me: "I can't seem to play ball when I am playing with fellows I know, like that bunch. I do much better when I am playing for the Stanley A.C. against some team in Dexter, Westland, or out of town." Accustomed to filling an inferior position, Frank was unable to star even in his favorite sport when he was competing against members of his own group.[8]

[4] Everett Cherrington Hughes and Helen MacGill Hughes, *Where People Meet* (New York: The Free Press of Glencoe, 1952), p. 39. See also Asghar Fathi, "Mechanisms for Maintaining Jewish Identity," *Pacific Sociological Review*, V, No. 1 (Spring, 1962), 44–47.

[5] Theodore M. Newcomb, *Social Psychology* (New York: Holt, Rinehart and Winston, Inc., 1950), p. 225.

[6] M. Sherif and C. Sherif, *Groups in Harmony and Tension* (New York: Harper & Row, Inc., 1953), pp. 160–161.

[7] See William Foote Whyte, *Street Corner Society* (Chicago: University of Chicago Press, 1955).

[8] *Ibid.*, p. 19.

Self control—social control. Motive decisions are one of the elements involved in the degree of harmony and stability of interaction. If any particular individual wants to do what the others involved want him to do, interaction proceeds smoothly. If mother wants her daughter to practice her piano lesson, and the daughter wants to practice, and even more, wants her mother to want her to practice, there is little likelihood of dissonance developing. Under such conditions, there is no need on the part of those in power positions to apply any negative sanctions to accomplish their goals. The fact that the relevant motive decisions are mutually supporting provides sufficient positive sanctions to keep "things running smoothly."

In the case of the newborn child or the newly arrived immigrant, the maintenance of established systems of interaction is facilitated if the new members learn to *want* to do the established behavior. Socialization or acculturation involves not only teaching individuals how to behave but teaches them to want to behave in that manner.

Further, if the maintenance of the way of life of a group requires among other things that, say, a certain number of surgeons, engineers, and square dance callers be periodically recruited to play the appropriate roles, easy continuity is effected if the requisite number of individuals can learn to want to play these roles. In a democracy the recruiting efforts of General Motors, General Electric, or a general of the Army usually involve emphasis upon aspects of the available positions which will harmonize with the established value definitions of potential candidates so that they will want to play the specified role. In a totalitarian society the recruitment patterns may be different, possibly revolving around the desire to remain alive rather than to play any particular role. Various degrees of "self control" and "social control" may be involved in different situations. The difference, however, is a matter of degree, as our previous discussions of *interactionism* have indicated.

Role taking involves assessment of the motive decisions of the others involved. In fact, the behavior of others would be relatively meaningless to us without such decisions. The ability accurately to make such decisions, however, is not shared equally by all individuals.

COLLECTIVE BEHAVIOR

In the absence of established norm-role definitions, individuals are likely to engage in behavior which they previously may have been motivated to perform but have refrained from since it was contrary to the established norm-role definitions.

These "repressed desires" may then be activated under the collective behavior situation in which they appear to be more appropriate. Collective behavior does not call forth animalistic or instinctive behavior which has been suppressed or repressed by society, but rather provides opportunity for the expression of learned behavior which was defined as inappropriate for other situations.

SUMMARY

Explanations in terms of reasons for or purposes of his own past, present, or future behavior, which an individual provides for himself, we have called motive decisions. Such explanations, a type of self definition, figure prominently in social interaction, although they are only one of the many causative elements involved. Data relative to motive decisions are secured through direct questioning or are indirectly inferred from the observation of other behavior.

Motive decisions may take into account an accepted value hierarchy, which frequently involves religious aspects. Decisions relative to high-saliency values may override lesser values, so that behavior unacceptable or "bad" in one aspect is nonetheless engaged in, in part, because other aspects are acceptable by higher level standards. There is, however, no universally accepted motive hierarchy.

Making motive decisions is learned behavior, and, therefore, subject to change. Well-established behavior patterns, however, tend to become motivationally autonomous. Certain types of motive decisions are viewed as appropriate to certain types of position, and interpreting motive decisions of others, although most likely a universal role-playing requirement, is differentially involved in various roles. Everyone is not equally skilled in this behavior.

Reference groups (which may or may not be membership groups) or significant others are involved, in that decisions about individual behavior are reached on the basis of perceptions as to how the behavior compares positively or negatively to that of certain actual or imaginary groups.

Shared motive decisions facilitate interaction and perpetuation of the group and serve to minimize the use of sanctions.

QUESTIONS

1. Does the definition of motivation provided in this chapter differ from that which you have previously used? How?
2. Analyze some of your recent behavior and identify motive decisions involved therein.
3. Concerning an examination you may have asked yourself, "Now why did he put that question in?" How did you go about providing an answer for yourself?
4. Explain the statement, "Motive decisions are not *the* cause of behavior."
5. How are value definitions involved in motive decisions?

6. How do you account for the fact that individuals do things which they consider to be wrong?
7. Lee suggested that physical survival has not actually been the ultimate goal of any group. Can you provide a sociological explanation for the widespread belief in the existence of a human "instinct for self preservation"?
8. Distinguish between a positive and a negative reference group.
9. How may motive decisions be related to definitions about one's ideal self?
10. How do certain motive decisions facilitate interaction?

PROJECT

Ask ten different students:

1. Why they speak English,
2. Why juvenile delinquents engage in deviant behavior,
3. Why college males attempt to kiss co-eds,
4. Why they worship or do not worship God.

Distinguish the different types of motive decisions which can be related to the same behavior.

SUGGESTED READING

BECKER, HOWARD S. "Becoming a Marihuana User," *The American Journal of Sociology*, LIX, No. 3 (November), 1953), 235–242.

DITTES, JAMES E. "Attractiveness of Group as Function of Self-Esteem and Acceptance by Group," *Journal of Abnormal and Social Psychology*, LIX (1959), 77–82.

FESTINGER, LEON. *A Theory of Cognitive Dissonance.* New York: Harper & Row, Inc., 1957.

FOOTE, NELSON N. "Identification as a Basis for a Theory of Motivation," *American Sociological Review*, XVI, No. 1 (February, 1951), 14–21.

GOFFMAN, ERVING. "On Cooling the Mark Out: Some Aspects of Adaptation to Failure," *Psychiatry: Jour-*

nal for the Study of Interpersonal Relations, XV, No. 4 (November, 1952), 451–463.

HUGHES, EVERETT C. "What Other?" in Arnold M. Rose (ed.), *Human Behavior and Social Processes.* Boston: Houghton Mifflin Co., 1962. Pp. 119–127.

KELLEY, HAROLD H. "Two Functions of Reference Groups," in Guy E. Swanson, Theodore M. Newcomb, and Eugene L. Hartley (eds.), *Readings in Social Psychology.* New York: Holt, Rinehart and Winston, Inc., 1952. Pp. 410–414.

LINDESMITH, ALFRED R., and ANSELM L. STRAUSS. *Social Psychology.* New York: Holt, Rinehart and Winston, Inc., 1956. Part III, pp. 267–367.

MacIVER, R. M. *Social Causation.* Boston: Ginn and Co., 1942.

SHIBUTANI, TAMOTSU. "Reference Groups and Social Control," in Arnold M. Rose (ed.), *Human Behavior and Social Processes.* Boston: Houghton Mifflin Co., 1962. Pp. 128–147.

16

Stratification

Most American college students are imbued with ideas of "improving themselves" or of becoming upwardly mobile, yet in moments of dorm or classroom discussions they talk, sometimes emotionally, about wanting everyone to be "equal." Even though any individual cannot be "better than" and "equal to" others at the same time, it is obviously possible to "believe in" both goals. Can you provide a sociological explanation for this phenomenon?

INTRODUCTION

In human interaction, no two individuals or groups consistently receive identical treatment from those with whom they interact. In industry, some receive more money than others for a day's work. Only certain individuals are invited to join specific clubs, such as sororities or fraternities. Some graduate from college, others only from high school, and some never get beyond the elementary grades. Some vacation abroad, some travel widely within their own country, and some never leave their home town. Differential treatment is one of the consistent facts of interaction with which we are all familiar not only because each of us is treated differently from other individuals, but because each of us is also constantly making decisions as to how he should relate himself to others and consequently making decisions as to who will or will not be given preferential treatment.

Giving preferential treatment involves ranking certain individuals above others, thereby creating a pattern or a hierarchy of levels or strata. The term "stratification" is often used to identify both the interaction which takes the ranking or strata definitions into account and the process by which the levels or strata are developed.[1]

[1] For a discussion of implications of various ways of conceptualizing social stratification see the following: Kingsley Davis and Wilbert E. Moore, "Some Principles of Stratification," *American Sociological Review*, X, No. 2 (April, 1945), 242–249; Wilbert E. Moore, "But Some Are More Equal Than Others"; Melvin Tumin, "On Inequality"; and Rejoinder by Moore, *American Sociological Review*, XXVIII, No. 1 (February, 1963), 13–28.

Stratification appears to be a universal societal characteristic, so that for any particular society there is really no question as to whether or not there will be stratification, but only what type of system there will be. Further, most Utopian views of the future envisage, as did Plato in his *Republic,* that the new society will be stratified according to some accepted criteria.

The goal of this chapter is to examine some of the factors which are involved in the development and perpetuation of the differential treatment of interaction systems. We will first, however, identify the major types of stratification systems.

CASTE SYSTEM

Societies in which specific differences are widely recognized and are felt to be relevant to most interaction are called caste societies or are said to have a caste system. Whatever the caste criteria—birth, skin color, occupation, or some other factor—they are constantly taken into account and accordingly are extensively involved in the norm and role definitions which are a part of the group's culture. In such a society, one is almost constantly aware of his caste definition (self definition) and the expectations which others have of his behavior as a result of this classification. Caste definitions are relatively permanent.

The fact that such definitions are consistently taken into account leads to and stems from beliefs that they are irrevocable or impossible to change. For such a system to persist for any great length of time, it must be tied to factors such as biological ones, which themselves do not change much. The facts of one's birth, one's sexual characteristics, pigmentation of the skin, or other physical features cannot usually be changed; such characteristics become permanent pivotal points upon which caste systems are frequently built.

The biological connection is clearly shown by the fact that one is usually seen as acquiring his caste label at the moment of birth, and spends his lifetime carrying that label. This classification is taken into account in decisions as to whom he marries, the occupation into which he enters, and where he lives. It has extensive influence upon most aspects of life.

Changing one's caste definition, or movement out of a caste group (mobility) is difficult and unlikely. Mobility from one caste level to another is not provided for in the norm-role definitions of the group, although it may be provided for in a religious system of beliefs about re-incarnation, which projects the change to another existence and consequently does not disrupt the on-going earthly interaction patterns. Acquisition by an individual at one level of the distinctive behavior patterns which are characteristic of other caste groups is difficult and unlikely. Caste systems are accordingly sometimes called "closed" systems.

Status Symbols

If individuals in interaction are to take stratification values into account they must in some way be able to apply the appropriate labels to each other. You need to be able properly to classify the others with whom you interact before you can enact the appropriate plans of action for that classification. Where the factor to be taken into account is a biological characteristic, say,

---

Caste and Self Definitions

In India, lower caste groups have a strong feeling of inferiority and self-abasement, and upper caste groups display a corresponding sense of superiority and self-satisfaction. The attitudes of each group toward the other(s) have a strong resemblance, as upper caste members look at themselves in much the same way as do lower caste members and vice versa.

—R. Rath and N. C. Sircar.*

---

* R. Rath and N. C. Sircar, "The Mental Pictures of Six Hindu Caste Groups About Each Other as Reflected in Verbal Stereotypes," *The Journal of Social Psychology,* LI, No. 4 (May, 1960), 277–293.

sexual makeup or the color of skin, the plans of action can be initiated when attention is paid to these characteristics. We can respond to these characteristics directly.

When, however, the more obvious characteristics of those involved cannot be used for identification purposes, special symbols are developed so that all involved (at least those who are "in the know") will be able to make the necessary distinctions in definitions and subsequent interaction. These symbols we call status or strata symbols.

When, for instance, Nazi Germany attempted to establish a caste distinction between Jews and "Aryans" but could not easily distinguish Jewish from non-Jewish individuals, they required that an armband bearing the Star of David be worn by the group defined as inferior. In India particular marks placed upon one's forehead serve a similar caste identification purpose. Such strata symbols permit others to treat those thus identified in what is defined as the appropriate manner.

However, if physical mobility is possible, or if the group is large enough for an individual to "lose himself" or disassociate himself from those who know of his caste or class identity, it is possible and likely that "unofficial" changes will be made. An urbanized, industrialized society provides opportunities for such anonymity. Maintenance of a rigid caste system under such conditions is difficult if not impossible, as India is discovering.[2]

Let us return for a moment to the involvement of biological factors in caste systems. Where caste is determined by biological characteristics, which in and of themselves are neither superior nor inferior, the group that takes them into account will usually superimpose upon them value definitions frequently of a religious nature, which effectively removes the responsibility for discrimination and inequalities from the humans involved and places it on the deities of the group. Such definitions likewise contribute to the belief that caste definitions are simply a reflection of

objective reality, or that they are merely a recognition of already existing and presumably always existing "facts of life."

With caste definitions being relatively permanent and widely applicable, those who share common characteristics are likely to receive somewhat consistent treatment from others of the society and accordingly define themselves as a caste group. They come to view their future as being intimately tied up to the future of the group. They develop group consciousness.

CLASS SYSTEM

A class system has many of the same characteristics as a caste system, only they are not applied with equal rigidity. In the first place, the criteria of class identification are more likely to be socially acquired than ascribed to biological characteristics. Class definitions are easier than caste definitions to change. Mobility is provided for in the norm-role definitions of the group and means are established whereby such mobility can, in fact, be effected. The extent of mobility may, of course, vary from one society to another and within one society from one time to another.

Whereas in a caste system the society is divided into recognizable caste groups for which society has developed identifying labels, in a class system the differences are not so distinct. Consensus may be somewhat limited as to the class to which a particular individual belongs, or even whether or not such "groups" actually exist. It is recognized that *differences* do exist, but they are viewed as shading from one level to another rather than being "grouped." They are viewed more as individual than group differences. Further, the characteristic involved may be seen as being relevant for certain types of interaction and not for others.

Since the criteria of classification are not seen as final and irrevocable, efforts may be made to secure change in the value system. Over a period of time specific factors may be de-emphasized or given more emphasis to harmonize with other changes going on in the group. Change is easier and more frequent in a class system than

[2] Kurt B. Mayer, *Class and Society* (New York: Random House, Inc., 1955), p. 70.

Figure 16.1   Recreational interests vary with class position.   (Wide World Photos.)

in a caste system. The young child receives his class position as a result of birth but, contrary to the caste pattern, may change it as he matures.

If class position is to be taken into account in interaction, one must be able to identify such position. Status symbols may be used for such purposes—symbols which are felt to reflect a number of characteristics which are somehow synthesized or lumped together. To the extent that there is consensus upon such symbols and their meaning, interaction is standardized.

In the armed services, for instance, an extensive system of such symbols has been developed, which are worn in prominent places so that those involved can easily identify them and plan their behavior accordingly. New recruits are expected very early to know the system "by heart," and are subjected to sanctions if errors are made. Such symbols are, in part, position symbols (role symbols) in that they inform those involved in a broad manner what the wearer does in the service, but they are also important status symbols,

TABLE 16.1

Characteristic	Class Pattern	Caste Pattern
Value definition of inferiority–superiority	Applied to any characteristic	Usually applied to biological aspect
Relevancy in norm-role definitions	Less than in caste system	More than in class system
Self definitions	Labels and awareness may be vague	Rigid labels and awareness
Change and mobility	Provided for and expected	Neither provided for nor expected
Material objects	Possession of valued objects increases as class position increases	Possession of valued objects increases as caste position increases
Justification of system (value definitions)	Pragmatic "this-worldly" justification	Strong religious endorsement

indicating who is superior or inferior to whom. That rank has its privileges is one of the basic facts of life in the armed services, as it is in any group.

In both caste and class systems differential treatment results in differential accumulation of material possessions, so that those with high rank accumulate more of prized possessions than those of lower rank.

In class systems, which are not as rigid as caste systems, the value definitions used to justify the differences involved are correspondingly less rigid. Existing differences are more likely to be attributed to human than superhuman factors. In class systems, justification for change must be incorporated into the value systems, whereas justification for non-change must be incorporated into the value system of a caste society.

Differences between ideal or typical class and caste systems can be summarized as shown in Table 16.1.

Any particular society may have a caste system, a class system, or a combination of both.

CLASS–CASTE IDENTIFICATION

If stratified (differential) interaction is to occur, it is necessary that those involved be able to classify individuals and/or groups according to their class–caste position. Likewise, if re-search is to be done on this aspect of behavior, the researcher must be able to make the appropriate identification.

Caste Identification

Caste identification is fairly easy. One of the characteristics of a caste system is that the criteria of classification are well known, since they are constantly taken into account in interaction. Thus, in a rigid caste system, one only has to ask those involved to provide the caste identification for themselves or others. Where the caste system is in the process of breaking down, such a technique, of course, requires modification.

Class Identification

Three major methods of identification which have been used in the measurement and the study of class are: (1) self identification, (2) the reputational approach, and (3) the objective approach. We are identifying the measurement of three different but correlated phenomena, not three different measures of the same thing.[3]

[3] Peterson found a fairly close relationship between the objective method and the subjective or self identification method in his study reported in Evan T. Peterson, "The Impact of Maternal Employment on the Mother-Daughter Relationship and on the Daughter's Role Orientation" (unpublished Ph.D. dissertation, University of Michigan, 1958), p. 77.

Self Identification. This approach, which is sometimes called the "subjective" approach, is essentially a measure of self definitions, in which the participants in the study are asked to respond to some form of the question, "To which social class do you feel you belong?" or "In which social class do you classify yourself?" In a 1940 study of Americans [4] it was found that when the following three categories were provided by the researcher, respondents' replies were divided as follows:

	Per Cent
Upper	6
Middle	88
Lower	6

However, in a 1945 study by Centers [5] the following categories were provided, and the pattern was:

	Per Cent
Upper	3
Middle	43
Working	51
Lower	1
Don't know	1
Don't believe in class	1

Where the replies are given by the respondent with no intent to deceive, they represent an accurate self evaluation in terms of the respondent's understanding of the categories utilized. The heavy concentration in the middle-class category may reflect the American dream of a great classless society or the reluctancy of respondents to place themselves in an extreme category, whatever the content of the question.

While such classifications reflect other factors—how others evaluate the respondent; objective characteristics such as amount of income, occupation, and type of residence—there is no *necessary* relationship among these factors. Subjective reality being what it is, it is entirely possible for one sincerely to classify himself in the middle class, while certain others classify him in the lower or upper class.

It should also be pointed out that such evidence does not suggest that those who place themselves in the same category, say, working class, necessarily see themselves as constituting a *group* whose interests are different from those of other Americans. They may or may not. Neither does it mean that they necessarily behave as a group in terms of voting or other behavior. They do, however, tend to have certain characteristics in common, as will be discussed later in the chapter.

What is identified with the self identification approach is self definitions. Since a class system is not as rigid as a caste system, one would expect varying definitions of just what constitutes one's class identification to be involved.

Reputational approach. The self identification approach or method asks the respondent to rank himself. The reputational approach asks others who know the individual to rank him on some class scale.[6] The scale is usually provided by the researcher, but could just as well be provided by the respondent. Easier tabulation and comparison are possible when the same categories are used by all involved. In this method, a few members of the community being studied—sometimes called judges—are provided with a list of names, each perhaps on an individual card, and are asked (1) to place each in one of a series of provided categories or (2) to rank them from high to low as each is compared with the others.

The use of this method is obviously restricted to relatively small communities in which the selected judges are familiar with the individuals they are rating.

---

[4] George Gallup and S. F. Rae, *The Pulse of Democracy* (New York: Simon and Schuster, Inc., 1940), p. 169.

[5] Richard Centers, *The Psychology of Social Classes* (Princeton: Princeton University Press, 1949), p. 77.

[6] Both the self identification and the reputational approaches are subjective in that individuals are called upon to provide subjective evaluations of class position. In the first, however, it is the individual who provides a subjective identification of himself; in the second it is judges who provide subjective evaluations of others. It was decided accordingly not to follow the widespread pattern of using the label "subjective approach" to identify the first type.

Comparisons of one community with another which involve this method should take into account the fact that somewhat different criteria may have been involved in each, even though involvement in the same larger national group would tend to develop similarities.

Both the reputational and the self identification approach permit the respondents to provide their own criteria of "social class" since the researcher does not specify any particular factors to be taken into account.

Warner and his associates used the reputational method in studies of a New England town of about 17,000 population which they called "Yankee City," [7] and a Midwestern town of about 6,000 called "Jonesville." [8] From these studies the following six-fold classification was developed, with a distribution of the population as shown:

	Yankee City	Jonesville
Upper-upper	1.4	2.7
Lower-upper	1.6	
Upper-middle	10.0	12.0
Lower-middle	28.0	32.2
Upper-lower	33.0	41.0
Lower-lower	25.0	12.1

Objective approach. The objective approach does not directly tap any value scale involved, but rather pays attention to objective characteristics which are believed to reflect prevailing value scales, or which singly or conjointly are used as a measure or index of the class structure. Class identification is determined by paying attention to objective factors upon which researchers would evidence high consensus such as amount of income, education, occupation (which would be ranked according to a previously established value scale), type of home or area of residence, which would be ranked according to criteria such as market value of the typical home therein.

[7] W. Lloyd Warner and Paul S. Lunt, *The Social Life of a Modern Community* (New Haven: Yale University Press, 1941), p. 88.
[8] W. Lloyd Warner and Associates, *Democracy in Jonesville* (New York: Harper & Row, Inc., 1949), pp. 50–51.

Use of objective criteria permits one to divide his universe of study into any number of categories. When amount of education is used, for instance, any number of different levels could be utilized although most such studies have used the conventional breaking points of grade school, high school, college, and graduate work. When amount of income is used as the class criterion, as it frequently is, two or two hundred different categories could be used.

One such distribution of income in the United States is shown in Table 16.2.

ESTATE SYSTEM

In the third type of system, the estate system, the important criterion of classification is land tenure which is related to military service. At the top is the royal family and a landholding, hereditary military aristocracy. The priesthood and the secular nobility are next in line, followed in turn by merchants and craftsmen, free peasants, and unfree serfs. Limited mobility is possible through such techniques as royal decree, marriage, military service, becoming artisans or tradesmen, or entering the clergy.[9]

In order to understand the systems of differential interaction involved in these systems, one needs to know, among other things, the way in which those involved define the salient factors—the value, norm, role, and self definitions involved.

VALUE DEFINITIONS

In the first place (although this does not *necessarily* precede other factors in any time sequence) the criteria of differential treatment must be determined. In over-simplified terms, the group in one way or another must decide what they approve of and therefore want to reward and encourage and conversely what they disapprove of and desire to penalize and discour-

[9] Peter I. Rose, *They and We* (New York: Random House, Inc., 1964), p. 6.

TABLE 16.2

Distribution of Total Money Income of Families and Unrelated
Individuals in the United States, 1963

Total Money Income	Families and Unrelated Individuals	
	Total Number: 47,436,000; Per Cent: 100.0	Cumulative Percentage
Under $1,000	3.8	3.8
$ 1,000 – $ 1,999	6.8	10.6
$ 2,000 – $ 2,999	7.9	18.5
$ 3,000 – $ 3,999	8.7	27.2
$ 4,000 – $ 4,999	9.0	36.2
$ 5,000 – $ 5,999	11.1	47.3
$ 6,000 – $ 6,999	10.2	57.5
$ 7,000 – $ 7,999	9.1	66.6
$ 8,000 – $ 9,999	13.4	80.0
$10,000 – $14,999	14.5	94.5
$15,000 – $24,999	4.4	98.9
$25,000 and over	1.0	99.9
Median Income	$6,249	

SOURCE: Compiled from *Current Population Reports*, Series P-60, No. 42, June 12, 1964, Table 1, p. 2.

age. Since at the human level such decisions are not provided by any biological process, the group must develop a NER value system or value scale for such purposes. Such scales are sometimes said to measure "social distance." It follows, then, that the value systems involved in stratified interaction will vary with the social experiences of the groups and even with the individuals involved. Since the value systems are NER in nature, the related stratification systems are not necessarily rational or logical from all perspectives.

Actually, any factors could be involved in the system. A group may, for instance, decide to evaluate certain biological characteristics as higher than others; in colonial America, the male was defined as superior to the female, and extensive plans of action were developed which took this differential evaluation into account. Any biological factors such as skin color, hair color, or physical build individually or collectively may be involved.

Economic factors may play a major role in some systems, although there is no justification for assuming, as did Marx, that they will always be the major class criteria. Other religious, educational, and occupational factors may frequently be involved. Various occupations may be valued differentially and those who hold a high-status position and play the accompanying role are given the corresponding status as individuals. Such differential evaluation of positions may be an important method of making sure that certain duties will be performed for the society. Further specificity may be introduced by granting greater prestige to those who play their roles in a particularly approved manner or who combine the role with other valued personal qualities.

Actually, any factor or combination of factors which the group for one reason or another decides to evaluate highly may be involved. It does not take much concentration to see the relationship governing the education-occupation-income triad in the American system. Some frequently included items are as follows:

Authority
Power (political, economic, military)
Ownership of property, relation to the means of production, control over land (the feudal estates)
Income—amount, type, and sources
Consumption patterns and style of life
Occupation or skill, and achievement in it
Education, learning, wisdom
Divinity, "control" over the supernatural
Altruism, public service, morality
Place in "high society," kinship connections, ancestry (i.e., inherited position), associational ties and connections
Ethnic status, religion, race
Age
Sex [10]

Evaluations of the various characteristics involved do not, of course, exist as separate and unrelated value definitions, but are rather interrelated, so that a somewhat consistent value *system* is developed. The system results not only from man's efforts to be consistent, but also from the fact that involving specific value judgments in interaction produces consequences which then have to be taken into account. If, for instance, the female is viewed as being inferior, the roles that she plays must logically be defined as inferior to those played by the "superior" male, and the rewards granted her varied accordingly. Actually in any society a whole network of interrelated value definitions and plans of action is developed and perpetuated.

Involvement of specific value systems in the interaction patterns permits those involved to explain to others and to themselves when the appropriate questions are raised that treating individuals with certain characteristics in a differential manner is good, proper, or right. Most members of a "college community" feel, for instance, that it is right and good that certain students receive A's in their sociology course while others receive B's, C's, and D's. Further, most Americans feel that it is only right and proper that the president of a company should be paid more than the bookkeeper of that company, and that it should be the president who is able to fire the bookkeeper, not the bookkeeper who is able to fire the president. Other explanations may be presented to justify the preferential treatment such as the fact that the president has more responsibility than the bookkeeper and is therefore entitled to his extra financial and prestige rewards. Such a statement, however, rests upon the value judgment (usually not stated) that increased responsibility is sufficient grounds for greater financial-prestige rewards. When we talk of *unequal* distribution of rewards, privileges, responsibilities, opportunities, and immunities, the term "unequal" refers only to the absence of identical qualities. No question is raised here as to whether any established system is *just* or *fair*.

Validation and perpetuation of established interaction systems are increased as the group reaches the decision that not only is its system "good" but that it has the endorsement of supernatural beings, or possibly that the system itself was initiated by supernatural beings for the wel-

---

Are the Stupid Discriminated Against?

But are the stupid really discriminated against and despised? Articles . . . seem to the writer to demonstrate that indeed they are. There is also the experience which may be observed over and over again of the denial of employment, of legal rights, of a fair hearing, of an opportunity, to the stupid because they are stupid (e.g., have a low IQ or show poor academic performances), and not because the stupidity is relevant to the task, or claim, or situation.

*—Lewis Anthony Dexter.**

---

[10] See Bernard Berelson and Gary A. Steiner, *Human Behavior* (New York: Harcourt, Brace & World, Inc., 1964), p. 454.

* Lewis Anthony Dexter, "On the Politics and Sociology of Stupidity in Our Society," in *The Other Side*, ed. by Howard S. Becker (New York: The Free Press of Glencoe, 1964), p. 40.

fare of society. This is one of the validating functions of religion to which greater attention will be given in a subsequent chapter on religion. Further, since established systems are usually viewed as having divine sanction, it is not surprising that those who come to challenge them likewise claim supernatural approval for the proposed changes. A somewhat parallel validating belief is that one system is *inherently* better than the other, and therefore should be perpetuated.

Decisions as to the fairness or the morality of a stratification system are not developed only after the system is established, as the above discussion might suggest. Rather, they are involved in the development of the system and are also a result of its development. The relationship between stratification systems (differential interaction patterns) and beliefs as to fairness is a reciprocal one.

NORM AND ROLE DEFINITIONS

The norm and role definitions related to the value definitions just discussed provide for a division of labor and indicate with varying degrees of specificity how members of the group are expected to behave in the situations which they cover. Such definitions are an integral part of any stratification system. Such definitions, for instance, specify who treats whom in specific ways. They specify who is expected and permitted to make certain types of decisions, and who is expected to perform certain types of tasks. They specify who makes occupational decisions as to how much money one receives for performing specified tasks and who makes decisions as to who gets promoted. These decisions, then, are important factors in the process by which some are able to accumulate economic surpluses which can, in turn, be influential in many other ways. The role and norm definitions further specify the criteria which will be taken into account in such decisions. Both formal and informal norm-role definitions are involved, and decisions as to whether or not Employee Jones is promoted may take into account not only his professional skills but his family connections as well.

If we define power as the capacity to control or at least to influence strongly the actions of others, and authority as power provided in the norm-role definitions, it follows that stratified (differential) interaction both results from and produces an unequal distribution of power and authority. Power to influence the behavior of individuals other than the members of one's own family is particularly important. Definitions of superiority usually are accompanied by plans of action which give the "superior" individual or group power and authority over the "inferior" individuals. Decisions by high-ranking individuals may have decisive influence upon the on-going and future behavior of others. Such decisions by one man or group may impose limitations upon the decisions which others are permitted to make. They also permit the favored individuals to treat others in ways which greatly influence their whole life pattern. The penetrating influence of decisions by those who control the means of production or the source of labor is apparent. Decisions as to who drops out of high school before graduation may have repercussions throughout the rest of the life of the "dropout." In the case of the military, role definitions indicate specifically who has the power to make decisions as to who lives and who dies.

SELF DEFINITIONS (CLASS AND CASTE CONSCIOUSNESS)

As the value and norm-role systems influence the behavior of the individual, it is inevitable that his definition of himself will be affected. Each of us is constantly making decisions (role taking) as to why others treat us in particular ways. Those who have characteristics specifically defined by the value system become aware of having these characteristics and apply the appropriate evaluations to themselves. Where several individuals enact norm-role definitions which call for similar behavior on their part and similar treatment by others, they develop somewhat similar individual behavior (personality) patterns. As they play their roles it would seem to be inevitable that they would become aware

Figure 16.2   Prestige differences may extend to pets.   (Wide World Photos.)

of characteristics which they share with others who are doing about the same thing and have about the same material possessions that they do.

In the process of interacting, individuals learn to "locate" themselves socially with relation to others. Most people know how they are rated by others and each person tends to adopt as self definitions the definitions that correspond to those of significant others. Definitions as to his class or caste are some of the most important self definitions which an individual acquires.

In a loosely structured class society where clear-cut definitions have not been developed, individuals may have only correspondingly hazy ideas as to just exactly how they "stack up" against others, but even here most know who is roughly above, below, and equal to them. In a society where clear-cut caste definitions are provided, there is no question as to just where one

fits in. Individuals know their caste labels every bit as well as they know their family and their occupational names. This is, in fact, one of the distinguishing features of a caste system.

SOCIALIZATION

Any established group has its class–caste system, the details of which are learned by those coming into the group. Those born into the group do not usually question whether the factors involved *should be* involved. The system is, at first at least, accepted by them as it is taught to them; it is *the* system. Harmonious beliefs and practices are accepted without much question. Since they know no other system, it is easy to accept the ethnocentric belief that the established system is the *only* way to behave. Later, when awareness of other systems is acquired, this belief is easily changed to acceptance of the established system as the *only proper* way to behave.

Members of a group may eventually learn to doubt the validity of their own system or even the desirability of any class–caste system. Such doubts, however, are usually acquired slowly. Whatever the pattern, whatever the changes, they are a result of human interaction.

ROLE PLAYING AND ROLE TAKING

A major function or result of stratification systems is that they facilitate interaction so that it is consistent and the· society can function. A functioning society is a complex phenomenon and differential interaction therein is a multi-faceted phenomenon. It involves role-norm enacting, the application of value labels, interpretation and re-interpretation of the behavior of others and self, and synthesizing all of these factors so that the whole experience more or less makes sense.

In this dynamic process, those involved have to make constant decisions as to which aspects of the people involved and which situational factors are to be taken into account, and which are to be ignored as irrelevant to the interaction sequence under way. In simple terms, decisions have to be made as to what labels will be placed upon the situation, the self, others, and objects involved, as well as relationships between these. Some characteristics are considered in most interactions, whereas others are brought into play under only limited situations. In crisis situations, for instance, many differences are ignored and those involved may be treated as "fellow human beings" with but little attention being given to stratification factors which under more normal conditions would greatly restrict interaction. Making such decisions as to which characteristics are relevant and which are irrelevant to the immediate situation is one of the dynamic aspects of interaction. Where such patterns are well established, we can say that the group has developed norms of relevancy which facilitate such decisions. Such norms are, in fact, developed as a part of the stratification system.

If a certain individual or group is defined as inferior (a NER definition) it is easier to maintain the definition if some empirical support for the belief can be found. It is hard to maintain that someone else is inferior to you so long as they behave as you do and have the same things you do. It is not surprising, then, that intentionally or unintentionally those defined as inferior are treated differentially in such a way that empirical differences will develop to accompany the non-empirical (NER) definitions. In many respects, applying a label of "inferior" to certain individuals becomes a somewhat self-fulfilling prophecy.

Interaction further involves recognition and evaluation of empirical differences which do obtain. If such differences are recognized and are felt to be important, man attempts to justify them on the basis of some moral code, which, of course, involves NER symbols. If, for instance, females are found to behave differently from males, efforts may be made to "explain" or "understand" such differences. When value definitions become involved in such explanations, stratification value scales may be developed which may then be used to perpetuate such differences and any interaction patterns which take them into account.

Actually the relationship between the two factors is a reciprocal one. Behavior tends to be patterned to harmonize with our value systems; conversely, value systems tend to harmonize with our behavior patterns.

The actual results of taking some value system into account in on-going interaction may extend, in a chain-reaction pattern, far beyond the immediate situation. The influence of decisions to grant military men greater prestige and financial reward than clergymen could, of course, be followed throughout the whole "warp and woof" of a society. Decisions as to the inferiority of females in colonial American society, to continue a previous illustration, resulted among other things in denying them admission to college, which in turn effectively excluded them from certain occupations, which in turn restricted their potential income, which in turn influenced their social life, which in turn influenced their marriage patterns, with the influence extending to their children and on and on throughout other activities and other generations. Individuals who have participated in the organization of a new group to move the discussion to a smaller scope and have had a chance to see the system of interaction become standardized become aware of the ramifications of early decisions as to who "outranks" whom upon what basis.

The limitations imposed by one's class position upon the decisions one can make and the actions in which he can engage provides cogent support to the anti-reductionist or interactionist position of sociology.

The same pattern may, of course, work in reverse. When "inferior" females are needed in certain "prohibited" occupations for a war effort, as during World War II, we have to change not only job restrictions but also at least part of our definition of inferiority. This in turn may weaken "generalized inferiority" definitions and result in changes in family, religious, sexual, and political behavior. It is difficult (but not impossible) to maintain "inferior" definitions in one area when equality has been established in another. Under such conditions, however, the norms of relevancy may be questioned and eventually changed.

Those who play different roles, formal and informal, engage in different types of behavior, endorse different sets of value definitions, and acquire different objects such as money, cars, and homes. Those who play similar roles develop similar characteristics. Further, the set of roles which any one individual plays is usually a somewhat consistent set, so that his behavior and possessions in one role harmonize with those in another. The fact that it is the same individual who plays the set of roles encourages consistency—even though a Dr. Jekyll–Mr. Hyde discrepancy may exist. Further, an individual is unlikely to seek to play roles which would cause him or others to question a prized position or possession. Consistency is further encouraged by the fact that many of the same individuals interact with Mr. X in many of his various roles, and expect to treat him at least somewhat the same in each of the roles.

By way of summary, then, differential definitions, involved in differential treatment, produce differential results, which are in turn involved in subsequent interaction. Our understanding of this dynamic process may be expanded if we figuratively stop the process, as one might a motion picture, and identify some of the inequalities which are to be found at a particular time, which we will now do with reference to the American society. What we are doing, then, is identifying or singling out for purposes of analysis, specific definitions (attitudes), behavior patterns, and objects which are involved in the complex interaction process. While this analysis is in terms of static quantities, it should be recognized that it pushes into the unrecognized background the dynamic manner in which the factors are involved in human interaction.

AMERICAN STRATIFICATION—AN OVERVIEW

As indicated, we will now utilize the preceding discussion and concepts in a brief analysis of the American society. While the discussion will be placed at the societal level, it should be recognized that these patterns of necessity ignore variations at the regional, community, neighborhood, and even individual levels, recognition of which may be important for other purposes.

Caste

The description of a caste system can be applied with a fair degree of accuracy to the system of relationships which obtains between the two major racial groups in America—Negro and white. The "fit" is at least sufficient to justify labeling the relationship semi-caste if not rigid caste. The white or Negro identity is acquired at birth, and is felt to be of sufficient importance that it is taken into account in most interaction throughout the lifetime of those involved. While there are exceptions, as in the case of those who "pass," usually the individual who is labeled a Negro at birth carries the label throughout his lifetime. Mobility within either caste group is common; mobility between caste groups is uncommon. Further, most marriages are racially

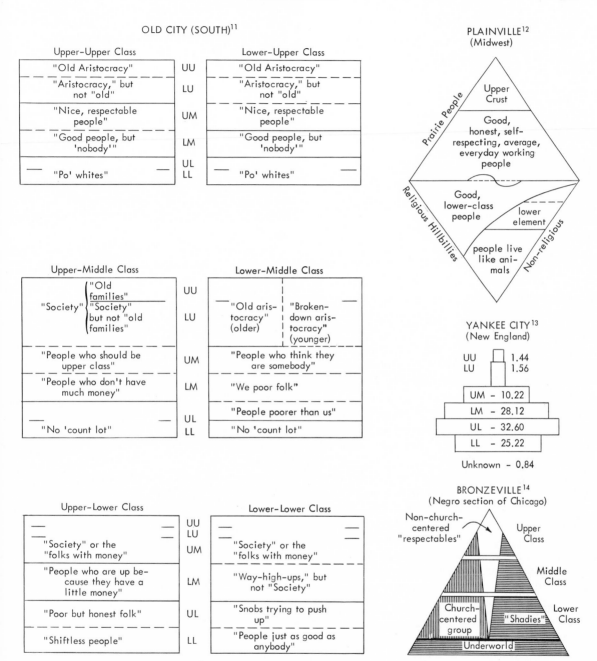

Figure 16.3

11 Allison Davis, Burleigh B. Gardner, and Mary R. Gardner, *Deep South: A Social-Anthropological Study of Caste and Class* (Chicago: The University of Chicago Press, 1941), p. 65.

12 James West, *Plainville, U.S.A.* (New York: Columbia University Press, 1945), p. 117.

13 Warner and Lunt, *op. cit.*

14 St. Clair Drake and H. R. Cayton, *Black Metropolis* (New York: Harcourt, Brace & World, Inc., 1945), p. 525.

endogamous—that is, they occur between individuals who share a common racial identity.

Change in the extent to which caste identity is taken into account in specific interaction patterns has been occurring at an accelerated rate, and the influence of the caste identity is weakened accordingly. However, the likelihood that Americans will, in the near future, cease to pay attention to racial identity does not appear to be great.

Class System

The percentage of Americans who are classified in various categories varies with the class criteria and the ones doing the categorizing. Graphic representations of the results of four studies of different populations in different sections of the country are shown in Figure 16.3. The Davis study of a southern city provides us with the labels used by the respondents in placing people in a six-fold classification, and emphasizes that the class structure may be viewed somewhat differently from different positions therein. The involvement of religion as a class criterion is evident in the Plainville and Bronzeville classifications. Stratification within the Negro caste is illustrated by the Bronzeville data.

The American class structure can also be visualized as a continuum, without clear, ready-made divisions therein. The continuum can be viewed as being a synthesis of, or an abstraction from, the interrelated factors involved. The following discussion of class correlates will utilize the continuum concept. The student should remember, however, that not all of the research summarized here used the same class criteria. Our discussion will assume that the correlation between the various criteria is sufficient to justify our talking about "class position" without specifying exactly what the criteria of the study were. A check of footnoted sources will provide more specific information about any specific correlation.

Further, while we will be talking about relationships, it should be clear that no causal relationship is implied. In this realm, as in most others, the principle of multiple causation applies. Most of the relationships identified probably reflect mutually interrelated factors, many of which will likely be suggested by a perusal of the list.

It should also be clearly understood that the correlations here identified merely indicate the direction of the relationship for *groups* of people; individual cases with contrary patterns most likely exist for each of the factors. In a sense, the correlation techniques average out the differences, which exist in reality. Our data, however, are sufficient to identify patterns in the relationships discussed and it is with these patterns that we are concerned.

Many relationships could have been introduced here. We will, however, use only enough to illustrate the extent to which these relationships are involved in human interaction. Other such relationships will be provided in the subsequent chapters which deal with specific institutions.

With these reservations, then, let us look at some of the factors which have been found to be correlated with class position.

Research studies in various fields have found that, in general, in the United States, as class position *increases:*

1. Infant mortality rate decreases.[15]

2. Life expectancy increases.[16]

3. Chances for survival in wartime in the armed forces increases.[17]

---

[15] Robert M. Woodbury, "Infant Mortality in the United States," *Annals of the American Academy of Political and Social Science,* CLXXXVIII (November, 1936, pp. 102–104; and M. E. Altender and B. Crowther, "Relation Between Infant Mortality and Socio Economic Factors in Urban Areas," *Public Health Reports,* LXIV (March 18, 1949), 331–339.

[16] J. S. Whitney, "Death Rates by Occupation Based on Data of the U. S. Census Bureau, 1930" (New York: National Tuberculosis Association, 1934); and L. Guralnick, "The Study of Mortality by Occupation in the United States" (National Office of Vital Statistics, Washington, D. C.: Government Printing Office, September, 1959).

[17] Albert J. Mayer and Thomas Ford Hoult, "Social Stratification and Combat Survival," *Social Forces,* XXXIV, No. 2 (December, 1955), 155–159.

4. Level of health increases.[18]

5. Number of visits to a doctor increases.[19]

6. Amount of yearly and lifetime income increases.[20]

7. Desire to "improve oneself" remains constant.[21]

8. Status of occupation increases.[22]

9. Likelihood of living in a "status" house in a "status" area of the city increases.[23]

10. Level of education increases.[24]

11. Facility in symbolic communication increases.[25]

12. Accuracy of role-taking ability increases.[26]

13. Selection of dating and marriage partners from *same* level remains constant.[27]

14. Age of first marriage increases.[28]

15. Likelihood of marriage being *unbroken* by divorce, separation, or desertion increases.[29]

16. Likelihood of being a virgin at marriage increases.[30]

17. Likelihood of parents treating children in warm, permissive manner and using praise and reasoning rather than physical punishment in socialization increases.[31]

18. Likelihood of voting in a presidential election increases.[32]

19. Extent of knowledge about political issues increases.[33]

20. Likelihood of identifying self politically as a Republican increases.[34]

[28] Warner and Lunt, *op. cit.*, p. 423.

[29] A. B. Hollingshead, "Class Differences in Family Stability," *Annals of the American Academy of Political and Social Science*, CCLXXII (November, 1950), pp. 39–46; Thomas P. Monahan, "Divorce by Occupational Level," *Marriage and Family Living*, XVII, No. 4 (November, 1955), 322–324; and William J. Goode, "Economic Factors and Marital Stability," *American Sociological Review*, XVI, No. 6 (December, 1951), pp. 802–812.

[30] Alfred C. Kinsey *et al.*, *Sexual Behavior in the Human Male* (Philadelphia: W. B. Saunders Co., 1948).

[31] Eleanor E. Maccoby and Patricia K. Gibbs, "Methods of Child Rearing in Two Social Classes," in W. E. Martin and C. B. Stendler (eds.), *Readings in Child Development* (New York: Harcourt, Brace & World, Inc., 1954); Robert J. Havighurst and Allison Davis, "A Comparison of the Chicago and Harvard Studies of Social Class Differences in Child Rearing," *American Sociological Review*, XX, No. 4 (August, 1955), 438–442; and Robert R. Sears *et al.*, *Patterns of Child Rearing* (New York: Harper & Row, Inc., 1957).

[32] Robert E. Lane, *Political Life* (New York: The Free Press of Glencoe, 1959), pp. 48–49; and Angus Campbell, Gerald Gurin, and Warren E. Miller, *The Voter Decides* (New York: Harper & Row, Inc., 1954).

[33] Campbell *et al.*, *op. cit.*; Bernard R. Berelson, Paul F. Lazarsfeld, and William M. McPhee, *Voting* (Chicago: University of Chicago Press, 1954); Arthur Kornhauser, Harold L. Sheppard, and Albert J. Mayer, *When Labor Votes: A Study of Auto Workers* (New York: University Books, 1956); and Gerhart H. Saenger, "Social Status and Political Behavior," *The American Journal of Sociology*, LI, No. 1 (September, 1945), 103–113.

[34] *Ibid.*

[18] "Illness and Medical Care in Relation to Economic Status" (Washington, D. C.: *The National Health Survey*, 1935–1936, Bulletin No. 2, 1938).

[19] *Ibid.*

[20] *Statistical Abstract of the United States: 1961* (Bureau of the Census, Washington, D. C.: Government Printing Office), Tables 142 and 143, pp. 110–111.

[21] LaMar T. Empey, "Social Class and Occupational Aspiration: A Comparison of Absolute and Relative Measurement," *American Sociological Review*, XXI, No. 6 (December, 1956), 703–709.

[22] *Current Population Reports*, Series P–60, No. 30, December, 1958, Table 8, p. 24.

[23] Joseph A. Kahl, *The American Class Structure* (New York: Holt, Rinehart and Winston, Inc., 1960), pp. 108–114.

[24] Elmo Roper, *Factors Affecting the Admission of High School Seniors to College* (Washington, D. C.: American Council on Education, 1949).

[25] Leonard Schatzman and Anselm Strauss, "Social Class and Modes of Communication," *The American Journal of Sociology*, LX, No. 4 (January, 1955), 329–338.

[26] Samuel Z. Klausner, "Social Class and Self-Concept," *Journal of Social Psychology*, XXXVIII, No. 2 (November, 1953), 201–205.

[27] Kingsley Davis, Harry C. Bredemeier, and Marion J. Levy, Jr. (eds.), *Modern American Society* (New York: Holt, Rinehart and Winston, Inc., 1949), p. 611.

21. Likelihood of belonging to voluntary associations increases.[35]

22. Likelihood of playing a leadership role in a church increases.[36]

23. Likelihood of having associates who are defined as "close friends" increases.[37]

24. Even though the likelihood of engaging in anti-social acts remains somewhat constant, the likelihood of becoming an official delinquent as a result thereof decreases.[38]

25. Likelihood of receiving "justice" in the courts of the land increases.[39]

26. Likelihood of endorsing principle of deferred gratification increases.[40]

27. Status anxiety remains somewhat constant except at Upper-Upper level.[41]

28. Likelihood of having racial and religious prejudice decreases.[42]

SOCIAL MOBILITY

Change in labels, related interaction patterns (role playing), and possessions are frequently referred to in sociological literature as well as in the popular press as *social mobility*. It is with such change that this section is concerned. Two major types of change are possible: (1) change of individuals within a stable society, and (2) change in the patterns of society. At a university, for instance, individual students may change from freshmen to seniors while the over-all system remains fairly constant. Likewise, in America, individuals may move from lower class to middle class while the society remains relatively constant. Change can occur, however, in the over-all university system or the over-all society, which may or may not be accompanied by marked individual change.

Caste Change

A major characteristic of a caste system is that there is no mobility between castes, although there may be mobility within any particular caste. Consequently, change in caste definitions and in the playing of the ascribed roles associated therewith takes place slowly. Motivation within such groups is in the direction of endorsing equilibrium rather than change. When change does occur, and it would appear to be inevitable that it will, it is most likely to be a result of contact with an out-group whereby value definitions are questioned, established interaction patterns are disrupted, and possessions such as money are redistributed. Such change can be painful since patterns and value definitions previously accepted without question and possibly with religious endorsement are subjected to question and possibly to reinterpretation.

[35] Charles R. Wright and H. H. Hyman, "Voluntary Association Memberships of American Adults: Evidence from National Sample Surveys," *American Sociological Review*, XXIII, No. 3 (June, 1958), 284–289; see also Genevieve Knupfer, "Portrait of the Underdog," *Public Opinion Quarterly*, XI, No. 1 (Spring, 1947), 101–118; and Joan Moore, "Exclusiveness and Ethnocentrism in a Metropolitan Upper-Class Agency," *Pacific Sociological Review*, V, No. 1 (Spring, 1962), 16–20.

[36] Jerome Davis, "A Study of Protestant Church Boards of Control," *The American Journal of Sociology*, XXXVIII, No. 3 (November, 1932), 418–431.

[37] Kahl, *op. cit.*, pp. 137–138; see also Peter H. Rossi, *Why Families Move* (New York: The Free Press of Glencoe, 1955), pp. 34–40.

[38] William C. Kvaraceus, "Juvenile Delinquency and Social Class," *Journal of Educational Sociology*, XVIII, No. 1 (September, 1944), 51–54; see also Austin Porterfield, *Youth in Trouble* (Austin, Texas: Leo Potishman Foundation, 1946).

[39] William F. Ogburn and Mayer F. Nimkoff, *Sociology* (4th ed.; Boston: Houghton Mifflin Co., 1964), p. 443.

[40] Louis Schneider and Sverre Lysgaard, "The Deferred Gratification Pattern: A Preliminary Study," *American Sociological Review*, XVIII, No. 2 (April, 1953), 142–149. Relationships between class position and other value definitions are found in Albert K. Cohen, *Delinquent Boys: The Culture of the Gang* (New York: The Free Press of Glencoe, 1955).

[41] William H. Sewell and A. O. Haller, "Factors in the Relationship Between Social Status and the Personality Adjustment of the Child," *American Sociological Review*, XXIV, No. 4 (August, 1959), 511–520.

[42] William McCord, Joan McCord, and Alan Howard, "Early Familial Experiences and Bigotry," *American Sociological Review*, XXV, No. 5 (October, 1960), 717–722.

Figure 16.4 "Home" means different things to different people. (Wide World Photos.)

Class Change

Class systems involve achieved roles, and are consequently predicated upon the premise that change or mobility is desirable and will occur. Different types of such change can be identified, such as (1) *vertical mobility*, which involves change of definitions to a higher or lower level; (2) *generational mobility*, which compares the class level of members of different generations, possibly fathers and sons; and (3) *career mo-*

bility, which involves change which takes place during the working lifetime of an individual.

In order for mobility to happen, the society must first of all be so organized that such change is possible, or so that individuals have a chance at least to have others relabel them and an opportunity to play the corresponding roles. Means must also be provided so that individuals can (1) acquire the desire to change (define change as possible and desirable) and (2) be permitted to do something to realize the desire.

Class Mobility in America

Some of the major characteristics of mobility patterns in the United States are as follows.

Historical foundation. *Frontier* conditions were conducive to mobility in that opportunities were provided for individuals to play new roles and accumulate possessions with few restraining social restrictions. A large supply of *immigrants,* who entered the society at the lower-class levels, came with desire to "better their lot," and were helped in their efforts by immigrants who followed, who were available for the lower-class roles, and who thus in effect "pushed" the older immigrants up. *Industrialization* substituted an economic frontier for the geographic frontier in that new positions and new industries were made available to members of the society.

Current factors. Americans still strongly endorse the desirability of upward mobility—the great "American dream." Further, avenues of change, particularly via increased education, are widely available.

There is, however, a lack of consensus as to the extent of actual change. Change does occur, but whether the rate of change is definitely accelerating or decelerating is the unanswered question. It is possible for individuals to move from a low position to a high one, but one thing is certain: the chances of a high position being one's terminal position are greater if he is born at that level than they are if he is born at a lower level. The Warner and Abegglen[43] study of the "business elite" concludes, for instance, that "Sons of the big business men . . . occupy nearly eight times their proportionate share of elite positions." Further, while various studies indicated that about 70 per cent of sons are engaged in occupations different from those followed by their fathers, a son is more likely to enter his father's occupation than any other *single* occu-

Upward Skidding

Everyone wants to go up; no one wants to go down. We have long cherished the illusion that we choose to go up, and are only forced to go down. It is time we wake up to the fact that Skid Row is actually a two-way street.

This idea is very hard to grasp for several reasons. First of all, in looking backward over our own lives, the admission, if we have moved up, that this might have been a mistake in choice or that we were coerced into it by outside forces is embarrassing or painful, depending upon how sharply we see it. Secondly, young people, who are still young enough to make a choice have insufficient experience on which to base it; and while their parents may have had the experience, it is not very often shared with their children in any meaningful way.

—William Bruce Cameron.*

pation, and most of the mobile sons do not go very far up or down the scale. Amount, but not extent, of intergenerational mobility is great.[44]

It may be interesting to speculate upon the question as to just what the results would be if the majority of Americans knew the exact extent of change. Quite possibly, ignorance of such facts is in itself a factor which contributes to the existing upward mobility.

Mobility is not achieved in a vacuum, and characteristics acquired in the struggle upward filter out to many tangential characteristics. Upward mobility, for instance, frequently necessitates leaving behind friends and maybe family members with whom satisfying relationships may have been previously established. Mobile individuals may become somewhat marginal and feel a degree of alienation and isolation, not knowing exactly where they belong and not being completely accepted at either level. The attention given to self "improvement" may produce coun-

---

[43] W. Lloyd Warner and James C. Abegglen, *Big Business Leaders in America* (New York: Harper & Row, Inc., 1955), p. 17.

* William Bruce Cameron, *Informal Sociology* (New York: Random House, Inc., 1963), pp. 95–96.
[44] Mayer, *op. cit.,* p. 70.

ter-balancing rejection from those who are most closely affected or from those who feel threatened by the mobile person. Movement to new neighborhoods or to different communities disrupts established satisfying relationships, which may appear in retrospect doubly desirable, since the establishment of new relationships takes time. Acquiring all or most of the appropriate behavior patterns, such as types of humor, types of speech and dress, and the appropriate objects of art to display in the home; gaining admission of children to the appropriate schools; finding marriage mates for them at the appropriate level, etc., takes time and certainly extracts its share of anguish.

Then there is always the question of what happens to those who aspire, try, and fail. Adjusting to "love's labor lost" is not always easy, and the process by which individuals finally settle upon a terminal position is most likely equally difficult.

America does have extensive class differences, but little or no *class* conflict has developed. The Marxian prediction with reference to such conflict has certainly not been fulfilled. Robin Williams [45] suggests that this is most likely related to the following identifiable characteristics:

1. The high level of real income and the relatively wide distribution of a "Comfort" level of living.
2. The actual incidence of upward mobility and the attendant hope of "getting ahead."
3. The existence of a large middle-income, middle-prestige aggregate.
4. Widespread legal and political rights, nominally equalitarian.
5. The accessibility of public facilities and services.
6. The prevalence of equalitarian symbols and behavior patterns.
7. Interaction heterogeneity in culture.
8. Mutual insulation of prestige classes.
9. Participation in common organizations and activities.
10. Persistence of a complex body of beliefs and values that lends legitimacy to the going system.

CLASSLESS IDEOLOGY

One of the interesting aspects of the American class system is the fact that Americans frequently deny that such a system even exists. In a study in Minneapolis,[46] for instance, it was found that when respondents were asked to what social class they belonged, a large proportion questioned the interviewer as to the meaning of social class. When a series of general questions about the existence of social classes and their characteristics were utilized before presenting the direct question, "Which one of these classes are you in?" 14 per cent of the group said "no class," 20 per cent said "Don't know" and 5 per cent refused to answer. Further, 27.5 per cent of a national sample in 1940, in reply to the question, "What word would you use to name the class in America you belong to?" answered "Don't know." Discussions of social stratification among

---

The Cost of Mobility

Another price of mobility is the feeling of never quite belonging, of never being fully accepted by the members of the class into which you have moved. With this feeling goes the fear of making a wrong move—of doing something that will cause people to say, "Well, what do you expect? After all, remember where she came from."

W. Lloyd Warner and
Mildred Hall Warner.*

---

* W. Lloyd Warner and Mildred Hall Warner, "Climbing the Social Ladder," in Read Bain (ed.), *Sociology: Introductory Readings* (New York: J. B. Lippincott Co., 1962), p. 191.

45 Robin M. Williams, *American Society* (2d ed.; New York: Alfred A. Knopf, Inc., 1960), p. 47.

46 Neal Gross, "Social Class Identification in the Urban Community," *American Sociological Review*, XVIII, No. 4 (August, 1953), 398–402.

college students usually provoke extensive consideration of the question as to just how you can tell to which class one belongs.

This uncertainty no doubt reflects the ideology endorsed by many Americans that we *should not,* and in fact, do not, have classes in America. But there would seem to be more to it than this. Certainly Americans have not developed any standardized terminology with accompanying definitions with which to identify different classes. Neither do we have any clear grouping of individuals, into class groups, although rough groupings are recognized by some, as Meltzer and Manis have shown.[47] Differences in many aspects of living exist and are well recognized, but it would appear to be questionable whether many Americans see these as *class* differences.

Part of the explanation of the uncertainty here apparently lies in the fact that for Americans to come to decisions about the class to which an individual belongs, they have to do some "translating." It is fairly easy to distinguish different amounts of income, different types of homes, or different amounts of education since these can be studied directly. But when asked to which class one belongs, an individual has to translate information about such direct characteristics into class information, and since the general public has not developed any clear-cut formula to do this, individuals frequently report that they don't know how to, or they question the legitimacy of even trying to do so.

Discrimination

"Why not treat each individual on his merits regardless of classification?" is a frequently heard plea, but is this really possible? Can you react to another without classification?

In a caste system, individuals are told from childhood to which caste they belong and are given the appropriate re-inforcing treatment. In the American open-class system, the interaction and the identification system are more subtle. Children are not provided with labels to identify their class membership in the same way they are told that they are, say, Methodists, Americans, or New Englanders. Even as adults they have difficulties translating the known characteristics into "class language." One cannot long escape awareness of the fact that extensive differences exist between people and groups of people, but many do not see these as class differences. And further, since we have not developed any clear consensus as to which terms we will use and how they will be defined, it is not necessarily illogical to have a belief in the classlessness of American society at the same time that, say, extensive economic differences are recognized.

Consciousness of existing class differences is also minimized by other characteristics of the society of which Williams [48] identifies the following:

1. The tendency in our society not to give clear recognition to invidious distinctions.
2. The rather marked diffusion of equalitarian social manners through a wide range of occupations, income levels, and positions.
3. The wide accessibility of such commonplace symbols of "respectable" position as automobiles, the less costly versions of fashionable clothing, or even the occasional opportunity to attend commercial amusements carrying prestige.
4. The many legal or political rights that are nominally universal; the franchise, the right to hold public office, the equal responsibility for military service and jury duty; the right to a public school education and the accessibility of college training, the availability of a wide variety of public services open to all citizens.

---

[47] Jerome G. Manis and Bernard N. Meltzer, "Attitudes of Textile Workers to Class Structure," *American Journal of Sociology,* LX, No. 1 (July, 1954), 30–35.

[48] Williams, *op. cit.,* p. 131.

5. Existing mobility.
6. The complexity of the occupational structure.
7. The crisscrossing of diverse criteria and symbols of position such as income, residence, religion, ethnic background, education, family prestige, organizational affiliations, manners, and so on.

Another interesting class phenomenon which to some appears to be a paradox is the acceptance of a strong belief in equality—"All men are created equal"—and an accompanying awareness of differences with an endorsement thereof. When pressed to reconcile the apparent contradiction, the answer generally secured is that one person is as good as the other, even though there are differences in money, education, etc. This, then, places the equality on the NER level and the inequality on the ER level. Since there are no empirical limitations upon the NER goodness of people, it may be entirely consistent to recognize empirical differences and endorse goodness (NER) equality.

SUMMARY

Stratified interaction, which is found in all societies, involves an established system of differential treatment, in which those who have certain objects, positions, or other characteristics are given preferential treatment. Value definitions and related religious definitions provide justification for the differential behavior patterns incorporated in the norm-role definitions, all of which are related to the self definitions of those involved. The specific definitions involved in any system originate from, are perpetuated by, and are changed by society-wide interaction, even though some aspects may be viewed by the participants as being biologically or supernaturally given. Stratified interaction involves learned behavior.

Various patterns have been developed by various groups. Rigid caste systems permit no mobility and the norm-role definitions involved specify extensive intra-caste interaction, whereas mobility potential and mobility motivation are built into the less rigid class systems. Where caste–class identification cannot be made by paying attention to biological differences, strata symbols are used.

The extensive involvement of the American stratification system in the interaction within the society can be identified by many of the correlates of class position.

The American class system is a continuum capable of being divided into any number of categories. There are three methods of class determination—self identification, reputational, and objective. Negro–white interaction in America exhibits caste-like characteristics. Americans are proud of the mobility which occurs and of the mobility potential of their system while at the same time they strongly endorse the principle of equality. No class conflicts have developed.

QUESTIONS

1. Speculate on what would have happened to the United States as a nation if early Americans had somehow decided to adopt Amish culture and rather than reward those who acquire higher education had discouraged any education beyond the eighth grade.
2. What effect do you anticipate your college experience will have upon your subsequent class position in society?
3. Distinguish between caste and class.
4. Can a research sociologist be scientific and use the reputational or subjective approach of class determination?
5. How are value definitions involved in stratified interaction?
6. Distinguish between prejudice and discrimination.
7. How are status symbols involved in stratified interaction?
8. What interconnections do you see between the various correlates of class position discussed in the text?
9. Do you think that mobility in the United States will increase or decrease in the next decade? Why?
10. What do you think would have to happen to the United States in order to change the class system into a caste system?

PROJECT

Indicate five types of discrimination of which you approve, and identify the value definitions which are related to this approval.

SUGGESTED READING

BARBER, BERNARD. *Social Stratification*. New York: Harcourt, Brace & World, Inc., 1957.

DOLLARD, JOHN. *Caste and Class in a Southern Town*. New Haven: Yale University Press, 1937.

GORDON, MILTON M. *Social Class in American Sociology*. Durham, N. C.: Duke University Press, 1958.

KAHL, JOSEPH A. *The American Class Structure*. New York: Holt, Rinehart, and Winston, Inc., 1957.

MAYER, KURT B. *Class and Society*. New York: Random House, Inc., 1955.

MILLS, C. W. *White Collar: The American Middle Classes*. Fair Lawn, N. J.: Oxford University Press, 1951.

REISSMAN, LEONARD. *Class in American Society*. New York: The Free Press of Glencoe, 1949.

SOROKIN, PITIRIM A. *Social and Cultural Mobility*. New York: The Free Press of Glencoe, 1959.

VEBLEN, T. B. *The Theory of the Leisure Class*. New York: The Viking Press, 1945.

WARNER, W. LLOYD, MARCHIA MEEKER, and KENNETH EELLS. *Social Class in America*. Chicago: Science Research Associates, Inc., 1949.

17

Primary–Secondary

Interaction

What sort of things do you expect your friends to do for you which you would not expect strangers to do? What sort of things do you expect your friends to expect you to do for them? What sort of things do you feel free to do with friends which you would not do with strangers, and conversely, what things do you feel free to do with strangers which you would not with friends? Why is friend–friend interaction so different from friend–stranger interaction?

INTRODUCTION

Human interaction is a complex, multi-faceted phenomenon of which many different characteristics can be identified and studied. In this chapter we expand our list of the characteristics under study to include primary and secondary relationships. In some discussions the term "primary and secondary groups" is used. We will use both terms, but will emphasize "relationship" to call attention to the dynamic, emergent aspects of such interaction. Primary and secondary groups can be identified, to be sure, on the basis of the types of interaction which take place within them.

As we will consider them, primary and secondary relationships are ideal or constructed types which can be viewed as falling at either end of a primary-secondary interaction continuum, pictured as follows:

Primary   Secondary

No actual relationship is likely to have *all* of the characteristics of either of these two ideal types. Stated in another way, no relationship would, when analyzed, be likely to fall at one end of

249

this continuum or the other, but rather would be placed somewhere along it.[1]

Our discussion of these two ideal types will concentrate upon the primary relationship, with the understanding that relationships of the secondary type have the reciprocal characteristics.

PRIMARY RELATIONSHIPS

Relatively "Whole Personality" Interaction

A primary relation is one in which the participants react to the "whole personality" of the other and realize that they, themselves, are being responded to in the same way. "Whole" personality interaction is impossible. Selective perception is always involved. However, what we are referring to here is the extent to which an individual's behavior patterns, both thinking and overt, are known and taken into account by the other involved. In a primary relationship each knows a lot about the other or others with whom he is interacting, including some details which the other would not be anxious or willing to have many people know. Those involved know of each other much that they have done and thought in the past, and consequently are able to anticipate much that they will do in the future. Those involved know the relative value definitions attached by primary others to important elements. Even secret value definitions are known. Participants in a primary relationship know of each other what "goes on in the heart," the "basic needs or feelings," or the "innermost thoughts." In interpreting the behavior of these others, one is able to give consideration to many more factors than he is in interaction with those with whom he has a secondary relationship.

Such understanding is not a one-way phenomenon. Participants in such a relationship are not only aware of these characteristics of the others involved, but are also well aware of the fact that these others know a corresponding amount about them. In a primary relationship, we interact with those who have extensive information about us. In such a relationship it is unnecessary to do much other than just "be ourselves." It is, in fact, difficult to fool these others by pretense or sham. They are able to see through such efforts. With them one "can't get away with much."

Whole personality interaction can be contrasted with secondary or segmental interaction, in which only limited segments of one's personality are taken into account. An extreme illustration of segmental interaction is that which involves one's "paper personality." This paper identity is that indicated on the many identification cards, credit cards, driver's licenses, membership cards, admittance passes, etc., which serve to identify the carrier for certain purposes. In such interaction the treatment one is accorded stems basically from the card he presents rather than from any manifest characteristics of the individual *per se*. Presumably certain behavior patterns were required to obtain the card in the first place, but the immediate

---

A Campus Clique

All eight members of this clique are from the same southern state, with four of the members being from the same community in that state. All of them are charming conversationalists well versed in the social ritual and niceties characteristic of their social class background. They enjoy bridge, horseback riding, and swimming. None belongs to a club whose concern is intellectual. They are very much at home at college teas and have proved themselves to be capable hostesses.

—Orden Smucker.*

---

[1] When sociologists use the term "ideal type," the word "ideal" is not used as a value judgment but rather to mean that the types are used for measuring purposes. They provide a "yardstick." "Constructed types" gives no such value implication.

* Orden Smucker, "The Campus Clique as an Agency of Socialization," *Journal of Educational Sociology*, XXI (November, 1947), 163–168.

interaction in which the card and the individual become involved does not take this into account. Very limited characteristics are taken into account with the major one being that the individual has the appropriate card.

Type of Communication

Since the knowledge about each other is extensive in a primary relationship, communication proceeds on an intimate basis. Verbal shortcuts, understood by those involved—and frequently only by those involved—are established. Communication on the non-verbal level frequently occurs. Those involved are, in fact, able to "read each other like an open book."

Size

It would follow from what has been said that in size a primary group is usually small, permitting frequent face-to-face interaction.[2] Maintenance of such relationships with a large group of people over a period of time would be difficult, and it is unlikely that the quality of the relationship could be retained beyond certain points. It is true, of course, that certain celebrities and leaders of the charismatic type behave in such a way that large groups of people feel that they have at least a semi-primary relationship with them. Reciprocal feelings, however, do not obtain.

VALUE DEFINITIONS

Individuals who have established a primary relationship not only share a common understanding of each other, but they also tend to see the rest of the world alike. They share a common culture, including a common set of

[2] Cooley, who first used the term "primary group," indicated that such a group was characterized by "face-to-face" relationships. Charles Horton Cooley, *Social Organization* (New York: Charles Scribner's Sons, 1909), p. 23.

value definitions. Shared value definitions contribute to the intimacy of the relationship.

The shared value configuration involves a positive value assessment of the others involved in the relationship. The over-all evaluation is a positive one, even though it may be punctured by negative aspects here and there. Participants in a primary relationship have definitions of mutual love and respect for each other. The word "love" is used here in a broad sense, which includes not only a sweetheart relationship, but also the broader family type and the friendship-clique relationship. Although sociologists do not make extensive use of the "love concept," in a broad sense a primary relationship is just that— a loving relationship.

The positive evaluations apply not only to the others involved, but to the relationship itself. Maintenance of the relationship, in fact, is frequently of major importance to the participants. The threatened loss of such a relationship due to geographic or social mobility may be viewed as intolerable. Economic opportunities may be passed by primarily on these grounds—although different reasons may be provided in explanations provided for public consumption. A primary relationship is valued as an end in itself. By way of contrast, a secondary relationship is valued as a means to another end. It is a utilitarian or instrumental relationship, in which individuals *use* each other to obtain certain goals. Such relationships are contractual in nature. In the literature, which at times becomes somewhat emotional, such relationships are described as those in which individuals are treated as "things" rather than persons. The relationship may be categorized as one of "dehumanization" or "alienation."

Expulsion from a primary group is defined by most as severe punishment. Threatened expulsion is an effective sanction in the control of the members thereof. Refusal to permit the usual interaction patterns for a period of time, such as the "shunning" practice of the Amish or the refusal of a group of college co-eds to speak to a roommate, is less severe but still a potent means of social control.

NORM-ROLE DEFINITIONS

Informal Norm-Role Definitions

It is highly unlikely that the definitions regulating primary interaction will be formalized and recorded. They will be developed, but will remain on the informal level. This does not mean that they are any less binding, but only that reducing the common understanding of the group to writing is seen as not only unnecessary but even as threatening to the very relationship which is so highly prized. The extent of the knowledge which each has of the other, however, permits of considerable flexibility and spontaneity within the group. Testing of new or different ideas and behavior patterns may be first undertaken within the safety of the primary group, and only extended beyond the group after they have been accepted therein.

Figure 17.1 Primary interaction is frequently face-to-face, as in this farm family. (Wide World Photos.)

Non-Transferability of Role Definitions

The behavior patterns involved in primary relations are essentially non-transferable. In secondary relationships such as the relationship between clerk and customer in the local store, the behavior patterns are transferable—so much so that any number of different individuals can play the role of clerk or of customer with equal facility. But when the clerk goes home at night to her husband and children, she plays the role of wife and mother in such a unique way (although even here there are similarities among various wives and mothers) that her behavior and expectations could not easily be transferred to another. Clerk behavior is usually secondary; family behavior is usually primary.

SELF DEFINITIONS

With such an extensive awareness of the extent to which one's past behavior is known and with the high evaluations of the others involved, it follows that such relationships would have considerable influence upon the establishment and perpetuation of self definitions. When we make decisions about what we are "really" like, we give greater attention to the definitions reflected by those with whom we have primary relationships than those with whom we have secondary relationships, although both are obviously involved. In the development of self definitions, primary groups frequently provide the significant others.

Continued affirmation of the appropriate self definitions which are provided by primary others is important in the maintenance of the self definitions that one values. Preservation of the primary group is important because in a very literal sense it involves the preservation of the individual. In some respects, decisions concerning the support of primary groups may involve the calculated weighing of alternatives, so that the desired primary support and protection can be obtained. However, in most cases behavior which does elicit the desired responses is engaged in because this is what those involved want to do anyway.

The pattern is a reciprocal one. While one is dependent upon others to provide him with the responses necessary for the maintenance of his self definitions, they likewise are dependent upon him for similar confirmation.

When one has some characteristic which is potentially "discreditable," to use Goffman's term, those with whom one has primary relations becomes involved in seeing that the secret is kept. We feel safe in our relationships with primary others. We feel that we are loved and appreciated, in spite of any characteristics which might be disruptive of satisfying relationships were they widely known. Members of primary groups are intimately involved in the management of self definitions.

SECONDARY RELATIONSHIPS

Secondary relationships or groups have characteristics reciprocal to those of the primary relationships we have identified. In summary form, secondary relationships as contrasted with primary relationships are characterized by:

1. Limited knowledge about the behavior patterns, including thinking behavior, of the others involved.
2. Low-intensity value definitions attributed to the relationship *per se* and the others involved, both of which are defined more as a means to an end than as an end in themselves. People are treated as "things."
3. Less willingness to protect known or potential stigma of others.

Love Therapy

Love received and love given comprise the best form of therapy.

—Gordon W. Allport.*

---

* Gordon W. Allport, *Becoming* (New Haven: Yale University Press, 1955), p. 33.

4. Limited involvement in development and maintenance of self definitions.
5. Interaction controlled more by formal norm-role definitions.
6. Positions more transferable.
7. Communication more impersonal.

DEVELOPMENT OF PRIMARY RELATIONSHIPS

The development of primary relationships is usually a time-consuming process. Despite the phenomenon which is called "falling in love at first sight," the establishment of durable primary relations takes time. In terms of love, one grows in love rather than falls in love and the act of falling in love does not of itself produce a primary relationship, although it may be a preliminary part thereof.

First contacts with others are usually of a secondary nature, in which only limited aspects of one's thinking and behaving patterns are exposed. If the relationship is defined as one having promise of developing some primary characteristics and if at least one of those involved decides that it is worth the effort to attempt such a development, then tentative overtures toward greater involvement may be made. Initially such overtures may be made in such a manner that one can gracefully retreat if it appears that the initiated efforts will not be returned in kind. Such overtures can be interpreted in different ways. They are somewhat ambiguous. The initiator then will evaluate the responses of the other and on the basis of this evaluation decide which of the alternate interpretations he will base subsequent behavior upon. If friendly gestures are coldly met, they will usually be curtailed, or at least withheld until a situation felt to be more promising is at hand. The interaction then proceeds as though a friendly response were not looked for in the first place.

If initial efforts are mutually satisfying, then the gates may be opened a bit further. Gradual opening, possibly coupled with temporary closures, may eventually lead to a relationship in which one's "whole soul" is exposed. Most individuals do not rush into such a relationship, since such exposure is potentially threatening. Things valued highly, including one's own self definitions, are protected from possible damage. Sharing of a crisis situation or some other out-of-the-ordinary experience may hasten the transition along the primary–secondary continuum.

Once such a relationship has been established, it is generally resistant to change. Change always occurs, however. Relationships never remain completely static. Over a period of time such a relationship may go through a transition into a secondary state. Or it may happen that unequal involvement and evaluation will develop. One individual may, in fact, desire to continue the relationship at the high-intensity, high-involvement level, while the other desires or is anxious to let the relationship move to a low-intensity, low-involvement level. This is an unreciprocated primary relationship.

A negative primary relationship is one in which there is high involvement of both, coupled with a mutual desire to abandon the relationship. The married couple who are seeking a divorce by mutual consent would evidence such a relationship. The fact of high involvement may be interpreted as a potential threat since exposure of intimate details of one's life might be damaging in several ways. Such potential threat, of course, varies with the content of the knowledge. It is not surprising that such negative primary relationships are terminated by separation where possible, or even at times by murder or suicide.

The "primaryness" of any relationship then may change over time, and the location of any relationship upon the primary–secondary continuum will always be relative to the situation involved.

SACRED AND SECULAR SOCIETIES

The primary–secondary concepts are useful in an analysis of a large group such as a society. A previous chapter distinguished between sacred and secular societies, or between *Gemeinschaft* and *Gesellschaft* societies, to use German labels which are frequently applied. In sacred societies the majority of the relationships evidence high primaryness. In secular societies the majority of relationships are secondary in nature. A sacred society is relatively small, so that many primary relationships can develop. The fact that sacred societies rely basically upon informally developed folkways and mores for social control

also encourages the establishment of primary relationships.

The primaryness of relationships in one Canadian comunity is suggested by the following excerpt from a study of a Quebec village:

Extensive interviewing of a 72 year old man and his wife revealed that they together recognized 1,518 persons through consanguinity and affinity. They could name 1,110 of these by their Christian names.

Figure 17.2 Impersonal evaluation by machines. Credit information on potential customers is provided in four seconds from this master electronic computer which holds information on 8.5 million Californians. Information secured from customers is passed along via TV screens, and operators like this one feed the information into the computer. (Wide World Photos.)

Of the 1,310 who were reported living, 254 were said to be in St. Justin itself, 828 in the province of Quebec, 66 in other provinces and 162 in the U. S. and elsewhere. This range of recognition is normal in St. Justin for persons over 60 years of age whose families have been settled there for at least four generations. Extensive interviews with two more married couples about 60 years of age gave kinship ranges of 1,325 and 1,278 persons respectively.[3]

A society such as the United States, where one out of every five individuals changes residence every year, would be considered to be secular. This does not mean that primary relationships are non-existent, but only that the majority of relationships which the typical member of the society has during the day would be of the secondary type. We are talking about the number of relationships.

In such a society individuals come into contact with many others, as fellow passengers on a train or street car, fellow shoppers on a street or within the stores of a large city, fellow spectators at a movie or sports event, and fellow worshippers at a religious service. With most of these individuals the relationship is secondary. Such a group of interacting individuals has been called a "lonely crowd." [4]

Male Dominance

Research has shown that in the middle-class couples studied, the husbands had greater influence than the wives in initiating friendships and in determining who the best friends of the couple would be.

—Nicholas Babchuk and Alan P. Bates.*

---

* Nicholas Babchuk and Alan P. Bates, "The Primary Relations of Middle-Class Couples: A Study in Male Dominance," *American Sociological Review*, XXVIII, No. 3 (June, 1963), 377–384.

[3] Philip Garigue, "St. Justin: A Case-Study in Rural French-Canadian Social Organization," *Canadian Journal of Economics and Political Science*, XXII, No. 3 (August, 1956), 301–318.

[4] David Riesman, Reuel Denney, and Nathan Glazer, *The Lonely Crowd* (New Haven: Yale University Press, 1950).

PRIMARY RELATIONSHIPS WITHIN LARGER SECONDARY GROUPS

A secondary society is, of course, an industrialized, urbanized society. In such a society, and especially within the large impersonal organizations which are its products, where individuals are identified by numbers and impersonal IBM machines make decisions on payroll deductions, the development of "islands" of primary relationships takes on increased significance to the individual. This is true in the United States today with reference to large industrial concerns, large educational institutions, large governmental agencies, large military installations, and large religious institutions.

Within such larger secondary groupings, smaller primary groups provide the individual with experiences which the larger group is incapable of providing. We refer to the small friendship groups, the cliques, the group of buddies, etc. Such relationships serve to counter-balance the impersonality of the large organization. Among the employees of, say, a United States Steel plant, each individual may be somewhat of a non-entity, a numbered employee, to be inventoried and treated in somewhat the same way as the machines in the plant. But within his clique of fellow workmen, he is more than just a worker who does a certain job each day. The intimate relationships of the primary group obtain. Within the primary group, allowances can be made for personal likes and dislikes. Compensations can be developed for shortcomings and rewards provided for strong abilities. More of the characteristics of the individual can be taken into account.

Within such groups, effective methods of evading the formal norm-role definitions can be developed. Friends can "cover" for someone. Output can be curtailed or increased to take particular circumstances into account. Regulations can be bent or even ignored.[5]

[5] See, for instance, J. Bensman and I. Gerver, "Crime and Punishment in the Factory: A Functional Analysis," in *Mass Society in Crisis*, Bernard Rosenberg, Israel Gerver, and F. William Howton (eds.) (New York: The Macmillan Co., 1964).

The strengths of the primary relationship can, of course, be used either to support the goals of the larger organization or to sabotage its program. It is certain that an organization wherein the majority of the primary relationships are not used in support of the larger program will never realize its potential.

Realizing the strength of such relationships, companies deliberately try to establish the fiction that the employees are all just one big, happy family. Picnics are held. Wives are invited to the plant on particular occasions (but are certainly not welcome otherwise). Journals or newspapers are established in which "folksy" (primary) language can be used and information of a more personal nature such as data about marriages, births, etc., can be disseminated. Primary relationships which support the company are useful to the company; even pseudo-primary relationships may help.

Such relationships develop at all organizational levels and have important consequences for top management, junior executives, or messenger boys.

C. Wright Mills discusses the manner in which adult cliques are involved in the military, economic, and political spheres, and suggests that they in fact constitute a power elite in the American society. The military cliques comprise the top military hierarchy of the armed forces—the warlords of the United States, as Mills refers to them.

He says:

There are, of course, cliques among the high military, variously related to one another, and variously related to given civilian policies and cliques. These become apparent when hidden tensions become open controversies—as at the time of MacArthur's dismissal from his Eastern command. At that time there was, in addition to the MacArthur school of Asia First, already declining in influence, the Marshall-set who gave priority to Europe. There was also the Eisenhower-Smith group, which had great influence but did not run the army; and there was the dominant group who did run it, the Bradley-Collins team. And there is the rather standard split between those who feel that the need of the services is for truly professional armed forces commanded by combat line offi-

cers and those who are happier about the rise of the new specialists and staff men.[6]

Mills also comments on the influence of business cliques in the ranks of business as follows:

Time and time again, in close-ups of the executive career, we observe how men in the same circles choose one another.... As future executives move upward and toward the center, they become members of a set of cliques, which they often refer to as a team. They must listen. They must weigh opinions. They must make snap judgments. They must fit into the business and social clique. Only in this way will they rise to the new expectations in the business world in promoting their interests as the new power elite.[7]

The influence of primary relationships was found in studies of soldier behavior during World War II, in which it was found that the primary relations among peers was a principal factor affecting soldier morale, loyalty, and willingness to fight.[8]

The network of communications established in primary groups, even though they may not be formally recognized by a company, are nonetheless an integral part of its communication system. Information through such means has an impact upon the effectiveness of the group and the accuracy of such information has to be taken into account in any accurate assessment of the functioning of the company. Individuals in leadership positions who make no effort to take the informal communication network into account are not as effective as those who are able accurately to assess this factor in the formula for organizational success.

The student at a large university need only recall his initial experiences as a member of the class of incoming freshmen to tie this discussion to his own past experiences. A group of several thousand freshmen who have not known

[6] C. Wright Mills, *The Power Elite* (New York: Galaxy Book Co., 1959), pp. 188–189.

[7] *Ibid.*, pp. 138–139.

[8] See, for instance, Edward A. Shils and Morris Janowitz, "Cohesion and Disintegration in the Wehrmacht in World War II," *Public Opinion Quarterly*, XII, No. 2 (Summer, 1948), 280–315.

each other before can be very impersonal. The satisfactions which are felt when the student is able to establish his own group of friends will serve to remind him of the importance of such relationships. Experiences with students who for one reason or another have been unable to establish primary relationships on campus will also provide first-hand illustrations of the contrasting experience. Such students usually "feel utterly miserable" and such conditions may make it increasingly difficult to behave in a manner that will facilitate the establishment of primary relationships. Such conditions may make study difficult and be a contributing factor to the subsequent dropout of the student.

Members of a secondary society may join one or more of the voluntary associations available to them, partly at least in an effort to establish primary relationships. They may be looking for a home—for a place where they can be accepted and feel that they belong. The "joiner" aspect of the "American personality" may stem in part from the "secondaryness" of the larger society. Erich Fromm [9] has suggested that this is a part of our effort to escape from the freedom which a secondary society provides, freedom which has not been found to be completely rewarding in terms of some of the goals which Americans desire. The freedom of the secondary relationship may not be exactly what is valued most highly.

Limited primary interaction may be particularly discomforting to the aged in a society which retires them from the active world of work at an age when some are not ready or willing to retire, and thus deprives them of the constant interaction with primary groups they have developed within their company and of the validation of self concepts afforded thereby. Further, such individuals, because of established value systems as well as the objective fact of limited housing facilities, may be frequently denied interaction with family members who could provide primary relations, and all of this at a time when death has made inroads into the other non-family groups of peers with whom primary relations have been previously established. Quite possibly the "lonely crowd" figure of speech is most applicable to elderly individuals.

No value judgments are implied in this discussion; its purpose has certainly not been to prove that primary relationships are good and secondary relationships, bad. Actually the influence of the primaryness or secondaryness of any relationship is always related to other social conditions. For one thing, it would be impossible to establish a large-scale, mass-production industry and maintain predominately primary relations therein. It would be impossible to develop a large-scale fighting force, political machine, or religious organization without developing such relationships or without bureaucratizing. It would be impossible to govern a democratic nation as large as the United States and rely upon unwritten, informally developed and transmitted norm definitions growing out of primary interaction. The United States could never have reached its position in the world community today without developing secondary characteristics.

Primary Relationships or Primary Group?

There is a difference between having established personal relations with several co-workers and being a member of a work group. . . . Tom and Dick are friends, and both have frequent contacts with Harry, who stands between them; but Tom also often talks to three fellows on his right, who are out of Dick's earshot, and Dick has friendly ties with two men on his left whom Tom hardly knows. There is no common network of social relationships that unites a number of workers and distinguishes them from others by furnishing a socially agreed-upon definition of the boundaries of the in-group.

—Peter M. Blau.*

---

[9] Erich Fromm, *Escape from Freedom* (New York: Holt, Rinehart and Winston, Inc., 1941).

* Peter M. Blau, "Formal Organization: Dimensions of Analysis," *The American Journal of Sociology,* LXIII, No. 1 (July, 1957), 58–69.

Further, once such a society has been developed, it is not surprising that its members seek satisfaction not provided by the larger society in intimate primary relations within the family, the clique, or some other small group.

UNIQUE, OTHER-WORLD-ORIENTED PRIMARY RELATIONSHIPS

A unique primary relationship may be developed by individuals who take into account definitions concerning a supernatural realm. The uniqueness of the relationship is two-fold: (1) the other or others involved in the relationship are believed to be superempirical or supernatural in nature, and (2) it is a one-way relationship, in terms of the extensiveness of knowledge about the "other" involved. Individuals who accept religious interpretations of behavior frequently believe in a god or gods who are all-knowing, or who know all about individuals "here on earth." God, to these individuals, is a being from whom one can keep no secrets. He knows what goes on in one's most confidential thinking. When viewed in this manner, God is certainly seen by the individual involved as a significant other and one with whom he has a primary relationship. The primaryness of the relationship is further evidenced by the fact that the relationship is positively evaluated by the individuals involved, and has many of the other characteristics inherent in primaryness.

The relationship, however, is generally viewed as a one-sided primary relationship: accompanying the belief that God knows everything about the individual is the contrary belief that the individual does not know all about God. On the contrary, God may be seen as a being who moves "in mysterious ways" and who does not permit man to know all about the supernatural realm and supernatural beings.

Such relationships may be seen as having tremendous reward and punishment potential, precisely because of the extent of the information believed to be available and the power attributed to God.

From the scientific viewpoint, an additional unique aspect of this relationship is that the objective existence of such a being or beings cannot be proved scientifically and thus, despite beliefs to the contrary, such a being or beings may not even exist. However, the *belief* that one has a primary relationship with supernatural beings can have a decided influence upon the behavior of natural man.

In a secondary society such beliefs may be involved in the maintenance of normal behavior patterns. Despite the treatment one receives in his interaction with other humans, he may be convinced that his primary relationship with the supernatural remains intact. Others may be against him but, he believes, God is on his side, providing love and appreciation. Maintenance of such a belief is easier if significant others reinforce its definitions.

MEASUREMENT OF PRIMARY–SECONDARY RELATIONSHIPS

The key factor in deciding whether a primary relationship exists between specific individuals is the type of definitions which each places upon the other and upon the relationship. Measurement efforts then involve asking questions about the relationship. Various methods have been used for this purpose. The sociogram is one of these.

A sociogram is a pictorial representation of the choices individuals make or report they would make for certain purposes. Members of a group may be asked, "From our group, which individual would you most like to have as a friend?" or "Which member of the group would you most like to have consider you as his or her friend?" or maybe "Which member of the group would you most like to have at a party you are giving?" Second or third choices can also be called for. Stated or actual choices are then plotted as shown on page 260.

Choices made to questions concerning hypothetical situations can be checked against the choice which those studied make in real situa-

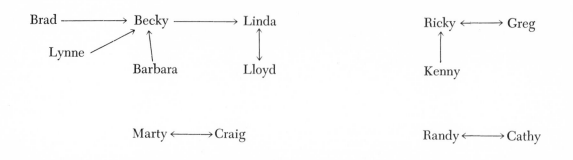

tions. Research has indicated that there is a close parallel between the two types of choices.[10]

A measure of empathic ability (ability to interpret the actions of others) can be included in a sociogram by asking each individual which of the others involved he would guess would select him. These guessed choices can then be compared with actual choices.

SUMMARY

The concepts "primary relationship" and "secondary relationship" are ideal types which are used to classify various relationships. The primary relationship involves voluntary, intimate interaction of relatively the whole personality, in which participants share mutual positive evaluations of the others and of the relationship *per se*. In popular terms it is a loving relationship. The intimacy of the relationship makes each one unique and non-transferable. Such interaction has a strong influence upon the development, maintenance, and change of self definitions, including any related stigma management. Primary relationships obtain in small groups in

which face-to-face contacts are the rule. Norm-role definitions are informal and include norms of reciprocity. Communication is frequently on the non-verbal level.

Such relationships usually develop slowly. Negative and unreciprocated primary relationships present particular problems to the participants.

Whole societies can be distinguished on the basis of the most frequent type of interaction that occurs. Urbanized, industrialized United States is a secular, *Gesellschaft*-type society.

Within any large organization such as a college or industry, small primary "islands" usually develop which serve to counter-balance the impersonality of the large organization by taking individual personal factors into account. Such groups with their own communication systems and value-norm-role configurations may either support or hinder the achievement of organization goals.

Neither type of interaction is *ipso facto* any better than the other. Each may be evaluated positively or negatively. However, certain goals can be accomplished with primary relationships and others with secondary relationships.

A unique one-directional type of primary relationship is frequently believed to exist between individuals and supernatural beings.

A sociogram provides a picture of the primary relationships within a group.

[10] See Helen H. Jennings, "Individual Differences in the Social Atom," *Sociometry*, IV (1941), 269–277.

QUESTIONS

1. Where would you place the class interaction of your sociology class on the primary–secondary continuum? What factors would you take into account in reaching this decision?
2. How do you go about making others feel like an "alien" or giving them a "get lost" feeling?
3. Under what conditions are definitions of alienation most like to develop? Least likely?
4. How intimate do you think student–teacher relationships should be? Can an intimate relationship hinder certain types of learning?
5. What happens to the new freshman and his loyalty to his university as he develops primary relationships on campus?
6. Provide illustrations of "primary pockets" in large secondary groups.
7. How would you classify the relationship which you see yourself having with God?
8. How are primary groups involved in stigma management?
9. Why doesn't a couple who are dating somewhat regularly formally decide upon rules and regulations to govern their interaction and write them down?
10. Why are primary positions or role non-transferable?

PROJECT

Analyze the development of a primary relationship which was discussed in a novel you have read recently.

SUGGESTED READING

CARTWRIGHT, DORWIN, and ALVIN ZANDER (eds.). *Group Dynamics*, 2nd ed. New York: Harper & Row, Inc., 1960.

FARIS, ELLSWORTH. "The Primary Group: Essence and Accident," *The American Journal of Sociology*, XXXVIII, No. 1 (July, 1932), 41–50.

HOMANS, GEORGE C. *The Human Group*. New York: Harcourt, Brace & World, Inc., 1950.

JENNINGS, HELEN H. *Leadership and Isolation* (2d ed.). New York: David McKay Co., Inc., 1950.

JOSEPHSON, ERIC, and MARY JOSEPHSON. *Man Alone: Alienation in Modern Society*. New York: Dell Publishing Co., Inc., 1962.

LAZARSFELD, PAUL F., and ROBERT K. MERTON. "Friendship as Social Process," in MORROE BERGER, THEODORE ABEL, and CHARLES H. PAGE, *Freedom and Control in Modern Society*. Princeton, N. J.: D. Van Nostrand Co., Inc., 1954.

SEEMAN, MELVIN. "On the Meaning of Alienation," *American Sociological Review*, XXIV, No. 6 (December, 1959), 783–791.

SHILS, EDWARD A. "Primary Groups in the American Army," in ROBERT K. MERTON and PAUL F. LAZARSFELD (eds.), *Continuities in Social Research*. New York: The Free Press of Glencoe, 1950.

SHILS, EDWARD A. "The Study of the Primary Group," in DANIEL LERNER and HAROLD D. LASSWELL (eds.), *The Policy Sciences*. Stanford: Stanford University Press, 1951.

THIBAUT, JOHN W., and HAROLD H. KELLEY. *The Social Psychology of Groups*. New York: John Wiley & Sons, Inc., 1959.

18

Racial and Ethnic Interaction

Some differences make a difference and some differences make no difference as far as interaction is concerned. Racial differences frequently make a difference; yet is there anything about these characteristics which in and of itself accounts for the differential treatment associated with them?

INTRODUCTION

In interaction any number of characteristics can be studied. This chapter introduces a new set of characteristics—racial and ethnic.

Our discussion here will contribute to our understanding of inter*personal* relations, in that the racial and/or ethnic identifications are applied to individual members of groups. Our perspective, however, is broader than the interpersonal view which was paramount in our discussion of primary–secondary relationships, in that we pay attention here to definitions which are developed to pattern the relationships of all those who share a group identity. Our perspective is similar to that used by the college student when he watches a football game. He sees individuals interact-

ing, but he also sees two *groups* of individuals interacting. The group identification is introduced into practically everything he sees. The behavior of the members of the home team is viewed in such a way that it is all tied together, rather than seen as unrelated patterns of individual behavior. The team (group) identification is only rarely forgotten by team members and spectators alike.

Likewise in life, racial and ethnic group membership is usually defined as being of such importance that it, too, is consistently taken into account. Those who share racial and/or ethnic identifications are subjected to essentially the same type of treatment under the same circumstances. Each member is defined as being but one representative of the larger racial or ethnic group.

The area of racial and ethnic intergroup relations is an area in which the significance of some other, previously discussed concepts frequently takes on increased meaning. Concepts such as subjective reality, objective reality, selective perception, value conflict, and our whole discussion of the manner in which symbols are involved in human interaction may take on new meaning, particularly if the student finds that his values are such that he feels a personal involvement in the area of discussion.

RACIAL GROUPS

Understanding of the area popularly called "race relations" requires that we make an initial distinction between "race" or biologically given racial characteristics (objective reality) and "racism" or man's definitions of racial factors (subjective reality). One determines the race of an individual or group by biological characteristics. The characteristics most frequently taken into account are skin pigmentation, head form (cephalic index), facial features, stature, and color, distribution, and texture of body hair.[1] If, on the other hand, one wants to study "racism," he pays attention to the way in which these racial characteristics are defined, including the plans of action accepted as appropriate for those with particular racial (biological) features, plus the value definitions woven into the cultural fabric.

Using the criteria of race given above, the most frequently distinguished racial groups are (1) caucasoid—popularly called "white," (2) mongoloid, or "yellow," and (3) negroid, or "black." It is difficult, however, to fit all groups of people into one of these three categories. Some seem to fall only marginally into any one group and others fall completely outside of the three groups. Experts in racial identification (physical anthropologists) have, in fact, divided the peoples of the world into as many as thirty distinguishable groups. Making racial classifications is not an easy task for those concerned with scientifically useful categories. This, however, does not deter others with other interests from rigidly classifying the individuals with whom they have contact into one of these three major categories.

Consideration of the history of any of these racial groups leads to the conclusion that individuals who are of "pure" racial stock are likely to be few and far between.[2] But again, this fact does not necessarily deter some from considering self and others as though they were "pure something-or-other" and engaging in plans of action which take these definitions into account.

How much direct influence does any one or combination of racial characteristics have upon the behavior of man? Does the color of the skin, head form, facial features, stature, or body hair directly *cause* people to behave in any particular way? Do racial features have any *direct* influence upon social behavior? According to the best evidence which we have today the answer to this question is a resounding "No." Further, with reference to biological characteristics which do have a direct relationship to man's behavior, such as intelligence, the best evidence today is that all racial *groups* are essentially equal. If group differences do exist, they are not great. Within any one group there are wide variations, there being, for instance, white geniuses and white morons, just as there are geniuses and morons within the negroid and mongoloid groups. Within a group, variation is great; between groups, variation is very small if it exists at all.[3]

Evidence from testing done during World Wars I and II can be used to illustrate this point. Examination of test scores made during World War I found that, as a group, Negroes tested substantially lower than whites. But Negroes from some northern states had higher scores than

---

[1] See, for example, Douglas G. Haring, "Racial Differences and Human Resemblances," in *American Minorities,* ed. by M. L. Barron (New York: Alfred A. Knopf, Inc., 1957), pp. 33–39.

[2] See Stanley M. Garn and Carleton S. Coon, "On the Number of Races of Mankind," *American Anthropologist,* LVII (October, 1955), 996–1001.

[3] See E. B. Reuter, "Racial Theory," *The American Journal of Sociology,* L, No. 6 (May, 1945), 452–461.

whites from some southern states. This would, obviously, be impossible if *all* Negroes were inferior to *all* whites.[4] During World War II, the Army Special Training Units for functional (non-biological) illiterates found that when level of prior education was held constant, Negro illiterates progressed as rapidly as did white illiterates.[5]

If differences in the *behavior* of racial groups exist—and they do—and we can find no biological characteristics adequately to explain this difference, how, then, can we account for the behavior? Learning experiences! If one racial group behaves differently from another, it is because its members have learned to do so. It is because they have had certain social experiences which have been productive of the behavior. Aspects of this learning process will be discussed in later sections of this chapter.

As a foundation for future discussions, let us establish, at this point, the racial composition of the United States. In 1960 the distribution was as shown in Table 18.1.

TABLE 18.1

Racial Groups in the United States 1960

Race	Number	Percentage of Total
White	158,831,732	88.6
Negro	18,871,831	10.5
Other races:		
Indian	523,591	0.9
Japanese	464,322	
Chinese	237,292	
Filipino	176,310	
All Other	218,087	
Totals	179,323,175	100.00

Source: Bureau of the Census, *1960 Census of Population, Supplementary Reports,* Pc (S1)-10 (Washington, D. C.: September 7, 1961), p. 3.

[4] See Otto Klineberg, *Race Differences* (New York: Harper & Row, Inc., 1935), chap. ix.

[5] H. Aptheker, "Literacy, the Negro and World War II," *Journal of Negro Education,* XIV (Fall, 1945), 595–602.

Ethnic Groups

Ethnic groups are distinguished from other groups not on the basis of biological characteristics but on the basis of social behavior of one type or another, such as religion, speech, and national origin. Members of ethnic groups share a unique social and cultural heritage which is passed on from generation to generation and serves as their distinguishing characteristic. The American Jews, Mexicans, Indians, Japanese, and Chinese are illustrations. In the United States some ethnic groups such as the American Indians are also racially distinctive. Some are not.

Behavior involving racial and/or ethnic groups stems from the definitions applied to them; thus, although much of our discussion will be about racial groups, the general conclusions derived will accordingly apply equally well to ethnic groups.

VALUE DEFINITIONS

Value definitions are involved in racial and ethnic group relations in much the same way they are in the stratified interaction, which we discussed in a previous chapter. The interaction patterns involve two factors: (1) recognition of differences, and (2) evaluation of these differences as superior or inferior. Such value definitions, of course, have no direct relationship to the characteristics evaluated, but rather reflect the past social experiences of those making the evaluations. In America, Negro–white interaction patterns involve not only an awareness or a belief that there are physical differences, but also an evaluation on the part of the dominant whites that those who are classified as Negro are somehow inferior.

Whether or not differences exist (objective reality) and whether or not there is any causal connection between existing racial differences and behavioral differences, so long as one group believes they exist and that one syndrome is superior to the other, then *to them* (subjective

Gringo

"In our neighborhood was an American family who owned the only grocery store. Their small son, Jonny, was the only non-Mexican playmate we had. From the older boys I often used to hear the word 'Gringo' which was used to identify this American family. Then, I didn't know what it meant for I was only five years old. Jonny and I grew very fond of each other and the older Mexican boys didn't approve because I was associating with a 'Gringo.' Many times I was given verbal and physical beatings by the older boys and denounced as an unworthy Mexican."

—Edward C. McDonagh and
Eugene S. Richards.*

reality) the differences do exist and to them the "out-group" or the "they" group is inferior. Interaction patterns are built upon this unquestioned premise.

The term "prejudice" is frequently used in discussions of racial and ethnic group relations and is usually defined as a negative definition or a definition of one group or set of characteristics as inferior. Some, such as Allport, suggest that it is a negative definition used without "sufficient warrant." Just what is "sufficient warrant" is hard to determine in some circumstances and impossible to determine scientifically in others. Two types of negative definitions can be distinguished as follows:

1. Belief that Negroes are intellectually inferior to whites.

2. Belief that Negroes are not as *good* as whites.

The first belief as to intellectual capacity is capable of being tested scientifically and on this

* Quoted in Edward C. McDonagh and Eugene S. Richards, *Ethnic Relations in the United States* (New York: Appleton-Century-Crofts, 1953), p. 61.

point all of the scientific evidence suggests that there is no foundation to the belief—Negroes and whites as racial groups can learn with equal facility.

Yet, subjective reality being what it is, it is entirely possible for one to believe that Negroes are innately different from whites in this respect despite all of the evidence to the contrary. If individuals holding such beliefs are called "prejudiced," prejudice in this case means maintaining a definition in the face of contrary scientific evidence. Such types of prejudice are, of course, frequently found.

The second belief, that Negroes are not as *good* as whites or that they are *inferior* to whites, involves when stated this way only NER definitions of goodness, and one could not scientifically prove that such a belief is held in the face of contrary empirical evidence. Such beliefs are rooted in social relationships and cannot be checked for accuracy by investigating the objects defined as inferior. In this case if the term "prejudice" is used it identifies a value judgment, the accuracy of which cannot be scientifically determined.

When we use the term "prejudice," we shall refer to negative definitions. However, we shall usually use "value judgment" rather than "prejudice," since this harmonizes with established usage in this book, and should by now make the reader aware of the NER nature of the definitions to which we refer. Understanding the NER nature of prejudice helps to understand (1) why the acceptance of prejudice stems more from contact with prejudice than from contact with the individuals toward whom the prejudice is directed, and (2) that the "prejudiced" individual does not define himself as "prejudiced." He sees himself merely as endorsing the right set of values.

There are, of course, two sides to any "coin" of prejudice. Defining one group or set of characteristics as inferior automatically defines the contrary or reverse set as "superior." In this sense, then, there is negative prejudice (prejudice against) and positive prejudice (prejudice for).

The Ideology of White Supremacy

A Southern state senator—Segregation is a natural order—created by God, in his wisdom, who made black men black and white men white. Each man should be proud of his race and should constantly strive to preserve its purity.

A Southern governor—It is useless for me to argue whether the racial instinct (for segregation) is right or wrong—it exists.

A utility executive—The Negro is irresponsible in every degree. I think it is a basic trait, although other conditions—environment, economics and education—contribute to his so-called lethargy.

A missionary association—We publish to the world that we protest the attempts being made to desegregate the races, because we believe such would inevitably lead into a hybrid monstrosity that would defy the word and will of God.

A U.S. congressman—I have yet to meet one (Negro) who told me they wanted their children to go to school with white children.

—James W. Vander Zanden.*

Value definitions may, of course, be so strongly endorsed that use of them may produce certain internal or emotional reactions, such as increased heartbeat and introduction of adrenalin into the blood stream. Interacting with members of a racial group defined as "inferior" may, then, produce noticeable physical reaction, which, in turn, influences the on-going interaction.

Definitions of inferiority may, of course, be accepted by the group toward whom they are directed, as well as by those who are defined as superior. In colonial America, for instance, there were apparently many females who accepted the belief that they were inferior to the males, just as some Negroes define themselves as inferior. Opposition to the emancipation of the female and of the Negro developed within the ranks of the "inferior" group as well as from the "superior" group. Such definitions can be changed, but the process is not always an easy one.

In this realm, as in all areas which the group learns to define as important, the key value definitions may be viewed as having supernatural endorsement, with the consequent rigidity of acceptance and difficulty of change. If such definitions lead to important differential treatment (discrimination), it is not surprising that religious endorsement is provided for the behavior.

One of the functions or results (consequences) of such value definitions, then, is to facilitate perpetuation of established systems of superiority–inferiority relationships.

It should not be assumed that all negative definitions exist without basis in objective reality. Not every individual or group is the same as the other, nor does everyone behave the same, or have the same things. Some may be negatively defined and discriminated against because they have "earned" the definition (to use Allport's term).[6] Becker[7] has also cautioned against what he calls "unconventional sentimentality." The unconventional sentimentalist, he says,

. . . assumes and refuses to examine the assumption that things are in fact "worse" than they might be. . . . He assumes . . . that the underdog is always right and those in authority always wrong. This tendency has been particularly noticeable in studies of race relations, where the possibility that minority groups have some of the faults attributed to them by bigots is systematically slighted. The same kind of sentimentality is sometimes found in the studies of deviance, manifesting itself in a tendency to refuse to admit that the deviants under study have done wrong.

---

* James W. Vander Zanden, *American Minority Relations* (New York: The Ronald Press Co., 1963), pp. 131–135.

[6] Gordon W. Allport, *The Nature of Prejudice* (Cambridge, Mass.: Addison-Wesley Publishing Co., Inc., 1954), p. 217.

[7] Howard S. Becker (ed.), *The Other Side* (New York: The Free Press of Glencoe, 1964), p. 5.

They

"Why, my brother-in-law was telling me that a friend of his, who works down at the office with him, had an aunt whose neighbor's sister once had a most unpleasant experience with one of them. Just what you'd expect. I've heard other stories, too. I know what they're like. I had a run-in with one of them myself a couple of years ago, and got a pretty good notion. And look at the way some of them live! You'd think they'd at least have a little decency. Not that I'm prejudiced against them, you understand. Give them their due, I always say, but don't let them go where they're not wanted either. You'd think they'd know without being told. But some people never understand. Maybe you can't expect them to."

—Robert Bierstedt.*

NORM-ROLE DEFINITIONS

Value definitions (prejudice) specify which group is "superior" or "inferior" to the other. Norm-role definitions move from the realm of *prejudice* to that of *discrimination,* and specify how the two groups or members of the two groups are expected to relate themselves to each other, with such relationships being structured to the advantage of the "superior" group. Value definitions provide the justification for the discriminatory practices incorporated in the norm-role definitions. Various types of differential treatment may be incorporated in the norm-role definitions, such as segregation and restricted interaction.

Norms of segregation specify that members of particular groups should be separated for particular activities. In the United States, for instance, individuals defined as Negro and white have been required by the formal and/or informal norm-role definitions at various places and at various times to be segregated for such purposes as:

School attendance
Movie attendance
Church attendance
Travel on public vehicles
Area of residence
Unit assignment in the armed forces
Use of drinking fountains
Use of public parks and swimming pools

Segregation involves physical separation. The norm-role definitions may also specify that when interracial interaction takes place it is to be restricted to particular types of behavior, such as that involved in a business relationship or a professional client relationship.

The norm-role definitions may be formal, as in the case of laws which prohibit marriage of individuals of different races, or laws which once denied American Indians voting and other citizen rights. Laws which denied certain racial and/or ethnic (nationality) groups equal immigration rights also fall in this category. Many informal norm-role definitions have also been developed, and in many respects the informal norm definitions are given the greatest priority by those involved. Even when formal legal endorsements of discriminatory practices are removed, as in the case of restrictive real estate covenants, the informal norm definitions have been of sufficient strength in the United States that the discriminatory practices have continued—without legal sanctions. And even though the legal norms of the land specified school integration as of May 17, 1954, by November, 1962, only 7.8 per cent of the Negro children who attended school in the 17 states where schools were previously segregated were in integrated schools. Where the laws and the mores conflict, it is difficult to enforce the laws.[8]

---

* Quoted in Robert Bierstedt, *The Social Order* (New York: McGraw-Hill Book Co., 1957), p. 435.

[8] *Statistical Summary* (Nashville, Tenn.: Southern Education Reporting Service, November, 1962).

Figure 18.1 A minority protest.
(Wide World Photos.)

Discussions of prejudice and discrimination frequently terminate in a rather blanket condemnation (value judgment) of discrimination. Making such widespread condemnation of discrimination may be an effective propaganda technique but cannot be taken seriously by the sociologist. It would, most likely, be impossible, as our discussion of stratification suggested, to have a society in which everyone was treated in an identical manner and in which no value judgments were made as to which types of behavior were given preferential definitions and which were given negative definitions. It is not a question of difference or no difference but only of what type of differences will be endorsed and

practiced. Problems arise for the society when its segments begin to question whether certain types of discrimination are compatible with important value definitions or other established behavior patterns. As long as everyone accepts the value judgments involved in the discriminatory patterns which favor whites and discriminate against Negroes, or vice versa for that matter, there are no problems for the society, any more than there are problems in America today in the maintenance of public rest rooms which are segregated on the basis of sex, or in granting parents control over their young children. Problems arise only when questions are raised about whether racial differences believed to exist actually do obtain in objective reality; or when conflict is seen between discriminatory values and norm-role definitions and other values such as democratic values which specify that all men should be treated equally; or Christian values which indicate that all men should be defined as brothers and treated accordingly.

Recognition of such conflict led Myrdal, a Swedish social economist who studied American race relations, to title the report of his study *An American Dilemma.* He suggests that with all its complexity the American race relations problem rests upon a value dilemma.

... Even a poor and uneducated white person in some isolated and backward rural region of the Deep South, who is violently prejudiced against the Negro and intent upon depriving him of civic rights and human independence, has also a whole compartment in his valuation sphere housing the entire American Creed of liberty, equality, justice and fair opportunity for everybody.... And these more general valuations —more general in the sense that they refer to all human beings—are, to some extent, effective in shaping his behavior.[9]

SELF DEFINITIONS

Since racial and ethnic identifications are of sufficient importance to be given attention in most interaction, it would be unlikely that members of such groups could long escape the fact that they were so classified by others, and with whatever degree of pleasure or displeasure associated therewith learn to apply the appropriate labels to themselves. The self evaluative dimension is usually not identical for the members of the minority group and the dominant group, but there is evidence that they tend to share the same evaluative aspects—the patterns at least are similar.

An important technic of racial and ethnic identification is the use of names which have come to be identified with such groups. Names such as Greenberg and Rothstein identify the named

Who Am I?

At fifteen I was fully conscious of the racial difference, and while I was sullen and resentful in my soul, I was beaten and knew it. I knew then that I could never aspire to be President of the United States, nor governor of my state, nor mayor of my city; I knew that I could only sit in the peanut gallery at our theater and could only ride on the back seat of the electric car and in the Jim Crow car on the train. I had bumped into the color line and knew that so far as white people were concerned, I was just another nigger.

—A. L. Holsey.*

as Jewish, whereas names such as Gonzales and Hernandes identify individuals as Mexican.

The practice of individuals deciding that they share in the fame or shame of others of their group is particularly prevalent among racial and ethnic groups, since such group membership is given such prominence by others in the society. Thus, when a Negro member distinguishes himself in some favorable way, other Negroes may feel a sense of pride and feel that indirectly they themselves have benefited from the act. The same pattern, of course, works in reverse, and the shame acquired by other members is seen as "rubbing off on" each member of the group.

When the members of a minority group, racial or ethnic, define themselves as inferior, this definition then becomes an effective barrier to the realization of economic, artistic, educational, or political potential of the group. To the extent that Americans see value in the full utilization of human resources, their perpetuation of definitions of inferiority of certain groups works against the realization of such goals. Likewise, to the extent that individual members define themselves as potentially productive in certain areas, but are prevented from realizing this po-

[9] Gunnar Myrdal, *An American Dilemma* (New York: Harper & Row, Inc., 1944), p. xlviii.

* A. L. Holsey, "Learning How To Be Black," *The American Mercury,* XVI (April, 1929), 421–425.

tential by the prejudice and/or norm-role definitions of the larger group, they are faced with the problem of living with the failure to achieve. No one should be surprised that individuals who are denied the opportunity to achieve goals which are presented to them by the larger group as being desirable and available to "any mother's son" have difficulty in adjusting to their situation and may develop counteracting reaction patterns which may be unacceptable to the larger group as individuals and to the goals of the larger society.

SOCIALIZATION

Our discussion thus far has emphasized that prejudice (value definitions) is learned, not biologically acquired. The value definitions of superiority and inferiority, the norm-role definitions which take these definitions into account, and the self definitions related thereto are all learned in interaction. Although myths have existed which suggested that members of different groups, particularly racial groups, were innately or biologically antagonistic to each other, all of the research evidence supports the contrary premise. We do not define particular others as inferior nor do we discriminate against them, unless we have learned to do so.

A social consequence of accepting myths of inherent antagonism is that those who accept the value definitions and engage in the discriminatory practices thereby view themselves as being absolved of any personal or group responsibility for the actions. After all, they conclude, man himself cannot be blamed for that which he acquired biologically. Once you accept such a belief you cease even to consider the possibility that there might be a different source of your behavior.

Development and acquisition of definitions unfavorable to certain racial or ethnic groups is not a simple process. Many factors such as economic interests, amount of education, social conformity, reactions to frustrations, authoritarian

personality structure, and the symbolic significance of the presence of particular minority members in certain areas may be involved in any particular pattern. We do not have space here to do more than acknowledge the importance of such factors in the study of racial and ethnic groups.

In America, in addition to the involvement of such factors as these, it is important to recognize that members of the society are confronted with many social conditions which lend support to the inferior definitions of racial groups, whatever their origin, and may, in fact, lead to conclusions about inferiority without individuals being specifically told that certain groups are inferior. There is, for instance, a disproportionately large percentage of Negroes and Indians in the lower class, which means that when compared to the whites as a group they have less income, fewer prestige occupations, less education, less desirable housing, all of the behavior patterns which go along with these inequalities. In addition, the mass media such as newspapers, magazines (even the advertisements therein), movies, and TV have, with some exceptions to be sure, typically shown the Negroes in inferior roles. Only rarely before the mid-1960's did the viewing public see a Negro play the role of the hero or heroine on the screen or on his TV set. Then there are the more subtle

---

Significant Others

Commenting on the story of "Jesus, the Jew," told to a Sunday-school class of ten year olds, a pupil declared that she had never known that Jesus was a Jew. After further elucidation by the teacher, this youngster declared that she had always known "that God was a Presbyterian, but not that Jesus was a Jew."

—Edward C. McDonagh and
Eugene S. Richards.*

---

* Edward C. McDonagh and Eugene S. Richards, *Ethnic Relations in the United States* (New York: Appleton-Century-Crofts, 1953), p. 32.

types of socialization involved in humor, such as the jokes about Sam or Rastus, and the "innocent" chants of children such as "Eenie, Meenie, Miney, Mo/Catch a nigger by the toe." One does not, in fact, have to look far to find many social supports to the belief that the Negro is inferior, since he is, in fact, different from whites in many respects. Those growing up in such a society do not need to be very smart to begin to wonder why these differences exist.

The key question, of course, is: Do these differences in behavior and possessions stem directly from the Negro's "Negroness" or from the social experiences he has had? Our previous discussion has emphasized that such differences cannot be adequately accounted for by biological (Negro) characteristics. If different racial groups behave differently it is because they have had the social experiences necessary to produce that particular behavior.

The implications of such a conclusion are tremendous for any nation experiencing so-called "racial" problems. In the United States or the Union of South Africa, for instance, it follows that if Negroes behave differently from whites it is primarily because of the experiences which the Negroes have had within that society. This does not, of course, put the "responsibility" (if one is interested in establishing responsibility) solely upon the shoulders of the white group, since the Negro group is obviously a part of the society also. However, if it is the dominant white group which has the dominant influence upon society, it also has the dominant influence upon "race relations." It follows, then, that if society-wide changes are going to be made which will result in changes in Negro behavior there must be changes in white behavior as well as in Negro behavior. Eradication of such racial problems, in fact, calls for greater change on the part of whites than Negroes. One might question on this basis, as did Myrdal,[10] whether the United States has a "Negro problem," a "white problem," or a "society problem."

[10] Ibid.

ROLE PLAYING AND ROLE TAKING

Racial and ethnic definitions are developed, perpetuated, or destroyed in the crucible of interaction. In some respects the development-perpetuation interaction sequence is somewhat circular, and can be viewed as what some have called, a "vicious circle," as shown in Figure 18.2 (see page 272).

Ignoring for the moment the question as to the origin of the negative evaluation, let us start viewing the "circle" at the point where the dominant group defines the minority group as inferior. This, then, leads to the development of norm-role definitions which specify that the "inferior" group should be treated in an inferior manner, such as being denied admittance to the best schools, the prestige and better-paying occupations, certain social organizations, or equal wages. This treatment produced individuals who are, in fact, inferior in that they do not have as much money, equal quality homes or clothes, or as good an occupation as the dominant group. This, in turn, reinforces the definition that they are inferior, which reinforces established norm-role definitions, which increases the likelihood that they will be treated in an inferior manner, which in turn produces marked differences between the two groups, which reinforces the negative definitions, which in turn—and around and around it goes.

Members of either group who desire to change the pattern may concentrate their attention at any of the five "stations" of the circle. It is difficult, of course, to change any one of the inter-related aspects so long as the others remain intact, and it is hard to change all five at once.

Behavior is never as simple as any introductory textbook makes it appear. The total pattern of intergroup relations has many complexities. Merton[11] provides a refinement to our over-

[11] Robert K. Merton, "Discrimination and the American Creed," in *Discrimination and National Welfare*, ed. by R. M. MacIver (New York: Harper & Row, Inc., 1949), pp. 99–126.

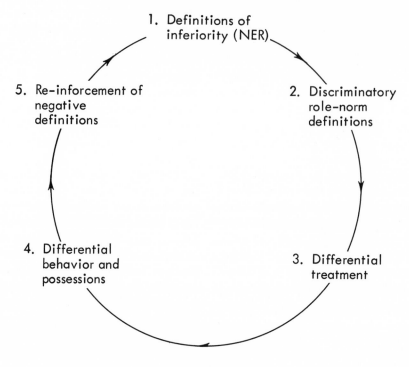

Figure 18.2

simplified discussion when he identifies four patterns of prejudice (value judgment) and discrimination as follows:

1. *Prejudiced discriminator,* in which the negative value definitions are accompanied by corresponding role playing. This is the pattern to which we have given most attention.
2. *Prejudiced non-discriminator*—the individual who defines the minority group members as inferior, but does not discriminate against them for such reasons as that he will be subject to a fine by the government if he does, or because he may lose his job, say as a teacher, or that he will lose customers if he does discriminate.
3. *Unprejudiced discriminator*—the individual who sincerely does not define particular others as inferior but does discriminate against them for other reasons, possibly to maintain a particular business clientele or to be accepted socially by a social group defined by him as desirable.

4. *Unprejudiced non-discriminator*—the individual who does not define the racial and/or ethnic group members as inferior, neither does he discriminate against them.

Interaction which takes racial-ethnic identifications into account involves the sometimes complex process of deciding exactly when such identifications will be taken into account and when they will not. Such decisions, of course, have to be made by all parties of the interaction. More than this, the member of the subordinate racial-ethnic group has the problem of anticipating the definitions of the other, and making decisions about his own behavior on the basis of such decisions. The Jewish individual who approaches the hotel desk to ask for a room faces the possibility of being denied a room because the hotel discriminates against Jews. However, he does not know until the interaction with the clerk is initiated whether he will be defined by the clerk as Jewish or otherwise. Those who have been subjected to prior discrimination are sensitive to

Racial Laziness

The distinguished French abstract artist, Jean Helion, once told the story of his life as a prisoner of war in a German camp, where, during the second World War, he was compelled to do forced labor. He told how he loafed on the job, how he thought of device after device for avoiding work and producing as little as possible—and, since, his prison camp was a farm, how he stole chickens at every opportunity. He also described how he put on an expression of good-natured imbecility whenever approached by his Nazi overseers. Without intending to do so, in describing his own actions, he gave an almost perfect picture of the literary type of the Southern Negro of slavery days. Jean Helion, confronted with the fact of forced labor, reacted as intelligently as southern Negro slaves, and the slaves reacted as intelligently as Jean Helion.
            —Samuel Ichiye Hayakawa.*

cues as to "which way the wind is blowing" and pattern their own behavior accordingly. Negroes are constantly faced with decisions as to just how far they can go in their interaction with whites, and those who have been subjected to discrimination are sensitive to the moment at which their racial identity begins to be taken into account. The interaction patterns may change subtly at first and then not so subtly if the Negro fails to respond in the manner the white person defines as appropriate to the situation.

Since any group may be involved in the stratification system of a society, racial and ethnic lines may also be class or caste lines.

CHANGE

Interaction involving racial and ethnic minority groups is, of course, subject to change. The racial turmoil experienced by the American society during the 1960's has provided those involved with evidence of the intensity of value definitions held by both Negroes and whites and of the difficulties which may be encountered as efforts are made to establish changed patterns. Techniques of change have included "freedom riders," "sit-ins," a freedom march on Washington, prayer meetings, legislative efforts, presidential pleas, and use of military forces to enforce integration in the schools.

Greater freedom and opportunity have been achieved by and for the Negro. Two general principles are applicable to change in this area. In the first place, it should be clear that prejudice (value definitions) and discrimination (norm-role enacting) are not both changed with equal effectiveness by the same techniques. Legislative efforts, for instance, may control or change discrimination without much influence upon the accompanying prejudice. Continued non-discriminatory interaction will, however, most likely contribute to changed value definitions, although the change may be gradual with only limited change during the lifetime of the "older generation." Interaction as equals is an effective means of prejudice re-education. Interaction as inferior–superior is likewise an effective way of developing and perpetuating prejudice.[12]

Another well-established point is that lectures and exhortation for "prejudiced" individuals to abandon their "prejudice" are usually not very effective. In the first place, they are likely to be interpreted as applying to the other fellow but "not to me." Such a conclusion follows from the fact that the prejudiced person, as we have said, does not define himself as "prejudiced"— only as one who holds the "right" value definitions. In certain respects value definitions are changed most effectively by a circuitous route rather than by direct confrontation.

"Passing" is one type of change which may be adopted by those who have the physical characteristics sufficient to accomplish the "pass."

* Samuel Ichiye Hayakawa, "How Words Change Our Lives," *Saturday Evening Post,* CCXXI, No. 26 (December 27, 1958), 73.

12 See, for instance, Samuel A. Stouffer *et al., The American Soldier: Adjustment During Army Life,* Vol. I (Princeton: Princeton University Press, 1949), pp. 586–595.

Passing involves permitting members of the "they" group to define you as "one of them" and behaving in the appropriate manner to confirm the definition. The Negro who passes as white, or in some cases the white who passes as Negro is an illustration. The passing may be done with the knowledge of members of the minority group, in which case it requires that the minority members cooperate in giving the right cues to the dominant group. In some cases, the passing may involve only occupational behavior wherein the Negro individual passes for white in order to get and hold a particular job, but returns to his minority status in non-occupational behavior. In other cases, the passing may be accomplished if the individual physically divorces himself from past associations and locations and establishes a new life in a new place. Understandably, such rejection of one's past is not always an easy accomplishment.

Figure 18.3   Interaction as equals is one way to reduce prejudice. (Wide World Photos).

Who Is and Who Isn't?

I was a Jew, until a few years ago. Now, I am not!

Many of you, the Jews whom I address as well as many gentiles, may scoff at the notion of a Jew ever becoming a non-Jew. And my former people may blame me bitterly for changing.

Fortunately, I cannot be reached. I have changed my name. I have changed my work. I have moved into a strange region and started afresh. My past is as finally sealed as though I had died and arisen with a new personality— for it is really necessary that a Jew change some important parts of his personality when he throws off his Jewishness.

—Anonymous.*

Exact figures are not available as to the extent of passing which has taken place in the United States. Estimates, however, range from a few thousand to tens of thousands.[13]

Changes in intergroup relations may lead to assimilation, amalgamation, or cultural pluralism. If assimilation takes place, the different groups merge so that only one group exists where two used to exist. Ethnic lines are wiped out. Racial identifications are no longer taken into account. The assimilation process might be called the "melting pot" process. Amalgamation is the process of erasing racial differences through interracial mating, so that the new generations are a biological mixture of the two groups. Despite laws and mores to the contrary, there has apparently been sufficient interbreeding between Negroes and whites that today it would be accurate to say that there are few, if any, "pure Negroes" in the United States.[14] During periods

* Anonymous, "I Was a Jew," *Forum*, CIII (January, 1940), 8–9. Quoted by Brewton Berry, *Race and Ethnic Relations* (Boston: Houghton Mifflin Co., 1958), pp. 489–490.

[13] James W. Vander Zanden, *American Minority Relations* (New York: The Ronald Press Co., 1963), p. 328.

[14] Peter I. Rose, *They and We* (New York: Random House, Inc., 1964), p. 9.

of slavery, such unions primarily involved white males and Negro females, since the white males who defined themselves as superior endorsed norm definitions which granted them sexual access to Negro females, while strongly rejecting any reciprocal sexual access to white females by Negro males. In fact, such behavior was given very strong negative evaluation and the belief (true or false) that such relationships had taken place was the premise upon which lynchings were most likely to occur.

In a society which follows a pattern of cultural pluralism, there is a recognition of differences. The differences, however, are not evaluated as one being better than the other, but rather as all having equal worth. Differentism *per se* is evaluated as desirable, and the society is seen as benefiting from the contributions of groups who are different and as gaining strength through this variety.

PRIMARY–SECONDARY RELATIONSHIPS

Racial and/or ethnic identifications are taken into account in both primary and secondary relationships. Secondary relationships and their related norm-role definitions may, in an impersonal manner, make those involved aware of the inferior–superior definitions involved. Interaction within the primary group may serve to develop counteracting patterns whereby individuals are able more effectively to live with the negative definitions and treatment. Within the primary groups, individuals may also devise ways and means of "getting around" the formal norm-role definitions, and utilize humor and serious discussions with a reverse set of definitions in which the minority group becomes the dominant group.

Interaction of members of different racial groups is most likely to occur in secondary relationships. The more personal the nature of a potential situation the greater are the barriers to primary, intimate intergroup participation. Primary relationships between minority–dominant group members are the last to be established. Intermarriage, which, of course, includes interracial sexual access, is usually the final equality leading to complete assimilation and amalgamation. In America, the key question which is supposed to "clinch" arguments about racial equality is, "Would you want your daughter (son) to marry a Negro?"

Marriage equality is the equality most feared by whites and least desired by Negroes, and consequently is the equality which will most likely not be approved and practiced until after the other types of equality have been obtained.

SUMMARY

There is a sharp distinction between racial factors *per se* and what one does about them, or how they are taken into account. Racial differences which exist have no direct influence upon man's behavior and it is biologically more meaningful to talk about the human *race* than the human *races*. Ethnic groups, unlike biological groups, are distinguished directly by socio-cultural factors. Interaction which takes either ethnic or racial factors into account stems from the labels involved plus the plans of action which man associates with them.

Racial and ethnic interactions are influenced by value definitions which label one group as superior and the other as inferior and thus provide justification for the discrimination involved. Norm-role definitions also specify discriminatory or differential treatment, and self definitions are influenced by such interaction and in turn also influence the behavior. Once discriminatory patterns are established, social differences in support of prejudice–discrimination develop and these differences may be viewed as proof of inferiority–superiority and used, in turn, to reinforce the established practices.

Racial and ethnic identifications are involved in stratification systems. Established patterns tend to be perpetuated, but change always occurs. The same technics of change are not equally effective in changing prejudice and discrimination. Change in either, however, facilitates change in the other.

Primary interaction is usually intra-ethnic and intra-racial interaction and may serve to counterbalance the prejudice–discrimination experiences in the larger society.

QUESTIONS

1. How is our previous discussion of subjective reality related to the material in this chapter?
2. Discuss the importance of labels (symbols) in interracial interaction.
3. Discuss the statement that with reference to racial groups there is more within-group variation than between-group variation.
4. What is the difference between racial and ethnic groups?
5. Distinguish between prejudice and discrimination.
6. List some of the types of non-racial and non-ethnic discrimination of which most Americans approve.
7. Describe the process by which you learned that you were different from others in some respect and how you adjusted to this information.
8. Relate this chapter's discussion of Negro–white responsibility for existing conditions to the discussion in Chapter 4 about interactionism.
9. Discuss the statement that prejudiced individuals do not view themselves as being prejudiced. How do you know when you are prejudiced?
10. Discuss the statement that "passing" requires a sociological rebirth on the part of the Negro involved.

PROJECT

Check the help-wanted ads in a large newspaper for one week, and identify any racial or ethnic limitations stated therein.

SUGGESTED READING

BARRON, MILTON L. (ed.). *American Minorities*. New York: Alfred A. Knopf, Inc., 1957.

BERRY, BREWTON. *Race Relations*. Boston: Houghton Mifflin Co., 1958.

FRAZIER, E. FRANKLIN. *Race and Culture Contacts in the Modern World*. New York: Alfred A. Knopf, Inc., 1957.

KLINEBERG, OTTO. *Race Differences*. New York: Harper & Row, Inc., 1935.

MENDELSON, WALLACE. *Discrimination*. Englewood Cliffs, N. J.: Prentice-Hall, Inc., 1962. Paperback. (A Spectrum Book.)

MYRDAL, GUNNAR, with the assistance of RICHARD STERNER and ARNOLD ROSE. *An American Dilemma*. New York: Harper & Row, Inc., 1944.

ROSE, PETER I. *They and We*. New York: Random House, Inc., 1964.

SIMPSON, GEORGE E., and J. MILTON YINGER. *Racial and Cultural Minorities*. Rev. ed. New York: Harper & Row, Inc., 1958.

SKLARE, MARSHALL (ed.). *The Jews*. New York: The Free Press of Glencoe, 1958.

VANDER ZANDEN, JAMES W. *American Minority Relations*. New York: The Ronald Press Co., 1963.

19

Societal Systems

During the past week, what influence would you say the following has had upon your behavior?

1. *The fact that you have been a member of a particular sociology class.*
2. *The fact that you have been a student at your particular university.*
3. *The fact that you participate in the activities of a particular community.*
4. *The fact that you live in a particular state and region.*
5. *The fact that you live in a specific nation.*

INTRODUCTION

Interacting individuals are able to relate themselves to each other in any number of different ways. Any particular individual, for instance, may be a member of many different groups, or may interact with a variety of different individuals. Group members can arrange and rearrange themselves into many different-sized groups, from a temporary dyad of two children playing hopscotch to the most complex relationships. For a large society such as the United States, the number of possible combinations is almost beyond comprehension, and the patterns are constantly in a state of flux. Groups are constantly being enlarged or diminished in size, they continue or are disbanded, they are organized and reorganized in many different ways, and any number of intergroup and intragroup relationships develop. The hourly rearrangement of students on a university campus, with the arrangement patterns themselves being rearranged every semester, is but one illustration of a constant, society-wide phenomenon.

Yet with all of this complexity and flexibility, behavior is sufficiently structured or systematized that the individual, the various subgroups, and the entire society all are able to function.

There are, of course, any number of characteristics of such groups and their interactions, and any number of ways in which these characteristics can be studied in our efforts to understand human behavior. This chapter directs attention to one of these, i.e., the influence of one of the largest, most inclusive groups into which man arranges himself—society, which is defined as a group of individuals who share a common culture and a related, relatively self-sufficient interaction system.[1] We will concern ourselves with the question of how societies are formed and maintained, and the integration of the behavior of their members and groups. Our major concern, however, is with the behavioral consequences of living in a society.

A society is composed of interacting human beings, so in this sense the whole text has been a discussion of society—or of certain aspects of society. However, an analysis which focuses attention on the broad concept of society and society-wide characteristics sensitizes us to factors to which only indirect prior attention has been given and thus helps to round out our sociological perspective.

Interaction is in many respects structured, organized, or systematized; the behavior of each of a number of individuals is interrelated in consistent ways. Various *systems* of interaction exist in any society and this chapter will discuss some of these systems. It may be helpful first to briefly discuss systems *per se*.

SYSTEMS

For scientific purposes it is more accurate to talk of systematized units or systematic behavior than to talk of "systems." Research attempts to determine the manner in which units are related.

With his ability to use symbols, however, man is able to talk about the arrangements themselves, and it is to these that one refers when he uses the word "system."

A system is an orderly combination or arrangement of elements, units, or "things" into a larger element, unit, or thing which functions, "works," or "runs" as an entity. The second entity is more than just an aggregate of parts, since the parts are interrelated in such a way that they can function as a unit. The major characteristics of the new unit stem from the interrelationships of the component parts; in combination they are more than they would be as a simple aggregate of non-related things. A simple illustration is the wrist watch which the typical college student wears, in which various wheels, gears, springs, and other parts all function together so that the watch "works." Certain elements may be more of a hindrance than a help in system functioning, and compensating mechanisms may accordingly be involved in the system. It may be that some elements involved in an on-going system make little or no significant contribution one way or the other. They are just there. Yet the system works, or the behavior of those involved is systematized.

Any number of different systems exist in the universe, with the systems evidencing an interlocking or interpenetrating relationship. Likewise, any number of different systems are directly and indirectly related to human interaction. Giving attention to any particular system, of course, selectively excludes attention at other levels. The systems most germane to our sociological interest are (1) individual or personality systems, in that they involve relationships with others, (2) intra-society group systems, and (3) society systems. Interest in biological systems is and has been only tangential to our concern.

With reference to any system such as that found in a wrist watch, a human cell, a transportation system, or a whole society, attention can be given to, among other things, the following: (1) the structure or the way the various elements are interrelated, (2) the functions or the consequences of having a particular element in the system, and (3) the requisites of system maintenance.

[1] When defined this way, "society" corresponds roughly to the modern concept of "nation." Not all nations, however, are self-sufficient.

FUNCTIONAL REQUISITES OF SOCIETY

A society is relatively self sufficient, but certain things must be accomplished for the society's maintenance. This discussion, which has society as its focus of attention, parallels a previous discussion of *needs* in which the individual was the focus of attention. Here we are concerned with identifying the conditions needed for a society's survival. We are not directly concerned with the related interaction patterns. Knowing the functional requisites of a society does not permit one to predict future behavior or the ways in which these "society needs" will be met. We know, however, that if the society persists, these functions will be met in some way. Any system may "run smoothly" or it may "limp along." Here we are concerned with the "bare minimum." Knowing these permits us to channel our interests and investigations into related problems.

Material Resources

If a society is to survive, food, clothing, and shelter sufficient for survival in the particular environment must be secured. Various biological and geographic factors are obviously involved, and have been seen by some as the "determiners" of behavior. The maintenance of society does not depend upon the survival of any one individual or any particular subgroup. The society maintains itself as members leave the group through death, expulsion, or other causes, and as new members are integrated into the group. Society, however, exists and maintains its identity and its interaction patterns beyond the life of the entire membership at any given moment. Physical survival of the members of the group, however, is a requisite for society.

Replacement of Members

If a society is to persist for long the members must in some way take into account the facts of death and the consequent societal depletion. There are two sources of new members: (1) sexual reproduction and (2) recruitment from outside the society. Since the supply of members from other societies is limited, sexual reproduc-

Biological Interaction

Most of the important things that happen in the body can no longer be explained simply as a result of interactions of two or more organs, but require the conception of a dynamic transaction which itself integrates the activities of the organs. . . . We are dealing here, therefore, not with the interaction of unchanged objects like billiard balls, but with events which can only be expressed in transactional terms. In other words, though physiology and pathology have to take account of what is happening in individual organs, the transaction as a whole is the important and unifying factor.

—Sir Russell Brain.*

tion is the major source of new members. Every society, if it is to persist, must then provide for sexual reproduction and for the care of the young. The norm-role-value definitions must be such that reproduction is permitted and possible. It would be an error to conclude, however, that any particular set of definitions involved was established for the purpose of maintaining society. The immediate intended function may have little if anything to do directly with awareness of such a requisite. Yet unless in some way, and for whatever purpose it may decide, a society provides for sexual reproduction, it will eventually cease to exist.

Culture

Previous discussions have emphasized the importance of symbols in human behavior, pointing out that symbolic interaction is the hallmark of human behavior, and that by its very nature it is a group or societal phenomenon. Society exists in communication. Single human beings might exist for a time without culture; interacting human beings could not. The plans of action

---

* Statement by Sir Russell Brain, a British neurologist, quoted by Hadley Cantril in *Conflict and Creativity*, ed. by Seymour M. Farber and Roger H. L. Wilson (New York: McGraw-Hill Book Co., 1963), p. 186.

associated with the labels which man uses are, of course, a major influencing factor upon the specific interaction which does take place. NER symbols are important in motive behavior.

Structured Interaction

If a system of interaction is to be maintained, the behavior of the participants must be at least somewhat harmonious. The method by which this harmony is achieved has been identified as (1) development of culture, which includes plans of action, the component parts of which are systematized or organized, plus (2) the actual enactment of the plans of action thus arranged, whereby differential activities are allocated to different individuals and groups within the society. The interaction must be productive of sufficient motivation to the members of society that they individually will want to do things which are necessary for group survival—but not necessarily for that purpose. Personality systems and social systems must be harmonious. With large numbers of individuals involved and many subsystems all integrated into the larger societal system, there are any number of different ways in which all of this can be accomplished.

Adjustment to Internal Change

Since the harmony developed by any society is always relative, some means of coping with conflict, disorganization, or loss of equilibrium must also be present. Conflict must be kept within manageable limits or the society will "come apart at the seams." Some adjustment is planned for and techniques of adjustment may be incorporated into the norm-role definitions. Equilibrium is never attained, however, and an unstructured, emergent aspect exists in all behavior.

Adjustment to External Change, Including Intersocietal Contacts

If intersociety contacts develop, the particular societies involved must establish some means of relating themselves to each other so that society identity or "boundary maintenance" is achieved. If societies refuse to leave each other alone, various adjustment techniques are possible, from complete destruction to enslavement, accommodation, or assimilation. Some means of meeting external change must be developed if the society is to persist.

Any of these functional requisites can be accomplished in a variety of ways. Differing social systems or structural arrangements have already been developed by man; new patterns will most likely follow. Individual behavior in any situation may contribute to or distract from the accomplishment of these "needs." Each society, however, if it persists, will develop its own unique pattern of behavior, the over-all consequence of which will be the meeting of these functional requisites. Sociologists are interested in identifying the patterns established by any particular society and assessing the consequences of any particular segment upon the larger social system and the other segments therein.

There are additional questions:

1. Whether any society will necessarily want to survive.

2. Whether any society will do everything to maximize its survival chances.

3. Whether any society will fully understand what is needed for survival.

4. Whether, if it does understand what is needed for survival, it will be able to or would want to do all of these things.

A society may not be able to nor even want to be able to do all of these things. It is important to recognize that consciously or unconsciously the society may do those things which will destroy it. The development of atomic power with its destructive potential has made us aware that the actual destruction of an entire society through such means is now a real possibility, and the deciding factor which will determine whether this power is used in this way would seem to be the manner in which men learn to define each other. It may well be true, as has been said, that the ultimate weapon is in symbol. Man is, however, less aware of the gradual changes introduced into his social systems, from which seeds could be planted which may be involved in the rise and fall of his empire (society). In any case, it would be wrong automatically to attribute affirmative answers to the above questions.

Neither has anything been implied about the value question as to the desirability of perpetuating any particular society, or of having completely harmonious interaction within a society. Most members of a society would endorse the value of society survival, yet it is also important to recognize, as Dorothy Lee[2] has indicated, that there would seem to be no society in which preservation of the society has been viewed as the one over-riding goal of man.

FUNCTION OR INFLUENCE OF SYSTEM COMPONENTS OR SUBUNITS

The function of any element in a system is the manner in which it influences the larger entity. In an analysis of functions of a subunit, attention is given to the consequences of having this particular unit as one subpart of the larger entity. The unit of attention may be anything from a goodnight kiss, the voting system of the United States, or a particular transistor in a rocket heading for Mars. With reference to socio-cultural systems, it is useful to distinguish among certain functions.

Manifest Function

This is the function or consequences which individuals tell themselves (subjective reality) that a particular behavior pattern has. These are the consequences of the act, which are manifest or apparent to the particular observer—usually the participant in the act. Interpretations may vary from individual to individual. Applying our previous discussions of subjective reality to this discussion leads to the conclusion that manifest functions may be seen differently by different individuals or by the same individual at different times and under different circumstances. What-

ever the content, these definitions are real to one holding them, in terms of their influence upon his behavior.

Latent Function

This is the "actual" function or consequences (objective reality) of the behavior regardless of whether it is understood or recognized by those involved. The latent function of an act may be determined by impartial, objective study. However, we never know what objective reality actually is—we only know what we experience. In operational terms, then, we define "latent function" as the consequences determined through scientific study.

A diabetic who is not aware of his condition may eat certain foods with the belief that they will contribute to his biological well-being (manifest function). The debilitating consequences of the act would be the latent function. Being the symbol user that he is, the individual concerned may attribute these results to any number of other factors. On a societal level, a group may similarly engage in economic, familial, or religious patterns believing that particular consequences will follow from such behavior; the actual consequences, whether they are aware of them or not, may be quite different and may

---

Functions of Social Conflict

Conflict within a group . . . may help to establish unity or to re-establish unity and cohesion. . . . Yet, we noted that not every type of conflict is likely to benefit group structure, nor that conflict can subserve such functions for all groups; whether social conflict is beneficial to internal adaptation or not depends on the type of issues over which it is fought as well as on the type of social structure within which it occurs.

—Lewis A. Coser.[*]

---

[2] Dorothy Lee, *Freedom and Culture* (Englewood Cliffs, N. J.: Prentice-Hall, Inc., 1959), p. 72.

[*] Lewis A. Coser, *The Functions of Social Conflict* (New York: The Free Press of Glencoe, 1956), p. 151.

weaken the society and contribute to its subsequent destruction.

Intended Function—Purpose, Goal, Motive

The intended function or purpose of any act is what the individual or group hopes to accomplish by engaging in that act. The decision may be related to a set of accepted value definitions. The purpose or motive is taken into account before the action occurs, but may be re-interpreted as the action progresses and after the action is completed.

There is a difference among (1) the intended function or purpose of an act, or what an individual tells himself about *why* he is doing the act; (2) the manifest function, or what he believes happens as a result of the act, which may be quite different from what he intended to happen; and (3) the latent function, or the actual consequence as measured by scientific study.

We are not concerned with the question of whether there is some over-all purpose to human existence which is manifest in actual behavior. Providing answers to such teleological questions falls outside the role definitions of the sociologist.

Sociologists and anthropologists have not been consistent in the way they have used the term "function." Some have defined it as we have— the influence of an activity or a unit upon the larger entity of which it is but one subpart. Others have used it to mean the contribution of an activity in meeting the needs of individuals; still others, as any relationship between one sort of activity and another.

Sociologists and anthropologists who have concentrated their attention upon the study of *function* have come to be called "functionalists" or "structural functionalists" or, collectively, the school of "functional analysis." Kingsley Davis [3] has suggested, however, that actually sociology *per se*, rather than just a "school" within sociology, has given attention to functional analysis. Structural–functional analysis is in effect, he says, sociological analysis. The two goals (intended

functions) of functionalism are (1) to relate the parts of society to the whole, and (2) to relate one part to another. Almost as common, he continues, is the specification of *how* it does this relating—by seeing one part as "performing a function for" or "meeting a need or requirement of" the whole society or some part of it. These are the functions (intended function again) of every science, since every science explains phenomena from the standpoint of a system of reasoning which presumably bears a relation to a corresponding system in nature.

Our whole text supports the Davis contention. Much of our previous discussion has been directly or indirectly related to the function of various elements in the larger social system.

Study of the latent functions or consequences of behavior makes us aware again that more than subjective reality is involved in behavior— the situational factors to which the particular behavior is related and in which it is "immersed" have an influence upon that behavior whether particular individuals are aware of them or not. Many people may not be aware, for instance, of the many direct and indirect influences which the larger systems of which they are a part have upon their behavior. Identification of these relationships is frequently left to the specialist. This chapter has as one of its purposes the discussion of such influences.

SOCIETAL SYSTEMS

The maintenance of a society, with its many subsystems and individuals, is a complex phenomenon. Even though specific individuals or subgroups within the society may not be aware of the complex manner in which their behavior is related to the larger society, in some way the basic functional requisites are being met. The over-all consequences of thousands of interaction patterns somehow harmonize so that the society is able to function. This harmonizing, integrating process is a societal one. It is not accomplished by any single individual, but rather by individuals in interaction.

[3] Kingsley Davis, "The Myth of Functional Analysis," *American Sociological Review*, XXIV, No. 6 (December, 1959), 757–772.

Figure 19.1 Structure refers to the manner in which various parts are related to each other. The various parts of social systems are related to each other in much the same way that the parts of this building come together. (The Dow Chemical Company.)

In his efforts to understand himself, man has provided many explanations as to just how this is accomplished. The explanation presented in this text is that the connecting link is the symbol, or rather a *system* of shared symbols. The fact that the system of symbols is shared permits humans to interact in a systematic way. The following discussion will point out some of the complex ways in which the mere existence of human society rests upon this shared phenomenon.

Individuals have, as one of the components of the configuration of self definitions, a society identification. We know to which society we belong; we have some idea as to what membership means and what is expected of members. The society definition is a broad, over-riding definition, making the individuals who accept it aware of their similarity with many others. For many individuals, particularly those living in a primitive society, the "society" label is synonymous (or almost so) with the "human" label. It it a label that ties many individuals together.

A society identification may also include a historical component. The fact that man responds to symbols permits him to take *a* past (which each individual considers to be *his* past) into account. Since man's response is to symbols rather than to past events *per se*, current members of a society share a past most likely more common in retrospect than when this past was the present. Sharing of definitions of the past contributes to the perpetuation of the society.

Society members also expect to share a future with each other. They plan and behave as though they will share a common future. There is, however, much more to the relationships between behavior and society membership than the self definitions involved.

Within any society, it is impossible for each member to interact directly with any degree of frequency with each other member. The influence of an individual, however, may be extended in ever widening circles. Individual *X* influences *A*, who in turn influences *B*, who in turn influences *C*, and so on. The influence is, of course, related to the extent that attention is also given by *A*, *B*, and *C* to the behavior of others. In any society there is most likely no direct interaction among all members, but rather interaction mediated through others. Complex mosaics of interrelated behavior patterns are, of course, found in any society. And since human behavior is behavior in response to symbols, this influence can extend into the future, being mediated again by its relationship to symbols which may have been originated far in the past.

This pattern of influence is illustrated in the report of the President's Research Committee on Recent Social Trends,[4] which in 1932 explored some of the consequences of the introduction of radio into the United States. The Committee provided a list of 150 different major consequences in such areas as transportation, educa-tion, dissemination of information, industry and business, occupations, and government and politics. In like manner, decisions in a labor–management conference, a tax cut, or a birth control pill may eventually permeate almost every major aspect of living.

It is likely that the society-wide influence of any particular interaction episode is not completely known, and since man, the symbol user, is involved, what the consequences are believed to be may not be very accurate when compared to what actually happens.

If our focus of attention is a group rather than an individual, we reach the same conclusion. The influence of any group in society may be felt in an ever widening circle, as Group *X* influences Group *A* which in turn influences Group *B*, and so on. The influence is, of course, related to the extent that attention is given by Groups *A*, *B*, and *C* to the behavior of other groups. Then, of course, groups may influence individuals and individuals may influence groups in other ways.

However, for a society to exist and function, it is not necessary (even if it were possible) for all individuals or groups to interact directly with each other. The important thing is that they share a common set of symbols—that they share a common culture. The particular set of symbols used by each individual or group need not be identical, but a common core of shared symbols is essential. Sharing of common culture permits systematic interaction.

We have defined a society as a self-sufficient group. The self sufficiency comes most directly from the fact that a "symbolic boundary line" is drawn around the group so that the members consider themselves as an entity. Plans of action associated therewith are restricted to this group. The decision of exclusiveness is only rarely decided because of complete physical isolation. It is "culture isolation" which is important. Decisions of self sufficiency may, of course, be reached slowly, being crystallized only when confronted with aggression or a crisis situation.

Sharing of common definitions leads to common behavior as common plans of action are followed. This similarity of behavior can then be recognized and responded to. Such responses serve to

---

[4] President's Research Committee on Recent Social Trends, *Recent Social Trends* (New York: McGraw-Hill Book Co., 1933).

reinforce the society identification, supporting the premise that people who behave this way "belong" together.

The basic similarity among society members is a similarity of culture and related interaction patterns which take this culture into account. There are many other differences among the various members of a society, but in many respects as far as societal functioning is concerned, these are differences which make no difference. With man's ability to see what he has been prepared to see, he may see greater similarity than actually exists, yet the belief in similarity *per se* helps tie society members together.

Once a society identification has been made, one of the immediate consequences is that interaction will be largely restricted to society members. Whatever subgroups are formed will be formed from members of the larger society. Subgroup and individual behavior will, of necessity, always be influenced by the fact that it is but one part of the larger society. The relationship is, of course, a two-way phenomenon in that individuals and subgroups influence society, while the society influences the subgroups and individuals. Society is composed of interacting individuals.

Efforts to integrate behavior usually stop at society's edge, as do efforts to develop subgroups, and many efforts to influence the behavior of others. Society is an "integrating label." Many plans of action are developed with societal limitations built into them.

The fact that man forms societies means that individual behavior becomes related to that of the other members of the society, and in effect each imposes limitations upon the other while at the same time permitting each to behave in ways and accomplish things which would otherwise be impossible. Without systematic interaction most of the things the individual does would be impossible of attainment. Efforts at group accomplishment, however, usually stop at society's edge.

In addition, various kinds of society-wide phenomena can be identified and taken into account by any or all concerned. Man, with his facility in symbol use, can pay attention to any configuration of phenomena that he learns to identify. He can pay attention to combinations of anything, and take these aggregates into account in many different ways. Such phenomena can be discussed, appraised, and re-appraised. Any pattern of value definitions can be applied. Man has the ability to see similarities and differences and to label these so that they can be taken into account. He is able to generalize from one phenomenon to another, selectively ignoring tremendous differences while paying attention to similarities. There is the complicating factor that he may see what he thinks he should see and may see order where none actually exists (his behaving as though there were order, however, may contribute to the establishment of the order); this is the self-fulfilling aspect of behavior. The crucial factor in social organization may be the fact that man believes that consistencies should exist.

Man can respond to the whole society as a "generalized other." When he decides that "they" would not approve of something, it is to the whole society that he is referring. Further, standardized ways of responding to society-wide phenomena can be developed, as in the case of national elections. The individual vote in a national election is just one vote, but so are all the other votes just one vote. Yet, in combination, they elect a president. A dollar spent at a local grocery store is just one dollar, but in combination with others influences a decision to stay in business. Plans of action are developed, the completion of which requires the efforts of more than one individual. Informal as well as formal means of assessing combined phenomena have been developed.

The President of the United States may concern himself with those in a particular economic bracket, and encourage legislation to affect all those in the category in certain ways. The President and Congress may not know how many are in the category, where they are located, or other statistics about them, but they can, nonetheless, legislate for this category in such a way that the whole society is influenced. Religious leaders can take "sinners" into account. Others may consider diverse categories such as Republicans,

Southerners, criminals, divorcees, or alumni. Labor unions can make decisions that influence workers throughout the land. Man can distinguish economic, religious, and familial behavior and take these broad definitions into account.

Man develops systems which require the integrated efforts and activities of many people. He develops goals which can be satisfied only through group efforts. The development may, of course, be of both a crescive or unplanned and a planned type.

Likewise, in the various subgroups and in society at large, particular positions may be established for the express purpose of system maintenance. Administrators from the President of the United States on down, devote considerable effort to making sure that interaction of individuals and groups is harmonious enough for the group to function.

Starting from the fact that certain things must be done to maintain a society, and that the maintenance of a society is necessary for the develop-

Figure 19.2 Society exists in communication. Without communication whether by pony express or telegraph, or more modern methods, the social system could not function. (The Bettmann Archive, Inc.)

ment of "human behavior patterns," this discussion leads to the conclusion that through the interaction of a tremendous number of human beings and the systematic interrelation of a tremendous number of other factors, self-sufficient or independent societies are developed. Each has its distinctive characteristics, "personality," or "national character," which not only results from the individual and subgroup characteristics of which it is composed, but which in turn exerts a reciprocal or return influence upon the behavior of the members of the society and the subsystems involved therein.

MULTIGROUP SOCIETY—MULTIGROUP MEMBERSHIPS

Within any society the individual is a member of several different groups and is involved in various socio-cultural systems. He is faced, then, with the task of somehow relating and integrating his multigroup behavior. Previous discussions of the various types of definitions which make up culture have provided insight into just how this is done. There are, of course, many different ways in which each individual can accomplish this interaction. Some, of course, are better "balanced" than others.

Society, on the other hand, if it is to persist, is faced with integrating the behavior of its various members so that harmony sufficient for the functioning of the group is obtained. The harmony is never complete. There may, of course, be islands or pockets of those who are different. If so, somehow society-wide decisions must be made as to which differences are acceptable—norms of relevancy and irrelevancy must be established.

At the society level, a minimum of integration between the various groups and types of interaction is necessary for the society's survival. No one at the moment appears to know just what the minimum integration is; it may be strictly an academic question. The minimum integration level may vary with the type of society and the configuration of the composite ingredients. So-

Level of Attention

Despite the sociologist's concern with social system analysis, he has gathered relatively little empirical evidence which would help him explain deviant games—dope addiction, homosexuality, delinquency, or crime—in the same terms the players would explain them. In research-action programs, especially, he has been concerned with setting up and measuring the outcomes of efforts to change individuals, not systems—personalities, not styles of play. Yet, suppose, instead of delinquents, we were interested in changing baseball players into professors. What chance of success would we have, especially if we concentrated on personality characteristics? How sensible, to the ballplayers, in the light of their present identities, would this intervention be? How meaningful would our actions seem? What would be the chances of recidivism?

—LaMar T. Empey.[*]

ciety is in a constant state of re-adjustment. No two societies have ever worked out identical internal relationships. Different emphases upon the various aspects of living are found. In some, it may be the religious leaders who "call the shots"; in others, it may be the military, the philosophers, or possibly, in a high-leisure society, the recreationalists. Anthropological and historical evidence makes us aware of the great variability in societal patterns which man has already developed. We can only speculate on future possibilities.

INSTITUTIONS

Another system found within a society is the system of institutions. An institution is a configuration of socio-cultural phenomena, which is

[*] LaMar T. Empey, "The Application of Sociological Theory to Social Problems Research," paper read at annual meeting of Society for the Study of Social Problems, Los Angeles, California, August, 1963.

related to a specific societal goal or purpose. An institution consists of the various definitions, including the related plans of action, which are oriented around this goal. Institutions are related to specific types of groups, which are involved in achieving the goal. The major institutions are as follows: [5]

Marriage, which is related to the goal configuration of reproduction, care of the young, and affectional security. The related group is the family.

Economic, which is related to the goal of "making a living." The related group is the "business group."

Education, which is related to the goal of socialization. The related group is the school.

Political, which is related to the goal of social control and protection. The related group is the government group.

Religion, which is related to the goal of making moral sense out of life, and to crisis adjustment by relating man to the supernatural. The related group is the church.

Since the socio-cultural phenomena involved in each institution have a common core orientation, it would follow that relatively systematic relationships would obtain between the various aspects of culture and the interaction patterns involved. The various institutions of any society are interrelated and integrated into the larger societal system. There is considerable overlapping of institutions, although each can be studied as an entity, and change in any one institution will have repercussions in the others. To take a simple illustration, if a society starts to divert a larger percentage of its income into artistic and religious channels than previously, the "economic pinch" will be felt in other areas.

[5] This listing is not exclusive. Hertzler considers the following as institutions: Language, Scientific-Technological, Familial, Economic, Welfare, Educational, Governmental, Stratification Systems (quasi-institution), Religious, and Art. See J. O. Hertzler, *American Social Institutions* (Boston: Allyn and Bacon, Inc., 1960).

If a society begins to give greater prestige to military leaders and military phenomena, other areas will experience a "prestige pinch." Individuals who devote more time than before to political affairs will have less time to devote to non-political affairs. Societies in which most members spend most of their waking hours working to "keep shoes on the kids" will have little time, money, or interest to invest in other pursuits such as art or philosophy.

Institutions are interrelated, and since it is the same individuals who are involved in the various interlocking systems and who move from one position to another playing a different role in each, there is a carry-over from one area or system to another. The various institutions generally *tend* to be harmonious with each other. The harmony is never complete and societies are constantly making efforts to resolve existing conflicts.

Not everyone pays attention to institutions as phenomena of concern. Those who provide for themselves an "individual" interpretation of behavior may not consciously study or analyze relationships between, say, economic and religious behavior. Rather, they give attention to relationships between individuals, and individual men are frequently given credit for great social phenomena. The study of institutions is frequently left to the specialists, such as the sociologist, the economist, or the political scientist. Such analysis is a major concern of the sociologist who studies institutions *per se* and the relationships of their various component parts, as well as the interinstitutional relationships. The course offerings of a sociology department at a university usually include separate courses in which particular attention is given to each of these major institutions.

How, asks the sociologist, does the religious system of a society influence the educational system? How is the family related to the government? What influence, for instance, does the income tax pattern have upon the family? How is the economic system related to the political system in such activities as strike mediation? Under what conditions do new religious groups spring into existence? Under what conditions does a society increasingly turn to formal schools to educate its members and under what conditions does it use the family for this purpose?

Not all societies make these distinctions. To some there is no distinction between religion and economic institutions, or between religious and government institutions. The distinction between church and state, of which Americans are very aware, is unknown to some societies where the state, the family, and the business organization are all religious. The fact that Americans make the state–church distinction is related to the type of society in which they live. The United States has become a nation of specialists; this fact is related to its size, the level of its economic development, its urbanization-industrialization patterns, and its educational levels. Specialization involves paying attention to particular phenomena. Institutional analysis is one of the specialized activities of the sociologist.

PERSONALITY OR INDIVIDUAL BEHAVIOR

The individual-personality theory and the group or social systems theory came together in "interaction." For one thing, the individual decides which role he is to play in a particular situation, and he chooses between roles which are individual-oriented, subgroup-oriented, or society-oriented. In one interaction sequence he is acting "for himself," in another, "for his company," in another, "for his church," in another, "for his country." In actual interaction these various roles frequently spill over into each other, but interaction episodes usually involve individuals with somewhat similar role orientations, and behavior becomes standardized. Labor union leaders interact with business leaders, each as representatives of large groups of people. Personality factors are involved, to be sure, but of more importance is the fact that while playing this role an individual represents a large group of other individuals, and interaction is taking place in the framework of an intricate set of definitions and plans of action which simultaneously imposes limits and creates possibilities.

From such an analysis, we gain increased awareness of the importance of symbols in this whole process. Such phenomena would be impossible if individuals were not able selectively to place different labels upon themselves, upon others, and upon various situations, and integrate the symbols they use into systems which can themselves be taken into account.

Out of such interaction are developed plans of action and sanctions which influence groups from the society on down. Interaction which involves formal role definitions and formal role playing has a counterpart of an informal nature, and the eventual outcome of any interaction episode involves a formal–informal configuration.

Personality is learned, and it is learned from interaction in a particular system. Personality deviance is both an individual and a social phenomenon, and those who are concerned with eliminating deviant behavior patterns may attempt to change "individuals" and leave the social system which produced the deviance intact.

Gyroscopic Stability?

The assumption is not made that persons strive to maintain either their self-concept or various habitual behaviors by virtue of some inherent "gyroscopic" force residing in these dispositions. Maintenance of intrapersonal structure occurs only when such maintenance is consistent with an ongoing interaction process which is in a state of congruency. That most individuals do maintain intrapersonal structure is a function of the fact that the behavior of others toward the individuals in question is normally overwhelmingly consistent with such maintenance.

—Paul F. Secord and
Carl W. Backman.*

---

* Paul F. Secord and Carl W. Backman, "Personality Theory and the Problem of Stability and Change in Individual Behavior: An Interpersonal Approach," *The Psychological Review*, LXVIII, No. 1 (January, 1961), 21–33.

The alternate approach would be to analyze the social system, exploring questions such as what, in the system or the organization, produces deviance. Deviant behavior may be an unintended or latent consequence of certain social aspects which in and of themselves may be defined as good, such as the rise in divorce rate which has followed female emancipation. The system may encourage members of the society to want certain things (develop certain motive patterns) which it is not set up to provide for at all.

Empey [6] has suggested that understanding of behavior involves knowing about the network of social relationships of which each game or episode of behavior is composed, the position of the players, when and how they play their positions, the moral imperatives which sanction them, what group context and social occasions initiate their games, or the persistent interactional structures by which the rules are maintained and transmitted.

Lack of constraints facilitates expression of deviant behavior, but does not account for the process by which it emerges. It does not explain the process by which deviant behavior systems are developed and perpetuated. Socialization affects the formation of personality, and interaction affects the expression of already formed characteristics. Further, role conflict may be a serious thing for the individual from his value perspective, but a good thing as far as the continuation of society is concerned.

Bales [7] and others have suggested that an individual's stability derives largely from his being able to count upon a stable social environment. All members of a group, whether their purposes are exploitative or cooperative, share a common need for being able to predict how other members will behave toward them. Out of this need

---

Experimental Sensory Isolation

After participation in an experiment in which he was immersed in a tank of water and isolated from all contacts except those necessary to maintain his life for a 4½ hour period, the subject at the end of his post isolation interview vehemently asserted, "I honestly believe, if you put a person in there, just kept him and fed him by vein, he'd just flat die!"

—Jay T. Shurley.*

---

for predictability come strong pressures on each member to assume certain stable relations with all other members. Behavior of individuals who for one reason or another are denied interaction with other humans rapidly becomes bizarre and capricious. Individuals who are denied the usual contacts with their physical environment reach a bizarre or disorganized state very quickly.

The individual and society are, as Cooley said, twin born and twin bred. Yet, as Parsons [8] has pointed out, "Personality and social systems are very intimately interrelated, but they are neither identical with one another or explicable by one another; the social system is not a plurality of personalities."

SUMMARY

Society is defined as a group sharing a common culture and a relatively self-sufficient system of interaction. The systematic or structured behavior within a society is one of the systems related to human behavior. The maintenance of society requires material resources, replacement of members, culture, structured interaction, and adjustment to internal and external change.

---

[6] LaMar T. Empey, "The Application of Sociological Theory to Social Problems Research," paper read at annual meeting of Society for the Study of Social Problems, Los Angeles, California, August, 1963.

[7] Robert F. Bales, *Interaction Process Analysis* (Cambridge; Mass.: Addison-Wesley Publishing Co., Inc., 1950).

* Jay T. Shurley, "Profound Experimental Sensory Isolation," *The American Journal of Psychiatry*, CXVII, No. 6 (December, 1961), 539–545.

[8] Talcott Parsons and Edward A. Shils (eds.), *Toward a General Theory of Action* (Cambridge, Mass.: Harvard University Press, 1952), p. 7.

If society persists, the elements of the system must together somehow serve these system requisites. There is, however, a difference between what the individual believes the consequences of his behavior to be (manifest function) and what the consequences are as determined by scientific study (latent function)—and both may be different from the intended function or motive with which he entered into the interaction sequence.

Self definitions which tie the individual to the society have an important influence upon behavior, as does the fact that putting a society definition upon a group imposes symbolic boundary lines which set limits upon interaction. Inter-action systems are integrated to stay within the society. Being a symbol user, man is able to take society-wide phenomena into account, to introduce such definitions into the interaction, and in the process to validate the society definition. Both individual members and component sub-groups are integrated in this manner.

Institutions, the configuration of definitions and plans of action oriented around a major goal of society, are interrelated and tend to be harmonious with each other.

Within a society, society-wide, subgroup, and individual systems are all intermeshed to form the functioning society.

QUESTIONS

1. Define "system."
2. Identify four different systems which are involved in human interaction.
3. How are the functional requisites of society similar to the biological needs which we have previously discussed?
4. Distinguish between manifest and latent functions.
5. How do you account for the frequent discrepancy between manifest and latent functions?
6. In what ways do you consider yourself to be like the majority of other citizens in your society?
7. Discuss the statement that a society identification includes an historical component.
8. Define "institution."
9. Why do the various institutions only *tend* to be harmonious with each other?
10. In what ways is deviant behavior not strictly an individual phenomenon?

PROJECT

Identify twenty ways in which the fact of your going to college has had an influence upon the behavior of your family. What does this illustrate about social systems?

SUGGESTED READING

ABERLE, D. F., *et al.* "The Functional Prerequisites of a Society," *Ethics*, LX (January, 1950), 100–111.

COHEN, YEHUDI A. *Social Structure and Personality.* New York: Holt, Rinehart and Winston, 1961.

DAVIS, KINGSLEY. "The Myth of Functional Analysis," *American Sociological Review*, XXIV, No. 6 (December, 1959), 757–772.

HERTZLER, J. O. *American Social Institutions.* Boston: Allyn and Bacon, Inc., 1961.

HOMANS, GEORGE C. *Sentiments and Activities.* New York: The Free Press of Glencoe, 1962.

KROEBER, A. L., and TALCOTT PARSONS. "The Concepts of Culture and of Social System," *American Socio-logical Review*, XXIII, No. 5 (October, 1958), 582–583.

LEVY, MARION J. *The Structure of Society.* Princeton: Princeton University Press, 1952.

MERTON, ROBERT K. *Social Theory and Social Structure.* New York: The Free Press of Glencoe, 1957.

PARSONS, TALCOTT. *The Social System.* New York, The Free Press of Glencoe, 1951.

SMELSER, NEIL J., and WILLIAM T. SMELSER. *Personality and Social Systems.* New York: John Wiley & Sons, Inc., 1963.

SOROKIN, P. A. *Society, Culture and Personality: Their Structure and Dynamics.* New York: Harper & Row, Inc., 1947.

Part V

Demographic and Ecological Foundations of Interaction

20

Population and Ecology

Being born and dying are very personal things, yet they always occur "on stage" and have important social consequences. One birth or death may make only a slight impact upon a society; yet this small impact joined with others may contribute to an explosion, the consequences of which may reverberate in all segments of society. What would be likely to happen to our way of life if the birth rate were suddenly to double or to be cut in half?

INTRODUCTION

In this chapter we turn our attention to a consideration of population characteristics and ecological variables (ecology is the study of the manner in which man distributes himself in space). Population factors, which are frequently called demographic factors, have already been given limited consideration. They have been viewed as being among the multitude of causative factors related to human behavior. In and of themselves they do not provide sufficient explanation to account for man's social behavior, but they are obviously necessary ingredients.

Such factors influence social behavior and are in turn influenced by it. Interacting human beings must in some way take these factors into account, provide identifying labels for the various aspects to which they are sensitized, and develop plans of action felt to be appropriate. We turn our attention now to a consideration of some of these variables; our major interests are to identify some of their current characteristics and trends and to indicate how social variables are related to them.

The particular aspects we will discuss are identified below and the empirical phenomena of observation involved in research are identified in the formulas provided for each concept.

Birth rate:

Crude birth rate—number of births per 1,000 population at midyear. Rate may be adjusted for birth registration practices.

Age specific birth rate—the number of births to mothers of a specific age group divided by the number of women of that age group multiplied by 1,000.

Fertility ratio (FR)—ratio of the number of children under 5 to the number of women of child-bearing age (15–44) multiplied by 1,000.

Death rate:

Crude death rate—number of deaths per 1,000 population at midyear.

Age specific death rate—number of deaths among specific age group per 1,000 population in specific age group.

Life expectancy:

The average length of life attained at the time of death by persons who were born during a specified time interval.

Life span:

Number of years lived by the oldest members of the group, or the age to which an individual could expect to live if protected from disease and injury.

Age composition:

Number and/or per cent of population in various age categories.

Sex ratio (SR):

Number of males in population per 100 females.

In this chapter, our attention is not directed primarily to interaction patterns *per se,* but rather to some of the measurable consequences of such interaction. Perception here is selective. Population figures are group figures and are not directly applicable to any one individual. Awareness of population characteristics can, of course,

affect interacting individuals. For instance, decisions about where to live or whether to have children may take demographic and/or ecological information into account. However, the influence or involvement of demographic factors is greater than this. These are factors which exist and influence (but do not determine) interaction whether or not individuals are aware of them, and whether or not they take them into account.

This chapter does not give direct attention to the interaction processes involved in or related to the demographic characteristics but concentrates primarily upon the identification of characteristics and changes which have taken place. Value definitions and motivational factors related to these changes, as well as their social consequences, will also be discussed.

Concern with demographic factors has probably always been a human characteristic. Malthus [1] (1766–1834) is remembered today as one of the first individuals to call attention through his writing to the importance of such factors. The important question raised by Malthus was whether the relationship between the rate of population increase and the available food supply was such that serious problems would arise. He viewed the population as increasing geometrically (2–4–8–16–32, etc.) whereas the food supply was seen as increasing arithmetically (1–2–3–4–5, etc.). Were such a pattern of increase continued for any number of generations, the seriousness of the relationship is apparent. Malthus was wrong in his predictions, but he did direct attention to this area, and current concern with the so-called "population explosion" finds modern man asking many of the same questions posed earlier by Malthus.

The United States has evidenced considerable interest and care in obtaining demographic data. The major sources today are the various publications of the Bureau of the Census. Census data are known to be not completely accurate, but

[1] Thomas Malthus published his "Essay on the Principle of Population, Etc.," in 1798. Other publications followed. See D. V. Glass (ed.), *Introduction to Malthus* (London: Watts & Co., 1953).

there are statistical means of determining the probable error involved and other types of "spot checks" have also been utilized to gauge accuracy. The first national census was taken in 1790. The first census of immigrants from Europe was made in 1820, and efforts to have the various states adopt a uniform system of birth registration were successful in 1915. Only since 1933, however, have birth and death figures been gathered throughout the entire country.

Taking a modern census is no simple task. The 1960 census utilized some 160,000 enumerators at a cost of approximately $100,000,000.

Let us look at some of the data available about the American society. Limited contrast with data from other countries and with world-wide figures will be provided. Further details about other countries are available from several sources.[2]

BIRTH RATE

Fertility refers to the actual number of children born in a group and is distinguished from fecundity, which refers to potential reproductive capacity. No exact measures of fecundity are available, but if we consider the child-bearing period of a female to be from about age 15 to 44 and take into account periods of infertility following childbirth, the fecundity of a physically normal female who mated regularly would be approximately 21–22. Obviously, in only a few cases does fertility approximate fecundity, and the differential is accounted for primarily by social and not biological factors. No society has all the babies it could have.

Various measures of fertility have been developed. The crude birth rate which is widely used makes no allowance for any particular characteristics of the over-all population. The crude birth rate of a mining town of 900 males and 100

females has the same base as the rate for an area with 500 males and 500 females. To compare the crude birth rate in these two areas would ignore an important difference. The age of females in the population is another factor which is not reflected in this measure. It does, however, provide a crude measure and is particularly useful for comparing large populations.

The age specific birth rate and the fertility ratio (FR) are more refined measures.

The over-all pattern of fertility in the United States has been one of gradual decline. However, in about 1940 the trend reversed itself and there was a general increase until about 1957. There was not, however, a return to large families, but rather an increase in the proportion of mothers bearing two or three children. There was also a marked decrease in the proportion of women bearing no children or only one child.[3]

With the "boom" babies of the late 1940's starting to produce their own babies in the late 1960's, Census Director Richard M. Scammon predicted another baby boom, indicating that a million more people would reach their eighteenth birthday in 1965 than did so in 1963. Half of this million would be women and by 1967, half of them would be married. Outcome—more babies![4]

Conceiving and giving birth to a child are obviously biological phenomena, but many non-biological factors are involved. When children are defined as an economic asset, as they were during colonial America, parents may attempt to have large families. In an urbanized center, children may be viewed as an economic liability, however, with such definitions contributing to a lower birth rate. Tax exemptions, family allowances, and other social devices may serve somewhat to counteract the economic liability involved. If men believe that their eternal reward will be determined by the number of chil-

2 See, for instance, Paul H. Landis and Paul K. Hatt, *Population Problems* (2d ed.; New York: American Book Co., 1954); William Petersen, *Population* (New York: The Macmillan Co., 1961); T. Lynn Smith, *Population Analysis* (New York: McGraw-Hill Book Co., 1948); and Dennis H. Wrong, *Population* (rev. ed.; New York: Random House, Inc., 1962).

3 Clyde V. Kiser, "General Mating and Fertility Trends," *Eugenics Quarterly*, VI (1959), 76.

4 Frederick Osborn, "The United States and the World Population Crisis," in *Report of the New England Assembly on the Population Dilemma* (Boston: World Affairs Council of Boston), April 16–18, 1964.

dren they produce, or if they gain temporal status from having large families, they may attempt to maximize the biblical commandment to multiply and replenish the world.

Further, social factors such as religion and racism are related to fertility patterns. The birth rate for Roman Catholic women in the United States is generally higher than that for Protestants, who in turn have a higher rate than Jewish women. Studies which have held other factors constant find that the relationship still exists, thus indicating that the differences are attributable to specifically religious factors.[5] The rate is higher for non-white women than for white women. The white population under five years of age increased 24.0 per cent between 1950 and 1962; the non-white increased 53.4 per cent.

Fertility patterns are related to value definitions relative to birth control and abortion, as well as to the availability and effectiveness of relevant methods. Both primitive and modern societies have attempted to control birth through such means as practicing contraception, sterilization, infanticide, and providing for periods of sexual abstinence. The effectiveness of such efforts, particularly through contraception, has increased over the years. Changing patterns are also related to increased emphasis upon individualism and the aspirations for higher education and higher standards of living for self and children. Norm-role definitions relative to age at marriage, remarriage, and sexual behavior both within and outside of marriage are also involved. Societies are less willing to accept technics for controlling birth than for controlling death, largely because birth control is more likely to conflict with established value definitions and because it requires individual decisions.[6]

Rural farm areas have higher fertility rates than rural non-farm areas, and both have higher rates than urban areas. There is a negative correlation between the size of the city and its fertility rate. Generally the lower-class families have evidenced a higher birth rate than the middle- or upper-class families. However, contrary patterns have emerged recently in that the higher classes have contributed more than their proportionate share to the increase. There is evidence that those in the highest brackets have greater fertility than those in the middle and medium high groups.[7] In the United States, fertility has also been found to be higher in periods of marked social change, in periods of prosperity, and among descendants of large families.

Quality

There is at present no sufficient scientific basis for believing that the higher birth rates of the people in the lower-income groups (but not including the socially inadequate) are causing a genetic deterioration from one generation to another.

—Frederick Osborn.*

DEATH RATE

The crude death rate in the United States has fallen from an estimated 17.2 per 1,000 population in 1900 to 9.3 in 1961. This death rate is lower than many other modern nations, but is higher than that of the Netherlands which has the lowest national rate in the world—7.6 per 1,000. Change has not been the same for all age groups, however. One of the more dramatic

---

* Frederick Osborn, "Qualitative Aspects of Population Control—Eugenics and Euthenics," *Law and Contemporary Problems*, XXV, No. 3 (Summer, 1960), 416.

[5] See Ronald Freedman and Others, *Family Planning, Sterility and Population Growth* (New York: McGraw-Hill Book Co., 1959), pp. 278–279; and Gerhard Lenski, *The Religious Factor* (Garden City: N. Y.: Doubleday & Co., Inc., 1961), pp. 212–219.

[6] Bernard Berelson and Gary A. Steiner, *Human Behavior* (New York: Harcourt, Brace & World, Inc., 1964), p. 595.

[7] Questions about the strength of the relationship have been raised by Charles F. Westoff *et al.*, *Family Growth in Metropolitan America* (Princeton, N. J.: Princeton University Press, 1962), p. 234.

changes has been in the infant mortality rate, as shown in the following figures:

Year	Infant Deaths (Under One Year) per 1,000 Live Births, 1915–1963
1915	99.9
1920	85.8
1925	71.7
1930	64.6
1935	55.7
1940	47.0
1945	38.3
1950	29.2
1955	26.4
1960	26.0
1961	25.3
1962	25.3
1963	25.2

Sources: Bureau of the Census, *Historical Statistics of the U. S., Colonial Times to 1957* (Washington, D. C.: Government Printing Office, 1960, p. 25; and Department of Commerce, *Statistical Abstract of the U. S.,* 84th Annual Ed. (1963), p. 62, and 85th Annual Ed. (1964), p. 57.

The extent of the change can be seen in figures indicating what the conditions would have been if the changes had not taken place. Thus, if the 1900 mortality rate had obtained in 1950, there would have been in that one year over a million and a half additional deaths, of which 400,000 would have been infants under one year of age; 420,000 between ages 1 and 24; 510,000 between ages 25 and 64; and 260,000 in the over-65 category.[8]

Such changes in the death rate reflect such factors as changes in diet, medical care, sanitation, famine, epidemics, and war. In the United States it has been found that mortality rates are (1) lower during periods of economic growth, prosperity, and a rise in the standard of living; (2) lower among the upper class; (3) lower for women than men; and (4) lower among the married than among the unmarried or divorced, especially among men. Since social conditions

only influence the manner and time of death, it follows that the death rate cannot continue to go down indefinitely. The record low of 9.2 per 1,000 achieved in 1954 may not be realized again. The 1962 rate was 9.5.

Osborn has pointed out that among primitive peoples over half of the children died before growing up. In Europe until about a century ago, one third of the children died in infancy. But among peoples of European descent today, less than 10 per cent of the children die before reaching age 30. In Asia, Africa, South America, and the Arab nations, the high death rates that prevailed until quite recently have now begun a rapid decline.

The influence of a change in death rate is shown by the fact that a reduction of infant death from 50 per cent to less than 10 per cent of all children born is equivalent to almost a doubling of births. When death rates decline and birth rates do not, the population continues to increase. Today, however, while deaths are decreasing in many areas of the world there are few signs of similar decline in births. The continued decline in death rates which will most likely occur in most of the world will, accordingly, contribute to an increase in world population.

LIFE EXPECTANCY AND LIFE SPAN

While the life span, as defined above, has remained much the same, the life expectancy of Americans has changed tremendously. Figure 20.1 portrays the changes from 1900 to 1955.

Death

In former times death was in the midst of life as the cemetery is in the middle of the village.
—Jean Fourastie.*

[8] "Age of Death in the United States," *Health Information Foundation Bulletin,* February, 1956, p. 3.

* Jean Fourastie, quoted in "Three Comments on the Near Future of Mankind," *Diogenes,* No. 32 (Winter, 1960), 1–16.

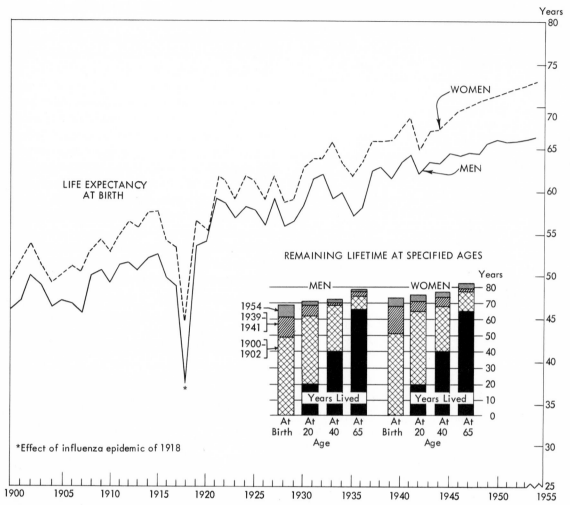

Figure 20.1 Changes in life span and life expectancy, 1900–1955. (From *Road Maps of Industry*, No. 1101, February 1, 1957. By permission of The Conference Board.)

The average life expectancy today of over 70 years is more than double that of 35 years which obtained in 1800. The average American born in 1962 could expect to live 70 years; the white girl, 74, and the white boy, 67; the non-white girl, 66, and the non-white boy, 61. The racial gap has been narrowing, while that between the sexes has been widening, as Figure 20.1 shows.

Life expectancy figures are, of course, influenced strongly by the death patterns of society, and by the social condition which influences the death rate.

Life expectancy will most likely continue to increase at a decreasing rate.

POPULATION SIZE

The size of any group is a result of the interplay of birth, death, and immigration and emigration factors, which in turn are influenced by

Population Change

Some very revealing facts have come to light in the preliminary results of the All-Union Population Census of 1959, published recently in the USSR.

The most striking revelation is how severely the male population was decimated during World War II. The loss was originally assessed at three million, but later seven million came to be generally accepted in the West. The census indicates that a loss of 15 to 20 million males, from all causes, is closer to the actual tragic fact.

—Robert C. Cook.*

---

many other factors including, of course, the size of the group. The mere or sheer size of any group is a factor which influences interaction of its members. In certain respects, children reared in a large family behave differently from the child with no siblings. The society with a population of 900,000 is unlikely to have as much influence in international power relationships as one with 900,000,000. The size of the population and the food resources obviously have a reciprocal relationship to each other.

The American colonies did not have enough population to do all they wanted to do, including protecting their "homeland" from the American Indians and from other nations, and developing their apparently limitless resources. Large families were the rule. Families of 12 to 15 were frequent, and the women who lived to middle age averaged eight children apiece. Almost one quarter of the children, however, died before they reached their fifth year. Immigration was extensively encouraged.

The population of the United States has increased from 275,000 in 1700 to approximately 180,000,000 in 1960. The balance of birth, death, and immigration and emigration factors has been such that increases of about two million per

* Robert C. Cook, "USSR Census: A Power Myth Exposed," *Population Bulletin* (July, 1959), 61.

year in the 1940's and almost three million per year in the 1950's have been experienced. The increase of population has been more and more due to the balance of birth and death and less and less to the immigration–emigration balance. In the first decade of this century, 39 per cent of the population increase resulted from an excess in the number of immigrants over emigrants, while in the 1950's only 10 per cent of the increase was accounted for by immigration. In the eighty years from 1880 to 1960, the proportion of the foreign-born in America decreased from 13.1 to 5.2 per cent and a further drop can be expected in the next few decades if the present patterns prevail.

The over-all pattern has been one of steady increase, but the rate of increase has been steadily decreasing, as shown in the following figures:

Year	Per Cent Increase
1790–1850	490
1850–1900	228
1900–1960	137

SOURCE: Murray Gendell and Hans L. Zetterberg, *A Sociological Almanac for the United States* (2d ed.; New York: Charles Scribner's Sons, 1964), p. 40.

Many variables have been related to the steady increase of population. Factors such as abundant new land, expansion of the railroads, industrialization, urbanization, a relatively high standard of living, a low death rate, the high proportion of young people in the original population, and improved public health were all involved.

Population of the World

World population has also experienced constant over-all increase as shown by the pattern in Figure 20.2. At the end of the Stone Age it is estimated that there were 10 million people in the whole world. At the time of Christ this had increased to from 200 to 300 million people, and at the beginning of the modern era (1960), to about 500 million. In 1964 the figure was over 3 billion. For thousands of years the rate of over-all increase was something less than 0.02 per cent per year. Some 300 years ago it

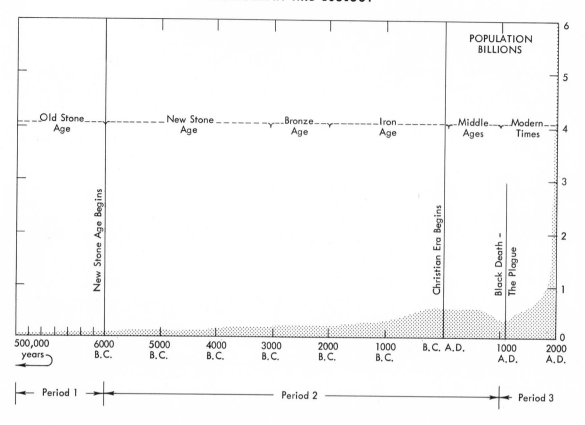

Figure 20.2 Increase in the population of the world. (From *Population Bulletin*, XVIII, No. 1, February, 1962), 5.

began to rise, slowly at first, then very quickly. From 1650 to 1930 the world population increased at an average of 0.5 per cent a year. Between 1930 and 1940 the increase averaged 1 per cent a year. Since the end of World War II it has averaged 1.6 per cent a year. At an increase rate of 1.6 per cent a year the population of the world would double about every 40 years. Estimates by United Nations demographers indicate that there will be a population of 6.2 billion by the year 2000. World population now increases in about 6 years as much as it did during the first 1,650 years following the birth of Christ. Every day over 165,000 people are added to the population of this planet.[9]

[9] Osborn, *op. cit.*, p. 6.

Two thirds of the world's people live in countries that are mainly agricultural and whose populations are growing at such a rate that they will double in less than 30 years. India's rate of growth is close to 2.5 per cent a year, which, if continued, would double her present population of 460 to 920 million in just under 30 years. Pakistan's growth rate of 2.6 per cent would double her 100 million people in 27 years. China's population has been estimated at over 700 million, and Chou En-lai is reported to have said that the Chinese population is increasing at the rate of 2.5 per cent a year, the same rate as that of India. Russia's population increase of 1.78 per cent annually is greater than that of the United States, 1.73 per cent.

Latin America has the fastest growing population of any continent. The most Europeanized

Years for Living

In mid-eighteenth century France, life expectancy was 25 years. About 440 out of 1,000 lived to marriage age. Half of the marriages reached their 15th year. At fourteen years of age the average child experienced the death of a parent. He was one of five children only half of whom lived to see their fifteenth birthday. Later, as the father of five children he saw two or three die before his own death at age 52. He had survived two or three families, long periods of serious food shortage, and several epidemics that cut down large number of persons in his community.

—Jean Fourastie.*

countries, Argentina and Uruguay, have the lowest birth rates, and the Central American countries have the highest. Costa Rica, El Salvador, and Venezuela are increasing at rates which would double their populations in less than 20 years. Present rates of growth in Guatemala, Jamaica, Mexico, Colombia, and Ecuador would double their population in 24 years. These latter rates are paralleled on the other side of the world, where the rates of growth of Egypt, Turkey, Tunisia, Ceylon, Hong Kong, Malaysia, the Philippines, Taiwan, and Thailand are also sufficient to double the number of their people in 24 years.[10]

Age Distribution

Changes in birth and death rates, as well as in life expectancy, change the age distributions of a population. The median age (the age at which half of the population is older and half younger) has been changing in the United States. In 1900 it was 22.9 years, in 1940 it was 29.0, in 1954 it had climbed to 30.6. It dropped to 28.9

* Jean Fourastie, "Three Comments on the Near Future of Mankind," *Diogenes*, No. 32 (Winter, 1960), 1–16. Quoted in J. Milton Yinger, *Sociology Looks at Religion* (New York: The Macmillan Co., 1963), p. 66.

[10] *Ibid.*, p. 7.

in 1962. It is anticipated that it will continue to decline, as the number of births increase, thus putting a larger percentage in the younger-age categories.

These figures give a deceptive picture, however, in that the proportions of the very young and the very old have *both* been rising, while the proportion in the middle period of life—the productive years—has been declining. Actually, the proportion of the population over 65 doubled between 1900 and 1959, from approximately one out of every 25 in 1900 to one out of every 12 in 1959. Previous assumptions that the trend toward an increasingly older population would continue for some time were modified by the sharp increase in the birth rate which started in the 1940's.

Several factors such as improved medical care, improved diets, and a high level of living have contributed to the increase in the life expectancy of the average American. Changes in this respect are likely to continue. Efforts to counteract the degenerative diseases which afflict the aged have not been very successful. Thus, more people continue to live to old age, and the death rate will most likely continue to rise in the years immediately ahead. It has been estimated that in approximately two decades the median age of the population will become higher accordingly.

SEX RATIO

Contemporary Patterns

The current sex ratio (SR) is approximately 98; in the over-all population, American women outnumber the men by one or two per hundred. The pattern varies, however, with age and area. The SR at birth is about 106, and at conception is even greater. More male than female babies are conceived and delivered with a steady decline in the difference as age increases. Women have a longer life expectancy than men, and the composite picture shows more females than males. Regionally, there is a surplus of males in the West, where the SR dropped from 105 in

1880 to about 102 in 1950. Alaska has a ratio of 132.

The sex ratio for all Negroes in the United States has been consistently lower than for whites. Further, the 1960 urban ratio of 94 is different from the rural ratio of 104. The urban–rural differential is greater for those in the marriageable age group. In the American urban centers which have surplus females, a certain number are likely to experience difficulty finding a suitable mate.

A sex ratio under 100 is a recent phenomenon, since the first census to show a female surplus was that of 1950. Change in this direction, however, had been taking place since the early 1900's.

The early SR above 100 reflects such factors as the high death rate for women in the child-bearing period and a heavy, predominantly male, migration from Europe. The SR for immigrants is usually above 100. Both of these factors have now changed. The death rate for men, which is now higher than that for females at each year of age, is likely to give the nation an even greater excess of females in the future.

In societies with monogamous marriage norm definitions, a surplus of either marriageable males or females could create a problem. However, in a society which permits plural mates, such problems need not materialize. Some groups practice infanticide (killing infants) to produce a sex ratio which harmonizes with their established marriage patterns.

RACIAL COMPOSITION

In the world there are roughly 1,300 million caucasoid, 800 million mongoloid, and 240 million negroid individuals. In 1960 the pattern in the United States was:

Caucasoid	88.6 per cent	158,900,000
Negroid	10.5 per cent	18,800,000
Mongoloid	0.9 per cent	1,600,000

For a number of years, the non-white population has made up about 10.0 per cent of the total population, but in recent years it has increased somewhat more rapidly than the white. The total United States Negro population went down from a high of 19.1 per cent of the total in 1790, to 14.1 per cent in 1860, to a low of 9.7 per cent in 1930. It rose to 10.5 in 1960 and is still rising.[11]

ECOLOGY

Human ecology is the study of how man distributes himself in space. Although other factors are obviously involved, where people live influences how they live, and how they live influences where they live. Knowing where an individual lives tells you something about how he lives.

Let us turn our attention first to an analysis of the community, which we define as a group of people living in a particular physical setting, having sufficient socio-cultural characteristics in common to be considered by themselves and others in the area as a recognizable unit, and whose interaction patterns take the community identity into account. No rigid limits as to size have been accepted.

Community members recognize community boundaries, at least in a rough sense, and figuratively or literally draw boundary lines around the area and then develop plans of action which take these boundary lines into account. In doing so, social systems get tied to the geographic area. As these plans of action are developed and enacted, they intermesh in such a way that the boundary lines become more solid and confining. Change in the "disintegrating" direction may occur, and communities may go through a process of re-alignment.

In interaction, community-wide patterns are established which both grow out of the interaction and in turn influence subsequent interaction. Various types of activity and various types of groups tend to concentrate in certain areas of the community. Segregation takes place. Once patterns of concentration are established, aware-

---

[11] *Ibid.,* p. 13.

Figure 20.3 Man distributes himself in space. How he distributes himself is influenced by his culture, while the available space also influences his culture, as in the case of this Hopi Indian community in the late 1800's. (The Bettmann Archive, Inc.)

ness of these area concentrations are taken into account in subsequent decisions involving those in the larger community which, in turn, further strengthen the concentration. Such areas have been called "natural areas," but the term should not be interpreted as implying that geographic factors (conditions of nature) *determine* the pattern. They are rather a "natural" consequence of established interaction patterns, which have established the areas and are involved in their perpetuation. Robert E. Park,[12] one of the first American sociologists to study the community, said, "In short, the structure of the city, as we find it, is clearly just as much the product of the struggle and efforts of its people to live and work together collectively as are its local customs, traditions, social rituals, laws, public opinion

[12] Robert E. Park, *Human Communities* (New York: The Free Press of Glencoe, 1952), p. 196.

and the prevailing moral order." The wholesale district, the downtown section, the manufacturing area, the railway area, the new shopping center, the slum, the ghetto, and even the "red light district" are examples of such areas.

In addition, man develops organizations designed to serve a particular area or restricted to it. A business may have certain limitations, such as the colonial restriction on how far a team could haul a load in one day. A pressure group in Congress, a school, or a church district may have community restrictions. Interaction then is entered into at various levels and in various places which take an area into account and respond to it as an entity. Those living in the area are treated as a group in such things as legislative decisions, school district decisions, and business decisions, whether they want to be or not.

Smaller areas have been given the name "neighborhood," which includes a recognizable area identification and at least a somewhat distinct "we" feeling or area identification on the part of the residents.

As people with similar value-norm-role definitions (culture) concentrate in an area it may take on a "particular flavor" in terms of religion, type of building, social class composition, type of national origin, language patterns, or more accurately a mosaic of interrelated characteristics.

Since such areas are all located within the same community and all share in certain community-wide systems such as government, utility, and transportation systems, the behavior and the groups within these areas develop *patterns* of interrelations. The ecologist sometimes speaks of the "biotic community" in which he includes all life forms which interact in that community. Biotic equilibrium is said to obtain when the interaction patterns are sufficiently integrated to provide smoothly working relationships.

No area, of course, is a complete island. Patterns of area interrelations obtain, with enough of a common culture, including ethnocentrism (loyalty) and common behavior patterns, to tie the various subparts to the larger community.

Competition between communities in athletic or other events also facilitates community self

identification for those involved as spectators or participants.

Over time, social conditions change. When viewed in their aggregate we can talk of "ecological *invasion*" in that there is a movement of people or organizations into areas already occupied by others. Again in a metaphorical sense, certain types of organizations *invade* an area of established concentration. In a growing city, for instance, the residential areas are invaded by the central business district. The expansion of the urban area has also been called an invasion of the rural areas. Through such a process, patterns of *succession* are established.

What happens in the local community also takes place in the larger regions. Many causative factors are involved—cost factors, breaks in transportation, location of other specific industries in the area—through which *regional patterns* of concentration or segregation are established. Interregional changes may occur, such as the movement of textile plants from the New England region to the South. Whole regions are likewise influenced by a concentration of say, defense-related industries, which in turn attracts other satellite industries. Through such processes a megalopolis may be established, such as some predict will extend in the future from Boston to New York.

One of the major community distinctions to which social scientists, among others, have given great attention is the rural–urban distinction. It was, in fact, an interest in urbanization which led the early sociologists at the University of Chicago to undertake studies that gave shape and substance to most of the current subdivisions of contemporary American sociology.[13]

Movement from rural areas to urban centers which has accompanied the increase of industrialization in America, has contributed to some profound changes in the American way of life. Many interrelated factors have been involved both as causes and as consequences of this migration. Without attempting to unravel the causal nexus we will identify some of the major rural-

[13] See Maurice R. Stein, *The Eclipse of Community* (New York: Harper & Row, Inc., 1960), chap. i.

urban differences which have been found to exist. Berelson and Steiner [14] identify these as follows.

1. More foreign immigrants in the cities than in rural areas.
2. More political and religious tolerance in the cities than in rural areas.
3. Less religious observance in the cities than in rural areas, especially in the form of church attendance by men.
4. More change in the cities, more stability in the country.
5. Higher level of education in the cities than in rural areas.
6. More severe mental illness in the cities than in rural areas (not conclusive).
7. More illegitimate births in the cities than in rural areas (not conclusive).
8. Fewer married people in the cities than in rural areas.
9. Lower birth rate in the cities than in rural areas.
10. More divorce in the cities than in rural areas.
11. More crime in the cities than in rural areas (not conclusive), although probably more crimes of violence, proportionately, in rural areas.
12. More suicide in the cities than in rural areas.

This modern list of rural-urban differences compares closely to the differences reported by the fourteenth-century Arab philosopher, Ibn Khaldun, for his society.

Migration

Modern Americans are either immigrants themselves or the descendants of immigrants, with the American Indians being the earliest immigrants to the American continent. Many factors both in the exit-land and the entrance-land are related to immigration patterns—famine, revolution, catastrophe, persecution, religious opportunity, freedom, favorable living conditions, occupational opportunity.

Early American immigration policy was a wide-open one with few restrictions. In 1875 "convicts and immoral women" were excluded. In 1882 a head tax of fifty cents was levied on

14 Berelson and Steiner, *op. cit.*, pp. 606–607.

Freedom

In the freedom of the city every individual, no matter how eccentric, finds somewhere an environment in which he can expand and bring what is peculiar in his nature to some sort of expression. A smaller community sometimes tolerates eccentricity, but the city often rewards it. Certainly one of the attractions of a city is that somewhere every type of individual—the criminal and the beggar, as well as the man of genius—may find congenial company and the vice or the talent which was suppressed in the more intimate circle of the family or in the narrow limits of a small community, discovers here a moral climate in which it flourishes.

—Robert E. Park.*

immigrants, and "lunatics, idiots, and other persons likely to become a public charge" were denied admission. The Office of the Superintendent of Immigration was created in 1891, and in 1917 the head tax was raised to $8.00.

Following World War I the restrictions were tightened, and a quota system established in 1921 was based on "nationality" and was proportionate to the number from a particular nation residing in the United States in 1910. The 1921 restrictions were aimed at countries outside the Americas and particularly at those in southern and southeastern Europe. The National Origins Plan of 1929 established a formula to favor the northern and northwestern nations of Europe and to decrease the immigration from other countries. Since then, 150,000 entries were prorated among the different countries according to their number from those countries or their descendants in the United States in 1920. Following World War II, 350,000 displaced persons were granted immigration permission.

From 1957 to 1961 the average number of immigrants per year to the United States from all countries was 253,000, nearly 50 per cent of

* Robert E. Park, *Human Communities* (New York: The Free Press of Glencoe, 1952), p. 86.

Rural–Urban Migration

Rural–urban migration is one of the most powerful and consistent forces in the world today. In numbers this movement is vastly more than international migration, and international migration itself is more often than not to the cities of the receiving countries.

—Dudley Kirk.*

whom came from Europe. A little less than one-sixth came from Canada and one-eighth from Mexico.

The net effect of the United States immigration policy has been to minimize impact of immigration upon size and composition of the population.

Internal Migration

A major movement of internal migration has been from rural to urban areas, some of the consequences of which we have just discussed. The urban population of 1790 comprised about 5 per cent of the total. By 1960 the percentage had increased to approximately 70 per cent. There were, in fact, actually fewer people living on farms in 1960 than in 1900. There has also been a general movement toward the West Coast and the industrial centers of the East from the agri-

* Dudley Kirk, "Major Migrations Since World War II," in *Proceedings of the 1957 Annual Conference of the Milbank Memorial Fund: Selected Studies of Migration Since World War II* (New York: Milbank Memorial Fund, 1958), p. 25.

cultural areas of the South and Midwest. The center of population moved westward twice as far from 1850 to 1900 as from 1900 to 1960.

On a smaller scale, about one in every five Americans moves from one home to another every year; the majority move only a short distance. Studies of migration have found that those who have moved once, by comparison with those who have not made that first move, are more likely to move again. Moves which cover a short distance are more frequent than those which cover greater distances. Further, there is evidence to suggest that migration is proportional to the number of opportunities at a given distance, and inversely proportional to the number of intervening opportunities.

Interaction always takes into account geographic conditions. It may be well to point out again in closing this discussion, however, that over the years man has increasingly developed ways of adapting geographic conditions to his own goals. He removes mountains, fills marshlands, cuts forests and reforests cut areas, dams rivers, irrigates arid lands. He changes but does not escape the geographic conditions.

SUMMARY

Various population measures can be identified and applied in the study of interaction. Some of the social correlates of these characteristics can also be identified. The characteristics of a community are recognizable as are the consequences of living in a community. Rural–urban differences and migration patterns have some significant consequences.

QUESTIONS

1. What factors do you see as contributing to the fact that the prediction of Malthus that the food supply would not keep pace with the population did not materialize?
2. Under what conditions would you think that fertility might approach fecundity?
3. What factors do you think influence the typical couple with a college education to limit the size of their families?
4. How do religious factors influence birth rate?
5. Explain the statement: The population of the United States has been *increasing* at a *decreasing* rate.

6. Explain the statement that life expectancy has increased markedly while life span has increased only slightly.
7. What do you see as some of the social consequences of the fact that the life expectancy of the female is greater than that of the male?
8. What might be done to reduce the population "explosion"? Which definitions held by a group of people would encourage and which definitions would discourage doing something about the "explosion"?
9. Why does a differential in the sex ratio of a society not necessarily create a social problem?
10. Which value definitions of a group do you think would have the greatest influence upon the birth rate and the death rate?

PROJECT

Check the births reported for the period of a week by
a large newspaper, and determine the sex ratio.

SUGGESTED READING

BUREAU OF THE CENSUS. *Current Population Reports, Population Characteristics*. Series P-20. Washington, D. C.: Government Printing Office, 1962–1964.

DEPARTMENT OF HEALTH, EDUCATION, AND WELFARE, NATIONAL OFFICE OF VITAL STATISTICS. *Monthly Vital Statistics Bulletin*. Washington, D. C.: Government Printing Office. Current issue.

GRAYBILL, WILSON H., CLYDE V. KISER, and PASCAL K. WHELPTON. *The Fertility of American Women*. New York: John Wiley & Sons, Inc., 1958.

HAUSER, PHILIP M., and OTIS DUDLEY DUNCAN (eds.). *The Study of Population*. Chicago: The University of Chicago Press, 1959.

LANDIS, PAUL H., and PAUL K. HATT. *Population Problems*. (2d ed.). New York: American Book Co., 1954.

MALTHUS, T. B. *An Essay on the Principle of Population*. New York: The Macmillan Co., 1909.

PETERSEN, WILLIAM. *Population*. New York: The Macmillan Co., 1961.

SMITH, T. LYNN. *Population Analysis*. New York: McGraw-Hill Co., 1948.

THOMPSON, WARREN S. *Population Problems*. 4th ed. New York: McGraw-Hill Book Co., 1953.

WRONG, DENNIS H. *Population*. Rev. ed. New York: Random House, Inc., 1962.

Part VI

Systems

21

Peers

Students are at times called upon to decide whether to follow the wishes of their college friends or their parents. It is not uncommon, to use a simple example, for students to decide to go to the show with their friends even though they know that their parents at home would not approve. Why this preferential treatment to peers? Under what conditions would you follow the wishes of peers rather than parents? Under what conditions would you give preferential treatment to parents?

INTRODUCTION

All individuals experience many different types of interactive relationships. This chapter is devoted to one major type, peer interaction, or interaction between individuals (1) who define each other as peers, or as being of about equal social status; (2) who interact voluntarily; (3) who frequently develop patterns of primary relationships. In many respects, then, peer interaction is the antithesis of stranger interaction. Since the social status of those involved is essentially equal, peer groups are sometimes called "horizontal groups." Peer interaction frequently, but not always, involves individuals of the same sex and approximately the same age. Our primary concern in this chapter is to identify the characteristics of peer interaction, and to discuss some of the consequences or functions of such interaction.

Interacting peers, considered as a group, are frequently classified into the following three categories.

Play Group

Interaction in a play group is, as the name suggests, primarily recreational or playful in nature and is relatively unstructured without a strong group identity. The term is usually used to refer to groups of children. Interaction in a play group is usually the child's first experience with peer interaction. Such interaction starts at around age three or four, and the children of this age seem to prefer group play to individual play. The size of the desired peer group generally increases with age. Such interaction may be initiated by adults, and is accordingly not strictly voluntary on the part of the children, but as they mature the interaction becomes more spontaneous and voluntary.[1]

The Clique

A clique is a peer group which has, through frequent interaction, developed an identity of its own. Members thereof recognize themselves as a group, with the identification being confirmed by non-clique members. Bossard describes a clique as follows:

A clique has a definite membership which may vary in number from two to as many as thirty. It may or may not be age graded and it may be unisexual or bisexual. Its organization is informal. It has no explicit rules of entrance or exit. The bond which holds it together is intimacy of interaction among the members, a strong sense of solidarity, and a common behavior pattern. Its significance for its members on the emotional side is very great. This expresses itself principally in two ways. First, as between members, it involves strong feelings of friendship and of responsibility to render mutual assistance in case of need; second, in regard to other groups and outside demands the clique is given preference, even over the family of its members.[2]

The Gang

A gang is a group of peers which is recognized as a group by the members and non-members alike. A gang has somewhat formal norm-role definitions which govern interaction of group members. McCormick, writing in 1912, indicated that a distinctive characteristic of gang interaction is that it is based upon conflict. "A gang can never thrive without another gang to fight with."[3] Thrasher, who provided one of the classical sociological studies of gangs, defined a gang as an "interstitial group originally formed spontaneously, and then integrated through conflict." To become a "true" gang, he said, the whole group must meet some hostile element which precipitates conflict.[4] Gangs thrive on independence from outside discipline and authority, and when they do join organized group programs, those in charge frequently complain that they disrupt the established programs. Gangs may be a cause of delinquent behavior, a symptom of delinquent behavior, or simply a case of delinquent individuals flocking together.

The degree of formal socio-cultural integration increases from play group to clique to gang, with the gang making most extensive use of identifying symbols such as names, slogans, passwords, grips, and uniforms. Some, but not all, more formally organized groups such as scout troops, clubs, and fraternities may also be peer groups.

In popular usage the term "peer group" is frequently restricted to young people. However, we will use it to identify groups of peers at all ages. Thus, a group of aged individuals who get together for companionship and recreation, a group of army buddies, a neighborhood "*kaffee-klatsch*," and a group of "top brass" at an exclusive metropolitan club are all peer groups.

Peer interaction has been attributed to an instinct for gregariousness, a gang instinct, or some other innate trait or tendency inside the individual. As our previous discussion has emphasized, such interaction today is considered to stem from the same social sources as other types of interaction.

---

[1] See Arnold Gesell and Frances Ilg, *The Child from Five to Ten* (New York: Harper & Row, Inc., 1946), pp. 359–373; and Elizabeth B. Hurlock, *Child Development* (New York: McGraw-Hill Book Co., 1942), p. 226.

[2] James H. S. Bossard, *The Sociology of Child Development* (rev. ed.; New York: Harper & Row, Inc., 1954), p. 526; see also August B. Hollingshead, *Elmtown's Youth* (New York: John Wiley & Sons, Inc., 1949).

[3] William McCormick, *The Boy and His Clubs* (Westwood, N. J.: Fleming H. Revell Co., 1912), as quoted by Bossard, *op. cit.*, p. 527.

[4] Frederic M. Thrasher, *The Gang* (2d rev. ed.; Chicago: The University of Chicago Press, 1936), pp. 54–57.

Peer interaction, of course, involves and is productive of shared definitions. Interaction which has progressed to an intimate peer stage has involved sufficient verbal exchange and feedback, plus individual "mulling things over," to provide those involved with common definitions of the objects, relationships, and situations which are related in any important way to the interaction. The intimacy of the relationship, in fact, contributes to the development of at least some unique definitions and language patterns, the meaning of which would escape the casual observer of the interaction. Special names and expressions are developed by and used exclusively within the group, and serve as a reminder to the participants that they are different from outside others.

VALUE DEFINITIONS

Peer interaction stems in part from the fact that those involved view each other as sharing similar value definitions—biases, prejudices, likes and dislikes, ethnocentrism, etc. Individuals who believe that they do not share many common value definitions about the phenomena related in significant ways to the interaction will find it difficult to develop an intimate relationship. Common value definitions likewise stem from the fact of frequent peer interaction. Those who view each other as equals are predisposed to view each other's value positions with favor. Acceptance is less critical than with those who view each other from a perspective or stance of inferiority or superiority.

Peer interaction is supported by the evaluations applied by the participants. Peer interaction is viewed as a consummatory end in itself rather than as a utilitarian means to an end. Peers get together frequently for the satisfaction obtained from getting together—they enjoy the companionship of each other and provide mutual support and stimulation. Those involved, then, come to realize that they themselves are valued not so much for what they can do for each other in a utilitarian sense, but rather for "what they are." Individuals secure a different type of satis-

The Play Is Not the Thing

The apparent importance of playmates ... suggests that "the play is not the thing" for the child comes to regard himself as a playmate who must share his toys with other children if he is to keep them as playmates. This compels him to see other characters in the playthings besides their immediate attraction to his play impulse and to that of possession. His plaything, as Mead has indicated, becomes a composite object; it is not only that which gives expression to his own impulse but something that keeps him with his cherished friends. Play becomes not merely an enjoyable personal experience—it is also a device whereby the child gains access and acceptance in the world of significant others.

*—Oscar W. Ritchie and Marvin R. Koller.**

faction from peer interaction than they do from, say, economic relationships in which the individual is evaluated in terms of what he can do for the other. The element of reciprocal value exchange is, of course, present in peer interaction, but those involved usually place higher value upon, and receive greater personal satisfaction from, interaction in which one "gives of himself" rather than renders some utilitarian service. Peer interaction is valued because it provides satisfying roles to play.

Since the goal of peer interaction is recreational in nature, it would follow that whatever value is attached to recreation would be generalized to the peer interaction. The value definitions involved, however, go beyond this.

By definition peer interaction involves individuals who define each other as equals. In peer interaction, the participants do not define the situation as one in which they must continually prove themselves to the others involved, or as one in which they must continually provide an expected service for others. In peer interaction,

* Oscar W. Ritchie and Marvin R. Koller, *Sociology of Childhood* (New York: Appleton-Century-Crofts, 1964), p. 203.

Figure 21.1 Peer group activities vary with age and location. The American boys (*above*) are playing basketball in New Mexico; the group of English boys (*opposite page*) is interacting outside a London pub. (Wide World Photos.)

participants can relax in a secure, comfortable relationship and just "be themselves." The shrinking modern family has increased the importance of peer groups for parents as well as children. Married couples associate with other married couples, and old folks frequently associate with old folks.

Peer interaction produces conformity of behavior, as well as providing a foundation for creative activity. The conformity is of a different type, however, than that found in secondary non-peer relationships. Peer conformity is conformity of "cooperation," to use Piaget's term, rather than conformity of "constraint." The personal satisfactions are valued—individuals want to conform; they are not motivated by a belief

that they will be formally penalized or sanctioned if they do not.

The sharing of values within the group and the high evaluation of the interaction *per se* provide a foundation out of which conflict with other groups may be supported. Value conflicts may exist between peer and non-peer groups. The conflict may be intergenerational or intragenerational in nature, and may involve the school, family, church, economic organizations, etc. With peer support members of the group can figuratively—and literally in some cases—"get away with murder." The peer group provides "guilt insurance" by protecting the members of the group with their own code of what is right and wrong.

As Redl has suggested,

"Gang psychology" enables the youngster to enjoy otherwise guilt-loaded or dangerous gratifications without the expense of guilt feelings and fear. It even offers him all the gratifications of "morality" at the same time; pride, moral indignation, the feeling of "being in the right" are still maintained, only they are carefully defined in terms of group code criteria.[5]

Individuals who appear to be out of step with one group may, in fact, be very much in harmony with a different one.

[5] Fritz Redl, "The Psychology of Gang Formation and the Treatment of Juvenile Delinquents," in *The Psychoanalytic Study of the Child*, Vol. I (New York: 1945).

NORM-ROLE DEFINITIONS

Interaction of peers is usually fairly structured interaction, although provisions may be made for considerable ad-libbing. Established norm-role definitions are of the crescive or informal type, having been developed in informal interaction rather than through formal deliberative procedures. Use of formal deliberative processes is greater in the gang than in the clique or play group. Peer membership is voluntary. Peer group roles (positions) are of the achieved type.

Peer groups place a group label upon themselves and consequently make distinctions between the peer group and other groups in which they may or may not hold membership. Awareness of group differences includes awareness of role-norm differences. It is through peer interaction that the young child, vaguely at first and then with some speed, becomes aware of the fact that norm-role definitions which apply to the family group may not or need not apply to his play group. It is from experiences in the family and the play group that he first begins to decide that norm-role definitions are relative to the situation rather than "just there" to be followed.

Learning to play games provides individuals with greater understanding of just how rules and regulations work, are developed, enforced (use of sanctions), evaded, and changed. Individuals, for instance, join or leave the game by particular processes, rather than just "barging in." Involvement in gaming behavior contributes to awareness that rules can be changed and that not everyone plays by the same rules. It may be in peer interaction that children first become aware of the fact that they can do something about changing norm-role definitions, and may have initial success in endeavors to do so.

Game participation may also contribute to greater understanding of the functions of rules (norm-role definitions). Such interaction cannot proceed smoothly unless there are rules upon which there is consensus. One can, of course, "pick up his marbles and go home" when confronted with problems. Peer interaction, however, most likely leads to an awareness that there are rules for life that cannot be avoided by "going home." Such behavior always takes place "on stage." There is no alternative.

Peer interaction also provides some awareness of the fact that conformity to the rules of the game provides greater flexibility or freedom for other types of behavior within the rules. As long as one haggles over the rules, other types of satisfactions are denied, such as playing the game and the creativity involved therein.

Experience within a peer group also leads to an awareness that people can be classified and experienced as *groups,* and that groups can be mutually supportive or non-supportive. It is within the play group that young children be-

---

Norm of Reciprocity

I suggest that a norm of reciprocity, in its universal form, makes two interrelated minimal demands: (1) people should help those who have helped them, and (2) people should not injure those who have helped them.
—Alvin W. Gouldner.*

---

come aware of conflict with their family group and are confronted with making decisions as to which set of norm-role definitions they will honor. Further, they learn that consequences of nonconformity to family norms can be influenced and maybe mitigated with the help and cooperation of peers. Norms of reciprocity may accordingly be established which specify, "I have helped you, now you will help me."

Awareness of these dimensions of interaction acquired in the play group are magnified in gang interaction, with its conflict dimension. In conflict, rules of conflict (combat) involving space, time, and interaction patterns are developed and followed. Norm-role definitions take on greater specificity, and group members are ranked according to some value scheme. At this stage the gang begins to take on characteristics of voluntary associations.

SELF DEFINITIONS

Peer interaction is intimate, first-name interaction involving maximum exposure of private self definitions. Such interaction has a double potential. Peer groups are important reference groups. Positive evaluation of intimate self definitions by others considered to be one's equal can be rewarding and satisfying, and encourages continued acceptance of such definitions even in the face of contrary reflections by others considered to be of lesser importance.

* Alvin W. Gouldner, "The Norm of Reciprocity: A Preliminary Statement," *American Sociological Review,* XXV, No. 2 (April, 1960), 171.

On the same basis, peer rejection is difficult, possibly traumatic. In less intimate interaction, less is invested and there is accordingly less likelihood of important self definitions being threatened. Where much is given, much is expected.

The norms of reciprocity of an intimate relationship involves mutual protection of self-definitions. Characteristics which could be defined by others as being a stigma may be covered up or ignored by mutual agreement, which may be unspoken, but nonetheless serves to avoid exposure of the characteristic to less accepting and potentially threatening others.[6]

Peer interaction provides those involved with information about themselves which is not likely to be secured through non-peer interaction. The ability to relate oneself to others on an intimate basis is an acquired, not a biologically given, phenomenon. Awareness of one's ability to participate in a loving, intimate relationship is learned in interaction. Typically, family interaction provides the initial experiences and awareness of such relationships and of the individual's ability to participate therein. Peer interaction provides the opportunity to expand such interaction, or maybe to compensate for lack of such family relationships.

Family relations, because of such factors as death, divorce, unavailability of a parent or parents, parental inabilities in relating themselves to the child, rejection of the other on the part of parent or child, or any number of other reasons, may be a contributing factor to an intense search on the part of familial members for a peer substitute. Individuals with such experiences, and even those with more normal family experiences, are frequently surprised at the intensity with which such peer relationships can be experienced.

In any such relationships, the individual not only develops skills in peer interaction but also becomes aware of his effectiveness therein. Such self definitions then become involved in subsequent interaction. Success in initial family and peer interaction contributes to subsequent behavior. Failure in family interaction may be compounded by failures in peer interaction or may be compensated for in such relationships, with the peer successes possibly being fed back into the family interaction and contributing to its subsequent success.

In any event, peer interaction provides the individuals involved with important self definitions, which by their intimate nature, become pivotal definitions involved in subsequent behavior.

Interaction in the family and in the peer group provides those involved with an awareness that different interaction experiences provide or contribute to different self definitions. Interaction with certain individuals makes one "feel ten feet high," while interaction with some others makes one feel insignificant.

From such interaction, decisions are reached as to the persons one feels comfortable with and conversely with whom one feels uncomfortable. Further, when two or more individuals decide that they share mutual acceptance, their interaction takes this into account and the interaction then supports and encourages a continuation thereof. Peer interaction is voluntary, and will accordingly be voluntarily discontinued unless it is mutually satisfying.

Awareness of the public evaluation of others who consider an individual to be their peer, serves to generalize this evaluation. Knowing how others who consider him to be their peer are evaluated by the society, provides him with a measure of how he himself is so evaluated. Knowing who treats him as a peer then tells him something about himself.

One of the major consequences or functions of peer interaction is that it provides important dimensions of the self definitions of those involved.

SOCIALIZATION

Peer interaction is, of course, learned behavior which involves the prior socialization of those involved. Such interaction is in itself a sociali-

[6] See Erving Goffman, *Stigma* (Englewood Cliffs, N. J.: Prentice-Hall, Inc., 1963).

zation experience through which many important things are learned. It is usually in the play group that children learn that they may be members of different and in some ways competing groups or interaction systems. Effective interaction involves the application of appropriate labels to those involved so that action appropriate to the situation and the actors can be initiated by all concerned, and so that the behavior of the others involved can be defined to harmonize therewith. As has been suggested, a child may, through peer interaction, learn that the behavior which his parents have directed toward him may be quite different from that which others present to him. A pampered child may have his first experiences in a non-pampering group; a harshly treated child may have contrary experiences of participating in friendly, accepting relationships.

Peer socialization is facilitated in an urbanized society by other agencies such as the school and the church. In school, individuals are grouped according to some criterion of equality, such as age or mental ability. Such action facilitates the development of peer groups within the larger secondary group in that students are required to spend many hours of the day and frequently of the night in close contact with each other. In schools and to a lesser degree in churches, students go through a process of "shuffling" wherein peer groups are developed. It is not surprising that lasting, highly valued relationships originate in this way.[7]

In terms of over-all subsequent behavior, it may well be that what students learn in peer interaction while in the formal educational system may be as important as what they learn in the formal classroom.

Efforts may be made, of course, by educators to involve peer groups in support of the formal program. Bronfenbrenner,[8] for instance, has de-

scribed the method utilized by Russian educators. Rather than start a new class with the instruction, "All sit straight," the teacher says, "Let's see which row can sit the straightest." One of the widely used manuals, *Socialist Competition in the Schools*, indicates that with such an approach:

The children not only try to do everything as well as possible themselves, but also take an evaluative attitude toward those who are undermining the achievement of the row. If similar measures arousing the spirit of competition in the children are systematically applied by experienced teachers in the primary classes, then gradually the children themselves begin to monitor the behavior of their comrades and remind those of them who forget about the rules set by the teacher, who forget what needs to be done and what should not be done. The teacher soon has helpers.

Records are kept for each row from day to day for different types of tasks so that the young children can develop a concept of group excellence. Great charts are kept in all the schools showing the performance of each row unit in every type of activity, together with their total over-all standing. "Who is best?" the charts ask, but the entries are not individuals but social units—rows, and later the "cells" of the communist youth organization. At first it is the teacher who sets the standards, but this pattern is soon replaced with the use of a series of peer monitors for each row, so that the row is evaluated by row members. Row members are further expected to take responsibility to help correct any behavior of other row members which does not conform to group standards.

By the third grade the row monitors are making public evaluations of the performance of their group, and at the beginning of a lesson the row leader may report, "Today Valadya did the wrong problem. Masha didn't write neatly and forgot to underline the right words in her lesson, Alyoshi had a dirty shirt collar." Further the teacher has the children enter into competition with the monitors to see if they can beat the monitor at his own game by criticizing them-

---

[7] See Hollingshead, *op. cit.*, p. 80.

[8] See Urie Bronfenbrenner, "Soviet Methods of Character Education: Some Implications for Research," *Research Supplement to Religious Education,* LVII, No. 4 (July-August, 1962), pp. S–45–61.

High School Peer Groups

In my high school there were two principal gangs. One was made up of the senior boys, the other, quite naturally, the junior boys . If a senior boy's hubcaps were missing the whole senior gang would "frisk" the whole junior gang. Quite ironically both groups had exactly the same number of boys in their membership. At times there was only friendly rivalry between the two peer groups but at times there was conflict. Both of these gangs had a leader. Both likewise had one person who would always be left to take the blame for anything they did which was wrong. Also in each group was one boy who tended to be just a little less anxious for the pranks than were the others. I often heard the boys remark, "Why do we put up with him? He ought to be shafted." But nevertheless he never was.

—From the author's files.

selves. "The results were spectacular: if the monitor was able to talk to only about four or five members of the row, there would be supplementary reports about their own shortcomings from as many as eight to ten pupils."

Bronfenbrenner reports a conversation which he had with three elementary school teachers he met by chance in a restaurant who were curious about the discipline technics used in American schools. After he had given them several examples the teachers asked, "But how do you use the collective?" And when informed that the classroom group was not used in any systematic way, he was asked, "But how do you keep discipline?"

ROLE PLAYING AND ROLE TAKING

Interaction with one's peers has different characteristics and different consequences (functions) than non-peer interaction. Such interaction, for instance, encourages and facilitates escaping or ignoring many restrictions of the larger society.

For children and teenagers such interaction provides some of their first opportunities to govern themselves or to make decisions which directly affect themselves. Great satisfaction may be obtained from being independent (even from defining themselves as being independent) even though at first for only short periods of time. Return to the security of the family following early periods of independence may take on increased significance and flavor.

Play groups, cliques, and gangs frequently seek to supplement their social isolation with physical isolation. They like to get away by themselves, to have secret hiding places, build club houses, or at least go to their rooms by themselves so that their physical isolation confirms their social uniqueness. Peer interaction is consummatory in nature, being defined as a desirable goal in itself. It is not surprising, then, that peers attempt to protect such interaction from control and possible disruption by others. Nor is it surprising that when threatened by others who attempt to impose their own standards upon the group the group of peers closes ranks against them, and develops its own technics and methods of avoiding the adult definitions as well as the adults themselves.

When individuals develop norm-role definitions which are different from those of the family or other larger group, they are faced with making decisions as to which set of definitions to follow in particular situations. It is not uncommon that such decisions are frequently made in favor of the peer group. Rosen's study of the decisions of adolescent Jewish males which involved conflict between adult and peer group norm definitions with reference to religiously related behavior, concluded that on the whole the peer group had greater influence upon the decisions of the boys he studied than did their parents.[9]

Peer groups develop their own norm-role definitions and expect members to conform. Appli-

[9] Bernard C. Rosen, "Conflicting Group Membership: A Study of Parent-Peer Group Cross Pressures," *American Sociological Review*, XX, No. 2 (April, 1955), 155–161.

cation of sanctions is made in efforts to insure such conformity. The family may decide how the child will dress, but the decision of the child as to whether he likes what he wears will be decided as he views himself through the eyes of his peers. "What will the gang (clique, my buddies) think?" is the decision he frequently considers as he decides whether he himself will approve. What is true about his dress is likewise true about his manners, his speech patterns, his relationships with the other sex, and many other matters.

Kirkendall's study of the circumstances associated with teen-age boys' visits to prostitutes provides additional evidence of the strength of peer groups. He found from interviews with college males who recounted their past experiences that the first contacts these boys had with prostitution generally were not a result of a "strong internal sex drive." Sheer physical release was, in fact, one of the least important reasons given as to why they engaged in such activities. Practically none of them had gone to a prostitute alone, but had been accompanied by one or more friends. He concludes that the major reason why such experiences occurred was the desire on the part of the boys to be a part of the group and to participate in the group experiences.

For these boys, going to a prostitute was essentially a male-group activity, and the prostitute was simply a vehicle through which the boys were trying to achieve a group purpose . . . many times boys who go to prostitutes are trying to prove to each other (and to themselves) that they are grown up, are dare-devils, and are worldly-wise and sophisticated.[10]

The social nature of the experience is further indicated by the behavior of the participants after the experience:

After their return, by a process of broad hints and discrete leaks (or sometimes by outright telling) boys not in on the experience are made aware that it oc-

curred. For a few days, the fellows who participated are the center of conversation. Jokes, questions, and perhaps envious comments come their way, and their position among their friends as sophisticated, worldly-wise "men about town" has been established.[11]

It is validation by one's peers which assures young people that they are, in fact, sophisticated men about town.

While peer interaction may deviate from the standards of the larger society, it may also be supportive to society. Peer interaction is, in fact, a two-edged social sword which can produce sharp divisions in a larger group, or can provide strong support. The society which has strong youth groups, with role-norm definitions which support the societal norms, in which peer interaction is experienced as desirable and rewarding, has internal support which greatly strengthens the whole society. Youth camps and youth programs have been established and supported by governments on such grounds. In the United States, youth organizations such as the boy scouts and girl scouts not only formally support the nation, but to the extent that peer interaction is fostered, provide informal support.

Peer interaction, then, may help to provide independence from adult controls, and provide experiences in decision making where conflicting definitions are involved.

Participating in peer groups provides underprivileged members of society with the opportunity to play roles and receive recognition which may otherwise be denied them. Participation in the gang, for instance, provides a chance to play the role of a leader and to make leader decisions. The complex role structure of a gang is identified by Barron as follows:

The organization of the gang usually calls for a leader, an inner circle, the rank and file, and finally the "fringers" or hangers-on. Gang leaders . . . are seldom elected. On the other hand, their elevation is not a matter of force, for the neighborhood bully is seldom the gang leader. . . . The well-organized conflict gangs also may have an officer who may be called

[10] Lester A. Kirkendall, "Circumstances Associated with Teen-age Boys' Use of Prostitution," *Marriage and Family Living*, XXII, No. 2 (May, 1960), 145–149.

[11] *Ibid.*, p. 147.

the war councilor. His task is to set dates and agree on battlegrounds for "rumbles" with enemy groups. He is also the master of war tactics and strategy. . . . Gangs, like other peer groups, also have their custodians of group membership, who are often members who themselves just "shaved in" and who rather quickly become "zealous keepers of the keys." Most of the groups have their "funny boys" whose irresponsible behavior is tolerated because of the humor they can contribute. Virtually every group has its "loudmouthed" member, the show-off or braggart, whose account of anything comes to be discounted by the gang. Then there is the aggressive member, an ambitious personality always reaching out for more territory, always willing to engage in a fight, provided that the others do the fighting. Every gang and most other peer groups have "goats." These are the boys of lower intelligence, slow of wit and frequently combining some special peculiarity of manner, speech or appearance with their subnormalities. They are the members who invariably are apprehended, or who are often sacrificed or used as a decoy by the group.[12]

Experience playing gang roles will invariably influence the subsequent behavior of those involved.

The various types of peer interaction take on increased importance in a society such as the contemporary urban, industrialized American society, in which family interaction involves a comparatively small range of activities. Parents are frequently relatively uninformed and unskilled in matters of style of dress, current favorites among popular songs, latest slang phrases, sports events, dating patterns, etc. Interaction which involves such activities becomes increasingly peer interaction which excludes family interaction. The distance between generations is great in any society since there are always differences in ages and roles. In contemporary society such differences become exaggerated. It is in interaction with peers that important decisions in these areas are made.[13]

The fact that those involved view each other as peers facilitates the role taking involved. Similar prior experiences which have produced "equal" individuals help them to understand each other, and to interpret the behavior of others. Research by the author involving a group of 827 boy scouts found that these boys viewed their peers as being more accurate in the evaluations of respondent goodness than parents, school teachers, or scoutmasters.[14]

Within peer groups, "silent" communication develops. Those involved do not define the situation as one demanding constant communication. Silent pauses are not viewed with alarm. Those involved feel that they know each other well enough that verbal communication may be ceased and picked up at a later stage with those involved having progressed to about the same point in the discussion. Empathic ability is high in peer groups.

SOCIAL CHANGE

Peer interaction is creative to the extent that it permits the development of new self, norm-role, and value definitions. Playing an established role in peer groups permits creativity within the role limitations. Individuals who may not have defined themselves as leaders may be so defined by their peers and given opportunity actually to play leadership roles and consequently to re-evaluate their ability and potential. Our previous discussions have suggested how peer interaction may be productive of new role-norm definitions.

The fact that peer interaction is, at times at least, relatively unstructured means that the group must decide what it will do and how it will do it. Increased leisure time provides opportunity to decide how to use it. Leisure provides not only *freedom from* established norm-role restrictions but also *freedom to do* particular things. The creativity of peer inter-

---

[12] Milton L. Barron, by permission of Alfred A. Knopf, Inc., from *The Juvenile in Delinquent Society* (New York, 1954), pp. 157–158.

[13] See David Riesman, Reuel Denney, and Nathan Glazer, *The Lonely Crowd* (New Haven: Yale University Press, 1950).

[14] Glenn M. Vernon, unpublished paper presented before the Utah Council on Family Relations, March 4, 1960.

action is in the *freedom to do* area, and an "idle peer group" is not necessarily the "devil's workshop." Dorothy Lee raises the question as to whether Americans have developed their creative abilities as fully as possible. Peer interaction in the future will help provide an answer to her question.[15]

Methods by which peer groups can be involved in planned programs of change can be seen in two therapy programs. The Highfields program in New Jersey and the Pinehills delinquency experiments in Utah have utilized peer interaction as a technic of changing delinquent behavior into behavior which conforms more closely to societal standards. Delinquents assigned to the programs by the courts participate with other delinquents (peers) in work programs and in group discussions, in which group-imposed sanctions are utilized to get delinquents to want to change delinquent patterns, and further to provide peer support for non-delinquent behavior. In group discussions with peers it is difficult to deceive others in description of behavior and motivation involved. Release from the group is obtained in two ways: (1) by being sent to the state "reform school" for failure to cooperate with the group or to change behavior, and (2) by convincing the group that delinquent patterns are being replaced by non-delinquent patterns. During the period of participation in the group the boys live at home and continue to participate in school or job activities. Con-

vincing one's peers, who know the "tricks of the trade," of a change when no change has actually taken place is difficult.[16]

A second effort to involve peers in change programs has been taking place in some mental hospitals. At the Utah State Hospital, for instance, patients are permitted and encouraged to participate in group discussions and in group decisions about the behavior of the group and individuals within the group. Decisions as to who gets various types of privileges including passes to leave the ward are made by the group. Decisions as to sanctions used when norm-role definitions are not honored are made by the group. Patients are involved in decisions at the ward, unit, and hospital levels. Involvement in such interaction appears to be an important type of therapy in the treatment of mental patients, especially when contrasted with the custodial type of care which many hospitals provide.[17]

STRATIFICATION

The stratification patterns of the larger society are reflected in the composition of peer groups. Decisions about one's class position are important variables in deciding whom one will define as his equal, and with whom one will establish peer (equal class) relationships. Class factors are operative in important antecedent decisions such as to which school one will go, to which church he will belong, or even whether he will belong to a church at all, and where one will live. Such decisions, of course, set limits upon the groups from which peers select each other.

The class factor operates at the adult level. Club membership reflects class lines, and while all members of any particular club may not establish peer relationships with each other, it is likely that such relationships will develop as club interaction takes place.

Religious Creativity

One would hardly expect a group of underprivileged boys to invent a glorious religion; but invent they will if the established churches pass them by.

                                        —J. Milton Yinger.*

---

* J. Milton Yinger, *Sociology Looks at Religion* (New York: The Macmillan Co., 1963), p. 27.

[15] Dorothy Lee, *Freedom and Culture* (Englewood Cliffs, N. J.: Prentice-Hall, Inc., 1959), pp. 53–58.

[16] LaMar T. Empey and Jerome Rabow, "Experiment in Delinquency Rehabilitation," *American Sociological Review*, XXVI, No. 5 (October, 1961), 679–696.

[17] See Eugene J. Faux, "Peer Expectation and Confrontation," *Provo Papers* (Provo, Utah: Utah State Hospital; Fall, 1962), pp. 9–18.

Even the extent of peer interaction is related to class position, with research indicating that the number of close friends, or those with whom one establishes peer relationships, increases as class position increases.[18]

Peer interaction is also involved in the process of upward mobility. The class position of a young child is essentially a family function. However, in an open-class society, the terminal position of individuals includes achieved as well as ascribed variables. It is, in fact, a part of the "American dream" that an individual can move above his original family position, and there are those who confirm the potential by actually doing so. In the process of upward mobility, peer interaction can be an important factor. This possibility is expressed in the popular cliché that "knowing the right people" helps. In reality the reciprocal aspect is equally important—being known by the right people. If we add to this, "and being accepted as an equal," we can see how peer relationships can be involved in upward mobility.

Class factors are important in gang behavior. Gangs are essentially a lower-class phenomenon, and are in effect a teen-age expression of the larger conflict of the class with society.

PRIMARY–SECONDARY INTERACTION

A frequent characteristic of the peer relationship is its primary nature. Our whole previous discussion of primary relationships applies to and supplements the discussion in this chapter. Involvement in peer interaction is an important means of counter-balancing (not necessarily escaping) the anonymity and impersonality of secondary relationships. Satisfying peer relationships may be sufficiently rewarding that the impersonal secondary experiences need not be defined as undesirable. If peer interaction is sufficiently rewarding, secondary relationships may in a complementary manner be experienced as desirable. The alienation of such relationships

[18] Joseph A. Kahl, *The American Class Structure* (New York: Holt, Rinehart and Winston, Inc., 1957), pp. 137–138.

need not necessarily be evaluated negatively.

Those without satisfying peer relationships most likely define and experience their secondary relationships quite differently.

There are also the limiting factors of time and space. In an urban setting where thousands may interact hourly, it would seem to be physically impossible to establish a primary intimate relationship with all. While it is no doubt true that one may "love his fellowmen," it is likewise true that the types of relationships he has with his peers will be quite different from those with his non-peers.

SUMMARY

Peer interaction, such as that found in play groups, cliques, and gangs is highly valued, voluntary behavior frequently of the primary type and defined by those involved as an end in itself. It is also a socialization experience, which takes on significance from the fact that it involves interaction of equals. Peer interaction frequently develops in conjunction with more formal experiences in schools and churches. While this voluntary interaction is frequently relatively unstructured, peer groups do govern their own behavior by establishing norm-role definitions. Gang interaction is the most highly structured.

In establishing their own "ground rules" peers develop awareness of how norm-role definitions are developed and enforced, and of the fact that they are relative to the situation. It is in peer interaction that initial efforts to play certain roles, such as leadership roles, are frequently made. Peers frequently attempt to isolate themselves physically and/or socially from the larger society.

The relative equality involved in peer interaction facilitates role taking and involves peers as significant others in the development of self definitions. Being of approximately equal class level, peers provide mutual support in mobility efforts. Peer influences have been successfully used in efforts to change delinquents.

Peer relationships are not necessarily any more important than other relationships, but do provide a particular type of experience which fits into a large configuration of interaction.

QUESTIONS

1. What kind of things does one learn from peer interaction?
2. What kind of sanctions do you use in interaction with your peers to try to get them to do what you think they should do?
3. Provide a sociological explanation for the fact that student cliques develop on all college campuses.
4. If there is a conflict between peer and faculty expectations on your campus, under what circumstances would you give preference to peer expectations? Faculty expectations?
5. How is social class related to peer interaction?
6. How is the discussion about peer groups in this chapter related to the previous discussion of primary groups?
7. Provide an illustration of how you have accurately anticipated (role taking) the behavior of one of your close friends.
8. Explain the statement that in peer interaction individuals have both *freedom from* and *freedom to.*
9. How does a clique to which you belong keep outsiders outside? What are your technics of exclusion?
10. Identify the group with which you spend most of your free time. What do you get out of the association?

PROJECT

Identify five individuals whom you consider to be your closest friends. List the characteristics you share with them, such as recreational interests, political interests, etc.

SUGGESTED READING

BOSSARD, JAMES H. S. *The Sociology of Child Development.* Rev. ed. New York: Harper & Row, Inc., 1949.

BRITTAIN, CLAY V. "Adolescent Choices and Parent-Peer Cross Pressures," *American Sociological Review,* XXVIII, No. 3 (June, 1963), 385–391.

COLEMAN, JAMES S. *The Adolescent Society.* New York: The Free Press of Glencoe, 1961.

EMPEY, LaMAR T., and JEROME RABOW. "The Provo Experiment in Delinquency Rehabilitation," *American Sociological Review,* XXVI, No. 5 (October, 1961), 679–695.

EPPERSON, DAVID C. "A Re-Assessment of Indices of Parental Influence in the Adolescent Society," *American Sociological Review,* XXIX, No. 1 (February, 1946), 93–96.

HOLLINGSHEAD, AUGUST B. *Elmtown's Youth.* New York: John Wiley & Sons, Inc., 1949.

MINNIS, MHYRA S. "Cleavage in Women's Organizations: A Reflection of the Social Structure of a City," *American Sociological Review,* XVIII, No. 1 (February, 1953), pp. 47–53.

PIAGET, JEAN. *The Moral Judgment of the Child.* Translated by MARJORIE GABIN. New York: Harcourt, Brace & World, Inc., 1932.

REMMERS, H. H., and D. H. RADLER. *The American Teenager.* Indianapolis: The Bobbs-Merrill Co., Inc., 1957.

THRASHER, FREDERIC M. *The Gang.* 2d rev. ed. Chicago: The University of Chicago Press, 1936.

22

Family

The fact that some type of family is found in all known societies has been interpreted as proof that there must be biologically given forces or drives which account for this. The conclusion does not necessarily follow from the evidence. Can you provide an alternate explanation which harmonizes more closely with the sociological perspective?

INTRODUCTION

Family interaction is interaction between individuals:

1. Who are related by birth, marriage, or adoption,

2. Who consider themselves (define themselves) as constituting a family group, and as being subject to family norm-role definitions of their group, whatever they may be,

3. Who engage in interaction sufficient to support this family definition.

Family interaction usually occurs between individuals who share a common living facility, although this is not an essential element for those who consider themselves to be a family. Students at college, for instance, usually define themselves as being members of their family, even though they live in the college dorm.

Three types of interaction are subsumed under the more inclusive "family" label: (1) husband–wife relationships, (2) parent–child relationships, and (3) sibling relationships. More than one generation of parent–child relationships, or what Americans would call grandparent–parent–child relationships, may be involved.

Although there is usually a biological relationship between family members, this is not a necessary condition. It is not biology which establishes a family but social definitions. Parents and their offspring, for instance, who are not aware of the biological relationship between them do not consider themselves to be a family. To interact as family members, family-identifying labels must be applied to those involved. Likewise, in the case of adoption, participation in legal rites of passage may be viewed as sufficient to establish a family relationship—sufficient to define those involved as though a biological relationship did exist. Legal action may further be viewed as sufficient to negate a biological relationship, at least for certain purposes, so that those involved are no longer considered to be, nor consider themselves to be, participants in a family relationship.

Just exactly who is included when one uses the label "family" varies from one group to another, and within one group different types of families can be identified. Those discussed here are as follows:

Nuclear (core) or conjugal family = husband and wife and their children if any.

Extended or consanguine family = husband and wife and their children plus one or more other persons related to these by biological descent.

Family of orientation = family into which the individual is born.

Family of procreation = family established by marriage ceremony.

Most individuals have experience in both a family of orientation and a family of procreation, with the relationships between these two families varying considerably as other social conditions vary. Either of these two types of families may likewise be nuclear or extended.

Death and the System

With high mortality rates, elaborate kinship systems are more likely to be ideal than actual, for the simple reason that there is a high probability that death will have left many nominal kinship positions unfilled. The implication of this circumstantial argument is that if kinship role requirements are really mandatory, and not simply contingent on the availability of role-players, additional duties will devolve on substitute kinsmen.

—Wilbert E. Moore.*

---

* Wilbert E. Moore, *Social Change* (Englewood Cliffs, N. J.: Prentice-Hall, Inc., 1963), pp. 14–15.

Family interaction, of course, is only one type of interaction occurring in any society. It is always but one part of a larger socio-cultural milieu. Our concern in this chapter is to identify some of the distinguishing characteristics of family interaction and the related social factors.

VALUE DEFINITIONS

Value definitions are, of course, extensively interwoven into family interaction. It could not be otherwise at the human level. A major definition, one, in fact, which is frequently accepted without question, is that the biological facts of parentage should establish grounds for a family relationship. Most societies believe that a different relationship *should* obtain between biological parents and child and between those not so related. Thus, an extensive set of reciprocal norm-role definitions are ascribed to those involved in such a relationship. Parents are supposed to "feel" and behave differently toward their own biological offspring than toward others. It is frequently assumed that such relationships are "natural" or biologically given. When contrary relationships do develop, they are viewed as abnormal or queer, and it is suggested that something is wrong with the "individuals" rather than with the social relationship. Even when comparable relationships exist between adopted parents and children, they are viewed as being somehow extraordinary or as exceptions to the rule.

With this set of norm-role definitions operating, parent–child relationships frequently do turn out to be different from adult–child relationships, which, of course, then provides confirmatory evidence that such relationships *really should* obtain, or even that the relationship is biologically given. The norm-role definitions which bind these individuals together are viewed as being more than just man-made. They are inherently good—or most likely God-given.

Value definitions can be applied to the family relationship *per se*, and to various types of possible and/or actual relationships as well as to any particular aspects of the relationship. Americans apparently value the marriage relationship highly, as evidenced by the fact that a higher percentage of the population is married than was true of any previous time. The percentage is also higher than that for any other western nation. Even though the divorce rate is high, the great majority of those who do terminate a particular marriage return for a second, third, or fourth (or more) try. Individuals may lose faith in a particular marriage, but not in marriage *per se*.

There have been societies in which the marriage relationship has been condemned, for example, the Shakers in early America; there have been others in which it has been tolerated, for example, among the early Christians, as is suggested by the statement of St. Paul: "But I say to the unmarried and to widows, it is good for them if they abide even as I. But if they have not continency, let them marry: for it is better to marry than to burn."[1] Virginity, asceticism, and celibacy were according to these standards valued above marriage.

American evaluation of the permanency of particular marriage relationships is changing. While a major family value definition is that a marriage *should be* a permanent (at least until death) relationship, increasingly the termination of a marriage has gained acceptance, and divorced individuals have been subjected to decreasing sanctions, including negative definitions. In colonial America divorced females were severely sanctioned; today, however, the divorced individual is accepted by society, many ministers will perform a marriage ceremony involving a divorced individual, and the divorced individual, male or female, actually has a greater chance of getting married again than has the single counterpart of the same age.[2]

The value, economic and otherwise, of a large family has for several reasons been decreasing. Availability of birth control information and devices and increasing acceptance of them have permitted the value definition to be realized.

Since World War II, however, the birth rate has increased, but we are as yet uncertain as to just what value definitions are related to this change.

The primary nature of the family relationship is usually highly prized, even in those families where it is not realized. Those who are unable to experience such a family relationship usually define themselves (and are so defined by society) as being deprived and unfortunate. In the case of the husband–wife relationship the previously discussed involvement in whole-personality interaction is augmented by sexual interaction, which is itself highly valued, thus creating in this relationship very extensive personal involvement.

The value of the extended family relationship is suggested by Jitodai's [3] finding that among the Detroiters whom he studied, 50 per cent interacted weekly with relatives, as contrasted with 32 per cent with neighbors, 28 per cent with friends, and 13 per cent with co-workers.

Family experience and identification are, in fact, so salient for most individuals that they influence and frequently determine religious membership, political party membership, and voting practices.

Value definitions are, of course, related to norm-role definitions, which we will discuss in a moment, and are reflected in other behavior patterns discussed throughout this chapter.

American marriage practices also mirror the high value placed upon individualism in the larger society. Choice of marriage partners is viewed as an individual matter, although the society is less willing to permit individual termination. Parents, particularly in the middle class, train their children to "be individuals," in fact, American families have been described as "child-centered."

NORM-ROLE DEFINITIONS

Every society of which we have records has regulated family interaction. Particular regulations are always relative to the situation, and

---

[1] I Cor. 7:8–9.
[2] Paul H. Landis, "Sequential Marriage," *Journal of Home Economics*, XLII, No. 8 (October, 1950), 625–628.

[3] Ted T. Jitodai, "Migration and Kinship Contacts," *Pacific Sociological Review*, VI, No. 2 (Fall, 1962), 49–55.

differing societal conditions have produced considerable variation in marriage norm-role definitions.

Differences in some of the most frequently established patterns are identified below.

Power Structure

Patriarchal—the husband-father (pater) makes most of the important family decisions. This was the most frequent pattern in colonial America, with the relationship being supported by legal definitions which prohibited females from owning property, entering certain occupations and schools, voting, or going into debt. Support was also provided by the religious definitions promulgated by male clergymen, which specified that the male god they worshipped recognized the inferiority of females and that the patriarchal family patterns thus had supernatural support. Under such norm-role definitions certain decisions were nonetheless left to the wife, who actually exerted considerable influence upon the family.

Matriarchal—the mother-wife (mater) makes most of the important family decisions. Such relationships in particular families have probably always existed, even when formal norm-role definitions were to the contrary. However, societies such as the Trobriand Islanders of northeastern New Guinea have standardized such power relationships as the normal accepted pattern.

Equalitarian—husband and wife share somewhat equally in decision making. Such an arrangement is viewed by contemporary Americans, particularly those in the early stages of marriage, as the most desirable. Most unmarried college students plan to establish such a relationship although the relationship will in most cases be at least somewhat patriarchal. In cases, for instance, calling for a decision to favor either the husband's or the wife's occupation, it is to the husband that preference is usually given.

To these types might be added the "child-centered" family, in which the child or children are defined as being of such importance that decisions are usually made to favor their position. It has been suggested that many American families in the 1950–1960's tended to be this type.

Mate Selection

Endogamous definitions—mates must be selected from within a particular group. American norm-role definitions specify, for instance, that mates should be selected from within the same social class, the same religious group, and the same racial group. Even in those states which do not legally prohibit Negro-white marriages, less than 5 per cent of the Negroes marry outside their racial group.[4] Studies have found that if American families are endogamous with reference to such factors as race, class, and religion, the likelihood increases that the marriage will not terminate in divorce (the durability of the marriage is increased).

Matriarchal Family Patterns

A housewife from a particular London suburb describes her day as follows:

"After breakfast I bathe the baby and sweep the kitchen and wash up. Then I go up the road shopping with Mum, Greta (one of this wife's married sisters) and the three children. After dinner I clean up and then round about two o'clock I go out for a walk if it's fine with Mum, Greta and the children. I come back at about a quarter to four to be in time for John when he gets back from school. He calls in at Mum's on his way home to see if I'm there. This is an ordinary day. If anything goes wrong, and I'm in any trouble, I always go round to Mum's."

—Peter Willmot and
Michael Young.*

---

* Peter Willmott and Michael Young, *Family and Class in a London Suburb* (London: Routledge and Kegan Paul, 1960), p. 30.

4 Ruth Shonle Cavan, *The American Family* (3d ed.; New York: Thomas Y. Crowell Co., 1963), pp. 208–209.

Exogamous definitions—mates must be selected from outside a particular group. Most societies, if not all, strongly disapprove of homosexual "marriages." Marriages within the "family" are also strongly disapproved, even though exceptions have been made in particular circumstances, as in the case of royalty. Such marital prohibitions are closely related to the sexual prohibition popularly known as the "incest taboo," which appears to be one of the most universally adopted regulations; nonetheless, exceptions have been provided, as in the case of the Thonga of Africa where the warrior husbands were expected to have intercourse with their daughters prior to going into battle. The act was viewed as a ritual, however, rather than as the usual sexual union. Further, there is no universal agreement as to the inclusiveness of the term "family." Marriage to half-siblings and to first cousins is prohibited by law in 29 states, and marriage between stepparents and stepchildren is prohibited in 23 states.[5]

Lineage

These definitions specify whether the child will be given the family name of the father or the mother, and provide for a set of duties and responsibilities, such as inheritance or providing help in times of crisis. The norm definitions may apply to a small or large group of relatives.

Patrilineal norms—the wife assumes the name of her husband and the children are "of his line."

Matrilineal norms—same as patrilineal, but centered around the wife.

Bilineal norms—both parents are involved. In terms of name ascription, the American pattern is patrilineal, but in terms of inheritance and relative obligations the pattern is bilineal.

Residential Patterns

Patrilocal—the newly married couple typically live with the family group of the husband. The Hindus in India have followed such a pattern, and the early American practice of the son receiving the "south forty acres" from his father and establishing his family of procreation there would fall somewhat into this category.

Matrilocal—the couple live with the parents of the wife, as did the Hopi Indians.

Neolocal or independent—the newly married establish their new or independent place of residence. Most Americans today define this as the preferred pattern, and those who do live with either set of in-laws usually hope that it will be only a temporary arrangement.

Number of Mates

Monogamy—each individual may have but one mate at one time. This, of course, is the accepted practice in the United States today. However, with a high divorce and remarriage rate a segment of the population actually experiences "sequential polygamy" or living with more than one mate—but in a sequence rather than at one time. Landis suggests that the percentage of the population following this pattern is approximately 15–20 per cent.[6]

Polygamy—the marriage involves plural mates. Any of the following patterns then, may properly be called polygamy.

In *polygyny*, the husband has more than one wife at a time. The early Mormons endorsed and a small percentage practiced this form of marriage. Although condemned by the Mormon Church and the state today, there are still a few who continue the practice.[7] *Sororal polygyny* is a particular form in which the norm defini-

---

[5] Clifford Kirkpatrick, *The Family* (2nd ed.; New York: The Ronald Press Co., 1963), p. 422. For a discussion of brother-sister and father-daughter marriages, see Russell Middleton, "Brother-Sister and Father-Daughter Marriage in Ancient Egypt," *American Sociological Review*, XXVII, No. 5 (October, 1962), 603–611.

[6] Landis, *op. cit.*, p. 628.
[7] For information relative to current definitions of this practice, see John R. Christiansen, "Contemporary Mormons' Attitudes Toward Polygynous Practices," *Marriage and Family Living*, XXV, No. 2 (May, 1963), 167–170.

tions specify that upon the death of a wife, her husband is expected to marry her sister.

In *polyandry,* the wife has more than one husband at a time. Levirate or "fraternal polyandry" norm definitions specify that upon the death of a husband, his brothers are expected to marry the widow and assume responsibility for her and the children. This practice was endorsed by the ancient Hebrews. Polyandry is a rare practice. Among the Marquesans of the South Pacific women of high status were permitted to take a number of unrelated husbands. In Tibet, plural husbands, usually brothers, were also found. The Todas, a tribe in India, practice female infanticide (killing of female infants) and permitted polyandry for the remaining females. The practice may be associated with conditions of economic deprivation or with certain types of occupation such as herding which required men to be away from home for long periods of time.

In *group marriage,* a group of males and a group of females all share reciprocal husband–wife relationships. This is a logical third type of polygamy but there is little evidence that it has been practiced extensively. The Community Perfectionists (1848–1876) of Oneida, New York, did follow a pattern in which each adult was given the right to have sexual relations with any adult member of the opposite sex. The basic family unit consisted of mother, children, and current sexual companion, and the sexual communism did not involve complete group marriage.[8]

An analysis by Murdock[9] of the available information about 250 societies provided the distribution of norm-role definitions shown in the tabulation in the next column.

Many factors are, of course, involved in development of and acceptance of any particular pattern. Value definitions relative thereto are NER as are all value definitions and are relative

	Number of Societies Approving	Per Cent
Monogamous	43	17.2
Polygynous	193	77.2
Polyandrous	2	.8
Group marriage	0	.0
No data	12	4.8
	250	100.0

to the situation. Scientific decisions cannot be reached as to the superiority of one type over any other. Neither do we have any conclusive evidence that there is an inevitable evolution from one type to another. Theories have been developed which viewed monogamy as the highest type and viewed it as evolving from inferior types such as group marriage–polygynous–polyandrous.

Duration of Marriage Contract

Temporary duration. A type of temporary marriage is referred to as trial marriage. Serious recommendations have, from time to time, been provided by individuals in America that a trial marriage would be desirable, in which the couple live as man and wife during a trial period and would be free to terminate the marriage if they so desired. Elsie Clews Parsons, before World War I, Melvin M. Knight in 1924, and Judge Ben B. Lindsey of Denver have supported and encouraged acceptance of such a plan. Acceptance of divorce and annulment practices involves endorsement of a temporary marriage pattern, in which the marriage can be terminated when specified requirements are met.

Lifetime or permanent duration. Many Americans define this as the most desirable pattern, and strive to realize it in their own marriages. Many do not, of course, realize this goal. As viewed by the Roman Catholic Church, "approved" marriages are lifetime agreements, and even though a civil divorce may be secured by a particular couple, in the eyes of the church they are still man and wife, and consequently not at liberty to contract a subsequent marriage. According to Roman Catholic teaching, such a marriage can be broken only by death.

[8] See Pierrepont Noyes, *My Father's House, an Oneida Boyhood* (New York: Holt, Rinehart and Winston, Inc., 1937), pp. 8–10.

[9] George P. Murdock, *Social Structure* (New York: The Macmillan Co., 1949), p. 28.

Eternal marriage. The Mormon Church defines a marriage which meets church regulations, including being married in a Mormon temple, as a contract to be in force "for time and all eternity," and views the marriage relationship then as one which will continue beyond the grave.

Other Expectations

An extensive system of duties, responsibilities, and privileges is involved in any family relationship. In a consanguine relationship, such relationships may become very complex. Some definitions with which the American family is familiar are as follows:

1. Rights of spousal sexual access. Refusal to grant sexual privileges is frequently accepted as adequate grounds for marriage termination.

2. Financial responsibility of husband for support of family. This obligation is tempered today with the increased earning power of the wife, and there have, in fact, been divorce cases in which it has been the wife who has been instructed to pay alimony to her divorced husband. The interinstitutional aspect of family interaction is shown here, in that the male economic role is also a family role. The male frequently is judged as a family man, on the basis of how he performs his economic role.

3. Care of the aged, or the financial responsibility of children for support and care of parents, tempered again with increased assignment of responsibility to society—state or nation.

4. Married couples are expected to have children, at least when they are mutually desired. Refusal to have children may be accepted as grounds for marriage termination.

5. Required legal procedures (rites of passage) before marital status can be assumed or terminated.

6. Family responsibility in times of crisis, with the responsibility extending into the consanguine area. At times of death or financial crisis the members of the family are expected to "rally around" and provide at least "moral support" if not more substantial support.

7. Marriage is expected to be founded upon and continued upon "love." To Americans a marriage without love is a marriage in name only.

As yet the seriously talked about possibility that test tube babies may be more than fanciful speculations has produced no serious efforts to develop value and norm definitions to handle such situations. Only in fiction, such as *Brave New World,* has this been done.

SELF DEFINITIONS

For most individuals the family group is an important reference group involved in the development of self definitions. A family name

---

Who Owns Your Body?

If we do not freely control the manner in which we use our bodies—and sexual activities are a prime area of dispute—then the question must be raised: "Who does own the bodies of citizens in a secular democracy?" To the extent in which sexual and other bodily activities are regulated by law, it must be concluded that the state owns (i.e., controls), at least in part, a person's body. There is nothing startling about this, for the state also owns a part of our earnings, through income and sales taxes; and it also controls our social conduct in a quite pervasive and general way, by means of laws and social customs.

—Thomas S. Szasz.*

---

* Thomas S. Szasz, "The Ethics of Birth Control, OR: Who Owns Your Body?" *The Humanist,* XX, No. 6 (1960), 334.

clearly ties the family members, conjugal and consanguine, together as one group and serves as a constant reminder of the family relationship to all concerned. The marriage ceremony bestows upon the bride a new name—a family name. The given name, of course, distinguishes a particular individual from other family members. Whatever fame or shame society associates with the family is generalized to individual members thereof, tempered, of course, with any relevant individual factors. For many, the family identity is an identity to be cherished and protected. Family honor is valued.

It is through family interaction that most individuals acquire their first vague self definitions. As interaction continues, and as the child acquires facility in symbol use, the labels used to identify him take on increased importance to him. Most likely his first evaluations of himself, as an object of which others approve or disapprove, are acquired through family interaction, with these self definitions providing the foundation through which subsequent self definitions are interpreted. Evidence concerning children who have experienced no or limited loving relationships suggests that without such experiences individuals are developed with behavior patterns markedly different from those we would consider to be normal. In fact, such experiences appear to be related to the likelihood of the child's remaining alive. There is much that we do not know in this area, however.

Since family interaction is primary interaction in which one's whole personality is involved, the experience plays an important role in the confirmation or rejection of self definitions acquired through non-family interaction. Conflicts may, of course, develop between the family group identity and such groups as peer groups, and individuals learn to shift self definitions to apply to the different types of interaction in which they participate.

Family interaction has important consequences for the self definitions of all participants. The acquisition of important self definitions is a parent as well as a child phenomenon. Parents find out important things about what kind of parents they are by interpreting the behavior of their children. As children mature and move into non-family interaction, approval and disapproval attributed to them are also generalized to the parents. When son John makes a home run, or the honor roll at school, society may reach conclusions about son and parent alike. The parents may, in fact, be more sensitive to such definitions than the son. Those who share a common family name share common social evaluations.

The family also serves an important editing function for information which is conveyed to non-family individuals. Family members usually define the relationship as one in which they should stick together, or in which socially unacceptable characteristics are minimized in their public aspects, and corresponding acceptable characteristics are maximized. Stigma management is an important family procedure which, of course, has an impact upon self definitions.

It is, in fact, within the family group that many Americans learn to take a "group first—individual second" perspective. The individualist ideology which permeates the American society, however, is reflected in typical statements such as, "I have a family," and "I have a sister," as though the family (and sister) were the property of the individual, rather than the shared identity of all. Among the Wintu Indians, the expression would be, "I am sistered," or "I live with my sister." [10]

Sexual behavior is, of course, universal, and in no society is sexual behavior exclusively family behavior. However, it is within the family context that many individuals reach important decisions as to their sexual abilities—acquire "sexual self definitions." In a society which highly values sexual vitality and performance, the family sexual experiences can contribute to over-all self satisfaction or dissatisfaction. Husbands and wives who facilitate the acquisition of definitions of sexual adequacy or maybe sexual sophistication on the part of their spouses, contribute to enhanced self definitions. Decisions as to sexual inadequacy can be generalized to other

[10] See Dorothy Lee, *Freedom and Culture* (Englewood Cliffs, N. J.: Prentice-Hall, Inc., 1959), p. 8.

self definitions. To decide that sexually one is a failure, can have strong impact upon other self identities. Much more than mere physical sensations are involved in sexual interaction.

The American norm definition that the establishment of a love relationship is a major criterion of mate selection has important ramifications as far as self definitions are concerned. Indirectly at least, this indicates that a major goal of establishing a family relationship is self enhancement, or the securing of emotional, including sexual, security. Individuals select as friends those who tend to maximize their self definitions, and from his group of friends one selects as a marriage partner an individual who, he believes, serves this function better than others in the group.

We "fall" or grow in love with those with whom we feel comfortable, or with those whom we idolize and feel unworthy to possess. This means, then, that if marriage decisions are made between such individuals (each idolizing the other), acceptance by such an idolized individual as a marriage partner results in increased self evaluation.

Role Conflict

The problem lay buried, unspoken, for many years in the minds of American women. It was a strange stirring, a sense of dissatisfaction, a yearning that women suffered in the middle of the twentieth century in the United States. Each suburban wife struggled with it alone. As she made the beds, shopped for groceries, matched slipcover material, ate peanut butter sandwiches with her children, chauffeured Cub Scouts and Brownies, lay beside her husband at night—she was afraid to ask even of herself the silent question—"Is this all?"

—Betty Friedan.*

---

* Betty Friedan, *The Feminine Mystique* (New York: W. W. Norton & Co., Inc. Copyright © 1963 by Betty Friedan. Reprinted by permission.

American emphasis upon the establishing of a loving relationship as the major criterion of marriage selection is not by any means a universal one. In fact, in some societies such a pattern would be defined as deviant or abnormal. Not that loving relationships are frowned upon, but using them as the foundation for establishing a marriage relationship hoped to be permanent is viewed with skepticism. Indeed, extramarital loving relationships may be highly valued. In such societies economic, political, power, or religious factors may be given priority as mate selection criteria.

SOCIALIZATION

For most neonates socialization begins in the family, and most societies specify that this is as it should be. In exceptional cases, nurseries or orphanages do the initial socializing, but family interaction is by far the preferred type. This, then, is one of the major functions of family interaction—the socialization of the young. A major function of the family is culture transmission.

Since family interaction usually antedates nonfamily interaction, it is easy to understand how established family behavior patterns will inevitably be involved in subsequent behavior, and why many have maintained that if given control of the young child during the formative years, say from birth to eight years of age, they will have established their adult patterns. "As the twig is bent, so grows the tree." Such statements are somewhat misleading. Behavior is constantly changing, within the limits of past learning experiences. It would appear that almost any type of change could be effected—given adequate control of the social experiences of the individual, including the type of confirmatory behavior which reference groups and significant others direct toward him. Change must, of course, always develop out of established patterns. But there is nothing irrevocable in early patterns. The dramatic (to some, frightening) changes which controlled experiences were able to produce in the American prisoners of war during the Korean War offer dramatic illustration of such changes.[11]

In family socialization the child is not just a passive recipient. He is an active member of the interaction team. Whatever past experiences he has had will, where relevant, be brought to bear upon the training his parents attempt to give him. Parents are, in fact, frequently frustrated in their efforts to get their children to conform to nice (i.e., parental) standards.

As our past discussions have indicated, family socialization includes both conscious and unconscious types of learning. Parents frequently teach their children things they did not intend to. Parental prejudices are frequently transmitted in just such ways.

Parental socialization involves more than verbal exchange. Parents also provide role models for the child to imitate. Watching his dad play his role as father, husband, breadwinner, and citizen provides Junior with a model as to how these roles should be played. Watching their mother play her roles provides the children, male and female alike, with indicators as to how mothers, wives—and possibly PTA members—are "supposed to behave." Older brothers and sisters, as well as other relatives, may also serve as models after which behavior may be patterned. The boy reared in a fatherless home may have problems learning how to play the male role in his society, without a male model around from whom he can learn many details through the innumerable exchanges which take place between father and son. A child's preparation for his own marital interaction starts at the time of birth, and continues as he progresses through his own family of orientation experiences.

ROLE PLAYING AND ROLE TAKING

Enacting the family norm-role definitions, or engaging in family interaction, has important consequences for the individuals directly involved and for society at large. Some of these have already been discussed. An additional con-

sequence follows from the fact that the husband–wife role definitions specify reciprocal sexual access, thus encouraging obtaining of sexual satisfactions (sensual) and reproduction. Although reproduction can and does take place outside the family, it is within-family procreation that is most widely endorsed and practiced. Further, most societies would prefer that non-approved or illegitimate parents get married so that a family name and family interaction can subsequently be related to the biologically related trio.

It would, however, be erroneous to suggest that the major function of sexual intercourse is reproduction. Increasingly Americans have emphasized the pleasure–emotional security aspect of sexual behavior, as an important consequence of such behavior, and as a desirable goal in itself. Sexual behavior can, of course, be interpreted in any number of different ways, and there are those who maintain that the only *proper* or *legitimate* (according to some set of value definitions, possibly religious in nature) reason for having sexual relations is reproduction. The Roman Catholic church endorses such an interpretation. The most common interpretation is suggested by a serious discussion of sexual behavior in a professional journal which carries the title "Sex as Play." [12] Only one out of approximately every thousand experiences of intercourse results in conception.[13] And most premarital relations have a definite anti-conception orientation. In other societies, however, a premarital pregnancy may be viewed as a prerequisite for marriage or as proof of marriageability.

The lack of reproduction is also reflected in the studies of abortion in the United States which indicate that the young married female is the most frequent patron of the abortionist and that 80 per cent of premarital and 17 per cent of marital pregnancies are terminated by abortion.[14]

---

[11] See E. H. Schein, "The Chinese Indoctrination Program for Prisoners of War," *Psychiatry*, No. 2 (May, 1956), 149–172.

[12] Nelson Foote, "Sex as Play," *Social Problems*, I, No. 4 (1954), 159–163.

[13] Alfred C. Kinsey *et al.*, *Sexual Behavior of the Human Female* (Philadelphia: W. B. Saunders Co., 1953), p. 327.

[14] Paul H. Gebhard *et al.*, *Pregnancy, Birth and Abortion* (New York: Harper & Row, Inc., 1958).

Figure 22.1 Family socialization, in which one may learn about bicycles, also teaches him something about himself. (Wide World Photos.)

It is usually in family interaction that individuals acquire their first experiences of giving and receiving love. Much of the language of love is a language of gestures. Learning to love involves learning how to interpret the gestures and other physical contacts of others. Individuals who, through family loving experiences, have not learned to express their love may find themselves handicapped when they enter their own family of procreation.

Family interaction is, of course, a dynamic process, founded in established norm-role definitions but developing far beyond these. The extensive intimate involvement of family members in the interaction provides a situation where role-taking ability can be maximized. Family members know so much about each other that interaction can take into account unique characteristics which are overlooked in not-so-intimate contacts. Where much is given, however, much is expected, and failure to take these into account in the family situation can be viewed with alarm by those who thus are "slighted."

Family interaction involves some of the critical incidents or critical decisions of many. The decision to unite two individuals in a family relationship is one of the most crucial decisions made. Once such a decision is made, its impact is radiated throughout most of the subsequent behavior of the individuals involved. Occupational success of the husband is related to the wife he has, as was shown in the *Fortune* study of junior executives which found that 20 per cent of junior executives of one large company who were viewed as personally qualified to be advanced to a senior executive position were denied promotion on the basis of the fact that they had a wife who was viewed as a deterrent.[15]

Likewise, the divorce decision when made is one of the critical decisions of a lifetime. Family interaction has no guarantee of smooth sailing and marriage relationships are terminated by those involved when interaction reaches what is defined by them as the necessary conditions. Societal approval may be granted if the formal stipulations are met. Individual separation or desertion may take place without societal approval.

Marriage relationships follow discernible patterns. Some following the formal ceremony develop increasing definitions of satisfying rewarding involvement so that the primary nature of the relationship gradually increases. Major trends may, of course, include temporary fluctuations as those involved move or perhaps bounce

from peaks to low points, but all in a general direction. Other interaction sequences proceed in the other direction in which one or both find that the expectations of the marriage relationship *per se*, and of the spouse, or maybe one's own self expectations, do not harmonize with the actual experience. Role conflicts of one type or another may develop and be handled in particular ways.[16]

SOCIAL CHANGE

Family interaction, while it has norm and role definitions which pattern it, is nonetheless a dynamic process. The creative aspect of family interaction which may appear of greatest significance to many observers is the socialization of the new baby. Of all newborn animals, the human neonate is most helpless and has the greatest potential. The process by which the child becomes an adult, functioning, member of society, is viewed by some as at least somewhat miraculous; actually, many sections of the text have been directly or indirectly related to this process.

A second important creative aspect is the development of a loving relationship between two or more individuals. Although the process by which the couple decide to get married is frequently described as "falling in love," "growing in love" more accurately identifies the process. The process by which the child–parent loving relationship is developed is likewise creative, in that it grows out of intimate family interaction. The process by which husband and wife or parent and child grow out of love is as much creative as the other, although it may be less deliberate and less rewarding. Latent consequences (functions) may be involved in such change.

Experiences within the family, of course, have strong influence upon the subsequent creativity level of the children.

---

[15] William H. Whyte, Jr., "The Wives of Management" and "The Corporation and the Wife," *Fortune*, XLIV (October, 1951), 86 ff., XLIV (November, 1951), 109 ff.

[16] For a discussion of adjustment patterns, see William G. Dyer, "Analyzing Marital Adjustment Using Role Theory," *Marriage and Family Living*, XXIV, No. 4 (November, 1962), 371–375.

Broad changes in family culture and related interaction patterns have been occurring right along, with the tempo of change increasing. The changes which we will identify are, of course, only one aspect of broader society-wide changes which have been progressing in previously established directions. Some of the major changes are given here.

1. *Shift of educational (socializing) responsibility from the home to the schools.* This is occurring at an increasingly earlier age in childhood. Kindergarten, nursery school, and pre-nursery school experiences are fairly common today. Occupational training has likewise been shifted to formal schools; parents in an agricultural environment are unqualified to provide their son with his vocational (agricultural) training, or their daughter with the training for her future occupation of housewife.

2. *Shift of care and responsibility for aged individuals from family to governmental agencies.* The widespread acceptance and use of social security is one of the best known illustrations of this change.

3. *Shift of recreational activities from family to non-family agencies.* Families do not play together as much as they used to.[17]

4. *Change in the role of the wife.* The formal and informal aspects of the wife–mother role have undergone extensive change since colonial times. Technological inventions such as dishwashers, electric cleaners, stoves, and ironers have in some respects made the actual housework easier while requiring the housewife to acquire skills of appliance maintenance and repair unknown to her colonial counterpart.

An important change has been increased participation in the "world of work" outside the home. The movement of the housewife into the factory and office received marked impetus during World War II, when the war effort provided the justification, acceptable to husbands and wives alike, for such a switch. The momentum thus initiated has not subsided. In 1958, for instance, 22 million women aged 14 or over were either employed or seeking employment. This was 35 per cent of the total female population aged 14 or over. Of these, slightly more than half were married and living with their husbands, one quarter were single, and one quarter had been married and were then widowed, divorced, or separated. The highest proportion employed was among the single, 45.4 per cent; employed women with children ages 6–17 and living with husbands totaled 37.6 per cent.[18]

Such a major change has not been accepted without adjustment problems. Husbands, although appreciating the increased income, have resented the home loss which the wife's absence entailed. Wives likewise have been subjected to social, including religious, criticisms and told repeatedly that the woman's (especially the mother's) "place is in the home." All sorts of social conditions, such as increased delinquency, many defined as "evils," have been attributed to the working mother. Research indicates, how-

---

Role Conflicts

"I am already assistant secretary of my corporation. In seven or eight years one of the vice-presidents of the corporation will retire. I am going to have his job. I am going to have it if it means we can't have children, if I have to spend every evening and every weekend to get it. It is the only chance I'll ever have like this, and it is the only really important thing in my life. I won't have such an opportunity again, but I can always get another wife!"

—James A. Peterson.*

---

[17] It is possible that families play together as much as they used to in terms of actual time involved; but with increased leisure they, in addition, engage in outside recreation.

* Quoted in James A. Peterson, *Education for Marriage* (2d ed.; New York: Charles Scribner's Sons, 1964), pp. 23–24.
[18] F. Ivan Nye and Lois Wladis Hoffman, *The Employed Mother in America* (Chicago: Rand McNally & Co., 1963), p. 9.

ever, that other things being equal the fact of a working mother does not account for the "evils" of delinquency.[19]

5. *Change in family interaction of aged individuals.* Definitions of responsibility have changed, with increased emphasis upon the responsibility of society (national and state and local) for the care of the aged. Such definitions have in general been accepted by the aged as well as those in other stages of family development. To the extent that the aged desire family relationships, to the extent that they want to be needed, loved, and involved in meaningful family relationships, experiences of alienation, with accompanying dissatisfaction, may result.

6. *Change in divorce patterns.* American divorce rates are high in comparison to colonial rates and other national rates as well. Divorce rates are frequently presented as a ratio of yearly marriages to yearly divorces. The ratio during the peak year 1946 was, for instance, one divorce for every three marriages. Such ratios, as a matter of statistical interpretation, are not sufficient to permit one to reach a conclusion about the *percentage* of marriages terminating in divorce. *Yearly* figures of divorces and marriages do not provide data about over-all divorce and marriage patterns.[20] The divorce patterns are also frequently stated as the number of divorces per a certain number of existing marriages. In 1946, there were 18.2 divorces per 1,000 existing marriages; in 1959 there were about half that many, or 9.4.[21]

Many couple the belief that individuals should marry for love with the corollary that without love a particular marriage should not be forced to continue.

Likewise, acceptance of an individualistic interpretation of religious salvation and eco-

---

The Courtship of Older Persons

In view of the therapeutic value of heterosexual love for all age groups—not just youth—it would appear that an effort should be made to develop more constructive and permissive attitudes toward the dating and mating activities of the older persons. Churches and other community services agencies, as well as families, need to rethink their attitudes toward this segment of the subculture of the older person.

—E. E. LeMasters.*

---

nomic salvation may be generalized to marital salvation. Decisions to marry and to terminate a marriage may be accordingly viewed as being strictly an individual prerogative.

What is implied here is that divorce has increased, not because individuals today are less trustworthy, sincere, or dedicated, but because, in part at least, they are born, live, marry, and sometimes divorce under conditions quite different from those of earlier low-divorce periods. Most people do not want to reverse any of the trends which have contributed to our national high divorce potential.

7. *Age at first marriage has been decreasing.* An 1890–1959 comparison for males is 26.1–22.3, and for females is 22.0–20.2 (from 1890 to 1959 the ages at first marriage for males moved from 26.1 to 22.3, and for females, from 22.0 to 20.2). Studies of American couples have found that in general as age at first marriage decreases, likelihood of eventual marriage dissolution increases. This pattern, then, has contributed to the high divorce rate discussed above.

8. *Change in sexual patterns.* An increase in the number of non-virgins at time of marriage is a major change. Studies by Terman [22] and by

---

[19] *Ibid.*, p. 280.

[20] See Glenn M. Vernon, "Misinterpreted Divorce Statistics," in *The Improvement Era* (Salt Lake City, Utah: L. D. S. Church, October, 1960), pp. 725 ff.

[21] Murray Gendell and Hans L. Zetterberg, *A Sociological Almanac for the United States* (2d ed., New York: Charles Scribner's Sons, 1964), p. 4.

* E. E. LeMasters, "The Courtship of Older Persons," *The Midwest Sociologist*, XX (December, 1957), 11.

[22] Lewis M. Terman, *Psychological Factors in Marital Happiness* (New York: McGraw-Hill Book Co., 1938).

Kinsey,[23] for example, have found that the increase is accounted for mainly by intercourse between couples who, at the time, at least, view each other as potential marriage partners. Random or promiscuous relationships have not increased greatly. These facts suggest that despite legal and religious norm definitions to the contrary, a sizable segment of young adults or young people have changed their definition of acceptable sexual behavior to include not only married couples, but couples planning or at least anticipating marriage. Moral standards have not been "abandoned"—they have been changed. Such change is viewed, however, by those who say that there is only *one* moral standard as an abandonment of morality.

STRATIFICATION

A child's initial class–caste identification is an ascribed one, provided by the fact of his birth, and shared by his whole family of orientation, at least its non-adult members. Our chapter on stratification has indicated that his whole experience in family interaction will be influenced directly or indirectly by the class position of the family. Research has shown that such behavior as the type of punishment parents use on children, the age at which toilet training is started, the extent of the family-approved play area, orientation toward sexual behavior, and self-defense methods are all related to class position.[24]

Further, one's choice of a marriage partner is essentially a class-related experience, in that such selection involves individuals from about the same class level. Where differences exist, the wife acquires the identification of her husband.

[23] Alfred C. Kinsey, Wardell B. Pomeroy, and Clyde E. Martin, *Sexual Behavior in the Human Male* (Philadelphia: W. B. Saunders Co., 1948).

[24] For discussion of class-related family patterns, see chaps. v, vi, and vii in Ruth Shonle Cavan, *The American Family* (3d ed.; New York: Thomas Y. Crowell Co., 1963); see also Robert R. Sears, Eleanor E. Maccoby, and Harry Levin, *Patterns of Child Rearing* (New York: Harper & Row, Publishers, 1957).

Mobility

Family experiences are related to the likelihood that the child will become upwardly mobile. Lower-class children, for instance, do not receive the parental encouragement of middle-class children to define higher education as valuable in itself and as a means of mobility. Lower-class parents frequently encourage children to become economically productive early, even if it means withdrawing from or foregoing formal education. Parental encouragement to better oneself is provided, but the perceived effective means of improvement is different. Mobility is viewed as primarily an occupational phenomenon, or a group phenomenon affected by the actions of labor unions or legislative means, rather than through the acquisition of education, before one moves into economic productivity.

The process of upward mobility has important family consequences. In the American society such mobility becomes somewhat individualized after an individual moves into the adult stages, and upward mobility of an individual which may mean likewise mobility for his family of procreation, may mean the creation of social distance or differences between the individual and his family of orientation, particularly his parents. Adjustment to these mobility-created family differences is not always easy, in that it involves at least partial rejection of individuals and values which were previously accepted. In a literal sense, it also involves rejection of aspects of one's prior "self definitions." Upwardly mobile individuals may become somewhat marginal as far as family of orientation is concerned. Efforts to seek old assurances and reassuring and satisfying interactions therein may prove to be upsetting and unfulfilled.

PRIMARY–SECONDARY INTERACTION

Family interaction is usually primary interaction. However, it is a somewhat unique kind in that it involves individuals, some of whom are not voluntary but rather captive participants.

This, of course, does not mean that the relationship necessarily loses any of its attractiveness to those involved, although it imposes limitations upon the relationship. It is not uncommon that as children mature they seek to escape from the family relationship, which only indicates that the primary relationship has never been realized or has deteriorated.

The family primary relationship takes on increased importance in an urbanized society, with extensive secondary contacts. In this sense, the "societal maintenance" function of the family takes on increased meaning, in that members get their "emotional batteries" recharged through such interaction.

ETHNIC MINORITY

An ethnic-minority identification, like a class identification, is an ascribed family label. The child's initial efforts to manage this identity are usually family-inspired or at least family-influenced. Many adapting patterns are unconsciously acquired through family interaction. Ways and means of living with or escaping, perhaps only temporarily, from discrimination and prejudice associated with ethnic-minority status are developed, tested, and discussed in family situations. For such groups, family interaction can be doubly significant since the inferior treatment received in the larger society can be counterbalanced by treatment as an equal or as a superior individual within the family.

One of the distinguishing features of ethnic-minority groups may be a distinctive family pattern. Frazier [25] has, for instance, identified distinctive features of the Negro family in the United States. One of the distinctive aspects of Jewish groups is their emphasis placed upon religious ceremonies which are to be performed within the home. These are frequently viewed as being of more significance than attendance at formal synagogue meetings.

[25] E. Franklin Frazier, *The Negro Family in the United States* (Chicago: The University of Chicago Press, 1939).

SUMMARY

Family interaction involves individuals related by birth, marriage, or adoption, who define themselves as a family and whose interaction confirms this definition. A biological relationship, while a frequent one, is not a necessary condition of family interaction, since it is to the family label which one responds in family interaction. The size of the group included under the family label may vary from the nuclear to the extended group. Most individuals are members of a family of orientation and a family of procreation.

Value definitions are applied to many aspects of family interaction—the family relationship *per se*, the permanency of a particular relationship, the primary nature of the relationship—and to the development of "individualism." The family-norm-role definitions specify patterns of power structure, mate selection, lineage, place of residence, number of mates, duration of the marriage contract, and various duties and responsibilities. Family interaction is intimately involved in the development and perpetuation of self definitions, including one's definition of his ability to give and receive love and his sexual ability. The last name by which the American identifies himself locates him in his family group.

Initial neonate socialization is usually a family affair, which involves considerable parental learning as well. Family socialization is always modified by non-family experiences.

Family role playing has many consequences such as "sex as fun" and procreation. Procreation within the family is the most widely endorsed form and it is generally to accomplish this goal that sexual regulations are established. Learning to participate in a loving relationship is a major potential of family interaction and one which is not always realized. The husband and wife have a reciprocal influence upon each other's success in non-family role playing, including the husband's occupational role.

Changing family patterns include the socialization of the child, recreational activities, working mothers, divorce, age at first marriage, and sexual behavior. Divorce statistics are frequently misinterpreted.

A child's initial class position is ascribed on the basis of his family connection. His terminal position is influenced extensively by family inter-

action. Mates are usually selected from a class level near one's own. Mobility has important family consequences. Family patterns also vary among ethnic and other minority groups.

QUESTIONS

1. Distinguish between the family of orientation and the family of procreation.
2. What evidence would support the hypothesis that mothers have an "instinct for mother love"? What evidence would challenge the hypothesis?
3. How are value definitions related to family behavior?
4. What is wrong with the statement, "One out of every four American marriages ends in divorce"?
5. What non-family social changes are likely to be related to the change from a patriarchal to an equalitarian family structure in the American society?
6. With reference to which characteristics are American families usually endogamous?

7. Is it logical to expect that couples who believe that the major criterion of mate selection is whether a love relationship has been established should expect to terminate marriages in which a love relationship no longer exists?
8. What are some of the potential role conflicts facing the contemporary wife?
9. Provide a sociological explanation for the fact that in the United States the family is no longer expected to socialize the child as extensively as it did during colonial times.
10. What social factors have contributed to the "sex as fun" orientation of the American society?

PROJECT

Interview a Protestant clergyman to determine whether the official position of his church has changed over

the years with reference to providing a church marriage ceremony for divorced individuals.

SUGGESTED READING

ANSHEN, RUTH NANDA (ed.). *The Family: Its Function and Destiny.* Rev. ed. New York: Harper & Row, Inc., 1959.

CHRISTENSEN, HAROLD T. *Marriage Analysis.* New York: The Ronald Press Co., 1950.

GLICK, PAUL C. *American Families.* New York: John Wiley & Sons, Inc., 1957.

GOODE, WILLIAM J. *After Divorce.* New York: The Free Press of Glencoe, 1956.

KIRKPATRICK, CLIFFORD. *The Family.* 2d ed. New York: The Ronald Press Co., 1963.

NYE, F. IVAN, and LOIS W. HOFFMAN. *The Employed*

Mother in America. Chicago: Rand McNally & Co., 1963.

PARSONS, TALCOTT, and ROBERT F. BALES. *Family, Socialization and Interaction Process.* New York: The Free Press of Glencoe, 1955.

RAINWATER, LEE. *And the Poor Get Children.* Chicago: Quadrangle Books, Inc., 1960.

STEPHENS, WILLIAM N. *The Family in Cross-cultural Perspective.* New York: Holt, Rinehart and Winston, Inc., 1963.

WINCH, ROBERT F. *Mate-Selection.* New York: Harper & Row, Inc., 1958.

23

Bureaucracy

Discussions of economic behavior frequently include terms such as "alienation," "man treated as a thing," "dehumanization," "red tape," "bureaucracy," "the vows of the organization." What would be likely to happen to the American way of life, and to the position of the United States in international relations, if somehow the conditions required to change these characteristics or to "unbureaucratize" the society could be instituted?

INTRODUCTION

Interacting individuals engage in a great variety of activities, and relate themselves to each other in many different ways. This chapter calls attention to a particular type of interaction—selective perception, i.e., bureaucratic interaction organized according to some formal, highly structured pattern, and to groups, sometimes called bureaucracies, in which such interaction takes place. Bureaucracies are found in many areas—political, economic, military, and religious. Not all groups or organizations in these areas, however, are bureaucratic. When we talk here about formal organizations or groups we refer, unless it is otherwise stated, to those with bureaucratic characteristics.

The term "formal" in the above definition calls attention to the fact that the interaction is patterned according to formally established definitions. All types of definitions, including of course the related plans of action, are included—value, norm role, self, object, and situation definitions. These definitions are developed in a rational, conscious manner, usually through some deliberative process, with the specific intention of governing future interaction. The definitions may be established in part because the laws of the society so specify, but even without such legal requirements it is likely that such procedures would be followed, since they facilitate the accomplishment of certain goals.

Once developed, the definitions are written down, possibly codified, and are given such labels as articles of incorporation, constitutions, bylaws, tables of organization, job descriptions, flow charts, and manuals of procedure. Considerations of behavior can then be referred to these formally established definitions, which may be available to members and non-members of the association.

In our study of bureaucratic interaction, we are concerned with cultural organization or the system of interrelated definitions (symbols) as well as social organization or systematized interaction or behavior. Formal, and informal, interaction is always a socio-cultural phenomenon.

Not all interaction in any such group, however, is formal. Informal interaction always develops. Organizations could be distributed along a "formal-to-informal" scale by the extent to which the interaction is formally patterned or bureaucratized. Our discussion here makes no pretense of specifying differing degrees of formality, but concerns only formal associations in general.

Individuals interact with individuals, and may be defined by each other in individualistic terms. Individuals, however, frequently band together or establish certain types of organizations under motivation as varied as the behavior itself. Whether intentional or not, such arrangements or organizations provide means whereby certain goals can be accomplished, many of which could not be accomplished by individuals working alone or working strictly for themselves. People can do collectively what they can't do alone.

Thinking About the Unthinkable

Bureaucracy makes possible "thinking about the unthinkable" (to borrow the phrase of one of the foremost authorities on thermonuclear war [Herman Kahn]) by making it rational; and having made it possible, impelled by new insecurities grafted on to old national rivalries, it finally makes it necessary.

—Bernard Rosenberg, et al.*

---

* Bernard Rosenberg, Israel Gerver, and F. William Howton, *Mass Society in Crisis* (New York: The Macmillan Co., 1964), p. 158.

A moment's analysis of how thousands of individuals are involved in operating a university should make the student aware that he could never get the education he is currently acquiring if others had not banded together in a formal manner to establish and maintain schools. Labor unions have accomplished what individuals working alone could not, as have business organizations, religious organizations, the American Camping Association, and many other formal organizations.

Individuals are members of the larger society and may be so defined. Individuals are also members of many subgroups, such as formal organizations, and their behavior in society or in some dyad is influenced by that membership.

That groups can accomplish what individuals alone cannot has tremendous implications, but this does not mean that groups can accomplish literally anything. Many limitations are imposed upon group accomplishment. As history so clearly illustrates, however, goals once believed impossible of human realization have been achieved by subsequent generations. The science fiction of one generation may become the scientific fact of the next. Every generation will likely be viewed by some future generation as ancient, provincial, and primitive. Conquering the American frontier was one thing; conquering the universe, another. Conquering the atom is still another, but not unrelated, phenomenon. What lies ahead in human achievement, social and material, can only be speculated now, but we can be sure that it will grow out of the present culture base and that the human achievement, even so-called "individual" inventions, will reflect the interactive behavior of many. Placing a human being on some other planet could not be accomplished without thousands and thousands of antecedent culture elements and interrelated behavior patterns.

VALUE DEFINITIONS

Any number of value decisions may be involved in the establishment and maintenance of formal, bureaucratic organizations. For those born into the society, participation in and at least general acceptance of formal organizations stem from their being there and being used by others. The way of life that involves formal organizations is in fact *the* way of life of the society. It is all that is known. Later, as different and possibly conflicting value definitions are learned, questions may be raised, and efforts may be made toward change. Social movements may develop. Formal organizations may even be established to reduce the extent and effect of formal organizations.

Once formal organizations are well established, the original organizational goals may be supplemented or replaced by the goal of self-perpetuation of the organization.

Be that as it may, a value frequently supporting the establishment of formal organization is technical efficiency. The organizers of formal government or economic, educational, religious, or recreational associations share, as Max Weber has indicated, the belief that bureaucratic organization has technical superiority over any other form of organization.[1] The complexity of the value definitions involved, however, equals that of interaction patterns. Efficiency of operation is frequently related to the second goal of profit maximation. There is, however, considerable evidence that the valued profit maximation is always tempered with many other related and at times even contradictory value definitions. The value premises supporting the behavior of leaders at various levels in formal organizations, for instance, may involve endorsements of such elements as power, prestige, security, creativity, adventure, identification with the group, playing the game for its own sake, and the desire to serve others. Gordon has suggested that money is becoming largely a "minimum condition for attracting the necessary supply of business leadership in the large corporation."[2] Hickman and Kuhn

also suggest that at a certain level (a "guaranteed security" level) breadwinning may stop being an occupation and become a sport, like mountain climbing. Why climb (the organizational mountain)? Because it is there![3]

Further, it is likely that, despite similarities of structure, the value foundation may vary from organization to organization.

The goal of "efficiency" is not as simple as it might at first appear. A question to which Americans have been giving increased attention is the value question as to where the greatest emphasis should be placed—upon the efficient utilization of (1) material resources or (2) human resources? All goal achievement has its latent or unintended as well as its manifest or apparent consequences. One, in effect, always "pays the piper" even though he may not be aware of the whole cost. One of the crucial questions today is exactly what happens to individuals as they become enmeshed in bureaucratic organizations.

In the United States, the value premise—that behavior should be rationally controlled—upon which bureaucracy rests has been of major significance not only in the economic realm, but in science, philosophy, and religion (particularly Calvinism) as well. In this respect the major institutions of the society have been mutually supportive.

Various types of value definitions are involved in any bureaucracy, i.e., various individual values, values of subgroups within the organization (departmental, divisions, informal peer groups, etc.), and the values of the larger organization. All of these are involved in the functioning of the organization. Some, however, have questioned whether "organizations" *have* values. They do. Organization value definitions can be identified by paying attention to official statements, written or verbal, provided by members of the organization, or they can be inferred from an analysis of behavior, which of course presents some problems of interpretation. Informal organizational values may also be se-

---

[1] Max Weber, from *Max Weber: Essays in Sociology*, trans. and ed. by H. H. Gerth and C. Wright Mills (Fair Lawn, N. J.: Oxford University Press, 1946), p. 214.

[2] Robert A. Gordon, *Business Leadership in the Large Corporation* (Washington, D. C.: The Brookings Institution, 1945), p. 313.

[3] C. Addison Hickman and Manford H. Kuhn, *Individuals, Groups and Economic Behavior* (New York: Holt, Rinehart and Winston, Inc., 1956), p. 60.

cured in the same way, although different degrees of rapport may be needed to obtain them.

The importance of understanding the official values of an organization is shown by the fact that individuals and groups do, in fact, pattern their behavior according to what are believed to be the goals or value definitions of the organization. Promotion or failure to get promoted may likewise be related to employee effectiveness in taking official and/or informal organizational value definitions into account. The organizational value definitions may also be involved in such activities as propaganda efforts, recruiting, and securing the cooperation of employees.

One factor which influences the functioning of an organization is the relationship between organizational value definitions and individual or other subgroup value definitions which may reflect non-organizational experiences such as those in the family, church, peer groups, lodge, or labor union. It would appear that relative harmony among these sets of value definitions would contribute to organizational effectiveness. However, there may be a point of diminishing returns where such identity becomes dysfunctional in that it hinders the accomplishment of goals of the larger society or of other organizations within the society, such as the family and the church.[4]

It is unlikely that the same type and extent of value harmony is required of employees at all levels. The effective functioning of the man on the assembly line or in the ranks of a military organization requires a different type of value identification than at the junior or senior executive level.

Leaders at the different levels of the organization usually operate upon the assumption that they know the salient value definitions of their employee. How true this is remains to be seen. One thing has, however, been demonstrated in repeated research—the fact that workers are not *primarily* motivated by economic goals. Eco-

Technology and Values

As an institution, technology has today, then, its own function: the rational control of man, space, and matter—and its own governing values. It is no stretch of meaning, I suggest, to hold that technology has sacred overtones in the minds of many. To contravene the values of technology in favor of, say, nationalism or economic profits can seem as impious to a scientist today as contravention of religious ends, in the name of economic gain, seemed to a medieval theologian.
—Robert A. Nisbet.*

nomic values do not always take precedence over others.[5]

NORM-ROLE DEFINITIONS

Division of Labor

The trade mark of a formal organization is the complex set of norm-role definitions which interrelate a large number, possibly thousands, of positions in such a way that the goal of the organization can be accomplished in what is viewed as the most efficient manner. Required activities are divided into identifiable units and configurations of behavior are assigned to certain positions or roles, all of which are interrelated according to some plan. In this division of labor, effort is made to free the organization from dependence upon particular individuals.

The behavior is associated with the position, not any specific individual who happens to play the role. In fact, an extensive division of labor can be worked out "on paper" before the organization ever starts to function, or before actual

* Robert A. Nisbet, "The Impact of Technology on Ethical Decision-Making," in Robert Lee and Martin E. Marty (eds.), *Religion and Social Conflict* (New York: Oxford University Press, 1964), p. 12.

[5] See, for instance, F. J. Roethlisberger and W. J. Dickson, *Management and the Worker* (Cambridge: Harvard University Press, 1939).

[4] See, for instance, Melvin M. Tunim, "Some Dysfunctions of Institutional Imbalance," *Behavioral Science*, I, No. 3 (July, 1956), 218–223.

people start to interact. Individuals who play the various roles then are expected to pattern their behavior in conformity with the previously determined plans.

Division of Authority and Power

We have previously distinguished between power as the ability to influence the behavior of others, and authority as *legitimate* power. Both power and authority are found in formal organizations, with effort being made to maximize the use of authority. It is the norm-role definitions which establish legitimate power. Such definitions specify, frequently in great detail, exactly who has the authority to make certain types of decisions, the factors to be taken into account in decision making and how the various types of authority decisions are expected to be related. Here again, the authority goes with the position, not the role player personally. Personal power will probably never be eliminated, nor would most organizations want to completely eliminate such power. Efforts are made, however, to maximize the formal authority. In such a system, subordinates are protected from arbitrary actions of superiors, and the actions of both are constrained by a set of mutually recognized norm-role definitions.

An important aspect of the authority structure is the specification as to who is authorized to use certain types of sanctioning behavior such as promotions, official recognition, reprisals, and dismissals. The role definitions also specify the qualifications required for specific positions, and

selection may accordingly be made in an impersonal and systematic manner. They specify the tenure arrangement associated with particular positions, as well as the requirements for promotion from one position to another, with efforts again to maximize the specific job-related, technical, and professional characteristics. Positions may also be organized so that a systematic means of upward mobility within the organization is established.

Standardizing behavior related to specific positions and synchronizing the behavior associated with many positions require that heavy attention be given to the time factor. Role definitions consequently specify such things as how long a particular activity should take, or the times at which individuals and material parts are to come together for particular purposes. The operation of a transcontinental railroad, for instance, at times requires split-second timing—at least if the railroad is run American-style. If interchangeability of parts—human and non-human—is maximized, time sequences are least likely to be disrupted.

Formal organizations also have another distinctive characteristic. Roles are developed in which major attention is given to organizational maintenance *per se*. Thus, superimposed upon the role definitions of those who actually produce the finished product, whatever it is, is a series of role definitions, arranged in some hierarchical fashion, in which attention is given to keeping the system and subsystems functioning efficiently. The amount of attention given to such activity is positively correlated with the size of the organization.

Number of Administrators

Bendix reports 8 administrative employees per 100 production workers in 1899, 18 in 1929, and 22 per 100 in 1947; in 1961 there were 36 per 100.
—Murray Gendell and Hans L. Zetterberg. *

---

* Murray Gendell and Hans L. Zetterberg, *A Sociological Almanac for the United States* (2d ed.; New York: Charles Scribner's Sons, 1964), p. 8.

SELF DEFINITIONS

Involvement in bureaucratic organizations with their formal norm-role definitions and standardized interaction patterns will inevitably influence the self definitions of those involved. Once the specific requirements for a particular role are delineated and formally written out, it is easier than in informal interaction to distinguish "what one does" from "what one is." It is easier to take

Figure 23.1 In a bureaucracy, a high-echelon decision may influence the lives of those "in the system" in important ways, as in the case of school desegregation. (Wide World Photos.)

an instrumental approach toward others and view them in terms of their contributions to the larger effort rather than "for themselves." It is easier, to use Buber's [6] term, to define the individual as a "thing" rather than a "person." It is easier to replace the name—the most personal, unique identification—with an impersonal number. In a sense the identity question changes from "Who am I?" to "What am I?"

[6] Martin Buber, *I and Thou* (1923), trans. by R. G. Smith (New York: Charles Scribner's Sons, 1955).

Those involved learn, perhaps reluctantly at first, that if they are applying such definitions to the others with whom they interact at the office or in the plant, these others are applying similar definitions to them. It is easy to view oneself as just one cog in a larger, rather impersonal machine. Since in interaction major consideration is given to the job one does, those with the same or similar jobs tend to be viewed as somewhat identical or at least interchangeable. Formal organizations are, in fact, established and maintained upon the premise that the human beings involved will be at least somewhat interchange-able, so that the "plant" may keep functioning in the absence of any individual or even any group of individuals.

In formal organizations there is the question as to exactly how the individual relates himself to the organization. There may be some sense of identity with the product, but it is of a differ-ent nature from that which the craftsman or artisan experiences, since the production-line worker may have difficulty relating his particu-lar contribution or production to the finished product. The individual contribution gets swal-lowed up in the finished product and becomes indistinguishable; in much the same way the individual gets incorporated into the corporation and becomes indistinguishable.

Personal identification has a motivational com-ponent. A relevant question, which is somewhat unanswered as yet, is whether individual work-ers find major personal identification with the aspect of the finished product with which they are personally related, with the finished product as a whole, with the company as a whole, with the physical plant in which they work, with the public "image" of the leaders of the company, or with the paycheck which they periodically re-ceive.

At the professional or semi-professional level, do these individuals define themselves as profes-sional first and company men second, or as com-pany men first and professional men second? Is the individual a chemist working for Dow Chem-ical, or a Dow official working in the area of chemistry?

In terms of the identity that influences the production rate of production workers, research indicates that identification with the immediate work group, in which primary relationships have been established, is a major factor, although cer-tainly not the only one involved.

Modern companies attempt to develop a strong employee identification with the company, so that at least at higher echelons, individuals will define themselves first as company men, and sec-ond as something else. This is reflected in the statement directed toward the wives of junior

management that their husbands *belong* to the company.[7] Organizational goals are, of course, facilitated to the extent that such self identifica-tions are developed—although it is most likely true that there is a point of diminishing returns, as is suggested by the technics by which individ-uals attempt to "get away from it all." Such escape may, of course, be physical, psychologi-cal, or even alcoholic.

New students at a large university may experi-ence similar feelings as they find themselves being just one "little fish in a big academic pond" and may have the feeling that no one cares for them "as an individual" but just as student no. 5682433.

Involvement in an urbanized society with its attendant extensive secondary relationships, or involvement in a formal organization with its secondary relationships, contributes considerably to the feeling of alienation from others which is a problem to many today.[8]

ROLE PLAYING AND ROLE TAKING

Organization role playing varies from level to level. At the upper-echelon level, an individual learns to play the role by learning not only the rights and duties of his position and the requi-site behavior, but also those of all other related persons in the system.

Such role playing at the lower levels, however, becomes standardized and routinized. Quotas are established, for instance, so that output is standardized. Everyone involved soon knows what constitutes a "day's work." Production lines are established, so that what one does becomes

[7] William H. Whyte, Jr., "The Wives of Management," *Fortune,* XLIV (October, 1951), 86 ff.

[8] See, for instance, Erich Fromm, *Escape from Free-dom* (New York: Holt, Rinehart and Winston, Inc., 1941); and Eric and Mary Josephson (eds.), *Man Alone: Alienation in Modern Society* (New York: Dell Pub-lishing Co., Inc., 1962). For a discussion of changing orientations, see Leonard G. Benson, *National Purpose* (Washington, D. C.: Public Affairs Press, 1963), pp. 116–124.

keyed to what others do, with the goals of those involved easily becoming to do what the quota or the production line requires and no more. In some jobs it, in fact, becomes almost physically impossible to do much more. On the production line, the actual work may become somewhat mechanical with the opportunity to "let one's mind wander," as a means of escape. Individuals behave according to the book, or "by the numbers."

Individual decisions are, of course, constantly being made, but the area in which they can be made and the types of decisions left open to individual decision are reduced to the extent that the formal "game rules" are developed.

Role definitions are established so that behavior can be standardized. Those, then, who play the same or similar roles have similar experiences which contribute to the development of similar personality or behavior patterns. Playing similar roles, treating others in similar ways, being treated by others in similar manner, and, in some cases, wearing similar uniforms, serves to standardize thinking and behavior patterns. Playing the role becomes a well integrated facet of the personality of those involved.

Playing a role at almost any level of the corporation requires that one learn to make authority or responsibility distinctions as well as behavior distinctions. Those involved have to learn which decisions are theirs to make and which have to be passed on up or down the chain of command. Here again the success of the organization depends, in part, upon how well the authority decisions harmonize as well as upon how the machine and parts come together. In this respect, then, it becomes important (again to the successful operation of the system) that the various right hands know what the corresponding left hands are doing, and various methods are developed to accomplish this. This usually involves paper work, such as providing six copies of all memos, which has become known as "red tape." With limited authority, limited perspective, and formal sanctions, limited decisions are necessary. Charges of inefficiency are frequently leveled against such organizations. Whether an

Zone of Indifference

Among all the orders a person in a particular position in an organization might conceivably receive, some he would consider unacceptable, some would be on the borderline of acceptability, and some would be "'unquestionably acceptable." These last fall within that particular person's "zone of indifference" and these he will readily obey.

—Terence K. Hopkins.*

abandonment of the system would result in more over-all inefficiency and duplication is at least questionable. Such organization may be more efficient than casual contacts with it may suggest.

The actual role playing, of course, is never completely mechanical. Opportunity for individual and group creativity is always present, as will be discussed shortly.

An important aspect of role playing in many formal organizations is the recruitment and training of new personnel at the various levels. At the upper echelons, this frequently involves a system of "in-service" training in which those in lower ranks are formally and informally being trained by those above, whom they may subsequently succeed. This is called "anticipatory succession."

Interaction in formal organizations involves making decisions as to when the formal norm-role definitions will be applicable and when they will not. Those involved quickly learn that the rules and regulations are not all equally applicable, enforced, or enforceable. Playing the roles for any length of time provides awareness as to just how far the regulations "can be stretched." Supervisors and supervised become aware that

* Terence K. Hopkins, "Bureaucratic Authority: The Convergence of Weber and Barnard," in Amitai Etzioni (ed.), *Complex Organizations, A Sociological Reader* (New York: Holt, Rinehart and Winston, Inc., 1962), p. 87.

the success or failure of the department is a joint affair, and that either can make the job miserable for the other. Homans has described such interaction in the following way:

In theory, the supervisor "bawled out" a girl if she failed for two days in a row to make the quota. In fact, he rarely had to, and when he did the bawling out was gentle. But neither did he praise a girl when she made a high record . . . the girls liked their immediate boss. He never tried to use "human relations skills." He was frank and outspoken when they broke the rules, but they felt they knew where they stood with him and said—which is the highest of all praise from workers—"He's fair." Or even, "He's a *man!*" For his part, he said, "I have a good bunch of girls working for me. I really don't think you could get a better one anywhere. They're not all equally fast. But they do a good job, even the slowest of them. Some of them are so good they really ought to have something better than they have now." [9]

Role playing in a bureaucracy involves selective perception as does all other role playing. In such behavior one has to learn the things he must pay major attention to, and what to ignore or push into the background. Decisions as to how individuals relate themselves to each other are based upon the utilitarian criterion: How does the behavior relate to the over-all organizational goals? Personal, individual goals have to be somewhat ignored, or considered as being only indirectly related to the immediate task, which is viewed as being related to the pay involved—"After all, that's what he's paid to do." How individuals relate their pay to their own personal goals is viewed as being beyond the scope of interest and authority of the organization.

Personal goals, of course, are always involved to a degree, and when they do receive major attention will frequently be defined in such a way that they appear to be furthering the goals of the organization—at least to those in superior positions who may have occasion to question the relevancy of the behavior.

Role taking involves learning through experience or otherwise how the "organization man" thinks. Accurate interpretation of his behavior involves understanding of his goals, his role, or his involvement in the organization. The "independent" has difficulty understanding "organization" behavior; those who have lived the "organization life" find the behavior of their co-workers easy to comprehend.

The complexity of organization role taking is suggested by the following statement of Winston Churchill:

It is always a misfortune when number two or three has to initiate a dominant plan or policy. He has to consider not only the merits of the policy but the mind of his chief; not only what to advise, but what it is proper for him in his station to advise; not only what to do, but how to get it agreed and how to get it done. Moreover, number two or three will have to reckon with numbers four, five, and six, or maybe some bright outsider, number 20. Ambition, not so much for vulgar ends, but for fame, glints in every mind. There are always several points of view which may be right, and many which are plausible.[10]

Following formally established rules and regulations imposes limitations upon those involved, but also opens the door to other creative possibilities.

SOCIALIZATION

Learning how to function in a formal organization obviously requires a different type of experience than learning how to function in a less formal group such as a family or peer group. Such skills are acquired in many ways. Many experiences may, in fact, be preparatory to formal organization functioning. The child who is socialized in a mass production school, possibly even in shifts, who buys items from a chain store, goes to the clinic for his medical checkup, attends a large urban church, again possibly "in shifts," and who attends big-league ball games

---

[9] George C. Homans, "The Cash Posters: A Study of a Group of Working Girls," *American Sociological Review*, XIX, No. 6 (December, 1954), 724–733.

[10] Winston S. Churchill, *Their Finest Hour* (Boston: Houghton Mifflin Co., 1949), p. 15, as quoted by Hickman and Kuhn, *op. cit.*, p. 66.

acquires in the process many of the general skills and perspectives which will be required of him as he moves into a mass production job, or joins a formal organization. Individuals reared in an urbanized, industrialized society find formal organization life, in fact, to be *the* way of life—*their* way of life.

Specific occupational skills may, of course, be acquired while on the job through participation in training schools maintained by the organization itself, or in the formal school system. Preparing large groups of individuals for somewhat interchangeable positions in an organization which values efficiency, logically becomes "efficient interchangeable" socialization involving a group rather than any one-to-one relationship. Training of this type has been referred to as "batch training" in which groups of new recruits from the outside or even from the inside are "run through" the training mill. Participants are first screened (and here individual differences are taken into account) so that they start out essentially as "equals." They are then treated as equals, given equal training, subjected to equal testing, and if they perform equally well, assigned to equal roles, in which they are expected to perform with equal skill and to endorse equal values. This equality is never actually obtained. The program, however, usually functions as though it were capable of realizing the equality. A high degree of uniformity is necessary if the organization is to function.

Training of employees involves not only the acquisition of job skills but job motivations as well. It involves not only learning how to do something but learning to *want* to do it. It would be a mistake, however, to assume that everyone at all levels in a formal organization is equally receptive to the same value orientation, or that those at different levels equally understand the motivation values involved at different levels. Workers on the line do not necessarily understand what "makes management run." Training programs usually include efforts to develop or stimulate the "appropriate" value orientation. Courses in "human relations," for instance, may provide those in the upper echelons with such an orientation, and those who play the higher-

echelon roles usually consider that they do understand the motivations of those whom they manage. Company programs, of course, reflect whatever set of definitions they hold.

At the higher echelons, when consideration is given to new appointments or to promotions from within the organization, greater attention is frequently given to finding individuals who share common values rather than other professional skills. We feel more comfortable with those who, we believe, share our values, even though they behave differently, than we do with those who behave as we do but who, we are convinced, do so for "other reasons."

Many informal socializing or preparatory schemes are used in formal organizations. Individuals who fill in for those above them during temporary absences or during periods of illness may be being groomed for the eventuality that they themselves will play that role in the future. Replacements are evaluated in such terms. Those at one level may also engage in individual "coaching" efforts whereby those below them are

---

Value Conflict

Middle East workers who have migrated to the city from villages where they had followed century-old customs and lived where their wants were relatively few frequently come to the factory on Monday, Tuesday, and Wednesday, and perhaps half a day on Thursday, but will not show up at all on Friday and Saturday. They see no point in working any longer because they have earned enough to maintain the standard of living they and their families have been accustomed to. It takes a bit of time for them to become aware of new standards and new potentialities which can relatively easily become theirs if they work the full week.

—Hadley Cantril.*

---

* Hadley Cantril, "The Individual's Demand on Society," in *Conflict and Creativity*, ed. by Seymour M. Farber and Roger H. L. Wilson (New York; McGraw-Hill Book Co., 1963), p. 195.

prepared to move up to a higher position. Important coaching goes on in the club room, on the golf course, and at the company party, as well as within the confines of the executive suite.

Socialization may, of course, extend beyond the organization itself. Those viewed as potential executive material, may, for instance, be sent at company expense to university workshops or to obtain an M.B.A. (Master of Business Administration) degree which emphasizes the acquisition of the "company" or "management" perspective rather than the acquisition of specific product-related skills.

Professionalization

Formal organizations involve a vast variety of roles, some of which are considered to be professional. Professional individuals may, of course, play their role in less formal organizations, or may be in private practice. Preparatory training for such roles, however, is usually accomplished in a formal organization, and those who play professional roles usually participate in extensive specialized training.

An important aspect of such training is the acquisition of the professional point of view—or learning how to make professional decisions. An important ingredient of this point of view is an orientation toward service to others, rather than the acquisition of personal goals such as money. The two goals are, of course, not mutually exclusive, and it frequently happens that in providing what is viewed as a valuable service to "mankind," the professional individual is able to acquire considerable personal wealth. The opportunity to acquire personal wealth is not the same in all professions, as a comparison of the income of surgeons and ministers illustrates.

The acquisition of a professional identity involves two major processes. First, individuals must learn to identify themselves with the appropriate label. They must be convinced that they are, in fact, qualified lawyers, medical doctors, artists. Acquisition of such an identity is an important result of professional training. Such an identity, however, must be confirmed by so-

ciety, and most likely by a specialized group of other professionals. A lawyer must pass the bar examination; some similar experience in other professions announces to the professional members and the general public that a new identity has been acquired by the neophyte. Maintenance of the professional identity following such an experience rests heavily upon interaction between the professional and those he serves. The surgeon whom no one will permit to perform an operation has difficulty in maintaining his "surgeon" identification. Acceptance into organizations with appropriate titles, such as "The American Medical Association," is also confirmatory evidence that one *is* what his title says he is—that he has *arrived*.

In a very literal sense the acquisition of a professional identity involves a "rebirth" of self definitions. The process may involve the "death" or abandonment of old self definitions, as well as the acquisition of the new, which may be facilitated by a literal stripping away of old identities or status symbols; an example is the new military recruits who are stripped to the skin and issued new clothes, usually just like those of everyone else going through the training. In such an experience it becomes difficult

---

Lawyers and Bureaucracy

Lawyers, who constitute about one-tenth of one per cent of the population of the United States, supply the majority of its decision-makers in government. For various periods, 70 per cent of all presidents, vice-presidents, and cabinet members have been lawyers and so have 57 per cent of all senators, 56 per cent of all members of the House of Representatives and 52 per cent of all state governors. This is not a recent trend.

—Murray Gendell and Hans L. Zetterberg.*

---

* Murray Gendell and Hans L. Zetterberg, *A Sociological Almanac for The United States* (2d ed.; New York: Charles Scribner's Sons, 1964), p. 9.

to take old identities (including self identities) into account. Physical or residential isolation may also force the establishment of new relationships which take the proposed new identity into account. The training program may also be so extensive that participants may have little opportunity to participate in extracurricular activities or even to want to participate. New recruits may, in fact, fall into bed at the end of a long day too exhausted to give more than a passing thought to past relationships and identities. Through some such procedure new professional identities are acquired.

The *method* of training may be the same for groups as diverse as regular army officers and clergymen.

CREATIVITY AND CHANGE

Rigid norm-role definitions are productive of rigid interaction patterns. Well established patterns tend to take on an aura of "rightness" which discourages change. However, it would be an error to conclude as do some "red-tape analyses" of formal organizations that creativity is thereby ruled out. Actually, while certain types of creativity are very effectively ruled out, the door is opened for other types. There is, of course, the creativity found in many such organizations involved in the development of ways and technics of avoiding the formal rules while maintaining the appearance of conformity.

But more importantly, it should be recognized that it is possible for people jointly to accomplish things which would literally be impossible to accomplish individually. An organization may, in fact, employ professionals and not only pay them to be creative, but also provide expensive physical facilities, workshops, equipment, and expert assistants, to help facilitate their creative work. Such types of creativity rule out individual creativity and it is not uncommon to hear complaints about the restrictions placed upon individuals in such situations. Making a value assessment as to which type of creativity provides the greatest rewards to the over-all society or its segments is difficult.

Each type of creative effort has its own limitations and problems. There is the question, for instance, of who has patent rights when an invention is produced in the company lab. There are also the restrictions imposed by "the administration" that is convinced (or behaves as though it were) that creativity takes place only between 8 and 5 o'clock. It should be recognized that in either case it is not a question of creativity vs. no creativity, but only of what type of creativity.

It is interesting to note that in a 1962 registration of "American science manpower," approximately 40 per cent of those responding reported that some phase of their work was being supported or sponsored by the federal government.[11]

The development of complex formal organizations is a creative act in its own right. Change is, of course, always experienced by formal organizations, and reorganization efforts are likewise creative. Failure or reluctance to change may lead to various types of adjustment, from the demise of the corporation, to merger, to acquisition of government support, to the acceptance of lower profits or even to operating "in the red." A capitalistic economy views the possibility of increased income as providing the incentive constantly to assess the on-going operation in terms of whether a more efficient method of production can be created.

Change today may be programmed change wherein efforts are made to standardize the change and eliminate what is defined as unhealthy side-effects. Efforts to adjust to automation are an illustration.

STRATIFICATION

The organizations to which one belongs, particularly the one for which he works, play an important role in the whole stratification system. Occupations within a society are ranked or evaluated differently, and those who occupy the occupational positions share this evaluation.

[11] National Science Foundation, *Scientific Manpower Bulletin,* No. 20 (March, 1964).

Change of position within one organization is also a change of position in the larger stratification system. The great American dream, in fact, envisions the possibility of an individual's moving from lower class to upper class while remaining within the same organization—going from office boy to corporation president.

Change of organizational position with corresponding class change may also involve physical mobility as an individual moves from the plant in one area to the office in another, to the regional office, and eventually to the home "executive suite"—if the final transition is made.

PRIMARY–SECONDARY RELATIONSHIPS

Primary relationships established within the larger formal organization have an important influence upon the performance of the organization. Loyalty to the primary group, the departmental clique, or the work group is given priority in many occupational decisions. Part of the strength of such groups, or the rewards of such relationships, is that they serve to counteract the impersonal relationships (alienation) experienced in the larger organization. Impersonal role definitions can be given individualized interpretation within the peer group. Individual factors can be taken into account.

The influence of peer relationships within the formal organization may be varied. Such groups can support or subvert organizational goals. Organizational goals may, in fact, be achieved by utilization of informal channels of communication, or by relying upon personal loyalties and "debts." Further, as Blau [12] has indicated, frequent participation in informal activities may not only increase the morale of individuals, but also contribute to their knowledge of the organization and to their self confidence and role-playing skill as well.

Primary relationships outside the organization, such as those of the family, may be important

[12] Peter M. Blau, *The Dynamics of Bureaucracy* (Chicago: The University of Chicago Press, 1955), p. 113.

factors influencing decisions to move into particular formal organizations.

SUMMARY

Goals which require the united efforts of many individuals and considerable technical skill can be most efficiently accomplished with formal, bureaucratic interaction. The socio-cultural milieu, of course, always imposes limitations upon what can be accomplished. Such activity requires an integration of norm, role, self, and value definitions so that the definitions, people, and material all come together in a harmonious manner. Attention must also be given to organizational maintenance as well.

Such interaction involves acceptance of different value-motivational definitions at various levels. Research has dispelled the notion that maximization of economic returns always is given top priority. Such interaction has frequently resulted in placing greater evaluation upon the efficient use of material than upon the maximum development of the individuals involved, particularly those on the production line. Those playing such roles with their secondary, instrumental relationships may come to define themselves as "being used," as "things," or as being "dehumanized." Such individuals work out some set of definitions and behavior patterns which take these definitions into account. They may attempt to counteract such relationships by becoming involved in primary relationships with fellow employees or by joining other voluntary groups such as clubs or churches, or they may escape via alcohol. Preparation for playing such roles involves "batch processing," which prepares for the interchangeability of individuals.

Socialization for higher-echelon positions may involve professional training, formal in-service training, and/or informal socialization on the job, at company parties, and at the country club. Self definitions are, of course, changed in the socialization process and their change may be facilitated by appropriate rites of passage. Playing a role which is integrated with many others requires a type of role-taking ability which

involves synthesizing various levels of authority and responsibility, skills and abilities, and
personal characteristics as well as anticipated
changes in any of these characteristics.

The class position of an individual is influenced by the company for which he works and
his position within the company. Intra-organi-
zational mobility is also societal mobility.

QUESTIONS

1. What interconnections do you see among family,
   religious, and economic behavior?
2. What is an "economic determinism" interpretation
   of behavior?
3. Why would it be impossible for the modern college
   to function as it does if there were no formal norm-
   role definitions developed?
4. List several different motive decisions which might
   be related to the same economic activity.
5. Is it possible for an organization to have an "official"
   set of value definitions? To what would you pay
   attention if you wanted to study this?

6. Describe the formal and informal power structure
   of some organization with which you are particularly
   familiar.
7. What types of behavior are involved in "organizational maintenance"?
8. How do standardized role definitions facilitate interaction in a large organization?
9. In what ways does informal socialization take place
   in a large organization?
10. Describe the formal and informal power structure
    of your sociology class.

PROJECT

Interview a business leader in the community to determine what he considers to be the major reasons why
he follows his professional role.

SUGGESTED READING

BLAU, PETER M., and W. RICHARD SCOTT. *Formal
Organizations: A Comparative Approach.* San Francisco: Chandler Publishing Co., 1962.

CAPLOW, THEODORE. *Sociology of Work.* Minneapolis:
University of Minnesota Press, 1954.

DUBIN, ROBERT. *The World of Work.* Englewood Cliffs,
N. J.: Prentice-Hall, Inc., 1958.

EISENSTADT, S. N. "Bureaucracy and Bureaucratization:
A Trend Report and Bibliography," *Current Sociology,* VII, No. 2 (1958), entire issue.

ETZIONI, AMITAI. *A Comparative Analysis of Complex
Organizations.* New York: The Free Press of
Glencoe, 1961.

HICKMAN, C. ADDISON, and MANFORD H. KUHN. *Individuals, Groups, and Economic Behavior.* New
York: Holt, Rinehart and Winston, Inc., 1956.

LIKERT, RENSIS. *New Patterns of Management.* New
York: McGraw-Hill Book Co., 1961.

MOORE, WILBERT E. *Man, Time, and Society.* New
York: John Wiley & Sons, Inc., 1963.

NOSOW, SIGMUND, and WILLIAM H. FORM (eds.). *Man,
Work, and Society.* New York: Basic Books, Inc.,
1962.

SCOTT, W. RICHARD. "Theory of Organizations," in
Handbook of Modern Sociology, ed. by ROBERT
E. L. FARIS. Chicago: Rand McNally & Co., 1964.
Chap. xiv.

SMELSER, NEIL J. *Sociology of Economic Life.* Englewood Cliffs, N. J.: Prentice-Hall, Inc., 1963.

WARNER, W. LLOYD, *et al. The American Federal Executive.* New Haven: Yale University Press, 1963.

24

Religion

Can you provide a sociological explanation for the fact that however varied they may be from group to group, the really important behavior patterns of a society are defined by the members of that society as having supernatural approval?

INTRODUCTION

In the culture of every group there are definitions which are religious in nature, and in the interaction of every society there is behavior which takes such definitions into account—religious behavior. This chapter analyzes the ways in which such phenomena are related to society in general and to the other particular segments of the socio-cultural milieu.

Although illustrations will be of specific religions in particular societies, our definition of religion will be sufficiently broad to cover the religion of the small primitive tribe and of a modern urbanized society as well. Greater comprehension of the material will result if the student remembers not to restrict his interpretation to his own particular religious experience.

Before we move into the discussion, however, let us briefly consider the religious composition

of the United States. The more than 250 different religious groups are frequently subdivided into three major categories—Protestant, Roman Catholic, and Jewish. Many different definitions are given to the label "church member." With the varied criteria as to just who is and who is not a member, and as to who should be carried on the official membership lists, comparison of membership figures is of limited value. However, the 1960 religious composition of the United States, according to the *1961 Yearbook of American Churches*, was as shown in the tabulation on the next page.

Religion, as a part of culture, consists of the configuration of definitions including, of course, the accompanying plans of action which in some way have to do with (1) the supernatural and/or (2) high-intensity or top-level value definitions, including definitions of sacredness. We include as a part of religion any knowledge, beliefs, or ideas which have to do with supernatural beings

Religious Group	Number of Members	Per Cent of Total United States Church Membership (Not Total Population)
Protestant	63 million	56
Roman Catholic	40 million	36
Jewish	5.5 million	5
Other		3

Source: Quoted from the *1961 Yearbook of American Churches*. Published by the National Council of Churches. Copyright 1960. Used with permission.

such as gods, angels, spirits, and related phenomena such as heaven and a life after death. The value definitions about which the group is most concerned are likewise included in our definition.

The specific content and the relationship between these two ingredients vary considerably from society to society. Whatever the pattern, however, we will, for sociological purposes, consider these definitions as a part of religion. The official configuration of such definitions of any religious group is their theology. Religious behavior is behavior which takes these definitions into account. We will use the term "religionist" to identify those who are deeply involved in religious behavior and who give strong attention to religious definitions. The term applies to leaders and laymen alike.

This definition is a sociological definition, and may be different from that used by others, including religionists, which may serve different purposes. Anything can be viewed in any number of different ways. Religion is no exception.

The culture of any group contains a pattern of religious definitions which share the characteristics of other definitions, in that they are passed on from generation to generation, are constantly changing, are man-made and learned through interaction, are the common property of the group, are cumulative, provide plans of action, and include ER and NER symbols. They relate to motivational and emotional behavior and are systematized. The religious segment of culture is unique in that it involves definitions which call attention to a realm believed to

be superempirical or supernatural, a realm believed to have an influence upon the empirical or natural world. This poses some questions about the applicability of the scientific method in the study of such definitions and behavior since the scientific method is restricted to the study of empirical phenomena.

In his study of religion, the scientist honors this limitation. The following discussion should be interpreted in this light. We are concerned with the empirical aspects of religion—not the superempirical. We are concerned with *man's* definitions *about* the supernatural, not with the supernatural *per se*. We are concerned with man's definitions of God but not with God's definition of man. We are concerned with the behavior of man—not the behavior of God. We are not, in our sociological discussion, even concerned with the question as to whether God exists or not, or the question as to which of the many available religious teachings is true *in the religious sense*. This restriction stems, of course, from the fact that his method of investigation does not permit the scientist to secure the second type of answer.

However, the fact that such answers cannot be secured scientifically does not mean that they cannot be secured by some other method—indeed they can. The same individual (or different individuals for that matter) uses one method to reach scientific decisions about a phenomenon of study, but in a different role may use a differ-

---

Secular Religion

"I suddenly realized that the devout Russian people no longer needed priests to pray them into heaven. On earth they were building a kingdom more bright than any heaven had to offer, and for which it was a glory to die . . ."
—John Reed.*

---

* Quoted in John Reed, "Conflict: The Brotherhood Grave," in *Sociology: Introductory Readings,* ed. by Read Bain (Philadelphia: J. B. Lippincott Co., 1962), p. 134.

Figure 24.1 Religious symbols vary considerably from society to society. This is the many-handed Indian goddess, incarnation of Shiva. (The Bettmann Archive, Inc.)

ent method to reach decisions about religious phenomena. Individuals may further integrate both types of answers into some meaningful larger picture. However, such integration is not the responsibility of sociology. Sociologists are, however, interested in how individuals do this type of integrating, without, again, being concerned with the question as to whether any integration is the right one, a good one, or a true one. Science has limitations.

What we have just said about religious decisions is also true about beauty decisions or justice decisions. The difference of method is the same as that between making a decision as to what happens when a set of chemicals are combined and a decision as to whether the resulting mixture is a beautiful mixture.

Religion as we have defined it is composed of two types of definitions: those concerning the supernatural, and definitions of sacredness—a type of value definition. Both of these are NER symbols. It follows that since man is the only animal who can use symbols, man is the only being who is religious. Religion is a uniquely human phenomenon.

The NER nature of religious symbols facilitates the development and perpetuation of religion. Since basically religious symbols have no empirical referent it is easy to see how explanation of their origin can translate "non-empirical" into "superempirical." Man appears to be reluctant to conclude that these NER symbols are man-made. Parents, in their efforts to get children to behave in the approved manner, are reluctant to simply make the statement that this "is our way."

The more frequent pattern is to say that the behavior is the *good* way, or to take it one step further, that the behavior is *God's* way. It is an oversimplification, but one of the generalizations stemming from a sociological analysis of religion is, speaking in monotheistic terms, that "our way is God's way" or at least our best or ideal way is God's way. This is true whatever the content of "our way" is.

There are some important social consequences of such practices, which we will merely identify at this point, but which will be elaborated as we proceed with our discussion:

1. Such definitions permit man, individually and collectively, to incorporate within his system of moral meaning or his value structure, a supernatural or top-level variable around which his whole configuration of value definitions can then be organized or structured into a somewhat consistent whole.

2. This system of moral meaning becomes involved in man's efforts to understand, adjust to, and justify those aspects of living which he experiences most intently—his successes as well as failures, frustrations, and insecurities.

3. Religious definitions about the *empirical world* may be used by man in the absence of or ignorance of scientific answers. History shows a frequent replacement of religious answers by scientific answers as the scope and acceptance of science have grown broader.

VALUE DEFINITIONS

Definitions of morality, righteousness, and goodness, and the reciprocal definitions of immorality, unrighteousness, and badness are a part of religion. Religion is not, however, the only source of such value definitions, but when such value definitions are given strong saliency, they become "religious" as we use the term. Every society and subsociety takes into account in its interaction a vast array of value definitions, with each particular definition being seen as having some degree of intensity or as falling somewhere along an intensity continuum. Those which fall at the high-intensity segment of the continuum are viewed as being different from those lower down, not only in intensity but also in origin. Their placement at the high-intensity pole of the continuum is justified by relating them not just to man, but to superhuman sources. Such definitions, of course, for those who accept them, serve to increase the likelihood that they will retain their saliency and be given important consideration in behavior decisions. If a group sincerely believes that a set of value definitions has been provided or at least endorsed by a Supreme Being, this increases the likelihood, but does not guarantee, that the group will take the definitions into account. For those who reject the idea of a Supreme Being (or at least of a particular Supreme Being) the involvement of these definitions may be quite different.

Our previous discussion of value definitions indicated that, in addition to the vast array of definitions which man develops about his empirical world, he develops a whole set of NER definitions which involve what we might call the moral world. He develops systems or ways of morally interpreting this empirical world, including, of course, the behavior of empirical beings, including himself. The set of value definitions is in a sense imposed upon or attributed to· this world. Value definitions identify the classifications or evaluations of the evaluator. Religious definitions are intimately involved in bringing order out of the vast congeries of value definitions held by a society.

Without biologically given drives or motivators to guide his interaction, man develops symbolic guides which he follows. He acquires definitions as to what he and others should do, and how they should relate themselves to each other. Approved patterns he calls good, fair, just, or moral. Disapproved patterns carry reverse labels. Man learns the moral system of his society and learns to *want* to have such a moral system. He learns to look for and to find a moral aspect of behavior.

Man seeks such answers not only with reference to the aspects of society or interaction which please him or which proceed smoothly, but also with reference to disruptive elements. He applies such definitions not only to health but to sickness; not only to peace but to war; not only to April showers but to April tornadoes. Once he accepts the premise that there is, in fact, a moral dimension, he is faced with the task of taking this dimension into account for the various aspects of living. Religious definitions are used by man to make moral sense out of his experiences. They may be involved in any and all aspects, but are particularly important in those aspects which he experiences most intently— either as intense pleasure or intense discomfort, as agony or frustration.

The intensity with which man may experience certain events is frequently surprising, startling, and somewhat unbelievable to many. When experiences reach such proportions, it is typical that they are viewed as being not just human but rather superhuman in origin; not just a result of interaction and internal responses, such as the influence of adrenalin in the blood stream. They are of supernatural origin.

The experiences which are extremely satisfying and rewarding to the participants are quite possibly more easily accepted as being *human* experiences. Those which are upsetting, disturbing, and calamitous are the ones most likely to be defined in religious or supernatural terms. Sapir has, in fact, defined religion in these terms, as "omnipresent fear and vast humility, paradoxically turned into bedrock security"[1] and Yinger his indicated that religion is "a system of beliefs and practices by means of which a group of people struggles with the ultimate problems of human life. It is the refusal to capitulate to death, to give up in the face of frustration, to allow hostility to tear apart one's human associations."[2]

Religious definitions, then, permit man to reach decisions about the moral nature of experience. They are used by man to find moral justification for whatever happens to him. The interpretation of this moral aspect may include sanction elements of reward and punishment. Certain experiences are, it is felt, the just, merited rewards for the related behavior, or they are the just, merited penalties for disapproved or evil behavior. In either event, they permit man to reach decisions about the morality of events and to fit these definitions into some structure or scheme. The typical use of religious definitions leads those involved to the decision that the experiences they have are morally justified or justifiable if man just searches hard enough for the correct interpretation.

The belief in the moral nature of the universe is related to man's awareness of the involvement of value definitions in his social world. He is aware that he does things which he defines as

[1] Edward Sapir, *Culture; Language and Personality* (Berkeley, Calif.: University of California Press, 1958), p. 123.

[2] J. Milton Yinger, *Religion, Society and the Individual* (New York: The Macmillan Co., 1957), p. 9.

good, and that those with whom he interacts are constantly making decisions as to whether X is good or bad. The child is early made aware of the fact that value definitions are given attention in human interaction. It is not difficult, then, to generalize awareness of the value or moral aspects of human interaction to the larger setting in which human interaction takes place, including, of course, the empirical world which provides the environment for his interaction, and the world or universe in which he views his particular world as being located. Since he is aware of the limited control he has over his empirical world, it is likely that the moral dimensions attributed thereto would be somewhat related to supernatural beings, powers, or entities.

NORM-ROLE DEFINITIONS

Beliefs in a supernatural realm are generally not just passively accepted. Instead, man attempts to relate himself to this realm in an active way. If supernatural beings are defined as powerful, efforts are usually made to direct this power toward the accomplishment of certain individual and group goals. The norm-role definitions developed by religious groups indicate with varying degrees of specificity what man should do to accomplish this. Praying (symbol manipulation) and other rituals are examples of frequently used patterns. Tremendous intergroup variability is evidenced in this respect.

The norm-role definitions which govern man–man relationships (as contrasted to man–God relationships) are also related to the high-intensity value definitions included in religion. The plans of action specified in the norm-role definitions represent man's efforts to actualize the value definitions of the group, particularly the top-level value definitions.

Our previous discussion of folkways and mores has indicated that the mores are always religiously reinforced. Members of a society are taught that these behavior patterns have not only societal approval but supernatural approval as well, with both societal and supernatural sanc-

The Role of Minister

In Springdale, the minister is expected to "get along with people" by being a "good fellow" and by being non-controversial and non-political. It is paradoxical that the Baptist minister, who represents the most controversial religious views, is also regarded personally as one of the best ministers in town. In his day-to-day relations with people he is friendly, personable, "says hello to everybody" and never discusses religion or politics.
—Arthur J. Vidich and Joseph Bensman.*

tions being related thereto. Acceptance of such beliefs increases the likelihood that the norm-role definitions will be followed. The important regulations of society are accordingly viewed as being more than the ordinary work of man. They are the best, the ultimate, the superior, the eternal. Acceptance of such definitions facilitates harmonious interaction. From a slightly different perspective we have been emphasizing that if our goal is to keep a group functioning, one way to facilitate this is to convince the members that the most important norm–role definitions are good or that they have supernatural endorsement—that they are of God.

The functional aspect, however, involves more than just a utilitarian device to keep established systems functioning and established leaders in power, although it may obviously help in such endeavors. Leaders themselves have convictions as to what is good, or of God. Leaders and followers usually seek what *to them* is the good life. Although we are certainly not endorsing a "great man" interpretation of leadership it is recognized that leaders are involved in interaction, and that it facilitates the leadership of leaders if they are convinced that their plans and behavior are good, moral, or just.

* Arthur J. Vidich and Joseph Bensman, *Small Town in Mass Society* (Garden City, N. Y.: Doubleday & Co., Inc., 1958), p. 244. (An Anchor Book.)

It is with reference to this function that it has been maintained that "if there were no God, man would invent one." The God concept is useful to man.

To the extent that leaders, followers, and any other groups within a society agree upon particular religious interpretations, religion helps to structure or integrate their interaction. Conversely, to the extent that there is disagreement, religion serves as a disruptive element which hampers society-wide harmony. Religion, in fact, is frequently a source of social conflict.

SELF DEFINITIONS

Top-intensity value definitions which are defined as being related to a supernatural realm and/or beings, could not long exist in a society

Figure 24.2 Symbol manipulation can take many forms: praying is an effort to influence the supernatural. (Wide World Photos.)

without influencing the self definitions of the members. If decisions are reached that harmonize one's behavior with "eternal" values and related norm-role definitions, self definitions are enhanced accordingly. If one is convinced that there is a divine or God-given plan which governs life on this earth and that his behavior serves to fulfill or enhance such a plan, his self definitions reflect this decision. Applying religious definitions to one's self permits the expansion of self definitions to infinite proportions—limited mainly by the religious concepts involved and the treatment received at the hands of significant others.

However, if one can be convinced that his behavior harmonizes with a supreme standard, he can also be convinced that it is at variance therewith. If one can be convinced that he is a saint, he can also be convinced that he is a sinner. If one can view himself as an exalted being he can also view himself as a fallen being. The decision that one has displeased society takes on increased significance if the belief is compounded with the conviction that one has displeased a Supreme Being as well.

Religion, then, may be involved in decisions, to state the extreme cases, that one is infinitely good or infinitely evil. Either definition may have tremendous consequences in the subsequent behavior of the individual.

Once negative self definitions are accepted, religion may be involved in the process by which the individual reaches decisions about forgiveness, reorientation, "cleansing," or "rebirth" of new self definitions. A religious experience may help to eliminate definitions of guilt. If one becomes convinced that he has done something wrong (NER definition) and that he himself is sinful or immoral, change in this NER self definition is facilitated if he is likewise convinced that there are established ways of changing it. Change in an NER definition may be facilitated if it is related to some particular procedure or ritual which provides evidence of an empirical change which may then be interpreted as indicative of an NER change. Actually doing something which one is convinced is related to NER

definitions facilitates changing the definition. Religious rituals may serve this purpose; other types of therapy may also be valid.

It is important to recognize the dual role of religion in this process. Religion may help to create the negative self definitions which it in turn attempts to change. Religiously oriented therapy has not proven equally effective in all cases.

Man involves religion in those aspects of living which he experiences most intensely—the experiences inevitably related to his self definitions. One such experience is death. While the patterns vary from group to group, frequently used adjustment technics are (1) providing plans of action which facilitate disposal of the body and re-integration of the family group which has been disrupted by the death, and (2) interpreting the experience in such a way that essential self definitions are not threatened. Death accordingly is defined not as the end but rather as the beginning of a new and different life. Individuals may see themselves as, in fact, being eternal, and when facing the death experience may echo the Biblical question, "Death, where is thy sting?"

The situation, however, is complex, as suggested by a study in which "religious" individuals were distinguished from "non-religious" individuals on the basis of whether they believed in a divine purpose in the operation of the universe, whether they believed in a life after death, and whether they accepted the Bible as revealing God's truths. It was found that the religious person (as thus defined), when compared to the non-religious person, was personally more afraid of death.[3] We cannot of course generalize from this limited evidence.

In any event, adjustment to death has been a perennial concern of religion, and the plea, "If I should die before I wake, I pray the Lord my soul to take," is familiar to many.

---

[3] Herman Feifel, "Attitudes Toward Death in Some Normal and Mentally Ill Populations," in Herman Feifel (ed.), *The Meaning of Death* (New York: McGraw-Hill Book Co., 1959), pp. 120–121.

SOCIALIZATION

Religious definitions and religious behavior are both learned, with both conscious and unconscious learning involved. While religious groups may believe that certain types of learning involve some kind of contact with the supernatural realm, they never stop at that point, but make conscious efforts to teach new members of the group their religion. Following religious rituals in the home, the church, or the synagogue are conscious efforts to teach religion, as are religious sermons, classes, and schools. Many aspects of religion are also transmitted unconsciously and may be woven into more secular behavior such as the discrimination patterns of the society. Much anti-Semitism, for instance, has been taught in this way.

Religion is also related to the socialization which takes place in the secular school systems. In the United States, for instance, many of the early schools, at all levels, were originally started by religious groups; Harvard, Yale, Michigan, Pennsylvania, Princeton, Columbia, Rutgers, Brown, William and Mary, and Dartmouth are illustrations at the university level.

The relationship, however, has not been a consistent one. Some religious groups endorse and encourage higher education while others do not. If a religious group is convinced that it has the "truth" and that secular education serves to contaminate that truth, it is easy to understand why they would not encourage such education.

In the United States various combinations of sacred–secular education have been worked out. The parochial school, sponsored and in general financed by the religious group involved, is well known. In such schools, education in a particular religion is provided along with secular subject matter, with the program of secular education usually meeting the government requirements. Roman Catholics, Jews, Seventh-Day Adventists, Lutherans, Methodists, and Quakers are among those involved in such programs. The Office of Education has estimated that in the 1959–1960 school year, 5,400,000 pupils in kindergarten through eighth grade out of a total national enrollment of 33,380,000 were enrolled in parochial and other private schools. It was also estimated that 1,100,000 out of a total enrollment of 9,590,000 in grades nine through twelve were in the same category. The percentage of American students enrolled in non-public elementary and secondary schools has increased from less than 10 per cent in 1930 to approximately 15 per cent in 1960.[4]

A second pattern is the released-time program in which students are excused from school classes for a period each day or each week to attend a class in religious instruction in a nearby church-controlled building.

Religious activities, including prayers and observance of major religious holidays, have been and continue to be frequently included in the state-supported school programs. Considerable attention has been drawn to such programs through the efforts of citizens interested in making the church–state separation more complete.

The reciprocal influence of religious and educational variables is suggested by the fact that the likelihood of an American's graduating from high school is related to his religious affiliation; Table 24.1 shows statistics from a study of 13,000 youth in Maryland in 1936. The figures are old ones and may have changed somewhat through the years, but not enough to have changed the pattern.

TABLE 24.1

Percentage of Youth Graduating from High School

Religious Affiliation of Parents	Per Cent of Youth Graduating from High School
Jewish	65
Protestant	40
Mixed	38
All	37
Roman Catholic	28
None	25

SOURCE: Leo Rosten, *A Guide to the Religions of America* (New York: Simon and Schuster, Inc., 1955), p. 235.

[4] See, for instance, Raymond A. Withey, Jr., "Role of Religion in Higher Education," *School and Society*, XXVI, No. 1975 (October 25, 1952), 257–261.

Lenski's 1958 Detroit Area Study distinguished among the educational attainments of white Protestants, Roman Catholics, and Jews. He found that the differences were not large. Jews were the most likely to have received some college education, and Catholics were the most likely to have received only a grammar school education. Catholics were as likely as Protestants to have received some college education, and Jews were more likely than Protestants to have received only a grammar school education. The findings are summarized as follows:

1. Catholics are more likely than Protestants or Jews to drop out of school without completing the unit of education they have begun;

2. Dropouts do not fare as well subsequently as those who complete an educational unit;

3. There is some evidence that the Catholic pattern of dropouts is a response to competitive difficulties encountered in the public schools;

4. Possibly the Catholic dropout pattern is a result of the positive attraction of earning one's own income and an unwillingness, or inability, to defer gratifications.[5]

An additional involvement of religion in the socialization process was found in a study of Mormon youth by Christiansen, Cowhig, and Payne. They found that the youth who were most active in their church were the ones most likely to positively evaluate a college education and, further, that they were the ones most likely to attend college.[6]

ROLE PLAYING AND ROLE TAKING

Playing roles which are primarily religious in nature and injecting a religious dimension into other more secular roles are bound to have effects throughout the whole society. Lenski concludes from his study of the Detroit area that the "religious factor" is of such importance that its con-

sequences parallel those of the social class factor.[7] The intricate weaving of this influence into the social fabric is suggested from Lenski's conclusion that religious affiliation is related to whether an individual will do each of the following things.

"Enjoy his occupation"	Jews, white Protestants, white Catholics, Negro Protestants
"Indulge in installment buying"	Negro Protestants, white Catholics, white Protestants, Jews
"Save to achieve objectives far in the future"	Jews, others
"Believe in the American Dream"	White Protestants, Jews, white Catholics, Negro Protestants
"Vote Republican"	White Protestants, white Catholics, Negro Protestants, Jews
"Favor the welfare state"	Jews, Negro Protestants, white Catholics, white Protestants
"Take a liberal point of view on the issue of freedom of speech"	White Protestants, white Catholics, Jews, Negro Protestants
"Oppose racial integration in the schools"	White Protestants, white Catholics, Jews
"Migrate to another community"	Negro Protestants, white Protestants, white Catholics, Jews
"Maintain close ties with his family"	Jews, white Catholics, Negro Protestants, white Protestants
"Develop a commitment to the principle of intellectual autonomy"	Jews, white Protestants, white Catholics, Negro Protestants
"Have a large family"	Negro Protestants, white Catholics, Jews, white Protestants
"Complete a given unit of education" (rather than drop out)	Jews, white Protestants, white Catholics, Negro Protestants
"Rise in the class system"	Jews, white Protestants, white Catholics, Negro Protestants

[5] Gerhard Lenski, *The Religious Factor* (Garden City, N. Y.: Doubleday & Co., Inc., 1961), pp. 235–240.

[6] John R. Christiansen, James D. Cowhig, and John W. Payne, *Educational and Occupational Progress of Rural Youth in Utah, a Follow-Up Study*, Social Science Bulletin No. 2, Brigham Young University, Provo, Utah, August, 1962.

[7] Gerhard Lenski, *The Religious Factor* (Garden City, N. Y.: Doubleday & Co., Inc., 1961). This summary form of Lenski's findings was taken from Bernard Berelson and Gary A. Steiner, *Human Behavior* (New York: Harcourt, Brace & World, Inc., 1964), pp. 395–396.

Note that he distinguished among Roman Catholics, Jews, white Protestants, and Negro Protestants. The rank order (high to low) of each of these groups on each characteristic is also shown.

These differences were found to hold true when other social factors were held constant, which provides evidence that they are related to the religious differences *per se*. Lenski also concluded that as a general rule, when there are differences of any magnitude between two socio-religious groups, internal differences are also present.

Other research has also found that religious affiliation is related to such factors as whether an individual will want to have a large family, actually expect to have a large family, and actually have a large family,[8] and even whether he will have a heart attack.[9]

CREATIVITY AND CHANGE

Creative activity is found in the religious realm as it is in all realms. Religion always exists in a constantly changing society. Religious creativity is akin to poetic and literary creativity in that the process involves paying major attention to NER symbols, and the product involves a new system of symbols related to the basic themes which we have identified in this chapter. Not everyone has equal facility in such creativity. Religious creativity is, in fact, restricted by unique aspects of religious definitions. In that religious definitions themselves are viewed as being divine, supernatural, eternal, ultimate, and unchanging, this very aspect discourages innovation. It is easy to accept the goal of defending established definitions rather than attempting to change them. If something is ultimate or final, it is final! If one feels he has the final truth he

---

[8] Ronald Freedman *et al.*, *Family Planning, Sterility and Population Growth* (New York: McGraw-Hill Book Co., 1959).

[9] Alan Muller, "Religion as a Factor in the Etiology of Chronic Diseases," paper presented at Pacific Sociological Association Meeting, April, 1963.

Conversion

A Study of the Galilean and Mormon missions among the Rimrock Navaho reveals that the Indians who wished to identify with white men were those who felt that they could not achieve satisfaction through the conventional Navaho patterns. Some were ignorant of the Navaho ways, and others who were familiar with them felt unfulfilled. The churches were filled with misfits.

—Robert N. Rapoport.*

---

may be reluctant to do anything which will "rock the boat."

However, since religious innovation involves basically NER symbols, which cannot be disproven by established scientific technics, professed innovators, if they present their message in a manner which appeals to others, may easily gain a following.

Religious innovators called prophets or messiahs do in fact constantly arise. Typically their initial following is small and is secured from among those who for some reason are dissatisfied with the established religious patterns and with their place in the secular world. Religious protest usually has more secular overtones as well.

Religious innovators are viewed as having particular relationships with the supernatural realm, with the prophet being viewed as speaking for and directly representing supernatural beings, and the messiah being defined as himself being divine. Defining a leader in this manner facilitates acceptance by the followers of the new religious definitions and the rituals which are introduced.

The label "sect" is used to identify small new religious groups which are somewhat "at war" with the world which they define as wicked, while "denomination" or church is used to identify a large, well-established group which has

---

* Robert N. Rapoport, "Changing Navaho Religious Values," *Papers of the Peabody Museum of American Archaeology and Ethnology*, XLI, No. 2 (1954).

TABLE 24.2

Characteristic	Sect	Denomination
Size	Small	Large
Relationship with other religious groups	Rejects—believes sect alone has "truth"	Accepts other denominations and is able to work in harmony with them
Wealth (church property, buildings, salary of clergy, income of members)	Limited	Extensive
Religious services	Emotional emphasis—tries to recapture conversion thrill; informal; extensive congregational participation	Intellectual emphasis; concern with teaching; formal; limited congregational participation
Clergy	Unspecialized; little if any professional training; frequently part-time	Specialized; professionally trained; full-time
Doctrines	Literal interpretation of Scriptures; emphasis upon other-worldly rewards	Liberal interpretation of Scriptures; emphasis upon this-worldly rewards
Membership requirements	Conversion experience; emotional commitment	Born into group or ritualistic requirements; intellectual commitment
Relationship with secular world	"At war" with the secular world which is defined as "evil"	Endorses prevailing culture and social organization
Social class of members	Mainly lower class	Mainly middle class

accommodated itself to the larger society. A cult is a loosely structured group sharing some focal interest. Individuals are not born into a cult, nor do they formally join one. The simple acceptance of the cult's beliefs is all that is required for membership. An *"ecclesia"* is, like the denomination, well established and accommodated to the world, but is also either national or international in scope.

Differences between the sect and the denomination are presented in summary form in Table 24.2.

STRATIFICATION

In small primitive societies, one set of religious beliefs and practices usually permeates the whole society and is accepted as *the* religion. Such societies are frequently referred to as "sacred" societies with the term suggesting that the whole way of life from economic activity to the stratification patterns is defined as

sacred. The efforts of Americans to separate church and state would not even occur to such groups, since to them the religious dimension of behavior is "just there," and cannot be separated from non-religious aspects.

At the other extreme is the secular type of society found in the United States. In such a society religious definitions and rituals are seen as more specialized, and distinctions are made between that which is religious and that which is secular. These distinctions are very sharp in some areas and rather blurred in others. In a secular society, the scientific method is used to make many of the decisions of interest to the group.

In such a society, religious diversity is frequently found, with the particular patterns being related to other social factors. If religion is involved in efforts to secure the goals previously discussed (top-level value definitions, thus contributing to social organization, crisis adjustment, securing scientifically unknown definitions), it would follow that different specific religious con-

TABLE 24.3

Per Cent of Religious Groups at Various Class Levels

Per Cent

	10	20	30	40	50	60	70	80	90	100

Episcopal

Congregational

Presbyterian

Jewish

Methodist

Lutheran

Roman Catholic

Baptist

	10	20	30	40	50	60	70	80	90	100

Upper Class - - - - -   Middle Class — — —   Lower Class ————

Religious Affiliation of Those Listed in *Who's Who*

	Representation in 1910-1911 *Who's Who in America* in Proportion to Church Membership (Fry)	Sample Cases per 100,000 Male Church Members, *Who's Who in the East*, 1942-1943 (Davis)
Unitarian	32.5	20
Reformed	6.25	—
Universalist	6.43	—
Episcopalian	6.07	4
Congregational	4.96	4
Quaker	4.40	—
Presbyterian	3.11	4
Christian Scientist	1.27	—
Methodist	0.89	1
Baptist	0.70	1
Disciples of Christ	0.61	—
Lutheran	0.32	—
Roman Catholic	0.31	0.1

Sources: C. L. Fry, "The Religious Affiliation of American Leaders," *Scientific Monthly*, XXXVI (March, 1933), 241–249; and B. Davis, "Eminence and Level of Social Origin," *The American Journal of Sociology*, LIX (July, 1953), 11-18.

figurations would not provide these goals equally well to those at all class levels. Research has found that religious behavior is related to social class in many different ways. Some of these have already been suggested in our discussion of the involvement of religion in role-playing behavior. Two additional findings are summarized in Table 24.3. The first reports the results of four polls taken by the American Institute of Public Opinion in 1946 and 1947 which related church affiliation and class position.[10] The second indicates the religious affiliation of Americans who were listed in *Who's Who in America*, with such listing being an indication of higher-class placement.

While members from all class levels are found in every church, the percentages of a given class in a group do vary characteristically with the group. Baptists and Roman Catholics have the highest percentage of lower-class members and the lowest percentage of upper-class members. The proportions of upper-class members is about equal for the four groups having the highest percentage of these, the Episcopal, Congregational, Presbyterian, and Jewish groups, whereas the percentage of lower-class members in these groups is less consistent. Methodists and Lutherans fall about midway between these extremes. Such a finding provides evidence of the fact that religion has a definite relationship to class structure but of course sheds no light upon why such a relationship obtains.

PRIMARY–SECONDARY INTERACTION

A modified type of primary relationship obtains between religious leaders and parishioners. Leaders are frequently granted special access to

[10] Studies of 1956–1957 data relating religious affiliation and education, occupation, and income found a pattern similar to the 1946–1947 data. See Bernard Lazerwitz, "Religion and Social Structure in the United States," in Louis Schneider (ed.), *Religion, Culture and Society* (New York: John Wiley & Sons, Inc., 1964), pp. 426–439.

Religion and Social Class

Among the socially elite of Hometown there is not a single Negro, Jewish, or Italian-American person. Members of the elite are native born of native-born parents. Catholics are rare in the inner circles, although some Catholic adherents are found in peripheral circles. Elite members are overwhelmingly members of prestigeful Protestant churches and are Republicans in politics.

—Robin M. Williams, Jr.*

the more intimate aspects of the behavior of their followers. Members may, for instance, confess their wrongdoing to their religious leaders or may seek counsel from them on personal problems. Leaders may, in fact, be defined as having great understanding or deep insight into human behavior. The lack of reciprocity, however, is evident from the fact that leaders do not typically confess their sins to parishioners, nor consult with them on personal or private matters. Intimate insight may, however, be provided in lessons and sermons delivered to the congregation. The primaryness of the relationship, however, is a one-sided one.

Man–man religious relationships are frequently of a primary nature. Within the sect the primaryness of the relationship is maximized. Within the local congregation of the larger denomination, efforts to approximate primary relationship are frequently initiated. As the primary relationship is approached, members of the same group feel free, possibly even obligated, to expose their "inner feelings" to each other. Meetings of the group in which members "bear testimony" of their religious convictions provide an institutionalized means of intimate self exposure.

Establishment of primary relationship within the religious group serves a control function, in

* Robin M. Williams, Jr., *Strangers Next Door* (Englewood Cliffs, N. J.: Prentice-Hall, Inc., 1964), p. 21.

that with intimate knowledge about each other, members are in effect constantly indicating to each other the extent to which they conform to group standards or confessing the extent to which they digress therefrom. In a sense, members of a small primary sect are constantly checking on each other, providing support to continued conformity and negative sanctions for non-conformity. As the group gets larger, more formal norm-role definitions are established. Although complete dedication to religious standards is still expected and encouraged, the process of "checking up on" members tends to become standardized or institutionalized around the established norm-role definitions, which most likely involve easily observable and possibly the least-involved behavior patterns, such as church attendance, payment of offerings, participation in established rituals, usually on the grounds that such criteria form an index of the deeper, more personal aspects of religious commitment.

ETHNIC MINORITY INTERACTION

If some configuration of characteristics is defined as of sufficient importance to the group that those who share the characteristics are considered to be a group and typically receive similar treatment at the hands of other members of the society, it would be surprising if the religious definitions of the society were not pertinent. In the first place, such distinctions with the discriminatory treatment related thereto must one way or another be justified. It would appear safe to hypothesize that the greater the degree of discrimination involved in interaction patterns, the greater the likelihood that religious sanction will be involved. If those with an ethnic identification are, for instance, denied admission to certain schools, certain occupations, certain residential areas, certain leisure-time activities or leisure-time areas, those doing the discriminating will attempt to provide for themselves as well as for new or potential members of the society moral justification for such discrimination. Well-

established patterns will be defined as having religious or supernatural sanction or justification.

In addition, if ethnic or minority identification is viewed as of enough importance to be taken into account in most interaction, it is likely that it will be taken into account as decisions are made as to membership restrictions of local religious congregations. In the United States, the local parish of the Roman Catholic Church, for instance, frequently reflects the Irish, Italian, Puerto Rican, or other identity of its members. Since such groups, particularly first-generation groups (in terms of residence in America), tend to live in the same areas, their living patterns facilitate religious segregation.

The Negro–white caste line in the United States during the first half of the twentieth century was likewise widely reflected in religious affiliation and worship practices. In fact, segregation was apparently most complete during church services, since less than one per cent of American Negroes regularly worshipped with white Americans. Religious leaders, however, have been active in the civil rights movement.

The Hate Stare

An author who passed for Negro reports:

The hate stare was everywhere practiced. . . . On Sunday, I made the experiment of dressing well and walking past some of the white churches just as services were over. In each instance, as the women came through the church doors and saw me, the "spiritual bouquets" changed to hostility. The transformation was grotesque. In all of Montgomery only one woman refrained. She did not smile. She merely looked at me and did not change her expression. My gratitude to her was so great it astonished me.

—John Howard Griffin.*

---

* John Howard Griffin, *Black Like Me* (Boston: Houghton Mifflin Co., 1961), p. 117.

COLLECTIVE BEHAVIOR

Religious factors may provide the major (although most likely never the exclusive) criteria taken into account in crowd and/or mob behavior. Acceptance of in-group members frequently accompanies strong rejection of out-group members. Well-established church groups have usually, in fact, been intolerant of other competing religious groups. The American patterns of recognizing religious differences and highly evaluating the very fact of religious pluralism are the exception rather than the rule, and, in fact, all patterns which grew out of considerable intolerance in the American colonies, most of which had an established or state-supported church. Intolerance is a factor contributing to mob–crowd demonstrations. As Lee has said, "It is too easy and even perhaps dishonest to think that the church is the solvent of social conflict. In a mood of confession we know that the church is often part of the problem and not merely the cure.[11] The crusades illustrate a major conflict involving religion.

Within-group religious behavior may also be used to demonstrate another aspect of collective or unstructured behavior. Religious services which call for extensive congregation participation such as singing, chanting, swaying, or rhythmic movements of one type or another, or which provide for individual expressions of the "working of the holy spirit" would be classified as expressive crowds. Revival meetings frequently follow the expressive crowd pattern. In such meetings, emotional contagion is particularly evident, and the "emotional pitch" of the interaction may reach a high level. Behavior such as jerking, shaking, dancing, or rolling on the floor may be encouraged, and this behavior may contribute to the use of a popular label such as "Holy Rollers" to identify such groups.

11 Robert Lee, "Introduction: Religion and Social Conflict," in Robert Lee and Martin E. Marty (eds.), *Religion and Social Conflict* (Fair Lawn, N. J.: Oxford University Press, 1964), p. 7.

SUMMARY

Religion, which involves NER definitions, is defined sociologically as the definitions and behavior which relate man to the realm of the supernatural.

Such definitions include high-intensity value definitions. So long as attention is restricted to religious definitions and the manner in which they are involved in man–man interaction, as contrasted with man–God interaction, religion can be studied scientifically. The scientist, however, is not concerned with questions as to the correctness of any religious definitions *per se*.

When man involves such definitions in his interaction he facilitates making moral interpretations of behavior. Such definitions, applied to intensely experienced behavior including successes and failures, may reduce the potentially disruptive aspects thereof, depending upon how well these definitions harmonize with the other aspects of the socio-cultural milieu.

Religious norm-role definitions specify how one may avail himself of supernatural power, and religious definitions further provide more and/or supernatural justification for the mores, which, again, may contribute to order or disorder depending upon how the religious aspects harmonize with the non-religious and whether the rate of religious change is somewhat comparable to that of the non-religious aspects. Religion, however, is traditionally conservative.

Religion is learned and is related to how one lives with himself and others. The influence of religious definitions and religious behavior extends the width and depth of interaction. Specific relationships which have been found by research can be identified: involvement in ethnic, racial, class, and caste behavior; secular education; and even the supposedly private act of having a heart attack.

Change in religion is related to the NER definitions involved. Splinter groups (sects) are led by a prophet, messiah, or other similar type of leader, and usually arise during periods of social unrest.

QUESTIONS

1. List three statements about religion which could be scientifically tested and three which could not.
2. Discuss Niebuhr's statement "Conscience is not purely individual. The individual is best able to defy the community when his conscience is informed and reinforced by another community."
3. Which is most capable of being realized—a universal religion or a universal science?
4. What does the text mean when it suggests that religion may expand the self to infinite proportions?
5. If it is true that religion endorses the mores of the group, what is the sequence of origin? Does society develop its mores, and does religion then provide sanctification for them, or does religion establish its value system and then society conform; or is there an interactive relationship between these two factors?
6. What are some of the consequences of including religious rituals and teaching in the programs of public schools?
7. In what ways might religious beliefs facilitate or hinder mobility in America?
8. Provide some illustrations of how individuals use religion in their efforts to adjust to crisis situations.
9. Provide a sociological explanation for the fact that all religious groups are not equally represented in *Who's Who in America*.
10. If man were somehow to lose his ability to use symbols, what would you speculate would happen to his religious beliefs and practices?

PROJECT

Analyze the content of a religious sermon or article and determine whether you think it contributed to positive or negative self definitions.

SUGGESTED READING

ARGYLE, MICHAEL. *Religious Behavior.* London: Routledge & Kegan Paul, Ltd., 1958.

DURKHEIM, EMILE. *The Elementary Forms of the Religious Life.* New York: The Free Press of Glencoe, 1947.

FICHTER, JOSEPH H., S. J. *Social Relations in an Urban Parish.* Chicago: The University of Chicago Press, 1953.

FICHTER, JOSEPH H., S. J. *The Dynamics of a City Church.* Chicago: The University of Chicago Press, 1951.

GOODE, WILLIAM J. *Religion Among the Primitives.* New York: The Free Press of Glencoe, 1951.

HERBERG, WILL. *Protestant-Catholic-Jew.* Rev. ed. Garden City, N. Y:. Doubleday & Co., Inc., 1960.

HOULT, THOMAS FORD. *The Sociology of Religion.* New York: Holt, Rinehart and Winston, Inc., 1958.

LEE, ROBERT, and MARTIN E. MARTY (eds.). *Religion and Social Conflict.* Fair Lawn, N. J.: Oxford University Press, 1964.

LENSKI, GERHARD. *The Religious Factor.* Garden City, N. Y.: Doubleday & Co., Inc., 1961.

SALISBURY, W. SEWARD. *Religion in American Culture.* Homewood, Ill.: The Dorsey Press, Inc., 1964.

SCHNEIDER, LOUIS (ed.). *Religion, Culture and Society.* New York: John Wiley & Sons, Inc., 1964.

VERNON, GLENN M. *Sociology of Religion.* New York: McGraw-Hill Book Co., 1962.

WEBER, MAX. *The Protestant Ethic and the Spirit of Capitalism.* London: George Allen & Unwin, 1930.

WEBER, MAX. *The Religion of China, The Religion of India, Ancient Judaism.* New York: The Free Press of Glencoe, 1951, 1958, 1958, respectively.

YINGER, J. MILTON. *Religion, Society and the Individual.* New York: The Macmillan Co., 1957.

Part VII

Social Changes

25

Creativity and Change

Writing a term paper, assuming that it was not directly copied from some one source, involves creativity on the part of the college student. Think through the process by which you wrote your last paper and decide (1) how the socio-cultural base of the college community was involved, (2) how much student creativity was involved, and (3) the different types of·creativity involved.

INTRODUCTION

Two major strands of thought have been woven into our previous discussions—(1) those having to do with stability and order and (2) those having to do with change or disorder. In this chapter, attention is directed to the changing aspects of interaction and the process by which change is produced—the process of creativity.

Creativity is defined as the process whereby something new or unique is introduced into the socio-cultural milieu. It is the process which produces "effective surprise," or which reveals "unsuspected kinship between . . . facts long known, but wrongly believed to be strangers to

one another." [1] Creativity is the process by which one goes beyond the common or established ways of experiencing the world. Other terms sometimes used to identify this process include "invention," "innovation," "inspiration," "revelation," and the "aha-experience."

The newness involved in the process may include or may result in (1) new predictiveness, whereby those concerned are capable of making predictions about phenomena of concern, which they were previously unable to do, (2) seeing new relationships which were not evident before, and (3) new combinations of symbols of a visionary, artistic, or metaphorical type.

[1] H. Poincaré, "Science and Hypothesis," in *The Foundations of Science*, trans. by George Bruce Halsted (Ephrata, Pa.: The Science Press, Inc., 1946).

377

The new perspective, the new behavior pattern, or the new empirical object will, of course, be composed of already existing elements. The newness is in the form or the combination of elements.

We might contrast creativity with discovery, which is the process of finding or paying attention to an existing object to which one did not previously pay attention. One discovers gold or uranium ore. Invention involves the active combination of elements into a new form. Discovery, planned or accidental, involves the passive perception of existing phenomena. Yet, as Nordskog has said:

> The two processes are, however, closely interrelated. Discovery of new facts or principles in physical or mental nature presupposes the invention of new methods of acting or thinking; on the other hand, invention of new influences and reactions, whether in nature or in society, is rarely devoid of newly discovered facts as assisting, inspiring, or even originating its conditions.[2]

Everyday Creativity—Emergent Behavior

While this chapter gives major attention to those acts or products which produce "effective surprise" or which differ sufficiently from the established forms and patterns to stand out, it should be emphasized that these are only the extreme examples of an everyday occurrence. Creative behavior is, in fact, an element in most interaction. If human beings were automatons with built-in mechanisms which routinely directed their behavior there would be no place for individual or group creativity. Human behavior, however, is not of this type. Previous discussions have emphasized that such behavior is orderly and systematic due, in part, to the culture which the group develops. It is, however, never completely routine and unimaginative. The process of labeling the phenomenon to which one pays attention is in part a creative act, as is the process of selecting, from all of the

---

Planned or Unplanned

When we come to creative thinking in the life of the individual, we are confronted with the most astonishing paradox of all: here, it usually seems, we do the least creative thinking, yet this is precisely the area in which we are best equipped for it and where the rewards of such thinking are greatest. Although it would be hard to establish quantitatively, experience suggests that we fall into an occupation, fall into marriage and other relations, fall into a way of living with alarming frequency, not stopping to ask ourselves: Is this the way of living for me? When we do think creatively in relation to our own lives, it seems most frequently to be in the sense of overcoming obstacles which stand between us and these so often unexamined goals. Even the creativeness of such thinking is limited by being in the service of an end, which has not been thought out. We limit ourselves to the solution of a problem which has much of the arbitrariness of the laboratory situation; we neglect to ask the creative question, to set the problem itself in its wider context.

—Mary Henle.*

---

elements in the universe to which one could pay attention, the ones to which he actually does pay attention.

The process of role taking or of arriving at decisions as to the meaning of the behavior of others likewise involves a creative aspect. Gaining understanding which involves integration of aspects to which one has been sensitized involves a creative aspect. Defining the situation is a creative act. Asking questions and determining which questions to ask have a creative element. Becoming aware of what one does not know is creative.

Interaction has its emergent, creative aspects—some experiences, of course, more than others.

---

[2] John Eric Nordskog, *Social Change* (New York: McGraw-Hill Book Co., 1960), p. 30.

* Mary Henle, "The Birth and Death of Ideas," in Howard E. Gruber, Glenn Terrell, and Michael Wertheimer (eds.), *Contemporary Approaches to Creative Thinking* (1962), p. 47. With permission from Atherton Press.

TYPES OF CREATIVITY

Change can take place in any aspect of anything. Three major types of change in which the sociologist is interested are as follows.

Cultural Change

Change in definitions, involving both ER and NER symbols and the plans of action incorporated into these definitions, is a major type of change. Creativity is found with reference to the philosophical, religious, ethical, poetic, mathematical, and humor systems and in the system of labels which man uses to identify the various aspects of the empirical world to which he pays attention. From the symbolic interactionist perspective, this involves "cutting up" the world in a different manner and applying new labels, or applying old labels to new aspects, so that they can be taken into account in a different way. It involves arranging symbols in a new manner so that the aspects of the world to which they refer can be experienced in a new way. It may involve inventing new symbols to use in the labeling process.

Social Change

Change may occur in the way in which individuals or groups relate themselves to each other. Creativity of this type would, of course, be related to culture change and would follow the new or revised plans of action involved therein. Thus, new types or aspects of governmental systems, educational systems, recreational and family interaction patterns, to mention but a few, are constantly being developed and practiced. Interaction patterns within any society are constantly being reorganized.

Actually, since the culture change and the social change are intertwined, it is simpler for some purposes to simply talk of socio-cultural change and include both under this one label.

Change in Culture Objects

Change in the empirical objects man utilizes is also a frequent occurrence. This is the type of change with which most people are most familiar. Man's history is one of constant and increasing invention. New "mousetraps" of one type or another have constantly been introduced into society. For many the word "invention" is first thought of as applying to empirical objects. In the United States today, invention in this area is proceeding at a rapid pace. Over a hundred-year period, the number of patents issued by the Commissioner of Patents increased from approximately 7,000 in 1860 to approximately 50,000 in 1960.[3] It is true, of course, that planned change in the empirical world is preceded by symbolic change. Man usually decides first what he wants to do, and then goes ahead with his plans of action. Changes and inventions may be worked out "on paper" before they are transformed into material objects or interaction patterns.

Taking into account all types of change, the contemporary world appears to be changing more rapidly than at any other time in history.

INDIVIDUAL AND GROUP CREATIVITY

It would be inaccurate to attribute change or creativity completely to an individual. Isolated individuals do not exist, and everything individuals do is directly or indirectly related to others both present and past. However, some innovations are more of an individual phenomenon than others. Thomas Edison, for instance, did much of his inventing while alone in his laboratory. Some individuals are better able to create while isolated from others, and quite possibly some things might be easier to create individually than in a group.

However, with increased industrialization and urbanization, group efforts at creativity have increased. Research laboratories are set up to permit such efforts. Bruner, a psychologist, describes his experience in a group which was

---

[3] U. S. Bureau of the Census, *Historical Statistics of the United States, 1789–1945*, pp. 312–313; and *Annual Report of the U. S. Commissioner of Patents.* (Washington, D. C.: Government Printing Office.)

Figure 25.1   The creativity of teen-agers reflects the social conditions in which they live.   (Wide World Photos.)

hired by an engineering consulting firm that designed such things as dams for India and atomic reactors for the government. "The group" as they called themselves worked apart from the rest of the firm, both physically and intellectually, and was actually somewhat autonomous in that the leader did the hiring and firing of its members. During the year under consideration the group consisted of Bruner, another psychologist, a highly skilled shop technician, and four others.[4] A high degree of group loyalty

[4] Jerome S. Bruner, in Howard E. Gruber, Glenn Terrell, and Michael Wertheimer (eds.), *Contemporary Approaches to Creative Thinking* (New York: The Atherton Press, 1963), pp. 1–30.

and *esprit de corps* developed. Once they were given a problem to solve they would start their discussion on rather trivial matters and then gradually lead into serious matters. Every session was taped and tapes were reviewed periodically to seek for insights and leads concerning their problem. Models were built and analyzed, then discarded and modified. The task at hand usually became an all-consuming one. They became deeply and personally involved in "it."

The group worked in relative isolation. They defined themselves as "elegant generalists" capable of doing the assigned task. They protected each other in their efforts at creativity—no idea was too absurd to be considered. They enjoyed being creative individuals and reject-

ing some of the conventional aspects of life. This group, as any group, developed its own norm definitions which patterned interaction and provided value judgments and rewards and punishments (sanctions) to support their activities. Products of their creative efforts were also rewarded by the larger society in the form of salary and prestige. The group was, of course, composed of creative individuals, but the resultant product was produced by the group; it could not be said to have been produced by any one individual.

SOCIO-CULTURAL BASE

The process of creativity, like any other process, always takes place in a social setting and is in some way related to the social factors present. Individual or small-group creativity is, in fact, but one aspect of the creativity of a society. Whole societies have characteristic patterns of creativity and the various correlates can be identified. Let us now turn our attention to some of these relationships.

Simultaneous Discoveries and Inventions

Telescope: Jansen, Lippershey, Metius, 1608

Sunspots: Fabricius, Galileo, Harriott, Scheiner, 1611

Nitrogen: Rutherford, 1772, Scheele, 1773

Oxygen: Priestley, Scheele, 1774

Water is H₂O: Cavendish, Watt, 1781, Lavoisier, 1783

Steamboat: Jouffroy, 1783, Rumsey, 1787, Fitch, 1788; Symington, 1788

Theory of Planetary Disturbances: Lagrange, Laplace, 1808

Telegraph: Henry, Morse, Steinheil, Wheatstone and Cooke, about 1837

and many others.

—A. L. Kroeber.*

As previously defined, creativity involves the recombining of already existing elements so that a relatively new product emerges. Something is not created from nothing. It would follow then that the condition of existing elements would always be related to the inventive process.

We would not expect the American pioneers to have invented rockets and satellites, because they had not at that time invented the requisite component parts. Automobiles could not be invented until there were wheels, gasoline motors, and gears to combine to produce the vehicle. Electric refrigerators could not be invented until man had learned how to produce electricity. The phenomenon of simultaneous inventions attests to this principle.

The same principle applies to the invention of new words, symbols, or symbol systems. If the student were to attempt such invention he would, of necessity, have to start where he is and work with what he has. For instance, before he can write a new novel, he must first master the fundamental norm definitions of grammar and novel development.

* From A. L. Kroeber, "Causes of Social Change," in *Sociology: Introductory Readings*, edited by Read Bain (Philadelphia: J. B. Lippincott Co., 1962), p. 44.

In like manner, efforts to establish democratic forms of government in societies which have not already developed the major component parts from which a democracy is built have not been very successful.

The inventive process involves chain reactions. New links are forged on the existing chains, not in isolation. One invention opens the door to another or more likely to *others*. In this manner, patterns of change develop which strongly influence subsequent creativity. The movement of change in a particular general direction has been referred to as cultural drift. The term "drift" suggests that the change is not all planned change, but rather the result of many established patterns of behavior. Inventions are made when the socio-cultural milieu is ready for them. The total social setting is more harmonious to the development of certain things than others.

The involvement of a multiplicity of socio-cultural factors in the creative process can be shown from an analysis of a hypothetical invention made by a scientist working for a large corporation on a government-financed grant. The invention *belongs* to

The scientist—after all, *he* invented it.

The corporation—they hired him and paid him for his services and provided other encouragement.

The government—they provided the money for the corporation.

His teachers—they taught him the basic foundation facts from which the invention grew.

His ancestors—they provided the culture for the teachers who taught the scientist.

His wife and family—they sustained him and encouraged him.

His religious group—they provided a value system which defined invention and the hard work which went into it as moral.

His society—which was organized in such a way that all of these variables could be interrelated so as to permit *him* to make the invention.

The interrelationships of all of these factors are more complex than is suggested by this analysis. These and many others are woven into a society-wide fabric, the details of which may be far from apparent to any inventor or other observer. A society is composed of a whole network of interrelated elements, with the level and types of creativity therein related to the over-all system, which involves many other subsystems. Every society has its own system of "checks and balances," all of which are involved. Individual interaction patterns, no one of which may make much direct impression upon the whole society, are all involved. In combination they produce society-wide reactions. It is true, of course, that some single invention may under certain conditions have tremendous social repercussions, but it is also true that the social conditions have as much influence upon the eventual outcome as the invention *per se.*

The influence of societal factors is further seen by the fact that the birth of a single child may have but limited consequences, but an increase in the birth rate of the society may be related to changes in most major institutions and organizations therein. One immigrant may have little society-wide influence but an increase in the

immigration of the nation may be felt throughout the land. One individual endorsing a new value system, likewise when compounded, influences the society and the individuals therein in many ways which at first glance are only remotely related to the specific value. The value systems of the society are related to many changes therein.

Whole systems of interrelated variables are found in a society. And while it may be difficult to trace a direct relationship between one element thereof and one particular invention or change, nonetheless patterns exist between the level of creativity of any society and the characteristics of the entire socio-cultural milieu. Composite patterns of economic systems, religious systems, family systems, educational systems, military systems, and many others provide the foundation from which social change emerges.

From another perspective, those concerned with promoting planned change quickly become aware of the limitations of individual efforts, and of the efforts of many individuals which are uncoordinated. When those who share common aspirations and interests become aware of this commonality, they may decide that "United we stand, divided we fall." Norm-role definitions may be developed, leadership arise, financing be secured, value supports provided, efforts made to integrate with other existing groups, and from such efforts a social movement may be born, nurtured, and sustained. Extensive societal change may or may not result.

The total socio-cultural milieu of any society then is more harmonious with the development of certain patterns than others. In the United States, for instance, long-established trends toward greater industrialization, urbanization, mobility, and secularization, to mention but a few, have been established. These of course reflect a long historical process involving the interaction and interrelationship of a multiplicity of factors. Efforts to reverse any of these trends could be expected to meet with only limited success. Inventions, both social and material, are likely to be made to harmonize with these established patterns.

Change Related to Change

Trends that are relatively impervious to attempts to alter them may offset deliberate planning— for example, trends in birth rates may be out of phase with respect to plans for improving schools. Slow and simple changes may intersect with rapid and complex transformations —for example, the steady rate of economic growth through private investment may be inadequate to meet sudden and complex changes in national defense needs and foreign-aid policies. Strains thus arise from lack of synchronization of types and rates of change.

—Wilbert E. Moore.*

---

* Wilbert E. Moore, *Social Change* (Englewood Cliffs, N. J.: Prentice-Hall, Inc., 1963), p. 3.

In addition to intrasociety factors, there are also intersociety relationships which are related to creativity and change. Boundary lines may be maintained as an "iron curtain" or an unguarded, unfenced line. Societies, on the basis of many internal factors as well as intersociety variables, go to war and may be conquered or may conquer—as a group, not as individuals. Societies may encourage "cultural exchange" or they may not. Culture borrowing or diffusion is impossible without intersociety contacts of some kind.

This discussion does not imply that the over-all pattern of change is one of harmony and stability. Indeed, it is not! Changes may be made which are rewarding to an individual or a group, but which are contrary to the goals of other individuals, other groups, or society. Criminal groups and individuals may invent new devices and/or organizational technics which may be used in support of their criminal activities but which are in opposition to the goals of the larger group. There are "good guys" and "bad guys" involved in creative processes as in all activities, and the decisions as to which individuals merit which label will also vary from group to group.

Every society includes conflicting elements, and every society develops its own technics of "tension management." One way or another all such factors are involved in the long-run direction the society takes. Whether the long-run (or short-term, for that matter) patterns are defined as progression or retrogression is likewise a matter of value definition and it is important to recognize that these definitions are also subject to change. What is today widely acclaimed as progress may, from the perspective of a subsequent generation, be viewed in quite different terms.

It is easy to underemphasize the influence of social factors such as those we have been discussing in the creative process, particularly for those who think in individualistic terms. Wallis [5] emphasizes this when he says:

The credit for epochal changes is ascribed to individuals, for cultural forces are usually personalized. The inevitability of gradual change, or the gradualness of the inevitable, is ignored. Individual men receive credit for the great forces of culture drift. There is always a tendency to overlook or, by implication, to deny the great sweep of evolutionary changes and the gradual accumulation of knowledge and skill. Culture epochs are sung in strains of arms and the man, with emphasis upon the man. As we must have our totems and scapegoats, so we must have our culture heroes, men of superhuman stature and ability. Mortals are assigned superhuman roles.

UNEVEN RATES OF CHANGE— CULTURE LAG

Changes in the various parts of the socio-cultural milieu do not occur at the same rate. In an existing value structure, change in one area may be viewed as more desirable than change in another. In urbanized America changes in science and technology are encouraged and rewarded more than changes in religion. New industrial inventions such as automation may occur and be adopted by "industry" before ways of living with the resultant change have been well worked out. "Culture lag" is a term which Og-

---

The Unit of Adoption

Many of the innovations in our society are adopted not by individuals or even by families but by organizations. The city-manager idea and the kindergarten were adopted by cities and by school boards respectively; automation is adopted by factories.

—Elihu Katz.*

---

* Elihu Katz, "Notes on the Unit of Adoption in Diffusion Research," *Sociological Inquiry*, XXXII, No. 1 (Winter, 1962), p. 3.

[5] Wilson D. Wallis, *"Messiahs: Their Role in Civilization"* (Washington, D. C.: American Council on Public Affairs, 1943), p. 3.

burn [6] used to identify such a condition, and the term has been widely used in sociological literature. Ogburn further suggested that change in one part of culture may require readjustments in the various correlated parts. He illustrated his point by an analysis of, among other things, the manner in which changes in education lagged behind changes in industry. The terms "technological lag" and "technological restraint" have also been used.

Human history has been one of adjustment to change and will continue to be so. Change in any aspect of a social system is likely to extend beyond that immediate aspect. Society is in a constant "process of becoming." If the term "culture lag" is used to identify conditions of uneven rates of change, one should not conclude that the aspect that is "out in front" or changing most rapidly should necessarily be there and consequently that the "laggard" should be brought "into line" as soon as possible. Implicit value definitions are frequently involved in such discussions.

One discussion in an introductory sociology text states:

The efficient use of the newly invented automobile required drastic improvements in the road systems, but the development and building of highways suitable for motor vehicles were long delayed. Traffic codes and techniques of traffic control have been worked out even more slowly, and an etiquette of automobile driving is yet to develop. The consequences are inefficiency, wasteful delay in utilizing new techniques, stress and maladjustment.[7]

The question this discussion raises is whether the "efficient use" of new inventions is the criterion to be used in determining "lag." A whole set of value definitions is involved in the adoption of new inventions, and it could be expected that few if any major innovations would be given complete societal acceptance. Whatever patterns are found in the acceptance of that which is new, they are the result of many antecedent sociocultural factors, and any changes therein will likewise reflect the interrelationships of a multitude of factors. Tracing the patterns of change and the relationships between the factors involved is one of the tasks of the sociologist.

We will now turn our attention to an analysis of some of the major elements involved in social change and conversely in social stability. These will be discussed individually. It is understood, of course, that they are all interrelated and together form a societal phenomenon which is itself involved in the creative process.

VALUE DEFINITIONS

An important aspect of the cultural system involved in the creative process is the configuration of value definitions incorporated therein. Individuals and groups tend to resist change in those aspects of life which they have come to define as good, with the strength of the resistance being directly related to the strength of the value definitions involved. Strong enthnocentrism discourages change. Prejudice and bias discourage change. If we feel that our way is the best way, there is obviously not much purpose in seeking any better way. If our system, our method, our product, our group is valued highly, we may be reluctant even to try to change it.

Change and creativity *per se*, however, can be evaluated highly with the accompanying plans of action also being endorsed. A democratic orientation, for instance, endorses and incorporates the element of planned change. Placing high value on change and creativity is positively related to high evaluations of freedom. Relative freedom to pursue individualistic goals would seem to be a requisite of inventiveness. Moore [8]

[6] William F. Ogburn, *Social Change with Respect to Culture and Original Nature* (New York: The Viking Press, Inc., 1950), pp. 200–213.

[7] Leonard Broom and Philip Selznick, *Sociology* (3d ed.; New York: Harper & Row, Inc., 1963), p. 82.

[8] Wilbert E. Moore, *Social Change* (Englewood Cliffs, N. J.: Prentice-Hall, Inc., 1963), p. 21.

suggests that "making constructive innovation a moral virtue is rare and mostly modern."

Creative individuals and groups are more at home with complexity and apparent disorder than are others. They believe that the irrational might generate some ordering principle if it is permitted expression and admitted to conscious scrutiny. Such individuals not only respect the irrational in themselves but count it as the most promising source of novelty. Creativity requires that one somehow go beyond already established boundaries.

The process of creativity is also related to the type of truth endorsed by the group and the individual. If certain types of answers or truths are defined as final, ultimate, and unchanging, then once such a definition is accepted, the door to any further change or redefinitions has been closed. If one has reached his goal, there is no longer any need to seek for it. Once he has

Figure 25.2 Culture lag? Not all things change at the same rate, as this scene at the airport in La Paz, Bolivia, indicates. (Photo: Linares.)

Creativity Lost

Graham Wallas relates the story of a man "who had so brilliant an idea that he went into his garden to thank God for it, and found upon rising from his knees that he had forgotten it, and he never recalled it."

—Mary Henle.*

found the final truth, his major goal (if he values truth) is generally to defend it from error, rather than to be critical and skeptical about it. Closely related to this is the method of obtaining truth which is endorsed. If one seeks truth from the "authority," then once the authority has spoken the truth has been established and there is little reason to search for new truths.

Answers incorporated in the religion of a group frequently but not always take on the final, ultimate aspects just discussed. Such answers are also frequently provided by authority. Established religious truths are hard to change. This is not to imply that creativity and change are not found in religion. Indeed they are. Certain religious values, however, are inimical to change. Science, as was described in an earlier chapter does not define "truth" as final and ultimate, but as tentative. Scientific truth is always subject to change. Innovation and change are in fact usually encouraged and rewarded. A religious orientation and a scientific orientation may each have a unique influence upon creativity.

It would be anticipated then that relationships could be found between religious variables and measures of creativity. Such relationships have been found. Lenski,[9] for instance, in his study of the Detroit area found that Protestant respondents were more inclined than Roman Cath-

olics to indicate that teaching their children to "think independently" was more important than teaching them to "obey." In that independent thinking is conducive to creativity, we would expect that those religious groups which encourage it would produce more creative individuals than those with a different orientation. This conclusion is supported by the fact that scientific creativity has been found to be more characteristic of Protestants than of Roman Catholics.[10] Part of the explanation for this relationship seems to be in the orientation Protestants are encouraged to take toward their world. Merton summarizes it as follows:

The positive estimation by Protestants of a hardly disguised utilitarianism, of intra-mundane interests, of a thorough-going empiricism, of the right and even duty of *libre examen*, and of the explicit individual questioning of authority were congenial to the very same values found in modern science. And perhaps above all is the significance of the active ascetic drive which necessitated the study of Nature that it might be controlled.[11]

Religion itself is a complex phenomenon and may be a source of creative innovation, as Parsons has pointed out.[12]

No value judgment is implied about the desirability of scientific creativity.

NORM-ROLE DEFINITIONS

Any group has a degree of stability, related in part to the configuration of norm-role definitions, which is developed to structure its interactions.

---

* Mary Henle, "The Birth and Death of Ideas," in Howard E. Gruber, Glenn Terrell, and Michael Wertheimer (eds.), *Contemporary Approaches to Creative Thinking* (1962), pp. 41–42. With permission from Atherton Press.

[9] Gerhard Lenski, *The Religious Factor* (Garden City, N. Y.: Doubleday & Co., Inc., 1961).

[10] See, for instance, Isidor Thorner, "Ascetic Protestantism and the Development of Science and Technology," *The American Journal of Sociology*, LVIII, No. 1 (July, 1952), 25–33. For a discussion of the interpretations of Max Weber and P. Sorokin, see Thomas Ford Hoult, *The Sociology of Religion* (New York: Holt, Rinehart and Winston, Inc., 1958), pp. 369–375.

[11] Robert K. Merton, *Special Theory and Social Structure* (rev. ed.; New York: The Free Press of Glencoe, 1957), p. 595.

[12] Talcott Parsons, "Religion as a Source of Creative Innovation," in *Religious Perspectives of College Teaching in Sociology and Social Psychology* (New Haven: Edward W. Hazen Foundation, Inc., 1951), pp. 29–34.

The rigidity of the plans of action incorporated therein is related to the extent of creativity in the group. Any situation in which norm-role definitions have been worked out in detail is not very conducive to change. Change and creativity are more likely with reference to behavior which has not been preplanned, and for which there is no set of group expectations. Once habitual patterns of action or thinking have been well established, they are difficult to change. Once we have learned to view the world or aspects thereof in particular ways, it is difficult to "shift gears" and take another perspective. Awareness of this fact is expressed in the ancient statement, "No man having drunk old wine, straightway desireth new, for he saith 'the old is better.' "

Change and creativity inherently involve nonconformity. John Dewey has said:

No one discovers a new world without forsaking an old one; and no one discovers a new world who exacts guarantee in advance for what it shall be, or who puts the act of discovery under bonds with respect to what the new world shall do to him when it comes into vision.[13]

In simple terms, one cannot be both creative and a conformist at the same time. Such a statement, however, over-simplifies since it fails to specify the aspects of behavior which are conformist and those which are not. Conformity in certain aspects of behavior is a necessary foundation to creativity and freedom in others. Thus, the fact that a group has developed norm definitions which specify how certain types of interaction will take place, frees those involved from any concern with behavior at the level covered by the norms and thus permits them to pay attention to other areas in which they may be creative. Only when norm definitions have been established is one free to enter into a much wider range of voluntary agreements with others in areas not covered by the norms.

Parsons illustrates this point by analysis of the barter system. Such a system, he points out, ties the individual down to the very limited opportunities available with partners willing to engage in the direct barter exchange. A market system, however, which involves money frees the participants from the constraints of barter with respect to items received in exchange. The individual can then decide later how and when he will spend his money. Such freedom exists only if the monetary system is widely accepted and if those involved conform to it, so that the expectations associated with the system are relatively stable. The individual is not free to establish his own monetary system, but once having accepted the system stabilized by the group he is free to do other things which he could not do otherwise.

The use of language provides another cogent example. Parsons indicates:

Language is one of the most crucial freedom-creating mechanisms in the whole human repertoire—its essence is that it is a medium in which almost any meaning can be conveyed—at least an immensely wide range of meaning. But one cannot speak intelligently and ignore the "conventions" of the language. Language is most definitely institutionalized—and without this institutionalization, "freedom of speech" would be meaningless. The way to increase freedoms of speech and of thought is not to abolish the constraints of language, but to utilize them.[14]

Creativity then does not incorporate the idea of complete abandonment of norm-role definitions and any value definitions associated with them. It is not the process of uncritical self expression. It is not the opposite of restraint. It is a matter of degree. By definition it involves changes in some areas, but not the complete abandonment of established practices. It is not complete self indulgence. Children upon whom no restraints are placed easily learn to do whatever they want to do and may learn to view the world as a place in which their wishes and desires take top priority. The creativity involved then may be only that involved in gratifying an

---

[13] John Dewey, *Experience and Nature* (Chicago: Open Court Publishing Co., 1925), p. 246.

[14] Talcott Parsons, "Comment," *Journal for the Scientific Study of Religion,* I, No. 1 (October, 1961), 26.

individual's unique desires. This, of course, imposes strong limitations upon the type of creativity involved and also the extent of creativity.

It has been suggested that creativity becomes fertile when each person takes the responsibility for it, both in himself and in others.

The power structure of the group, which of course is related to the norm-role definitions, is also related to the likelihood of innovation, as well as the source of innovation. Democratic organizations encourage creativity and change by all who actively participate in the decision making of the group. Lewin, for instance, in his laboratory study of democratic, laissez-faire, and authoritarian groups, found that the level of creativity was higher for the democratic groups than for either of the other groups.[15]

Vested interest groups within any society may also serve to discourage change and innovation in any aspect of their society which they feel would work to their disadvantage in terms of economic, political, power, or other factors.

The popular saying which maintains that "Necessity is the mother of invention" contains only a partial truth. Inventions do not result just because someone feels they are needed. The atomic bomb was needed as much during World War I as during World War II. The requisite cultural base, however, was not ready. It is true, however, that conditions of stress and loss of equilibrium may provide added incentive to the whole creative process.

Sanctions

The norm-role definitions of a group usually include a sanction system which is related to the extent of creativity. Where creativity is endorsed, sanctions are developed and used to encourage such creativity. It is important to recognize that sanctions are not granted to any and all creativity to the same degree. Only certain types gain the positive sanctions of the group. The

[15] Kurt Lewin, R. Lippitt, and R. K. White, "Patterns of Aggressive Behavior in Experimentally Created 'Social Climates'," *Journal of Social Psychology*, X, No. 2 (May, 1939), 271–299.

young child may, for example, invent new words and may incorporate them into *his* vocabulary. How long are they tolerated by his family and peers, however? Usually after an initial period of praise or joking approval which may include adults' use of the words themselves, the novelty wears off and the new words are discouraged or forbidden in efforts to maintain the flow of communication within the group or to avoid the disapproval of out-group members.

Intricate innovations, both technically and socially, may be developed by criminals and delinquents, which while they may gain positive sanctions from their own delinquent or criminal reference groups, may result in negative sanctions from the society at large.

Sanctions can be used to encourage or discourage creativity. In terms of a previous discussion, encouragement or endorsement of particular self definitions may be one of the most potent sanctions available.

SELF DEFINITIONS

The self definitions of an individual or a group are related to creativity in several ways. In the first place, the individual (or the group) must usually define himself as being capable of the creative act before he will attempt to engage therein. Such definitions are socially secured (as are all self definitions) and may involve a chain reaction of "definition-success-reinforced," "definition-increased success-reinforced" definitions, etc. "Nothing succeeds like success." The reverse pattern would, of course, serve to inhibit creativity.

In addition to these definitions, it is likely that individuals who are insecure as far as self definitions are concerned, or who are not sure just what they are or what skills and talents they have and who consequently spend much time and effort worrying about themselves and their future, are not likely to be creatively productive. Creativity requires that attention be focused upon the phenomenon of concern—not upon the creator or the potential creator. Creative persons then tend to have a realistic, secure definition of themselves.

Creativity—A Parable *

A pedant for a long time had a nightingale and he was gladdened by its song. Then the bird died. The pedant, finding the silence and loneliness uncomfortable, went out to buy another bird. But only a few nests had been brought to market; the dealer did not know whether the eggs had been fertilized, and in any case would not guarantee that males would be hatched from the fertilized eggs; besides the young, when hatched, would still require attention and care before they would grow into singers. This seemed too hazardous to the pedant, and he went away saying that he would rather keep his dead nightingale. This was acting conservatively; but for what use? It was possible that the trouble of raising the young would go for nothing, but it was certain that the dead bird would never sing.

In addition, creative individuals usually develop a commitment to find something new. Their self definitions may in fact become intimately related to the new phenomenon. Achieving the desired goal becomes a highly prized goal. The individual is accordingly willing to let this goal take precedence over other goals. The individual's life may become dominated by the search or the effort to create the "thing." This need not necessarily be a search for immediate culmination. Completion may, in fact, be deferred for some time. Such individuals become creativity-oriented. Some "fall in love with" or "become obsessed" with the task at hand. The task takes on primary saliency.

Creativity is accomplished at the price of other unattempted or unfinished tasks. This applies to creative groups as well as creative individuals.

PLANNED AND UNPLANNED CHANGE

Playing a creative role may involve various types of behavior. Some change may be consciously planned while much change is of the unplanned type. Rarely is planned-for change likely to materialize exactly as it was planned. Most change involves both planned and unplanned aspects. Planned change is, of course, a uniquely human phenomenon, closely related to the fact that man can use symbols which permit him to take into account both the past and the future. Lower animals cannot do this.

Whether or not planned change is endorsed by any particular group depends in part upon their value system. Democracy rests upon the premise that planned change is not only desirable, but also that the average man is capable of making the "right" choices for his group. In a democracy, groups meet often in a council situation in order consciously to plan future changes for themselves.

Unplanned change is an ever present phenomenon. There is, of course, the question as to just how extensive planned change can ever be. Many theories have been developed which view change as being essentially unplanned. Some have viewed it as being predetermined or automatically built in, by some process that is most likely unstated. Thus, some writers such as Sorokin [16] and Toynbee [17] have theorized that society is always changing in a cyclical fashion. Others such as Comte [18] and Spencer [19] have also endorsed the premise of constant change, but have endorsed a linear theory which views the change as always occurring in a positive or upward direction. Scientific limits remove from our concern the question as to whether any change pattern is a "positive one," or one of improvement. Discussion which takes this ap-

---

* Jacob Henle, *Handbuch der rationellen Pathologie* (2d ed.; Braunschweig: F. Vieweg u. Sohn, 1846), quoted by Mary Henle, "The Birth and Death of Ideas," in Howard E. Gruber, Glenn Terrell, and Michael Wertheimer (eds.), *Contemporary Approaches to Creative Thinking* (1962), p. 60. With permission from Atherton Press.

[16] Pitirin A. Sorokin, *Social and Cultural Dynamics*, 4 vols. (New York: American Book Co., 1937–1943).

[17] Arnold J. Toynbee, *A Study of History* (Fair Lawn, N. J.: Oxford University Press, 1947).

[18] Auguste Comte, *Cours de Philosophie Positive* (Paris: Rouen, 1830–1842).

[19] Herbert Spencer, *First Principles* (New York: Appleton-Century-Crofts, 1890).

proach tells us more about the people evaluating the change than about the change *per se*. Major concern now centers upon the identification of different types of change and of the configuration of social correlates of each.

The contacts one group has with another, as well as those one individual has with another, are a major factor in the creative process. Contacts with others would appear to be the major source of change and innovation. The term "diffusion" has been used to label the process by which the interchange of cultural and/or social phenomena takes place. It is, in simple terms, the borrowing process.

The extent to which the American way of life has been influenced by the diffusion process is suggested in the following quote from Ralph Linton.[20]

Our solid American citizen awakens in a bed built on a pattern which originated in the Near East but which was modified in Northern Europe before it was transmitted to America. He throws back the covers made from cotton, domesticated in India, or linen, domesticated in the Near East, or wool from sheep, also domesticated in the Near East, or silk the use of which was discovered in China. All of these materials have been spun and woven by processes invented in the Near East. He slips into his moccasins, invented by the Indians of the Eastern woodlands, and goes to the bathroom, whose fixtures are a mixture of European and American inventions, both of recent date. He takes off his pajamas, a garment invented in India, and washes with soap invented by the ancient Gauls. He then shaves, a masochistic rite which seems to have been derived from either Sumer or ancient Egypt. . . .

On his way to breakfast, he stops to buy a paper, paying for it with coins, an ancient Lydian invention. At the restaurant a whole new series of borrowed elements confronts him. His plate is made of a form of pottery invented in China. His knife is of steel, an alloy first made in southern India, his fork a medieval Italian invention, and his spoon a derivative of a Roman original. He begins breakfast with an orange, from the eastern Mediterranean, a cantaloupe from

Persia, or perhaps a piece of African watermelon. With this he has coffee, an Abyssinian plant, with cream and sugar. Both the domestication of cows and the idea of milking them originated in the Near East, while sugar was first made in India. After his fruit and first coffee he goes on to waffles, cakes made by a Scandinavian technique from wheat domesticated in Asia Minor. Over these he pours maple syrup, invented by the Indians of the Eastern woodlands. As a side dish he may have the eggs of a specific bird domesticated in Indo-China, or thin strips of the flesh of an animal domesticated in Eastern Asia which have been salted and smoked by a process developed in northern Europe.

When our friend has finished eating, he settles back to smoke, an American Indian habit, consuming a plant domesticated in Brazil in either a pipe derived from the Indians of Virginia, or a cigarette, derived from Mexico. If he is hardy enough he may even attempt a cigar, transmitted to us from the Antilles by way of Spain. While smoking he reads the news of the day, imprinted in characters invented in Germany. As he absorbs the accounts of foreign troubles he will, if he is a good conservative citizen, thank a Hebrew deity in an Indo-European language that he is 100 per cent American.

Borrowed cultural or social elements are incorporated into an already existing social structure and may take on some unique aspects in their new setting.

SUMMARY

An adequate explanation of human behavior must, in addition to accounting for the stability of social systems, also account for the change, the novelty, the "effective surprise" therein. To do this is the goal of this chapter. Attention has been given to change in culture, cultural objects, and society, as well as to individual and group creativity. In that all aspects of society are interrelated, change in any one part will, in chain reaction, permeate the rest of the socio-cultural milieu. Broad patterns of change called "culture drift" become established and themselves influence subsequent change. Differential rates of change (socio-cultural lag) are experienced, however.

[20] Ralph Linton, *The Study of Man* (New York: Appleton-Century-Crofts, 1936), pp. 326–327.

Value definitions as well as the religion in which they are incorporated may support conformity or non-conformity, as do the types of truth which society endorses.

Norm-role definitions, including sanctions incorporated within them, as well as self definitions, inhibit or facilitate certain types of creativity.

QUESTIONS

1. How are value definitions related to creativity?
2. Why does an interactionist question the "great man" theory of change?
3. Under what conditions have you experienced greatest creativity?
4. How does conformity at one level facilitate creative behavior at another?
5. Identify some of the types of creative behavior which are observable in your sociology class.
6. What would happen to a group if its members gave equal encouragement to *all* types of creative behavior?
7. What differences do you see between religious creativity and scientific creativity?
8. How is change in one type of behavior related to other types?
9. What types of change are most easily accepted by Americans?
10. Discuss the statement that all interaction has its emergent, creative aspects.

PROJECT

Interview ten students to find out what types of religious change they would be most willing to accept. Do the answers suggest anything about religious change as contrasted with, say, technological change?

SUGGESTED READING

BARNETT, H. G. *Innovation: The Basis of Cultural Change.* New York: McGraw-Hill Book Co., 1953.

GINSBERG, MORRIS. "Social Change," *British Journal of Sociology,* IX (September, 1958), 205–229.

GRUBER, HOWARD E., GLENN TERRELL, and MICHAEL WERTHEIMER (eds.). *Contemporary Approaches to Creative Thinking.* New York: The Atherton Press, 1962.

LINTON, RALPH. *The Tree of Culture.* New York: Alfred A. Knopf, Inc., 1955.

LIPPITT, RONALD, *et al. The Dynamics of Planned Change.* New York: Harcourt, Brace & World, Inc., 1958.

McCLELLAND, DAVID C. *The Achieving Society.* Princeton, N. J.: D. Van Nostrand Company, Inc., 1961.

NORDSKOG, JOHN ERIC. *Social Change.* New York: McGraw-Hill Book Co., 1960.

OGBURN, WILLIAM F. "How Technology Changes Society," *Annals of the American Academy of Political and Social Science,* CCXLIX (January, 1947), 81–88.

PARSONS, TALCOTT. "Comment," in *Journal for the Scientific Study of Religion,* I, No. 1 (October, 1961), pp. 22–29.

ROGERS, EVERETT M. *Social Change in Rural Society.* New York: Appleton-Century-Crofts, 1960.

Glossary

Glossary

Accommodation. The process of mutual revision of definitions and behavior patterns so that conflict is reduced.

Acculturation. The process by which individuals or groups from one society acquire the culture and behavior patterns of another.

Amoral. Behavior which does not involve making moral (value) decisions. Science is amoral.

Assimilation. The process by which the culture and behavior of two groups are merged into one, so that old distinctions are lost.

Attitude. That which is measured by an attitude scale—usually a value judgment for or against something.

Audience. Individuals toward whom a particular communication effort is directed.

Authority. Plans of action incorporated in the norm-role definitions which specify the types of decisions one can make to influence others.

Bureaucracy. A large organization or association in which interaction is extensively controlled by formally developed and formally administered norm-role definitions. Relations tend to be impersonal, although personal (primary) relationships usually exist within the organization.

Caste. A category of individuals for which particular norm-role definitions specify rigid differential treatment, particularly with reference to marriage and frequently with reference to occupation. A caste system provides for no mobility or change between castes.

Class. A category of individuals which receives differential treatment (discrimination) specified in the culture of the group. In a class system, individuals can rise or fall from one class to another. Criteria of differential treatment are arbitrary and vary from group to group.

Continuum. A device or scheme which permits an ordering of data in uninterrupted and graduated degrees ranging from lowest to highest.

Correlation. A co-relation between two or more variables which is such that change in one is related to change in the other or others to a degree which permits prediction of one from knowledge of the other.

Creativity. The process by which new culture, culture objects, and behavior patterns are introduced.

Crowd. A group of persons who react to a common focus of attention and engage in relatively unstructured interaction.

Culture. The culture of a society is the totality of the definitions, including plans of action, held by the society. Culture is defined by some as also including, in addition to the definitions (knowledge and beliefs, etc.), the learned behavior patterns and man-made objects.

Culture lag. An uneven rate of change of elements of a culture.

Definition. The meaning of a label (symbol) including referent identification, plans of action, and value aspects associated therewith, used to identify some phenomenon.

Demography. The study of population characteristics, such as sex ratio, birth rates, death rates, size, etc.

Denomination. A religious group which is usually large in size and is accommodated to the society. Contrasted with a *sect*.

Dichotomy. A classification scheme or device which permits of classification only into one of two categories.

Diffusion. The process by which culture spreads from one group to another.

Discrimination. Differential treatment, rights, and privileges based upon some accepted criteria.

Ecology. The study of how people distribute themselves in space, and how such distributions are related to interaction patterns.

Empathy. Role-taking ability, or the process by which one comes to a decision about the meaning of the behavior of others.

Empirical. That which exists outside of and independent of the observer. Science requires that attention be given to empirical phenomena, which are accordingly available for shared observation and verification.

Ethnocentrism. Value definition that one's own way is the best way. Evaluating others by the standards of your own group.

Fad. A temporary change in behavior patterns, usually with strong support from its adherents.

Family. A group related by birth, marriage, or adoption who define themselves as a family.

Fashion. A distinctive type of behavior which has widespread support in the group. More permanent than a *fad*, and may in fact become permanently established in the culture of the group.

Feral individuals. Humans who have had little human contact, and who were presumably nurtured by animals, so that they were not socialized.

Folkway. A norm definition of moderate intensity, contrasted with *mores* which have high intensity.

Function, intended. What an individual or group expects to accomplish by engaging in an act. Purpose or goal of the act.

Function, latent. The consequences of an act as determined by scientific observation. May be different from *manifest function*.

Function, manifest. The consequences which individuals tell themselves a particular act has. May be different from the actual or latent consequences.

Group. Two or more human beings in reciprocal communication.

Group, ethnic. A group having some distinctive characteristics so that they receive differential treatment by the larger society. They have common ancestry, usually unique language patterns and maybe national origin. Sometimes used as meaning any minority group.

Group, primary. A group in which the relationships are of a primary nature, that is, of an intimate, very personal type, and in which the relationship *per se* is valued.

Group, reference. A group whose value-norm-role definitions are used in making decisions about one's behavior. Need not be a membership group.

Group, secondary. A group in which the relationships are of a secondary type, i.e., of a non-intimate, segmental type. Relationship is instrumental or a means to an end, and not valued for itself as in case of *primary relationship*.

Ideal type. Hypothetical configuration of characteristics, with which actual behavior can be compared.

In-group. The label applied to a group by the members thereof who identify strongly therewith, and thus distinguish themselves from members of the out-group. The in-group for one individual may be the out-group for another.

Institution. A configuration of socio-cultural phenomena related to a societal goal or purpose.

Intensity continuum. A measuring device which permits one to distinguish the various value definitions applied to something.

Interaction. The behavior of two or more individuals mutually influencing each other.

Invention. Combination of two or more existing socio-cultural elements into something new.

Law. A formally derived and enforced norm definition. Contrasted with *folkways* and *mores* which are informally derived and enforced.

Looking-glass self. One's conception of himself based upon his decision as to what the behavior of others "mirrors" or informs him about himself.

Marginal. Being neither completely in nor completely out of a group. A marginal individual accepts parts of two or more sets of definitions and does not consistently follow either of them.

Matriarchal. Type of family in which major authority rests with the mother.

Matrilineal. Type of family in which lineage is only from mother's family.

Mobility, social. Change of culture and interaction patterns which results in their being classed in a higher or lower category. Movement through "social" space.

Mores. Strongly endorsed, informally developed norm definitions. These plans of action are defined as "must" behavior and given religious endorsement.

Motivation. The explanations an individual gives to himself as to why he does what he does. Defined differently by different disciplines.

Multiple causation, principle of. Any behavior has multiple antecedent factors related to it in a causal manner.

Norm definitions. Plans of action (expectations, script) which members of a society are generally expected to follow. Includes *folkways, mores,* and *laws.* The term "norm" is sometimes used to mean both the expected behavior patterns and the actual behavior patterns.

Norm-role definitions. A broad term used to include both the norm definitions which are society-wide in nature and the role definitions, each of which is restricted to a particular position.

Objectivity. The ability to view phenomena in a scientifically verifiable manner, thus presumably seeing what is there rather than what one might wish were there.

Operational definition. Definition stated in terms of the operations through which one goes in order to observe the defined phenomenon.

Patriarchal. Family type with father-invested power.

Patrilineal. Family in which descent is traced from father's family only.

Peer group. Group composed of one's equals.

Personality. Totality of the definitions including plans of action of an individual. Frequently defined to include also the totality of an individual's behavior patterns.

Polyandry. Marriage pattern in which one woman marries two or more men.

Polygamy. Marriage pattern involving a plurality of mates. As a term it may include *polygyny* or *polyandry*, or both.

Polygyny. Marriage pattern in which one man marries two or more women.

Power. The extent to which a person or group can control the behavior of another. May be related to formal and informal norm-role definitions.

Prejudice. Negative value definitions and/or definitions accepted despite contrary empirical evidence.

Primary relationship. Relationships in a primary group, characterized by intimate knowledge of those involved plus a high evaluation of the relationship *per se.*

Propaganda. Efforts to persuade others to accept particular definitions.

Public. Those concerned (pro or con) with a particular issue. Need not be in physical proximity.

Race. A main biological division of the human species.

Reference group. See *Group, reference.*

Referent. That to which a symbol refers. Need not be empirical.

Religion. Definitions which relate man to the supernatural and the top-level value definitions (including definitions of sacredness). Religious behavior is behavior which takes these definitions into account.

Role definition. Expected behavior patterns, or the plans of action which are associated with a particular position. See *Norm-role definitions.*

Role playing. Role enacting, or role performance. Actually engaging in the behavior specified in the role definitions, plus the emergent behavior related thereto.

Role taking. The process of interpreting the behavior of others.

Sacred. A definition man attaches to phenomena which are believed to be related to the supernatural in an important way, and are consequently highly valued.

Secondary relationship. Relationship within a secondary group.

Sect. A religious group which is usually small, and is at odds (non-accommodated) with society.

Selective perception. Process of paying attention to only a segment of the total available to be perceived.

Self definitions. Definitions attributed by an individual to that individual—to himself.

Significant others. Persons to whom special significance is given in the process of reaching decisions. Reference groups are composed of significant others.

Situation, definition of. Definition of a configuration of elements so that both the larger configuration as well as component parts thereof make sense, with the interpretation of each being related to the interpretation of the other. Involves synthesizing.

Social movement. Collective efforts to bring about a major change in the culture and the behavior patterns of the society.

Socialization. The process by which the individual acquires his human behavior patterns—the learning process.

Society. A group of people who share a common culture and a relatively self-sufficient interaction system. They also share a common territory.

Socio-cultural. A term used to designate a combination of social (society) and cultural (definitions). Interaction is socio-cultural in that it involves individuals (society) interacting on the basis of culture.

Sociology. The scientific study of human interaction.

Status. Value judgment as to rank or standing in the group. Sometimes used to mean position.

Stratification. Process of developing a system of differential rewards and punishments or the resulting system itself which constitutes a status hierarchy.

Subculture. The distinctive culture (definitions) held by a subgroup.

Subjective reality. Whatever an individual or group believes to be real, contrasted with objective reality or that which is real regardless of how it is defined.

Symbol. Anything which stands for or represents something else. ER symbols have an empirical referent; NER symbols have a non-empirical referent.

Value definition. Definitions as to the relative worth of phenomena. These are attributed by man to the phenomena, rather than qualities or characteristics existing in the objects. NER symbols are involved.

Indexes

Index of Names

Index of Subjects